Praise for Philip Dray's

THERE IS POWER IN A UNION

"One of the great values of this beautifully written book is that it shows the centrality of labor and working-class organizations to America itself. . . . Dray comes into the ring with fists flying, and he doesn't let up for a moment. If you love Howard Zinn's *A People's History of the United States* you'll probably love Dray's history, too." —*San Francisco Chronicle*

"Dray provides a grand context for thinking about labor-management relations in a society beset by bad will within millions of workplaces. . . . He is a refreshing chronicler of history." —*Minneapolis Star Tribune*

"Insightful. . . . An exhaustive and surprisingly lively account of the integral role labor has played in American life." —*The Plain Dealer*

"A stirring study. . . . Packed with vivid characters and dramatic scenes, Dray's fine recap of a neglected but vital tradition has much to say about labor's current straits." —*The Washington Examiner*

"An exemplary history of the American labor movement, from its time-shrouded beginnings to its murky present . . . in the tradition of Eric Foner and Studs Terkel."
—*Kirkus Reviews* (starred)

"The unending struggle between unions and big business has never been more vividly told. Philip Dray is a marvelous storyteller who brings history memorably alive, and you will not soon forget the tales of murder and greed, commitment and sacrifice that fill these pages. But this is more than history; the compelling saga of labor as a crucible for social change should prompt some honest and hard debate about what's happening to working men and women today."
—Bill Moyers

"Sobering. . . . This unusually interesting book delivers on the promise of its subtitle. . . . [Dray] offers a balanced and comprehensive coverage of a force for American progress that is now in danger of becoming a relic of our storied past."
—*America Magazine*

"Philip Dray's big and bold history of organized labor in America splendidly retells a story—or a multitude of stories—badly in need of retelling. The labor movement's decline in recent decades has accompanied a great national amnesia about all that the movement achieved for the nation. That amnesia threatens those achievements, so Dray's book is timely as well as gripping."   —Sean Wilentz, author of
The Rise of American Democracy

PHILIP DRAY

THERE IS POWER IN A UNION

Philip Dray is the author of *At the Hands of Persons Unknown: The Lynching of Black America*, which won the Robert F. Kennedy Memorial Book Award and was a finalist for the Pulitzer Prize. His book *Capitol Men: The Epic Story of Reconstruction Through the Lives of the First Black Congressmen* was a *New York Times* Notable Book and received the Peter Seaborg Award for Civil War Scholarship. He lives in Brooklyn, New York.

*Capitol Men: The Epic Story of Reconstruction Through the
Lives of the First Black Congressmen*

*Stealing God's Thunder: Benjamin Franklin's Lightning Rod
and the Invention of America*

*At the Hands of Persons Unknown: The Lynching of
Black America*

*We Are Not Afraid: The Story of Goodman, Schwerner, and
Chaney, and the Civil Rights Campaign for Mississippi*
(with Seth Cagin)

THERE IS
POWER
★ IN A ★
UNION

THE EPIC STORY OF
LABOR IN AMERICA

PHILIP DRAY

• ANCHOR BOOKS •

A DIVISION OF RANDOM HOUSE, INC.

NEW YORK

FIRST ANCHOR BOOKS EDITION, SEPTEMBER 2011

Copyright © 2010 by Philip Dray

All rights reserved. Published in the United States by Anchor Books,
a division of Random House, Inc., New York, and in Canada by Random House of
Canada Limited, Toronto. Originally published in hardcover in the United States
by Doubleday, a division of Random House, Inc., New York, in 2010.

Anchor Books and colophon are registered trademarks of Random House, Inc.

Pages 743–44 constitute an extension of this copyright page.

The Library of Congress has cataloged the Doubleday edition as follows:
Dray, Philip.
There is power in a union : the epic story of labor in America / Philip Dray.—1st ed.
p. cm.
Includes bibliographical references and index.
1. Labor unions—United States—History. 2. Labor movement—United States—History.
3. Industrialization—Social aspects—United States—History.
4. United States—Social conditions. I. Title.
HD6508.D73 2010
331.880973—dc22
2010002357

Anchor ISBN: 978-0-307-38976-3

Author photograph © Mindy Tucker

www.anchorbooks.com

Printed in the United States of America

10   9   8   7

For my sister Alison

There is pow'r, there is pow'r
In a band of workingmen.
When they stand, hand in hand.
That's a pow'r, that's a pow'r
That must rule in every land—
One Industrial Union Grand.

—Joe Hill, "There Is Power in a Union"

★ CONTENTS ★

THERE WAS NO WORK, AND NEW YORK CITY'S unemployed were desperate for food, coal, the means to pay the rent and provide milk to the children. The trouble had started a few months before, in September 1873: a sudden financial panic. The brokerage firm of Jay Cooke and Company went first, then all of Wall Street collapsed, taking with it banks and investments, fortunes, jobs. On the chilly morning of January 13, 1874, they huddled fifteen thousand strong in Tompkins Square to demand government relief and public jobs. Stamping their feet to stay warm, they smoked and waited. Speeches were to be made. Mayor William Havemeyer, who knew of their difficulties, had agreed to address them.

But something was wrong: police on horseback had appeared at the edge of the square, sent by city officials worried about the large number of people who'd recently taken to marching in the streets. Fear had been stoked by the newspapers, which described the protestors as "reds" and "Communists" and warned that they might revolt.[1] Only three years earlier French Communards had seized the eastern precincts of Paris in the name of the dispossessed, thrown up barricades, and had then been crushed by soldiers in an orgy of horrific street fighting and drumhead executions. "There is a dangerous class in New York, quite as much as in Paris," the *New York Times* advised the city, "and they want only the opportunity or the incentive to spread anarchy and ruin."[2]

Certainly those in Tompkins Square had done their cause little good by naming their coordinating group "the Committee of Safety," a phrase borrowed from the Commune as well as the French Revolution. Nor had they set civic minds at ease a week earlier, when on January 5 a delegation from the Lower East Side visited city hall. There they asked for work on municipal projects such as street-paving, an advance of either money or food for the poorest families, and a temporary ban on evictions. When the aldermen offered no immediate remedies, some of the unemployed in anger offered to "throw those whelps out of the windows," and threatened to go all the way to the legislature in Albany and throw officials out of the windows there as well.[3] And so the authorities had had second thoughts about the gathering in Tompkins Square; they had canceled Mayor Havemeyer's speech and withdrawn the permit for the rally. No one, however, had informed the event's organizers.

The police commissioner, Abram Duryée, strode into the park to order the crowd to disperse, a squad of officers walking behind him and using their batons to prod the reluctant. Two German workers who resented being shoved struck back, prompting police on horses to enter the square. The crowd panicked and rushed to the gates, but the pathways were narrow and the horsemen came on swiftly, charging "like Cossacks," one Russian immigrant recalled, swinging their clubs and chasing the protestors out of the square and through the nearby streets as far as the Bowery. There were injuries from the policemen's blows and numerous arrests.

One group of organizers hurried to city hall. "All we want is work!" they assured the mayor.[4] Havemeyer was sympathetic but explained, "It is not the purpose or object of the city government to furnish work to the industrious poor. That system belongs to other countries, not ours."[5]

When they implored him to honor his promise to address the unemployed, the mayor demurred. "I have heard what occurred this morning, and I do not desire to address crazy or excited people, who might be anxious to send brickbats flying."[6]

When industry appeared in the United States in the early years of the republic, the country dared hope that its democratic virtues would forge sufficient regard between labor and capital that scenes like Tompkins Square would never come to pass. Now the police, with the use of unnecessary force, had added to the workers' outrage by denying their right to free speech and assembly. "What citizens were those who wanted to meet on Tompkins Square on the 13th of January?" demanded Augusta Lilienthal of the German Free-Thinkers Union at a public meeting convened two weeks later at Cooper Union. "They were a portion of positively the best class of our citizens. They were the true taxpayers. They were working men! (Cheers.) They had assembled to ask for work, and for that they were knocked down! (Hisses.) What a condition of affairs is this?"[7]

A Dr. Emil Hoeber spoke in answer, noting that although "favorable auspices" had attended the long-ago founding of the nation, now the country "is situated as if placed atop a volcano, the present circumstances tending to make some rich while consigning hundreds of thousands to permanent poverty. There must, sooner or later, be a change."[8] Journalist and labor advocate John Swinton reminded the hall that "twenty years ago 'Abolitionist' sounded as terrible as the word 'Communist' does today. . . . Let us not wait in this case till our tongues are tied and our hands are manacled. Let us not lie supine till our chains are forged, but let the forgers be warned and thwarted in advance."[9]

The audience understood these allusions all too well—slavery, the division of classes, of bosses and laborers, of "haves" and "have-nots." The hint of impending struggle—that, too, had a familiar ring. A generation earlier the country had been warned that an "irrepressible conflict" was coming, a titanic struggle over the issue of slavery. The result had been civil war more devastating than anyone had imagined, a trauma from which recovery was yet incomplete. Would another such "irrepressible conflict" be required to right all that had gone wrong in the relations between those who provided work and those who relied on it, between capital and labor?[10]

I N THE CROWD IN TOMPKINS SQUARE had been two men destined for far different roles in the nation's labor struggle. Samuel Gompers, a twenty-three-year-old member of a New York cigar makers' union, had fled the police charge and narrowly avoided a crack over the head by diving into a cellar stairway. Justus Schwab, a resident of the Lower East Side, had reentered the park after the police had cleared it and raced across the grounds waving a red flag. Tackled and taken into custody, he was brought to the nearest precinct house, where, to the annoyance of the arresting officers, he defiantly began singing "La Marseillaise."[11] Gompers within a decade would become the president of the American Federation of Labor, and would cite the riot at Tompkins Square as having convinced him of the futility of radicalism; disgruntled people confronting authority in public places was not the means of bettering the lot of the workingman. Labor's rights could best be won through negotiation and the careful use of the workers' leverage over profits and production. Schwab, who would have further brushes with the law, went on to operate a saloon on East First Street popular with neighborhood radicals, including anarchists Emma Goldman, Alexander Berkman, and Johann Most, who wished to abolish the wage system, saw capitalism as a useless, inhumane form of social organization, and advocated violence where necessary to awaken insurrectionary fervor.[12]

As Gompers and Schwab's divergent paths suggest, the saga of organized labor in America is not one story but many. It is also much more than a catalog of strikes, picket lines, and flailing police batons. The debate about work and industry and the struggle for workers' rights and dignity have been consuming subjects since the birth of our nation; they have shaped laws and customs, acted as a crucible for social change, and ultimately helped define what it means to be an American. This book attempts to relate that remarkable account by exploring the tension between skilled and unskilled labor, the impact of immigration, and the changing role of government in labor issues. It focuses on the evolution of labor's hopes and expectations from the introduction of industry in America in the 1820s to the modern labor movement's decline in the 1980s, and considers what kind of future workers in every era believed in for themselves, their families, and their country. It examines what they felt they were entitled to, what they demanded, and how their tactics for realizing those objectives evolved.

T HAT SOME PEOPLE THOUGHT UNIONS to be an obnoxious and unwelcome intrusion in the workplace dawned on me for the first time one weekday morning in March 1976. I was sitting in the office of Evelyn Johnson, an advertising manager at the *Minneapolis Star and Tribune,* who was about to become my boss. Evelyn was a soft-spoken older woman, kindly, and I could tell she wanted me to have the part-time job for which I'd applied. I had told her how when I was eight or nine I'd sometimes gone out in the freezing predawn darkness to help my big brother deliver the *Tribune*, the paper's morning edition, and she and I had lapsed into a typical Minnesota conversation about the harshness of the past winter. Then suddenly she was talking about a recent attempt to unionize the workers in the advertising department; she wondered if I'd ever be inclined to join such an effort. I knew at once that the "correct" answer was "No." Still, it caught me off guard that so direct and obviously determinative a question had come from this otherwise pleasant-looking person, who, as I remember, was wearing a pastel blue sweater.

Having grown up in the late 1950s and 1960s, at the end of what some now call labor's golden era, I had always been given to understand that labor unions were valuable and necessary to society. They fought for workers, brought dignity to people's lives, decent hours, the five-day week, benefits, and paid vacations. The photographs I'd seen in my junior high school social studies textbook of strikers marching or picketing seemed images of American heroism no less exemplary than the illustrations of "Washington Crossing the Delaware" or pioneer families making their way west along the Oregon Trail. The labor giants—the AFL-CIO, the Teamsters, the United Mine Workers, and historic ones like the

Industrial Workers of the World or the Knights of Labor—these were venerable institutions, part of our nation's heritage.

My own limited experience as a union worker, when I was sixteen and worked as a busboy in a suburban supper club, had been a positive one. New hires were required to join a local hotel and restaurant workers' union, which extracted monthly dues from our paychecks. The shop steward, a burly cook named Larry, made sure the staff punched in and out on time, reminded us to take our allotted breaks, advised the cocktail waitresses how to politely fend off unwanted advances from customers, and acted as a buffer between the employees and the often erratic demands of the club's owner and its executive chef. I didn't doubt that the few dollars I contributed in dues were worth having Larry, my coworkers, and the union officers downtown perceive me as someone with needs and rights—someone who might have a grievance with a boss, require a sick day, or want to be transferred off the Sunday brunch shift. That sense of belonging is the very essence of labor unionism.

Later I came to know that labor leaders themselves were often difficult, argumentative people, and that strikes could involve sharp differences of opinion and conflict, but these I assumed to be less failings than manifestations of a process that, however tumultuous, was good for America. It was democracy at work. No one could expect labor unions to behave like the Boy Scouts or a church choir; they were dynamic organizations that took on life-and-death issues: economics, government policy, workers' health and safety, and fair pay. To do this they stood up to the powerful. They made demands and caused inconvenience. Yet they did so as parties to a kind of covenant: behind their strong language and equally strong actions, they shared the same goals as management—productivity and national prosperity.[13]

I N THE BEGINNING THE ARTISANS, apprentices, tradesmen, and farmers of the youthful American republic—long restricted by the British in the Colonial Era from developing manufacturing—were unsure if they wished to welcome the factory. Work indoors regulated by the chiming of bells was a new type of regimen; gone were the intimacy of the small workshop and the autonomy and gratification of making a living with one's own hands.

After a brief initiation, workers began to react and rebel, casting back to the American Revolution for inspiration to declare their own independence from the brutal conditions and sameness of industrial work. Organizing into workers' associations, they demanded fair wages and hours and challenged unjust regulations. While not all Northern workers opposed slavery on moral grounds, their concern for its extension into the West bolstered the spirit of "free soil, free labor, and free men" that swept Abraham Lincoln and the Republican Party to power in 1860 and helped bring on the Civil War. From workers' ranks came the soldiers for that war, as well as the call for land that fostered the homestead movement.

In reaction to the economic injustice of the Gilded Age, workers helped transform the vistas of reform by bringing new concern for the underclass of urban poor. They inspired and guided Progressives to challenge the reigning ethos of laissez-faire, and to address the problems of crowded tenement housing, sweatshops, child labor. Where industry was cruel or uncomprehending of the human beings it employed, labor insisted on the ten- and eight-hour day, time for leisure and the enjoyment of life, and ultimately health benefits and insurance that would protect workers and their families; none of these achievements came easily, indeed all were resisted fiercely, yet in time they became standard features of American life.

Labor unions also exerted a civilizing influence on politics, government policy, and corporate behavior, by either forcing beneficial changes like regular factory inspections and fire laws, or inspiring accommodating developments such as the creation of Henry Ford's "Five Dollar Day" and the Wagner Act of 1935, which guaranteed workers the right of collective bargaining. Unions also helped assimilate new arrivals to America, serving as the social and political organizational apparatus of choice for waves of immigrants—Irish miners, German craftsmen, Russian and Italian garment workers—while left-leaning unionists such as the IWW and the Socialists fought for free speech and challenged the nation's sedition laws, conscription, and war-making itself.

Early on, however, American workers learned something unfortunate about their country: it did not care much for labor unions. In no other nation has organized capital so resisted organized labor, perhaps because in contrast to England and Europe, powerful American corporations developed before the emergence of strong centralized government or "overt class politics," as scholar Nelson Lichtenstein writes. By the time unions came to strength and legislatures took an interest in industry's affairs, the "most critical decisions about the direction of American economic development were in private hands."[14]

The courts also proved unfavorably disposed toward the idea of associations of ordinary people standing up against corporate might. The right to property, to own and conduct a competitive business—these were concepts held sacred—while the notion of an independent group of workers leveraging power, impacting economic and social policy, was not. "A union movement in America will always be a scandal," labor lawyer Thomas Geoghegan has said, for "the subversive thing about labor is not the strike, but the idea of solidarity."[15]

Employers leveled charges of foreign radicalism against labor with devastating effect. Business lobbyists such as the U.S. Chamber of Commerce and the National Association of Manufacturers learned to play on such fears, vilifying workers' groups by invoking cherished American ideals of individualism, personal freedom, and liberty. Workers *did* occasionally couch their unhappiness in revolutionary terms. But there was a painful irony to the fact that the labor movement was regularly tarred as an antisocial conspiracy when it was the corporations, the railroads, and the government that most often acted in collusion, frequently with the aid of the courts, the police, and at times soldiers' bayonets.

Organized labor would sometimes prove its own worst enemy—excluding minority workers with whom they might have formed useful coalitions, paying inadequate attention to the needs of workingwomen, aligning with the worst tendencies of cold war anti-Communism, succumbing to corruption and racketeering, and mimicking the arrogance of big business. The fundamental urge behind labor organizing, however, the idea that workers have a right to be equitably paid for the work they do, to be treated with dignity, and to believe their efforts might better their own prospects and the lives of those dear to them, has always been legitimate and just. Against the gathered power of moneyed interests, the state, the ideology of the free market, and often public opinion, they clung tenaciously to the faith that they deserved to be seen as human beings, not cogs or commodities, and that America would be the better for it if they were. In this they were certainly right.

For a century or more labor leaders like Eugene Debs, "Big" Bill Haywood, "Mother" Jones, Samuel Gompers, John L. Lewis, Sidney Hillman, and Walter Reuther were names respected in millions of American homes, their opinions in the newspaper or their words carried over the radio as important as those of leading politicians and even presidents. No less vital were the Haymarket martyrs and the Molly Maguires; Ira Steward, the so-called Eight-Hour Monomaniac; William Sylvis, America's original itinerant labor organizer; the "soldiers" of Coxey's Army; young Elizabeth Gurley Flynn, the Wobblies' "Red Flame," who once brought an entire city to a standstill from her jail cell; and of course the garment workers, autoworkers, steelworkers, and other rank and file who risked everything to strike and protest and give union demands authority.

These were in a very real sense the makers of our world. Yet most today are little known, if they are remembered at all. That is unfair to them, and to us. Organized labor today may have been reduced to a whisper of its former greatness, and no one can divine or guarantee its future, but we can know its past. It is this book's faith that there *is* power in a union, as the old labor song goes, and that in neglecting the valuable history of unions we risk losing something worthwhile in ourselves.

CHAPTER ONE

THE OPPRESSING
HAND OF AVARICE

I**T SEEMS FITTING THAT ONE OF THE FIRST** renowned activists in the titanic struggle between labor and capital on this continent, Sarah G. Bagley, was an unassuming young woman off the farm, initially no different from any of the thousands who emerged from rural New England in the 1820s and 1830s to become "operatives" in the textile mills of Lowell, Massachusetts, the nation's earliest industrial city. This original population of American factory workers was, for a generation, the pride of the youthful United States, and Lowell a model of enlightened industrialism that visitors were drawn from across the country and around the world to behold with their own eyes.

Bagley, like most of her peers, shared in the public's fascination; only after many years did she grow concerned about the system's injustices. In an era when few if any women spoke publicly she found her voice, first as a writer, then as a labor organizer, eventually leading the Lowell Female Labor Reform Association, which she helped create, in its historic fight for decent work conditions and a ten-hour day. At turns eloquent and caustic, her challenge to the status quo brought her into open conflict with Lowell's powerful mill and banking interests, the legislature of the state of Massachusetts, and even many of her cohorts and friends.

Born in Candia, New Hampshire, in 1806, where her parents, two brothers, and a sister farmed and operated a sawmill, Bagley worked as a schoolteacher before moving to Lowell in 1837. Beyond those few facts not much is known of her early life, although there are what may be intriguing glimpses into her background in two stories she wrote for the *Lowell Offering*, the independent literary journal published by women mill workers and celebrated here and in Europe as evidence of the superiority of America's factory culture. In one tale Bagley describes a young farm girl unhappy with her fate as a household domestic, who, smitten by "Lowell fever," dreams of being a worker in the booming mill city thirty miles distant. So poor she doesn't own a pair of shoes in which to travel, the little heroine nonetheless defies her cruel mistress and runs away. A kindly stagecoach driver takes pity on the barefoot child he encounters walking along the road, her few possessions in a knotted bundle, and, asking no fare, delivers her to Lowell. There, within days, she is reborn, with new acquaintances, a job in a mill, and even the beginnings of a modest bank account. In the second story, a Lowell mill hand named Catherine B., suffering from dire homesickness, receives the terrible news that her mother and father have both died. Stricken by grief but determined to save her younger brother and sister from poverty, she rededicates herself to the steady job she is fortunate to hold in a Lowell factory. For her brave display of "practical benevolence," Catherine is wooed for marriage by a desirable man.[1]

"Lowell fever"—the lure of the textile mills, of factory work at good wages, was remarked upon by many who flocked to the teeming little city. Not only did mill work pay better than the other jobs open to Yankee farm girls, chiefly those of teacher, nanny, or domestic, it offered escape from the other common alternative—grueling, unpaid labor on the family farm. The role of independent worker better suited the freeborn American women of Bagley's time. The first young people to come of age in the postrevolutionary era, they "expected to make something of them-selves and of life," Lucy Larcom, a Lowell operative who entered the mills at age eleven, later remembered.[2] Young women like Larcom and Bagley, no less than John Greenleaf Whittier, a Lowell resident, Henry W. Long-fellow, Nathaniel Hawthorne, and Ralph Waldo Emerson—who would write that "the children of New England between 1820 and 1840 were born with knives in their brains"—were swept up in the intellectual ferment, heightened spirituality, and openness to new ideas that characterized the nation in the age of Jackson.[3] These expectations led increasingly from the countryside to the civilization of the industrialized town.

For young women the initial benefits of the transition were abun-dant. The Lowell factory/boardinghouse system offered a safe living environment (a reassurance to their parents), a peek at the wider world, the chance to meet like-minded young people, as well as a sort of under-graduate education in its after-work classes, reading rooms, and occa-sional lyceum lectures. A girl from Maine reported that she was drawn to Lowell chiefly for access to the town's lending library, from which she was observed to withdraw as many as four novels per week. Some arrivals hailed from illustrious New England families. Harriet Curtis, editor of the *Lowell Offering*, traced her lineage to Miles Standish; Harriet Robinson's great-grandfather had sold Thomas Brattle the land on which much of Harvard College stood; Harriet Farley was descended from a long line of famous New England clerics, including the eccentric Joseph "Hand-kerchief" Moody, whose practice of hiding his face behind a black veil inspired a Nathaniel Hawthorne short story. Curtis, even before arriving at Lowell, had made her reputation as the author of a popular novel, *Kate in Search of a Husband*, although, as an historian notes, "the earnings of a mill operative . . . were larger and more dependable than any she could expect from the writing of fiction."[4]

Bagley mentions these advantages and more in "The Pleasures of Factory Life," published in the *Offering* in 1840. She writes of the mill girls' wages assisting distant relatives, the broadening experience of meeting women from other states and towns, and exposure through the lyceum lectures to the likes of Emerson and John Quincy Adams. But it was the busy factories, the enormous workrooms of looms and spindles synchronized as one giant, interlocking mechanism, that most impressed her. "In the mill we see displays of the wonderful power of the mind," she wrote. "Who can closely examine all the movements of the complicated, curious machinery, and not be led to the reflection, that the mind is boundless, and is destined to rise higher and still higher; and that it can accomplish almost anything on which it fixes its attention!"[5]

T HOMAS JEFFERSON WOULD HAVE LIKED Lowell. The humming mill town that grew up at the confluence of the Concord and Merrimack rivers, with its systematized production methods and lending libraries, might have struck the Sage of Monticello as an acceptable solution to his concerns about the development of manufacturing in America. He had prized the ideal of the United States as a pastoral world, its citizens enriched by their closeness to the soil, free of the drudgery and regimentation of industry. "Those who labor in the earth are the chosen people of God if ever he had a chosen people, whose breasts he has made his peculiar deposit for substantial and genuine virtue," he had written in *Notes on the State of Virginia*, published in 1787. "While we have land to labor . . . let us never wish to see our citizens occupied at a workbench, or twirling a distaff."[6]

His vision of America as a perpetual garden was not far-fetched in the 1780s, for nine of ten Americans still lived on farms, land was available and affordable, and to the west of the Colonies lay vast unsettled territory. Large-scale manufacturing, he believed, might best remain in Europe, as the cost of importing factory goods would be worth the benefit of preserving the American landscape, its people and government, from the baleful influences of industrial development already seen in British manufacturing cities. An immigrant who crossed the ocean hoping to make his mark in industry would quickly transfer his ambition to farming once he saw firsthand the benefits of such an independent calling.[7]

Jefferson, however, was also known for his interest in anthropology, science, and mechanical innovation. To love America as he did was to love its clockmakers, gunsmiths, shed-bound dreamers of a thousand tinkered mechanical schemes, as well as its "natural philosophers," men like John and William Bartram of Philadelphia, who traipsed the Appalachians for plant specimens and Indian relics. As president, Jefferson filled the East Room of the Executive Mansion with mastodon bones collected at Big Salt Lick on the Ohio River. He appreciated, too, the ingenious homespun textile crafts of diligent American women.

These fabrics were also favored by George Washington, who spun cotton himself at his home at Mount Vernon and who disparaged the wearing of imported fabrics by Americans as a symbol of continuing reliance on Great Britain. "I hope it will not be a great while before it will be unfashionable for a gentleman to appear in any other dress (except homespun)," remarked the first president. "Indeed, we have already been too long subject to British prejudices. I use no porter or cheese in my family, but such as is made in America."[8]

Gradually Jefferson accepted that his belief in a "permanently undeveloped, rural America" was more a cherished ideal than an actual program for the country's future; by 1789 he was, in a letter to a friend, describing Virginia as a likely site for the development of textile mills.[9] Manufacturing in the Colonies had been suppressed during the decades of British authority, including such edicts of Parliament as the Hat Act of 1732, intended to keep Americans from exploiting the New World's ample supply of beaver pelts, and the Iron Act of 1750, meant to keep the Colonies reliant on imports.[10] Reaction to such arbitrary laws and to British rule in general had inspired self-recognition on the part of American workers as well as the first organized efforts to use consumer habits to thwart English profits. It was in the period of resentment over the Stamp Act in the 1760s that artisans and craftsmen began calling themselves "Mechanicks," coinciding with their growing presence as a political force. In the 1770s appeared the first "Buy American" campaign, as from Boston to Charleston the cry arose to eschew the purchase of British-made objects and sell and buy only indigenous manufactures.

The Revolution and then the War of 1812 revealed starkly America's lack of industrial self-reliance. "To be independent for the comforts of life we must fabricate them ourselves," Jefferson was writing by 1816. "He, therefore, who is now against domestic manufacture, must be for reducing us either to dependence on that foreign nation, or to be clothed in skins, and to live like wild beasts in dens and caverns. I am proud to say I am not one of these. Experience has taught me that manufactures are now as necessary to our independence as to our comfort."[11]

One of the more prolific early boosters of American industry was Tench Coxe, a Philadelphia merchant, former delegate to the Continental Congress, and leading spokesman for the Pennsylvania Society for the Encouragement of Manufactures and the Useful Arts, a group whose founders had included Benjamin Franklin. Although not a member of the Constitutional Convention that gathered in Philadelphia in 1787, he shared with its members copies of his recent speeches and writings urging commerce, manufacturing, and "every measure that will give to our newborn states the strength of manhood."[12] Coxe appreciated, as did Jefferson, the fruitfulness of the American countryside, but saw in it not a nation of small farmers; instead he perceived its limitless natural resources, its mighty rivers turning machines and powering industry. Workers at times hardly seemed to figure in Coxe's vision, so substantial was the earth's raw power. "Horses, and the potent elements of fire and water, aided by the faculties of the human mind," he wrote, "are to be, in many instances, our daily laborers."[13] Manufacturing, he enthused, would be a comprehensive economic, social, and moral force able to:

Consume our native productions . . . teach us to explore the fossil and vegetable kingdoms . . . accelerate the improvement of our internal navigation and bring into action the dormant powers of nature and the elements . . . it will [restore] frugality and industry, those potent antidotes to the vices of mankind; and will give us real independence by rescuing us from the tyranny of foreign fashions and the destructive torrent of luxury.[14]

As evidence that Americans could distinguish themselves as world-class innovators, he spoke of Franklin's discoveries in electricity and of David Rittenhouse's orrery, a clocklike marvel that showed the workings of the solar system. Addressing the concern that burgeoning American industry would attract an unpropertied class of workers from across the Atlantic, Coxe reminded the Constitutional Convention that the United States had, if anything, too few people residing in its remote interior. The sprouting of industry, joined with the considerable appeal of a new and virtuous nation already known as an "asylum for mankind," would lure not only workers but also skilled technicians, who would bring with them knowledge of ever more advanced forms of technology. To facilitate this, he proposed that Congress make available quality lands to be given as rewards to foreigners who brought valuable manufacturing concepts to American shores.[15]

Much as the delegates hoped to produce a Constitution that improved upon Old World methods of government, Coxe insisted, so would the American spirit, applied to manufacturing, remake the habits of industry and labor. This appealing idea—that the purity of America, its virtuous and revolutionary outlook, would democratize and morally sanitize its factory system—resonated deeply within the young nation, and became a guiding first principle of early American industrialization.[16]

Coxe found an important ally for his ideas in Alexander Hamilton, who in 1791 as secretary of the Treasury submitted to his government the influential treatise *Report on the Subject of Manufactures*. Hamilton echoed Coxe's view that American industry would be exceptional for being shaped by American ideals, and that both industry and agriculture would thrive as progress in one sphere encouraged productivity in the other. Men would surely leave farming to work in factories, Hamilton conceded, but the activity of the factories would cause more farms to be tilled, and as workers and tillers of the soil came to share in the wealth produced, America herself would become a greater power, the interdependence among its citizens helping to stabilize the country and enable its self-sufficiency. "The extreme embarrassments of the United States during the [Revolutionary War], from an incapacity of supplying them-selves, are still matter of keen recollection," Hamilton wrote. "A future war might be expected again to exemplify the mischiefs and dangers of [that] situation . . . unless changed by timely and vigorous exertions. To effect this change as fast as shall be prudent, merits all the attention and all the zeal of our public councils." Hamilton urged his countrymen that indus-trialization was "the next great work to be accomplished."[17]

So it was that among optimistic men of government, of business, shipping, and manufacture, there emerged a compelling faith that the new nation might write its own destiny in the industrial realm as assur-edly as it had written its own founding documents. But could such a thing as a humane factory system exist? And how would machines, entire rooms of machines, in all their deafening, repetitive authority, impact the lives of the Americans who tended them?

T HE ANSWERS LAY WITH TWO EMERGING FORCES—the bankers, businessmen, and visionaries, most scions of old Boston families, who built the new industrial city of Lowell, and the young women like Sarah Bagley who responded to the tocsin of this New Age. Francis Cabot Lowell was a Harvard graduate and an importer of British goods whose business had been interrupted by the Napoleonic Wars and the War of 1812. On a visit to England in 1810, he had toured the textile mills of Man-chester. Industrial espionage on the part of would-be American entre-preneurs was not uncommon, indeed it was encouraged by "friends of manufacturing" groups in the United States and the luggage of visitors was often searched for drawings and blueprints before they were permit-ted to embark on their return voyage. Lowell, according to legend, man-aged to assign to memory the workings of the power looms he witnessed in operation at the Manchester mills.[18]

Back in Boston in 1812, he joined his brother-in-law, banker and for-mer seaman Patrick Tracy Jackson, known as "P.T.," and financier Nathan Appleton, a New Hampshire native and one-term United States congress-man, to form the Boston Manufacturing Company; by 1814, with the help of mechanic Paul Moody, they had opened the nation's first fully integrated textile mill on the Charles River at Waltham. All manufacturing processes—from bale to loom to fabric bolt—took place under one roof, with every mechanical device in the plant driven by water power.

Never in good health, Lowell died in 1817, and in 1821, with three mills at Waltham using the available water force, the remaining "Boston Associates" sought a larger site with river access. They found it at East Chelmsford, a village at the meeting of the Merrimack and Concord rivers, twenty-seven miles northwest of Boston. The site boasted the dynamic Merrimack Falls, which fell thirty-two feet over the course of a mile, as well as two useful canals, the modest Pawtucket Canal, and the larger Middlesex, dug in 1804 to link the East Chelmsford area with Boston and the first man-made waterway in the United States to carry both goods and people. The Merrimack and the Concord were meandering streams compared with the great inland seas of American destiny—the Hudson, the Mississippi, the Ohio—but it was in these New England backwaters that the country's industrial revolution began.[19]

To supervise construction of a mill at East Chelmsford, renamed Lowell by the partners, they chose Kirk Boott, an American engineer, surveyor, and Anglophile who had bought a commission in the British army and served in the Napoleonic Wars under the Duke of Wellington. Soon the Merrimack Valley rang with work sounds, as the Irish immigrant crews Boott assembled from Boston and marched out to Lowell dredged and widened the Middlesex Canal and constructed the first large mill, called the Merrimack. Boott was feared by the locals. "Though not an Englishman," recalled Harriet Robinson, "he had . . . imbibed the autocratic ideas of the mill owners of the mother country, and many stories were told of his tyranny. The boys were so afraid of him that they would not go near him willingly."[20] He had apparently bought neighboring farmlands for transformation into mill property without revealing the true nature of his interest, and the victimized East Chelmsford farmers who'd sold cheap thereafter nursed a warm hatred for him. The mill workers likewise were displeased with the 37½ cents he deducted from their pay packet each month to support an Episcopalian church he had built and insisted they attend, regardless of their faith.[21] The only recorded thwarting of his iron will came when he raised both the British and American flags on July Fourth, with the Stars and Stripes *beneath* the Union Jack. So great was the outcry, the mill owners commanded Boott to reverse the banners at once.[22]

The new industrial town grew swiftly. East Chelmsford had been little more than a hamlet in 1820, with two hundred residents; by 1836 the city of Lowell boasted a population of eighteen thousand and was on its way to becoming the largest manufacturing center in the United States. In the shadows of the Merrimack Mill soon rose nine other mill complexes, including the Hamilton, the Appleton, the Lowell, the Middlesex, the Tremont, the Boott, and the Massachusetts. Citywide, about ten thousand young men and women were employed, sequestered in no fewer than 550 local boardinghouses, constituting an industrial workforce unprecedented in America.[23]

As historian Thomas Dublin reports of one of the large Lowell mills, about 95 percent of the workers were native-born; and as many as 75 percent were women between the ages of fifteen and thirty. Men tended to be supervisors or had skilled jobs, while women worked the looms and other machines, or toiled in the carding room. Workrooms typically had two male supervisors, eighty women workers, and two children who served as helpers.[24] The entry point for the least experienced girls was the carding room, where the cotton was "roved," turning it into a thick strand that was wound around wooden cylinders. In the next chamber, the spinning room, a worker spun the roving into warp, a workable thread ready for the looms. The material was then further cleaned and refined before entering the weaving room, where the thread was made into cloth. In the final stage the finished cloth was trimmed, perhaps printed, then baled and made ready for shipment.[25] By the 1840s Lowell was producing tens of millions of yards of cloth annually and was the nation's undisputed capital of textile manufacture, while the Boston Manufacturing Company made a small fortune selling the patent rights to the loom and machine processes it used.

Lowell's rapid growth and output were remarkable, but equally notable was the company's determination—in keeping with the vows made in
the era of Tench Coxe and Alexander Hamilton—to limit the nefarious
effects of industrial labor on workers. "God forbid that there ever may
arise a counterpart of Manchester in the New World!" an American who
had returned from that bleak, crowded English industrial city had written:[26] Hamilton had suggested as early as 1791 that this might be assured by
enlisting as laborers the women and girls who were not otherwise engaged
in any but home crafts, and whose ability for the first time to earn a salary
would be welcomed by their families. "The husbandman . . . experiences
a new source of profit and support from the increased industry of his wife
and daughters," Hamilton advised. "In general, women and children are
rendered more useful, and the latter more early useful, by manufacturing
establishments, than they would otherwise be."[27]

Women mill workers received an average of between $2.25 and $4.00
per week, as compared to the men, who got $4.00 to $12.00, with the mills
deducting $1.25 per week from all for room and board. This left some
female workers clearing about a dollar a week, or less than two cents an
hour for seventy-two hours of labor, but even this represented a substantial leap in women's earning power in rural areas. "Since I have wrote
you," as one mill hand informed her sister, "another pay day has come
around. I earned 14 dollars and a half, nine and a half dollars beside my
board. The folks think I get along just first-rate, they say. I like it well as
ever and Sarah don't I feel independent of everyone! The thought that I
am living on no one is a happy one indeed to me."[28]

U NLIKE MILLS THAT COMPENSATED workers in scrip redeemable
only at a company store, the Boston Associates paid cash wages,
giving girls off the farm the first real spending money they'd ever had.
Most of the young women spent a portion of this initial income in the
dry goods stores and dress shops of Lowell, making themselves over from
bumpkins into fashionable belles, a transformation much commented
upon by visiting dignitaries. "After the first pay-day came," recalled Robinson, "and they felt the jingle of silver in their pockets . . . their bowed

heads were lifted, their necks seemed braced with steel, they looked you in the face, sang blithely among their looms or frames, and walked with elastic step to and from their work." Having come to Lowell in homespun, possibly barefoot, speaking queer rural dialects and introducing themselves as "Samantha, Triphena, Plumy, Kezia, Aseneth, Elgardy, Leafy, Ruhamah, Almaretta, Sarpeta, and Florilla," some switched to more citified names like Jane or Susan. They purchased new bonnets (known as "scooters"), began applying rouge to their faces, and even adopted a more urban style of speech. A few were emboldened to buy company stock.[29]

Nathan Appleton of the Boston Associates is credited with drafting Lowell's policy of paternalistic concern and humane treatment for workers. The good motives of Appleton and the other managers toward the girls were genuine, although it was apparent that maintaining a workers' society free of squalor was also sound business policy. Conveniently, the farm girls of New England came to the mills already inured to long hours of toil, and having been trained from the cradle to spin and weave, most were to some degree conversant with the techniques of textile manufacture.[30] The bosses also lived up to their commitment to safeguard the young women's moral life, controlling the boardinghouses where carefully screened managers, "mature Christian women," served as surrogate parents to homesick mill girls. The houses were often crowded, with women sleeping six or eight in a room and often three in a bed, but workers could select the house where they would live and thus house managers' livelihoods were reliant on their maintaining a quality environment. Some houses had fancy parlors, well-stocked bookcases, and other special amenities; all provided substantial meals of biscuits, potatoes, puddings, and, as one impressed English visitor, the novelist Anthony Trollope, recorded, "hot meat."[31] Strict rules monitored the women's social lives, while "the habit of profanity and Sabbath breaking" were strongly discouraged.[32]

The women were, by most reports, adamant themselves about maintaining their reputations, for in an age when the question of how an independent young woman would support herself led easily to speculation of sexual compromise, there was distinct pride in a pay envelope gained through honest labor. The female editors of the *Lowell Offering* made quick work of the Boston cleric Orestes Brownson when, despite his other good words and works on behalf of labor, he recklessly suggested that life in a factory demeaned the virtue of young women.[33] The mill workers knew better. Their character remained flawless at Lowell, nurtured by "a moral atmosphere as clear and bracing as that of the mountains from whose breezy slopes" they had come.[34]

I T DID NOT TAKE LONG for the curious world to ride a Middlesex Canal boat up from Boston to see the "Lowell Miracle" for itself. One of the greatest successes of the mill operators was in selling the concept of Lowell and its mill girls. Images or silhouettes of tidy women at their looms often appeared on labels of Lowell cotton goods, and their reputation was widely promoted. So dynamic was the phenomenon that the young female operatives became themselves admired "products" of the Lowell system, returning home after a few years of fruitful work enriched monetarily, spiritually, and intellectually, and "daily carrying gladness to the firesides where [they] were reared," as Massachusetts congressman Edward Everett put it in a July Fourth oration at Lowell in 1830. Everett's speech was warm praise for Nathan Appleton and the other Boston Associates who had poured heart and muscle into Lowell's success. Responding to the anxieties of an earlier generation, and to Jefferson specifically, Everett recalled how "reflecting persons, on this side of the ocean, contemplated with uneasiness the introduction, into this country, of a system which had disclosed such hideous features in Europe; but it must be frankly owned that these apprehensions have proved wholly unfounded."[35]

One of the first visitors to Lowell was Basil Hall, a British naval officer, whose *Travels in North America in the Years 1827 and 1828* found the factories' "discipline, ventilation, and other arrangements . . . excellent," and the mill workers "healthy and cheerful." Awakened at dawn by the beckoning bells of the mill, he glanced from his window to see the whole space between the factories and the village speckled over with girls, nicely dressed, and glittering with bright shawls and showy-colored gowns and gay bonnets, all streaming along to their business, with an air of lightness, and an elasticity of step, implying an obvious desire to get to their work.[36]

In June 1833 President Andrew Jackson arrived, walking among the beaming mill workers for almost a mile, congratulating them and inquiring their names. "The exhilarating experience of being made the target of thousands of dazzling smiles and arch glances shot out from under the green-fringed parasols moved the chivalrous old hero almost as much as the barrage of British bullets that shrilled past his head at the Battle of New Orleans," according to a contemporary account. "By the Eternal," Old Hickory was heard to exclaim after his perambulations around the town, "they are very pretty women!"[37]

Frontiersman and Tennessee congressman Davy Crockett also beat a path to Lowell to see for himself how "these Northerners could buy our cotton and carry it home, manufacture it, bring it back, and sell it half for nothing; and in the meantime, be well to live and make money besides." In his popular book, *Account of Col. Crockett's Tour to the North and Down East*, he reported,

the dinner-bells were ringing and the folks pouring out of the houses like bees out of gum. I looked at them as they passed, all well-dressed, lively and genteel in their appearance, indeed the girls looked as if they were coming from a quilting frolic. . . . I went in among the young girls, and talked with many of them. Not one expressed herself as tired of her employment, or oppressed with work; all talked well, and looked healthy.[38]

Such impressions ensured Lowell's reputation as a model for industrialization. But the opinion that they "all talked well, and looked healthy" represented only the beginning of the repute the mill girls of Lowell were to enjoy. Abel C. Thomas, a young Universalist minister who led an "improvement club," a reading and discussion circle for the women, had noticed that some hesitated to speak up in the club's meetings. He began providing a box into which they could anonymously place their stories, poems, and articles; the literary quality of some of these "offerings" led him to suggest they be published. In October 1840 he and the women launched *The Lowell Offering: A Repository of Original Articles, Written Exclusively by Females Actively Employed in the Mills.* Just as the improvement clubs were among the first women's literary gatherings in America, so the *Offering* was, in turn, the first magazine in America edited by women.[39] Recognizing the journal's significance, the mill workers reminded subscribers,

> Other nations can look upon the relics of a glory come and gone, upon their magnificent ruins. . . . We have other and better things. Let us look upon . . . our Lyceums, our Common Schools . . . the Periodical of Our Laboring Females; upon all that is indigenous to our Republic, and say, with the spirit of the Roman Cornelia, "*these, these are our jewels.*"[40]

No less an authority than the British writer Charles Dickens soon came to pass judgment. His visit to Lowell in 1842 was much anticipated, as he was not merely a famous personage but had spent part of his childhood working in a factory and had written of the corrosive effect of industrial society's evils on the young. In *American Notes*, the memoir Dickens wrote of his journey, he did not hesitate to criticize what he found in the United States; he was particularly disgusted by the institution of slavery, and reprinted numerous slave auction advertisements and notices about runaway slaves. Thus his wholehearted praise for Lowell—he crowed that the operatives had pianos in their boardinghouses, subscribed to circulating libraries, and had started their own literary magazine—was seen as hard-won approval from the toughest of critics. Dickens went so far as to insist that the *Lowell Offering* was as good as comparable English literary periodicals; he was no doubt being gracious, but his fellow British writer Harriet Martineau was sufficiently moved to see that the magazine was shown to Queen Victoria and to arrange for the publication of an English anthology of its contents, produced in 1844 under the title *Mind Among the Spindles*. In Paris the novelist George Sand performed a similar role, hailing the *Offering* as an example of how enlightened industrialism in the United States made possible intellectual endeavors among working-women. Perhaps it was Sand who sent a copy to the French Chamber of Deputies. There, one official was sufficiently impressed to assure a visiting American, "Sir, yours will be the greatest country in the world!"[41]

I F ANYTHING VOUCHED FOR the editorial independence of the *Lowell Offering*, it was the occasional appearance in its pages of bursts of worker unhappiness. The most common complaint had to do with the punishing hours of work in the mills, which allowed inadequate time for meals and rest. With no preexisting American industrial model available, management had fixed the workers' hours to resemble those associated with farm labor, basically dawn to dusk. In summer this could mean standing at a loom or carding machine twelve to fourteen hours per day, six days a week; in the winter for eleven hours a day. The midday dinner break was thirty minutes. "The time we are required to labor is altogether too long," explained an operative. "If anyone doubts it, let them come into our mills of a summer's day, at four or five o'clock in the afternoon, and see the drooping, weary persons moving about, as though their legs were hardly able to support their bodies."[42] Wrote "Ellen" in the *Offering*:

> I object to the constant hurry of everything. We cannot have
> time to eat, drink, or sleep; we have only thirty minutes, or
> at most three quarters of an hour, allowed us, to go from our
> work, partake of our food, and return to the noisy clatter of the
> machinery. Up before day, at the clang of the bell—and out of
> the mill by the clang of the bell—into the mill, and at work, in
> obedience to that ding-dong of a bell—just as though we were

living machines. I will give my notice tomorrow: go I will—I won't stay here and be a white slave.

With abolitionist fervor on the rise in New England by the early 1830s, the analogy between downtrodden mill girls and Southern Negro field hands was heard frequently. But in the case of "Ellen," her bitter outburst is answered by a trusted friend, who convinces her to stay in the mills by reminding her that the farmyard at home, with its animal smells, noise, and drudgery, also offers no picnic of a working life, and that a job in Lowell will at least promote her independence and develop her intellect.[43]

Of more serious consequence to the workers were company production innovations such as the "stretch-out," an increase in the number of machines for which a worker was responsible; the "speedup," foremen running the machines at a faster pace; and "the premium system," by which supervisors whose workers were most productive were rewarded with substantial cash awards. The unsurprising result of the premium system was a tyrannical attitude on the part of some floor-bosses, leading, according to worker Josephine Baker, to "many occurrences that send the warm blood mantling to the cheek when they must be borne in silence, and many harsh words and acts that are not called for."[44]

At the same time the workers' health often appeared at risk. The factories' poor ventilation, the cotton lint that floated in the air, stifling temperatures in summer, and the acrid smoke from whale-oil lamps in winter made breathing difficult. Some workers chewed tobacco snuff as a means of limiting the ill effects of the airborne lint, but many suffered from a persistent grippe the women called "mill fever."[45] It was never proven that the Lowell mills were unhealthy, nor was a comprehensive medical inquiry ever conducted. By and large the girls were youthful and robust enough to convince observers that "probably no town since the Amazons had presented so uniform a population of sturdy young women."[46] But as early as the 1830s a New York labor newspaper beseeched "the farmers of our country not to permit their daughters to go into the mills at all, in any place under the present regulations, if they value the life and health of their children,"[47] and there was no shortage of cautionary anecdotes. "Malvina was brot home dead from Manchester, N.H. where she had been at work at a factory," a farmer's wife wrote in 1851. "She was sick of Typhoid fever only eight days. Her sister Columbia has also been very sick at the same place. . . . Seven years ago Amanda the sister next older was bro't home a corpse from Lowell."[48]

There had been, even in the first cheery days of "the Lowell Miracle," sporadic acts of rebellion, usually by individual workers. Mill records indicate that as early as 1826 women were fired for "misconduct," "impudence to overseer," "circulating false stories," "levity," and complaining about their pay. One woman was terminated for "mutiny," while another was let go because she "was hysterical and the overseer was fearful she would get caught in the gearing." The name of one particularly uncooperative worker was appended, "Regularly discharged forever."[49]

The lack of any planned insurrection was likely due to the fact that the mill hands were willing, to an extent, to *own* the features of the Lowell experience, both good and bad, and to endure unwanted conditions as temporary imperfections, hardships to be borne. No doubt the employer's absolute power to blacklist workers from hire in any of the Lowell mills was also an influence, as was the fact that labor unions—"combinations" of workers making demands of employers—were still technically illegal. Then there was the workers' impermanence; many viewed the mill experience as an intense, short-term way to make money, and stayed only a year or two before returning to their families to go to school, take a teaching position, or to marry. The term used by the mill owners to refer to expressions of worker discontent was "New Jersey feelings," a reference to an outbreak of labor unrest at Paterson in 1828 and a way of suggesting such discord was alien to Lowell.

Thus it was more than a decade into the enterprise at Lowell before the first organized labor action struck in February 1834.[50] One of the triggering elements was an item in the *Lowell Journal* stating that, due to corporate financial setbacks, "many of the directors and stockholders of the Factories in this town, are upon the point of deciding to stop the mills," and warning portentously, "The effect upon thousands of our people will be indescribable. Laborers of every class, and artisans of every trade, must go, they know not whither, to seek in vain for subsistence, and all the inhabitants who depend upon them for support will be left destitute."[51] It soon was established the *Journal* had overstated the case, but there was some truth to the rumor: due to disappointing profits, it was made known, supervisors in Lowell would need to impose a 15 percent wage reduction. (This was substantially less than the 25 percent cut initially suggested by the mill owners in Boston, but it is not clear the employees knew this.)

When supervisor William Austin learned that women in a spinning room were holding a meeting about the anticipated pay cut, he went to investigate and was challenged by "a dictatress" who was in the midst of addressing her fellow workers. Finding the woman unruly and intractable, Austin offered her an honorable discharge from the mill, which she refused. He left the spinning room, but when, a bit later, he saw the same woman preaching again to her peers and noted that she "continually had a crowd around her," he fired her on the spot. She was soon sighted outside the mill, waving "her calash [bonnet] in the air as a signal to the others, who were watching from the windows, when 800 immediately 'struck,' and, exiting the building, assembled around her."[52] The crowd then marched off the mill property and paraded through the little industrial city, shouting to other mill workers looking down from their windows and beckoning them to join the exodus. "A procession was formed," according to the *Boston Transcript*, "and they marched about the town to the amusement of a mob of idlers and boys, and we are sorry to add not altogether to the credit of Yankee Girls." At the Lowell Common, "one of the leaders mounted a pump and made a flaming Mary Woolstonecroft [sic] speech on the rights of women and the inequities of 'monied aristocracy,' which produced a powerful effect on her auditors, as no one could recall a woman ever giving a public speech before in Lowell. The strikers determined 'to have their own way if they died for it.' "[53]

A great number of the women then headed for a local bank known to be used by the mill owners and withdrew all their savings. This would tide them over in case of a protracted strike and force the owners to replenish the bank's funds. They then issued a formal proclamation embracing "the spirit of our patriotic ancestors" and vowing that while "the oppressing hand of avarice would enslave us, as we are free, we would remain in possession of what kind Providence has bestowed upon us, and remain daughters of freemen still."[54] The women's claim on America's revolutionary heritage was characteristic of the period, as the events of 1776 were often then recalled as a struggle waged and won by workingmen—Emerson's "embattled farmers" at Concord Bridge, Franklin's "leather apron men," and independent artisans like silversmith Paul Revere. Urban workers' associations of the era regularly based their own founding documents on the Declaration of Independence. Moreover, the inland villages from which the Lowell girls hailed tended to be deeply Yankee places with an intrinsic sense of Americanism.

Accounts of the 1834 turnout note the mill owners' disappointment at the unfortunate display of worker resentment.[55] The happy balance of the Lowell industrial model hinged on the reliability that the young female workers of New England would not morph into the angry proletariat that troubled English mills, but would remain content, cosseted by the owners' patronage. Now, suddenly, they'd acted out, become ungrateful daughters. One mill agent, describing the turnout as an "amizonian display," informed a colleague, "This afternoon we have paid off several of these Amazons and presume that they will leave town on Monday." He bemoaned the fact that despite the caring guidance of the men who ran Lowell, "a spirit of evil omen . . . has prevailed" among the women and "overcome the judgment and discretion of too many."[56] A Lynn, Massachusetts, labor paper, *The Mechanic*, suggested the boldness of the demanding females resulted from a warping of gender traits, for which industry was responsible:

> From some cause or another, either from the despotism exercised over them, or from a too great familiarity with males . . . the

factory girls exchange some of their feminine qualities for the masculine—she becomes too *bold*. Her naturally fine tones of voice are from loud speaking made coarser. There are various causes which produce this *manly* appearance, and which spoils their manners.[57]

The Awl, a journal for shoemakers, was more sympathetic:

The story of her wrongs is full of bitterness, and the guilty wretch who caused them [the factory boss], trembles in his shoes lest she will expose him. Hitherto he has found her tame, submissive, at times almost crouching—but now she dares look him in the eye, and every such glance is a dagger to his soul.[58]

This was all a bit exaggerated. Women mill workers were not turned into unrecognizable hellcats by the ardor of mill work; in truth few dared challenge shop supervisors for fear of dismissal. And the mills' reaction to the women's outbursts, even to the 1834 turnout at Lowell, was in fact relatively muted. Perhaps concerned that the image of Lowell as a showcase of industrial progress be as little blemished by disruption of any kind, and sensing that the women's strike fervor would die out quickly given the lack of job alternatives and the fear of blacklisting, the owners neither sought repression by police or militia, nor invoked the courts to punish the turnout as a criminal conspiracy, as strikes were then often defined.

Indeed, despite its dramatic beginning and the women's defiant march to the village green, the 1834 strike proved of short duration. The mills had substantial inventory of finished cloth, and the workers lacked the will or organizational discipline to sustain a work stoppage that would threaten profits. There also was something of a leadership vacuum, since nothing prohibited the mills from sacking workers found to be difficult or outspoken; this proved effective at weeding out potential agitators. Notably absent, too, were the well-funded treasuries, the "strike funds" that would become crucial to the support of later unionization efforts.

In the end, management simply refused to reconsider the 15 percent pay cut, and within a few days most of the women had accepted the new lower wage and gone back to their looms.

That the tactics of organized labor resistance could be learned, however, became clear in 1836, when a second turnout at Lowell proved more successful. The mill owners had traditionally deducted $1.25 per week from their employees' wage packets to cover the cost of room and board, but recently the boardinghouse proprietors had cited rising expenses. When the mills announced their intention to take an additional 25 cents per week for this purpose from each paycheck, two thousand workers, a third of Lowell's female mill hands, rebelled. Declaring the new reduction tantamount to an unwarranted pay cut, fifteen hundred attended a spirited strike meeting. As in 1834, they linked their cause to their fathers' valor in the Revolution, vowing "never to wear the yoke which has been prepared for us,"[59] although now they had devised an actual strategy. Instead of a single large turnout, the women targeted one workroom at a time, rotating their absences and thus judiciously slowing the mill's output. And rather than linger in town and attempt to subsist without a paycheck, many simply returned to their family farms to await word of the mills' capitulation. The *Boston Transcript* mocked them as ingrates for having "kicked up this bobbery,"[60] but the mills, caught off guard by the women's actions and lacking the inventory that had protected them in 1834, eventually conceded and restored the 25 cents to the workers' pay.

THE VICTORY RESULTED FROM the women's own experience, but also from their awareness that the assertion of laborers' rights in the Merrimack Valley was of a piece with larger regional political and cultural movements. The 1830s were a time of dynamic change in New England, as railroads initiated a market revolution in the way goods were produced and transported, and the religious revival known as the Second Great Awakening promoted the democratizing idea that individuals were responsible for making moral choices. Transcendentalism, a philosophical and literary movement celebrating nature and emphasizing human intuition over reason, emanated from nearby Concord and a circle of influential writers, ministers, and reformers that included Emerson, Henry David Thoreau, Margaret Fuller, and Bronson Alcott. The elements of religious life, "the idea of God, of duty, of immortality," they believed, were "given outright in the nature and constitution of man, and do not have to be learned from any book or confirmed by any miracle."[61] Human beings possessed an "inborn capacity to perceive truth and right."[62]

A generation after the introduction of the Lowell experiment, many workers had come to believe less in the paternalistic care of the governing mill proprietors and to see their own plight increasingly in the context of societal injustice. They identified more readily with contemporary causes such as abolition, temperance, universal free education, the utopian Socialism of the French thinker Charles Fourier, and the stirrings of a nascent feminist movement. "The elements are truly in motion which are destined to work out a greater moral, physical and mental revolution than the world ever conceived of," predicted a Lowell labor journal in 1845.

> The strong band of Abolitionists . . . are making visible
> inroads upon the foul and heaven-cursed institution of
> black slavery. . . . Our Temperance reformers are on the
> alert . . . bringing joy and hope to the drunkard's once
> desolate home. . . . The Workingmen have put on the whole
> armour . . . combating the powers of white, as well as black
> slavery. . . . God speed these noble reforms which . . . are all
> acting in harmony, and will usher in a day of peaceful industry
> and happiness to our degenerate world.[63]

Slavery was a particularly discomforting, morally intrusive fact at Lowell, for mill workers, no less than the Boston Associates and the plantation owners of Virginia, Georgia, and the Carolinas, were links in a chain daily brightened and enriched by the South's slave economy. "The lords of the loom and the lords of the lash" was the memorable expression the Massachusetts abolitionist statesman Charles Sumner used to forcefully connect Lowell to the Southern disgrace.[64] The dilemma for the mill workers was that they insisted on comparing their lot to that of plantation slaves, even as they worked the very cotton the actual slaves had picked, although, according to worker Lucy Larcom, since the cloth produced at Lowell was worn by even "the most zealous antislavery agitators, the question was allowed to pass as one too complicated for us to decide."[65] Many of the mill workers felt that their low pay and status exonerated them from culpability, while, to most abolitionists, comparisons between Northern "wage slavery" and Southern chattel slavery were offensive. Unlike Negro bondsmen, after all, mill employees were citizens; if poorly paid or unfairly treated, they were free to leave their job. The mill owners themselves were not immune to feelings of complicity. Nathan Appleton as a young man had seen a slave auction in South Carolina and been sickened by it, but while continuing to regard slavery as "a tremendous evil," he rationalized that the question was one the South must address.[66]

Debate over the worker/slave analogy roiled the first several issues of William Lloyd Garrison's abolitionist weekly, the *Liberator*, which debuted in January 1831, a month before the founding in Boston of the New England Association of Farmers, Mechanics and Other Workingmen. Garrison brusquely minimized the possibility that wage workers' suffering was anywhere near on par with that of Southern slaves; labor's grievances were, if anything, exaggerated, even sensationalized. "An attempt has been made," he wrote,

> to enflame the minds of our working classes against the more opulent, and to persuade men that they are contemned and oppressed by a wealthy aristocracy. It is in the highest degree criminal . . . to exasperate our mechanics to deeds of violence or to array them under a party banner; for it is not true, that, at any time, they have been the objects of reproach. Labor is not dishonorable. The industrious artisan, in a government like ours, will always be held in better estimation than the wealthy idler.[67]

William West of the Boston workingmen's group took strong exception, replying to Garrison that there existed "a very intimate connection between the interests of the workingmen's party and your own. You are striving to excite the attention of your countrymen to the injustice of holding their fellow men in bondage and depriving them of the fruit of their toil. We are aiming at a similar object." West pointed out that, like slaves, working people were kept in a state of serfdom, ignorance, and dependence, and that capital did not truly share the bounty of production with the producers, but rather strove to obtain workers' labor at the cheapest possible rate. "The value and the price of labor have been rated not by the *worth of their product*, but by the *power* of those who command its proceeds, or for whom it is performed—*to obtain it*, and enjoy its benefits."[68]

Garrison responded that it was unjust to indict the wealthy as behaving cruelly toward labor, since it was wealth that created commercial enterprises, manufacturing, and employment. He wrote:

> There is, no doubt, an abuse of wealth, as well as of talent, office and emolument, but where is the evidence that our wealthy citizens, as a body, are hostile to the interests of the laboring classes? It is not found in their commercial enterprises, which whiten the ocean with canvas, and give employment to a useful and numerous class of men; it is not found in their manufacturing establishments, which multiply labor and cheapen the necessities of the poor. . . . It is a miserable characteristic of human nature to look with an envious eye upon those who are more fortunate in their pursuits, or more exalted in their station. . . . Perhaps it would be nearer to the truth to affirm that mechanics are more inimical to the success of each other, more unjust toward each other, than the rich toward them.[69]

West then asked Garrison why, if wealthy men harbored no hostility for the laborer and all men in a republican nation shared equal opportunity, it was the workingman who was found living in the poorest hovels or meanest dwellings—subsisting on the humblest fare—working in all weather, exposed to every evil—and enjoying but little leisure or opportunity for the cultivation of heart or intellect. Would this be so if they were equitably paid for their labor? Is it not obvious that the process[es] of mechanical and agricultural labor are altogether too low, when an idle libertine, who produces nothing, can command the proceeds of the labor all around him, and live at the cost which would support a hundred industrious working citizens and their useful families?[70]

West's argument had a distorted echo in the writings of Southern apologists like George Fitzhugh, who insisted in two popular books of the era that the paternalism of plantation slavery was superior to the supposedly enlightened attitudes of Northern mill owners, since Negro slaves were valued and looked after, while in the North's system of "wage slavery" the individual was left to struggle alone against uncaring corporations and the unknowable forces of economic fate.[71]

The discussion soon receded from the *Liberator*'s pages. But West's remarks would prove prescient. Labor advocates increasingly compared their fate to that of Southern chattel slaves as labor militancy hardened in the 1840s. "Much has been written and spoken in [the slave's] behalf," said the *Boston Bee* in 1844,

and the horrors of his situation have been depicted in a most glowing and heart-stirring manner. But where are the advocates of the oppressed among *us*—here at the north? In our eagerness to cast out the mote which is in our brother's eye, have we not overlooked the beam which is in our own? . . . Yes, reader, we have oppression in our very midst—a slavery even worse than that endured by the poor negro, in that it bears the *semblance* of freedom.[72]

Such opinions raised but did not answer a fundamental question: Who were the workers of America to be—members of a permanent proletariat, or free people earning their way to economic independence, property, and security? With many young men heading west to seek opportunity and land, and mill girls returning to their communities to marry and raise families, it was possible to maintain, up to a point, a vision of factory labor as a transitory stage rather than a life condition. But the ideal of the decent man or woman's incremental rise through honest toil to prosperity had begun to feel less assured; at the same time it was becoming harder to dismiss its opposite—a life of labor at killing hours for low pay—as the industrial worker's more or less fixed predicament. For many, the latter was a prospect too dire for citizens of a supposedly democratic republic to accept. "At one time, they tell us our free institutions are based upon the virtue and intelligence of the American people, and the influence of the mother form[s] and mould[s] the man," observed Sarah Bagley, "and [in] the next breath, that the way to make the mothers of the next generation virtuous, is to enclose them within the brick walls of a cotton mill from twelve and a half to thirteen and a half hours a day."[73]

While the analogy between Northern factory work and Southern plantation slavery was never entirely convincing, labor reformers might be forgiven for believing their problems to be at least equally systemic. What the women mill workers of Lowell had learned in the turnouts of 1834 and 1836 was that they were no longer the special daughters of New England serving in the nation's industrial showplace, but "had become full-fledged members of the working class."[74] Was not the factory's exploitation of poor workers a "peculiar institution" all its own?

Bagley's hardening views embodied this change, for her experience in the Lowell mills had by the mid-1840s brought her a long way from the rosy optimism of "The Pleasures of Factory Life." The *Voice of Industry*, a labor periodical she wrote for and later edited, openly mocked those visitors to Lowell who, after a cursory tour provided by management, compared the young women's lot favorably to that of industrial workers in England.

Bagley and her activist colleagues found the assessment maddeningly premature. While in England, warned the *Voice*, "the whole system of factory labor is unnatural, oppressive and unjust," in America it had "not yet reached its climax," but "that gloomy era approaches—in our manufacturing towns we see more than premonitions of its coming—when the pale sky of New England shall look down on men, women, and children ground to the very dust by feudal monopoly."[75]

MILL WORKERS WHO QUESTIONED the conditions of industrial labor could not help but be intrigued by the advent of rural workers' collectives. These idealistic efforts offered to resolve the issue of how a self-respecting individual might fit into industrialized society, as the self-supporting communities were removed from the rigors of the urban factory as well as the sin and hubbub of the outside world. By the early 1840s they were based increasingly on the theories of Charles Fourier, a Parisian businessman and minor bank official "appalled at the monotony and waste that a free-market economy engendered."[76] Publishing a series of innovative tracts that examined the deficiencies of capitalism, Fourier prescribed a distinct alternative—a collective model of societal organization that freed man from the wage system and allowed him to develop his true aptitude and interests. Fourier had died in 1837, but his ideas were avidly promoted in the United States by a well-to-do American, Arthur Brisbane, who had met Fourier in France and paid the master for tutorials on his unique philosophy.

Fourier envisioned rural agricultural and industrial units of approximately fifteen hundred individuals gathered in a collective he referred to as a "harmonic group" or *phalanstery*; the members would serve the larger entity according to one's personal aptitude or expertise, what Fourier termed one's *passion* or *association*; the adherents of such projects were known as *associationists*. The collectives were to be economically self-sustaining, offering humane conditions for members along with the uplifting benefits of education, community, and engagement with the arts. A Fourierist world of hundreds or thousands of *phalansteries*, it was believed, would ultimately render states and nations as well as wages obsolete. Fourier was meticulous in his planning, devising procedures and schedules for all aspects of life in his communities, even down to the marching order of barnyard animals.[77]

While history has generally cast a dubious eye over these undertakings, they proliferated throughout early and mid-nineteenth-century America—forty *phalanxes* with approximately eight thousand members came into existence during the 1840s—and were viewed seriously as potential alternatives to factory life. "We are a little wild here with numberless projects of social reform," Emerson wrote to Scottish historian and philosopher Thomas Carlyle in 1840. "Not a reading man but has a draft of a new community in his waistcoat pocket." It didn't harm their appeal that the communities harkened back to a familiar American ideal, the Jeffersonian faith in the virtues of agricultural endeavor and closeness to the land.

As Emerson's comment suggests, there was in America even prior to Brisbane's efforts on behalf of Fourierism already an active interest in self-sustaining communities set apart from the immoral, wasteful world. The goal, according to George Ripley, founder of Brook Farm, a 170-acre dairy farm near West Roxbury, Massachusetts, one of the best-known secular "Transcendentalist" collectives, was "to insure a more natural union between intellectual and manual labor [and] to guarantee the highest mental freedom by providing all with labor adapted to their tastes and talents, and securing to them the fruits of their industry." Begun in 1841, Brook Farm attracted such notable participants as Nathaniel Hawthorne, Charles Dana, and Orestes Brownson, as well as visitors like Margaret Fuller and Bronson Alcott. Members earned their keep by performing work in their chosen field of labor or through an investment in the farm. The collective operated a successful school attended by the children of many prominent liberal New Englanders (one student was Robert Gould Shaw, later to attain immortal glory leading the all-black 54th Massachusetts Infantry in the Civil War) and produced its own literary journal, *The Harbinger*. When Brook Farm struggled financially it reorganized in early 1844 as a Fourierist entity, bringing dozens of new membership applications, thanks to Brisbane's advocacy and his popular publication of *Social Destiny of Man*, an accessible account of Fourier's thought. Brisbane gained a critical ally in *New York Tribune* editor Horace Greeley, who beginning in 1842 gave Brisbane space for a front-page column in which Brisbane expounded on Fourier's ideas.[78]

Most Fourierist communities foundered within a few years, or at the longest a generation, the enterprises culturally out of sync with American notions of private property and individual autonomy. In addition, the romantic men and women such ventures tended to attract were often ill-suited for the daily rigors of industry or agriculture. Hawthorne, resident at Brook Farm, has a protagonist in his novel *The Blithedale Romance* sour on "the spiritualization of labor," and conclude, "The clods of earth, which we so constantly belabored and turned over, were never etherealized into thought. . . . Intellectual activity is incompatible with any large amount of bodily exercise. The yeoman and the scholar . . . are two distinct individuals, and can never be melted or melded into one substance." Amid mounting financial woes, tensions between the original and later-arriving participants, and a debate as to whether the enterprise should be Christian in orientation, the Brook Farm experiment flamed out quite literally in 1846 when the main communal structure burned to the ground.[79]

A brief flirtation of sorts did ensue between mill workers and collective farmers. The women of Lowell were interested in an alternative to wage labor, while the associationists were drawn to the workers' efforts to ameliorate inhumane mill conditions. Sarah Bagley immersed herself in the Lowell Union of Associationists, which advanced information about Fourier projects, and spoke on behalf of the group at a gathering in Boston in 1846. The Fourierists, however, were soon convinced their aims could never be conjoined with wage earners who passed their days within the confines of a traditional factory. The Lowell mill hands did respond to the spirit of the movement by joining local consumer cooperatives—at one point there were eight cooperative stores in the city with almost a thousand members—and associationist speakers were frequent visitors at the local lyceums, even as their theories over time seemed increasingly quaint. "We often heard the Brook Farm community talked of, and were curious about it," Lucy Larcom recalled, "as an experiment at air-castle building by intellectual people who had time to indulge their tastes." Of course, Lowell workers were hardly immune to the appeal of other faddish trends. They contemplated water cures and the dietary philosophy of the Connecticut vegetarian guru Dr. Sylvester Graham, father of "the Graham Cracker," and listened earnestly, like many in the Northeast, for spirit noises and rapping on tables.[80]

American workingmen and -women of the 1840s found a far more pragmatic and relatable cause in the crusade for land reform. One of its guides, George Henry Evans, former editor of the *Working Man's Advocate*, believed that "if man has any right on the earth, he has the right to land enough to raise a habitation on." Not only did Southern slaves deserve emancipation, he insisted; without land ownership neither would white laborers ever attain a respected place in society.[81] The land movement went through a brief Fourierist-like phase in which it demanded free land for the establishment of "rural republican townships," but it morphed eventually into a call by Evans, echoed by Greeley, for land out west as, among other things, a possible solution to the nation's labor troubles.

"An idealistic Yankee" who "had come to New York as a farm boy to enter the printing trade," Greeley "was a familiar figure at labor gatherings ... his round moon face, with its fringe of whiskers known to thousands of workers."[82] Along with his support of collectives and the people's right to free land, he supported the idea of legislatures setting limits on hours worked, and even the heretical notion that the government had a responsibility to provide people jobs.[83] Greeley disliked strikes or any expression of class conflict, insisting on the possibility that harmony could prevail between worker and employer, both sharing in the benefits of production and progress in a capitalist system.[84] The prospect of land ownership, he and Evans believed, would act as a kind of societal safety valve, drawing off surplus workers and keeping management honest by offering workers an alternative to factory life.

Greeley's editorial advocacy of the "free soil" homestead idea, joined with the efforts of Evans's National Reform Association and its explicit slogan, "Vote Yourself a Farm," led in 1844 to the introduction of several land-granting bills in Congress. This effort was particularly important for its thematic alliance with the antislavery cause, and because homesteading offered a distinct economic alternative to the spread of plantation slavery to the western territories, it became known as the "free soil" movement. Predictably, it was anathema to the Southern bloc in Congress, who stifled any possibility of the legislation's passage. "Free soil-ism," however, became the common plea of both antislavery forces and laborers seeking freedom from wage slavery, a useful political platform championing the freedom of social mobility and the dignity of labor as well as the restricting of slavery from the new western states. This broad political viability provided the genesis in 1848 for the Free Soil Party, whose members, upon the party's dissolution in 1854, joined Northern Whigs and antislavery Democrats to found the Republican Party.[85]

For many Americans, especially low-wage industrial workers, westward migration would remain something of a dream. The western wilderness was isolated and dangerous. Transporting one's family and worldly possessions hundreds of miles to begin a farming enterprise from scratch would be a struggle for even an experienced tiller of the soil, and most laboring poor lacked the know-how or capital to make the transition from eastern mill towns to a life clearing and working a plot of land in the west. But few were unaffected by the ideal the homestead concept represented.

I T HAD BEEN SHOWN at Lowell that Yankee farm girls and gentlemen capitalists could attain a balance of mutual regard and enrichment, a superior American version of industrialization. But the ardor of life in a textile mill, the two turnouts of the mid-1830s, and the financial pressures felt by the Boston Associates from a series of economic downturns gradually eroded that fragile ideal. Each year there were new tensions, new worker resentments. As yet there existed no respected structure for the hearing of grievances or constructive compromise between employees and management (what would later be known as collective bargaining). The courts held labor unions to be unlawful "combinations" or "conspiracies," and mill owners tended to dismiss work stoppages as illegitimate, while workers had no recourse against firings or the blacklist.

"We are destined to be a great manufacturing people," the Reverend Henry A. Miles reminded readers in *Lowell, As It Was, and As It Is*, written in 1845, one of the first retrospectives of the city. He cautioned, however, that "the influences that go forth from Lowell will go forth from many other manufacturing villages and cities. If these influences are pernicious, we have great calamity impending over us." Miles vowed that he would "prefer to have every factory destroyed" than lasting harm done to "our sons and daughters"—the working people of the country.[86]

Not that the working people were passive in this regard. Each season saw the founding of new groups and publications furthering the labor cause, and ever-larger yearly petitions to the Massachusetts state legislature demanding relief from the crushing work schedule in textile mills and other factories. The most prominent of these was the Ten-Hour movement. In 1835 the labor pamphleteer Seth Luther, who'd emerged from a carpenters' guild, published a seminal treatise, the "Ten-Hour Circular," which posited that men and women were citizens before they were workers, and that as citizens they had the right—a "natural right" akin to those enumerated in the Declaration of Independence—to do something *other* than work twelve- and fourteen-hour days.

The Ten-Hour cause was both popular and to a degree irrefutable, for it had the advantage of being primarily about time, not money. Its argument that providing workers more leisure time so that they might become literate and educated, in short, better citizens and workers, was compelling, and was not as easily brushed aside as a demand for higher wages. "What are we coming to?" asked a New Hampshire textile worker named Octavia. "Here am I, a healthy New England Girl, quite well-behaved, bestowing just half of all my hours including Sundays, upon a company, for less than two cents an hour, and out of the other half of my time, I am obliged to wash, mend, read, reflect, go to church, etc. I repeat it, what are we coming to?"[87] Workers recognized the irony that just as they had gained access to the benefits of the manufacturing economy through the wage system, they were denied the time and opportunity to buy the objects they produced. "We are free, but not free enough," was a Massachusetts shoemaker's lament. "We want the liberty of living."[88]

They were encouraged by the fact that shorter-hour measures had been enacted in the past. The ten-hour issue was at the heart of what some consider the first labor confrontation in U.S. history, when in June 1827 Philadelphia carpenters mounted an unsuccessful strike. The defeat prompted the carpenters to reach out for allies among the city's weavers, printers, and other journeymen, and to found in 1828 the nation's first urban labor federation, the Mechanics' Union of Trade Associations.[89] By 1835 the Philadelphia common council had established the ten-hour day for municipal workers, and in 1840 President Martin Van Buren issued an executive order making ten hours the standard for contract workers and employees of the federal government.

The plea for reasonable hours of work struck directly at the question of whether the wealth created by industry was truly to be shared, and revived the debate that had prevailed in the early years of the republic as to whether industrialism would be a more just and equitable affair in America than abroad. It was an issue that mattered greatly because workers increasingly recognized the industrial revolution's permanence, and, in seeking to define their place in it, resisted vehemently the possibility that they were to be mere cogs, a laboring peasantry, not citizens. "*We* have erected these cities and villages," a spokesman for a Boston area workingmen's committee told an 1840 labor rally:

> *Our* labor has digged the canals, and constructed the rail-
> ways. . . . *We* have built and manned the ships which navigate
> every ocean, and furnished the houses of the rich with all their

comforts and luxuries. Our labor has done it all, [yet] we toil on from morning to night, from one year's end to another, increasing our exertions with each year, and with each day, and still we are poor and dependent.[90]

Rallying around the ten-hour day, the New England labor movement grew in size and determination in the mid-1840s, with Sarah Bagley emerging as a leader in the fight. In December 1844 she and dozens of other women pressed into a Lowell lecture space appropriately named "Anti-Slavery Hall" to create the Lowell Female Labor Reform Association (LFLRA), a branch of the New England Workingmen's Association (NEWA), founded that same year by shorter-hour advocates. "When men begin to inquire why the Laborer does not hold that place in the social, moral and intellectual world, which a bountiful Creator designed him to occupy, the reason is obvious," insisted the women's constitution. "He is a slave to a false and debasing state of society. Our merciful Father in his infinite wisdom surely has not bestowed all his blessings, both mental and moral, on a few, on whom also he has showered all of pecuniary gifts. No! To us all has he given minds capable of eternal progression and improvement!"[91]

When workingmen gathered in Boston in June 1845, Bagley was there to speak for the daughters of New England, standing beneath a banner she had presented to the men that proclaimed UNION FOR POWER—POWER TO BLESS HUMANITY. "For the last half a century," she said, "it has been deemed a violation of woman's sphere to appear before the public as a speaker; but when our rights are trampled upon and we appeal in vain to legislators, what shall we do but appeal to the people?" Promising the cooperation of the female operatives of Lowell, she told the men, to warm applause, "may no differences ever arise to check the great work so well commenced."[92]

The women brought a distinctive touch to labor reform, capably staging social events and fund-raisers with speakers, bands, and singing groups, as well as hosting a lecture series that brought to Lowell notables, including Horace Greeley, William Lloyd Garrison, and the attorney Robert Rantoul Jr., hero of the Massachusetts legal case *Commonwealth v. Hunt*, which had challenged the courts' denial of the workers' right to form unions. Their entry into the Ten-Hour struggle, however, much as the Lowell turnouts of the 1830s, was viewed uncharitably by the mill owners; some were threatened with the blacklist. "What!" exclaimed Bagley,

> deprive us, after working thirteen hours, of the poor privilege
> of finding fault—of saying our lot is a hard one! Intentionally
> turn away a girl unjustly persecuted . . . for free expression
> of honest political opinions! We will make the name of him
> who dares the act stink with every wind, from all points of the
> compass . . . he shall be hissed in the streets, and in all the cities
> of this widespread republic; for our name is legion though our
> oppression is great.

Bagley's words appeared in the labor periodical the *Voice of Industry* (devoted to "the abolition of Mental, Moral, and Physical Servitude") because she'd fallen out with her former colleagues at the journal *Lowell Offering*, who had spurned as too radical articles Bagley had recently submitted. She took the rejection poorly, indicting the literary journal as willfully blind to the need for agitation. "Led on by the fatal error of neutrality, [it] has neglected the operative as a working being," Bagley wrote. "The very position of the *Offering* as a factory girls' magazine precludes the possibility of neutrality."[93]

The Ten-Hour movement's objective remained elusive, but the militancy stirred by the cause was about to claim its first victim. The *Lowell Offering* had come to represent, in Bagley's eyes, "the mincing prudery, the saccharine pieties, and the rest of the Victorian nonsense then considered suitable for female readers," according to Harriet Robinson.[94] While the *Offering* let itself be used as a prop so the owners "could convince the world that factory girls can write sentimental tales," alleged the *Voice*, the actual workers had "discovered an inherent evil in the present organized system of factory labor, which like gangrene is secretly eating away upon the physical and mental constitutions of a large portion of our people."[95]

The high point of the dispute came when Bagley lambasted the *Offering* before an audience of two thousand at an outdoor gathering at Woburn, Massachusetts, on July 4, 1845. After alluding to her years of service in the mills, Bagley accused the *Offering* and its editors of misrepresenting the truth about the hardship of the workers' lives and glossing over the mill owners' inhumanity. "Miss S.G. Bagley of Lowell, so spell-bound [the] large auditory . . . that the rustling of the leaves might be heard playing softly with the wind between the intervals of speech," noted one account. After vowing that she and other mill workers would intensify their fight for ten hours, Bagley "took her seat amidst the loud and unanimous huzzas of the deep-moved throng."[96] When the *Offering*'s editor, Harriet Farley, defended herself against Bagley's harangue in the pages of the *Lowell Courier*, Bagley denied she had meant to abuse Farley personally, but couldn't resist one pointed thrust, advising, "I have not the least objection to a controversy with Miss Farley, although she has literary talents to which I lay no claim; but I have facts, and that is better."[97]

Given the intense feeling growing in New England industry over workplace conditions and hours, Bagley made a strong argument that Lowell workers should no longer be represented by a "literary repository" that tended to "varnish over the evils, wrongs, and privations of factory life."[98] Badly stung and unable to shed the barbs launched into its flanks, the *Offering*, so recently the pride of the Lowell Miracle, struggled on briefly, then ceased publication. "Whatever the overblown claims of patrons or admirers," historian Benita Eisler points out, "the *Offering* itself [was], finally, as modest as its title suggests . . . ultimately it could not survive when its basic worldview had been shattered."[99]

SETH LUTHER HAD LEFT New England in 1817 to wander and work his way across the West and the South. The young pioneer, still in his early twenties, was deeply impressed by the rough-hewn egalitarianism of the frontier, where nature played no favorites and each man proved his worth. It was fifteen years before he returned to New England and he was aghast at what he found: the so-called civilized Northeast had succumbed to the evils and injustices of the industrial system.[100] His indignation can perhaps best be understood by considering the region's socioeconomy. Unlike the plantation South, the Northern United States historically had less amassed capital, and as a result the lines between social classes were not broadly demarcated. When, with industrialization, factory owners emerged as a powerful new force in society—Sarah Bagley called them "the mushroom aristocracy of New England"—the new hegemony felt wrong, un-American, especially to citizens like Luther, son of a Revolutionary War veteran.

Taking pen to paper, he produced a forcefully argued paper, *An Address to the Working Men of New England*, published in 1832, that averred that the rights of American workers had been secured "by the blood of our fathers, shed on our battlefield in the War of Revolution."[101] Luther drew inspiration from 1776, as did most of his working-class peers; but he went further, insisting that the Revolution would remain unfinished so long as a class of industrialists subjugated their fellow Americans. "The Workingmen bared their arms and bosoms in '76, and they are about to do it again in '36," he vowed.[102]

Equally offensive to Luther was the courts' continuing suppression of labor unions. Common law tradition dating back at least to the early eighteenth century perceived trade unionism as an illegal "combination," since workers leveraging their demands in an organized way, as in a strike, would unjustly impact commerce by threatening profits and hindering competition. Yet clearly the advent of large manufacturing concerns with workforces of several hundred men and women, as at Lowell, made recognition of workers' collectivization inevitable. "Men of property find no fault with combinations to extinguish fires and to protect their precious persons from danger," Luther pointed out. "But if poor men ask justice, it is a most horrible combination. The Declaration of Independence was the work of a combination, and was as hateful to the traitors and Tories of those days, as combinations among workingmen are now to the avaricious monopolist and purse-proud aristocrat."[103] He asserted that the very vehemence with which unions were attacked on grounds of conspiracy was sound argument for workers to seek sanctuary in a trade union.[104]

The issue had been at the center of a well-known case in Philadelphia in 1806, when eight boot-makers were indicted for having formed a combination and conspiracy. At trial, the prosecution asserted that the boot-makers belonged to an organization that conspired to demand higher wages and to injure their employer's business by withholding their labor; they also were accused of threatening other shoemakers who would fill their jobs and of agreeing among themselves not to work for any employer whose hiring or wage-paying practices violated their group's rules. The boot-makers were, in other words, behaving as would a labor union. In court, the defense showed that the wage increases demanded were not out of line with rates paid elsewhere, and that the boot-makers society had existed for fifteen years and was accepted by most employers as an association whose aim was the betterment of shoemakers' lives. It was also pointed out by the defense that the employers themselves had "conspired" by agreeing on mutual protection and the setting of prices. More technically, the defense noted that labor unions in England were prohibited by statute from demanding a wage higher than that fixed by law, while no such statutes existed in Pennsylvania. Wages were a matter between employer and worker.

The boot-makers failed to overcome the court's bias against labor combinations; unfortunately, the Philadelphia decision became the precedent in law for several decades, leading to as many as twenty indictments in the United States against similar groups of workers. The situation grew increasingly intolerable. In 1834, several thousand Boston journeymen and wage employees—masons, shipwrights, rope makers, printers, and bakers, among others—ignored prevailing judicial sentiment to create a citywide workers' trade union. After all, Frederick Robinson, a Massachusetts state legislator from Marblehead, asserted, "How can an unaided individual without wealth, without education, ignorant of the world, and even of the value of his own labor, who must command immediate employment or starve, enjoy this right as an individual right. If he enjoy it at all, the interests of others engaged in the same or other employments must secure it for him."[105]

A Boston court took up a reconsideration of the issue in 1842 in the case of *Commonwealth v. Hunt*, which like the earlier Philadelphia case involved boot-makers. Jeremiah Horne, a member of the Boston Society of Journeymen Bootmakers, had performed some extra work for his employer, Isaac Waite, without pay. This went against the Journeymen's rules and Horne was fined one dollar. When he refused to honor the fine, his fellow workers threatened to walk off the job unless Waite fired him. Waite, seeking to avoid trouble with his workers, offered to cover Horne's fine, but when Horne refused, Waite had no choice but to dismiss him to keep the peace with the Bootmakers. Horne denounced the society in rather explicit terms, so irritating the members, they insisted that for full reinstatement the deviant would have to pay $6 in addition to his fine as punishment for slandering the group. Horne then filed a complaint with the district attorney, who leveled a charge of criminal conspiracy against John Hunt, president of the Bootmakers.

The society's lawyer, Robert Rantoul Jr., who had once represented Gloucester in the state legislature, insisted the group had done nothing harmful or illegal, and vowed a spirited defense. Rantoul came from a family of reformers—his father had helped found Unitarianism in America and had started the nation's first Sunday school—and the son was a staunch believer in free education and workers' rights.[106] A few years earlier, when a conspiracy conviction against organized tailors in New York City led to a near riot and the burning of the deciding magistrate in effigy, the younger Rantoul had denounced publicly the lie that trade unions were conspiracies.[107]

Things at first did not auger well for Rantoul's arguments in *Commonwealth v. Hunt*. The initial case was presided over by Judge Peter O. Thacher, a jurist so unfriendly to labor he had once listed trade unions as societal evils along with "mobs, insurrections, and other civil commotions."[108] The trial began with employer Isaac Waite's testimony that the workmen's organization posed no harm, and thus hardly represented a criminal conspiracy; other witnesses representing local employers told the court the Society of Journeymen Bootmakers had, if anything, exerted a positive effect on employees, motivating better work habits and encouraging temperance. Thacher, however, instructed the jury that labor combinations would "convulse the social system to its center," making "a frightful despotism" of "this happy and free commonwealth."[109]

Rantoul begged the court to ignore the great volume of judicial anti-labor precedents as ill-adapted to the current times. The Bootmakers, he insisted, could hardly be defined as an illegal organization; only its acts could be so viewed if they were criminal in effect or intent. He argued that the states had not adopted English common law ("they were part of the English tyranny from which we fled"), and that, unlike the English legal precedents, there were no laws in America fixing wages that one could conspire to violate. He also, in a clever courtroom maneuver, managed to forbid any testimony from Jeremiah Horne on the basis that Horne was an avowed atheist. The strong-willed Thacher nonetheless pushed the jury toward a finding of guilty.[110]

Rantoul appealed the decision to the Massachusetts Supreme Court, where the case came before the influential Lemuel Shaw, a veteran jurist who, like Thacher, was known to be inimical to trade union combinations. Shaw had recently handed down a ruling that employers were not responsible for a worker's workplace injuries if it could be shown that another employee was partly at fault. Rantoul and the Bootmakers were not optimistic to go before Shaw, but to their surprise the judge showed considerable sympathy for Rantoul's arguments. He agreed that the English legal precedents regarding conspiracy were noncontrolling, and that in the new, more interconnected and competitive market ruled by free trade, both business and workers' associations would arise. While conceding that, in a free market, the actions of a labor union might have injurious effects, Shaw thought the means and objectives of the union were not themselves illegal. Workers, Shaw granted, had the right to organize and deny employers their labor, so long as they did not violate work contracts and went about their affairs peaceably. He went on to suggest that the pressures brought by labor unions amounted to a form of competition that likely benefited the public.[111] Just as a commercial enterprise would never be charged with conspiracy for selling a product more cheaply than another, and perhaps driving that competitor out of business, no labor union could be accused of ruining their employers through a legitimate pursuit of fair wages or better working conditions.

To the main point of whether a labor association was itself criminal, Shaw declared that in order to qualify as a conspiracy, a combination would either have to have as its goal "to accomplish some criminal or unlawful *purpose*, or to accomplish some purpose, not in itself criminal or unlawful, by criminal or unlawful *means*."[112] Thus, unless a trade union was formed with hostile or threatening intent, or turned to criminal methods, it could not be a conspiracy. In the case of Jeremiah Horne and the Society of Bootmakers, there was clearly nothing criminal about an organization seeking to exact fines from its members.

It seems likely that Shaw, by reputation suspicious of labor unions, was moved to change course not solely by Rantoul's words but by the clear perception that industrialism and the end of the old master-apprentice system had created a need for workers' organizations. The social and political clout of such entities was growing stronger. "Since it was obvious that open suppression of labor unions by the judiciary would not endure for long, and that the prestige of the judiciary would suffer in the eyes of organized labor," historian Elias Lieberman comments, "it was imperative to find a legal basis for tolerating the existence of labor unions."[113] Whatever the precise motivations, Judge Shaw chose to see the young country's diversity of opinions, even the push and pull between labor and capital, as healthy, not threatening.

For its legitimization of labor unions *Commonwealth v. Hunt* is sometimes termed the "Magna Carta of American trade-unionism."[114] The decision gave unions a legal leg on which to stand, surely, and was soon copied in other states, although it reserved the possibility that certain behaviors by unions could be judged criminal, thus leaving an opening for determined prosecutors.

I N SEPTEMBER 1845, Sarah Bagley and other women of the LFLRA took an important step, traveling from New England to attend a mass meeting of the Ten-Hour movement in Pittsburgh, where a labor newspaper described them as "white slaves of capital employed in cotton factories . . . pale poor looking creatures whose health has been undermined by the slavish toil that makes their employers wealthy."[115] The Ten-Hour cause had reached across trades as well as state and regional boundaries, and its emergence as a national labor campaign marked a notable advance. Among the strategies discussed at the gathering was a possible general strike for shorter hours and the reinvigoration of petition campaigns to state legislatures. The *Voice of Industry* announced soon after that "at Pittsburgh, Lowell, Manchester, and other places, the operatives are laying their plans, and if the Factory Lords will not voluntarily adopt the Ten-Hour System, a general turn-out will take place no later than the 4th of July, 1846." Workers, assured the *Voice*, were determined "that every factory shall rot down rather than that the long-hour system shall any longer be enforced."[116] Continuing the outreach they had begun by going to Pittsburgh, Bagley and some of her colleagues traveled to Manchester, New Hampshire, in December 1845 to lead a well-attended meeting at the town hall where more than a thousand workers, chiefly women, applauded the speeches of the Lowell committee and the organizational constitution Bagley presented. Within six months the Manchester Female Labor Reform Association boasted three hundred members.[117]

Meanwhile, in a coordinated effort, Bagley's group submitted a petition bearing several thousand names of Lowell operatives (it was reportedly 130 feet in length) to the Massachusetts state legislature, demanding the official mandate of a ten-hour day. Similar efforts came from Fall River, Andover, and other manufacturing towns. The Lowell petition complained of workers

toiling from thirteen to fourteen hours per day, confined in
unhealthy apartments, exposed to the poisonous contagion of air,

vegetable, animal, and mineral properties, debarred from proper
physical exercise, time for mental discipline, and mastication
cruelly limited; and thereby hastening us on through pain,
disease, and privation, down to a premature grave.

The mill owners countered that fewer hours worked would result in
lower wages paid, and argued further that a long day's work was actually
beneficial to workers; shorter hours, by making possible greater leisure time,
would leave them more susceptible to corrupting influences. "The morals
of the operatives will necessarily suffer, if longer absent from the whole-
some discipline of factory life," they warned, "leaving them thus to their
will and liberty, without a warrant that this time will be well employed."[118]

Bagley and her peers lampooned such objections, noting that where
the mills had added a quarter hour to the workers' mealtimes, lengthen-
ing them from thirty to forty-five minutes, the young women had been
observed to chew rather than swallow their food. "This system of placing
a quantity of food in the mouth and swallowing it almost without any
mastication whatever is one peculiar to the Working Classes of this country," deadpanned the *Voice*, "and we do believe it to be one of the principal
causes of the mortality existing among them." Some workers, it related,
had begun using the extra minutes after dining for other pursuits. "And
what horrible things do you suppose they were doing? Most of them were
reading books or newspapers, others were chatting with their friends or
greeting newcomers, and all seemed to be enjoying themselves rationally
and happily."[119] The longer lunch hour no doubt helped allay the fears
of Lowell clergyman Henry A. Miles, who had worried that the women
would grow so listless from lack of nourishment that they would suc-
cumb to a "morbid hankering" for candy.[120]

The petitions submitted for the ten-hour day in Massachusetts
proved historic, in that they led to the first legislative hearings ever conducted in America to examine the conditions of labor. Lowell's state representative, William Schouler, owner of the corporation-friendly *Lowell
Courier* and briefly a publisher of the *Lowell Offering*, led the investigating committee, which called upon six women and two men, including

Bagley, to testify in person. This may have been an attempt at intimidation, as it was still unusual for women to speak in public forums. Sarah and Angelina Grimké, white daughters of South Carolina who had toured New England in the 1830s in opposition to slavery, had stunned the public by doing so, and the "flaming Mary Woolstonecroft speech" delivered by a female mill hand from atop a water pump on the Lowell Common in 1834 was still recollected as something of a scandal. But such concerns did not deter Bagley and the others from testifying before the legislature's committee. They told of fourteen-hour workdays, beginning at 5 a.m. and extending to 7 p.m., with short breaks allowed for meals, 150 people made to work side by side in close quarters, and women standing on their feet all day. They spoke of prolonged exposure to the noxious atmosphere in the workrooms, the airborne cotton dust, the smoke from whale-oil lamps, and the fact that the windows were often nailed shut. The legislators of the investigating committee duly went to see the Lowell mills for themselves, interviewing owners' representatives and observing firsthand conditions in the workrooms.

The committee's conclusion was that Massachusetts factory workers enjoyed circumstances superior to those in Britain, where "the whole family go into the mills as soon as they have sufficient bodily strength to earn a penny [and] never come out until they die." By comparison, the Lowell girls "are farmers' daughters," well raised and educated New Englanders of strong constitution, who earn a few hundred dollars in the mills, then "depart for their homes, get married, settle down in life, and become the heads of families." The health of the operatives at Lowell, they decreed, was generally as good as elsewhere in the population. The committee's most sympathetic finding was an acknowledgment that abuses existed, but its report insisted that "the remedy is not with us." In any case, legislative intervention in the workplace was deemed inappropriate because resulting reforms would harm the ability of Massachusetts industrialists to compete with mills in other states not burdened with such mandates; similarly, the committee proclaimed that matters relating to hours and wages were not the state's business but private issues to be resolved between the workers and the company.[121]

Bagley and her cohorts interpreted the rebuff as an affront to female workers. They believed they had been patronized and ultimately refused by the legislature because women lacked the vote, and thus could have little impact on the elected officials who manned the committee. Their turnouts, aimed at affecting the mill owners economically, had taken them only so far; in the political sphere, as well, they now concluded, their lack of suffrage severely limited their impact. "Your actions are in perfect keeping with the ruling spirit of the times," a mill worker wrote with evident sarcasm to the legislature. "You are no doubt, true to the interests of wealth and monopoly. . . . Your sapient heads are very busy in forming laws to protect, uphold and upbuild the rich."[122] A *Voice* article noted that women workers had "at last learnt the lesson which a bitter experience teaches, that not to those who style themselves their 'natural protectors' are they to look for the needful help, but to the strong and resolute of their own sex."[123] Part of their ire turned on William Schouler, who they believed had helped torpedo their petition. The LFLRA targeted him for special retribution, caricaturing him as "the tool sent by the Lowell Corporations to the Massachusetts Legislature," and took credit soon after when Schouler lost his bid at reelection, thus "consigning him to the obscurity he so justly deserves."[124]

Further efforts to gain a statewide ten-hour law, including one Massachusetts petition bearing ten thousand names, persisted throughout the 1850s. But it proved difficult for the workers to maintain any leverage against the mill owners because European immigrants, who were far less likely to make demands or sign a petition, were increasingly being hired in the mills. While New Hampshire, Pennsylvania, Maine, and Connecticut did produce some version of a ten-hour law by the 1850s, and some manufacturers independently reduced hours, a law shortening the workday to ten hours was not enacted in Massachusetts until 1874.[125]

MILL WORK HAD BROUGHT American women out of the home and into the workplace, and their resolve to have a say in their treatment, in particular their advocacy for the ten-hour day, had now carried them into the public sphere. Increasingly their activism was concerned with issues other than fair wages and decent hours of work; articles about education, marriage, equal pay, and women's suffrage began to appear in the *Voice of Industry*. There was more to life than "a dress, a pudding, or a beau," Huldah Stone, secretary of the LFRA, asserted,[126] while her colleague, Mehitable Eastman, placed the advocacy for women's working rights in the context of broader social reform. "Never while we have hearts to feel and tongues to speak," she told the group,

> will we silently and passively witness so much that is opposed to justice and benevolence. Never, while a wretched being is crying to us for succor, from the alleys and dens of our cities—from our crammed manufactories, and workshops, from poverty-stricken garrets and cellars . . . Never shall we hold ourselves exempt from responsibility.

While the impetus for the historic founding of the American women's movement at Seneca Falls, New York, on July 19 and 20, 1848, came largely from individuals active in the abolition cause, the struggle of women workers was both an inspiration and a relevant part of the agenda; as Seneca Falls was a manufacturing town, young female workers from a local glove factory filled seats at the gathering. Organized by Elizabeth Cady Stanton, Jane Hunt, Lucretia Mott, and Mott's sister, Martha Coffin Wright, the meeting at the town's Wesleyan Chapel was hailed by Stanton as "the first organized protest against the injustice which has brooded for ages over the character and destiny of one-half the race,"[127] although in deference to the perceived impropriety of female-led public meetings, Mott's husband, James, was drafted to serve as chairperson.

Property rights for women; the right to make contracts, to bring lawsuits, and to testify in court; equality in marriage; the moral double standard affecting men and women; and improved access to education and employment were among the many challenges addressed in the discussions. Women's suffrage, though controversial, was also included. A hundred people—sixty-eight women and thirty-two men, including Frederick Douglass, who was vocal in supporting the plank for the women's vote—signed the convention's Declaration of Sentiments and Resolutions. Abolitionist periodicals, as well as Horace Greeley's *New York Tribune*, applauded the event, although many daily papers mocked the gathering as aggressive and improper, calling the participants "sour old maids," or worse.

The Seneca Falls convention laid an agenda for the women's rights movement in America. As that campaign developed throughout the 1850s and beyond the Civil War, and as more women left the home to toil for wages, the transformative experience of New England female textile workers would frequently be repeated, the travails of industry for women workers reinforcing the obvious link between the struggle for equality on the job and women's desire to confront gender inequity in its myriad forms.[128] An influential book by the reformer Caroline H. Dall, *Women's Right to Labor*, which appeared in 1860, advanced the idea that women's "economic emancipation" ultimately relied upon their access to paid work. "Women have, from the beginning, done the hardest and most unwholesome work of the world," Dall wrote; calling the notion that men must take care of women "an absurd fiction," and citing as an example of female fortitude the report that the previous winter several women had ice-skated on the Merrimack "from Lowell to Lawrence, with a head wind; and one or two made the ten miles in forty minutes."[129]

Having done much to propel women's issues out of the factory, Sarah Bagley began to extricate herself from the world of textile mills and labor politics by the late 1840s. In February 1846 she met Francis Smith, a representative of the telegraph service about to be introduced in Lowell. Impressed with her facile language skills and comfort with the new technology, Smith hired Bagley as the first female telegraph operator in America. On February 21, when service was initiated in Lowell, Bagley tapped out the town's first messages to the outside world. Disarming concerns that women couldn't be trusted to work in telegraph offices because they were unable to keep secrets, Bagley excelled in the position, and was soon relied upon to assist people in not only sending but writing their telegrams. Later she ran the telegraph office at Springfield, Massachusetts, although she left upon discovering that she was being paid two-thirds what her male predecessor had received. Relocating to Philadelphia, where she joined the staff of a Quaker home for prostitutes and disadvantaged women, she met and married James Durno, a manufacturer of herbal medicines. The pursuit of homeopathic cures and other alternatives was at the time a kind of reform campaign itself—a concerted departure from horrendous standard medical practices such as purging, blistering and bleeding, and the reliance on morphine and laudanum as anesthetics. In 1851 the couple became homeopathic physicians and promoters of alternative, nonobtrusive forms of healing, working out of their brownstone home in Brooklyn Heights, New York.[130]

Lowell's golden age also dwindled to an end, as a downturn in the national economy in the late 1850s brought a slowdown, as well as layoffs, to the mills. The fame of the Lowell girls and of Lowell as an industrial showplace continued to draw both American and foreign visitors, but by the time of the Civil War, "the town finally ceased to exercise its former charm on the curious."[131] Now when female mill workers went home to their farms and families, they and their younger sisters did not necessarily return, as textile jobs went increasingly to newly arrived immigrants from Ireland, Poland, and French Canada. Whereas in 1836 native New Englanders made up about 95 percent of the employees at one large Lowell mill, by 1860 the figure was less than 40 percent, and by 1900 only 8 percent of the Lowell workforce was nonimmigrant.[132] A tragic marker of the waning of New England's industrial innocence came on January 10, 1860, when a building collapse and fire at the Pemberton textile mill in nearby Lawrence, Massachusetts, killed eighty-eight workers and injured hundreds more. An investigation revealed that the Pemberton's owners had disregarded warnings about the mill's structural deficiencies.

The Lowell Miracle, which had turned New England's "pie-fed angels" into workers, then into labor activists and even proto-feminists, had provided, in ways the town's founders never dreamed of, a convincing demonstration of how American workers would respond to industrialization. In terms of actual union organizing, however, the results were germinal at best. Strikes took place, with little gain, the ten-hour petitions met limited success, and in the end no enduring trade unions were formed.[133] The experience of the immigrants who took over the looms of Lowell would differ greatly from that of their Yankee predecessors. Instead of being prominently displayed as examples of fair industry in a democratic republic and accorded a degree of respect as equals, the immigrants became an anonymous, interchangeable labor force, much like the Irishmen who'd been brought by Kirk Boott to build the mills in the 1820s and relegated to a ramshackle "paddy camp." It was this less trusting, less generous relationship between mill owners and workers that would characterize the nation's industrial labor relations in the coming years.

CHAPTER TWO

HELL WITH THE LID OFF

T HE LIVES OF THE SHOEMAKERS OF LYNN,
a Massachusetts seacoast town, differed markedly from those of the textile mill operatives of
nearby Lowell. Whereas in Lowell large-scale industry had arrived all at once in the 1820s, Lynn and the
surrounding towns of Marblehead and Salem had a
workshop tradition of shoemaking dating back to the
seventeenth century; Lynn was well known as a shoemaking capital by the time the first treadle sewing
machine appeared there in 1852. The mini-industrial
revolution set in motion by that technological event
produced in turn the first nationally watched labor
battle in U.S. history. Twenty thousand shoe workers
abandoned their workbenches for three months, the
largest and longest work stoppage in pre–Civil War
America, in what one headline termed the "Beginning
of Conflict Between Capital and Labor."[1]

Because shoemaking was originally a home-based
craft, it had been natural for the head of the household, in fulfilling his orders, to enlist family members
to assist; women's familiarity with garment-making
made them natural partners. The men, known as

"cordwainers" or "jours," short for "journeymen," cut the leather and cobbled the basic shoe, while the female outworkers, known as "stitchers" or "fancy stitchers," sewed the delicate leather "uppers." The women toiled in farm kitchens while the men and boys worked together in small outbuildings known as "ten-footers."

The sewing machine rudely disrupted this long-established system by greatly increasing the pace at which uppers could be sewn. Shoe factories furnished with rows of sewing machines opened in Lynn; uniform shoe sizes were introduced, as were shoe boxes to safeguard the product on its way to market. There had been centralized workshops before, known as *manufactories*, where the old traditions of apprentice, journeyman, and master still held sway; but the newer term "factory" implied something different, a place of workers and bosses, ordered by strict hours and oversight and the hum of machines. These "shoe mills" exercised the same effect on rural New England women as had the Lowell textile industry, drawing them to Lynn; as "machine girls" working the treadle devices, they earned substantially more than the women who stitched shoes at home. By 1860, only 25 percent of the shoe workers were Lynn natives, and many of the local journeymen and skilled home stitchers had been driven from the family hearth and backyard ten-footers to occupy factory benches in town. The transition was resisted, but local shoe production doubled as a result of the new technology.[2]

This transformation coincided with the advent of the railroad and the opening of new national markets for Lynn shoes, and brought dramatic social and economic changes to the town. At Lowell, the intent of the Boston Associates had been to safeguard manufacturing's reputation by shielding workers from its deleterious effects; in Lynn the emphasis was on meeting industrialization's challenges and ensuring needed levels of production with a strengthened communal sense of morality, diligence, and hard work.[3] The custom of shoe workers to enjoy daily portions of rum mixed with raisins and sugar, or "black strap," a concoction of rum and molasses, was done away with, as were the festivities that had traditionally marked the days upon which apprentices reached their majority and became journeymen. Lynn became one of the first communities in New England to enforce a total prohibition on liquor. Temperance was urged as a cure for malingering and other vices ranging from thievery to domestic abuse. New laws also went on the books prohibiting gambling, profanity, and swimming in the nude.

The impulse to rein in unproductive habits joined a heightened intolerance for the indolent and the poor. Families of modest means were no longer allowed to draw goods on credit, authorities enforced compulsory school attendance, and life in the almshouse became more unpleasant. Even the physical world constricted. Between 1830 and 1860 developers nibbled away at the public lands around Lynn, turning nearby sea reaches into a summer haven for the Boston gentry. Some of the areas overrun were beaches long favored for swimming and clam-hunting. To make matters worse, it was soon evident that the affluent newcomers had no wish to mingle with the town's residents, one estate owner going so far as to install a pack of vicious dogs in order to keep the locals away.[4]

In the pre-factory era a worker looked forward to his "competency," the amount of savings that would carry him into old age or disability. With the new system factory owners, not independent workers, controlled hours and wages as well as the availability of work, and a "competency" was no longer a sure thing; in its stead loomed the potential humiliation of living one's aged years as a pauper, supported by the church or public relief. Lynn shoemakers were displeased by this loss of egalitarian balance, angry that they, the actual producers of the town's wealth, were forced to see their share of the shoe business's material rewards diminish even as their futures grew more uncertain.

At stake was what economists call "the labor theory of value," the idea that capital is dependent upon labor, and would not be created at all without labor's exertions. Certainly enterprise played a role organizing the workplaces, offering jobs, and paying wages, but it was labor that made things and in so doing fulfilled human needs. This dynamic could only suffer as industry grew and came to employ hundreds rather than dozens of workers. At the same time, when craftsmen entered the mass production factory they forfeited their individuality as well as the creativity of self-directed work; their new jobs called on their muscle and brains but less often their skill or judgment. "The image of the artisan seemed to dissolve before their eyes," writes Alan Dawley, "and in its place they saw an image of the industrial worker taking shape."[5]

All of these tensions were in play during the 1850s as the expansion of shoe manufacturing built a sizable business concentration at Lynn. Toward decade's end, however, the nation entered a precipitous economic recession. When Lynn factories announced wage cuts, the shoemakers proposed instead a mutually governed work stoppage, in which the factories would contribute financially to the subsistence of idle employees while the businesses reconstituted their operations and sold off their sizable inventories. Owners backed away from any such pact, and instead began running their plants at reduced pay rates. Outraged workers saw an effort to degrade permanently the wages paid shoemakers in Lynn and declared a strike, demanding a standardized wage.[6]

On Washington's Birthday, February 22, 1860, the shoemakers marched in protest, holding aloft placards bearing images of the first president along with American flags and a banner that declared, OUR CAUSE IS JUST AND OUR UNION PERFECT. Arriving trains brought sympathetic workers from nearby towns, including a shoemaker from nearby Marblehead wearing a paper hat that read, "I HAVE STRUCK." He was immediately hoisted into a wheelbarrow, the crowd pushing him along a sidewalk in imitation of a visiting dignitary.[7] As fire companies rang their bells, a sea of ten thousand people flowed through the streets to a nearby park, where the Lynn Cornet Band entertained between rallying speeches.

The next day was far less jubilant. The factories, it was said, were secretly sending shoes to market. A wagon driver from Marblehead suspected of hauling the contraband was roughly pulled from his rig, and cases of shoe stock were removed from another vehicle and strewn about. City Marshal Thomas Thurston had his hat knocked off and his coat torn while trying to restore order. Soon, a large crate was noticed at a loading dock by the train depot. "Shoes! Shoes!" the cry went up. A town constable who intervened was mobbed, knocked down, and dragged along the ground; he escaped only by drawing his gun.[8] Lynn took pride in being an enlightened New England town, with several newspapers, bookstores, lyceums, and a record of staunch abolitionism (citizens had once come to Frederick Douglass's rescue when a local railroad tried to evict him from a first-class train car). Thus the violence connected with the strike was deeply troubling.

The following day Lynn sustained an even worse insult, when a squad of thirty Boston policemen arrived by train. "They were a fine looking set of men," the editor of the *Bay State* wrote. "But good citizens, it was outrageous to bring the Boston police here."[9] The paper recorded that "groans and hisses" greeted the officers as they marched, followed by a crowd that chanted in derision, "Brass Buttons! Brass Buttons!" When the police reached the corner of Washington Street and Railroad Avenue, a stone was thrown that struck one of them, an Officer Fogg, on the head, sparking a melee in which several people were bludgeoned by police clubs or trampled by their own fleeing comrades.[10]

The next day the Boston police were withdrawn, to widespread relief, and the remaining strike events were spirited if far less menacing. Almost every day there were rallies and speeches. Town historian Alonzo Lewis contributed his "Cordwainers' Song," written expressly for the strike:

> *The workman is worthy of his hire,*
> *No tyrant shall hold us in thrall;*
> *They may order their soldiers to fire,*
> *But we'll stick to the hammer and awl.*
> *Yes, we'll stick to the hammer and awl.*[11]

One grand march in Lynn—described by the *Bay State* as "an all-pervading, animated wave of humanity"—featured twenty-six American flags and boisterous delegations from nearby South Danvers, Saugus, South Reading, Stoneham, Beverly, and Salem.[12] When not parading, the strikers kept their morale up with potluck suppers, clambakes, and even a "candy party," to which each Lynn neighborhood brought its own kettle and distinctive sugary recipe. Three thousand men, women, and children, it was said, danced and ate "the lasses' candy," as the Lynn Cornet Band, who alone seemed to be enjoying full employment, "discoursed sweet music."[13]

But the lasses intended to do more than watch candy thicken in a pot. When the newly formed Lynn Mechanics Association convened in Lyceum Hall, founder and president Alonzo Draper requested the support of the female shoemakers. "Remember, ladies, especially you young and blooming ones," he said, "that if you want husbands, wages must go up, for no one can get married at present prices."[14] He was voicing the not-unfamiliar refrain that women's role in labor disputes was to help safeguard, by the withholding of their own labor, a decent wage for male workers. The women, particularly the factory workers, saw the situation differently. They *also* demanded a raise. Clara Brown, a twenty-one-year-old machine stitcher, advocated using the factory girls' numbers and strong bargaining position to break the exploitive practices of the factory owners. She astutely questioned the town's professed "industrial morality" of temperance and hard work, when the local capitalists were guilty of the far greater immorality of driving rates down, causing hardship for workers and their families. Brown said that very morning she had visited a friend's place of work where the going rate was 8 cents per pair of uppers. "Girls of Lynn! Girls of Lynn!" she cried. "Do you hear that and will you stand for it? Never, never, never! Strike then—strike at once; demand 8½ cents for your work when the binding isn't closed and you will get it. Don't let them make niggers of you!"

"Shame," someone said, "there are colored persons here."

"I meant Southern niggers," corrected Brown. "Keep still; don't work your machines; let them lie still till we get all we ask, and then go at it, as did our mothers in the Revolution."[15]

At a follow-up meeting of women and girls on February 28, President Draper repeated his suggestion that female factory hands wield their power on behalf of their husbands. A dispute ensued between the machine girls, who were younger women, often not native to Lynn, and the outworkers, many of whom were older residents. After several minutes Willard Oliver, the chair, demanded: "Ladies! Stop this wrangling. Do you care for your noble cause? Are you descendants of old Molly Stark or not? Did you ever hear of the Spirit of '76?" Hundred of voices assured him they had. Molly Stark, whose name was often invoked during the Lynn strike, was a regional heroine of the American Revolution whose fame rested chiefly on an utterance made by her husband, General John Stark, at the Battle of Bennington in August 1777. "There are your enemies, the Red Coats and the Tories," General Stark had urged his men. "They are ours, or this night Molly Stark sleeps a widow." The American forces had been victorious, and Molly Stark's name entered into legend.[16] "Well, then," said Draper, "do behave yourselves. There ain't nobody nowhere who will aid you if you don't show them that you're regular built Moll Starks over again."[17]

Draper, concerned that the demands by Clara Brown and the other factory girls would derail the men's strike, reconvened the women the following night. Mary Damon and Mrs. William Graham, home workers, insisted that backing the men should take precedence. Graham said 7 cents per pair of uppers was the best they could get, and that, in any case, talk of 9 cents was out of the question, while others worried that higher wages paid at the factory would bring an end to all piecework, or that manufacturers would simply take their businesses elsewhere. Brown accused her sisters of timidity; she was sure a higher wage was within reach. "Only the Lynn girls can bind shoes as they should be bound and the competition of the girls from out of town is no account," she said. Another young woman echoed Brown, urging the pieceworkers, "Don't be bluffed. We shall get our prices if we are not faint-hearted."[18]

By the time a fourth meeting of the women gathered on March 2, sentiment appeared to have turned against the factory girls and their demands; the Mechanics Association had worked with the women loyal to the home workers to submit a lower wage demand for female labor. The home stitchers were so confident of their strength that they even invited the hated reporter from the *New York Times*, who signed his pieces "HOWARD," to attend. HOWARD had made himself unwelcome in Lynn by writing that if the local women didn't settle with the factories soon, they'd be impoverished and forced into prostitution; as a result, he reported to his readers back in New York, clumps of mud were being thrown at him each time he ventured from his hotel. But before the March 2 gathering one of the home workers told him "they were going to have high old times, and if Clara B dared to open her head, she was to be kicked down [the] stairs."[19]

Clara Brown, however, continued to argue that the women had greater power over the local shoemaking establishment than they knew, and that if they would remain militant they could assert their will. She said she and other factory women would not support a lame bill of demands. "Where is the use of striking," she asked, "if you gain nothing by it? It has come to a pretty pass if the machine bosses of Lynn were to govern the girls as they chose. If Mr. Fred Ignalls—the meanest man in Lynn—can rule us as he pleases, then where is the use of the strike? His machines are worth nothing if he can't get his girls to work them; and if they only hold out, the list would have to be met by the bosses." There were cheers for Brown but also some booing. Mrs. Damon stood to remind the room that unity with the men's strike was a priority, words that enraged Brown, who leaped to her feet, declaring, "For God's sake, don't act like a pack of fools!" Her words were greeted by hisses. "Mr. Oliver," stated Brown, holding her ground, "I say if we are going to strike for anything, let's strike for something worth having."

But James Dillon, vice president of the Mechanics Association, then rose and appealed effectively to the conservative hearth-and-home contingent. "We rest on you; you, who suckle us in our infancy," he assured the women, "who court us in our prime, who succor, support, and comfort us in our old age and declining powers, we rest on you to help us here, now, at this time; give us, journeymen shoemakers, your encouragement and cooperation, and we'll go on, on, on even to Death's grim door."[20] Dillon's allusions ultimately trumped Brown's stridency and quieted her supporters, and approval was voted for the lower women's wage demands. "Come," said Oliver, urging the women to join a women's march on March 7, "come without your silks, your satins, or your furbelo riggin'; come in your modestest attire, and the great God above you will be on your side; your bosses will give you the rates, and your beaux will be pleased."[21]

On March 7, as many as eight hundred women trudged in falling snow through the city's main streets, bearing a banner that vowed, AMERICAN LADIES WILL NOT BE SLAVES: GIVE US A FAIR COMPENSATION AND WE WILL LABOUR CHEERFULLY. But another better reflected the spirit of the women's compromise, WEAK IN PHYSICAL STRENGTH BUT STRONG IN MORAL COURAGE, WE DARE TO BATTLE FOR THE RIGHT, SHOULDER TO SHOULDER WITH OUR FATHERS, HUSBANDS, AND BROTHERS.

The 1860 Lynn shoemaker strike against the authoritarian dictates of the factory system proved something of a last gasp. Technically it gained little in terms of better wages or working conditions. The manufacturers refused to sign any blanket agreement with the strikers, partly out of fear that if one factory signed others would not, although wages did soon increase. The manufacturers had benefited from the production slowdown created by the strike by selling off six hundred thousand pairs of shoes at a higher price than they would have ordinarily obtained, and the outbreak of the Civil War the following spring proved a boon to Lynn's recovery, as the federal government turned to the town to provide boots and other leather goods for the Union army.

As in the Ten-Hour movement and the earlier turnouts at Lowell, the Lynn shoemakers' strike of 1860 can be judged a success more for its display of worker militancy and the free public discussion of labor issues than for any specific results. "The experience left an indelible mark on folk memory," notes Dawley, "and for a generation it was recalled with the frequency and vividness people usually reserved for earthquakes and hurricanes."[22] Fifteen thousand male and two thousand female shoemakers had entered the fold of organized labor, and lasting connections had been made between workers of neighboring manufacturing towns.[23] Politically energized, the local jours and stitchers soon founded a workers' party that in fall 1860 elected a shoemaker to be the new mayor of Lynn. "The strike was a noble act on the part of the shoemakers," concluded the *Bay State*, "and will show to the world that they know their rights, whether they obtain them or not; they strike for a principle, as our revolutionary fathers did who struck for self-government."[24] Those storied ancestors would have likely been gratified by one banner held aloft by the Lynn workers: LET TYRANTS TREMBLE WHEN THE PEOPLE RISE!

O N MARCH 5, 1860, Republican presidential candidate Abraham Lincoln was campaigning in Hartford when a reporter asked his opinion of the shoemakers' strike then under way at Lynn. Lincoln's chief opponent, Democrat Stephen A. Douglas, had cited the Lynn turnout as an example of the potential disruption caused by free labor, but Lincoln scoffed at that view. "I am glad to see that a system of labor prevails in New England under which laborers can strike when they want to," he said, "where they are not obliged to labor whether you pay them or not. I like a system which lets a man quit when he wants to, and wish it might prevail everywhere."[25] Lincoln believed American workers deserved to participate fully in "the race of life," and that the country and its citizens would best grow and prosper in a free marketplace. Joined with the related ideas that land should be available to those who would till it, and that the western states and territories entering the Union be kept nonslave, the belief in "free labor, free soil, free men" helped that fall to secure Lincoln and the Republican Party the presidency.

With the firing on Fort Sumter in April 1861, Northern workingmen returned Lincoln's goodwill, some unions enlisting in their entirety so that members could fight shoulder to shoulder, much as they worked together in mine or mill. "This union stands adjourned until either the Union is safe or we are whipped," one labor leader told his followers. Partly due to the policy that allowed men of means to satisfy Northern conscription orders by purchasing the services of a replacement for $300, the foot soldiers in the resulting federal victory were to a large extent drawn from America's toiling class—immigrant Irish, Italians, and Jews from the North's teeming cities, German and Scandinavian farmers from the wheat belt, as well as African Americans, free blacks but mostly freed slaves, who filled soldiers' ranks in higher proportion to their overall population than any single group.

The Northern victory sealed at Appomattox four years later served as a powerful vindication of the right of place in American society of even the most humble worker and citizen. Although not every laborer had agreed with the abolitionists or approved of equal rights for the freed slaves, the war had given America's still-young industrial working class "a memorable vision of class struggle."[26] What had been secured for the wage earner, no less than the entrepreneur, was the dream of personal independence and the right to pursue property, mobility, and economic well-being.

The conflict had also spurred an unprecedented wave of industrialization in the North, the vast war-spending reinvigorating a national economy staggered by the recession of 1857. Large monopolies took shape in oil, steel, and sugar, as the economic doctrine of laissez-faire allowed a concentration of wealth and power the likes of which the country had never known. Congress actively supported big business—making huge land grants to railroads, raising tariffs on foreign goods, and authorizing employers to import immigrant laborers. In response there occurred in the months after the war a parallel expansion of workers' organizations, from fewer than one hundred in 1860 to nearly three hundred, corresponding with the explosive increase of industrial workers overall. Between 1860 and 1870 the number of factory hands grew from 1.3 million to 2 million, at which point the country's manufacturing personnel for the first time surpassed the number of people working in agriculture. In addition to these, there were 3.6 million other wage earners active in various enterprises, creating a total of 5.5 million nonfarm workers out of a national population of 35.2 million.[27]

Many of the new trade unions strived for national stature, most notably the National Typographical Union, the Iron Molders' Union, the Machinists and Blacksmiths, the Brotherhood of Locomotive Engineers, and the ironworkers, who organized as the Sons of Vulcan. Labor organizing, apace with manufacturing, crossed state lines and even branched into Canada. Much as industrialists found themselves in competition with factories hundreds of miles distant, so now did workers in Chicago and Philadelphia vie for wages with workers in Massachusetts and New Hampshire. The surge in unionism was sympathetically covered by *Fincher's Trades' Review*, the era's leading labor newspaper, which urged in partisan prose "one common platform, pledging ourselves, as fast friends, to scrupulously adhere to that unity of action which can alone enable us to successfully counteract the wily machinations of those heartless moneyed despots."[28]

While trade unions grew in strength and character, the abolitionist arm of the Republican Party's formative years showed signs of fatigue. To many of those who had so ardently opposed slavery, emancipation represented the long-sought-for triumph. Further vindication arrived with the Reconstruction Acts, which called for new, democratic constitutions in the former Confederate states, and soon the ratification of the Fourteenth and Fifteenth amendments, granting rights of citizenship and universal male suffrage, respectively. After decades of activism and the trauma of a devastating war, few of the abolitionists sought the less morally absolute arena of labor conflict.

A notable exception was Wendell Phillips, the patrician "Golden Trumpet" of the antislavery cause, who saw clearly the importance of labor unions. "My ideal of civilization is a very high one," he related. "It is a New England town of some two thousand inhabitants, with no rich man and no poor man in it, all mingling in the same society, every child at the same school, no poor-house, no beggar, opportunities equal, nobody too proud to stand aloof, nobody too humble to be shut out."[29] Instead the country was headed in the opposite direction, he feared, toward a condition in which an affluent minority would possess all the nation's power, most of its opportunity, and a great deal of its property. Capital, with its corporations, banks, railroads, courts, and easily bought legislatures, would reign supreme. Phillips "wrapped his cloak once more about him [and] went forth to meet a greater enemy," a contemporary wrote;

he declared himself for "toilers' rights" and joined the emerging call for an eight-hour workday sounded by mechanic and fellow Bostonian Ira Steward.[30]

During the war numerous state and local eight-hour leagues had been organized, fifty in California alone, mostly through the single-handed efforts of Steward, who was known as the Eight-Hour Monomaniac. Described as a "brown, gnome-like man," Steward, then in his early thirties, could apparently "speak of little else. . . . Meet him any day as he steams along the street," wrote a contemporary, "[and] he will stop and plead with you until night-fall."[31] Steward in 1863 had won an eight-hour resolution from his own union, the Machinists and Blacksmiths, and had created the Grand Eight Hour League of Massachusetts. Allied with Wendell Phillips, Steward made Boston a center for eight-hour agitation. His wife coined the movement's slogan:

Whether you work by the piece or work by the day
Decreasing the hours increases the pay.

Not all Northern middle-class reformers were swayed. They tended to lack familiarity with labor groups, which were often composed of recent immigrants, and held a bias against strikes or any other potential interference with business or production. "Let not him who is houseless, pull down the house of another," Lincoln had cautioned workingmen during the war, "but let him labor diligently and build one for himself."[32] Horace Greeley, writing in a similar vein, warned against "Jacobin ravings in the Park" as a means of resolving class issues[33]; many prominent voices urged laborers to resist rebellion and instead pull themselves up within the capitalist system, and to do so by minding their own temperance and self-discipline.

ORGANIZED LABOR'S FIRST CHALLENGE after the war was to flex the strength of its new national unions, and in William Sylvis, president of the Iron Molders' International Union, it had a man uniquely devoted to the task. The son of a wagon-maker, born into humble circumstances in rural Pennsylvania, Sylvis "never went to school six days in his life," but he "could not long remain in the bondage of ignorance," for, as the *New York Sun* explained, "perseverance and determination are as plainly written in his countenance as if the words were penned there with indelible ink."[34] Sleeping in lonely train depots awaiting his next connection to Buffalo, Canton, Milwaukee, or wherever iron molders awaited him, at times cadging rides in locomotive cabs from sympathetic trainmen, Sylvis was America's original indefatigable traveling union organizer.

He was energized by the conviction that the nation's workers only needed to know of labor's united cause to join it wholeheartedly. Often neglectful of his wife, four children, and his own health, stricken by recurring nerve and gastrointestinal problems likely related to his itinerant existence, he drove himself feverishly, consumed with the prophecy he spread. When no audience of workingmen was handy, he turned to lecturing the young at Sunday school classes. "Suffering from permanent indignation, he was not a cautious man and if he thought a thing he would say so," it was noted. "His bright blue eyes seemed to flare with hotness when he was angry, which was most of the time."[35]

Organized labor, in the analogy Sylvis frequently offered his hearers, was a powerful locomotive, sitting in readiness on a track, but without sufficient fuel to move forward. Only a unified movement of workers could do that, could wield the power needed to confront capital. There was no alternative because industry, as he saw it, was a cheat. "If workingmen and capitalists are equal co-partners, why do they not share equally in the profits?" he demanded. "Why does capital take to itself the whole loaf, while labor is left to gather up the crumbs? Why does capital roll in luxury and wealth, while labor is left to eke out a miserable existence in poverty and want? Are these the evidences of an identity of interests, of mutual relations, of equal partnership? No . . . on the contrary they are evidences of an antagonism . . . a never-ending conflict between the two classes, [where] capital is in all cases the aggressor."[36]

He had taken charge of the Iron Molders' International shortly after its founding in 1863, when many of the union's leaders were still at war; indeed, the organization almost collapsed when its financial officer was killed in combat without having repaid the $62 he had borrowed from the union's funds. By 1865, however, under Sylvis's tireless promotion, the group was on its way to becoming the strongest trade union in America, with seven thousand members and fifty-three locals. Much of this growth resulted from three lengthy organizing trips he made to the South, Midwest, and Northeast, covering ten thousand miles. The welcome he received from his beloved molders usually made the jaunt worthwhile, although more than once he left a town one step ahead of an inhospitable foundry boss.[37] "He wore clothes until they became quite threadbare and he could wear them no longer," his brother recalled of Sylvis's wanderings. "The shawl he wore to the day of his death . . . was filled with little holes burned there by the splashing of molten iron from the ladles of molders in strange cities, whom he was beseeching to organize."[38] Despite his vagabond appearance, Sylvis was a superb detail man, standardizing the collection of dues and compiling an extensive card index that was probably America's first national "database" of union membership. It led to an expanding roster of members as well as a bulging union treasury.[39]

Because he believed all workers belonged in a union, he had little patience for those who resisted the call to organize, and he could become apoplectic on the subject of replacement workers, those men so lacking in the spirit of brotherhood and class consciousness they would take over another man's job. He kept what he called a "scab album," in order to track the names and movements of these dangerous creatures. "What can be done with such trash?" he once asked. "You cannot call them human without libeling the whole human race."[40] Yet it was characteristic of Sylvis that he also reached out to scabs wherever possible, in the hope of making them reconsider their folly and adding them to the union fold.

This ambitious, inclusive embrace of all toiling men led to his founding of the National Labor Union (NLU), the country's first national labor federation, in the summer of 1866. Sylvis was to his last breath an iron molder, devoutly faithful to his union, but the NLU was the far more original undertaking, an entity dedicated not to any specific trade but to all, to the cause of labor itself, to both skilled and unskilled workers, as well as to farmers, women, and African Americans. The NLU's agenda, laid out in its *Address to the Workingmen of the United States*, highlighted worker and consumer cooperatives as well as monetary reforms that would shift the country away from the gold standard to legal tender currency based on actual wealth, theoretically making more "greenbacks" available for workers and small businesses. But its major issue was the eight-hour day, which Sylvis embraced as a moral crusade. Work in industry turned human beings into automatons who did little other than sleep, eat, and work. What they required, he declared, was "time to breathe, to rest, to repose, to think—a little time transferred from the busy workshop to the quiet family circle . . . time to think of our Creator's bounty, to forget man's tyranny, to remember heaven's promise and to refresh the weary soul with prayer."[41] Shorter hours of work held the potential to remake society, for with their new leisure time, workers would become consumers, closing the gap with the affluent; at the same time their expenditures would invigorate manufacturing and create jobs. The faith that the nation's economy functioned best when workers were able to afford and enjoy the objects they made would be echoed by several generations of labor activists, and most famously by no less a captain of industry than Henry Ford.

Some of the popularity of the eight-hour crusade in the wake of the Civil War derived from the prospect that a shortened workday would create more jobs for returning soldiers. Private industry, however, proved resistant to the reform, although New York, Boston, Detroit, and Baltimore had at war's end enacted eight-hour regulations for municipal employees, and half a dozen states ushered in similar laws; in June 1868 the federal government decreed an eight-hour day for workmen and mechanics in the federal arsenals and navy yards. As with any regulation, the trouble came with enforcement. Private work contracts, where eight-hour codes existed, could still stipulate whatever hours employer and worker agreed upon, and employers, even those covered by Washington's mandate, did act where possible to either reduce wages or cram more work into the shortened day. The NLU had established the nation's first permanent labor lobby in Washington, and when Sylvis and others suspected the Grant administration of laxity in applying the eight-hour rule, it lodged a forceful complaint. In response, President Ulysses S. Grant issued a proclamation in May 1869 affirming that "from and after this date, no reduction shall be made in the wages paid by the Government by the day to such laborers, workmen, and mechanics, on account of such reduction of the hours of labor." The NLU's intervention was one of the first examples of labor successfully politicizing an issue at the federal level, and helped set in motion the process by which all government workers were eventually granted eight-hour rights.[42]

I T WAS CHARACTERISTIC OF this phase of labor history that workers' organizations perceived the leveling of American society to be both possible and necessary, and the creation of a permanent wage-earning class unacceptable. Sylvis saw a means to address the problem in cooperative ventures, both manufacturing enterprises and consumer-run stores. If workers could sustain themselves independent of wages, they would not be marginalized in society or held in industrial peonage. As cooperationists they would sell the products they manufactured and subsist off the profits. Worker-owned industries would spawn land and home associations, worker-friendly banks, and lending institutions, as well as the means to distribute food and other necessities at reasonable prices. This, like the eight-hour fight, was couched as a moral issue; wages were the buying of a man's labor, nothing more, and wage-workers would surely become demoralized, indifferent, and lazy, if never challenged to develop business sense or the ability to rely on their own resourcefulness. It could not be healthy for society, noted the *Nation*'s E. L. Godkin, "when the master's recklessness or dishonesty bring on a financial crash . . . [and] the working classes, on whom the heaviest burden of the woe falls, meet their fate in blind and helpless ignorance of its causes."[43] While Godkin thought trade unions valuable, because the individual worker could not "bargain with the capitalist on equal terms,"[44] the better cure, as *Fincher's* opined, was "Labor being its own employer. When the producer becomes the seller, [this] ceases the confliction of interests. Then Capital and Labor become mutual friends, which otherwise they can never be."[45]

Sylvis's own Iron Molders' Union showed the way, opening an iron foundry cooperative at Troy, New York, and soon others in Albany, Rochester, Cleveland, and Pittsburgh. The molders became so smitten by the cooperative program that at one point they formally changed their organization's name to the Iron Molders' International Cooperative and Protective Union.

Such trends were watched with caution by the country's editorial pages, for there was fear that the leaders of such communistic enterprises, namely those of the increasingly powerful NLU, would place undue demands on state legislatures or Washington to make special fixes for industrial projects unable to compete in the open market.[46] These concerns were borne out when the molders' foundries hit rough financial water and Sylvis approached the federal government about supporting worker cooperatives with gifts of money and public lands, much as it had railroad interests. Godkin, writing sympathetically of the cooperative effort, nonetheless cast doubt as to its survival in America. Unlike Europe, where the collective impulse was intrinsic to how citizens viewed their governments and themselves, America was devoted to the individual—a person's freedom to compete and to succeed or fail based on his or her own merits and abilities. So ingrained was this quality, Godkin predicted, that impatience with cooperative ventures would persist even if they proved successful. "By many, [cooperation] is still regarded as an offshoot of communism . . . hostile to property and therefore to civilization; by others, simply as an expression of political discontent, part of a great leveling process which will end in something very destructive."[47]

In less ideological terms, what ailed the cooperatives was that they were undercapitalized; sales of their manufactured products were inadequate, and they lacked the money necessary to grow and sustain a large industrial enterprise. Nor was workers' faith in such projects absolute. Union molders grumbled when Sylvis tried to shift money from a standing strike fund to cover the needs of one teetering foundry; workers at other sites rebelled when managers were forced to cut wages to cover outstanding overhead costs, and they rejected the co-ops' effort to introduce profit-sharing as a substitute for the missing pay. A more fundamental problem was that cooperative businesses, because of their stress on democratic decision making and the absence of traditional managerial control, often lacked the market-savvy leadership needed to compete with ordinary enterprises. "The business of production is the most difficult kind of business," advised Godkin. "Raw materials have to be bought at the lowest prices, worked up with economy, and sold at the right time, in order to keep the concern going; and this requires a combination of qualities which are as yet not readily found amongst workingmen."[48] Industrial cooperatives didn't die off overnight. Some managed to creep into the twentieth century, and the cooperative store movement, always easier to maintain, fared better than its industrial cousin, although there, too, enthusiasm gradually dropped off.

The NLU also broke new ground in its inclusion of women and blacks in its membership rolls. While Sylvis personally believed women's primary roles were as nurturers of children and keepers of a civilized home, he recognized that insomuch as they had been forced into the workplace, they had the right to unionize no less than men. "How can we hope to reach the social elevation for which we all aim," he asked, "without making women the companion of our advancement?"[49] He knew the hardships workingwomen endured, sewing and laboring at piecework from dawn to dark for less than $3 a week, "steeped in a gulf of mental and moral darkness, such as make angels weep." He believed such conditions "ruined more innocent girls than all the libertines and roués of the land."[50]

Not all the male members of the group shared Sylvis's attitude; some were made apprehensive by the influx of female industrial workers that had occurred during the war and by the possibility that their presence in the workforce would drive down wages. Many simply did not believe women deserved wages equal to those given a man. Women's role in the NLU was also thwarted by strong differences of opinion about female suffrage. They had played a crucial part in the abolition movement, and at war's end had been angered to find their male colleagues, including Wendell Phillips, William Lloyd Garrison, and Frederick Douglass, willing to set the campaign for women's vote aside in order to prioritize the immediate interest of advancing black citizenship and suffrage. The women were insulted not merely because they felt they had priority, but because they considered themselves more qualified to cast votes than recently freed slaves, a high percentage of whom were illiterate. When Susan B. Anthony and Elizabeth Cady Stanton appeared at an NLU gathering on September 21, 1868, it was recorded by the *New York Herald* that Anthony's assured demeanor impressed "the bearded delegates," but that Stanton was greeted with derision because she came from a women's suffrage group, and thus her cause was political and not labor-oriented.[51] There was a motion to admit Mrs. Stanton only as a "corresponding delegate," but Sylvis, calling her "one of the most brilliant writers of the age," assured his fellow workingmen that he would "admit the devil himself" to the NLU if that personage was a great reformer and labor sympathizer as was Stanton. Anthony suggested that the degradation of women workers was related to their not having the vote, and pointed out that if they were politically equal to men, that would benefit labor overall, for when a boss paid women less, workingmen's pay and opportunity, too, was diminished.[52] The situation in the hall became unruly as members of the building trades threatened to walk out of the gathering over the suffrage issue. One delegate complained that "a woman is a very strange kind of being," who might nullify her husband's vote in an election just out of marital spite.[53] Sylvis's fiery speech in Stanton's defense notwithstanding, she was allowed to remain only under an agreement that the NLU "does not regard itself as endorsing her peculiar ideas" on women's suffrage.[54]

Anthony, encouraged by Sylvis's personal commitment, and by the NLU's embrace of women workers, if not their voting rights, told a founding meeting of the Women's Typographical Union a month later, "Girls, you must take this matter to heart seriously now, for you have established a union, and for the first time in woman's history in the United States you are placed . . . on a level with men . . . to obtain wages for your labor. I need not say that you have taken a great momentous step forward. . . . Keep at it now girls, and you will achieve full and plenteous success."[55] Unfortunately, the relationship between women workers and the NLU soon fractured irreparably during a strike by the male-dominated Typographical Union No. 6 of New York City. It was discovered that women had appealed directly to employers to teach them the skills of the striking workers. At a meeting in August 1869, Anthony addressed the allegation, saying that the opportunity for women to learn the skill was valuable and that they would have readily abandoned their seats back to the male union members once the strike was resolved. The men, however, rejected this explanation. NLU leaders attempted to intervene, but the women's status in the NLU was already too tentative to be salvaged.[56]

Similarly, after a promising start, the NLU also stumbled in its efforts to include black workers. "What is wanted," Sylvis had once said, "is for every union to help inculcate the grand ennobling idea that the interests of labor are one; that there should be no distinction of race and nationality; no classification of Jew or Gentile, Christian or infidel; that there is one dividing line, that which separates mankind into two great classes, the class that labors and the class that lives by others' labor."[57] Karl Marx, founder of the International Workingmen's Association (IWA) and a foreign booster of the NLU, had encouraged the organization's inclusion of the freedmen as a way in which American trade unions might embody the true meaning of the Civil War, and the IWA had tried to lead by example, showcasing black labor organizations in a parade held in New York City in 1871. But as early as its founding convention of 1866 the NLU wrestled with the attempt to make black inclusion a reality, and by 1869 it had asked black delegates to form their own all-black organization. The result was the Colored National Labor Union (CNLU), whose 214 delegates gathered in Washington, choosing Isaac Myers as its president; Frederick Douglass headed the organization after 1872. "It is not without interest," historian Rayford W. Logan notes, "that the first large-scale exclusion of Negroes by private organizations in the postbellum period was the handiwork of organized labor."[58]

African American workers figure prominently in the nation's history. It was the South's defense of slavery, the ultimate system of cheap labor, which came to dominate the region's politics and to influence public morality in America through the abolition movement. The debate over whether newly added territories and states would be slave or free, whether slavery would move west with the country's expansion—at first troubling, then divisive and rancorous—led to the Civil War. Reconstruction (1865–1877) saw the freedmen become citizens, voters, elected officials, and, to a small extent, owners of property. Officers of the Freedmen's Bureau (formally the Bureau of Refugees, Freedmen, and Abandoned Lands) assisted in the negotiation of wage contracts between the former slaves and their former masters; the bureau's chief, General O. O. Howard, and others worked to obtain confiscated Confederate lands for the former slaves, but under President Andrew Johnson official support for land redistribution withered, and most former slaves remained propertyless, unable to escape the peonage of hired farm labor or the sharecropping system.

One of the CNLU's first acts, after Myers had undertaken a cross-country organizing tour much as Sylvis had done, was to renew appeals to Congress to make land available to former slaves through low-interest loans. But these various efforts, however just and poetic—"owning a piece of the land that had once owned them"—ended in defeat, a misfortune in that it denied blacks economic equality, frustrating the kind of broader democracy in the region that might have enabled greater mutual interest and coalition among workers of both races.

As had been evident in its efforts with women workers, there remained a traditionalist strain within the NLU. It didn't help that Sylvis, despite his enlightened thoughts on labor, held fairly conservative ideas on race and Reconstruction. He thought Congress's efforts to reconstruct the South were excessive, accepted the prevalent Southern view that Northern politicians and businessmen in the South, the notorious "carpetbaggers," were dishonorable, and favored the soonest possible reconciliation between the North and the former Confederacy. Having become enamored of the South during his peripatetic years as a labor organizer, he had been heard to speak of his interest in eventually relocating his family there.

But the real weakness in the effort to include blacks in the NLU was likely the fact that worker equality was not the chief motive; rather it was the need to deny employers the option of hiring blacks as scabs or as low-cost wage competitors. African Americans, of course, had little choice but to take what they could get; excluded from white trade unions, they were also refused access to quality jobs generally. This created a cyclical problem, in that the ordinary aspirations of black workers appeared inimical to white workers' interests, their actions "disruptive," which in turn diminished the ideal of their equality as men and potential union cohorts.[59] While Sylvis didn't hesitate to couch the appeal for racial solidarity among workers as "a second Emancipation Proclamation,"[60] his and the NLU's efforts had less in common with that glorious document than with the anxiety that a black peasantry would be exploited by capital to the detriment of white labor.

The NLU's solution of encouraging equality but not integration, urging the formation of separate black trade unions, "was a first halting note," according to W. E. B. Du Bois. "Negroes were welcomed to the labor movement, not because they were laborers but because they might be competitors in the market, and the logical conclusion was either to organize them or guard against their actual competition by other methods. It was to this latter alternative that white American labor almost unanimously turned."[61] The recommendation of a specially formed NLU Committee on Negro Labor reveals the hamstrung quality of the members' deliberations: "While we feel the importance of the subject, and realize the danger in the form of competition in mechanical Negro labor," the committeemen concluded, "yet we find the subject involved in so much mystery, and upon it so wide diversity of opinion amongst our members, we believe that it is inexpedient to take action on the subject."[62] Du Bois cites the NLU's failure to bridge the divide of race as a fatal misstep.

Relegating the black worker to a role as "a competitor and a prospective under-bidder" and asking him, "when he appeared at conventions . . . to organize separately; that is, outside the real labor movement," was nothing less than "a contradiction of all sound labor policy."[63]

Thus the NLU proved no better than the rest of the nation at fulfilling Reconstruction's ideal of integrating America's newest citizens into society, and the mistrust and disunity between white and black laborers only deepened as Reconstruction itself flagged and ultimately collapsed in the late 1870s. One supplemental problem was that blacks were politically aligned with the Republican Party, the party of Lincoln and Grant and of Emancipation and the franchise, while many white laboring men adhered to the Democratic Party, which was strong in cities and had stood up for immigrants against nativist parties such as the Know-Nothings. "It is useless to attempt to cover up the fact that there is still a wide gulf between the two races in this country," a labor writer of the era concluded. "For a time at least they must each in their own way work out a solution to this labor problem."[64]

Given these divisive issues, as well as an organizational platform unsuited to the rough-and-tumble of the post–Civil War economy, the NLU's survival would have been doubtful under any circumstances, but its leadership suffered an unanticipated blow in late July 1869 when William Sylvis died suddenly at age forty-one. "Sylvis! The National Calamity!" a labor newspaper exclaimed at his abrupt disappearance, noting that his passing "cast a veil of despondency upon the whole working class." It was said he had worn himself out by his monumental exertions on behalf of workingmen, although one biographer offered the more prosaic explanation that his end had come due to "his nervous habit of rapid eating."[65] Whatever the cause, he was borne to his grave as one of the nation's original labor martyrs, having so completely committed his resources to his work that his widow was forced to borrow money to pay the undertaker.

In the year of Sylvis's death, the NLU drifted to the cause of monetary reform as a panacea for struggling workers and farmers, and in 1872 it made alliance with the greenback contingent that joined a doomed presidential challenge by publisher Horace Greeley. The NLU's turning away from its signature labor campaigns confused and alienated many of its members; black affiliates, of course, almost exclusively remained loyal to Grant. With the labor base of the organization fractured, the NLU soon dissolved.

Some eulogized the departed Sylvis as "Our Lincoln" and remembered wistfully when such an allusion had not seemed at all far-fetched, for there had indeed been talk of promoting him for national office. He had, it so happened, been the first American laborite to suggest the creation within the government of a national Department of Labor. Alas, such attainments were not to be, but Sylvis *had* done much and performed heroically. With the iron molders he had cobbled together elements of the modern national labor union—the administration of geographically far-flung locals; the staging of massive labor conventions; the maintaining of union officials on salary. He had established standards for membership and the management of union finances. Having suffered both a workplace injury (molten iron had spilled into his boot) and a family crisis (his first wife had died of typhoid at age twenty-nine), he had also helped pioneer ways in which unions could serve as benevolent agencies for injured or sick workers and their families. His efforts within the NLU were similarly groundbreaking, promoting broad union inclusion and solidarity across all trades. Finally, he was likely the first national labor leader around whom there grew a cult of personality—his tireless wanderings over America, his unbending faith in the potential of organized labor, contributing to his becoming a legend in his own lifetime.

MINERS PERFORMING the arduous task of extracting anthracite coal from the mountains of eastern Pennsylvania could rely on one very dependable ally: *the rat*. When the rodents were seen scurrying toward a mine's surface, the men inside knew a collapse of the ceiling or its support timbers was imminent. But a disaster at the Avondale mine just south of Scranton on the morning of September 6, 1869, caught even the rats off guard, when a wooden structure encasing the entryway caught fire and tumbled into the shaft, filling the tunnel with smoke. Avondale being a single shaft mine, the trapped miners below had no other means of exit. As word of the accident spread, wives and children from the miners' village came on the run, as did brother miners from nearby sites. Frantic efforts began at once to dig an alternate way into the Avondale, to no avail. By early afternoon it was certain all 179 of those below ground had perished by asphyxiation.

One of the only labor officials on the scene was John Siney. An Irish immigrant who had come to the anthracite region during the Civil War, Siney had founded the Workers Benevolent Association (WBA), the area's first miners' union, which by the time of the Avondale fire had thirty locals and thirty thousand members. On the day of the tragedy he rushed to the site directly from an NLU meeting in Philadelphia. Mounting a box to address the dead miners' kin and colleagues, he did not disguise his fury that all the victims would be alive had the mine operator taken the precaution of providing an emergency exit. "Men, if you must die with your boots on, die for your families, your homes, your country," Siney exclaimed, "but do not longer consent to die like rats in a trap for those who take no more interest in you than in the pick you dig with." Would the mine's owners themselves "unhesitatingly" go down in their own mine? No, Siney assured, they would surely not do so without another avenue of escape. "What they would do for themselves," he insisted, "they must be compelled by law to do for their workmen."[66]

The agony of the Avondale disaster was compounded by the fact that a few months earlier reformers had introduced in the state legislature a bill to mandate better ventilation of coal mines and to assign mine inspectors for each mining county in Pennsylvania. Samuel G. Turner, the senator from Luzerne County, where Avondale was located, had done the coal operators' bidding and helped engineer the measure's defeat in committee. In the wake of the fire, Turner, knowing his political career and perhaps even his life were at risk, joined with Siney of the WBA to push through the Pennsylvania Mine Safety Act of 1870, which, among other features, demanded that every mine have at least two means of entrance and exit.

Despite the legislature's swift response to Avondale, mine cave-ins and other disasters in the region continued to take their toll. In Schuylkill County, which lay at the heart of the anthracite region, 556 mine deaths occurred in the years 1870–1875, with more than a thousand men left injured or maimed. Visitors to southeast Pennsylvania's five-hundred-square-mile coal district frequently described the miners' villages not just as poor and tumbledown, but as uneasy, haunted places where women prayed and watched fearfully as their men headed toward work each morning. Every child knew the popular rhyme,

> *Oh Daddy, don't work in the mines today,*
> *for dreams have so often come true;*
> *Oh Daddy, dear Daddy, please don't go away;*
> *I never could live without you.*[67]

Prior to industrialization, miners carried their own tools and worked relatively autonomously all day at the coal face, often hiring their own laborers. But the old craft skills had been rendered obsolete by the coming of machines that blasted and undercut the rock. At the same time, the mining companies' demands on an individual worker's daily tonnage increased. Where a miner in the 1860s might be expected to personally extract 2.5 tons of coal per day, within a generation this amount had grown to 9 tons per day, and ultimately, in the 1920s, to 16.5 tons. Technology, instead of making the miner's life easier, gave mine operators the ability to squeeze more coal from their property, and greater effort from the men who daily descended into the earth.

John Siney and the WBA brought much-needed relief and comfort. In addition to the Mine Safety Act, Siney's union helped establish the first miners' hospital in Schuylkill County, arranged for union funds to pay sick or injured miners, or their burial costs, and supported the widows and families of men killed or stricken. It also oversaw enforcement of a new state-approved eight-hour-day law and worked to abolish the use of scrip payment to miners.

But Siney and the WBA were not the only organization important to the miners. An Irish fraternal order, the Ancient Order of Hibernians (AOH), was active in the social and cultural life of the region. Several of its leading members owned popular crossroads saloons; some were colorful outsize figures, known for their physical daring, a few claiming roots in the Irish independence struggle. In the WBA the Irishmen tended to be the most defiant, lobbying the union to take strong positions. Like many a fraternal lodge, the AOH practiced secretive membership rituals that piqued public curiosity and suspicion. When the Hibernians gathered one night in a village school, local residents feared they had come "to deliberate upon the business of house and head smashing," an assumption fueled by the hill country tradition of fierce Irish American resistance to authority associated with a ruthless gang known as the Molly Maguires.

The original Molly Maguire, a legendary Irish nationalist rebel and anti-landlord vigilante, according to journalist Louis Adamic, "was a barbaric and picturesque character [who] blackened her face and under her petticoat carried a pistol strapped to each of her stout thighs."[68] She reputedly led her followers to commit anti-British terrorism, sometimes disguised as women. Historians disagree as to whether such a person ever really existed, but Molly's inspiration accompanied Irish emigrants to the New World. Beginning with the large Irish emigration to America in the late 1840s, there were rumors of the appearance of "Molly Maguires" in New England, and in southeast Pennsylvania "Molly Maguirism" became a euphemism for any mayhem or violent disorder suspected of having been carried out by rebellious Irish (although the malefactors were sometimes known by other names, such as the Buckshots, the Ribbonmen, the Sleepers, or the White Boys).

The terrain of Schuylkill County, desolate, forbidding, its coal settlements linked by lonely mountain roads, proved ideal for tales of shadowy characters and midnight knocks on the door. As in their native land, the identity of the suspected outlaws was guarded by a prevailing code of silence among fearful residents. Benjamin Bannan, editor of the *Miners Journal*, published in Pottsville, the seat of Schuylkill County, became in

1857 the first to record that "Molly Maguires" were active in the anthracite region. A few years later, with the coming of the Civil War, they were alleged to be involved in aiding local Irish lads to resist conscription, the young men hiding in the hills until the contemptible army "enrollers" departed. Once, the story was told, Molly Maguires forcibly stopped a trainload of hapless conscripts headed down the mountain for Harrisburg, freeing them to return home.

This rebellious spirit entered into labor matters as well. In December 1862 a force of "Mollies" invaded a mine, roughed up scabs, and shut down a company store. But the desperadoes also preyed on miners. "If we are called upon to work after dark, these rascals lie in wait for us on our way home, and with the treachery of an assassin pounce upon us in the solitude of the night," complained a miner worried about being relieved of his pay packet. Thus the name Molly Maguire became associated with almost every variety of mischief in the coal lands, from petty crime to labor troubles to the treasonous harassment of government officials.

By giving hard-luck miners a voice in their conditions of work, Siney and the WBA brought relative stability and a respite from terrorism. There had been fifty unsolved murders in Schuylkill County in the years 1863 to 1867, but crime fell sharply during the years of the union's operations, 1868–1874. A highlight of the WBA's tenure came in July 1870, when the union and the regional operators' association, the Anthracite Board of Trade, signed the nation's first written pact between mine operators and miners. Since the WBA's thirty thousand members represented 85 percent of the coal region miners, the contract was a significant recognition of the WBA and might have served to further pacify labor relations. Siney and his union, however, had a determined nemesis in Franklin B. Gowen, the president of the Philadelphia & Reading Railroad. Gowen, whose dynastic vision and heavy-handed tactics soon came to dominate the region, wanted no trouble from labor unions or Molly Maguires, and he would eventually find ways to undermine both.

Although raised in Pennsylvania, Gowen hailed from a family of Confederate sympathizers, and had purchased a substitute to take his place in the Union army. He was well educated, charming in a blustery way, and devoted to such elitist pastimes as cricket and translating German poetry. After a stint as a coal trader he tried his hand at operating a mine, then served as district attorney for Schuylkill County; he worked as a lawyer for the Reading before becoming its president in 1869 at age thirty-two. As historians are fond of observing, Gowen's swift advancement brought him the ultimate symbol of Gilded Age status—a private railcar.

Coal being not only the essential fuel for his railroad but a profitable cargo, Gowen set out to control the anthracite mines so as to monopolize its transport. Under the Reading's state charter the railroad was not allowed to own coal mines, but Gowen got around this by creating landholding entities to do so. The Reading also bought the Schuylkill Canal, which carried coal barges and small passenger boats from Schuylkill County to Philadelphia, and ordered it closed, thus making the region more dependent on rail. Once the Reading controlled the means and could set the rates charged for bringing coal off the mountain to market, it could also determine the price of coal tonnage and, by extension, miners' wages. This positioned Gowen as the "arbiter of labor relations in the anthracite region," striking bargains with the mine operators and Siney's WBA to fix the wage scale to fluctuating coal prices.[69]

But this much authority proved insufficient. Even though the WBA was functioning in the best spirit of labor unionism, and opposed Molly Maguirism, Gowen willfully blurred the distinction between the two by playing on prevailing stereotypes of the working Irish. Press and public knew them as natural agitators who enjoyed their liquor and thought with their fists, and mine operators disliked them because they often took the lead in the most fractious labor battles; Gowen's contention that they all were incorrigible outlaws thus fed a ready-made preconception, enabling interests inimical to the WBA to conflate legitimate union activities with membership in the AOH and the specter of the Molly Maguires. He had a key ally in editor Bannan of the *Miners Journal*, who accepted Gowen's argument that the WBA was likely thick with "Mollie terrorists."

Gowen also managed to manipulate the state legislature when, in March 1871, it convened an investigation into the Reading's price fixing.

In a lengthy and theatrical speech, Gowen turned scrutiny away from his own possible misdeeds to alleged obstructionism on the part of the WBA, painting an elaborate word-portrait of intrigue in Schuylkill County, in which tyrannical union leaders worked secretly with Molly Maguires, who used violence and threats to keep workers in line. Gowen was convincing in outlining a conspiracy that

> votes in secret at night that men's lives shall be taken, and
> that they shall be shot before their wives, murdered in cold
> blood. . . . There has never been, in the most despotic government
> in the world, such a tyranny before in which the poor laboring
> man has to crouch like a whipped spaniel before the lash, and
> dare not say that his soul is his own. . . . I do not charge the
> [WBA] with it, but I say there is an association which votes in
> secret, at night, that men's lives shall be taken . . . for daring to
> work against the order.[70]

The legislators, brought around by Gowen's lurid tale, pivoted the focus of their inquiry and called Siney to testify. He adamantly denied any link between the WBA and the Mollies. "I wish to be placed upon my oath," he said. "As workingmen we are stigmatized as a band of assassins; anything coming from our lips is supposed not to be believed . . . [but] we are an organization . . . first chartered by the county, next by the legislature; today we have neither sign, password, oath nor pledge."[71] But Siney's defense of his union failed in the face of Gowen's hyperbole, and the idea that the WBA and Molly Maguirism were connected took hold.[72]

That same month Gowen pushed through the legislature his scheme to allow the Reading to buy up coal land. Within three years the Reading—through its front company, the Laurel Run Improvement Company—would own one hundred thousand acres and control extensive mining operations; as a result many mine owners chose to sell to the increasingly omnipotent Reading, those who stayed on serving as mine superintendents or land agents for the company. Two years later the railroad's grip tightened further when Gowen and the heads of four other regional railroads met in New York City and fixed the price of transporting coal at $5 a ton. The consortium also agreed on limits to how much coal would be carried by each railroad, thus granting the roads more leverage in determining coal operators' profits. Bannan of the *Miners Journal* now grew concerned about the power Gowen had acquired. An old-line free labor advocate, he regretted seeing the region's smaller coal operators forced aside, leaving only large capital to vie with the local miners, a struggle he saw as hopeless.[73]

Another paradoxical result of Gowen's reckless ambition was that by weakening the "treacherous" WBA, he spurred a resurgence of actual Molly Maguirism. After a relative lull during the years of greatest WBA activity, there were new reports of mine bosses being roughed up, suspected arson at mine sites, railcars being vandalized, as well as threatening notices left on miners' doors:

> This is to give you the Gap men a cliar understanding that if
> you don't quit work after this NOTICE you may preper for your
> DETH. You are the damdest *turncoats* in the *State*—there is no
> ples fit for you bute *Hell* and you will be soone there.
>   MOLLY
> Sind by the real boys this time—so you better loocke oute.[74]

Because of such disruptions, Gowen in 1873 asked the legislature to allow the Reading to create its own law enforcement agency, the Reading Coal and Iron Police. Equipped with their own train car, the Coal and Iron cops were capable of responding quickly and aggressively to reports of strikes, worksite violence, or vigilantism. But to break the insurrectionary spirit of Irish resistance once and for all, Gowen decided he would also need to work from the inside.

THE NINETEENTH-CENTURY DETECTIVE Allan Pinkerton was a Scottish immigrant and barrel-maker once active in the abolition movement in Illinois, who built a second career in law enforcement by coordinating teams of "spotters" on Illinois railroads to catch conductors who embezzled ticket proceeds. He went on to become chief of security for the Philadelphia, Wilmington & Baltimore Railroad, where, in early 1861, he claimed to have discovered a plot to assassinate President-elect Abraham Lincoln as Lincoln's train passed through Baltimore en route to his inaugural in Washington. The genuineness of the plot has been questioned by some historians, but Lincoln himself—who had been a railroad attorney and knew Pinkerton from Illinois—believed it was real, and in any case Pinkerton did manage to get Lincoln safely to the capital.[75] He was soon hired by General George B. McClellan to lead the Union military's secret service. After the war, when city police forces were often substandard and law enforcement was inadequate along remote rail lines away from urban centers, a number of detective and protective agencies appeared to offer security services. Pinkerton's "cinder dicks" distinguished themselves on the sprawling railroads, including the Reading, and increasingly were hired for workforce-oriented espionage and union-busting.[76] Like Franklin Gowen, Pinkerton chose to see little difference between unions and criminals, only perhaps that union men were less scheming than simply foolish. In his view, workers who formed "associations for compelling from their employers what their employers cannot afford to yield, assume[d] a position of open antagonism to the existence of the very interests upon which they are utterly dependent for their own sustenance."[77]

Now Gowen sought out the renowned sleuth for a special assignment. A cutthroat group known as the Molly Maguires, he explained, infested the coal region, "making sad havoc with the country." Municipal laws, county sheriffs, and local police were helpless to bring the culprits to heel.[78] Pennsylvania, the entire nation, "wherever anthracite is employed," Gowen explained, remained in "the vise-like grip of this midnight, dark-lantern, murderous-minded fraternity."[79] Pinkerton, who was said to have "an almost personal hatred for all criminals," listened carefully to Gowen's description of the deadly Mollies. After brief deliberation he chose to send to the troubled coal hills one of his most promising young agents, James McParlan, a twenty-nine-year-old Irish immigrant who had worked the Chicago streetcars, gathering evidence against dishonest conductors. McParlan was to blend in with the Mollies and learn their secrets.[80]

McParlan entered Schuylkill County under the alias James McKenna and obtained work in a mine, making himself conspicuous at suspected Mollie roadhouses by singing Irish ballads and dancing jigs, brawling with local bullies, and drinking to realistic excess. To fool the desperadoes he hoped to entrap, he devised the compelling cover story that he was laying low for having committed a murder in Buffalo, and was living off disability payments from his Civil War service and occasionally "passing the cheat" (circulating counterfeit money). McKenna's outlaw bona fides, his convincing roughness, and his ardent love of the mother country eventually endeared him to his new coal country friends. He became a confidant of several "bodymasters," alleged ringleaders of the region's criminal underworld, including Patrick Dormer, a saloon keeper in Pottsville, and John Kehoe, a tavern owner in Girardsville known as "The King of the Mollies." Michael "Muff" Lawler, so nicknamed because he had two beards, one on each side of his chin, welcomed McKenna into his home as a boarder. In April 1874 Lawler, believing McKenna might be helpful to the AOH because he could read and write, inducted the detective into the Order. Soon McKenna was made an officer of the group.

Later that year, in December, a showdown ensued between Gowen and the WBA when the rail baron announced a 20 percent wage cut in Reading-controlled mines, prompting the WBA miners to strike as of January 1, 1875. Management fought back with scabs imported and protected by the Coal and Iron Police, while twenty-six members of the WBA leadership were arrested on trumped-up charges. Conditions in the mining towns were atrocious that winter, as the bosses worked to literally starve the strikers and their families into submission. During the course of what became known as "the Long Strike," which lasted from January through June 1875, the WBA finally weakened and collapsed. With the union's influence in the region now obliterated, a new round of violence broke out between former WBA rank and file and Gowen's police and vigilantes. An anonymous note sent to a local newspaperman stated:

> I am against shooting as mutch as ye are. But the union is Broke up and we Have got nothing to defind ourselves with But our Revolvers and if we dount use them we shal have to work For 50 cints a Day. And I tell ye the other nationalateys is the same as we are onley thay are to Damd cowardley. Ye can think and say what ye Like it is all the same to us. But I have told ye the Mind of the children of Mistress Molly Maguire.[81]

McKenna had meanwhile gathered information on several crimes, including the murder of Tamaqua police chief Benjamin Yost, as well as the killing of miner William Uren and mine bosses Thomas Sanger and John Jones at SM Heaton & Company's colliery at Raven Run. Yost, who had been warned that his head would be made "softer than his ass" for poking around in AOH affairs, was killed early one morning while dousing the Tamaqua streetlamps.[82] Sanger's final transgression had been to ignore a "coffin notice" warning him to leave Schuylkill County. He, along with Uren and Jones, had died in a blaze of gunfire at the hands of five strangers who showed up at SM Heaton's mine pretending to seek work.

The undercover detective ultimately provided Gowen with the names of 347 people he suspected of involvement in various criminal plots. Using this intelligence, Gowen in September 1875 ordered two dozen men arrested and accused them of belonging to a terror group known as the Molly Maguires. The first case prosecuted, a January 1876 conviction of Michael Boyle for the murder of John Jones, did not require McParlan's testimony, but suspicions had been aroused among the Mollies that someone was talking. A secret AOH membership list had mysteriously been made public, suggesting a spy was at work, and early in 1876 a railroad conductor who had had a previous run-in with McParlan recognized and exposed him as a Pinkerton. In March 1876 a very lucky "McKenna" managed to slip out of the region before the Mollies he'd double-crossed could lay hands on him.

The first of what would be a series of show trials began in spring 1876 featuring the testimony of McParlan (whose true identity was now revealed), and that of a Mollie turncoat, Jimmy Kerrigan, who stood only four feet eleven inches and was known even to his own wife as "a little rat." She testified that it had been her husband who had murdered Officer Yost, not the men accused of the deed.

By now the story of McParlan's undercover feat and the shady workings of a clandestine gang of Irish outlaws had reached New York and Philadelphia, and big-city reporters were drawn to the Schuylkill County Courthouse in Pottsville ("Murder County," *Miners Journal* editor Bannan had dubbed the community). Much as disturbing tales of Southern Ku Klux Klan violence had once titillated newspaper readers, the Molly Maguires and the intrepid detective who'd fooled them in their lair also made for compelling copy. The appeal of the Molly Maguire allegations, of course, as Gowen well knew, was that they piqued existing public fears that labor organizations, particularly clannish ones based on ethnic identity, were radical and probably dangerous. The *Irish World* and the *Labor Standard* denounced the "Molly" stories, suggesting the gang's alleged exploits had been concocted by the Pinkertons and the railroads, and Terence Powderly, Grand Master Workman of the Knights of Labor, asserted that the accused men might have in fact been led by McParlan, "under the guise of friendship," to commit "deeds of desperation and blood."[83] Gowen himself was likely surprised at how effectively his evocation of Irish brigands riding the Pennsylvania hills played with the press, for a few years earlier he had tried with far less success to peddle the story that the Hibernians were "Communists." As for Powderly's allegation, it's never been entirely clear how much of McParlan's reporting was accurate, or whether Gowen helped embellish some of the tales. Perhaps, as one scholar suggests, "the world believed it all because it was just too good to be false."[84]

At the time a private citizen had the right to serve as prosecutor in a criminal case, and Gowen announced that he, a former district attorney, would lead the prosecution. He proceeded to fill the jury box with Pennsylvania Dutch, conservative farm folk known to regard the working-class Irish as hooligans. The height of the melodrama came on May 12, 1876, during the trial of Tom Munley for the murders of Thomas Sanger and William Uren, when Gowen delivered a stirring oration that bordered on the hallucinatory but effectively sealed the fate of the Molly Maguires. He declared:

> This very organization that we are now, for the first time,
> exposing to the light of day, has hung like a pall over the people
> of this country. Behind it stalked darkness and despair, brooding
> like grim shadows over the desolated hearth and the ruined
> home, and throughout the length and breadth of this fair land
> was heard the voice of wailing and of lamentation. . . . Nor is
> it alone those whose names that I have mentioned, but it is the
> hundreds of unknown victims, whose bones lie mouldering over
> the face of this county.

Gowen, pacing before the jury, made a mournful face and indicated with a sweep of his arm the world beyond the courtroom, saying, "In hidden places and by silent paths, in the dark ravines of the mountains, and in secret ledges of the rocks, who shall say how many bodies of the victims of this order now await the final trump of God?"

But, he warned:

> There is not a place on the habitable globe where these men
> can find refuge and in which they will not be tracked down. Let
> them go to the Rocky Mountains, or to the shores of the Pacific;
> let them traverse the bleak deserts of Siberia, penetrate into the
> jungles of India, or wander over the wild steppes of Central Asia,
> and they will be dogged and tracked and brought to justice, just
> as surely as Thomas Munley is brought to justice today.[85]

Gowen ended his three-hour lecture with the ludicrous proposal that if any of the Mollies present wished to assassinate *him* as they had so callously snuffed out the lives of decent policemen and mine officials, they should do so now. The speech sold briskly in pamphlet form.

Several additional cases were heard, McParlan's testimony leading to the conviction of eleven men for murder and arson. In addition to Jimmy Kerrigan's perjured testimony, a convict known as Kelly the Bum, who was already in prison on a murder charge, was brought forth to offer incriminating evidence against alleged Mollies in exchange for leniency in his own case. It was reported that he had confided to a cellmate at the trial, "I would squeal on Jesus Christ to get out of here."[86]

Against the onslaught of public outrage, rigged testimony, and Gowen's theatrics, lawyers for the accused men faced an almost impossible task. "For God's sake give labor an equal chance," one defense attorney exhorted the jury. "Do not crush it. Let it not perish under the imperial mandates of capital in a free country."[87] But the juries' verdicts were a foregone conclusion. On June 21, 1876, ten Mollies were hanged in Pottsville and in nearby Mauch Chunk, the executions heavily guarded by armed soldiers to discourage possible rescue. Soon after, nine other men were executed and two dozen sent to prison.

So remote was the area where the Mollies allegedly held sway, and so grandiose did the sensationalized claims of their abuses become, that it is difficult even to this day to ascertain their actual history. While the tradition remains that the Molly Maguires were a treacherous gang of labor sympathizers who terrorized the anthracite district for a generation or more, it is likely that Gowen's conflation of the Mollies with the WBA, his bare-knuckle investigative and prosecutorial tactics, along with hundreds of sensationalized news articles, are more truly responsible for their enduring legend—an early example of capital energizing the courts and the press to paint labor with the broad brush of treason and criminality. Even in the midst of the trials, local Pottsville folk assured a *New York Times* reporter that it was common knowledge that Gowen had brought the prosecutions "for the purpose of breaking up a labor organization that was hurtful to his business interests"[88] and had allowed popular prejudice against the Irish to do the rest.

The Mollies, in the end, were not above creating legends of their own. Convicted outlaw Tom Fisher placed a handprint on the wall of his jail cell as he awaited execution at Mauch Chunk in March 1878, and predicted it would remain there forever as a sign of his innocence. The hand's outline was visible as late as the 1930s, it is said, when it was plastered over to discourage the curious.[89]

I N 1873 AMERICA TRIPPED OVER its own hurrying feet. With the failure of the banking house of Jay Cooke and Company and the ensuing collapse of other financial firms, the post–Civil War economic boom in stocks, railroads, and new national markets seemed suddenly to have run its course. The panic's effects rippled out from the East Coast to farms, mines, and retailers across the country, halting construction and slowing manufacturing. Even the thriving steel mills were quieted, prompting one veteran of that enterprise to predict that "within a few years, the furnace-stacks of the industry [will] only be useful as observatories for the study of astronomy."[90]

Labor, which had struggled to find a cogent answer to the swift buildup of industry and the dehumanizing organization of factory work, now faced the challenges of slashed wages and massive layoffs. Unionization itself was jeopardized. As of 1870 there had been thirty-three national unions, but there were only nine by 1877, with overall union membership down from three hundred thousand in 1870 to fifty thousand in 1876. William Sylvis's NLU, which had once boasted six hundred thousand members, had folded in 1872, three years after the death of its guiding force. The eight-hour cause, cooperatives—each had thrived in turn, but neither had adequately answered the question of whether American workers could shorten the economic distance between themselves and their employers, or could themselves become producers of wealth. The Knights of St. Crispin, a shoemakers' union organized in 1867, gained prominence and built a membership of fifty thousand, but collapsed within a decade, having dissipated much of its energy opposing new manufacturing technology and the unskilled immigrant labor that operated it. The Noble and Holy Order of the Knights of Labor, a pan-trades organization started in 1869 that somewhat replicated the broad agenda of the NLU, had by the mid-1870s gathered no more than five thousand members, while the strongest railroad union, the Brotherhood of Locomotive Engineers, was largely a benevolent society with little taste for confrontation; its craft elitism tended to minimize even the likelihood of collaboration with fellow rail workers.

Hard times offered little traction to workers but were especially punishing to the indigent. Reconstruction, the federal government's effort to guide the former Confederate states' reentry into the Union with new state constitutions, the vote for the freedmen, and equal rights, was increasingly derided as hubristic social and political engineering; federal "occupying" troops and remaining carpetbag governors sympathetic to Reconstruction's aims were chased from the South by 1877. Out of sheer weariness with war- and race-related issues, and also from impatience with Reconstruction's perceived excesses, the American public had largely surrendered its postwar idealism; it now evinced scant interest in programs to relieve the plight of the distressed, especially Southern freedmen. At the same time, in response to the influx of immigrants from Germany and other European nations with turbulent political histories, such as France with its recent Paris Commune, authorities became concerned that any unified expression of worker grievances might not be homegrown, but rather a brand of insurrection drummed up in the cafés of Berlin, Paris, or Vienna.

Such misapprehensions were not the only obstacles to arriving immigrant workers as they struggled to gain a foothold in their adopted land. A trend of thought known as Social Darwinism (unfair to its namesake, the British naturalist Charles Darwin) contended that social inequalities were inevitable, that the well-off deserved their station in life as the poor deserved theirs. In a sense this was the ideology of free labor taken to its cruelest extreme: each person was to be unhindered in their quest for

wealth, security, and independence; but when fate or ill fortune intervened they were left to their own devices, their plight no one else's fault
or responsibility. "It is not the purpose or object of the city government
to furnish work to the industrious poor," New York mayor William Havemeyer had reminded a delegation of unemployed men after the Tompkins
Square riot of 1874. "That system belongs to other countries, not ours."[91]
From his Brooklyn pulpit, the Reverend Henry Ward Beecher expanded
on the concept:

> We look upon the importation of the communistic and like
> European notions as abominations. Their notions and theories
> that the government should be paternal and take care of the
> welfare of its subjects and provide them with labor, is un-
> American. It is the form in which oppression has had its most
> disastrous scope in the world. The American doctrine is that
> it is the duty of the government merely to protect the people
> while they are taking care of themselves—nothing more than
> that. "Hands off," we say to the government. "See to it that we
> are protected in our rights and our individuality. No more than
> that."[92]

But with 5 million unemployed nationwide and their families suffering in hunger and squalor, demonstrations like the one in Tompkins
Square had become a distressing feature of life in large cities such as Chicago, Cleveland, Philadelphia, and New York, a reality no philosophy of
self-reliance, however eloquently stated, could erase.

Soon workers' frustration found an appropriate and vulnerable target:
the railroads. The reach of the nation's rail network, built on aggressive
expansion and fat government land grants, now extended to more than
seventy thousand miles of track, a development crowned by the 1869 linking of the two coasts with the driving of the golden spike at Promontory,
Utah. The railroads' growth created new national markets for beef, wheat,
and other goods shipped by freight, along with faster and more efficient

modes of passenger travel. States such as Maryland, Pennsylvania, and Illinois became busy national crossroads, hubs of a system that served the entire country and was maintained by tens of thousands of workers.[93]

The rights of these workers had for the most part failed to expand along with the industry. The "roads" were notorious for delayed payment of salaries or offering only scrip transferable at company stores; there was no sick pay, and in some instances even fines for days or hours of missed work. Workers were frequently made to sign what they called "obnoxious contracts," pledging to abide by company rules and to not attempt to hold management responsible for injury. The latter was a dreadful stipulation in an occupation so routinely dangerous that "a brakeman with both hands and all his fingers was either remarkably skillful, incredibly lucky or new on the job." The implementation of safety measures in the coupling of trains alone would have greatly reduced rail yard injuries, but, as the trainmen said, "Condolences come cheaper."[94]

But for once labor held a key potential advantage. Unlike most businesses, railroads were geographically "infinite," their property stretching across vast miles of open countryside, while their trains ran on strict timetables, connecting and intersecting at hundreds of hubs and junctions. Even the most localized work stoppage or disruption had the potential to halt freight and passenger service over entire regions. Nor could owners protect railway equipment from those who knew best how it ran; striking workers might commandeer dispatch towers, cripple trackside switches, disable locomotives, or carry out other forms of sabotage.

A preview of the trouble that might ensue came in March 1874, when the Erie Railway fell behind in paying workers at its machine shops in Susquehanna Depot near Scranton. On March 15, a day upon which the Erie had promised that wages would be paid, the railroad announced that it had suffered recent financial reversals and could not make good until the twenty-fifth. The workers agreed to the ten-day grace period but warned they would cease all work if the extended deadline was not met. On the twenty-fifth came word that the company was still short and that it had been forced to prioritize payment to workers elsewhere in the Erie system, as those wages were in even greater arrears.

Their patience exhausted, the Susquehanna workers seized the company premises, drove away the managers, and vowed that if they were not paid within twenty-four hours they would begin halting trains. The Erie's response was to fire the leaders of the threatened strike, an act so infuriating to workers that they attacked a number of locomotives, disabling and detouring them into a roundhouse, leaving one thousand freight cars loaded with coal and petroleum and other goods stranded on adjacent sidings. In some cases the trainmen removed crucial mechanical parts of the engines and held them hostage, stashing them elsewhere in the town.

"The people and press of this section are in sympathy with the men," reported the *New York Times*, "and the opinion among all classes is that the company [has] acted in very bad faith with all the employees."[95] Even Sheriff M. M. Helme sided with the strikers, refusing the Erie's demands that he chase them off railroad property or seek the help of the state militia. Pennsylvania governor J. F. Hartranft told the railroad only Sheriff Helme could make a formal request for troops, while five leading citizens of Susquehanna signed a telegram to the governor assuring him soldiers were not needed. Governor Hartranft, however, did feel obliged to warn the strike's leaders:

> As an individual, I may sympathize with your people in their misfortune in not receiving prompt payment of their dues, but, as the Chief Executive of this State, I cannot allow creditors, however meritorious their claims may be, to forcibly seize property of their debtors, and hold it without due process of law. Much less can I allow them to take and hold illegal possession of a great highway, and punish the innocent public, either as passengers or transporters, for the default of a corporation with which they have no concern.[96]

Railroad lawyers scrambled for a solution: reports were already coming in of delays and stalled trains elsewhere down the line. As the chaos around the depot showed no sign of abating, Sheriff Helme, under mounting pressure from the Erie, did eventually call in the militia. Two

thousand soldiers bearing thirty pieces of artillery arrived at Susquehanna, ordering all persons from railroad property. The angry workers cursed the militiamen, but allowed themselves to be herded off the
tracks. The company then extended an olive branch, offering to rein-
state all employees except the strike spokesmen, whom they deemed to
be agitators. When the workers denounced the offer the railroad played
its trump card, threatening that if the strike didn't end at once it would
relocate the Susquehanna rail shops permanently to Elmira, New York.
Local businesses, alarmed by the economic catastrophe inherent in such
a threat, hurriedly withdrew their support of the strikers, one merchant
even handing to the Erie's representatives a list he had compiled of those
who had egged on the strike. Within hours the workers began drifting
back to their jobs.

The Susquehanna standoff held lessons for both labor and management. Rail workers had glimpsed how fully the country's railroads could
be delayed, the public inconvenienced, and corporate revenues hurt by
a well-timed and strategically located strike. Railroads took away from
the crisis the certainty that such disturbances must be terminated in
their earliest phase and that clearing railroad tracks of belligerent people
required soldiers with guns.[97]

T HE UNITED STATES OBSERVED the centennial of its birth in July
1876, with a world's fair in Philadelphia and patriotic commemo-
rations in virtually every city and town, as citizens recalled the nation's
heroic beginnings and regarded with awe the various social and technological attainments that marked the distance it had come. But it was also
a year of division across a land still recovering from civil war and diminished by economic distress. The administration of President Ulysses S.
Grant was by now associated with several scandals—the Crédit Mobilier's
overbilling for the construction of a Union Pacific roadbed that had lined
the pockets of stockholders and politicians; the Whiskey Ring, centered
in St. Louis, in which distillers withheld federal liquor taxes and bought
official complicity; and the Belknap scandal, wherein Secretary of War

William Belknap and his wife "Puss" were found to have taken payments in exchange for the lucrative appointment of a military post tradership. Even the much-admired Reverend Beecher had been exposed as a charlatan and seducer.

The presidential election itself in that centennial year would be deeply flawed and bitterly contested; with results in several key states in dispute, it played out with backroom deals as well as promises of federal money for a Southern railway, the restoration of white rule in the South, and the setting aside of equal rights for the freedmen in the interest of national reconciliation. When all the trade-offs were in place, Democrat Samuel Tilden, who had probably won the election, was turned aside, and the Republican governor of Ohio, Rutherford B. Hayes, thereafter known as "His Fraudulency," was installed in the White House. The powerful influence of the railroad interests, led by Thomas Scott, a U.S. senator and president of the Pennsylvania Railroad, had a role in producing the final bargain.

As scandal, compromise, and chicanery tainted the highest and mightiest, the lower classes "brooded on the oppression of labor, the arrogance of capital, the wild inequality of fortune, the misery of tenement life, [and] the fear and hunger and degradation of hard times. Whenever quitting time poured thousands into the streets," wrote the *Nation*, "there stood the mob, ready-made."[98]

The railroad operators sensed something volatile brooding along their thinly extended system, and the end of the centennial year brought an unsettling portent—one of the most horrific train wrecks in the country's history. On the snowy night of December 29, 1876, a Lake Shore Road Pacific Express with hundreds of passengers aboard broke through a trestle bridge just east of Ashtabula, Ohio. The wreckage collapsed into a ravine and caught fire. Those fortunate enough to excise themselves struggled in the pitch darkness and freezing water, listening to the screams of those trapped inside the overturned cars, many of whom burned to death. Survivors related the ghastly story of a woman pleading that her leg be severed with an ax that she might escape the flames. One hundred of the 160 people aboard perished, including a prominent Cleveland minister, a pair of newlyweds from Buffalo, and a female cousin of Rutherford B. Hayes.[99]

Three months later the railroads faced a different kind of setback when in March the United States Supreme Court upheld the right of the states to regulate private enterprise used by the public, meaning that the railroads alone would no longer be allowed to set the highly profitable rates they charged for the storage and transport of goods. The case, *Munn v. Illinois*, was the result of efforts by farmers united in the National Grange of the Patrons of Husbandry; the farmers sought to reduce price gouging by the railroads that controlled the flow of agricultural products to big-city markets. The high court, in a 7–2 ruling, established the constitutionality of the so-called Granger laws—the right of state governments to restrict commerce on railroads, ferries, bridges, waterways, and other facilities, on the grounds that when one puts "property to a use in which the public has an interest, he, in effect, grants to the public an interest in that use, and must submit to be controlled by the public for the common good."[100] The decision was a blow to the autonomy of the railroads and the first step toward the creation of the Interstate Commerce Act of 1887 and the Interstate Commerce Commission to regulate national transport.

Chastened by *Munn* and contemplating declining revenues due to the court's ruling, the major railroads agreed to halt their self-destructive rate wars. The heads of the big eastern roads—John W. Garrett of the Baltimore & Ohio, William H. Vanderbilt of the New York Central, Hugh J. Jewett of the Erie, and Tom Scott of the Pennsylvania—held a series of meetings in which they worked out ways to pool their freight schedules and adjust shipping rates for their mutual advantage. They also discussed the need for wage cuts and how any ensuing strikes might be combated. The Susquehanna debacle of 1874 was still a fresh memory, and in 1876 the Boston and Maine had been challenged by a potent walkout of the Brotherhood of Locomotive Engineers, a strike crushed only through attrition of the Brotherhood's funds.

It was also recalled, however, that Franklin Gowen's Reading had survived a recent work stoppage because it happened to have a pooling arrangement with other coal carriers; its share of the annual business secured, the railroad was less affected by a short-term strike and could afford to wait out disgruntled workers. The four major roads are believed to have agreed on a similar arrangement—what some critics dubbed "strike insurance." When one railroad cut workers' wages and suffered a strike, the other three would cover its lost traffic for the strike's duration. Once that strike had been broken or resolved, the next railroad could roll back wages, with the same guarantee of support from the others. It was a surefire plan to limit the potential losses from labor disruptions and render rail employees's striking power nil.[101]

This self-serving strategy allowed the firms to conveniently avoid dealing with the very real grievances simmering among rail workers— exhausting work schedules, the lack of overtime pay, an unacceptable frequency of on-the-job injuries, and a seniority system that was exploited to underpay new hires. By choosing the subterfuge of "strike insurance," the corporations neglected the opportunity to address the simple fact that workingmen were being pushed by the rail system to work longer for less pay in a dangerous occupation that in every way treated them as replaceable cogs. "Drive a rat into a corner and he will fight," warned the *Irish World* at the end of June 1877. "Drive your serfs to desperation . . . and in their desperation they will some day pounce upon you and destroy you."[102]

THE LONG-ANTICIPATED CONFRONTATION began two weeks later, on July 16, at Martinsburg, West Virginia. That day the Baltimore & Ohio had announced a 10 percent wage cut, the second since fall 1876. Firemen were to be lowered from $1.75 to $1.58 per day, brakemen from $1.50 to $1.35. The company also said it planned to reduce the number of days available for work. For several hours unhappy trainmen milled about the Martinsburg yards discussing the cuts; then the crew of a cattle train abruptly stopped work, leaving their live cargo stranded. When management sought other workers to replace the crew, the crowd of employees announced that the yard was to be frozen. To emphasize the point, B & O brakeman Richard Zepp led his fellow workers in uncoupling trains so they could not be moved. Mayor A. T. Shutt arrived on the scene and ordered three men taken into custody, but the arresting police were themselves quickly surrounded and made to free the prisoners. Railroad officials in Wheeling, the state capital, learning by telegraph of what had occurred, implored West Virginia governor Henry M. Matthews to order the Beverly Light Guards, a local Martinsburg militia, to secure the B & O yards at once.

The militia, under the command of Colonel C. J. Faulkner, entered the yards early the next morning and attempted to move the cattle train that was still standing in the station from the previous day, but no engineer would cooperate. Soldiers then took charge of the locomotive. When the cars began to move a striking fireman named William Vandergriff threw a track switch, diverting the train. Private John Poisal of the Berkeley Guards confronted Vandergriff, rifle in hand, at which Vandergriff drew a pistol and fired, grazing the soldier, who immediately returned fire, as did other militiamen, mortally wounding Vandergriff. Other strikers then shot Poisal, bloodying his right hand. Most of the militiamen were locals who were halfhearted about policing the strikers in the first place, and the exchange of gunfire and the wounding of two men seemed to permanently sour them on the mission. Many walked away, ending the militia's brief effort to break the strike, while the cattle were off-loaded and driven to graze in a nearby pasture.

Frustrated by the militia's abandonment of its duty, the B & O demanded that Governor Matthews request federal troops, the rail bosses assuring President Hayes in a separate telegram that "this great national highway can only be restored for public use by the interposition of U.S. forces."[103] Hayes, installed recently as president on a Republican promise to formally end Reconstruction by withdrawing federal troops from the South, stood at an historical crossroads.[104] Although the fourth article of the Constitution, which promises each state a republican form of government, required the president to send troops at the request of a state's governor to quell domestic violence, not since the time of President Jackson had the president dispatched federal soldiers during peacetime to settle a labor dispute.[105] Hayes's immediate predecessor, President Grant, had had numerous opportunities to weigh the requests of Republican governors in Southern states for emergency military aid; often Grant had complied; more recently he had refused; but the resounding sentiment that accompanied the end of Reconstruction, as Hayes confided to his diary, was that the time had come to "put aside the bayonet," in effect to cease the practice of using federal troops to intervene in local affairs. Still, what was happening to the B & O was no longer local politics or civil rights but *business*. With governors and leading railroad men beseeching Washington's help, citing the complete disruption of America's railways and the inability or unwillingness of local militia to put down the rebellion, Hayes concluded he had no option but to direct three hundred troops to Martinsburg.[106]

The soldiers, led by Major General W. H. French, were apparently under orders to avoid bloodshed; one observer said it looked as though they hoped to intimidate people simply by allowing sunlight to gleam off their bayonets.[107] With help from those militiamen who had remained loyal, the federal troops were able to make it possible for trains to pass through the town, although they were unable to convince B & O employees to move stranded trains.

Those trains that did pass through were not having an easy time. In sympathy with Martinsburg, other workers in the vicinity—ironworkers, canal men, miners—had begun a campaign of harassment, hurling stones at trains, blocking the tracks, and occasionally skirmishing with crews. These trackside ambushes were impossible for even the army to detect or defend against, as they could come from the cover of woods or bushes, at blind curves, or from beneath rail bridges. The entire countryside, it appeared, was in rebellion against the railroad.

Hoping to head off further outbreaks, B & O brass on July 20 asked Governor John Lee Carroll of Maryland to provide armed assistance at Cumberland, a key rail junction in western Maryland, about forty miles from Martinsburg, where a strike was imminent. Carroll wanted to avoid the mistake of Martinsburg—sending local militiamen who would prove timid and useless against their own neighbors—so he ordered two regiments of the Maryland National Guard to entrain at Baltimore. The march of the Guard's Fifth Regiment from its armory to Baltimore's Camden Station coincided with quitting time at local factories. At first the workers gathering along city streets instinctively cheered the passing soldiers; when word spread of their mission, however, the crowd's temper changed. Ugly words and curses fell on the uniformed men, a hail of stones and brickbats followed, and in a moment the proud, orderly procession had become a rout, as the Guardsmen quick-marched, then ran toward the depot, covering their heads from airborne missiles.

Worse was to come. An officer of the other regiment ordered out, the Sixth, began leading his troops through the same streets where the Fifth had been attacked; by now nearly fifteen thousand protestors lay in wait. The regiment's 150 troops—cursed at, spat upon, showered with bricks and stones—ran and then panicked under the bombardment; nearly half the troops deserted. Some who gamely remained in ranks fired their rifles into the air to scare off their tormentors; when that proved ineffectual, they leveled their guns at the crowd. Ten men and boys were killed by the soldiers' fire.

The depot itself proved no safe haven. A mob swarmed around the station and began vandalizing empty cars and equipment; one group of rioters commandeered a locomotive and managed to drive it entirely off the tracks, while another set fire to wooden freight cars on the south end of the train yard. Governor Carroll, who was himself trapped inside the station along with other state officials and National Guard officers, urgently telegraphed President Hayes for the army. Without hesitation, Hayes dispatched several federal units to the scene.

By now the White House telegraph was clattering almost nonstop, as the workers' insurrection—unguided by any organized trade union, yet abetted by throngs of angry citizens—spread from the B & O to the Pennsylvania Railroad. Trouble started on the Pennsylvania when the road announced that all freight trains bound east would be "doubleheaders"—a train with two locomotives and extra cars. Ordinarily a freight train was considered complete with seventeen cars, but doubleheaders often hauled as many as thirty-six. The doubling-up required one train crew to perform the work of two, allowing the railroad to discharge another crew from duty. Pittsburgh-based trainmen for the Pennsylvania had been following word of events in Martinsburg, and when at eight o'clock on the morning of Thursday, July 19, the call came to "shape up a doubleheader," a flagman named Gus Harris refused. Other railroad workers in the Pittsburgh yard were appealed to, but they chose to follow Harris's example. When trainmaster David Garrett asked flagman Andrew Hice to get a train moving, Hice replied: "It's a question of bread or blood, and we're going to resist. If I go to the penitentiary I can get bread and water, and that's about all I can get now."[108] Within an hour of Hice's declaration, other trains were stopped and a formidable crowd of men and boys had gathered in the Pittsburgh yard.

Railroad work stoppages in places like Martinsburg or Cumberland were inconvenient, to be sure, but Pittsburgh was a major rail crossroads and the nation's leading industrial city. With its oil refineries, glass factories, iron mills, and steel rolling mills in almost continuous operation, the town by night, its smokestacks belching flames, was said to resemble "Hell with the lid off."[109] The ramifications of a strike there would be felt within a few hours across the entire country.

At first, efforts by local authorities to contain the situation were almost comical. Pittsburgh police ranks had been thinned by recent layoffs, so no more than eight officers were available for emergency duty in the train yards; meanwhile, a militia unit that showed up soon stacked its weapons and began mingling amicably with the strikers. "The laboring people . . . will not take up arms to put down their brethren," a striker told a reporter. "Will capital, then, rely on the United States Army? Pshaw!" He warned that even federal forces "would be swept from our path like leaves in the whirlwind."[110]

The rapidly spreading railroad strike was difficult for authority to confront for the simple reason that it was unorganized—the largely spontaneous acting out by embittered workers of "mischievous passions . . . easily wrought to excess and desperation."[111] But the circumstances did create instantaneous leadership. In Pittsburgh, a rail federation called the Trainmen's Union had emerged in early June, its spokesman a twenty-five-year-old brakeman named Robert Ammons. The union sought to organize all railroad men under one flag, a departure from the traditionally stratified and not always cooperative brotherhoods of engineers, firemen, brakemen, and conductors. On the evening of July 19 Ammons's group rallied at Phoenix Hall on Pittsburgh's Eleventh Street, where resolutions were struck to continue opposition to the Pennsylvania's doubleheader policy. The list of other demands drawn up included a restoration of wages as received prior to June 1, rehiring of men dismissed for strike activities, and the equalizing of pay for certain job classifications. A visiting mill worker assured the railroaders of his support: "We're with you. We're in the same boat. I heard a reduction of ten per cent hinted at in our mill this morning. I won't call employers despots, I won't call them tyrants, but the term capitalists is sort of synonymous and will do as well."[112] By the next night, the elite Brotherhood of Locomotive Engineers had joined the Trainmen's Union, evidence of growing worker solidarity against the major roads.

Meanwhile, the brief holiday of Pittsburgh militia setting aside their duties and their guns came to an end. City officials had arranged to bring in six hundred troops of the First Division of the Pennsylvania National Guard from Philadelphia, a crack militia unit composed in part of Civil War veterans. There was a tradition of antagonism between the western areas of Pennsylvania and the city of Philadelphia, and the First's "invasion" of Pittsburgh—it arrived in a convoy of two trains with several pieces of artillery and a Gatling gun—was vehemently resented. Even as the troop trains came into view at the outskirts of Pittsburgh, they already showed extensive damage from the stones, bricks, and chunks of coal with which they'd been bombarded as they'd passed through Harrisburg, Altoona, and other towns. Many of the trains' windows were broken and debris covered the rooftops.

The welcome was equally hostile at the corner of Liberty Street and Twenty-eighth, where the soldiers faced a crowd of six thousand strikers and spectators who pelted them with a barrage of projectiles. The troops, hemmed in by the infuriated crowd, fired into the air, but a second volley was far more lethal, mowing down scores of people and killing twenty, including an eighteen-year-old local militiaman. The wounded included women and small children.

The town seethed in reaction. "Shot in Cold Blood by the Roughs of Philadelphia. The Lexington of the Labor Conflict Is at Hand," blasted one local headline. As the dead were grieved over and carried away, "howling crowds paraded the streets, and it was not safe to say a word against the strikers, as a blow would follow its utterance," reported the *New York Times*, which headlined its coverage "A Terrible Day in Pittsburgh."[113] James Bonn & Sons, a prominent weapons dealer, was sacked of guns and ammunition. Some protestors managed to lay hands on rifles abandoned earlier by the local militia. These armed citizens then laid siege to the roundhouse, where the Philadelphia soldiers had taken cover after the shooting. The mob captured the soldiers' rations wagons, thus denying them food and water, but more dramatic measures were deemed necessary to deal with the cowards who had fired upon and killed innocent people.

The roundhouse, to the misfortune of those inside, lay at the bottom of an incline, and the crowd, unable to lure the invaders out, seized freight cars loaded with oil and coal, set them ablaze, and pushed them downhill toward the building. By Sunday morning the roundhouse was on fire and the captive guardsmen had no choice but to evacuate as best they could. "It was better to run the risk of being shot down than burned to death, and so we filed out in a compact body," one recalled. "It was lively times, I tell you, reaching the U.S. Arsenal. . . . I thought we should all be cut to pieces."[114] Some had changed into civilian clothes in the hope of blending into the crowd. Several soldiers were struck by bullets as they headed for the safety of the arsenal, prompting a commander to order a Gatling gun fired to disperse those who continued to harass the troops. The mob, its fury unquenched, then turned on the railroad's property and the downtown area, burning, looting, and destroying.[115] More than a hundred locomotives and two thousand freight cars were savaged, along with a grain elevator and the city's main passenger depot.

Residents awoke the next day to the sight of a huge plume of smoke over the rail yards and the newspaper headline "Pittsburgh Sacked—The City Completely in the Power of a Howling Mob." In truth the mob, having rioted itself to exhaustion, had largely gone home, but two square miles of America's greatest industrial city lay in near-total ruin.

B Y NOW THE GREAT STRIKE OF 1877 had taken on a life of its own, causing violence and turmoil on a scale unprecedented in America's peacetime history. In many places it assumed the form of spontaneous turnouts, as laborers at pipe works, tanneries, hog yards, mines, and rolling mills walked off. In Galveston, black longshoremen led a strike action demanding $2 per day, and were soon joined by whites. At Louisville, black sewer workers attacked the Louisville and Nashville Railroad while a marauding group of white strikers closed some factories and besieged others, urging textile workers, carpenters, and mechanics to join them. Sympathy strikes and sabotage tied up railroads from Worcester to San Francisco. So quickly did the fracas become widespread, a newspaper in Chicago telling of the rebellion's arrival required only the succinct headline "It Is Here!"

Chicago could hardly expect a reprieve. It was the nation's key rail hub, and its large and impoverished working class provided a tinderbox of discontent. The Workingmen's Party (WP), the first Marxist-influenced political party in America, organized in Philadelphia in 1876, was active there with a substantial following of foreign-born laborers. It was led by two well-spoken Americans, Philip Van Patten and Albert Parsons. Van Patten was educated, a draftsman by trade. Parsons was an ex-Confederate officer driven from the South for his liberal ideas;

and in Chicago he had been drawn into politics, running unsuccessfully for alderman.

With Parsons and Van Patten at the lead, the WP channeled the strike's energy coming out of the East with local resentment against railroads and authority in general. On the evening of Monday the twenty-third, Parsons went before a crowd of thirty thousand on Market Street to appeal to unemployed war veterans; he urged the heroes of the Grand Army of the Republic—now soldiers in what he termed a "Grand Army of Starvation"—to join "the Grand Army of Labor."

"A mighty spirit is animating the hearts of the American people today," he declared of the rail strike. "When I say the American people I mean the backbone of the country . . ."

The crowd responded with boisterous cheers.

" . . . the men who till the soil, who guide the machine, who weave the fabrics and cover the backs of civilized men. We are part of that people . . ."

"We *are*! We *are*!"

" . . . and we demand that we be permitted to live, that we shall not be turned upon the earth as vagrants and tramps."

The thousands roared their approval, taking up the chant, "Pittsburgh! Pittsburgh! Pittsburgh!"[116]

Local commerce boarded up its storefronts as if in anticipation of a hurricane and waited in fear as the violence grew overnight in fervency, spreading rapidly from the rail yards to the packinghouses, to clothing plants, brickyards, and streetcars. The Chicago Board of Trade, a committee of businessmen led by retailers Marshall Field and Levi Leiter, hired Pinkerton guards, organized private militias to keep watch over affluent residential areas, and authorized the use of their store delivery wagons to transport police reinforcements.

By Tuesday, July 24, the police elected to meet rabble with rabble, hiring unemployed toughs as "special deputies" and arming them with clubs to clear the rail yards. Into the next day there were skirmishes, the beating of rioters by police squads and vigilantes, and several fatalities.

Thursday morning found a squad of police surrounded by a mob of five thousand on the west side near a viaduct where Halsted Street crossed Sixteenth Street. "The mob began to gather, and surged up and down on the sidewalk and in the street—a howling, yelping mob of irresponsible idiots," said *Harper's Weekly*. Hand-to-hand combat ensued, as the cornered police swung their clubs, "hitting to hurt."[117] The struggle with fists, batons, stones, and pistols lasted into the afternoon, claiming numerous lives. That evening the police, now barely discriminating in their attacks, stormed a meeting of the Furniture-Workers Union at Vorwaerts Turner Hall on Twelfth Street. The hall's proprietor, a Mr. Wasserman, was knocked down by the police as they charged into the gathering; the laborers, caught by surprise, defended themselves with the only weapons available: pieces of furniture. A worker named Tessman was slain by gunfire, bringing the total number of victims in the Chicago violence to thirty.[118]

If the Great Strike was convincing of anything, it was that the shift of national concern from Reconstruction to the North's festering labor problems had been prescient. The whiff of class upheaval in the smoke wafting from burning train yards, the bloody encounters between rioters and police or soldiers, the dead being carried away from the barricades, appalled the entire country. Equally distressing was the relative ease with which the rebellion had halted the nation's business. Less than a decade before America had celebrated its new transcontinental rail network; now railmen and their allies had shown that they, too, could unite coast-to-coast; extraordinary as the country's transportation system was, it was now revealed to be only as impregnable as its least contented workers.

One clear lesson that might have been drawn from the disturbances was that capital would be better off if strike actions were brought by "established" workers' organizations, so that corporations and authorities could deal openly with such groups. While the rhetoric of organized strikers could be fierce, even insurrectionary, what they generally were after was respect, recognition, and the acknowledgment (and acceptance) of their demands. Such things could be discussed and negotiated. The alternative—armed boys and men, as well as some women, unaffiliated with any union or subject to group discipline, rioting, and vandalizing— brought only chaos.

But no such analysis emerged from the powerful. Instead, B & O president John W. Garrett was indignant that soldiers did not more willingly shoot rioters; Jay Gould, who had built up the Erie and now was developing the Union Pacific, suggested that perhaps what the nation most needed was a monarchy. Tom Scott of the Pennsylvania Railroad suggested that the hungry strikers try "a rifle diet for a few days and see how they like that kind of bread."[119] The nation's editorial pages were filled with similarly indignant sentiments.

While the 1877 strike is recalled chiefly for its extreme violence and destruction, it actually attained what may have been its fullest fruition in a relatively peaceful general strike at St. Louis. With its eighteen-mile stretch of flour mills, breweries, foundries, and meatpacking plants abreast the Mississippi River, the city was one of the nation's busiest ports. For years it had been a portal to the frontier West; now, with the advance of the railroads, it had assumed more the identity of a shipping crossroads. But the economic downturn of the 1870s had hit the town particularly hard. The National Bank of the State of Missouri had been forced to close in early 1877, and many other businesses followed. Thousands were left jobless. As a local paper warned, the city's poor and out-of-work didn't fully understand what had "struck them down and blasted their lives," yet "they see the sharp contrast between their sufferings and the splendor of the rich; they have been made desperate by want, they are ready to follow any leader."[120]

Unlike Baltimore, Pittsburgh, and Chicago, there was no street fighting in St. Louis, but because the general strike—probably the country's first—so thoroughly choked off the town's commerce and industry, it was the more frightening to established interests. The possibility of "an American Commune" became quite real to local merchants and men of property when the Workingmen's Party led ten thousand in phalanx down the city's broad avenues singing "La Marseillaise," and a speaker reminded the crowd of "a time in the history of France when the poor found themselves oppressed to such an extent that forbearance ceased to be a virtue, and hundreds of heads tumbled into the basket. That time may have arrived with us."[121] Dismayed by what was occurring and being said in the streets, the *St. Louis Republican* lost no time in concluding, "It is wrong to call this a strike, it is labor revolution!"

Racial solidarity was achieved when black stevedores joined the ranks of the strikers. At one point a black man astride a muscular white horse galloped through the factory streets, beseeching workers to set their tools down and come out. Even the town's newsboys struck, declining to peddle newspapers. "All you have to do, gentlemen, for you have the numbers," a strike leader exhorted a rally, "is to unite on one idea—that the workingmen shall rule the country. What man makes belongs to him, and the workingmen made this country."[122]

The strikers did "have the numbers," and so St. Louis employers, stunned by their militancy and made uneasy by the allusions to the guillotine's efficacy, hastily agreed to some wage hikes and shorter hours without a loss of pay. In a double cross, however, many of the offers were rescinded after the U.S. Army arrived, martial law was declared, and eighty strike leaders were arrested; these included several prominent Workingmen's Party figures seen leaping from the windows of their headquarters in a futile attempt to evade the police.

T HE UPHEAVAL OF SUMMER 1877 has always eluded easy explanation. The first labor revolt in American history to spread into a national civil disorder, it channeled not only the exasperation of the eighty thousand rail workers who walked away from their jobs, but the anger and sympathy of countless other workers and the unemployed. "The Republic had celebrated its Centennial in July, 1876," historian David Burbank offers. "Exactly a year later, the industrial working class of the nation celebrated *its* coming of age."[123]

There was an effort by a stunned nation to pin the disturbances on "communistic influences" imported by foreigners, but while this charge may have been somewhat applicable to the St. Louis movement, it was an inadequate characterization overall, given the large number of participants and the inability to find any organization responsible for the strike or even a specific objective. More likely it was simply reassuring to assume that a disturbance that so resembled a class uprising could not possibly be American in origin. As a few editorialists quipped, most of the rioters could not, if queried, have explained what a "Communist" was, and even President Hayes poured cold water on the idea of alien influence by pointing out that the people's vengeance had been directed primarily at the railroads, not property per se. Still, the "Communist" label, once affixed to workingmen, would prove difficult to peel off. "War between labor and capital has begun in earnest," said the *New Orleans Times* of the summer's events. "America's first experience in communism is now the most significant episode of the most extraordinary year in our political history."[124]

It is a revealing measure of how serious the threat posed by labor radicalism seemed in 1877 that a concerted response to the railroad troubles was to expand the National Guard and improve ways to coordinate its equipment and readiness. With the urging and support of leaders of commerce, Northern cities undertook to build armories in concentrated urban industrial areas, for as *Harper's Weekly* noted, "The country has learned the necessity of a thorough and efficient local armed organization."[125] Over the years Americans have come to think of these dour, substantial buildings as historic rallying places for troops in the case of foreign threats to U.S. soil, but their original purpose was to allow the rapid deployment of the militia to keep workingmen in check.

Were the armories necessary? Were the fears of "labor revolution" and "an American Commune" legitimate? At the time the answer appeared far from certain. Historically, U.S. business interests, the courts, the press, have been overly quick to discern conspiracy and foreign influence in labor's struggle for fundamental goals such as better pay, hours, and working conditions. Nonetheless, some conservative anxiety was perhaps understandable in 1877, given that what workers appeared to be challenging were the laissez-faire principles upon which the nation's economy rested. And although labor technically "lost" the railroad strike, its actions inchoate and its gains temporary or few, there was no denying that the scope and vehemence of the outburst had changed perceptions of laboring people and the poor in ways that surprised the whole country, including the workers themselves. What labor had won was a new appreciation of its own strength, and of the power of the strike.

"The calcium light that illumined the skies of our social and industrial life," Socialist George Schilling termed the upheaval[126] opening the country's eyes irrevocably to the frustrations of a large underclass of its own citizens—those who lived on the margins, enduring joblessness, inadequate housing and sanitation, at times facing starvation. It was increasingly evident this was an American dilemma, that there was something fundamentally wrong with the persistence of such dire want in the midst of the world's greatest democracy. "Middle class people began at last to realize what 'survival of the fittest' implied, and to reject it," notes historian Robert Bruce. "More than that, they began to question its corollary of rugged individualism."[127] Harper's Weekly, a barometer of middle-class opinion, fretted that the strike had revealed "a vast movement of the poor against the rich, of labor against capital, which is nothing less than absolute anarchy,"[128] but went on to suggest it was high time this suffering became "the business of the State, that is, the people, to prevent disorder of the kind that we saw in the summer, by removing the discontent which is its cause."[129] Voters appeared to agree. That fall the Workingmen's Party in Louisville elected five men to the Kentucky state legislature, and with the news from Kentucky serving as a catalyst, Workingmen's groups organized around the nation, running candidates for offices across the electoral spectrum. "The laissez-faire policy," one newspaper concluded, "has been knocked out of men's heads for the next generation."[130]

For longer than that many Americans would look back to the summer of 1877 as a turning point, a season whose disruptions helped stir to life multiple strains of reform—the muckrakers' exposé of corruption and corporate excess, the settlement house movement and its determination to educate and lift up the immigrant worker and poor urban dweller, and the growth of oppositional political consciousness in both city and countryside. Even in the sanctum of the White House the momentous change in outlook found expression. "The strikes have been put down by force," President Hayes confided to his diary, "but now for the real remedy."[131]

CHAPTER THREE

WE MEAN TO HAVE EIGHT HOURS

TO TERENCE V. POWDERLY, GRAND MASTER
Workman of the Knights of Labor, the
group's philosophy, "an injury to one is a concern
to all," always held special meaning. His conversion
to the necessity of labor unity had occurred on September 6, 1869, as he watched the bodies of the 179
victims of the Avondale mine disaster brought to
the surface and returned to their grieving families.
A twenty-year-old railroad machinist, Powderly had
until that moment felt "no more cause for complaint
of ill-treatment in the shop I worked in than hundreds of other young men, and had I considered my
own selfish interests alone it is quite likely I would
never have affiliated with any labor organization.
[But] when I saw a mother kneel in silent grief to
hold the cold, still face of her boy to hers, and when
I saw her fall lifeless on his dead body, I experienced
a sensation that I have never forgotten." John Siney
of the Workers Benevolent Association spoke to the
gathered sufferers, and Powderly thought he saw
Christ in Siney's face and heard a new Sermon on
the Mount. "I there resolved to do my part, humble

though it may be, to improve the condition of those who worked for a living."[1]

Five years later, in 1874, Powderly joined the recently founded Knights, which had grown out of a small Philadelphia tailors' union, and whose guiding light, Uriah S. Stephens, shared Powderly's conviction that bettering workers' lives was a sacred cause. A garment cutter and aspiring Baptist minister, Stephens had been inspired by the Freemasons and other mystical orders in devising a structure of elaborate titles and offices for the Knights (he declared himself Grand Master Workman) as well as secret rituals, such as never writing out the organization's name, but instead designating it with five asterisks.

As their name implied, the Knights insisted on the inherent nobility of labor. Like the National Labor Union, they believed the amassed power of capital could be met successfully only by an organization representing the broadest possible community of workingmen. To their ranks Stephens and Powderly welcomed men and women of any race, of all crafts and levels of skill, as well as previously unorganized laborers such as laundresses and tobacco harvesters. So certain was their belief that Americans of good conscience shared the desire for sweeping reform in the dynamic between labor and capital, even employers were encouraged to join.[2]

Powderly succeeded Stephens as Grand Master Workman in 1878 after Stephens, disavowing his usual contempt for politics, ran and lost in a bid for a congressional seat on a Greenback-Labor ticket. Stephens departed the Knights (and died a short time later), although his ideas survived under the leadership of Powderly, who shared Stephens's doubts regarding the wage system and hopes that working citizens might own the means of production. Like Stephens, Powderly had also succumbed to politics, in 1878 becoming the mayor of Scranton.

Powderly, as the labor reporter John Swinton wrote at the time, hardly looked the part of "the leader of a million of the horny-fisted sons of toil."[3] With his small build, bookish mien, and delicate features, he more closely resembled a country parson. In the mode of Rutherford B. Hayes's wife, Lucy, known as "Lemonade Lucy" for her banishment of liquor from the

White House, Powderly was a strict teetotaler and obsessed with the need for temperance among union members. He eschewed giving speeches in casual settings where workers might be drinking beer, warning his aides, "I will talk at no picnics."[4]

The Knights reprised some of the objectives of the NLU, such as cooperatives, land and currency reform, an end to child labor, and economic parity between male and female laborers. In lieu of strikes, which Powderly associated with the railroad troubles of 1877 and considered "a relic of barbarism," the group pursued what he called "uplift," the gradualist improvement of workers' lives through long-term goals like public ownership of the railroads and the disciplining of wayward employers through worker boycotts of consumer products. They established 135 manufacturing cooperatives in areas as diverse as coal mining, cooperage, printing, and shoe-making. Unfortunately all struggled and eventually sank under the same general lack of financing and market skills that had doomed similar NLU experiments. These mostly fruitless efforts drained the Knights' treasury, while the organization's ambivalent and inconsistent attitude toward strikes made its course difficult. Particularly infuriating to members was Powderly's habit of tentatively backing strike actions, only to then withdraw support and recommend conciliation with employers. He also kept the rank and file on edge with his flair for melodrama, announcing frequently that he could no longer carry on the responsibilities of his office, but then fiercely defending his leadership when others appeared willing to accept his departure.

In spite of Powderly's quirks and distaste for work stoppages, the group did claim several strike victories against the railroads beginning in 1882. These led ultimately to a showdown in 1885 with the nation's most powerful railroad financier, Jay Gould. When Gould tried to smash a regional railroad union affiliated with the Knights, Powderly heroically demanded and won a face-to-face meeting, the first time the leader of an American workers' organization had been granted such an encounter with a major capitalist. Gould, no friend of labor, was notorious for the remark, "I can hire half the working class to shoot the other half," but the meeting with Powderly resulted in a significant breakthrough—Gould's agreement to stop targeting the Knights and to accept their right to organize. For his part, Powderly vowed that the Knights would not strike Gould's railroads again without first engaging in direct consultation with management. This unprecedented bringing to terms of as feared a monopolist as Gould greatly enhanced the Knights' reputation, sending their membership soaring from one hundred thousand to seven hundred thousand in just one year. With lighter hearts and a new swagger they sang,

> *Storm the fort, ye Knights of Labor,*
> *Battle for your cause;*
> *Equal rights for every neighbor—*
> *Down with Tyrant laws!*[5]

So completely did the Knights, with this membership surge, assume domination of the U.S. labor movement, there were rumblings of concern among business interests and in editorial pages at the prospect of a national labor organization so powerful it would be capable of launching strike campaigns potentially crippling to commerce. Particularly worrisome was the group's long-term agenda items such as the nationalization of the railroads and other industries. Labor union activity confined to workplace issues was vexing enough; messianic movements fostering economic revolution were unacceptable.

Such anxiety on the part of the establishment proved premature, for the group was soon humbled at the hands of the same Jay Gould whose earlier capitulation had led to its overnight rise. The trouble began when a Knights-federated rail union struck without Powderly's say-so, taking three thousand trainmen off their jobs. Gould responded swiftly, accusing the Grand Master Workman of abnegating the nonstrike agreement; Gould then called in Pinkerton detectives and state militia, and hired anti-labor toughs to safeguard replacement workers. He ordered strike meetings broken up and labor-sympathetic journalists intimidated. The strikers, and the Knights leadership, came in for criticism for inconveniencing the national rail system and selfishly "trying to introduce into modern society a new right . . . the right to be employed by people who do not want you and who cannot afford to pay what you ask."[6] Powderly offered to negotiate, but Gould, sensing he'd gained the upper hand, remained aloof. Ultimately, with the rail workers beset by Gould's hired guns and the rail baron refusing to once again join Powderly at the bargaining table, the latter withdrew the Knights' formal support of the strike and demanded the trainmen return to their jobs. It was an all-out defeat for the Knights, as dispiriting to its members as it was heartening for critics.

An equally serious blow to the Knights' prestige was workers' disappointment with the group's lackluster support of the revived crusade in the 1880s for an eight-hour day. That cause had waned since the collapse of the NLU, but in 1884 the Federation of Organized Trades and Labor Unions, a new trade union conglomerate led by Samuel Gompers, chose eight-hour agitation as a means of galvanizing and growing its membership. Short-hour campaigns were always popular with rank-and-file workers and suited Gompers's philosophy of organized labor's proper aims. Although he's often quoted as having responded cutely to the question "What does labor want?" with the single word "More!," as if his federation's aims were solely pecuniary, Gompers's actual statement, published in 1893, was both visionary and humane, stating in part,

> What does labor want? It wants the earth and the fullness
> thereof. . . . Labor wants more schoolhouses and less jail cells;
> more books and less arsenals; more learning and less vice; more
> leisure and less greed; more justice and less revenge; in fact,
> more of the opportunities to cultivate our better natures, and to
> make manhood more noble, womanhood more beautiful, and
> childhood more happy and bright.[7]

To give workers an objective to rally around, the federation chose May 1, 1886, as a fixed date beyond which no American trade unionist would ever again work more than an eight-hour day. Plans were set for a general strike to take effect on that date—*der Tag* it was called, in anticipation, by German American workers—and the revived movement buzzed with fervent editorials, poetry, and music, including the infectious "Eight-Hour Song."

> *We mean to make things over;*
> *we're tired of toil for naught,*
> *But bare enough to live on:*
> *never an hour for thought.*
>
> *We want to feel the sunshine;*
> *we want to smell the flowers;*
> *We're sure that God has willed it,*
> *and we mean to have eight hours.*
>
> *We're summoning our forces*
> *from shipyard, shop, and mill:*
> *Eight hours for work, eight hours for rest,*
> *eight hours for what we will!*[8]

Although Powderly gave the crusade his halfhearted approval, he cautioned his supporters away from direct conflict with employers or strike talk, urging them instead to seek change through legislation and other peaceful means, such as writing short essays on the benefits of the eight-hour day for their local newspapers.[9] As had become a pattern with the Knights, many of its unions listened politely to Powderly's cautious instructions but then went their own way, unable to resist the broadening surge of the eight-hour crusade. Gompers's federation, as well, found it could not keep pace with its own members' zeal for the reform. Indeed, enthusiasm proved so universal it brought even doubting anarchists and other radicals into the fold. What neither Powderly nor Gompers could have foreseen was that the growing call for eight hours would spark an incident so emotional and divisive it would not only paralyze the eight-hour cause, but change forever the way America viewed organized labor.

THE WORKINGMEN'S PARTY, PROMINENT in the St. Louis General Strike of 1877, is often viewed as the first tangible political representation of the Socialist impulse in America. Its seven thousand members were mostly German American craft workers but the group favored worker unity across ethnic and racial lines. Where the organization foundered was on the question of advancing Socialism's cause through electoral politics. Some members, composing the so-called Lassallean faction, followers of the ideas of the German theorist Ferdinand Lassalle, envisioned a Socialist political party that would incrementally develop support based around appealing core ideals, much as the Republican Party had done in the 1850s. Marxian Socialists, adherents of Karl Marx, did not believe it worthwhile to engage in party politics. There would be no progress until man's labor was fairly valued, and toward achieving that goal Marxians promoted strong trade unions, strikes, and boycotts that would reveal the weaknesses of capitalism and private property.

Having renamed itself the Socialist Labor Party (SLP) shortly after the 1877 rail strikes, it achieved its most notable electoral success in Chicago, where in 1878–1879 its candidates won slots for a state senator, three state representatives, and four city aldermen. But within a few years many in the Chicago SLP became disillusioned with the frightful degree of local political corruption. Particularly galling was an 1880 incident in which two crooked election judges tried to deny reelection to Frank A. Stauber, a Socialist alderman popular for his efforts to open public bathhouses for workingmen. He was eventually given his post, but only after a lawsuit that cost his supporters $2,000 and effectively kept Stauber from office for a full year. The two election officials were tried but set free. Such outrages greatly offended Albert Parsons, who had led the Workingmen's Party in the trying days of 1877 and who had previously placed his faith in the ballot as a means of alleviating the workers' plight. "It was then I began to realize the hopeless task of political reformation," Parsons said of the Stauber scandal, and among many Chicago workers, he recounted,

> the conviction began to spread that the State, the Government and its laws, was merely the agent of the owners of capital . . . that the chief function of all Government was to maintain economic subjection of the man of labor . . . and that the element of coercion, of force, which enabled one person to dominate and exploit the labor of another, was centered or concentrated in the State . . . [and] in the last analysis . . . force was despotism, an invasion of man's natural right to liberty.[10]

Chicago authorities had kept their eye on Parsons ever since his rousing Market Street speech, which was blamed for having helped trigger the violence in the city during the railroad upheaval. What worried them was not solely that he was devoted to workers' rights; it was that he was an American, gentlemanly and articulate, and his family background denied critics the usual means by which they might smear him as a "labor radical." Parsons was descended from one of the oldest Anglo-Saxon families in America; his ancestors had arrived in New England in 1632. The Reverend Jonathan Parsons of Newburyport, Massachusetts, a fervent resister of British occupation forces in the 1770s, became the inspiration for the popular American caricature "Brother Jonathan." An anti-British sermon he delivered from his pulpit in early June 1775 led to the forming of a military company that distinguished itself at the Battle of Bunker Hill. Another relation, Major General Samuel Parsons, lost an arm in the fighting.

Albert was born into a large family in Montgomery, Alabama, in 1848. Both of his parents, who were religious reformers, died before he was five, leaving him to the care of his eldest brother, William Henry Parsons. A skilled horseman and crack shot by age thirteen, Albert ran away to join the Confederate forces in 1861, eventually serving as a scout attached to a cavalry brigade led by his brother, who was known during the war as "Wild Bill" Parsons. After the peace Albert apprenticed as a printer, and following the example of both William and the renowned Confederate general James Longstreet, became a Republican, accepting Reconstruction and its efforts to assist the former slaves. Such views soon came to be held as traitorous by his neighbors, particularly after he "took to the stump to vindicate my positions," and Parsons was forced to cease operation of a small newspaper he published.[11] In 1869 he began work as a traveling correspondent and agent for a Houston newspaper, and in his meanderings through rural Texas met Lucy E. Gathings, a head-turning beauty who claimed mixed Mexican and Native American heritage but was in all probability part black. They married in Austin in 1871. Two years later, after a brief stint as an internal revenue agent, he and Lucy went north, first to Philadelphia, then Chicago.

Parsons had been a member of the Typographical Union while still a teenager in Texas, and in Chicago he joined local Typographical Union No. 16, working as a printer and compositor at both the *Chicago Inter-Ocean* and the *Chicago Times*. His special empathy for issues affecting working people probably dated from 1874, when he became involved in protests against a local relief agency that in the aftermath of the Chicago Fire of 1871 had taken funds meant for the destitute and diverted them to stock market speculation and other unauthorized investments. The city's newspapers declared the rumors false and tried to tar those who'd raised suspicions as "Communists, robbers, loafers, etc." As Parsons wrote:

> I began to examine into this subject, and I found that the complaints of the working people against the [agency] were just and proper. I also discovered a great similarity between the abuse heaped upon these poor people . . . and the actions of the late Southern slaveholders in Texas toward the newly enfranchised slaves. . . . It satisfied me there was a great fundamental wrong at work in society and in existing social and industrial arrangements.[12]

Parsons joined the Workingmen's Party in 1876 and, believing their admirable socialistic aims were misunderstood partly because many members spoke less-than-perfect English, volunteered to become their tribune as a writer and speaker. That same year he gained the distinction of being the first person in Chicago to join the Knights of Labor, serving the organization in various official roles while contributing pieces to the Knights' periodical, the *Journal of United Labor*. After he came to national attention during the railroad strike of 1877, he was regularly sought as a lecturer.[13]

In fall 1877 Parsons garnered eight thousand votes for county clerk in Chicago on the Workingmen's Party ticket, narrowly losing, then went on to the national convention in Newark, New Jersey, where the party's name was changed to the Socialist Labor Party. At an SLP convention in 1879 he was nominated for president of the United States; deeply honored, he nonetheless declined, reminding the delegates that he had not yet reached the qualifying age of thirty-five, as required by the U.S. Constitution. However, he did accept appointment as the head of the Council of Trade and Labor Unions of Chicago, and later broke away to help found the city's Socialist-oriented Central Labor Union.

Parsons's counterpart—another rising star in the Chicago labor firmament—was August Spies, a skilled upholster and saddle maker who had come to Chicago from his native Germany in 1872. Two years later he "went on a tramp" of the West and South, then returned in 1875 to Chicago, where he became a convert to Socialism. Said to possess "a warm heart controlled by a cold, philosopher's brain," Spies was as impressive to look at as he was to listen to, an exceedingly handsome man and physical fitness devotee who belonged to a local *turnverein*, a German American gymnasium. In 1877 he became business manager of a German-language daily, the *Arbeiter-Zeitung*, and a year later its editor. Spies gradually made the paper's tone more radical, his anger toward authority deepening in 1884 after one of his brothers was shot dead in a fight with a policeman.[14] In December of that year he challenged the police directly when he aided a local German family in bringing charges against an "Officer Patten," who had allegedly taken advantage of their daughter, sixteen-year-old Martha Seidel, a domestic jailed on an accusation of household theft. In what the *Alarm* termed "an unparalleled crime," Patten, aware that her family was too poor to post bail for the girl, removed Martha to his own home and, "there, during the long moaning night," forced her to endure "all that a mountain of bestial flesh insane with lust, restrained by no fear, secure of immunity, could inflict upon her shuddering helplessness."[15]

Despite Parsons's outrage over the Stauber affair and Spies's cynicism about the Chicago police, both men retained a tenuous faith in the ballot as an instrument of change; but increasingly they found themselves alone among more adamant colleagues at national gatherings of the Revolutionary Socialist Party, an anarchist splinter element whose New York wing advocated direct actions including terrorism as a means of harassing the ruling elite and emboldening the masses.[16]

T HE VIEWS OF JOHANN MOST, a German émigré and resident of New York's Lower East Side who published the nation's best-known anarchist paper, *Die Freiheit*, typified the radicals' estrangement from "routine" labor-management solutions. "Extirpate the miserable brood!" he declared of the lords of capital. "Let us rely upon the unquenchable spirit of destruction and annihilation which is the perpetual spring of new life. The joy of destruction is a creative joy."[17] The aim was to disrupt the world of commerce and government, not to gain such "petty reforms" as shorter hours or higher wages, which Most dismissed as "sops thrown to the proletariat."[18] As one anarchist paper explained, "Right and wrong cannot arbitrate. The wage laborer who resorts to arbitration condones the wrongs, practiced by capital upon himself, and compounds the capitalistic felony which robs him of his labor product."[19]

Most had emerged from childhood with a mysterious "cancer" of the cheek, and a botched operation to repair it left his face "a wrinkled, malformed, lurid knot" that gave him a freakish jawline, which as an adult he attempted to disguise with a bushy beard. Ostracized by his peers on account of his disfigurement, he pursued a life of the mind, reading deeply in politics, history, and philosophy and becoming a Socialist scholar and politician. He served two terms in the Reichstag, although his own father, who had brutalized the boy when young, disliked his progeny to the extent that he gave speeches on behalf of Most's political opponents.[20] Eventually he surfaced in London, where he was jailed in 1881 for publishing an article approving of the assassination of Tsar Alexander II.

In America Most lectured widely and spread his views through *Die Freiheit* and other publications, including a seventy-four-page booklet called *The Science of Revolutionary Warfare*. Subtitled *A Little Handbook of Instruction in the Use and Preparation of Nitroglycerine, Dynamite, Gun-Cotton, Fulminating Mercury, Bombs, Fuses, Poisons, etc.*, this "manual for the extermination of the bourgeoisie"[21] denigrated police, capitalists, clergy, and government officials and recommended they be killed by whatever means came to hand. It offered detailed information on arson, poisoning, the use of knives, guns, and letter bombs, and waxed rhapsodic about the day when massive annihilation might be visited on the powerful by dropping bombs from hovering airships, particularly into the midst of military processions. *The Science of Revolutionary Warfare* sold well in anarchist circles and its contents were often excerpted by radical newspapers. Thanks in part to Most's exhortations, allusions to dynamite, a substance possessing an almost mythical power to equalize society, became frequent in radical journals. Inexpensive to make, easy to conceal, it was technology's gift to the have-nots of the world. A disciple of Most's, a "Professor Mezzeroff" of New York City, reported that he took a dynamite bomb with him wherever he went. "If you carry two or three pounds with you people will respect you much more than if you carried a pistol," Mezzeroff advised.[22]

Popular in late-nineteenth-century America primarily in the immigrant enclaves of large cities, anarchism centered around the view "that all forms of government rest on violence, and are therefore wrong and harmful as well as unnecessary."[23] There were no *better* forms of government. Whether organized as a dictatorship of the left or right, or as a democratic republic, each ruled by force, each was a means for the fortunate to safeguard their property and privilege, and all were at odds with natural principles of human social organization. Anarchists, like Socialists, believed that private control of the means of production was unfair to labor, but while Socialists envisioned the end of capitalism and the creation of a revolutionary proletariat through worker solidarity and either electoral politics or trade union agitation, anarchists sought more immediate means of displacing the state apparatus. "Rather than contracting with governments to ensure his well-being, as in the Lockean tradition that informed the American Declaration of Independence," writes scholar Miriam Brody, "the individual liberated from state tyranny enters into free associations with other individuals, these associations forming the social networks of public life."[24]

The anarchist thinker Peter Kropotkin, a Russian aristocrat and geologist, promulgated the idea that all living creatures have the capacity for self-organization "in response to natural conditions," and that "free of the constraints of government, [they] would continue to do so."[25] The New England anarchist Bartolomeo Vanzetti, who would later, along with Nicola Sacco, be executed for their anarchistic beliefs, described it as a living philosophy, an insight that guided one to a state of buoyant liberation. "The anarchism is as beauty as a woman for me," Vanzetti wrote, "perhaps even more since it includes all the rest and me and her. Calm, serene, honest, natural, virile, muddy and celestial at once, austere, heroic, fearless, fatal, generous and implacable—all these and more it is."[26]

But what always remained somewhat vague (even to anarchists) was precisely how the desired future would come into being. Pierre-Joseph Proudhon, an early-nineteenth-century French founder of anarchistic thought, saw widespread proletariat cooperation geared to a world of artisans and small craftsman; he didn't account for large-scale industrialization. Mikhail Bakunin, Proudhoun's Russian compere, saw "an apocalyptic breakdown of society, a purifying and regenerating baptism by fire out of which, phoenixlike, the voluntary and autonomous network of workers' federations would emerge."[27] Bakunin's vision gained adherents in the radical wing of anarchism peopled by the likes of Johann

Most, but Karl Marx deemed such notions so unacceptable that in 1872 he drove Bakunin's followers out of the First International, the original version of the International Workingmen's Association, founded in London in 1864.

The prospect of an "apocalyptic breakdown" that would shock societies into self-recognition and change, likely through acts of terror the anarchists called *attentats*, or "propaganda by the deed," was likely better suited, if at all, to authoritarian societies in which citizens had little other opportunity, such as the ballot or the courts, to effect change. The fact that the United States possessed such options, and that anarchism was more an ideal than a program, diminished its appeal to pragmatic Americans, and indeed frightened many. The daily press took a dim, condescending view of the anarchist fringe, which it considered juvenile and maladjusted. *Harper's Weekly* advised:

> The present situation has shown that there are two very different kinds of so-called labor movements. There are those which seek redress for real grievances, when the demand for redress is so reasonable that it commands general sympathy and support, and there are those which spring from certain social theories, and seek the violent overthrow of the existing social order. These last are mainly led by foreigners who scarcely speak our language, and who have no knowledge of the country nor comprehension of American institutions.[28]

Yet it is a measure of how deeply alienated many workers felt in American industrial society of the Gilded Age that anarchy, despite its lack of clarity, attracted both serious devotees and the merely curious. "We are the birds of the coming storm," August Spies liked to say, "the prophets of the revolution."[29] Even for the generally clearheaded Albert Parsons, notes a biographer, "principles of anarchism, socialism and equalitarianism were hopelessly entangled." He recognized inherent value in each and tended to use the concepts interchangeably, as his memberships in various causes and groups overlapped. "We are called Communists, or Social-ists, or Anarchists," Parsons conceded. "We accept all three of the terms."[30]

BY 1884 CHICAGO'S CENTRAL LABOR UNION had two thousand members, chiefly Germans and Poles, and a lively journal, the *Alarm*, edited by Albert Parsons,[31] which urged readers to "join with your comrades in the warfare against your deadly foe—poverty—and against the accursed system that rewards industry . . . and makes of this fair earth a slave pen." The *Alarm* enjoyed a subscription list of twenty-five hun-dred, although its pass-along readership was likely much higher.[32] Parsons was also a popular soapbox speaker, his appearances at rallies and meet-ings regularly attracting substantial audiences of keen-eared listeners; like his friend August Spies, he exhorted workingmen to arm themselves. Both men did so in the context of advocating workers' self-defense, but the *Alarm*, per Johann Most, carried a regular column dealing with the tech-nical aspects of bomb-making and the various properties of dynamite and nitroglycerin, the articles provocatively titled "Explosives: A Practical Les-son in Popular Chemistry; The Manufacture of Dynamite Made Easy,"[33] or "Bombs! The Weapon of the Social Revolutionist Placed Within the Reach of All."[34] Even Parsons's wife, Lucy, got into the act, allowing herself to be quoted by the *Chicago Tribune*, "Let every dirty, lousy tramp arm himself with a revolver or knife and lay in wait on the steps of the palaces of the rich and stab or shoot the owners as they come out."[35]

But was this all talk? Most, Spies, and Parsons clearly used the sym-bolism of dynamite as an expressive metaphor, a means of articulating their utter contempt for authority; yet none of them ever personally acted on the principle, or urged others to do so in a specific instance. Of course their exaggerated threats—including Most's prediction that "sooner or later the red flag of the revolution will wave over Independence Hall" in Philadelphia—were understandably troubling to Chicago businessmen such as Marshall Field and Cyrus McCormick Jr., as well as the police.[36] Such flaming rhetoric tended to make even the most legitimate demands of organized labor dangerous and insurrectionary, so that "every striker was a foreigner and every foreigner a Communist, Anarchist, Socialist or

Nihilist."[37] No less an authority on lethal conflict than General William Tecumseh Sherman saw looming in the anarchists' speech "an armed contest between Capital and Labor ... [who] will oppose each other not with words and arguments and ballots, but with shot and shell, gunpowder and cannon. The better classes are tired of the insane howlings of the lower strata, and they mean to stop them"[38]; the *Chicago Tribune* reassured its readers that "Judge Lynch is an American by birth and character" and that "every lamp-post in Chicago will be decorated with a communistic carcass if necessary."[39]

The anarchists were playing a dangerous game, one frightening enough to Chicago's business and government elites that Illinois in 1878 prohibited all paramilitary organizations not part of the state militia. But in fact, any such official restrictions were routinely ignored. Among German workingmen in nineteenth-century America, self-defense belonged to a proud tradition. Recreational *Schutzengesellschaften*, or shooting clubs, where members took target practice or carried their guns into the countryside on weekend outings, were a corollary to the popular gymnasiums, or *turnverein*, which emphasized physical fitness and were central to German American social life. The German community even had its own American military hero and patron saint, the Prussian militarist Baron Friedrich von Steuben, who had joined General Washington's staff in 1777 and trained the Continental army at Valley Forge, and who was honored in annual festivities. During the Civil War many *turnverein* in Northern cities such as New York and Chicago had sent German American fighting units to the Union army, and they proudly retained their flags, uniforms, and soldierly customs.

No doubt the idea of a coming "workers' society" seemed almost tangible at the massive picnics held on the southwest side of Chicago at Wright's Grove, in the north side at Ogden's Grove, with its revolving stage and a band shell, or along Lake Michigan. For these events entire neighborhoods emptied out of a Sunday afternoon to eat, drink, lounge, watch acrobatics and shooting contests, and mingle in the sunshine. Especially popular were the annual March 18 celebrations marking the anniversary of the Paris Commune, events that were martial in character and featured neighborhood "defense corps" parading with guns and bayonets to the rousing sounds of "La Marseillaise" and shouts of "*Vive la Commune!*" A highlight was occasional appearances by actual survivors of the Commune itself.[40]

In April 1885 there was an incident even radical Chicagoans likely did not dare expect—a violent confrontation with capital in which the workers came out on top. Located south of town, the McCormick Reaper Company was, with its two thousand employees, the world's largest farm implement manufacturer. Workers had struck McCormick over "poor pay, long work hours," and their frustration with "the insulting and dictatorial bearing of the foremen and superintendent." The company responded by bringing in scabs protected by detested "Pinkerton pups." When a rumor spread that strikers had been fired upon, a group of them boldly ambushed two wagons being used by the Pinkertons, dragging the detectives to the ground and beating several of them senseless. Inside one of the vehicles the strikers discovered two cases of Winchester rifles and twenty-five Colt revolvers, which they seized.

McCormick executives were caught off guard by the workers' terrorizing of the Pinkertons, and with their great factory largely idle and the roads leading to it blocked by strikers, they asked for a parlay. A company spokesman met with a workers' delegation and, after "dealing in palaver and taffy until it disgusted the committee," offered terms of compromise and acceded to many of the employees' demands, including a wage increase. The *Alarm* cheered the victory as "the most exciting, serious and determined struggle between capitalists and wage laborers that has occurred in Chicago in several years," and termed McCormick's capitulation "an unconditional surrender." Both Parsons and Spies emphasized the heroic example the McCormick workers had given in conquering force with force.[41]

But the episode would have serious ramifications. As a result of the workers' bravado, Mayor Carter Harrison, who had dedicated his efforts to maintaining a relative calm between workers and the police, came under pressure from local businessmen to institute stronger checks on radical agitation. In October 1885 he promoted to police inspector one of the city's toughest cops, Captain John Bonfield, who was so feared in the city's ethnic enclaves, he was known as "Black Jack" or simply "The Clubber."

The decision certainly was not typical of Harrison, a joyful rustic from Kentucky who was popular with voters and famously in love with his job and his city—his "bride," as he called Chicago, "who laves her beautiful limbs daily in Lake Michigan and comes out clean and pure every morning."[42] He was often to be seen riding through the streets on a black bay mare, cigar in hand, his shirt festooned with tiny diamonds, hat at a rakish tilt. "He was thrilled with the sensation of being on parade," recalled a memoirist, "and never grew weary of seeing himself pass by."[43] Born into a family that claimed descent from Pocahontas, Harrison had been educated at Yale, had traveled widely in Europe, and had done exceedingly well in Chicago real estate; as mayor he had secured the loyalty of the city's working neighborhoods by learning a smattering of several immigrant languages and showing up regularly at block parties and ethnic celebrations. Unlike some politicians who did such things stiffly and out of a sense of obligation, Harrison actually appeared to be enjoying himself. Influential Chicagoans such as *Daily News* publisher Melville Stone tolerated the mayor so long as his outgoing demeanor kept the working class quiet, but in the wake of the McCormick violence they demanded a firmer guarantee of protection.[44]

Bonfield, the man who embodied the new policy, had been with the police since the 1877 railroad disturbances and had won several promotions for his willingness to take on assignments in areas of the city considered dangerous. These lonely postings led to Bonfield's suggestion for a unique innovation—a system of call boxes so that a patrolman walking a beat in a remote area could notify headquarters for backup if trouble arose. The concept, which made use of the then-emerging technology of the telephone, was implemented in Chicago and soon replicated elsewhere in America. Bonfield's real value, however, was his courage in aggressive street actions. During a July 1885 confrontation with striking trolley car employees, he had ordered his men to clear protestors from a street, and when demonstrators had refused to budge, deriding the officers as "scabs" and "rats," an infuriated Bonfield had personally led his troops directly into the crowd. He was seen pounding protestors into submission, even gashing the heads of two strikers' representatives who had approached him, seeing his captain's uniform, in hopes of calming the situation. One of Mayor Harrison's own sons was among the many hundreds of people bruised by cops that afternoon.[45] There was some pro forma grousing over Bonfield's excessive behavior in the affair, but in truth his performance had made a very favorable impression.

RADICAL LABOR ELEMENTS HAD INITIALLY disparaged the plan by Samuel Gompers and the Federation of Organized Trades and Labor Unions to use May 1, 1886, as a day of nationwide demonstration and a general strike in support of the eight-hour cause. They derided the campaign as "soothing syrup for babies, but of no consequence to grown men,"[46] with Johann Most predicting the "eight-hour fraud" would never squelch "the revolutionary tension,"[47] and the *Alarm* writing it off as "literal foolishness."[48]

The eight-hour cause had proven a compelling rallying cry, however, as recently as September 5 1882, when it was one of the themes featured in a "monster labor festival" in New York City. The daylong event, scheduled in early September so as to flex labor's strength at the opening of the fall political season, brought ten thousand trade unionists from Manhattan, Brooklyn, and Jersey City to Union Square, many in their work uniforms or shop aprons. Five hundred jewelers marched tapping canes along the pavement, the cigar makers' unions distributed free stogies, along with numerous bands and floats as well as a sizable turnout from Typographical Union No. 6, which had helped in the event's preparations along with the Knights of Labor. The workers, "determined to show their numerical strength in order to satisfy the politicians of this city that they must not be trifled with," marched around the square's perimeter behind Grand Marshal William McNabe and a multitude of banners declaring LABOR CREATES ALL WEALTH and LABOR BUILT THIS REPUBLIC AND LABOR

SHALL RULE IT. Other signs denounced convict labor or demanded the closing of stores at 6 p.m.; one in particular that caught the attention of the city's editorial writers, PAY NO RENT, was a tribute to the Paris Commune. Assorted clergy and union dignitaries watched approvingly from a reviewing stand at the northern end of the square. It was reportedly one of these impressed observers who dubbed the passing spectacle "Labor Day," the beginning of the American tradition honoring an annual workers' holiday.[49]

By February 1886 the *Alarm* had come around to the view that the popular "eight-hour movement is a sign of the progressive ideas underlying the entire labor movement,"[50] and Parsons and his fellow anarchists embraced it for its potential to humiliate and inconvenience the industrial system. "Winning the eight-hour day would give the workers more leisure in which to train for the greater task of emancipating themselves from capitalism," he wrote.[51] Always fond of lacing his arguments with statistics (and sharing them with an audience), Parsons soon became enamored of data suggesting that, historically, shortened hours led to increased wages, "more leisure from mere drudge work," and the opportunity for workers to "minister to their higher aspirations."[52]

However, it appeared that something other than "higher aspirations" preoccupied the *Alarm* in the week before Chicago's big May 1 eight-hour demonstration, when the paper ran the headline "To Arms! American Workingmen Are Called Upon to Arm Themselves." The article that followed discounted existing options for progress in electoral politics, religion, and industry, and demanded to know if the present generation had the audacity of early American revolutionaries such as Paul Revere.[53] The conservative *Chicago Mail*, apparently deciding it had had enough of the *Alarm*'s provocations, replied: "There are two dangerous ruffians at large in this city, two sneaking cowards who are trying to create trouble. One of them is named Parsons; the other is named Spies. . . . Mark them for today. Keep them in view. Hold them personally responsible for any trouble that occurs. Make an example of them if trouble does occur."[54]

There were other public warnings that any radical shenanigans on

May 1 would be quashed at once by Inspector Bonfield and his men, but in fact the day's events were largely calm and orderly, despite Chicago's having the nation's largest eight-hour rally and parade, with nearly one hundred thousand people marching down Michigan Avenue. Tens of thousands also turned out in New York, Detroit, Milwaukee, and other cities, and more than a thousand factories across the country suffered strike actions in observance of the day's event. While there was some friction elsewhere, the mammoth Chicago outpouring was fairly anticlimactic. "Expecting Armageddon," notes an historian, "Chicago felt a little cheated at getting only peace."[55]

Monday, May 3, however, brought a far different result: another riot at McCormick Reaper. The company was still smarting over its capitulation to the workers the previous spring. That settlement, in which the company had agreed to boost wages, had proved a bitter pill for the firm's executives, who had to suffer the annoyance of hearing radical propagandists cheer "the people" for humbling the mighty McCormick. In early 1886 it chose to once again move aggressively against employees, dismissing a large number of skilled iron molders so they could be replaced by new pneumatic molding machines. Other workers walked out in sympathy, demanding the rehiring of the molders and higher pay for unskilled employees. McCormick replied by importing three hundred scabs to take the strikers' jobs, but this time, instead of Pinkertons, the firm arranged for a special 350-man force of police organized by Inspector Bonfield to protect the scabs and the firm's property. Even with this police coverage tension persisted; there were several brawls and exchanges of insults between the ousted workers and their replacements.

On May 3, August Spies was in the vicinity of the McCormick factory at an unrelated rally of lumber workers, when shots were heard coming from the McCormick site: a shift change was under way and the usual taunting of scabs had apparently escalated. Some of those in Spies's audience were McCormick workers, and they immediately ran toward the scene of the fighting. In the ensuing fracas, Bonfield's police savagely beat dozens of workers and shot four men to death. Enraged, Spies returned to his newspaper office and produced what would become known as "the

Revenge Circular." Under the single word "Revenge" ran the bold head-line "Workingmen, to Arms!!!" and a text that was equally fiery:

> You have for years endured the most abject humiliations; you have endured the pangs of hunger and want; you have worked yourself to death; your children you have sacrificed to the factory lords. . . . If you are men, if you are the sons of grand sires who have shed their blood to free you, then you will rise in your might . . . and destroy the hideous monster that seeks to destroy you. To arms, we call you. To arms![56]

To protest the slaughter at McCormick a rally was called for the next evening at Chicago's Haymarket Square. "Good speakers will be present to denounce the latest atrocious act of the police, the shooting of our fellow-workmen yesterday afternoon," it was promised.

Perhaps because many workers had marched only a few days before in the big eight-hour rally, or due to fears of police violence after what had occurred at McCormick, only about three thousand people rather than the twenty-five thousand organizers had hoped for materialized the evening of May 4 in Haymarket Square. The square was far too large for the modest turnout, so those in charge maneuvered an empty wagon into an alley to provide a platform for the speakers. The gathering was peaceful, and Mayor Harrison came and mingled with the crowd as Spies and Parsons spoke. It was a breezy evening, threatening rain, and Harrison was forced to strike several matches in order to keep his cigar lit; when someone advised him that in doing so he'd give himself away to the crowd, he insisted that he didn't mind because "I want the people to know their mayor is here."

Before heading home, Harrison stopped at the nearby Desplaines Street police station house where Bonfield had his troops in readiness if it became necessary to confront the group in the Haymarket. The police had wisely elected not to have a uniformed presence in the square, but Bonfield had sent observers there to monitor the event and report back if words became inflammatory or the crowd troublesome. Mayor Harrison informed the inspector and other police officials that the rally was lightly attended, not at all boisterous, and even suggested that some of the reserve officers on duty be allowed to go home.

Back at the rally, Spies was speaking from the wagon, accusing the McCormick bosses of murder although cautioning against thoughtless retaliation. Parsons, who had arrived back in town only that evening from a speaking engagement in Cincinnati, came to the square with his wife, Lucy, and their two small children, Lulu and Albert Jr. He urged the workers to arm in self-defense, but otherwise devoted his remarks to the prospects for international Socialism. After speaking, Parsons left the Haymarket with his family to join friends at nearby Zepf's Saloon.

Last to address the gathering was Samuel Fielden, a former English lay preacher who worked as a teamster. Rugged and bearlike in appearance, with a full bushy beard, Fielden was a favorite speaker at such events, known for his sense of humor and occasional use of quaint Briticisms. Rain had begun to fall and people had started to drift away, leaving Fielden with a crowd of only a few hundred. He proposed to speak briefly. His remarks were not unlike those already made from the wagon, but one of the plainclothes detectives noted that Fielden was counseling his listeners to defy the law. "Keep your eye upon it, throttle it, kill it, stab it, do everything you can to wound it—to impede its progress," he advised. "Socialists are not going to declare war; but I tell you war has been declared on us, and I ask you to get hold of anything that will help to resist the onslaught of the enemy and the usurper. The skirmish lines are met. People have been shot. Men, women, and children have not been spared by the capitalists and minions of private capital. They had no mercy, so ought you?"

Something of these remarks was transmitted to Bonfield, who ordered his men out of the station house. As Fielden was closing his remarks and the rally was moments away from adjournment, Captain William Ward walked to the speaker's wagon at the head of a column of police and told Fielden, "In the name of the people of Illinois, I command this meeting immediately and peaceably to disperse." Fielden replied, "We *are* peaceable," and was stepping down from the wagon when suddenly there was a terrific explosion, the square lit by a blinding white light.[57] A bomb had been thrown at the police. One, Mathias Degan, was killed instantly; many others fell wounded, some mortally. Those officers who could quickly unholstered their guns and "swept the sidewalks with a hot and telling fire." Several workers were struck, a few may have returned fire, and in the smoke and confusion the police also shot into their own ranks.[58] It all happened within seconds, and just as swiftly the crowd was in full flight, some helping to carry away bleeding and injured comrades.

The police retreated en masse to the Desplaines Street station house, where the scene was one of carnage, the floor slick with blood, as dying policemen and the wounded writhed in pain and volunteers tried frantically to administer aid. Seven policemen ultimately died from wounds received in the Haymarket; sixty-seven were badly hurt. Of the workers, four had died and fifty were wounded. Samuel Fielden was led away by companions, a police bullet lodged in his knee.

T HE NATION WAS OUTRAGED over the incident, a deadly assault on uniformed police by anarchists. Commentators reached back to the murder of Lincoln for a comparable act as horrendous.[59] The *New York Times* began its excited coverage, "The villainous teachings of the Anarchists bore bloody fruit in Chicago . . ." and blamed "the doctrine of Herr Johann Most."[60] *Harper's Weekly* saw the terror bombing as the result of passions "plainly gathering for several days . . . an outburst of anarchy; the deliberate crime of men who openly advocate massacre and the overthrow of intelligent and orderly society."[61]

Chicago Daily News publisher Melville Stone did more than editorialize. He contacted William Pinkerton, son of the detective agency's founder, and urged him to at once "put shadows" over Spies, Parsons, and Fielden—"the same little coterie [that] had been preaching anarchy for months."[62] In fact, Chicago police, in some cases assisted by Pinkertons, had already reacted, descending on dozens of homes, businesses, and meeting halls frequented by workingmen. "There is hardly an Anarchist in the city . . . not in a tremor for fear of a domiciliary visit from the police," it was reported. "Search warrants are no longer considered necessary, and suspicious houses are being ransacked at all hours of the day and night."[63]

While the much-published assumption was that the bombing was "a concerted, deliberately planned, and coolly executed murder,"[64] it became apparent to investigators within several hours that there was little proof to support such a theory. Police hauled in dozens of men (and a few women), along with cartons of suspicious papers and other items, but wound up letting most of those arrested go free. The seven men they had quickly swooped up and held in custody as ringleaders of the plot—August Spies, Adolph Fischer, George Engel, Louis Lingg, Michael Schwab, Samuel Fielden, and Oscar Neebe—were all known as committed radicals. Only Fielden and Spies had been at the Haymarket when the bomb was thrown. Albert Parsons, who had left the square with his family before the explosion, had had time to evade the police dragnet. His first thought upon learning of the bombing was that it had been the work of an agent provocateur; he knew, nonetheless, that he would be among those blamed, and he left town on a midnight train to seek refuge with friends in northern Illinois. Rudolph Schnaubelt, an anarchist suspected by the police of having hurled the bomb, had likewise disappeared.

The other men in custody were deeply implicated by their participation in local anarchist or workingmen's causes. Louis Lingg was a twenty-two-year-old German immigrant carpenter, in America only one year. "Fearfully, dangerously handsome, the image of manly health and beauty . . . the lion of the ballroom,"[65] Lingg was also known for being somewhat deranged, and was said to bear a grudge against authority because his father had been fired from a job after having sustained a debilitating workplace injury. Lingg had not been in the Haymarket, but he was known to tinker with bomb-making and was, according to one friend, "crazy on the labor question and wanted to kill everybody that did not agree with him."[66] Lingg struggled fiercely with the police sent to arrest him and had to be forcibly subdued.

George Engel, the owner of a toy store and an earnest Socialist, had been at the meeting held on the evening of May 3 at Greif's Hall, where the Haymarket rally was planned, although on the night of the bombing he was at home playing cards. Adolph Fischer was a printer at Spies's paper, the *Arbeiter-Zeitung*, and had also been at Greif's. Unable to find Rudolph Schnaubelt, the police and prosecutors had made Fischer the chief suspect for having thrown or triggered the explosive.[67] Oscar Neebe, an organizer with a beer-wagon drivers' union, was a Socialist whose chief offense seemed to be that he had kept the *Arbeiter-Zeitung* in operation after Spies and the others had been arrested, while Michael Schwab, an associate editor of the paper, had the bad fortune to have published a rabble-rousing piece about resisting capitalism on the very day of the bombing. Nor could it have helped that the bearded, thin-faced Schwab appeared to investigators and journalists "very untidy . . . his general appearance that of a fanatic, half-insane," and that it was known he was "married to a woman in free-love fashion."[68] Schwab had been in Haymarket Square on the fateful night but had left early.

Sifting through the scant evidence and interviewing witnesses, investigators could not agree on whether the bomb had been thrown at the police from the speakers' wagon, the sidewalk, or a window overhead. Nonetheless, over several days the outlines of a conspiracy emerged. The radicals, hungry for revenge after the killings at the McCormick factory, had met at Greif's Hall on Monday night and laid plans to murder as many police as possible. The rally at Haymarket would begin with reasonable-sounding speeches but slowly intensify in order to lure the police from their nearby station house. When the hated "Black Jack" Bonfield and his men entered the square, the conspirators would detonate their "deadly Nihilist bomb."[69] Lost in this scenario was the question of whether Bonfield's decision to march a large body of police into the Haymarket had been necessary, whether the alleged plotters could really have predicted it, and the possibility the bombing might have been the work of someone other than an anarchist; also disregarded was the fact that most of the policemen's wounds had resulted not from the bomb but from shots fired by fellow officers in the first panicked moments after the explosion.[70]

Official interrogations of the detained men added little new information, for with their practiced contempt for the law, the radicals easily resisted efforts to coerce their cooperation. Fischer, told by a police lieutenant that August Spies had confessed to the conspiracy and had named Fischer as the bomb thrower, replied coolly, "If Spies has really told you that, then he has lied. Either you lie or Spies does. That Spies has told an untruth I do not believe. Therefore you are the liar." When Cook County prosecutor Julius S. Grinnell took a turn with Fischer, counseling him that "a brave man does not lie," Fischer snapped back, "Is that so? Then you must be the greatest coward in the world, for you are a lawyer, which signifies a liar by profession." Fischer also refused Grinnell's offer of leniency in return for his cooperation, angering the prosecutor. "Then we'll hang you!" Grinnell shouted. "Very well," replied Fischer, "then hang me, but don't degrade me with any more of your rascally propositions."[71]

Discussions between Grinnell and city attorney Fred Winston as to the difficulty of proceeding without proof of the bomber's identity came to include publisher Melville Stone. "They were in trouble," Stone recalled. "No one knew who had actually thrown the bomb, and they both felt that this was important in the conduct of the case. I at once took the ground that the identity of the bomb thrower was of no consequence, and that, inasmuch as Spies and Parsons and Fielden had advocated over and over again the use of violence against the police and had urged the manufacture and throwing of bombs, their culpability was clear." The prosecutors warmed at once to Stone's idea. It would not be necessary to link the men held in custody with the bomb; their words had created the atmosphere in which the assault had taken place. They were as guilty as if they had thrown it.[72]

Unfortunately for the accused, the trial was set to proceed within weeks, meaning it would take place in a Chicago still furious about the wanton murder of its policemen. The seven defendants (neither Parsons nor Schnaubelt had been found, despite a nationwide manhunt) hired two attorneys—William Perkins Black, a Civil War hero and recipient of the Congressional Medal of Honor, and criminal defense lawyer William

A. Foster. (Black, it was said, was displaying more courage in representing the most despised men in America than he had in meeting the Confederate advance at the Battle of Pea Ridge.) The sitting judge was Joseph Eaton Gary, a twenty-year veteran of the Cook County Superior Court bench not known for his sympathy to the interests of workers or radicals. Black, citing the judge's own known prejudices and the mob atmosphere surrounding the impending trial, asked that Gary recuse himself from the bench; he also sought a change of venue and separate trials for the defendants. All these requests were denied.

On June 21, 1886, the trial opened with a dramatic flourish when through the doors of the courtroom walked Albert Parsons. After going underground in northern Illinois, he had moved on and spent several weeks laying low at the home of a sympathizer in Waukesha, Wisconsin. When the considerable buzz in the chamber had been quieted, Parsons informed Judge Gary in a clear tone, "I have come to stand trial, your honor, with my innocent comrades."[73]

Attorney Black had been instrumental in convincing Lucy Parsons that Albert should return and face the charges; he was convinced the prosecution would not be able to make the case that men who gave speeches and published newspaper editorials, however inflammatory, were responsible for a bombing with which they had no physical connection, and that Parsons's hiding out only implied his guilt. Through Lucy, Black also had gotten the sense that Albert was too honorable a man to be content to long remain a fugitive, and too committed an anarchist to pass up the opportunity to use the trial and the accusations against him to make public his beliefs.

Parsons didn't fully share Black's optimism about winning acquittal, and likely recognized that, even if miraculously set free, he and Spies and the others would be hunted down by vengeful police, relatives of the dead officers, or vigilante groups, some of whom had already issued warnings to that effect. Still, for a combination of reasons, some known only to himself, Parsons made a fateful decision, one consistent with how he had always lived his life, and surrendered to the judgment of the law.

———

THE HAYMARKET TRIAL has been viewed for well over a century as a remarkable travesty of justice. With the city and the nation's fulsome contempt for the accused at his back, Judge Gary gave himself broad latitude to bring the case to the resolution demanded. The compromises to expediency began with the jury selection. As it was virtually impossible to find potential jurors in Chicago not already convinced of the defendants' guilt, or even willing to say they might keep an open mind about crimes allegedly committed by anarchists, the judge sought only a dubious guarantee that they would be objective in a murder trial, and then determinedly closed off the defense's peremptory challenges. This was significant, since the trial would ultimately turn not on evidence of murder but on whether the defendants held anarchist beliefs. The result was a jury of twelve white men, not a single one of whom was a laborer or an immigrant, a few of whom even said they were friends of policemen present at Haymarket Square. Once so grossly biased a jury had been seated, Judge Gary's denial of Black's plea for a change of venue seemed ever more obtuse and unjust.

The trial got under way on July 15 with the county's Julius Grinnell laying out the prosecution's case, abetted by extensive readings from anarchist and Socialist tracts and the testimony of compensated informants. He placed August Spies at the head of a network of bomb-throwing anarchists. According to Grinnell, Spies had orchestrated the violence at the McCormick plant on May 3 as a way to provoke outrage and violence among the city's workmen, and had then immediately issued the "Revenge!" flyer calling for violent resistance and the next night's rally in the Haymarket. At the gathering at Greif's Hall on the night of May 3 the conspirators had agreed to hurl bombs at the police if they made a show of force. Samuel Fielden's speech at the Haymarket, Grinnell explained, was intended to agitate the police and bring a response; the bomb had been thrown from the vicinity of the speakers' wagon after the police had been drawn there. The conspirators' ultimate hope, he asserted, was that the spilling of police blood would in turn trigger a citywide uprising of workingmen and other citizens. While the state had not been able to identify the bomber, Grinnell told the jury that "it is not necessary in this kind of case . . . that the individual who commits the particular offense—for instance, the man who threw the bomb . . . be in court at all. He need not even be indicted. The question for you to determine is, having ascertained that a murder was committed, not only who did it, but who is responsible for it, who abetted it, assisted it, encouraged it."[74]

Interestingly, a case heard in New York City the year before might have been instructive. In early 1885 Justus Schwab (the man arrested in 1874 for racing across Tompkins Square waving a red flag) had been charged with inciting to riot after an incident at an anarchist lecture in which a police captain had been crowned over the head with a chair. Dozens of police reinforcements had then rushed into the hall shouting, "Drive the loafers out!" and bludgeoning men and women audience members as they tried to flee. Schwab was an ideal target for the prosecution—a known trouble-maker who ran a saloon on the Lower East Side that was a gathering place for radicals. But there was no evidence indicating Schwab had "incited" the fighting in the hall. The district attorney harped instead on the allegation that he was a Socialist, until Schwab himself demanded, "Is Socialism on trial here, or is Justus H. Schwab on trial?" In the end the charges were dismissed after the jury declined to convict a man solely on his beliefs.[75] Few if any people associated with the Haymarket trial, however, antici-pated so enlightened a verdict.

The Chicago trial carried on through the warm, humid days of sum-mer 1886. Despite the intense heat and closeness of the courtroom, there was a daily demand for seats. The fortunate who gained entry packed their lunches, intent on sitting through every moment of the drama. The result, in the sultry atmosphere, was a courtroom "fragrant" with the smells of meat sandwiches, boiled potatoes, oranges, and bananas, and noisy at times with the crinkling of food wrappers. So desirable were good viewing places that Judge Gary opened his own riser each day to special guests, often society women of his acquaintance, who sat in chairs at his rear; the judge frequently passed personal notes to his visitors, or shared the contents of a candy dish.[76]

As the trial progressed, the defense succeeded at presenting witnesses who contradicted the conspiracy Grinnell had described. The meeting at Greif's Hall could hardly be characterized as a gathering to plot a bombing since it was open to the public, and Albert Parsons had not even been there, for he was in Ohio that evening making a speech. He had only learned of the Haymarket gathering upon arriving back in Chicago on May 4, and when he dropped by the rally, where he was glad to make a few remarks, he had with him his wife and children, curious behavior for someone aware a bomb was about to be exploded and a riot instigated. Louis Lingg had been neither at Greif's Hall nor at the Haymarket rally, and even though it appeared he had manufactured bombs, there was no evidence linking him to the bomb in the Haymarket. It was tempting to connect the vanished Rudolph Schnaubelt to the crime, since his flight suggested guilt, but the defense was able to show that his involvement was little more than speculation, as was the prosecution's attempt to place the bomb in the hands of either Adolph Fischer or another man, Reinhold "Big" Krueger, who could not answer for himself because he had been killed in the Haymarket.

Unionist Oscar Neebe's connection to the other defendants and the cause of anarchy was sufficiently vague that, as one observer put it, all the accusations against him, even if true, "would not justify a five-dollar fine."[77] Neebe tweaked the prosecution by testifying that, yes, he had committed many crimes—the "crimes" of organizing bakers so that instead of working fourteen- and sixteen-hour days they now worked only ten, and that he had committed the same "crime" for brewers and grocery clerks, many of whom now had Sundays off. "That," he conceded, "is a great crime."[78]

Confronted by the state's apparently weak case, Albert Parsons tried turning the tables on the prosecution by offering his own version of the disaster. Rather than an anarchist plot to stoke revolutionary violence, he declared, the bomber was likely a Pinkerton agent or other kind of spy dispatched to cause an incident that would license a sweeping crackdown on anarchists and labor advocates. As the labor journalist John Swinton had observed, "The bomb was a godsend to the enemies of the labor movement. They have used it as an explosive against all the objects that the working people are bent upon accomplishing, and in defense of all the evils that capital is bent on maintaining."[79] Parsons's claim that the bombing had been a kind of reverse conspiracy, a deliberate provocation, was unproven but not far-fetched; it was, to its credit, as compelling an explanation of what had occurred as the state's largely conjectural story.

The defense also assaulted the state's claim that the anarchists intended the rally in the Haymarket to trigger "a revolution," since any intelligent person knew that when anarchists spoke of *revolution* they were referring to an ideal—a change in the economic and civic conditions of society that would someday replace government authority with greater individual autonomy. Workers might arm and prepare for that day of deliverance, but no anarchist leader was so naive as to think a single act of terrorist violence would compel it into being. "Anarchists do not make the social revolution," as Parsons explained. "They prophesy its coming."[80]

Black's closing argument begged for the jurors' objectivity and perspective, reminding them that Jesus had also been a Socialist, in a sense no different from the defendants. Grinnell wrapped up for the state, saying there could be no place for anarchism in America's free, egalitarian society.

On August 19, after ensuring they understood his instruction that the defendants could be found guilty of murder even though no physical evidence linked them to the victims, Judge Gary sent the jury off to deliberate on the men's guilt as well as their sentence, as was the practice in Illinois. The culpability and punishment of all the defendants was agreed upon quickly by the jurymen—an hour into their deliberations they were glimpsed through a window relaxing and smoking cigars—the only sticking point being whether Oscar Neebe, whose role was tangential, deserved execution. The jury ultimately recommended his conviction and a sentence of fifteen years; the others were all sentenced to die on the gallows.

There was widespread approval of the verdicts, particularly in Chicago, where shouts of celebration were heard in the streets surrounding the courthouse and the *Tribune* trumpeted its extensive coverage, "Nooses for the Reds."[81] Fearing an outbreak of anarchist protest, Inspector Bonfield sternly advised against any public demonstrations in support of the condemned, warning that "if any violence is done by the friends of these men the lamp posts of Chicago will bear fruit . . . [and] the police will be powerless to quell the popular rage."

It is not recorded whether Bonfield appreciated the irony of his words: lynching would be tolerated if anarchists misbehaved.[82]

T HE LABOR MOVEMENT, like the rest of America, had been stunned by the Haymarket carnage, and out of concern for its image in the face of public anger it had initially condemned the attack and the men who stood accused of the crime. But the biased trial and convictions produced a slow but certain change of heart, as outrage grew that men who had defended and championed workers could be indicted, convicted, and sentenced to death solely for their opinions. As Adolph Fischer offered, "I was tried here in this room for murder, and I was convicted of Anarchy. This verdict is a death-blow to free speech, free press and free thought in this country."[83] No sooner had the fatal verdicts been rendered than a process began by which the condemned were transformed into heroes, martyrs to the First Amendment and the rights of labor. Even Samuel Gompers, who detested radical influence in labor's affairs, vowed that working people would never willingly surrender Spies, Parsons, and the rest to the "vengeance of the common enemy."

This trend was abetted by second-guessing over the way in which the trial had been conducted—the judicial shortcuts taken by Judge Gary, the lack of physical evidence, and the fact that under the circumstances in which the trial was held no other result was possible. The *Chicago Express* dared print what many people privately believed, that it was not the anarchists but Inspector Bonfield who was most directly to blame for the tragedy, as he had foolishly marched his police to disperse a nonviolent gathering that was only moments away from its peaceful conclusion.[84]

The defendants were themselves allowed to comment on their precarious fate when, at a hearing in October, defense attorney Black's call for a new trial was formally rejected. Spies defended his innocence and mocked the prosecution's conceit that in hanging seven men the cause of laboring people would be stilled. "If you think you can stamp out the labor movement, then hang us!" he demanded, but the protests of dissatisfied working people would not be silenced. "Here you will tread upon a spark," he warned, "but here, and there, and behind you and in front of you, and everywhere, flames will blaze up. It is a subterranean fire. You cannot put it out. The ground is on fire upon which you stand."[85] Parsons criticized the judge for upholding convictions obtained in a trial that had taken place in a hostile atmosphere, calling the jury's decision "a verdict of passion, born of passion, nurtured in passion . . . the sum total of the organized passion of the city of Chicago." He defended anarchists as people who sought the humane goal of an egalitarian society without oppressive authority, and complained that the police, Chicago businessmen, the press, as well as the court, had conspired to muzzle the community's true sentiments. "Think you the people are blind, are asleep, are indifferent? You deceive yourselves! I tell you, as a man of the people, and I speak for them, that your every word and act . . . are recorded." He assured Judge Gary, "You are being weighed in the balance. . . . I, a working man, stand here, and to your face, in your stronghold of oppression, denounce . . . your crimes against humanity."[86]

Gary's rejection of the retrial motions led the defense to appeal the case to the Illinois Supreme Court and ultimately to the United States Supreme Court on the grounds that the trial had been conducted improperly. The Illinois court examined the issue for months before announcing it saw no procedural unfairness, while the high court in Washington in turn refused to hear the appeal, saying no federal issues were involved.

The thwarted appeals did succeed at least in helping to publicize the wrongs of the trial and in encouraging a worldwide movement protesting the death sentences. Pleas for Illinois governor Richard Oglesby to exercise clemency—to change the death sentences to life imprisonment—came from former U.S. senator Lyman Trumbull, architect of the Fourteenth Amendment; former Massachusetts congressman Benjamin F. Butler; reformer Henry Demarest Lloyd; and the influential editor William Dean Howells, who thought the defendants not guilty of "anything but their opinions" and termed the convictions "the greatest wrong that ever threatened our fame as a nation."[87] Lucy Parsons took to the road, visiting sixteen states to plead her husband's and the others' innocence and to raise funds in support of the clemency campaign. She also conducted a one-woman letter-writing crusade, targeting notable figures in the United States and overseas. Partly as a result of her activity, petitions arrived from as far away as England bearing the signatures of Oscar Wilde, William Morris, George Bernard Shaw, William Rossetti, and Friedrich Engels.

The appeals for mercy soon overwhelmed the office of Governor Oglesby. One petition arrived bearing one hundred thousand signatures, and several delegations of prominent people trooped to the capital at downstate Springfield in an attempt to persuade the state's chief executive to delay or halt the executions. Samuel Gompers told Oglesby that if Jefferson Davis, the traitorous president of the Confederacy, could be granted amnesty, a group of anarchists whose only crime was to be labor activists were deserving of reprieve as well. Gompers also cautioned that putting men to death for their words and associations, not for a specific misdeed, was bound to turn them into eternal martyrs to radicalism and encourage further violence. From prison, August Spies wrote to Oglesby to suggest that the state of Illinois execute him alone, since "if legal murder there must be, let one, let mine suffice." The governor also heard from Albert Parsons, who pointed out that if he was to be hanged for coming to Haymarket Square on the evening of May 4, so should his wife and two small children, as they had also been present. "My God, this is terrible!" blurted Oglesby to an aide, upon reading the Spies and Parsons letters.[88]

Once the convictions had been handed down and the fate of the guilty sealed, the tone of the press coverage had also changed markedly: newspapers which had gleefully vilified the accused, began to record their prison lives as if they were celebrities, noting their every visitor, guessing at their mood, and reporting extensively on their private business. Parsons's wife, Lucy, and their children were frequent visitors to the jail, while Spies and Lingg both had admiring female friends. Spies's romance took a turn for the sensational when he and Nina Van Zandt, a local woman from respectable society who'd come to know Spies only since his arrest, announced their intention to wed. The press was happy to mine this development for its compelling copy, but nonetheless feigned outrage that a condemned killer of policemen would be allowed to marry a woman of decent reputation. Even Spies's attorneys advised against it, fearing it would harm any chance of appeal. But the two lovers were undeterred, Spies's brother Henry standing in as proxy for him in an exchange of vows with Van Zandt when the authorities refused to release Spies to attend his own wedding.

In Springfield the clemency decision continued to weigh upon Governor Oglesby. A decorated Civil War veteran and confidant of Abraham Lincoln (he had been at Lincoln's deathbed), Oglesby was genuinely sympathetic to the labor cause, having signed Illinois's first eight-hour law in 1867. The compromise he finally offered was that he would commute the Haymarket sentences to life in prison if Chicago's business leaders—men like retailer Marshall Field and Cyrus McCormick Jr.—approved of the measure, and if the condemned anarchists would, in turn, disavow in writing their words and actions. Schwab and Fielden did so, and had their sentences commuted to life imprisonment; Parsons, Spies, Engel, Fischer, and Lingg refused, Parsons quoting Patrick Henry's famous words, "Give me liberty or give me death."[89]

Oglesby was not alone in his prevarication. Some prominent Chicagoans, including the conservative *Chicago Tribune*, had begun to question the need for the executions. The paper argued that law had triumphed, convictions had been sought and won. Hanging the condemned would only create martyrs to the cause of anarchism, whereas a public recommendation for commutation coming from the city's business elite would, as a gesture, go a long way toward easing the city's persistent labor troubles. Marshall Field, however, harbored a powerful enmity toward those who fomented labor unrest, an attitude dating from the railroad strike of 1877. Following that debacle, he had led an effort by the city's business leaders to buy a 632-acre site for the construction of a new military base thirty miles north of Chicago on Lake Michigan (soon named Fort Sheridan), as well as the construction of a new thoroughfare linking the fort with the city (the Sheridan Road), in order to enable the rapid intervention of federal troops in strikes and riots. With the local aristocrats of commerce, led by Field, remaining unmoved by the defendants' plight, and Oglesby hemmed in by five of the condemned's refusal to accept his offer and apologize, it was announced that the sentences would be carried out on the morning of November 11, 1887.

As that date approached, public outcry over the impending hangings was muted somewhat by the sudden (and suspicious) "discovery" of bomb-making materials in Lingg's jail cell. How bomb-related items got into the heavily guarded lockup was never established. Author Louis Adamic suggests a "sweetheart" of Lingg's was responsible, but the evidence is unclear.[90] However, on the night before the executions Lingg managed to commit suicide by cracking a dynamite cap open in his mouth. His death left only four of the original eight defendants for the gallows—Parsons, Spies, Engel, and Fischer—all of whom remained steadfast. Fischer assured Johann Most, "I am ready to deposit my life at the altar of the good cause,"[91] while Engel, echoing Fischer's sentiment, reassured friends, "Any man who is a true socialist, thoroughly imbued with its glorious principles, can go bravely to the scaffold and die for them."[92]

Near the end Parsons was visited by Dyer Lum, his successor at the *Alarm*, who asked whether he now regretted returning from hiding in Wisconsin to surrender to Judge Gary's court. "No, I still believe I did right," Albert replied. "My comrades, like myself, were unjustly charged. They did not shirk the issue; honor demanded that I should share their fate. Even under all the experience of the year past I honestly believe I could do no otherwise today."[93] When Lucy Parsons and her children were denied a final visit, Parsons turned to his love of poetry to console himself during his last night on earth. He found a sympathetic listener in a jailhouse deputy, and read to him John Greenleaf Whittier's "The Reformer":

> *Whether on the gallows high,*
> *Or in the battle van*
> *The noblest place for man to die,*
> *Is where he dies for man.*

"That song," Parsons assured his companion, "will go ringing down the corridors of time."[94]

HAYMARKET UNIQUELY CHALLENGED LABOR by forcing it to decide what long-term message to take away. There was of course great indignation at the verdicts and at the premise of the trial itself, but there was also frustration that the eight-hour crusade that had indirectly led to the affair was now discredited, and that anarchists had so badly sullied labor's name. The bomb-throwing radical had become a popular caricature of worker unrest, newspaper cartoons depicting "The Anarchist" as a gnomelike, bearded figure (likely modeled after Johann Most), secreting a bomb behind his back or in his coat. One entrepreneur ventured to cash in on the sensationalist interest in anarchy by exhibiting the remains of Louis Lingg, offering $10,000 for the privilege and promising to return the corpse in good condition when he was through.[95] Labor leaders were unsure whether to defend the principles for which the men had died, strive harder to distance themselves from anarchism, or simply move on.

The Knights of Labor were an especial victim of Haymarket fallout: the group had formally offered only tepid support for the giant eight-hour rallies of May 1, and had been quick to condemn those rounded up after the May 4 bombing. "Let it be understood by all the world," stated the group's Chicago house organ, "that the Knights of Labor have no affiliation, association, sympathy or respect for the band of cowardly murderers, cut-throats and robbers, known as anarchists. . . . Better that seven times seven men hang than to have the millstone of odium around the standard of this Order in affiliating in any way with this element of destruction."[96] When, at a national conference of the Knights in October 1886, the rank and file demanded a resolution to the effect that the Haymarket condemned were not guilty, Terence Powderly led an effort to defeat it; the meeting did, however, vote to request that those convicted receive leniency, and Powderly belatedly agreed that the court's work in the case had been hasty. Johann Most called Powderly a "scoundrel" guilty of "wretched trickery" for having withheld more full-hearted support for Spies and company. "It [was] within his power to bring the whole organization of which he is the head to declare itself against the judicial murders," Most said. "But Powderly did the very opposite. . . . The blood of our murdered comrades sticks forever to his hands."[97] The Master Workman felt deeply the sting of such criticisms; in October 1887 he confided his fear that anarchists were plotting to kill *him*.[98]

On the scaffold, moments from death, August Spies had cried out, "The time will come when our silence will be more powerful than the voices you strangle today." The backlash from Haymarket, per Spies's prophecy, did prove considerable, and the ever-ambivalent Powderly was among the first to be diminished by it.

But it was in more substantial ways not a good season for the Knights. In fall 1886, twenty thousand Knights struck the Chicago meatpacking plants for an eight-hour day. Management brought in scabs and special guards under the direction of the Pinkertons. The strikers, who stayed off the job for three weeks and believed they were close to wringing concessions out of the employers, were blindsided when Powderly unexpectedly ordered the strikers back to their jobs, threatening those who disobeyed his edict with dismissal from the union. With the support of the Knights national leadership withdrawn, the strikers capitulated and returned to the plant's ten-hour regimen, but were furious at their own organization's faintheartedness.

Rank and file began to depart the Knights. It increasingly appeared that their huge membership, erratic leadership, and inability to focus on the needs of a specific trade were a poor means of carrying forward the struggle for better hours. From a membership of seven hundred thousand prior to Haymarket, the Knights lost members steadily after 1886, until it could claim only seventy-five thousand members in 1893, the year Powderly was deposed. Unfortunately his replacement, James Sovereign, also signed on to gradual reformist programs that had come to be seen by many as chimerical. Like Powderly, Sovereign seemed willing to ignore the fact that the Knights' remarkable growth had come not through programs involving manufacturing cooperatives or land reform, but from standing up to Jay Gould and other employers on the basics of wages and hours.

The U.S. labor cause has always been an extended conversation between ideology and pragmatism, and in the wake of Haymarket, pragmatism spoke the loudest and clearest. "No more powerful blow was ever struck for capitalism than when that bomb was thrown on Haymarket Square," lamented a Socialist journal in 1909, causing the labor movement "to come definitely under the control of its most conservative element."[99] With the Knights in decline and Socialists and anarchists hobbled by their association with so traumatic a series of events, a new spirit asserted itself in American unionism epitomized by the 1886 founding of Gompers's American Federation of Labor (AFL). Gompers's group harbored no illusions about shaping a new world more favorable to the proletariat; it focused instead on wages, hours, and working conditions, and the effective power of trade unions fighting for these goals within the industrial status quo. It followed a philosophy that many workers found reassuring, one "based upon wage consciousness rather than class consciousness," with "no idea of trying to change the economic system, let alone seeking to overthrow it."[100] As a federation spokesman had famously stated in testimony before Congress in 1883, "We have no ultimate ends. . . . We are fighting only for immediate objects that can be realized in a few years. We are opposed to theorists. . . . We are practical men."[101]

While there were occasional efforts to create bridges of respect and friendship between the Knights and Gompers's federation, the groups became increasingly distrustful of one another, particularly as the latter surged to greater national prominence. It probably didn't help that the organizations' leaders were of opposite dispositions. The devout, temperance-minded Powderly took exception to Gompers's obstreperousness, his love of saloons, stogies, and beer; he once referred to him as a "Christ-slugger."[102] Powderly had in turn angered Gompers with the Knights' effort to make the Cigar Makers' International into a group more embracing of unskilled immigrants.[103] Gompers thought the movement was simply not ready for the large-scale organizing of immigrant workers, men and women who knew little or no English and brought alien beliefs from across the Atlantic. Unions, Gompers believed, "survived only where the public would tolerate them, in the small shops and in artisan trades where craft unions seemed to uphold American individualistic values."[104]

Gompers was himself an immigrant, of Dutch-Jewish heritage, born in London in 1850, and brought to America as a child, arriving with his family in 1863. As a young man he followed his father's trade as a cigar maker, a proud craft tradition unique in that it was performed in quiet, not in the proximity of pounding machines. Cigar makers' workrooms famously served as informal schools for workers; young Sam was often assigned the job of reading from books and newspapers to the other cigar makers as they worked. Precocious and socially adept, Gompers was groomed as a future leader in the Cigar Makers' International, headed by Adolph Strasser and Karl Ferdinand Laurrell; both were Socialists who had wearied of the endless bickering and dogmatism between various cells and belief systems; they impressed upon young Sam Gompers the importance of sticking to the hard business of trade unionism, with a minimum emphasis on Socialist politics. "Go to their meetings, listen to them and understand them, but do not join the Party," Laurrell warned him. Gompers later called Laurrell "my mental guide through many of my early struggles,"[105] and all his life was fond of quoting Laurrell's words of admonishment: "Study your union card, Sam, and if the idea does not square with that, it ain't true."[106]

One can imagine how valid Laurrell's words must have sounded to Gompers by the time he presided over the founding of the AFL. William Sylvis with his iron molders and the NLU had frittered away precious organizational resources on political causes, cooperation, monetary reform, women's issues; Terence Powderly had offered inconsistent leadership; the Knights of St. Crispin had railed in vain to preserve skilled labor and the craft tradition. Gompers, in contrast, had absorbed these and other valuable lessons. Having once joined an unsuccessful strike against the introduction of a newfangled cigar-rolling device, he came away believing that one could not strike effectively against technological progress; one could only adapt to it, safeguarding workers' interests in the transition as best one could. Another observation he made was that strikes against wage cuts rarely worked if carried out in tough economic times, for management simply turned to scabs and strikebreakers. Strikes had a better chance where employers were doing well and workers' demands could be linked to overall profitability, and where work disruptions would have a more telling effect. So strongly did Gompers feel about inappropriately timed strikes that when he ran the Cigar Makers' local in New York he was known to discipline wildcat strikers by helping to provide employers with replacement workers. This could be perceived as a nasty bit of double-dealing, but as he liked to say in defense of his tactics, "The trade union is not a Sunday School."[107]

While cautious about strikes, Gompers nonetheless defended the right to withhold one's labor; strikes were a "sign that the people are not yet willing to surrender every spark of their manhood and their honor and their independence." He liked an analogy of a strike as a natural release of energy, like a thunderstorm. "No man would think of trying to invent some machine by which the thunderstorms could be abolished," Gompers asserted, for they are "the result of noxious gases or different gases in the atmosphere that come together and crush, and they simply purify the atmosphere, and make us feel reinvigorated and with renewed hope."[108] Picking its battles carefully paid off for Gompers's Cigar Makers' union; it received 218 applications for strikes from its locals between 1881 and 1883 and approved 194 of them, winning about 75 percent of the time.[109]

Gompers also placed great value on fat strike funds and the high dues required to sustain them. Once employers knew his cigar makers had an ample purse and could hold out in case of a strike, they became more inclined to treat worker demands seriously. "There is not a dollar which the working man or woman pays into a labor organization," he often said of his dues policy, "which does not come back a hundredfold."[110]

Gompers had joined the Federation of Organized Trades at its founding in 1881. The influence of the group remained slight until 1886, when the power of the Knights began to wane and Gompers and his allies saw their opening. At a federation gathering in Philadelphia at the end of May 1886, just after Haymarket, many of the delegates had gone out of their way to appear in conservative garb, "a silk hat and a Prince Albert coat," Gompers later recalled, the better to emphasize their dignity and self-respect as trade workers.[111] This conclave led to a gathering at Columbus, Ohio, that fall at which trade union representatives of 150,000 workers from the Cigar Makers, Iron Molders, Carpenters, Mine Workers, and others founded the AFL and elected Gompers its president.

Haymarket's aftermath played a role in Gompers's later inclination to keep electoral politics at arm's length. In fall 1886 he backed the candidacy of Henry George for mayor of New York City on the United Labor Party ticket. George was a movement literary celebrity, having in 1879 published *Progress and Poverty*, a seminal account of the impact of industrialization in which he linked the growing gap between affluent and poor in America to the disproportionate ownership of land by a handful of individuals and corporations. George suggested a "single tax" that would address this imbalance. The amount of available land in America was shrinking steadily, he pointed out, an observation that had a chilling effect on readers' faith in the ideal of land for all and of an ever-westward growing nation. Gompers campaigned hard for George, who won almost a third of the vote in a three-way race, but ultimately lost to Abram Hewitt, who as an ungracious winner had the cheek to describe Gompers and other George supporters as "anarchists."

The next year George disappointed his followers by denouncing clemency in the Haymarket case. He had initially criticized the trial's unfairness, but either to protect his political ambitions or out of pique at Socialist associates, he was by October 1887 recommending that the ruling of the Illinois Supreme Court rejecting the Haymarket defendants' appeal be respected.[112] Bitter over George's failure at the polls and at the changeable nature of the candidate's views, Gompers ever after tended to regard immersion in party politics as a waste of one's efforts, efforts better directed toward the actual workaday needs of labor. His federation might advance a legislative program, but tended to steer clear of any fixed alignment with political parties. It would swing support to politicians who aided its causes and deny support to those who offended it on a case-by-case basis.

The AFL offered well-defined independence to its individual trade unions, yet a central leadership that was run like a smart company, carefully controlling policy, benefits, dues, and the flow of funds to distressed locals. Gompers provided much of the energy for the operation of the AFL in its earliest days—writing and answering correspondence, handling the organization's accounting, and running its headquarters with the help of his son Henry, who served as office boy for $3 a week. He was adamant about knowing personally the details of the work in which he was engaged; once, when the Cigar Makers were preparing an appeal to the state legislature about the need to regulate tenement workplaces, Gompers had gone door-to-door through the tenements of the Lower East Side pretending to be a salesman of the collected works of Charles Dickens, in order to get a firsthand view of existing household cigar factories.[113] Where an effective labor organization succeeded, he recognized, was in such thorough awareness and control—not necessarily in bold undertakings like strikes; what mattered was the day-to-day routine of negotiating small matters with disparate unions and labor councils, examining grievances, administering benefits—actions that did not make headlines but were the real building blocks of labor justice and peace.

Gompers recognized that industrialism was not an aberration; it was rather the logical result of history's advance. Thus, defeating industrialism outright was unlikely, particularly through the pursuit of utopian fantasies. The earth was not going to revolve backward to a simpler time of small artisan businesses and the family farm. He thus shied away from visionary fixes like currency reform, land programs, and cooperation that had spellbound the National Labor Union and the Knights of Labor, as he chucked aside the naive notions that laborers everywhere would rise up as one against authority or were likely even to share a single unifying national purpose. Workers might curse bosses and "property beasts," but most believed firmly in their own eventual ascendance, in property rights, and in the rule of law. Far from disrespecting capital, they were faithful to the promise of individual attainment. "There is a certain principle inborn in every man. . . . That principle is hope," one AFL official told the *Alarm*. "Men must be permitted to better their condition by individual exertion or civilization will perish of dry rot."[114]

Thus, far more effectively than groups like the NLU or the Knights or the Socialists, which were in a sense organizations devoted to labor-related *ideas*, the AFL appealed to its members with the targeting of fundamental and achievable goals. "It endured not because it had a blueprint for a new world, or for a return to an old one," notes Gompers's biographer Harold Livesay, "but because it best managed to protect the cherished rights of its members against the inroads of the new industrial age." It did this by confining itself "to economic and political methods sanctioned by the prevailing system."[115]

★ CHAPTER FOUR ★

PULLMAN'S TOWN

THE COMMANDER OF THE U.S. ARMY REGI-
ment at Fort Keogh in eastern Montana peered
through his binoculars, scanning the railroad track
and the limitless prairie for any sign of movement.
It was April 25, 1894, and he had urgent orders from
Washington to stop the oncoming Northern Pacific
freight train at all costs. This was no ordinary freight
loaded with lumber or cattle, but a hijacked train carrying five hundred armed and angry men. They were
the unemployed miners, teamsters, and rail yardmen
of Idaho and western Montana, and had announced
they would ride the stolen train, and carry their protest, all the way to the nation's capital. Already they had
used their superior numbers to beat back attempts by
authorities to retake the train. At Billings, just hours
before, there had been an exchange of gunfire and a
bystander killed, but now there were no more sizable
towns in Montana and the track looking east was clear.
Up ahead, the soldiers from Fort Keogh crouched by
the roadbed, unseen, readying their weapons.

Only seven years shy of the twentieth century,
such was the absurd character of the struggle for

workers' rights in America—desperate men on a hijacked train determined to cross the country to petition Congress for relief, and heavily armed soldiers waiting in ambush to stop them, prepared to shoot and kill their fellow citizens, if need be.

Since the onset of a severe financial crisis the year before, the nation had entered the most precipitous economic depression in its history. Laboring men everywhere were in despair; farm income had dried up; the Union Pacific and Erie railways were in arrears; banks had closed, as many as four hundred in the West and South. While no official numbers of unemployed were kept, it was estimated there were as many as 200,000 without work in New York, 100,000 in Chicago; in Philadelphia, 62,500. In lieu of public assistance, private charities could do only so much. Families slept in public parks, parents improvising each morning a way to find food and milk for their children, while less fortunate urchins scrounged in the streets. Husbands left home in search of work, some never to be heard from again, joining the permanent ranks of jobless wanderers. There is "something wrong," the *Cleveland Plain Dealer* lamented, "when such a large number of people are thrown up like driftwood on the shore, out of place, out of use."

If there was any silver lining in these troubles, it was that they reinvigorated reform efforts under way in the cities to address the conditions of slum dwellers, the jobless, and the poor. On the labor front, the struggles of recent years—the 1877 railroad strikes, the Haymarket affair, and now the 1893 economic crisis—had had the effect of honing a sharper, more pragmatic outlook among the large national organizations. The AFL, the Amalgamated Association of Iron and Steel Workers, and the American Railway Union, recognizing the enormous sway of the corporations, were coordinating thousands of members and union locals. Public and official concern about the accumulating power of both capital and labor would soon bring the federal government and the courts into the fray; there was uncertainty as to what their role would mean for industrial society, but none as to its potential significance.

———

CARNEGIE STEEL'S HOMESTEAD WORKS, America's largest steel-making complex, sat on the Monongahela River southeast of Pittsburgh, occupying fifty acres and containing three separate mills, a port, and a private railroad. Of the plant's thirty-eight hundred workers, 750 skilled laborers most essential to the mill operations belonged to the Amalgamated Association of Iron and Steel Workers. They had a solid contract and enjoyed a say, through a multitude of negotiated rules and guidelines, in how the plant functioned and work was done. In 1889 the Carnegie Company had set out to defeat the Amalgamated, but the workers, surprising Carnegie with their degree of organization and resolve, formed an impenetrable human barrier around the plant and successfully drove away the company's scabs and detectives. Faced with such unexpected solidarity—as well as sympathy strikes at related Carnegie operations, including the railroads on which Homestead relied—the firm surrendered; it agreed to the work rules and set wages on a sliding scale to reflect the prevailing market price of steel products.

Although the 1889 pact—good for three years—had bought both sides time, the company had not relinquished its aim of destroying the union. This contradicted the public statements of its president, Andrew Carnegie, who in two articles in *Forum* magazine in 1886 had expressed sympathy for the rights of workingmen. Carnegie, himself an immigrant to America, prided himself on knowing many of his German, Italian, and Bohemian workers by their first names, and encouraged them to be similarly informal toward him. "There can never be any hopeless troubles . . . as long as they call me 'Andy,' " he liked to tell business colleagues.[1] Carnegie's avowed respect for his workers extended to their right to organize, and even to their distrust of scabs. "To expect that one dependent upon his daily wage for the necessaries of life will stand by peacefully and see a new man employed in his stead is to expect too much," he'd written. But Carnegie was known to occasionally sacrifice truth in order to appear reasonable before the press, and in 1892, when the union contract expired and another showdown with the Amalgamated loomed, he had conveniently departed on an extended vacation to Aberdeen, Scotland, where he maintained one of his many homes. Bill Jones, a Carnegie manager who had traditionally handled employee relations and was popular with the workers—his benevolence included the introduction of eight-hour shifts at one plant—had unfortunately been killed not long before in a blast furnace accident.

The man left to assume Jones's duties, Henry Clay Frick, was far less empathetic. He was said to have once bodily picked up a disputatious striker and thrown him and all his belongings into a creek. Known as "the King of Coke," Frick was a millionaire in his own right. His H. C. Frick Company had been one of the nation's leading vendors of iron-smelting coke until the firm was absorbed by the Carnegie enterprise. It was Frick who had suggested to Andrew Carnegie that all the steel magnate's concerns be merged under one rubric, Carnegie Steel, of which Frick was now chairman. Frick considered Carnegie's oft-spoken solicitude for workers, whether genuine or not, to be antiquated and softheaded, and he was eager to demonstrate his own management style and willingness to trim costs.

The Amalgamated, concerned about the imminent expiration of the earlier contract, had proposed a new pact that would align the wage scale with the greater prices being had for steel products and the increased production of the Homestead mills. Henry Clay Frick paid little heed to the offer. He wanted to undo Carnegie's bonds to the Amalgamated, make Homestead a nonunion plant, and allow the firm to set wages as it saw fit, with no sliding scale. The Carnegie Company couched this desire in democratic-sounding language, saying it wished to deal with the majority of its workers, those who were unskilled and nonunion, rather than the more "elite" skilled members of the Amalgamated. But this was misleading; the unskilled employees largely supported the Amalgamated because plant conditions overall benefited from the union's success.

Carnegie later claimed that the first reports of bloodshed at his mills "came on me like a thunderbolt in a clear sky."[2] A New York paper as early as mid-June, however, had printed the headline "A Bitter Struggle Coming" above a story about the deteriorating situation,[3] and Frick's elaborate measures to prepare for violence as the showdown approached could not have been unknown to Carnegie, even in far-off Scotland. The King of Coke had ordered a ten-foot fence built around the plant, topped it with barbed wire, cut holes in it for rifles, and installed searchlights on a series of watchtowers. He arranged for barges to be at the ready to ferry Pinkerton agents to the site, if needed. Workers, nervously eyeing the extensive preparations, renamed the Homestead plant "Fort Frick."

On June 28 Frick locked out the entire workforce and announced that as of July 1 Homestead would be operated as a nonunion mill. The Amalgamated immediately went on strike, taking the nonunion workers with them. Having anticipated the company's moves, the union divided one thousand employee volunteers into watch committees to keep an eye out for scabs, spies, or other interlopers; it also rented a small boat, the *Edna*, to patrol the river approach to the plant. When, on July 5, Allegheny county sheriff William H. McCleary showed up with a detachment of deputies to "secure" the Homestead works, he and his entourage were intercepted by one such committee of strikers, escorted onto the *Edna*, and taken back to Pittsburgh. McCleary's visit was in all likelihood a bit of play-acting, the strikers' "rejection" of the sheriff and his men serving as a pretext for Frick's use of Pinkertons and armed force.

That very night, at about 2 a.m., the union was informed by telegraph that barges were on the river headed toward Homestead. The Carnegie Company had purchased two vessels for use by the Pinkertons—the *Iron Mountain*, which served as a floating dormitory for three hundred agents, and the *Monongahela*, which held a kitchen and dining area. A tugboat, the *Little Bill*, had been engaged to tow them into position. The crew of the union's boat, the *Edna*, shoved off to engage the intruders in the river, firing warning shots in the direction of the *Little Bill* before turning back to alert the workers. Not only strike volunteers heard the *Edna*'s shrill whistle of alarm. The town adjacent to the mill stirred to life and its residents descended to the riverfront. Some were armed with shotguns and pistols; others had hoes, rakes, or similar implements. As the barges came within hailing distance someone in the crowd warned: "Don't step off that boat; go back, go back, or we'll not answer for your lives!" An instant later a Pinkerton, Captain Frederick Heinde, appeared, and was told by Hugh O'Donnell, one of the strike leaders, "In the name of God and humanity, don't attempt to land! Don't attempt to enter these works by force!"

"We were sent here to take possession of this property and to guard it for this company," replied Heinde. "We don't wish to shed blood, but . . . if you men don't withdraw, we will mow every one of you down"—a somewhat audacious threat considering the crowd greatly outnumbered the men aboard the barges. "Before you enter those mills," vowed a striker, "you will trample over the dead bodies of three thousand honest workingmen."[4] A few strikers moved to block any attempt by the Pinkertons to disembark. One, William Foy, lay down upon the gangplank and drew a revolver; Captain Heinde, coming toward him, swung at Foy with his baton and then, accidentally, stepped on an oar that bounced upward and struck another worker in the face. Suddenly shots were fired, wounding both Foy and Heinde. After a momentary pause there was more shooting, knocking down several Pinkertons and causing the rest to retreat belowdecks.

As the sun rose the detectives made another effort to land, which brought a second exchange of gunfire; this time it was the Pinkertons' aim that was accurate, killing and wounding several strikers. Further engaging the crowd which, having been fired upon, now appeared dangerously agitated, seemed an exceedingly poor idea, and the invaders gave up the effort to land the barges. As the *Little Bill* began to tow them away from shore, the tug's captain raised an American flag, perhaps thinking the mob would hesitate to shoot at the Stars and Stripes; the workers, however, opened a withering fire on the tug, injuring a crewman and sending both the captain and pilot scampering for cover. The *Little Bill* then steamed away, abandoning the Pinkertons' barges.

"Men of Homestead and fellow strikers," declared a worker, "our friends have been murdered—our brothers have been shot down before our eyes by hired thugs! Yonder in those boats are hundreds of men who have murdered our friends and would ravish our homes! Men of Homestead, we must kill them! Not one must escape alive!"[5] His listeners, requiring little urging and seizing on their sudden tactical advantage, began at once trying to oust the agents from the barges, using small skiffs to come up alongside the vessels, shooting and hurling small projectiles. The Pinkertons struggled to mount a defense. Only forty of the three hundred agents were full-time Pinkerton men; the rest were recent recruits who had signed on to stand guard duty at a steel mill, and were inadequately trained (or motivated) to suppress an armed mob. But even the veteran agents began to recognize the hopelessness of their position when a white flag they raised in surrender was blown to tatters by the strikers.[6]

Sheriff McCleary, alerted to the detectives' predicament, wired Pennsylvania governor Robert E. Pattison at once for the militia, but Pattison, cognizant of the fact that Carnegie wanted an excuse to bring in troops and suspecting McCleary's earlier visit to the mill had been staged, hesitated to intervene. "The sheriff has employed but 12 deputies up to the present time," Pattison replied. "If the emergency is as great as alleged, he should have employed a thousand. It is not the purpose of the military to act as police officers."[7] The governor told McCleary that at Homestead he was facing a local challenge to law and order, and that as sheriff he must deputize a force to counter it.

As appeals for military help went unanswered, the Pinkertons' dilemma became grave, for some in the crowd had initiated an effort with potentially ghastly results, pouring oil on the water around the barges in an attempt to set them alight, which would surely incinerate those on board. Fortunately, senior officials of the Amalgamated had by now arrived on the scene. "Men, for God's sake and your families' sake, and for your own sake, listen to the pleadings of cool-headed men," urged union president M. M. Garland. "We have positive assurance that these [Pinkertons] will be sent away, and all we want is a statement that you will not do any more firing." But even as Garland spoke, workers were lighting fireworks near the barges in an attempt to ignite the oil. Hugh O'Donnell of the Amalgamated had better luck with the crowd, obtaining an agreement that would allow the Pinkertons to surrender their arms to the workers and submit to arrest by Sheriff McCleary on charges of murder.[8]

The Pinkertons came ashore under a flag of truce. The crowd, however, ignoring the entreaties of the Amalgamated leaders, set upon the bewildered agents, beating them mercilessly with clubs, stabbing, and in some cases shooting them. Not a single Pinkerton escaped the mob's punishment. As the agents were being roughed up, demonstrators boarded the now-abandoned barges and stripped them of beds, quilts, and cooking utensils, then set both vessels on fire.

Nor was the crowd's fury yet spent. Even after authorities took control of the Pinkertons and attempted to lead them through the town, men, women, and children emerged from their homes to heap further beatings and indignities on the already hobbled captives, hitting them with kitchen utensils, garden tools, and whatever came to hand. Eventually, the bruised and bleeding agents were secured in the local opera house and, in the middle of the night, put aboard a special train and taken away.

There was widespread condemnation of the sadistic attack on the surrendering Pinkertons and, more generally, of the idea that a union-led mob would use deadly force against agents whose presence was legitimate in that they had been hired by the property's management. "Men talk like anarchists or lunatics," opined the *Independent*, "when they insist that the workmen at Homestead have done right."[9] Thus, even though a number of workers had been killed, the incident played into the company's hands. "This outbreak settles one matter forever," announced a Carnegie executive, "and that is that the Homestead mill hereafter will be run non-union and the Carnegie Company will never again recognize the Amalgamated Association nor any other labor organization."[10]

On July 12, with the strikers still occupying the site, Governor Pattison, responding to a request by Frick, finally consented to send in the militia. The Amalgamated workers welcomed the soldiers with cheers and an impromptu band concert, proudly telling commanding officer General George Snowden how they, the workers, controlled the plant by virtue of having fended off the invasion of the company's hirelings. But Snowden rudely punctured the strikers' mood. "Pennsylvanians can hardly appreciate the actual communism of these people," he commented. "They [the strikers] believe the works are theirs quite as much as Carnegie's."[11] His militia, eight thousand strong, easily managed where the Pinkertons had failed, taking control of the mills and safeguarding the arrival of hundreds of replacement workers. The Amalgamated countered by convincing some of the scabs to leave the plant—many, it seemed, had been lied to about the work they were accepting—but by early fall, Homestead was back in operation with two thousand new nonunion workers.

In mid-November the Amalgamated admitted defeat, those members who returned forced to accept a nonunion wage structure. While events at Homestead had played out, an equally depressing labor setback had occurred in the silver and copper mine region of western Idaho at Coeur d'Alene, where a miners' union violently resisted the importation of scabs, only to be crushed in turn by soldiers and a declaration of martial law; hundreds of strikers had been rounded up and imprisoned in a crude detention camp.

The confrontations at both Homestead and Coeur d'Alene in 1892 showed corporations willing to act with ever-greater deliberation in confronting labor unions—supplanting workers with new technology, importing scabs in large numbers, and relying on the quick insertion of Pinkertons and soldiers to overwhelm local opposition.[12] During the coming decade the Amalgamated would steadily lose membership as technology reduced the number of employees needed to run the Homestead plant, and union activism was squelched there and at other area mills by the firing or blacklisting of suspect employees. Carnegie and its corporate descendant, the United States Steel Company, would successfully inhibit labor organizing in the Pennsylvania steel mills for many years to come.

THE INTENSITY OF THE HOMESTEAD CRISIS was unsettling to anyone mindful of the precarious state of labor-industrial relations in America, although it's probably fair to say no one responded more dramatically than two young anarchists, Emma Goldman and Alexander Berkman. Goldman, born in Russia in 1869, had emigrated in 1886 to live with relatives in Rochester, New York; like many young intellectuals of her generation, she had been enraged by the Haymarket trial and executions. Acting on her deepening political commitment, she left a youthful marriage and came to New York City in 1889, ingratiating herself with the Lower East Side anarchist milieu dominated by men like Johann Most and Justus Schwab. She first encountered the peculiar and excitable Berkman, a young Lithuanian Jew, wolfing down his dinner in a bohemian café. Both Goldman and Berkman became adherents of Most; Goldman briefly was his sexual partner and Berkman worked in Most's publishing business. Like their mentor, they were intrigued with the idea of the *attentat*, the violent "propaganda by deed" of anarchist philosophy.

Poring over news accounts of the Homestead lockout and strike, they were outraged by Carnegie's heavy-handed actions. One worker's pregnant wife, they were horrified to learn, had been evicted from her house by sheriff's deputies and left in the street. They resolved to go to Homestead at once to aid the workers in confronting so diabolical a creature as the Carnegie Company and its badge-wearing minions. They would compose an anarchist manifesto for the Homestead strikers, for while they saw in the Amalgamated's resistance an inspiring "awakening" of anticapitalist fervor, it seemed a "blind rebellion," one lacking "conscious revolutionary purpose." In their view, "anarchism alone" could shape discontent into meaningful insurrectionary expression. "The dissemination of our ideas among the proletariat at Homestead," Berkman later wrote, "would illumine the great struggle, help to clarify the issues, and point the way to complete ultimate emancipation."[13]

Before the two could advance their plans, however, news reached New York of the terrible battle that had taken place at Homestead with the Pinkertons. "We were stunned," Goldman would recall. "We saw at once that the time for our manifesto had passed. Words had lost their meaning in the face of the innocent blood spilled on the banks of the Monongahela." Berkman's fervency was transformed immediately from the aim of educating the workers to exacting revenge on Henry Clay Frick. "Frick is the responsible factor in this crime," he decided, "[and] must be made to stand the consequences."

With Goldman agreeing that "a blow aimed at Frick would re-echo in the poorest hovel" and show the world "the proletariat of America had its avengers,"[14] the couple hatched a scheme to murder the villain. Frick would be killed, and Berkman, while fully expecting to be executed for his crime, would use the opportunity of his trial to denounce the Carnegie dynasty and defend the anarchist cause. Goldman insisted she be taken along because as a woman she might have an easier time getting close to Frick without raising suspicion, but Berkman argued there was no use in two people sacrificing themselves in an *attentat* when one would suffice, and that her skills as a public speaker made it important she remain free to be able to defend and explain the purpose of the deed.

Planning an act of revolutionary terrorism, they soon discovered, did not come as easily as revolutionary thought. Having chosen a time bomb as the best way to kill Frick, Berkman purchased the raw materials and assembled it based on information contained in Most's guidebook, *The Science of Revolutionary Warfare*. A friend led him to an abandoned field on Staten Island where he could test the homemade device; but after several hours of trials, an exasperated Berkman returned to Manhattan to tell Goldman he couldn't get the gadget to detonate. They had wasted $40 on a nonexploding bomb.

Goldman, meanwhile, having exhausted the generosity of friends who could loan her money to pay Berkman's train fare to Pittsburgh and other expenses, decided that if he was willing to give his life for the cause, she would not be above selling her body to raise the needed funds. Putting aside her spectacles and usual modest garb, she outfitted herself in a gauzy dress and makeup and joined the streetwalkers on Fourteenth Street. After a long while she managed to attract the attentions of an elderly man-about-town. He took her to a nearby saloon and bought her a beer, but soon sensed Goldman's nervousness and lack of expertise. After eliciting from her the fact that she was a novice, he handed her $10 and advised her to go home.[15]

Berkman soon left New York, a portrait of Frick clipped from a newspaper in his wallet so he would know his victim on sight. Riding west alone, gazing from the window of the train and musing on the role history had allotted him, he reminded himself that "the removal of a tyrant is not merely justifiable; it is the highest duty of every true revolutionist . . . and what could be higher in life than to be a true revolutionist? It is to be a *man*, a complete MAN."[16]

On July 23 the "complete man" was in the reception area of Frick's office on the second floor of the Chronicle-Telegraph Building on Pittsburgh's Fifth Avenue, fingering the inexpensive pistol in his pocket. According to the *New York Times* account, Berkman may have attempted to see Frick at least once before, showing a secretary a phony business card bearing the name "Simon Bachman," an "employment agent" seeking to know if Carnegie needed assistance arranging for replacement workers at Homestead, but had been turned away.

Now, as on the previous occasions, Berkman was told by a porter that the boss was unavailable, but this time the assassin caught a glimpse of Frick in an adjoining room. Brushing past the porter, he ran inside and "with a quick motion I [drew] the revolver," he later recalled. "As I raise[d] the weapon, I [saw] Frick clutch with both hands the arm of the chair, and attempt to rise. I [aimed] at his head. . . . With a look of horror he quickly avert[ed] his face, as I pull[ed] the trigger."[17] Berkman managed to fire three times at the startled executive, striking him twice in the neck, before being tackled by Carnegie vice president John G. A. Leishman, who had been in the room consulting with Frick. A crew of carpenters working nearby also responded to the gunshots and helped subdue the assassin, although during the struggle Berkman managed to break free and stab Frick. Despite his multiple wounds, Frick dragged himself to his desk chair, where he sat immobile as police swarmed into the building. "Don't shoot!" Frick is said to have called to the arriving officers, who placed Berkman under arrest. "Leave him to the law, but raise his head and let me see his face." Doctors were summoned who dressed Frick's wounds and removed several bullet fragments from his neck.

In captivity, "the foreign crank," as the newspapers called Berkman, declared he had attacked Frick because he was "an enemy of the people." The would-be assassin's clothes, soaked with Frick's blood, were removed;

"when stripped, the crank was five feet 3½ inches high and weighed 116 pounds," reported the police. "He was of slender frame and showed no evidence of having been engaged in a laborious occupation. His lips were thick, his nose large, and he was a typical Russian Jew in appearance."[18]

Berkman surprised his captors by evincing a singular cool. A day after the attack "the crank" was observed passing time in his jail cell smoking cigarettes and whistling show tunes from the New York variety houses.[19] Back in that city, however, his recent movements were being closely investigated. There were calls for the arrests of Goldman and Johann Most; police broke into Goldman's apartment and made off with some revolutionary pamphlets. But the investigators somehow failed to detect her role in the incident, so she remained free, worrying about "Sasha," her pet name for Berkman, and attempting to rally the city's anarchist community in support of the *attentat*.

"It is stated by Berkman's acquaintances that of late he had been the lover of a German girl named Goldman," reported the *Times*, misstating her nationality. "This girl attended a meeting . . . held at Paul Wilzig's saloon, 85 East Fourth Street, on Saturday night. The Goldman woman exulted in the deed of her lover, and made a speech to the assembly. She deplored the fact that Frick had not been instantly killed. It was evident that she had no advance knowledge of Berkman's intended deed."[20]

To Goldman's extreme irritation, it was soon evident that Berkman's courageous revolutionary act had not particularly inspired their fellow anarchists. Berkman had, of course, failed to assassinate Frick; nor did it help that he was not highly regarded in anarchist circles, as his views were considered extreme and his behavior immature. Then, in an August 27 article in *Die Freiheit* came the ultimate betrayal: Johann Most, America's best-known anarchist, repudiated Berkman's assault on Frick. Goldman was livid, replying to Most with an article in the *Anarchist* insisting that Most explain his blatant disloyalty. When Most ignored her, Goldman showed up at Most's next public lecture with a horse whip concealed in her coat. As the speaker approached the lectern, Goldman suddenly leaped to her feet and shouted, "I came to demand proof of your insinuations against Alexander Berkman," and began horsewhipping the older man. "Repeatedly I lashed him across the face and neck," she later said, "then broke the whip over my knee and threw the pieces at him. It was all done so quickly that no one had time to interfere."[21]

Back in Pittsburgh Berkman's day in court did not go well. The standard sentence for attempted murder was seven years, but he received a sentence three times as long—"twenty-two years in a living tomb," as Goldman characterized it.[22] As for Frick, the "King of Coke's" brush with death at the hands of an anarchistic zealot had the unintended effect of making him appear both heroic and indestructible, and served the Carnegie Company as a useful distraction from the otherwise unfavorable coverage it was getting over the Homestead fracas; certainly it reinforced the impression that radical elements had infiltrated the forces of organized labor.

Andrew Carnegie was not so fortunate; editorials in the mainstream press noted that he had left the dirty work of ousting the Amalgamated in the hands of subordinates while he conveniently absented himself on the other side of the Atlantic, and that the extremely messy consequences had been the violence involving the Pinkertons and the assault on Frick. Even his much-vaunted philanthropy could not help him. "Ten thousand 'Carnegie Public Libraries' [will] not compensate the country for the direct and indirect evils resulting from the Homestead lockout," commented the *St. Louis Post-Dispatch*. "Say what you will of Frick, he is a brave man. Say what you will of Carnegie, he is a coward. And gods and men hate cowards."[23]

BY THE 1890s, an era historian Rayford Logan has famously termed "the nadir" of the black experience in America, Southern state legislatures had begun the devious process of eliminating black voting across the former Confederacy. Other rights of citizenship granted African Americans by the postwar amendments were also stripped away. Meanwhile, reports of the lynching of African American men began appearing in newspapers almost every other day; magazines ran insulting caricatures of blacks and published articles of pseudoscientific nonsense about Negroes' genetic backwardness; finally, in 1896, the U.S. Supreme Court in *Plessy v. Ferguson* certified Jim Crow segregation as the law of the land.[24] Black inferiority appeared beyond question. As for the worker of color, now formally a second-class citizen, "separate but equal," his position had never been more precarious.

Part of the problem was demographic. Until 1900 no more than 10 percent of black Americans resided in the North, which was rapidly industrializing; the percentage in the mining and agricultural empires of the West was even smaller, less than one half of one percent.[25] At the same time the perception of the Negro as an agricultural serf, a "carrier of water and a hewer of wood," had been so firmly established by slavery and the sharecropping system, and now by law, many factory owners treated it as an article of faith that blacks were physiologically unsuited to industrial work.[26]

Neither had the labor movement shown itself willing to accommodate African American workers, except under the most rigid, piecemeal terms. In the decades after the Civil War all three major federations—the National Labor Union, the Knights of Labor, and to a lesser degree the American Federation of Labor—gave lip service to the idea of creating and maintaining a biracial labor coalition. Of the three, the Knights were probably the most committed to a program of inclusiveness. That they did make occasional strides toward black organizing in the South is perhaps best revealed in the ferocity with which the Knights were targeted by white vigilantes, including the Ku Klux Klan. As the Knights faltered in the late 1880s, however, so did their outreach to African American members. The People's Party, the Populist urge that swept the South and West in the 1890s, was nominally dedicated to a biracial coalition of workers and farmers, but it was undone, in part, by an inability to achieve biracial trust and parity within its own ranks, and to put its enlightened ideals into practice.

It was apparent to the AFL's Sam Gompers, as it had been to William Sylvis, that keeping blacks out of unions had the effect of creating an available pool of cheap labor that industry could and did exploit, using blacks as replacement workers and strikebreakers. It was equally clear that only unity across racial lines would guarantee labor the fullest bargaining power. "Wage-workers like many others may not care to socially meet colored people," Gompers said, "but as working men we are not justified in refusing them the right of the opportunity to organize for their common protection. . . . If organizations do, we will only make enemies of them, and of necessity they will be antagonistic to our interests."[27] Four delegates from black workers' organizations attended the founding convention of the AFL in 1886; there, attendees resolved that the new federation would include "the whole laboring element of this country, no matter of what calling," and vowed "never to discriminate against a fellow worker on account of color, creed or nationality."[28]

Gompers, however, was limited in how much he could do to dictate policy to unions within his federation, and the AFL response remained inconsistent. An 1890 AFL convention passed a resolution expressing the federation's displeasure with unions that excluded members due to their race, but many locals refused to desegregate under any terms. Some opted for parallel unions—white and black butchers, white and black plumbers, white and black miners—although even when working side by side at the same location and for the same employer, white union locals frequently shrugged off opportunities for joint labor bargaining. White-controlled unions were often unwilling to allow black locals to be represented on central labor councils, the local committees that coordinated strategy and were often the liaison to the national federation's leadership.

By 1895 Gompers appeared to weary of the fight. The decline in the nation's economy had placed greater pressure on workers to find and retain employment. Whites were, if anything, less inclined to elevate blacks—whom they perceived as competition willing to accept lower wages—onto an equal platform from which they could negotiate with employers. At the same time the AFL itself became more lenient toward those unions that barred black membership. As a half-measure, Gompers asked unions to at least not carry exclusionary "whites-only" language in their constitutions. This condition received a test of sorts in the mid-

1890s when the Brotherhood of Locomotive Firemen considered joining the AFL. The railroad brotherhoods tended to be of such strong social and fraternal character that the inclusion of blacks was unlikely and in some instances explicitly denied. When Gompers suggested that the AFL's only stipulation was that no statements of racial bias appear in the union's documents,[29] the firemen decried the condition as unacceptable temporizing. "The brotherhood protested that it did not want its 'honor' compromised by affiliation with a labor federation that pretended to oppose the exclusion of nonwhites," relates scholar Herbert Hill, "but in reality would allow Negro exclusion to be practiced discreetly as a reward for new members."[30] Several nationally prominent unions, including the Cigar Makers, the International Typographical Union, the Bricklayers, and the Carpenters and Joiners, were, in contrast to the AFL, open in their stated exclusion of blacks.[31]

Interestingly, and as a sign of what might have been, AFL locals—white and black, skilled and unskilled—came together in 1892 to mount an historic action in New Orleans. A walkout by streetcar drivers demanding a twelve-hour day (instead of being made to work sixteen-hour shifts) had been resolved by arbitration in the drivers' favor; other local workers, inspired by the breakthrough, began pursuing further possibilities for labor reform. Thirty new AFL locals were chartered and a Workingmen's Amalgamated Council was established that included both black and white workers from the teamsters and warehouse industries. On October 24, 1892, this biracial force struck their industries for a ten-hour day, overtime wages, and exclusive union bargaining authority. The town's conservative Board of Trade retaliated with calls for the militia and court injunctions, and commercial leaders and the press used race-baiting and warnings of "Negro domination" to try to split the coalition, but the biracial coalition held firm and called a general strike. On November 8 an estimated twenty-five thousand people halted work, bringing the city to a four-day standstill as even nonindustrial workers such as musicians, store clerks, printers, and utility workers went out in sympathy. "I am sorry you are not down here to take a hand in it," one organizer enthused in a letter to Gompers. "It is a strike that will go down in history."[32]

Ultimately, Louisiana governor Murphy J. Foster's threats to deploy the militia and declare martial law brought the strike to an end, but the wage and hour demands of the biracial shipping unions were met, although businesses refused to recognize them as sole representatives of the workers. The Board of Trade, furious that union solidarity had led to such a widespread stoppage, saw to it that numerous strike leaders were indicted for violating an injunction under the Sherman Antitrust Act, setting a controversial precedent.

That the two races could unite as wage earners to present a strong front to employers in a major Southern city spoke volumes about how worker bargaining power might, under ideal circumstances, be multiplied; however, New Orleans would remain a tantalizing exception.[33] Gompers saw the strike as "a very bright ray of hope for the future of organized labor" and often mentioned it in later years as proof positive of what worker unity could achieve, but in the main he and other AFL leaders had little choice but to adhere to the existing policy of informal acquiescence to individual unions' racial bias.[34] While sticking to its policy of not chartering unions that had discriminatory language in their constitutions, the federation began recommending that such restrictions simply be transferred to other membership rituals; and locals found their own methods of keeping blacks away—requiring skills that few had had an opportunity to acquire, or charging exorbitant dues. In many Southern communities, maintaining a "lily-white" local was perceived as a sign of strength and regional loyalty, and was an inducement to employers who thought likewise and wished to retain a "preferred" body of able workers.

"The history of the labor movement from 1886 to 1902 so far as the Negro is concerned," W. E. B. Du Bois observed, "has been a gradual receding from the righteous declaration of earlier years."[35] Of course, given the reality of race relations in the country at the time, which were essentially nonexistent, and black citizenship rights, which had become invisible, labor's success at cracking so intractable a problem would have been remarkable, if not miraculous. As Philip Foner points out, labor's inability to achieve integration was more truly a national failure. Gompers could thus with a clear conscience relinquish the effort when it became evident it was impractical; he had even begun to fear that too persistent a devotion to black labor would likely doom his own federation, the survival of which was his primary obligation.[36] "We cannot overcome prejudice in a day," he concluded, and seemingly oblivious to the fact they had no other options, took to lashing out at black workers for their willingness to serve as strikebreakers.[37]

Confounded by their own inhibition and intolerance from realizing what should have been a natural alliance, white unionists could only rage at blacks for undercutting union bargaining, for being, in Logan's phrase, "cheap men."[38] Black workers, angry at being shunned and refusing to be blamed for the situation thrust upon them, understandably became cynical about organized labor generally. There may be no better example of the mounting disillusionment than Tuskegee educator Booker T. Washington, a former member of the Knights of Labor, who in 1895 delivered his famous Atlanta Compromise address in which he advised black Americans to relinquish their efforts to attain the constitutional promises of Emancipation and Reconstruction and focus on becoming dependable workers. By 1897 he was criticizing the AFL openly, warning that the federation's racial policies left him no choice but to side with employers against labor unions. He pointed out to factory owners the benefits of hiring the black worker who, unlike a white unionist, was "almost a stranger to strife, lock-outs, and labor wars . . . is law-abiding, peaceable, teachable . . . [and] has never been tempted to follow the red flag of anarchy."[39] Washington, upon the death of Frederick Douglass in 1895, had become America's most influential spokesman on race, and his counsel on the union racial divide resonated widely, in black newspapers and among employers happy to justify their use of black nonunion labor.

WHEN THE RAILROAD INNOVATOR George Mortimer Pullman introduced his elegant new sleeping car in the 1870s, advisers called it impractical: travelers, they feared, would never respect such opulent furnishings. Pullman, however, maintained that his insistence on quality would be appreciated, and that the very behavior of passengers would be transformed by the experience of riding in a luxurious railroad car. His faith in what he termed "the commercial value of beauty" soon proved correct: consumers were grateful for the Pullman cars, and didn't mind paying more to ride in comfort. In 1889 he applied a similar philosophy to his employees, creating a model community for them near Chicago meant to alleviate the hardship and insecurity in the lives of workers and their dependents.[40] The Pullman sleeper would become synonymous with the indulgence of superior rail travel; the model town of Pullman, Illinois, was destined to be the source of one of the most infamous labor disputes in American history.

Born in upstate New York in 1831, Pullman left high school to become a cabinetmaker, and soon entered the employ of his father, Lewis, a mechanic who specialized in hoisting and moving buildings and who had patented a device for rolling a lifted structure on wheels. George proved an adept and diligent apprentice, the first to volunteer to crawl into the tight places beneath lifted buildings to remove impeding stones. Upon Lewis Pullman's death in 1853, George assumed control of the enterprise, supervising a contract to move twenty warehouses along the Erie Canal.

In 1859 he was hired to relocate the five-story Matteson House, a prominent Chicago hotel whose foundation was threatened by water seepage from Lake Michigan. It was the largest building ever raised by mechanical means. Additional work of this kind was offered him, crowned by a unique challenge the following year in which Pullman lifted an entire city block of buildings and stores, a feat brought off with the coordinated help of six hundred workers. Chicagoans considered it such a marvel of technology, a popular lithograph was struck of the achievement. In another impressive lift, he directed an army of twelve hundred men in moving a four-story hotel, the Tremont House, without breaking a single pane of window glass.

Pullman's abundant ingenuity was soon drawn to the technical challenges confronting America's railroads. Train travel over great distances was still something of a marvel, but the trip between New York and Chicago took three and a half days and followed a roundabout route that added five hundred miles to the journey. Passengers were forced to purchase tickets on several connecting railroads and endured layovers for hours in small junction towns; once aboard, they sat on hard wooden benches and often breathed soot from the locomotive blowing in through open windows. Carriages were too hot in summer, too cold in winter; sleep was near impossible due to the train's vibration. Pullman knew firsthand the suffering of the long-distance rail passenger, and became intrigued by the idea of building a workable sleeping car, or "land barge," as some called it, that would offer greater comfort. Working with cast-off cars that he refurbished, he produced several prototypes, one of which, the "Pioneer," was used in May 1865 as part of the funeral train carrying the remains of President Lincoln from Chicago to Springfield, Illinois.[41]

Pullman shrewdly saw opportunity in the westward expansion of railroads. Transcontinental rail travel, a reality after 1869, required trains that could serve as self-contained communities, offering amenities for sleeping, eating, and leisure. In addition to his sleepers, Pullman introduced the first successful rail dining car, the "Delmonico," as well as the first parlor car, which was touted as "a hotel lobby on wheels." Because Pullman retained ownership of and operated the sleeping cars that were leased by the railroads, he was able to maintain his own high standards for quality and cleanliness. The Pullman Palace Car Company quickly became the gold standard for railroad car construction, while George Pullman was hailed as a rising star of engineering and industry, a levelheaded young corporate visionary who "refers his speech to his mind before he utters it."[42]

He also soon displayed a social conscience. Like many, Pullman had been stunned by the upheaval of the 1877 railroad strikes, and perceived the poverty and deprivation of city slums to be not only a blot on America, but a potential breeding ground for anarchists and other unwanted influences. On a transatlantic voyage, he had read and been impressed by a novel titled *Put Yourself in His Place* by Charles Reade, in which a skilled inventor applies scientific thought to the problems of production, increasing profits while simultaneously bettering working conditions and hours. The idea of humane reforms acting in tandem with sound business principles appealed to him, and he became intrigued by the possibility of allaying labor strife by improving the workingman's environment. He was about to open new car shops south of Chicago and began making plans to build a factory town for the workers who would be drawn there. "Seeing nothing wrong in a society oriented toward the profit motive," writes historian Steven Buder, "his intention was only to apply principles of business efficiency to meet the needs of his own workers. These ideas were promoted with the same verve as earlier had been lavished on the sleeping car."[43]

Pullman had also taken an interest in what was known as the Model Tenement Movement, championed by Alfred T. White, an affluent Brooklynite who in 1879 published a pamphlet entitled *Improved Dwellings for the Laboring Classes: The Need, and the Way to Meet It on Strict Commercial Principles*. White, who erected two model housing compounds, was convinced that many of the social hardships afflicting urban workers could be alleviated by freeing them from predatory landlords. Clean, well-ventilated, affordable housing would help stabilize workers' lives and inculcate virtues of thrift, for a key aspect of White's movement, and one that appealed greatly to the conservative Pullman, was that all hint of charity was avoided; tenants were expected to keep their apartments in good condition and pay a reasonable but not discounted rent, on which the landlord realized a 7 to 10 percent income.

To create the model town and a new site for his car works, Pullman purchased four thousand acres of former marshland along the shores of Lake Calumet, about twelve miles south of the Chicago business district. The town, completed in 1889, offered in addition to worker housing numerous amenities such as schools, a theater, a shopping arcade, and a man-made lake. To honor the community's place in the vanguard of industrial development and provide power for his factories, Pullman purchased the huge Corliss engine, which had been exhibited at the Philadelphia exhibition of 1876. He mounted the great machine in a glass case, where workers and visitors could admire its muscular churning.

Rents in the company town were no bargain—they were slightly higher than what was charged for comparable housing outside the community—and many of the residents were forced to share WCs and bathtubs. Pullman also charged for conveniences such as use of the town library, to which he donated his own collection of five thousand books. But his "workers' city," with its parklike atmosphere, its planned streets bearing the names of great inventors—Fulton, Stephenson, Watt, and Pullman himself—became a popular side attraction for the crowds drawn to the Columbian Exposition, the Chicago World's Fair of 1893. After a day viewing the fair's futuristic exhibits, the curious could take a fifteen-minute interurban ride to what must have seemed like the future itself—a functioning corporate town, with neatly trimmed hedges, a village square, and seemingly contented residents. Nearly thirteen thousand people lived in Pullman, roughly five thousand workers and their dependents.

The development of the Chicago World's Fair and the need to transport fairgoers to Chicago—27 million visitors were drawn to the fair during its six-month run—had brought an increased demand for Pullman railcars. This delayed the effect of the national economic downturn of 1893 on the Pullman works,[44] but by late summer 1893 orders for sleepers had diminished. The firm let go more than three thousand workers and reduced the hours and wages of those who remained, although it managed to reemploy two thousand of those dismissed by spring 1894, albeit at lower pay.[45] The wage reductions averaged 25 to 33 percent, and in some cases 50 percent; for example, a carpet-cutter's pay-per-piece rate fell from $3.00 to $1.50; a mattress-maker's from $2.25 to $1.40; a seat-maker's from $1.25 to $0.79.[46] This economic adjustment might have allowed Pullman and his employees to endure the downturn together, but his strong ethical views about charity led him to insist that the workers continue to pay a competitive rent for their housing. This was ruinous for the employees, as their rents were no longer near commensurate with their reduced pay. The company had all along deducted rent and the costs of utilities like water and illuminating gas from workers' paychecks; now, because rents remained the same even as pay levels dipped, many workers were left a pittance in weekly salary. "The wages he pays out with one hand, the Pullman Palace Car Company," stated a formal grievance issued by the employees, "[but] he takes back with the other, the Pullman Land Association."[47]

Philosophically unsympathetic to unionization, Pullman had joined other major Chicago employers in the aftermath of Haymarket to demand that the alleged perpetrators be held to the fullest account. This group, which also consisted of meatpacker Philip Armour, retailer Marshall Field, and farm equipment manufacturer Cyrus McCormick Jr., gave $100,000 to aid the families of policemen hurt or killed in the terror explosion, funds that were redirected in subsequent years to assisting local authorities to suppress radicals. Pullman's anxiety about labor strife and his identification with the concerns of big business tended to distance him from his own rank-and-file workers, a trend that intensified as his wealth and influence grew. Increasingly he relied on foremen and department heads to deal with employees. These intermediaries, knowing of Pullman's perfectionism and bouts of temper, often chose not to impart to him the actual difficulties experienced on the shop floor. When he did choose to intervene, the results were often harsh, as when he banned meetings by workers in his town who had joined the Knights of Labor and arranged to fire those men he considered organizers of the movement.[48] He had become confident of his ability to keep the "chronic kickers," as he called labor activists, in check.

Pullman's control over what types of associations might gather in the town was just one aspect of the village's feudal character. He had imposed strict sanitary regulations, banned alcohol and prostitution, imposed a curfew, and restricted the consumption of tobacco. A legion of spies and informers kept him abreast of residents' activities and made sure rules were obeyed. All structures including workers' homes were subject to company-only maintenance and inspection. No one, not even a group that approached him wanting to form a church, was allowed to buy property. "Just as no man or woman of our 4,000 toilers has ever felt the friendly pressure of George M. Pullman's hand," the workers reported, "so no man or woman of us all has ever owned or can ever hope to own one inch of George M. Pullman's land."[49] This controlling governance had become unwieldy, as the town increasingly was home to immigrant workers who didn't share Pullman's personal ideas about drinking beer or how they spent their leisure time. "We are born in a Pullman house, fed from the Pullman shop, taught in the Pullman school, catechized in the Pullman church, and when we die we shall be buried in the Pullman cemetery and go to the Pullman hell," one worker protested.[50]

With the firm demanding rent (and back rent) from the very workers whose pay had been cut, the cruelest aspect of the town's organization was made apparent. As work and paychecks diminished over the cold winter of 1893–1894, families suffered from want of basic necessities such as coal for heating. The desperation and lack of solutions were especially acute, as historian Ray Ginger points out, because "the town had no mechanisms for public relief," for such would have been "contrary to the owner's ideas of individual self-help."[51] The city of Chicago could be of little assistance, as it was facing its own crisis of homeless unemployed. Hordes had been drawn to the glittering Columbian Exposition by the possibility of work, and failing to obtain it had become something akin to a large refugee population, shuffling from church to relief agency in hope of a hot meal, sleeping in doorways, police stations, and saloons.

By spring 1894 some Pullman workers and their families were meeting outside the town in order to discuss their predicament, away from the ears of company spies. Compounding their concern was the report that Pullman, while slashing workers' pay, had not reduced his own or his top executives' salaries, and had maintained the high level of dividends paid to the firm's stockholders. On May 7 they sent representatives to meet with company vice president Thomas H. Wickes, who asked them to submit their grievances in writing and return for another conversation on May 9, at which George Pullman would be present. In that meeting—one of the first in years Pullman had had with his employees—Pullman explained that he had cut wages because orders were down and that he was attempting to manage the amount of work available so as to limit layoffs; he asserted that the firm had agreed to several low-bid work contracts expressly to maintain employment levels. He offered to let workers examine the company's financial records to verify this, and vowed that there would be no reprisals against the workers' representatives who had come forward with grievances.

Due to an apparent misunderstanding or extremely poor timing, however, three of the men who had conferred with Pullman and Wickes were let go the very next day in what the company cited as previously ordered staff reductions. Whatever the intent behind the firings, the word among Pullman employees was that the men had been discharged for daring to lead a potential strike committee, and that George Pullman himself had gone back on his word. Two days later Pullman employees, fed up with the sleeping car magnate's greed, obstinacy, and apparent double-dealing, set their tools down.

T HE CRISIS AT THE NATION'S LEADING sleeping car manufacturer was not the only labor-related headline of spring 1894. Only a few months earlier, an uprising had begun the likes of which had never occurred in the United States, as armies of unemployed citizens—emanating from dozens of cities, villages, mines, and lumber camps—commenced a march on Washington to demand work.

The instigator was Jacob S. Coxey, owner of a quarry in Massillon, Ohio. For several years he had lobbied Congress to enact legislation that would assist the unemployed by creating jobs to build roads and other public infrastructure. In promoting a public works program that would put an economically depressed America back to work, Coxey was anticipating elements of the New Deal, still half a century away, but this being the 1890s, such a broad-ranging plan of direct government aid was decried as wishful, if not eccentric. Another man might have filed away the last rejection letter from Congress and let the matter rest, but Coxey, convinced that the solons in faraway Washington simply required stronger convincing, announced a plan to walk in protest from Ohio to the nation's capital with one hundred thousand of his fellow citizens—"a petition in boots," he called it—in order to demonstrate both the need and the available manpower for his program of federal jobs.[52]

The march departed Massillon on March 25, 1894, with five hundred participants, far fewer than the tens of thousands Coxey had imagined, but raising enough dust to bring out crowds in every hamlet through which it passed. Coxey and his coleader, Carl Browne, had an innate sense of spectacle that worked in their favor. Browne resembled, and had garbed himself, like the star of a Wild West show. Coxey, a mild-looking fellow in a suit and glasses whom no one would mistake for a revolutionary, dressed his seventeen-year-old daughter, Mamie, in red, white, and blue and named her the "Goddess of Peace." His eighteen-year-old son, Jesse, was adorned in an outfit that combined equal amounts of Confederate gray and Union blue—a sartorial expression of the sectional reconciliation that was another of Coxey's pet aims. His two-month-old son, Legal Tender, named in honor of monetary reform, was also along for the march, and was at each stop held aloft by Coxey's wife to cheers and applause.

Press and public at first doubted whether such a ragtag bunch would really cover by foot the four hundred miles from Ohio to Washington, but as the little army approached the Potomac on April 30 curiosity turned to concern; authorities declared a full alert, for no one could be sure what angry, unemployed people who had trekked hundreds of miles would do. The result was decidedly anticlimactic; Coxey and his fellow leaders were arrested within hours of their arrival for trespassing on the lawn of the Capitol, but not before he had managed to give to reporters a statement he'd intended to read from the building's portico.

> Up these steps the lobbyists of trusts and corporations have passed unchallenged on their way to the committee rooms, access to which we, the representatives of the toiling wealth producers, have been denied. We stand here today in behalf of millions of toilers whose petitions have been buried in committee rooms, whose prayers have been un-responded to, and whose opportunities for honest, remunerative labor have been taken away from them by unjust legislation, which protects idlers, speculators and gamblers.[53]

Though technically a failure, the strange pilgrimage had succeeded in garnering at least the momentary attention of elected officials. It also inspired the launching of dozens of other "armies" of the unemployed, sometimes known as "industrials," that began walking or riding east toward the capital during the late spring and summer of 1894 from as far west as San Francisco. This sudden, mobile crusade, self-generated from countless locales, was startling in its determination. One departed from Portland, Oregon, and made it as far as Cokeville, Wyoming; a Polish American "army" stepped off from Chicago; others began in St. Louis, Boston, Omaha, Reno, Fargo, Los Angeles, and Seattle. Some Coxey loyalists in Montana hammered rafts together and floated down the Missouri River. Author Jack London joined a group out of California and traveled with it into the nation's heartland, while fellow West Coast writer Ambrose Bierce derided the "pickpocket civilization" that America had become, a society in which the affluent few exploited the labor of the many and the kind of useful public policy Coxey advocated was throttled by the strangulating grip of laissez-faire.[54]

Most alarming were the hijacked trains. In Montana, a state hard hit by a mining industry collapse that had thrown twenty thousand men out of work, as many as five hundred followers of an unemployed teamster named William Hogan seized a Northern Pacific freight train in Butte on April 24 for the journey east. Federal marshals attempted to halt the stolen train and take Hogan into custody, but Butte citizens rallied to the hijackers' defense. Similar scenes were enacted at Bozeman, Livingston, and Columbus, as local crowds that turned out in support of the Hoganites proved too great for lawmen to overcome. At Billings on the morning of April 25 guns blazed between marshals and Hogan's followers; one bystander was killed and several people wounded before the authorities withdrew and allowed the train to steam out of the depot under the hijackers' control. Hogan and his comrades, having escaped Billings, the last sizable town in Montana, assumed they had cleared the last obstacle on the way to Washington. But just west of the present-day town of Forsyth in Rosebud County they found the tracks barricaded by federal troops. U.S. attorney general Richard Olney, having learned from Montana's governor by urgent telegram of the shooting at Billings, had called out the army stationed at Fort Keogh to block the track. "General" Hogan and his men were forced from the train and arrested.[55]

"Coxeyism teaches a bad lesson," one newspaper concluded, "the most dangerous lesson indeed that can be taught to the American people—the lesson of dependence on the Federal government."[56] It was particularly disturbing that many "industrials" had originated in the West, the part of the country long identified with the creed of individual reward won through determination and hard work.

The phenomenon of legions of jobless people traipsing across the land was in itself unnerving, for America had developed a particular distaste for tramps, the term used generally to refer to the wandering unemployed. Lounging in public parks, riding the rails, appearing at the outskirts of small towns, begging for work or for food, the "tramp" was the national bogeyman of the late nineteenth century, an object of both scorn and fear. Newspapers carried cautionary tales of alleged "tramp mischief," from chicken-stealing to the snatching of pies left on windowsills.

The actual risk tramps posed was no doubt exaggerated, but the public's disdain—expressed in anti-vagrancy laws and vigilantism—could not have been more genuine. "War on the Tramps," as one headline stated.[57] No one wanted tramps passing through their community; no one wished them to stay. Some towns fought the affliction by giving food and shelter to passing jobless "armies" on the condition they move on; but many citizens would have concurred with the simpler solution offered by Chicago reformer Mary A. Livermore, "The sooner they are dead and buried the better for society."[58]

At heart, the critics of Coxey's Army, and of tramps generally, seemed bothered not so much by the real threat of lawlessness, as by the reality that there were large numbers of dispossessed people in the first place, and that, in the case of the Coxey industrials, they appeared to want something they had not earned. Their demands implied that poverty and unemployment did not stem from laziness or even bad luck, but rather from larger, systemic problems in the economy, in society—factors that were beyond any one person's control.[59] Such a claim raised vexing questions. Self-reliance, resourcefulness, individual initiative—these traits were intrinsic to the ideal of what it meant to be American. Americans always made do. If government took greater responsibility for people's well-being, would that not alter the very essence of the United States, seduce and possibly corrupt its character? Was that not the aim of those foreign theories spread in workers' enclaves in the big cities—anarchism, Communism, Socialism?

Coxey's sympathizers couldn't help note the irony that government largesse *was* acceptable to manufacturers protected by high tariffs, to railway corporations receiving massive land grants, to homesteaders, to black voters protected from the Ku Klux Klan, to governors who called in federal soldiers to quell labor unrest. Why then shouldn't workers, *the people*, enjoy the same deference and concern, and be comforted in knowing that those in authority saw the hardships they endured and would act to ameliorate them?[60]

Such questions were for the moment unanswerable; the government's response to the demands of the Coxeyites had been muted, to say the least, although federal authorities had not hesitated to call out the army to confront "General" Hogan and his railroad mutineers. The Pullman Strike, however, was about to draw Washington more fully and irrevocably into the nation's deepening labor conflict.

BUILDERS OF LUXURY PULLMAN CARS were not railroad workers, but because there was a short railroad track at the Pullman shops south of Chicago, they were deemed eligible for membership in the American Railway Union (ARU), the country's newest and most innovative labor organization. Founded in 1893, the ARU was national in scope and inclusive of all railroad workers; its unification across all crafts was meant to break the tradition of solitary railway brotherhoods that had long complicated effective worker representation, and better equip rail workers to meet the expanding power of the major railroads. Its founder and president, Eugene V. Debs, was a veteran trainman, an officer of the Brotherhood of Locomotive Firemen, and the well-regarded editor of its magazine. Intimately familiar with the virtues and shortcomings of craft orientation, he had championed the need for an industrial railroad union.

A grocer's son from Terre Haute, Indiana, Debs seems to have been destined from childhood for a life in the public arena. He was smitten as a youngster by the power of the spoken word, the fierce oratory of Patrick Henry and John Brown; while still in his teens he began organizing visiting lectures by men of national stature such as Wendell Phillips and the freethinker Robert Ingersoll. As if in coordination with his promising intellect, Debs's body sprouted like an Indiana beanstalk; he emerged into adulthood gangly and storklike, six and a half feet in height, a Lincoln-esque combination of sinew and brains, hardened by years of physical labor on the railroad. Bald at an early age, with a distinctive egg-shaped head, he was unmistakable in appearance, with a kindly face and warmth of character that made him seem more seminary graduate than railroader.

Beginning in 1880, Debs's union work as grand secretary of the firemen's brotherhood was "one perpetual organizing trip" of overnight train rides, stump speeches, meeting halls, saloons, and the shops and round-houses where railway men could be found. His devotion to the cause was unquestionable, but what began to make Debs truly memorable was his giving nature, a passion for identifying with the lost, the desperate, or underprivileged. He became known for simple Christ-like acts of generosity, such as presenting clothes from his own valise to those in need, or making impulsive gifts of money. "While there is a lower class I am in it; while there is a criminal element I am of it; while there is a soul in prison I am not free," he once declared. By the time the ARU emerged in 1893 he was one of America's most admired labor leaders, a man surely marked in the eyes of his followers for glory and greatness.[61]

Initially he had viewed the firemen's brotherhood he led as a benevolent society, looking after sick and injured workers and occasionally their widows and families. Violence and confrontation were not in his nature, and he heartily disliked the idea of strikes and the vandalism and carnage that too often accompanied them. He was a student of the railroad upheavals of 1877, and saw in that terrible uprising little practical gain. But over the years he'd become disabused of the assumption that capitalists were willing to be instructed by judicious argument and transformed by reason; he'd also learned that rank-and-file workers expected their union to be comfortable with the strike as an ultimate weapon, and to be ready for its use. It was a failed 1888 strike by a brother union, the locomotive engineers, against the Chicago, Burlington and Quincy Railroad, that first suggested to Debs the need for one large rail workers' union; his hunch was confirmed in 1892 when a strike by railroad switchmen in Buffalo fell flat because other rail brotherhoods withheld support. By fall of that year Debs was urging the nation's six hundred thousand rail workers to make better use of their collective might.

The response to the birth of the ARU was favorable, thousands seeking membership, including unskilled laborers previously excluded by the brotherhoods.[62] "There was never a time in the history of labor when it was so enlightened, so defiant, and so courageous as now," Debs wrote. "It is organizing and every lodge is a school and an army post. These schools are educating and sending forth leaders and champions of labor. They are voices in the wilderness, and they are blazing a new pathway."[63]

A second surge of interest came in spring 1894 after the ARU, in the first flexing of its strength, struck successfully against the St. Paul–based Great Northern Railroad. Workers shut down the road for two weeks, leading the St. Paul Chamber of Commerce to pressure the company and its powerful owner, James J. Hill, into arbitration. The strikers won nearly all of their demands, including a pay hike. There had been no violence, no bloodshed, only a disciplined and coordinated strike action. Even Hill wound up congratulating Debs and the other ARU leaders for their principled handling of the affair. At the strike's conclusion, Debs glanced from a window as his train departed St. Paul to return him to Indiana and saw hundreds of track workers doffing their hats in his honor; it was a "tribute," he would later recall, "more precious to me than all the banquets in the world."[64]

The ARU victory over the Great Northern had a galvanizing effect on the labor movement much as had the Knights of Labor in 1885, when the momentarily brilliant Terence Powderly stayed the mercenary hand of rail baron Jay Gould. "The unskilled workers had been unprotected, underpaid, exploited," wrote biographer Ray Ginger of Debs and the ARU's accomplishment. "Now the dikes snapped and a reservoir of bitterness and hope drove men pell-mell into the ARU.... The [union's] officials did not have to coax or persuade; their main job was to sign cards and issue charters."[65] An ebullient Debs posed the question of the hour: " 'What can we do for labor?' It is the old, old query repeated all along the centuries, heard wherever a master wielded a whip above the bowed forms of the slaves . . . but [now] our ears are regaled by a more manly query . . . '*What can labor do for itself?*' "[66] Encompassing all white rail workers, skilled and unskilled, with an active membership of 125,000, the ARU was soon larger than the four existing rail brotherhoods combined.

On June 12, 1894, exactly a year after its founding, the ARU opened a two-week convention at Chicago's Uhlich's Hall. Pullman workers, having joined the ARU in March, appeared before the gathering of four hundred delegates on June 15 to urgently request the union's help. As of May 11, all but 10 percent of Pullman's thirty-eight hundred workers had walked out. "We joined the American Railway Union because it gave us a glimmer of hope," their spokesman told the conclave. "Twenty thousand souls, men, women, and little ones, have their eyes turned toward this convention today."[67] One disgruntled Pullman worker, a father of four, rose before the gathering. "I think that when a man is sober and steady, and has a saving wife, and after working two and a half years for a company he finds himself in debt for a common living," he said, "something must be wrong."[68] Most affecting were the words of seamstress Jennie Curtis, the youthful head of a women's local at the Pullman works, who told the convention that after her father, a thirteen-year Pullman employee, had passed away, she had been made to pay the $60 in back rent he had owed the company at his death. Her story elicited oaths from the ARU men as to how "the bloodsucker" George Pullman had mistreated and robbed "a girl."[69] It was another blatant example, all too familiar to workers of the 1890s, of what

Samuel Gompers had termed "the barbarity of capitalism."[70] Debs left the convention to tour the Pullman village and came away distressed by what he saw—a model town meant to reveal the future, sadly revealing all too much about the present. "The paternalism of Pullman is the same as the self-interest of a slaveholder in his human chattels," he assured the strikers. "You are striking to avert slavery and degradation."[71]

On behalf of the workers, the ARU appealed to Pullman to submit its issues with the employees to arbitration. When the company refused, Debs faced a dilemma: he detested Pullman's arrogance, but was unsure how deeply to involve the ARU and hesitated to make strike threats in its name. Despite the Great Northern victory his organization was still new and unproven, and had little money on hand. Yet the more George Pullman remained unwilling to compromise the more he became the object of intense worker resentment, an evil assailing the life of young Jennie Curtis and thousands like her. The nation's railroad men were spoiling for a fight with the "management" of America; unlike 1877, now they were not only angry but organized, and in Eugene Debs they saw their crusader.

On June 21 the convention voted that its members who were switchmen would not handle Pullman cars after June 26 unless the company agreed to arbitration. Pullman again refused, and with the switchmen's work stoppage the great Pullman Strike began. The sides quickly formed, the big railroads aligning with Pullman and, as a deliberate provocation to labor, declining to remove his sleeper cars from their trains. The once-splintered rail brotherhoods gathered for the fight, while friendly unions of carpenters, mechanics, and warehousemen signaled their intended support. "The sons of toil must stand together, shoulder to shoulder," urged Knights leader James Sovereign, and for once reality appeared ready to match labor's hopeful rhetoric.[72]

THE ARU BOYCOTT OF Pullman's railcars and, by extension, America's railroads, was, in the eyes of commerce, a far more reprehensible act than a run-of-the-mill trade union strike. Because it engaged diverse groups of train workers across occupational boundaries, as well as sympathetic backing from other unions, it had more the feel of a full-fledged rebellion. The potential harm to business and the economy as a whole, which was now reliant on rail transport even more than it had been at the time of the 1877 troubles, was almost beyond measure, "a particularly flagrant intrusion by society into the hallowed preserve of the market."[73] And while 1877 had been frightening for its violence and destruction, that insurrection had been spontaneous; the threat that now loomed appeared darker for its being coordinated by centralized leadership.

The switchmen's refusal to handle trains with Pullman cars multiplied swiftly over the next few days, as rail workers in twenty-seven states and U.S. territories joined the action. One hundred thousand men had voluntarily stopped work nationwide. Soon both freight and passenger train traffic in and out of Chicago was at a standstill, and had slowed to a crawl as far west as San Francisco. News bulletins from Chicago reported that

> the Illinois Central, Wisconsin Central, Chicago Great Western, Baltimore & Ohio, Chicago and Northern Pacific, and the lines interested in the Western Indiana System are tied up completely. Seventy-five cars of perishable freight tonight lie side-tracked. One hundred carloads of bananas are between New Orleans and Chicago, and it is not thought they can be delivered.[74]

"The railroads were paralyzed," reported Eugene Debs. "The people demanded of the railroads that they operate their trains. They could not do it. Not a man would serve them."[75] The complications quickly spread to the major cities of the East, with the *New York Times* relating on July 4 that

> the big ice companies have been making almost superhuman efforts today to avoid suspending operations, but they gave up tonight, and thousands of sick and suffering in hospitals, public institutions, and private homes, will be added to the already

gigantic roster of innocent victims of the strike. Just outside the city there are miles of loaded cars with their contents rotting in the sun.[76]

Editorial pages lost no time in naming the villain responsible for the tie-up. "King Debs" he was dubbed—the would-be "dictator" who sought to grind the nation to a halt, deny families their meat and coal, children their milk, all in the name of making false promises to several hundred disgruntled Pullman workers. He was "a lawbreaker," certainly, averred one paper, but also "an enemy of the human race." To the *Chicago Herald* he was a "reckless, ranting, contumacious, impudent braggadocio." A much-reprinted cartoon pictured Debs as a misbehaved man-child, wearing a cheap crown, straddling the Chicago rail yards.[77] The *Times* was so agitated it abandoned its usual journalistic standards, and stunned readers, with a 210-word lead sentence:

> Eugene V. Debs, who within one week has sprung from obscurity to a position of the most absolute and potential power over all classes, millionaires, merchants, and mechanics, who by a mere nod controls and closes the business of great railway systems as if these were but his toys, who commands a fairly well disciplined and blindly obedient army of about 1,000,000 desperate and determined men, who now controls all the traffic of fourteen states, and coolly notifies the railway officials of all other states that he will attend to their cases unless they are very careful how they behave themselves, who has halted and sidetracked upward of 200 railway trains at various points of a territory far greater than all of Europe, who has crippled the commerce and manufactures of twenty great cities, who has halted the United States mail in hundreds of places and defied the federal government even to molest him, who spends $400 a day in telegraphic orders to his subordinates, who commands all of his great army of followers to cease all labor and to give up all their

daily wages, who is costing the great railways and cities a loss in trade and traffic of fully $10,000,000 each day, is yet a young man.[78]

The paper went on to scrutinize Debs's personal life, publishing an account by a physician who claimed to have treated the ARU president for alcoholism.[79] "Those who knew Debs well while he was in this city," the *Times* reported, "believe that his personal conduct is in large measure, if not wholly, due to the disordered condition of his mind and body, brought about by the liquor habit. . . . Indeed, serious doubts are expressed by them as to his responsibility as a rational individual."[80] The confidence that intemperance was at fault formed the basis for a sermon titled "The Strike and Its Terrors," which was delivered from one prominent New York pulpit, lamenting the passing of labor's reins from the moderate Terence V. Powderly to the "saloon-trained men of the Debs pattern."[81]

The assault on Debs's character was one thing; more harmful was the press's willingness to exaggerate the strike's impact. "Mob Is in Control, Law Is Trampled On, Strike Is Now War," blared the headlines of the *Chicago Tribune*, while a *Washington Post* article, "Chicago Is at the Mercy of the Incendiary's Torch," fed a rumor that the entire city of Chicago, not just its rail yards, was under siege.[82] "Meat Famine Near at Hand," the *Times* threw in for good measure, ratcheting up public fear.[83]

While press and pulpit thrashed Debs and his union, the railroads were also taking concerted action against the embargo. Much as the ARU represented an unprecedented coalition of rail workers, the rail corporations had their own consortium—the General Managers Association (GMA), founded in 1886—which consisted of all twenty-six railroads that served Chicago. The GMA had in recent days transformed itself into an antistrike task force. Deciding that the ARU had entered the Pullman standoff somewhat recklessly and that it was not truly capable of administering a sustained national labor stoppage, the GMA resolved to crush the adolescent organization; to do this, it quickly settled on a strategy to bring the federal government into the fray.

Washington, it was clear, shared the country's outrage at the crisis Debs and the ARU had made. As William Howard Taft, judge of the U.S. Court of Appeals for the 6th Circuit, denounced "the gigantic character of the conspiracy of the American Railway Union" for "the starvation of a nation,"[84] Attorney General Richard Olney moved to take back control of the railroads. He had spent the spring of 1894 dealing with the outlandish "borrowing" of trains by the misfit soldiers of Coxey's Army, and had played a decisive role in stopping the freight train–stealing Hoganites in Montana. Olney was determined that such abuse of the nation's railroads would not be again tolerated and that "the ragged edge of anarchy" would be trimmed promptly and completely.[85] He believed it essential that the government make its stand in Chicago, "the origin and center of the demonstration," in order to "make it a failure everywhere else, and to prevent its spread over the entire country." Himself a veteran railroad lawyer, he quickly appointed a former colleague, Chicago attorney Edwin Walker, to the position of special federal attorney in Chicago. Walker, after receiving instructions from Olney, sought a court injunction against the ARU based on the Sherman Antitrust Act of 1890, as well as the law against interfering with the U.S. mail.

The defense of the mail's sanctity was based on the fact that it was handled by a federal agency using federal equipment and employees, as well as the assumption that the contents of any given mailbag likely contained missives involving government business; any interference with it potentially threatened the ability of the government to function. President Grover Cleveland bought wholly into this construction, vowing, "If it takes every dollar in the Treasury and every soldier in the United States Army to deliver a postal card in Chicago, that postal card shall be delivered."[86] Debs and the ARU saw this for the trap that it was—turning the mail into a sacred cow whose defense could justify strong reactive measures—and expressly informed its members everywhere not to impede the movement of mail cars.

As for injunctions under the Sherman Act, the government's intended use of the antitrust law, which had been designed to curb the excesses of corporations, not labor unions, offered a convenient end run around ordinary rights of due process. It gave the government a convenient lever with which it might hold individuals in contempt, and perhaps put them in jail, without having to meet the higher bar of indicting them for specific criminal acts. The violated court injunctions could also serve as an argument for federal military involvement. The success of the army in halting "General" Hogan's hijacked train of unemployed miners in Montana that spring, when all attempts by local lawmen had failed, had helped convince Olney of the efficacy of deploying federal soldiers. Such extreme measures were justified, the attorney general and the GMA contended, because the ARU boycott was not simply a labor action against a specific employer, but an assault on the nation's business, "an exercise of tyrannical power by a labor union," as the *Times* wrote, "such as would not be tolerated on the part of public authority in any civilized country."[87]

Debs naturally saw the crisis through a different lens. To him the unprecedented extent of the boycott was an impressive act of solidarity and goodwill by labor's rank and file; he had only praise for the ARU members and trainmen across far-flung regions and state boundaries who had thrown their lot in with the Pullman workers. Rejecting the charge that he had assumed dictatorial powers over the nation's railroads, he warned President Cleveland by telegram that "a deep-seated conviction is fast becoming prevalent that this Government is soon to be declared a military despotism."[88] Cleveland heard similar protests from Illinois governor John Peter Altgeld. Citing Article IV of the Constitution, which permits federal troops to enter a state only if a condition of insurrection exists and the state's executive specifically requests such aid, Altgeld explained that reports of strike-related violence had been greatly overstated and warned against sending soldiers. As for the city of Chicago being under siege, Altgeld reassured the president that news reports to that effect were barefaced lies. Chicago mayor John P. Hopkins, it so happened, had given $1,500 to a fund to benefit the families of Pullman workers, and had been seen conducting the city's business with a white strike ribbon in his lapel.[89]

Altgeld echoed Debs in warning that real violence would begin if and when soldiers were introduced, reminding Cleveland that "local self-government is a fundamental principle of our Constitution. Each community shall govern itself so long as it can and is ready and able to enforce the law."[90] He also took the opportunity to upbraid the president on his attorney general's misuse of court injunctions under the Sherman Act. "This decision marks a turning point in our history," the governor stated, "for it establishes a new form of government never before heard of among men; that is government by injunction. . . . Under this new order of things a federal judge becomes at once a legislator, court and executioner."[91] Cleveland was said to be furious—fed up with the Pullman workers, who, on what seemed to him little foundation, had joined with the ARU, but also with the resistance of a troublesome Illinois reform governor whose thinking appeared to be in step with "Dictator Debs."

JOHN PETER ALTGELD'S NAME is synonymous with the dawn of the Progressive era. Like his hero Abraham Lincoln, he saw resilience and character in the American people, believed some of their better qualities too often went untapped, and wished for all a greater say and a role in the life of their country. Because a society based on the idea of "the survival of the fittest" was, in Altgeld's view, inherently unjust, the so-called lower classes must be lifted up and educated in the values of cleanliness, good health, and temperance, as well as the virtues of citizenship. Labor unions had a vital role in this transformation, he believed, providing a counterforce to big business and giving workers a foothold on democracy, a means to organize, to seek redress and a fair wage.

Immersion in the problems of the Pullman Strike came naturally for the governor, for after arriving in the Midwest from Germany as a young man, he, too, had swung a hammer on a track crew before going on to work as a teacher and lawyer. He had been on hand for the building boom that followed the Chicago Fire of 1871, diverting part of his income into the purchase of real estate. In 1884 he came out as a public man, winning a seat in Congress and publishing a small but incisive tract on penal reform, *Our Penal Machinery and Its Victims*. Altgeld's essay argued that rather than reform youthful first offenders, incarceration was turning them into hardened criminals. He suggested that the well behaved be permitted to work outside of the prison each day, railed against the system of paying fees to police based on the number of arrests they made, and decried as unjust the practice of holding indigent prisoners for long periods before trial because they lacked the means to make bail.

Through his efforts on behalf of prison reform, Altgeld met and befriended Clarence Darrow, a young criminal attorney from Ohio whose family had roots in the abolition movement. With Altgeld's help, Darrow became corporation counsel for the city of Chicago. Among the advice that Darrow gave his friend when Altgeld won the Illinois governorship in 1892 was the recommendation that Altgeld alleviate the shame still hanging over the state from the Haymarket case and free the men still in custody—Oscar Neebe, Samuel Fielden, and Michael Schwab. August Spies, in his last words upon the gallows, had declared, "The time will come when our silence will be more powerful than the voices you strangle today." Darrow and Altgeld were among those who still "heard" that silence, and were troubled by it.

Since the trapdoors had opened beneath the condemned Haymarket martyrs on November 11, 1887, it had become widely recognized that the convictions had been unfair and the executions a gross mistake. With an Amnesty Association active on behalf of the prisoners, countless briefs and petitions had been submitted to Springfield, and such influential men as former U.S. senator Lyman Trumbull and banker E. S. Dreyer, who had been foreman of the grand jury that had originally indicted the Haymarket defendants, had demanded a pardon on the grounds that the three men still imprisoned were either innocent or had by now been sufficiently punished. Darrow reminded Altgeld that, unlike most people who resented this awful blemish on American justice, he had the power to actually do something about it. Both men understood, of course, the tremendous potential cost to the governor of any act of commutation or pardon. "If I do it I will be a dead man politically," Altgeld acknowledged. Yet, he vowed, "By God, if I decide that these men are innocent I will pardon them if I never hold office for another day."[92]

Altgeld proceeded carefully. Although already familiar with the case, he took a hard second look, researching it closely and writing his own detailed legal analysis; he reviewed the method of jury selection, Judge Gary's rulings against defense motions, and the possibility that incriminating evidence had been obtained through bribery and threats. He also questioned the trial's essential premise that men could be convicted of murder for their words, when no physical connection had been made between them and the crime. One insight Altgeld offered was that even if sentiments published by Parsons, Spies, and the others were inflammatory, there was no evidence that the bomb thrower, whoever that person was, had read those words or acted upon them. Finally, Altgeld excoriated Judge Gary for conducting the trial "with malicious ferocity," for his numerous prejudicial remarks against the defendants, and for his general disregard for fairness and the law. The governor's not unexpected conclusion was that those executed and those remaining behind bars had been convicted solely for their political beliefs, and that the means used to convict them represented "a greater menace to the republic" than anything the accused may have actually done.[93]

Full pardons were granted by Altgeld on June 26, 1893. The timing of their issuance was symbolic, for only the day before, eight thousand people had gathered in Chicago's Waldheim Cemetery for the unveiling and dedication of a heroic "martyrs" monument at the executed men's graves.[94] At Joliet State Prison, Neebe, Fielden, and Schwab, who had had no advance warning of Altgeld's possible ruling, were suddenly notified of their good fortune and summoned to the office of Warden R. L. Allen. There they were given new clothes along with envelopes containing a railroad ticket and "a snug bundle of crisp bills." After a brief sit-down supper with the warden, who distributed cigars and offered to vouch for their characters if they should ever require job references, the three men, still in a state of stunned disbelief, were chauffeured to the depot to catch the evening train for Chicago.[95]

Altgeld's act, as expected, stirred a fierce reaction. By issuing the pardons and offering explicit official acknowledgment of the fraudulency of the Haymarket convictions, the governor had "insulted" the memory of the policemen killed in the bombing, undermined the leverage the courts had grown accustomed to using against labor unions, and punctured, at least for a moment, the public's reflexive attitude toward anarchists and other radicals.[96] "In every street car, in every place of public meeting, and on sidewalks as people hurried homeward," it was reported, "could be heard expressions of intense disgust with the governor."[97] Newspapers questioned Altgeld's patriotism, reminding readers the governor was not American-born; he was an alien much like the men he'd set free. But Altgeld, knowing he had acted in good conscience, managed to remain stoic in the face of such criticism. "Let them pitch in and give me the devil if they want to," Altgeld confided to a friend. "They could not cut through my hide in three weeks with an axe."[98]

Altgeld's reputation clearly suffered, however, complicating his stance with the ARU against federal intervention the following summer in the Pullman Strike. "Having pardoned Anarchists who murdered the police of that city," observed a Philadelphia paper, "it is only reasonable to assume that he is wholly in sympathy with the mob that now rules Chicago and shames his great state."[99] Some writers went so far as to link both Altgeld and Debs with Alexander Berkman, the would-be assassin of Frick, who was still in prison in Pennsylvania.[100] Thankfully, the *Baltimore Sun* assured readers, even if the governor of Illinois was a fool and the plaything of radicals, the country could still rely on President Grover Cleveland, "the big, strong man and sturdy patriot whom the people have placed in the White House."[101]

T HE GOVERNMENT'S LEGALISTIC TRAP designed by President Cleveland's attorney general, Richard Olney, was set to close on the ARU. The railroads of the GMA had begun placing both Pullman sleepers and mail cars strategically in regular trains in order to provoke a violation. The union did make a good-faith effort to allow the U.S. mail through, as the ARU sent hundreds of telegrams to far-flung locals with instructions not to disrupt the mail; at one point it proposed to the railroads that crews might be assembled for special "all mail" trains, an idea that would have sounded reasonable to the railroads if their actual concern was the transmittal of the mail. Instead the railroads ignored the offer and, inevitably, mail cars *were* delayed in the strike.

On July 2 federal district court judge Peter J. Grosscup issued an injunction banning the ARU from interfering with the mails or other rail movement in interstate commerce, or from attempting to convince rail workers to stop work. The invoking of the interstate commerce law was a perversion of its original intent, which had been to protect small businesses and farmers from price manipulations by the railroads, and the injunction was so broadly written as to disallow Debs and his colleagues from having anything to do with the maintenance of the boycott. Under threat of arrest and incarceration, they were not to send telegrams or respond to questions about the labor action, or to encourage others who were involved in the boycott. "A Gatling gun on paper," one newspaper termed the edict from Grosscup's pen.[102]

On July 3, "a mob of from two to three thousand" surrounded U.S. marshal J. W. Arnold in the Chicago rail yards as he read the injunction aloud; at one point he was interrupted by a voice that shouted, "To hell with the United States court!"[103] Afterward Arnold wired Olney:

> The reading of the writ met with no response except jeers and hoots. Shortly after, the mob threw a number of baggage-cars across the track, since when no mail train has been able to move. I am unable to disperse the mob, clear the tracks, or arrest the men who were engaged in the acts named, and believe that no force less than the regular troops of the United States can procure the passage of the mail trains or enforce the orders of the courts.[104]

Soldiers arrived later that day from nearby Fort Sheridan, the outpost created in the aftermath of Haymarket to have federal troops available "not so much to quell a riot as to crush labor unions," in the view of Detroit mayor Hazen S. Pingree, who had hurried to Chicago bearing telegrams from the mayors of more than fifty U.S. cities urging an arbitrated settlement to the Pullman Strike.[105] The army troops—eight companies of infantry, one troop of cavalry, and an artillery battalion, constituting a federal force of about two thousand—spread out along the railroad tracks leading into Chicago and encamped by the lakefront near the business district.

The next day, July 4, as both Debs and Altgeld had warned, the federal troops' presence sparked violence. "All the bitterness, the hoodlumism, the despair, stored up at the bottom of Chicago's soul . . . boiled over into the railroad yards," notes a popular history of the city. "Here and there engines were crippled, capsized on tracks; whole trains of standing freight cars were overturned, tower-men were dragged from switch-towers."[106] As in 1877, the main antagonists were not so much Pullman strikers or even rail workers, but large crowds of belligerent citizens—the poor, the unemployed, families of railroad men, other sympathizers—provoked by the appearance of federal uniforms and "inflamed by passion and frequent draughts from the neighboring saloons." They catcalled and cursed at the soldiers, and hurled brickbats, stones, and rail spikes. So determined and numerous were they, the rioters even managed to uncouple the cars of an army troop train.[107]

Hopelessly worsening the situation was the introduction of two thousand "special deputies" hired by the federal marshals. As was often the case with men enlisted as last-minute enforcers in strike disputes, the deputies were for the most part untrained toughs, who despite their muscular physiques tended to be the first to panic when confronted with large groups of protestors. Police chief John Brennan described them as "thugs, thieves, and ex-convicts" willing to trade their brawn for some quick cash, and criticized "their careless use of pistols."[108] In the chaos at the rail yards they were also not above helping themselves to the contents of some of the stalled freight cars.[109]

The following day a mob estimated at ten thousand men and women advanced from the packinghouse district to the rail yards, destroying property and setting railroad cars afire. After roughing up a railroad official and pushing freight cars off the tracks, one group of protestors entered the World's Fair site and attempted to vandalize buildings. More volatile crises arose on July 6, when a trigger-happy Illinois Central manager shot two rioters, inspiring numerous acts of revenge, including arson. Seven hundred freight cars were put to the torch, as well as bridges and railroad buildings. Telegraph lines were cut. On the outskirts of Chicago, crowds gathered on the tracks to temporarily halt passenger trains from entering the city. By sunset thirteen people had been killed and fifty-three injured. Similar scenes were reported at rail yards across the country.

Chicago's organized labor movement did not sit idly by as these developments occurred; talk of a general strike in support of the rail workers had been bandied about for days, and intensified once the president committed the troops from Fort Sheridan. In an urgent call, two dozen national labor leaders including Samuel Gompers were summoned to an emergency conference at Chicago's Briggs House hotel to help steer labor's course. Representatives of the nation's labor press, the so-called knights of the notebook, gathered downstairs in the lobby, ready to transmit the conclave's decision. Many of the Chicago unions continued to back the idea of a general strike, as did Eugene Debs; AFL locals from across the country advised Gompers that they stood ready to join any such action at his word. Had the order for it emanated from the conference, there's little doubt a general strike on a national scale would have been attempted.

While Gompers had joined Debs and Governor Altgeld in cautioning President Cleveland about the government's improper use of the courts and the military, he had been convinced by the reversals at Homestead and in the Coeur d'Alene two years earlier that labor could not launch successful actions against the combined might of industry and government. Particularly now that federal injunctions had been issued and troops put in place in the Pullman Strike, Gompers believed the cause was lost. The conferees passed a resolution that damned George Pullman as "a public enemy," praised the ARU boycott as a "vigorous protest against the gathering, growing forces of plutocratic power and corporation rule," and applauded the nation's trainmen for exposing "the hollow shams of Pullman's pharisaical paradise," but noted with regret that

> the present conflict has become surrounded and beset with complications so grave in their nature that we cannot consistently advise a course which would but add to the general confusion. . . . The public press, ever alive to the interests of corporate wealth, have . . . so maliciously misrepresented matters that in the public mind the working classes are now arrayed in open hostility to federal authority. This is a position we do not wish to be placed in.

The document concluded: "We declare it to be the sense of this conference that a general strike at this time is inexpedient, unwise, and contrary to the best interests of the working people."[110]

Gompers's role at the gathering would become as controversial as the resolution produced there. Surely a nationwide general strike would have been a momentous "act of war" on the part of labor against both the government and private capital, and it's not clear what strategies its advocates were considering that would have avoided further mass arrests of protestors or greater physical upheaval. Gompers's opposition to the general strike, nonetheless, became to some critics part of a larger pattern of compromise, even betrayal, unforgivable to many in the left wing of the movement. It was known that Gompers had questioned the ARU's wisdom in rushing into so major an undertaking as a national rail boycott so soon after its own founding, and rumored that as he had boarded a train to attend the Briggs House meeting he had told an aide, "I am going to the funeral of the ARU."[111]

The labor movement had stepped back from the precipice, but the federal government had no such hesitation. On July 10 it arrested Debs and three of his top aides on a charge of interfering with the U.S. mail and obstructing interstate commerce. Released on bail, they were rearrested a week later on the more serious charge of contempt of court for disregarding the sweeping injunction against the ARU sympathy strike Judge Grosscup had issued under the Sherman Act. In protest Debs and his lieutenants refused to offer bail and were detained indefinitely behind bars. "If I happen to go to jail don't worry," Debs had written to his parents back in Terre Haute. "I would rather a thousand times be a *man* in prison than a free poltroon. Thousands of the world's best and noblest have occupied prison cells. After all, I shall go into history right."[112]

THE USE OF THE SHERMAN ACT OF 1890 to restrict the actions of organized labor in the Pullman Strike was a hugely contentious issue, since to many people's understanding the law's avowed purpose was to curb trusts and monopolies. The legislation's namesake, Ohio senator John Sherman, had in fact once offered the Pullman Palace Car Company, with its vast market influence, as an example of why such a law was necessary. Samuel Gompers later recalled having had numerous meetings with members of Congress while the act was being discussed, and that the restriction of illegal trusts was its object, not labor unions. But in 1892, Senator George F. Edmunds, who was credited with having provided the act's wording, insisted it was meant to

> cover every form of combination that seeks to in any way interfere or restrain free competition, whether it be capital in the form of trusts, combinations, railroad pools or agreements, or labor through the form of boycotting organizations that say a man shall not earn his bread unless he joins this or that society. Both are wrong. Both are crimes, and indictable under the antitrust law.[113]

Its initial use against labor appears to have come at New Orleans in March 1893, in a case resulting from that city's biracial general strike the previous fall. The defendants in *U.S. v. Workingmen's Amalgamated Council* asserted that the Sherman Act involved only capital trusts, but a federal court established a precedent disastrous to organized labor by concluding that while the statute "had its origin in the evil of massed capital . . . [the] subject had so broadened in the minds of the legislators" by the time the law was passed, its restrictions were understood to include excesses of labor.[114] An opposing definition of the law, however, was rendered that same year in a Massachusetts case, *United States v. Patterson*, involving the marketing of cash registers, where the court ruled that the "restraint of trade" clause in the Sherman Act referred to monopolies, and warned against its "careless or inapt construction" to include labor strikes or boycotts. But it was the New Orleans ruling that served as the commonly used precedent.[115]

In December 1894 hearings related to the Pullman Strike, an Illinois federal judge ruled that while Congress had discussed but not acted on a provision to exempt farmers and laborers from the antitrust law, the only logical interpretation was that Congress did not countenance any such exemption. This argument was a reference to the so-called Sherman Amendment, a proposed addition to the bill crafted by the legislation's namesake that pointedly exempted labor unions; the amendment was left off the final draft of the bill, suggesting to some that Congress *did* mean for the legislation to reach labor unions. But others insisted it had been left off because the final draft of the bill was so written as to make any such amendment superfluous.[116]

The confusion about the proper application of Sherman stemmed in part from the fact that the law had been conceived initially more as a sop to public concern than as an actual weapon to be deployed. "Trust-busting" was a nice-sounding term, but capital had sufficient control over the press, the legislatures, and the courts to keep it from becoming the fearsome instrument of anticorporate reform its advocates envisioned. Several prominent legal cases of the period demonstrate why. One was the U.S. Supreme Court's ruling in *United States v. E. C. Knight Co.*, known as the "Sugar Trust" case. In 1892 the American Sugar Refining Company had taken over E. C. Knight and other sugar refining firms, giving it a near monopoly over the nation's production of sugar. The Cleveland administration asked for a government suit against Knight under the Sherman

Act. In a questionable opinion issued in January 1895, the Supreme Court ruled that Sherman had been intended to address the activities of corporations only as they pertained to interstate commerce, and that issues relating strictly to the behavior of large manufacturers were more properly the responsibility of the states. Coming at a time when Sherman was being misused against labor unions, the court's willingness to nitpick the act's language in this manner to protect big business was especially maddening.[117] It was, quipped one observer, a decision "based upon Webster's Dictionary rather than upon economic reality."[118]

Another revealing history was that of Standard Oil, which dominated the U.S. oil trade through its methods of buying up smaller companies, fixing rail rates, monopolizing oil pipelines, and corporate spying. In 1890 the Ohio Supreme Court ordered the Standard Oil Trust dissolved. Instead it "retained its character," notes historian Patrick Renshaw, "and in 1899 reincorporated under the laws of New Jersey as a holding company. In 1907 it was fined almost $30 million (which was reversed on appeal) and in 1911, in *Standard Oil Co. of New Jersey v. United States*, the U.S. Supreme Court ordered its dissolution." But in doing so the high court set new limits on the Sherman Act, saying its restrictions must be interpreted with an eye for only those violations that constituted "undue restraints" against commerce, thus softening the act's initial thrust and creating an invisible bar of what might be termed a "reasonable" monopoly or an "unreasonable" restraint of trade.[119] This left only a marginal possibility that misbehaved trusts would actually be brought to heel.

In a separate opinion in *Standard Oil Co. of New Jersey*, Justice John Marshall Harlan alleged that the new, flexible criteria amounted to "judicial legislation," that is, the court's succumbing to pressures from the business community to reverse laws that duly elected legislators had put in place. "By mere interpretation," Harlan wrote, the Court had "modified the act of Congress, and deprived it of practical value as a defensive measure against the evils to be remedied." He went on to warn against "aggregations of capital in the hands of a few individuals and corporations controlling, for their own profit and advantage exclusively, the entire business of the country, including the production and sale of the necessities of life."[120]

To say the use of antitrust injunctions against labor unions remained controversial would be an understatement; it became a major preoccupation, figuring in hundreds of labor cases in the coming years. In the Pullman affair there was never a doubt that the government had wielded it to devastating effect, validating the fear Gompers had expressed at Briggs House that labor risked being overwhelmed by the mix of judicial and executive powers the railroad interests had arrayed against the ARU. The injunctions that allowed the government to arrest Debs and other strike leaders and hold them behind bars, depriving the insurrection of its guidance, and the introduction of soldiers to disrupt the roving crowds and in some cases help man trains, had had the effect of breaking both the Pullman Strike and the ARU boycott. Two hundred rank-and-file strikers had also been arrested under the injunctions, joining several hundred ordinary citizens rounded up for rioting in the rail yards. "I have broken the backbone of this strike," reporters quoted General Nelson Miles of the U.S. Army.[121] As the mobs dispersed, train lines gradually reopened, troops safeguarding locomotives and riding shotgun on trains exiting big-city yards.

George Pullman had stayed largely out of public sight for most of the strike, only emerging once the Debs forces had been routed. "The public should not permit the real question which has been before it to be obscured," he advised. "That question was as to the possibility of the creation and duration of a dictatorship which could make all the industries of the United States and the daily comfort of millions dependent upon them, hostages for the granting of the fantastic whim of such a dictator."[122]

P ULLMAN WAS CORRECT IN implying that the strike that bore his name had been a defining moment for American labor. The movement learned decisively that it had no friends in Washington, and that the federal government would not hesitate to send soldiers to confront workers pressing legitimate grievances. Most disturbing was the government's use of an antitrust law to halt union organizing and even gag communication from a union's leaders to its members, a throwback to the supposedly discarded notion that routine labor union activity represented a "combination" or "conspiracy" dangerous to society. Not unexpectedly, the business community and the conservative press widely praised President Cleveland's firmness in putting down "Debs' Rebellion" and setting organized labor in its place.

Far from convincing workers of the error of their ways, the means the authorities had used had the effect of radicalizing many unionists. As Debs acknowledged:

> We have no power of the government behind us . . . no
> recognized influence in society on our side. . . . On the other
> side the corporations are in perfect alliance; they have all of the
> things that money can command, and that means a subsidized
> press . . . the clergy almost steadily united in thundering their
> enunciations, then the courts, then the state militia, then the
> federal troops.[123]

Among moderate laborites like Gompers, of course, the Pullman experience reinforced cautious attitudes about the efficacy of boycotts and strikes; the ARU's fate was proof that, given the opposition's strength, a more judicious advocacy might be preferable for securing functioning agreements with capital.

If it was any solace to the whipped ARU, Pullman and his company did not emerge unscathed. The events of summer 1894 brought criticism of the very notion of company towns, most prominently Pullman's. One Chicago cleric, the Reverend William H. Carwardine, denounced the model community as so thoroughly undemocratic as to be un-American, as well as an affront to God, since Pullman himself, not God, ruled the community and the lives of its inhabitants. Within a decade the town, many of its once-impressive amenities grown shabby with neglect, was declared by the Illinois State Supreme Court to exist in opposition "to good public policy and incompatible with the theory and spirit of our institutions." The court cited the Pullman Company's ownership of it as being in violation of the community's own articles of incorporation, and the state ordered the firm to relinquish all parts of it not essential to manufacturing. Pullman, Illinois, per se ceased to exist, some of its structures were altered or disassembled, and what remained was incorporated within the city of Chicago.[124] Although company towns would not cease to spring up, as they often did in mining regions, the term increasingly took on a pejorative meaning, and the Pullman experience had the effect of dissuading the wiser planners of such communities from assuming absolute control over their residents. Many corporations in the Progressive Era and beyond, guided by the unhappy fate of Pullman, turned the responsibility for company housing of workers and other employer-employee relations over to an emerging class of sociologists and industrial relations experts who could serve as "buffers between capital and labor."[125]

While the press continued to belittle Debs, and wipe its collective brow that a "dictator" of labor had been stymied in his harmful ambition, a more considered appraisal of the Pullman Strike came, ironically, from a commission of inquiry set to work by President Cleveland. George Pullman, Eugene Debs, and numerous others testified before the panel. The commission's report bemoaned the fact that both capital and labor had become so concentrated that they were capable, in times of strife, of wreaking great havoc with the entire economy; it noted that the strike had caused the deaths of thirty people, engaged fourteen thousand soldiers and police, and had cost railroads $4 million in revenues and workingmen $1.6 million in lost wages. While challenging the wisdom of the ARU's decision to allow Pullman factory employees into a railroad union, the report saved some its strongest criticism for George Pullman for assuming the dual role of employer and landlord and for his refusal to submit disputed issues to arbitration; most surprising, it scolded the rail barons and their GMA for scheming to destroy the ARU as an illegitimate labor combination when it was itself a combination, albeit one of business. It also held the government responsible "for not adequately controlling monopolies and corporations, and for failing to reasonably protect the rights of labor and redress its wrongs." As Debs testified, employers would reduce workers to a state of near slavery if no one ever stood up to them. "If it were not for resistance to degrading conditions," he offered, "the tendency of our whole civilization would be downward."[126]

In its challenge to management's reflexive hostility toward organized labor, the commission pointed out that "capital abroad prefers to deal with these [labor] unions rather than with individuals or mobs, and from their joint efforts in good faith at conciliation and arbitration much good and many peaceful days have resulted." It pondered whether in America it would not also be "wise to recognize them by law, to admit their necessity as labor guild protectors, to conserve their usefulness, increase their responsibility and to prevent their follies and aggressions by conferring upon them the privileges enjoyed by corporations, with like proper restrictions and regulations."[127]

Such rumination pointed toward a question that would become central in the post-Pullman decades: What was the proper role of government in labor disputes? In the eyes of the ARU, governmental interference of the wrong kind had been the grievous error of the Pullman Strike. Debs was convinced that had his union been left alone to deal with management, it could have wrought concessions peacefully and in a way far less disruptive to commerce and public convenience. Reformers would soon argue that government's obligation in industrial relations should not be to rush to aid private enterprise, but would best be directed toward passing legislation and creating enforcement agencies to safeguard employee rights, improve conditions, and ameliorate labor abuses. If a third party was to be involved in resolving labor strife, it should take the forms of neutral government boards of mediation or similar entities made up of nongovernmental actors. One of the Cleveland commission's recommendations was that a permanent three-person U.S. strike commission be created to intervene in and mediate future railroad strikes.[128]

Pullman was a deeply patriotic man who cherished his image as a benevolent giver of convenience and value to society, so he was wounded by the perception that his actions had in any way endangered the country, or that he was to blame for the strike. Usually meticulous at managing his own image and that of his business—he was known for the lavish junkets for reporters and VIPs who attended the formal rollouts of his new railroad cars—he seemed to not have appreciated the bad press that could adhere to a company or an individual as the result of poorly handled labor relations. He had "won" the strike but lost the public's favor; no longer was he the admired innovator and knight of commerce. For a perfectionist of his bent this was maddening, humiliating even in that he had been taken down, exposed as cold and self-interested, by his own lowly shop workers; they had "found the chink in his armor," as one historian suggests, and for the first time in a career largely triumphant, "opened him to criticism, something he could not abide." Pullman tried to recover his reputation through various charitable works, with limited success. That the shock of the strike had disoriented him and vanquished some of his habitual confidence was evident to leading company stockholders, who briefly considered asking for his resignation as head of the firm.[129]

In fall 1895 there were two amateurish, easily foiled attempts on Pullman's life. Already in poor health (he suffered from a heart ailment), he became convinced that his former employees were behind the assassination plots. He likely knew the rumors about Franklin B. Gowen, the onetime president of the Reading Railroad and titan of the Pennsylvania anthracite fields, who had been found dead in a Washington hotel room in 1889, an apparent suicide, although it was whispered he'd met his end at the hands of vengeful Molly Maguires.[130] Pullman eventually became prey to an even more macabre obsession—that upon his death, ex-employees of the Pullman Palace Car Company would steal or desecrate his remains. Wealthy enough to act on such fears, however irrational, he left strict orders regarding his anticipated internment in Graceland Cemetery in Chicago, designing a burial vault fortified to resist all forms of forced entry. Drawing one last time on his passion for innovative engineering, the man who had hoisted whole city blocks and redefined American rail travel arranged for his coffin to be lined in lead, set in concrete, covered with asphalt, then protected from any attempt at excavation by a set of heavy iron bars laid across the top of the vault.[131]

A far more important product of the Pullman Strike was the political evolution of Eugene Debs. As president of the Brotherhood of Locomotive Firemen, Debs had disdained strikes; he believed the purpose of unions to be largely benevolent, providing hospitalization and death benefits for men in a dangerous occupation. Even the staid Gompers was initially more "radical" than Debs, insisting on unions' right to strike and bargain, a power Debs had only slowly come to accept. What the Pullman debacle had shown him was that not only corporations were capable of wrongful, unprincipled actions; the government and its federal judges, the "ermined sycophants," as Debs called them; President Cleveland, for whom he'd campaigned in 1892; as well as the military and powerful newspapers—all, in their disdain for workers' just demands, were willing to twist facts, to scheme, and to employ blunt force.

Like George Pullman, he, too, had been personally wounded by events. Turning his back on mainstream politics, he denounced all but the Populists' People's Party, which had called for a number of labor-related reforms, including the enforcement of the eight-hour day in government jobs and the suppression of the "hireling army" known as the Pinkertons; to this list of objectives the party would soon add the demand for an end to the use of court injunctions against labor unions. "I have been a Democrat all my life and I am ashamed to admit it," he said at the last ARU gathering he addressed before beginning a six-month jail term for contempt. "I want every one of you to go to the polls and vote the People's ticket."[132]

Debs had to deal with two separate legal proceedings against him. His six-month prison sentence arose from his violation of the July 2 anti-trust injunction (his codefendants were each sentenced to three months). All appealed their conviction to the U.S. Supreme Court. While awaiting the high court's ruling, they also had to answer to charges of conspiracy emanating from the ARU's alleged blocking of a mail train on the Rock Island Railroad. That trial began in January 1895 and was presided over by none other than Judge Peter Grosscup, who had issued the original edict against the ARU. Clarence Darrow, defending Debs, tried to put the GMA's lawyers on trial, accusing them of "persecution not prosecution," and pointing out that there was not a scintilla of evidence that Debs or any other ARU official had conspired to halt mail traffic. The executives of the GMA were vague and seemed forgetful, no doubt because a true accounting of their actions would reveal their conspiratorial intent to defeat the labor organization; notably, George Pullman left the state so as to be unavailable to testify. The case dragged on for a month, and many observers felt Darrow was getting the better of the government, but then a juror fell ill—mysteriously, in Debs's opinion—and Judge Grosscup discharged the jury and continued the case, but it was never reopened. Debs later wrote that the members of the jury had privately assured him of their intent to acquit.

The July 2 injunction case eventually did get a hearing before the Supreme Court in spring 1895, and for Debs's forces the Court's ruling was a disappointment. In *In re Debs*, the Court essentially dodged the critical issue of whether the federal government had the right to issue an injunction based on the Sherman Act against a labor union, and instead reaffirmed unanimously that a federal injunction was valid where interstate commerce and the U.S. mails were disrupted. The Supreme Court's consideration of the validity of antitrust injunctions against labor would not be resolved, and then unfavorably for labor, until the Court's decision in *Loewe v. Lawlor* in 1908.[133]

Debs's six-month incarceration at a jail in rural Woodstock, Illinois, has become a legendary chapter in the story of his long progress from railroad unionist to Socialist Party presidential candidate. "My imprisonment is very much to arouse the public conscience," Debs wrote to his father,[134] but the time also proved to be one of self-discovery and reevaluation. Debs exercised, received visitors, made friends of the sheriff and his family, and charmed the small town's residents, many of whom took the opportunity to stop by to meet and befriend the celebrity prisoner. He told stories of his days on the railroad. He read a great deal in Socialist and Marxist texts sent to him, and was particularly taken by a book called

The Cooperative Commonwealth by Laurence Gronlund, who as "Peter Lofgreen" had been active in the St. Louis Workingmen's Party at the time of the 1877 general strike in that city.

By the time he completed his term in November 1895, Debs had developed a keen interest in Socialism. He was convinced that what was required was not more of the labor struggle's give-and-take with management, or largely futile opposition to government hirelings, but a reordering of American society on the scale of the revolution that had toppled chattel slavery. Returning to Chicago, he received a hero's welcome. "Go Wild over Debs," the *Tribune* headlined its coverage.[135] Hatless, somewhat thinner, he was borne along by a throng of one hundred thousand from the depot to a speakers' stand. "That's our boy, Gene!" "Tell the bosses now!" urged the workingmen who pressed in from all sides, as Debs, touched by the adulation, accepted telegrams of congratulation from Western Union boys who had to be lifted over the crowd.

His ARU had lost its boycott (and would not recover any meaningful semblance of organization), but the power of an industrial union had been demonstrated. Armies and bogus court rulings could not repress it. "They might as well try to stop Niagara with a feather as to crush the spirit of organization in this country," Eugene Debs believed with all his heart. "It may not come up in the form of the American Railway Union, but this spirit of resistance to wrong is there, it is growing stronger constantly."[136]

CHAPTER FIVE

INDUSTRIAL DEMOCRACY

THE PULLMAN STRIKE HAD DEEPENED UNDER-
standing on both sides of the labor-management divide. Labor perceived that even well-run work
stoppages would face not only corporate might and
determination, but industry's powerful handmaidens—the anti-labor bias of the courts, as well as
military force. As for capital, it had learned that
successfully breaking a strike could prove a hollow
victory, in that it still meant consequential financial loss and inconvenience. As the economic desperation of the 1890s lifted and relative prosperity
returned, there arose a constructive impatience with
the status quo in industrial relations and its by-now
visible shortcomings, while technological progress
and the rise in living standards that accompanied the
dawn of the new century helped spawn a desire for
more workable solutions. Persistent unemployment
and urban poverty, the inability to peacefully resolve
labor-management issues, the intractability of business barons—might not all such issues be enabled by
society's willingness to grant them greater empathy
and closer, wiser analysis?[1]

The Progressive viewpoint that produced such questions had gathered energy throughout the last two decades of the nineteenth century. Driven initially by the church-based reform movement known as the Social Gospel, which rejected Social Darwinism's cruel formulas and worked to reverse the determinative influences of fate on the poor, Progressivism had expanded on numerous fronts. These included efforts to study and reform factory conditions and to intercede in a range of unacceptable factors of modern life from tainted food to child labor to the conditions of urban tenement slums and corruption in municipal government.

Adding to the crises of the cities was the tremendous influx of new immigrants in the years around the turn of the century, all record-setting years, which peaked at 1,285,000 in 1907.[2] The newcomers helped overwhelm the civic resources of many communities, resulting in the urban corruption and slum conditions cataloged in the work of the muckrakers—Lincoln Steffens's *The Shame of the Cities*; Jacob Riis's *How the Other Half Lives*; and William Stead's *If Christ Came to Chicago*—among numerous others. The muckrakers went beyond shaming readers with the squalor of urban life; they introduced America to an underworld of racketeers, political bosses, and red-light districts; they described a fallen nation, one whose redemption demanded nothing less than a rediscovery of the country's fundamental values. These insights were reflected in the literature of the day, inspiring Theodore Dreiser, Stephen Crane, Jack London, and Frank Norris, among others. Of particular interest was Edward Bellamy's *Looking Backward: 2000–1877*, published in 1888, an innovative novel about a futuristic Socialist utopia in the United States; the book proved such a sensation that "Bellamy Societies" sprang up across the country to weigh its implications.

Progressivism has been described as an attempt by the rising middle class to readjust the chief organizing principles of society; this included a call for a new public morality, one that recognized that great wrongs could result not solely from conscious acts, but also from decisions made by faceless institutions, corporate boards, the courts, and neglectful government agencies.[3] For labor, it meant a new openness to the idea that workers and capital might acknowledge the other's necessity, that trade unions had a role to play in standardizing decent wages so as to alleviate the need for relief or charity, and that some form of mutualism, the working out of problems, could replace the cyclical tradition of hurtful strikes and class antagonism. In this evolving process government would be asked whether, if it was to be involved in labor disputes, it might find more constructive methods than urging court injunctions and dispatching regiments.

A valuable influence on Progressivism and the labor front in particular was a brand of English Socialism associated with the Fabian Society, a group that included playwright George Bernard Shaw and the sociologists Sidney and Beatrice Webb. Fabianism sought to reform society gradually through enlightenment of the individual, but the Webbs, authors and social critics, also promoted the idea that major institutional forces in the industrial age—capital, government, and labor organizations—all had important roles to play in maintaining a semblance of balance. In *Industrial Democracy*, published in 1897, the Webbs described unions as entities that would check the excesses of impersonal, large-scale capitalism. They coined the term "collective bargaining" to designate the method by which industry and labor would together rectify their relationship's inherent inequalities. The phrase that served as the title of their book, "industrial democracy," would come in America to represent the idea that the democratic principles and "basic civil and political rights embedded in the Constitution and its post Civil War amendments" should apply to the issues of labor and industry as much as they informed the nation's political system. Industrial democracy implied the recognition that neither side in labor disputes held all the answers, and that neither was entirely in the right. It also came to mean the inclusion in conflict resolution of not only workers and employers but legislatures, reformers, and public relief agencies, as well as scholars, the press, and the public.[4]

One indirect force behind the Progressive yearning for moderate solutions was the relative vibrancy and popularity of Socialism. In the years surrounding the turn of the century, U.S. readers could select from eight foreign-language Socialist dailies, five English-language Socialist dailies, and 262 English- and 36 foreign-language Socialist weeklies. By 1904 the most prominent weekly Socialist periodical, the *Appeal to Reason*, published in Kansas, had a circulation of 500,000,[5] while a special antitrust broadside it published in late 1905 sold 3 million copies.[6] By May 1912, the nation had 1,039 Socialists in elected seats of authority, including fifty-six mayors, 160 councilmen, and 145 aldermen. Eugene Debs, the five-time candidate for president of the Socialist Party, racked up 897,000 votes in the 1912 election, 6 percent of the national vote; in 1920 he garnered more than a million votes even as he sat in an Atlanta penitentiary. "When the Socialist said that the grievances of the people could be relieved only under Socialism," offers historian Richard Hofstadter, "the typical Progressive became the more determined to find ways of showing that these grievances were remediable under capitalism. In [this] way the alleged 'threat' of Socialism, much talked about in the Progressive period, actually gave added impetus to middle-class programs."[7]

This impetus, guided in part by the Webbs' influential ideas, begot a new willingness to view the challenges of modern society, and of labor and industry in particular, as resolvable by a kind of science—*social science*. If the social and economic problems confronting workers could be studied, measured, rationalized, and improved, went the reformers' hope, they would cease to assume the form of radical class struggle.[8] Labor unions were to have a functional, helpful role in American life, treated for the first time, suggests labor scholar Richard Greenwald, as "constructive institutions rather than economic obstacles."[9]

There were even artistic links between labor and the Progressive sensibility, such as the emergence of the British arts-and-crafts movement, which was welcomed in America by a group associated with the Museum of Fine Arts in Boston headed by Charles Loring, and heralded in a prominent exhibit at Copley Hall in April 1897. Arts and crafts represented both an aesthetic response to the dehumanizing effects of the modern factory and an attempt to rediscover the pleasures of craftsmanship, the loss of which to mass production, art critic and reformer John Ruskin had warned, would wreak a destructive effect on mankind. Through the influence of the English designer and Socialist William Morris, arts and crafts spread through architecture (often in the form of bungalow or cottage building), furniture-making, and decorative arts such as pottery and tile-making. A parallel development in America was the movement known as City Beautiful, an aesthetic that emphasized urban beautification and architecture on a monumental scale as a means of instilling values of moral and civic virtue in urban residents. The City Beautiful ideal was first notably explored at the World's Columbian Exposition of 1893 in Chicago under the hand of architect Daniel Burnham and the sculptor Augustus Saint-Gaudens, and its influence was widely seen in major American cities during the early decades of the twentieth century, often in the design of government buildings such as 20 Centre Street in New York City, the approach to the Manhattan Bridge, Grand Central Station, and various public statuary and fountains, as well as features of the New York subway system.

Notably, the Progressive impulse was all-encompassing enough that it did not belong exclusively to muckrakers, reformers, social scientists, or artists. Directors of corporations joined the striving for moderation with a new kind of managerial paternalism, known as welfare capitalism, an effort to turn workers and their families into members of the middle class, stabilizing workforces through the provision to employees of benefits such as pensions, profit-sharing, and a variety of social, financial, and recreational perks. By 1914 an estimated twenty-five hundred firms nationwide were using welfare capitalism as a means of worker retention. So pervasive was the movement that even U.S. Steel, which had since Homestead worked assiduously to snuff out unionization in its plants, became one of the first large corporations to offer its workers pension plans and stock participation. Of course welfare capitalism, while revealing a kinder corporate face to workers, also was aimed at diminishing the need for labor unions.[10]

The National Cash Register headquarters in Dayton, Ohio, were the site of one of the nation's leadings efforts in this field. The cash register itself was a symbol of the emerging era of commercial automation, as was the city of Dayton considered a kind of Silicon Valley of its day. Technologically blessed, this small municipality in the early years of the twentieth century gave the world, in addition to the cash register, the airplane, the crankless automobile, leaded gasoline, and the folded ice cream carton, among other innovations. "The Cash," led by its dynamic young president, John H. Patterson, strove to apply Progressive ideas to the workplace, introducing free child care, after-work education, organized sports teams and facilities, an on-site medical clinic, as well as split shifts for female employees so they could arrive and depart the plant independently of men. Patterson was also active in bringing to Dayton the reformist city manager system of municipal government, which was intended to undo the traditional bossism and city corruption of American cities exposed in the muckraking of Lincoln Steffens. In addition to municipal reform, Patterson led a campaign for city parks, libraries, concerts, new health and sanitation rules, and—following a devastating flood that struck Dayton in 1913—measures to improve levees, bridges, and roads. His study of his own workers' needs was so detailed that it included ideas for specific types of bushes to be planted on company grounds and the colors most appropriate for employees' houses.

While some unionists distrusted welfare at work for its tendency to put the incentive for labor organizing to sleep, and to permit management excessive involvement with workers' financial and even personal lives, others, mostly business and social conservatives, worried that mothering workers ran against America's ingrained individualism. "Patronizing and coddling grown men and women is not looked upon favorably by the Infinite Power which governs us all," commented the cereal manufacturer Charles W. Post. "It is intended by the Creator that mankind obtain 'welfare' as the result of service and often-times hard service. It is not to be fed to him in a silver spoon and his chin held up while he takes it."[11]

Another influential voice was that of Philadelphia engineer and business consultant Frederick W. Taylor, famous for his emphasis on disciplined plant efficiency, a concept that became known as "scientific management" or "Taylorism." Born in 1856 to an affluent Philadelphia Quaker family, Taylor overcame debilitating problems with his eyesight to study mechanical engineering, and grew wealthy in his own right by devising a precision method of calibrating the temperatures at which steel can be cut and manipulated. In resolute defiance of the health issues that had plagued his youth, he devoted himself to a life of physical fitness, becoming a cricketer, a better-than-average golfer, and, in 1881, one of the first doubles champions in the history of the U.S. Lawn Tennis Association.

His ideas for industrial reform started from the position that the craft tradition, and its reliance on the expertise of veteran workers, had been made obsolete by automation, and that a standardization of methods was needed to redefine the factory worker's role. Shop foremen were to lose their on-site authority in favor of company-level planning committees. Rule-of-thumb approaches to performing a particular work task were to be discarded in favor of practices based on the scientific analysis of that task. Employees would be assigned a job based on their aptitude and ability, then trained specifically for that position so that it could be performed with maximum efficiency. "The greatest permanent prosperity for the workman, coupled with the greatest prosperity for the employer," Taylor insisted, "can be brought about only when the work of the establishment is done with the smallest combined expenditure of human effort."[12] By the 1890s he was an expert on shop-efficiency methods, conducting time and motion studies of men performing tasks such as loading pig iron and shoveling coal; he also urged the importance of worker retention and of keeping the factory employee's mind stimulated.

The term "scientific management," although always associated with Taylor, actually originated with a devotee of his ideas, the prominent Boston attorney Louis D. Brandeis. The future Supreme Court justice, in testifying on behalf of shippers before the Interstate Commerce Commission concerning a desired increase in railroad freight charges, suggested that a preferable way for the railroads to save money would be to adopt

Taylor's innovative methods.[13] "Roads Could Save $1,000,000 a Day" declared the next day's *New York Times*, one of many news articles that sparked curiosity about Taylor's love of efficiency and his determined efforts at "weeding waste out of business."[14] At a time when corporations were growing larger and industry more automated, there was something reassuring about the idea that such changes might be understood scientifically, that issues like worker contentment, increased production, and the betterment of labor-management relations could be solved through greater scrutiny and analysis. As Taylor had proposed, "What constitutes a fair day's work will be a question for scientific investigation, instead of a subject to be bargained and haggled over."[15] This sounded very good to capital enterprises weary of expensive, wasteful disputes with employees and labor unions.

But it sat less well with organized labor, for the AFL and other unions could hardly abide Taylor's emphasis on taking decision-making away from the worker. Taylor had not hesitated to suggest that workers generally were unqualified to adjudge their own labor from a scientific standpoint, and that such perspective need be left to management. Particularly troubling to laborites was his proposal that differential wages be paid to those workers who showed themselves most efficient, as such a principle reeked of the hated bonus system used in textile mills, emphasized individual workers rather than employees as a group, and threatened to defeat the rationale for collective bargaining. Taylor countered that because employers often lowered the piece rate when individuals demonstrated initiative, which only demoralized the best workers, a sliding scale would put more money in the pockets of the most adept workers and benefit the employer by encouraging rather than discouraging maximum effort. "An establishment running under the principles of scientific management will confer far greater blessings upon the working people than could be brought about through any form of collective bargaining," he insisted, but by 1911 the AFL had adopted a formal resolution denouncing his policies.[16]

Samuel Gompers feared that "wage-workers" might come to be viewed as "mere machines," and mocked the idea that workers' jobs should be "standardized and [their] motion-power brought up to the highest possible perfection in all respects, including speeds." The result would be that "science would thus get the most out of [workers] before [they] are sent to the junk pile." Taylor angrily resisted such caricature as "the worst falsehood," insisting that his goal was to spare the worker unnecessary effort. Labor twice managed to force Taylor to appear before congressional committees to justify his methods; already infamous for lacing his guest lectures at Harvard with "profane shop language," he became so outraged in one congressional hearing at the barbed questions from representatives sympathetic to labor's concerns, much of his testimony had to be stricken from the record.[17]

Few workplaces ever implemented Frederick Taylor's recommendations to the letter, and after an initial public infatuation with scientific management, critics were heard to declare it a pseudoscience, mocking some of its more laughable concepts such as "scientific shoveling."[18] But the concept had obvious and lasting implications for the coming era of mass production, and in the early years of the century business itself eagerly embraced the idea that its methods were scientific. In addition to innovative labor-saving mechanisms like the cash register, new paper-based control systems proliferated, including "departmental cost-tracking, standard paying and receiving systems, data tabulation and performance reporting," according to historian Charles R. Morris.[19] Countless books and articles about management techniques and other aspects of business appeared, as did a new type of educational institution, the business college.

And while labor initially resented the systematizing of work, even the AFL by the mid-1920s had grown accepting of the need to define the parameters of a job in terms of its role in production, efficiency, and employee well-being. Certainly, Taylor's belief in the equitable treatment of workers and worker retention complemented unions' high estimation of labor's value. What remained to be seen was how the enlightened principles of industrial democracy would work in practice, and if they could abide independent unionism.

O NE OF THE FIRST TRIALS of the idea that Progressive ideas might enable the resolution of labor disputes came at the turn of the century, when the nation was repeatedly threatened by the prospect of a lengthy coal strike. The United Mine Workers had expanded from the bituminous or soft coal regions of western Pennsylvania and the Midwest into the rugged anthracite region of eastern Pennsylvania, a place known for its railroad feudalism and the violent legends of the Molly Maguires. Much change had come to the anthracite lands in the generation since Franklin B. Gowen of the Reading had persecuted John Siney's mine union and the Mollies. The long Irish dominance of the region had receded before a polyglot wave of Italian and Eastern European immigrants, whose many languages and customs brought cultural variety but whose willingness to work at low wages complicated union organizing. Nonetheless, when in 1900 the UMW began talking strike in anthracite country, tens of thousands of miners, immigrant and native alike, signaled their readiness.

This development worried Marcus Alonzo Hanna, U.S. senator from Ohio and the chair of the Republican National Committee, who was busy trying to secure the reelection of President William McKinley. Based in Cleveland, Hanna had made a fortune shipping coal and iron on the Great Lakes; for years he had been the managing force behind McKinley's career, boosting the two-term Ohio governor to the White House in the election of 1896 with a promise to workingmen of a "Full Dinner Pail." The slogan was reprised for McKinley's reelection campaign of 1900 as "Four More Years of the Full Dinner Pail," assuring labor he would continue to safeguard its interests. The incumbent was expected to withstand the challenge from Democrat William Jennings Bryan, whom he had defeated four years earlier, but Hanna, ever cautious, feared the political ramifications of a protracted coal strike, pitting miners against big business and possibly creating a fuel shortage in the chill autumn weeks before the election.

Hanna shared the Progressive perspective that by showing labor organizations respect, management fostered greater productivity and minimized potential disruptions from Socialists and other radical elements. "A man who won't meet his men halfway is a God-damn fool!" he exclaimed. "My plan is to have organized union labor Americanized in the best sense, and thoroughly educated to an understanding of its responsibilities, and in this way to make it the ally of the capitalist, rather than a foe with which to grapple."[20] He put his beliefs on the line as a labor conciliator for the National Civic Federation, founded in 1896, a group of businessmen, reformers, and mainstream labor leaders that sought to improve America's industrial relations. The NCF's roster was a decidedly mixed bag, including powerful men of means like industrialist John D. Rockefeller Jr. and financier August Belmont, laborites Samuel Gompers of the AFL and John Mitchell of the UMW, as well as former president Grover Cleveland and the president of Harvard, Charles W. Eliot. The NCF represented an effort to insert a moderate public or "conference" sensibility into the labor-capital relationship—the faith that no issue was too divisive to defy rational dialogue—but because of its diverse makeup, the organization never fully gained either labor or management's trust.

Hanna typified that ambivalence; he stood at the nexus of the country's politics and business, and while he may have sincerely believed in a "full dinner pail" for labor, his ambitions were large and he knew how to use money to serve them. For McKinley's 1896 presidential run he had raised unprecedented sums of money, staging what many historians regard as the original "modern" American political campaign, with slick promotional materials, an army of volunteers, and a corps of effective surrogate speakers. Not for nothing was he known as "Dollar Mark."

He set out with like determination to protect McKinley in 1900 by seeing to it that a coal strike did not invigorate Bryan's candidacy. Through negotiation with J. P. Morgan, the leading coal and railroad financier who had tremendous financial influence with the anthracite business, Hanna was able to obtain a settlement for the miners of a 10 percent pay hike. The mine owners refused to formally recognize the UMW, but the union ordered its forces back to work, staving off a coalfield insurrection and helping ensure McKinley's reelection.[21]

Less than a year into his second term, in September 1901, McKinley was assassinated by the anarchist Leon Czolgosz, putting Vice President Theodore Roosevelt in the White House. Roosevelt and Hanna shared little of the rapport that had characterized the Hanna-McKinley partnership, and the new relationship was sorely tested in May 1902 when the 1900 coal agreement expired and the UMW made new demands. Wages remained unacceptable, the miner's ten-hour day was too long, and workers resented the operators' practice of laying men off and rehiring them based on short-term need. In addition, safety measures in the mines were inadequate, and the company towns in which the miners and their families lived were generally degraded, unsanitary hovels, where already thin salaries were gouged at company stores. Some miners described their lot as a Northern variation of the sharecropping system. On their behalf the UMW demanded a 20 percent pay raise, an eight-hour day, and a more just method of measuring coal production where it was used to adjust pay scales.

Roosevelt was as contemptuous of industrial tycoons as he was of radical change-seekers; he did, however, accept the ideas that the conciliatory adjudication of labor's legitimate demands would be of great benefit to the nation. "I strongly favor labor unions," he had once said. "If I were a wage worker in a big city I should certainly join one."[22] The avoidance of labor disruptions, he insisted, was "really in the interest of property, for it will save it from the danger of revolution."[23] While he believed that government might serve as an honest broker in labor-management crises, he had his own prejudices; he was inclined to form a favorable view of a labor union only if he respected and felt personally at ease with its leading spokesman.

In confronting the 1902 UMW demands, Roosevelt had reason to distrust Hanna, who had become a force in the Senate and was thought to harbor presidential ambitions for 1904. It would suit Hanna's aims to once again deliver labor peace to the nation, and there was no doubt heroic measures would be called for in the face of a devastating coal strike. A walkout by the UMW would affect 357 collieries and nearly

150,000 miners in eastern Pennsylvania, with the capacity to cause inconvenience and suffering for millions of citizens for whom coal was an essential commodity.[24] The loss of anthracite coal in particular would be a hardship, as it was superior to the softer bituminous variety as a burning fuel.

When the strike began on June 2 the mine operators reverted to the labor-busting methods of the 1870s, sending replacements and industry cops into the mine region, although one factor in the union's favor was that Pennsylvania now required that miners be licensed, thus limiting the number of scabs who could step easily into the job. Another advantage was the character of UMW president John Mitchell. A mine worker since age thirteen, he had, like Eugene Debs, advanced precociously through organized labor's ranks, becoming master workman of his Knights of Labor local before he turned seventeen. An attractive man known for his assured personal style, Mitchell had ingratiated himself with the ethnically diverse groups that each day descended into the nation's mines, and was widely respected by his union's rank and file, as Debs had been by the ARU. Mitchell also got on well with President Roosevelt, who considered him "a gentleman."[25]

Mitchell used all his skills to sustain public support for the striking miners, the first time "a labor organization tied up for months a strategic industry," historian Selig Perlman explains, "without being condemned as a revolutionary menace."[26] He didn't inflate the crisis by insisting UMW workers from the soft-coal regions strike in sympathy, and he agreed to submit the entire dispute for arbitration to the NCF or another impartial entity. Probably the biggest help to Mitchell and the UMW was the presence on management's side of a "tailor-made villain,"[27] the unyielding George F. Baer, a sixty-four-year-old attorney and president of the Philadelphia & Reading Railroad, who was adamant that no labor union would dictate terms to mine owners. Baer was "the master-spirit of the anthracite industry," according to a contemporary account, "foremost among the commanding generals, on active service, fighting the battle of vested interests against the advancing forces of radicalism." The military analogy was not offhand; he was a Civil War veteran, and his manner when in full antiunion mode was said to resemble that of a Prussian officer planning a siege, complete with the habit of pacing deliberately up and back in a room as he spoke. The sole humanizing quality of this "cold-tempered" man appeared to be horticultural—an enthusiasm for engineering chrysanthemum hybrids. But he wanted no part of any "sentimental" fix to the coal strike, such as the help of the NCF, nor would he deal directly with or even condescend to acknowledge the UMW.[28] That Baer and the mine operators turned aside the UMW's call for fair arbitration played poorly with the public, suggesting indifference to the real suffering that would result from a "coal famine" and raising suspicion that the anthracite profiteers wouldn't mind a prolonged strike that drove up prices.

At the heart of the coal operators' refusal to recognize the UMW was the issue of the closed shop, a union's exclusive representation of all labor working in any particular job site. To unionists the closed shop was seen as essential to collective bargaining, as it alone granted a union the ability to speak for all workers, unifying them with regard to their demands, strike votes, and ultimate acceptance or rejection of management's offers. As dear as the concept was to labor, however, capital experienced it as potentially ruinous. Indeed, employer groups such as the National Association of Manufacturers (NAM), founded in 1895, worked assiduously to ensure that the very term "closed shop" came to carry negative, un-American associations in the public mind, at odds with sacred notions of individual liberty.

The NAM boosted instead "the open shop," a workplace in which unions would not be allowed to collectively "dictate" workers' desires and goals. This controversy, so easily linked to emotionally powerful terms like "freedom" and "choice," cut to the very core of labor's struggle, as there was perhaps no issue more critical in unionization than the question of the ability of workers to amass their strength in such a way as to present a solid bargaining position to an employer. Management, historically, seeks to disrupt that process. The "closed shop, open shop" debate took place in this context, with both sides realizing early on the significance of the relevant terminology. Samuel Gompers, keenly aware of the unfortunate connotation of "closed shop," always made a point of substituting the phrase "union shop," which he believed rang more pleasantly in the ear. "It is absurd to consent to, or give assent to the organization of labor, and deny the logical result—the union shop," he affirmed.[29]

Of course, George Baer was not simply parsing words. He sincerely believed that mine owners deserved to retain authority over their workers, and went so far as to suggest this might be a matter of divine appointment. "The rights and interests of the laboring men will be protected and cared for—not by the labor agitators," he proclaimed, "but by the Christian men to whom God in His infinite wisdom has given the control of the property interests of this country."[30] Baer was only paraphrasing the common adage that "the best men should rule," but at a moment when it appeared likely Baer's obstinacy might cause a coal shortage, his assurance that God was on his side stunned and offended many Americans.[31]

Baer's imperious remark would be recalled as the cold nights of fall came on in the big cities, and the strike-induced shortage of coal sent per-ton prices climbing from $5 to $20. While punishing to large institutions such as schools, factories, hospitals, and hotels (coal was not only a source of heat but also powered gas illumination), the crisis fell most heavily on the poor, as they were accustomed to buying coal in small amounts, sometimes a pailful at a time. Newspapers warned of "no more coal in sight" and printed ominous headlines such as "Darkness Threatens Chicago."[32] With the UMW and Baer's operators checkmated it was the public that finally pressed for resolution, clergymen gathering their congregants and other citizens in parlors and church basements to call for government action. "A conflict between employers and employed which involves the interests of every home and business establishment," a statement drafted at one such meeting declared, "can no longer be regarded as a private quarrel."[33]

The operators, led by Baer, had begun thinking similarly, although their idea of government participation was for President Roosevelt to assist in procuring a court injunction against the striking miners under the Sherman Antitrust Act. The president demurred, believing that organized labor deserved a hearing and should be viewed as a partner in seeking resolution to workingmen's difficulties. Moreover, conscious of Mark Hanna hovering over his shoulder, willing to jump in and resolve the strike should Roosevelt falter, he wanted his own involvement to be perceived as constructive. After the president dispatched his commissioner of labor, Carroll D. Wright, to investigate the strike's origins and causes, Wright reported back that the miners' working hours probably *were* too long and that a fair bargaining scenario would be the best approach, despite the operators' reluctance. Roosevelt, fearing "untold misery . . . with the certainty of riots which might develop into social war" in case of a continuing fuel shortage, called a Washington conference of all parties to take place on October 3.[34]

Such a gathering was newsworthy—a president had never before offered to help mediate an industrial strike—and on the day of the meeting, reporters and a "snapshot brigade" of press photographers hovered as the representatives of coal and labor were welcomed to a building adjacent to the White House. Roosevelt was incapacitated as the result of an accident a few weeks earlier when his carriage had been struck by a trolley car, and it was from a wheelchair that he called the event to order. He got straight to business, reminding his guests that the coal crisis affected not only the interests in the room but the public and the economic health of the country. Mitchell of the UMW, flattered by the conference's implied recognition of the UMW, fell in at once with Roosevelt's conciliatory tone, offering to put his miners "back to work immediately, provided the operators would agree to leave the [strike] issues to President Roosevelt to decide, and agreed to abide by his decision or the decision of a tribunal to be appointed by him."[35]

Baer and his associates would have none of it. They still resented Hanna's intrusion into the 1900 strike and scorned the notion of putting wage issues into a third party's hands, even if those hands were those of the president of the United States. Instead they sought to jog Roosevelt's memory about the Pullman Strike of 1894, when President Cleveland had not hesitated to send the army to deal with turbulent workers and rioters; they suggested that he follow his predecessor's example and "put federal troops in the field." Baer, according to one account, spoke with such "great earnestness" that at one point he brought his fist down on a table with force enough "that the blow could be heard even across the street."[36] Roosevelt, who didn't care much for Baer to begin with, was displeased by his audacity and lack of etiquette. "Bitter language was used, and fists were waved in the air," it was reported. "The President's chair was so near the window that from across the street he could be seen at intervals making gestures and every time that he did a clinched hand was seen waving above in counter-gesticulation."[37] Roosevelt later said of Baer's arrogance, "If it wasn't for the high office I hold, I would have taken him by the seat of the breeches and the nape of the neck and chucked him out of the window."[38]

Despite the thorough airing of views, not even the hint of a breakthrough emerged from the conference. The coal operators agreed to deal with the miners generally, but not with the UMW. During the meeting Baer and the others actually refused to address Mitchell directly, even as he sat a few feet away, for fear so ordinary a courtesy might grant legitimacy to the miners' union. Roosevelt, however, did not have the luxury of ignoring any further the mounting public pressure for a solution. As a sop to the operators he did send troops to the anthracite region, at one point even suggesting he would, if necessary, have the army take over the mines and operate them. But this development had little effect on either the owners or the miners, who held steadfast to their positions. Determined at all cost not to involve Hanna as an emissary to the coal interests, Roosevelt dispatched Elihu Root, his secretary of war, to consult J. P. Morgan, who had reportedly begun to share the president's and the public's concern. Root, a successful attorney whose impeccable reputation included fighting political corruption in New York City, met with

Morgan for five hours on October 11 aboard Morgan's yacht, *Corsair*, in New York harbor, an unusual place to resolve a coal strike but one chosen to evade reporters.

Morgan's interests controlled railroads and valuable coal lands throughout the coal region, and while he was accustomed to allowing the operators a free hand to control the mines, he agreed with Root that the nation would only suffer from any further destabilization of the anthracite industry. The question, after the ruckus at the meeting Roosevelt had convened, was how the various parties—especially the prickly Baer—could be brought into mediation without the owners formally recognizing the UMW. Root and Morgan discussed a proposal in which the mine owners would request that the White House create an Anthracite Coal Strike Commission, its members to be selected by the president. A few days later in Washington, Morgan reiterated the idea directly to Roosevelt, who approved.

The owners and the miners also consented to the plan, the owners imposing the caveats that they would not be forced to recognize the UMW and that no labor representative would take part in the arbitration. Roosevelt agreed to their demands, although he did manage to save a chair on the panel for an "eminent sociologist," and into that slot installed a union man, Edgar E. Clark of the Order of Railway Conductors, who did his best to fulfill the masquerade by dressing and acting professorial. Once seated, the commission worked swiftly. On October 23 a deal was outlined that awarded the miners a 10 percent wage hike, reduced their working hours from ten to nine, or eight in some instances, and established a permanent six-man mediation board to handle future disputes with management.

Although the process had been far from smooth, Roosevelt, with the help of Mitchell, Root, and Morgan, had achieved a significant advance by demonstrating the efficacy of a new means of managing labor disputes. There had been no court injunctions, no violence; no one had been driven from the street at the point of a bayonet. The mining of coal, so essential to the nation's well-being, had been peacefully restored. The UMW failed to gain recognition from the Baer forces, but the operators had at least bought into the conference system, implicitly acknowledging miners as persons whose demands deserved attention and resolution. Whether they would concede the point or not, the operators had participated in a process that affirmed the legitimacy of labor unions.[39]

THE CONTEST BETWEEN LABOR AND CAPITAL had found its way to the conference room, but it was, with increasing regularity, also beginning to turn up in court. The government's decisive use (or misuse) of the antitrust laws in the Pullman Strike had helped stir this trend, and in the early years of the new century, arguments regarding controversial issues such as the closed shop and the regulatory powers of state legislatures, and the rights of organized labor, would frequently be heard and decided there. "What chance," Samuel Gompers complained to attorney Louis Brandeis in 1902, "have labor and the laborers for fair play when the whole history of jurisprudence has been against the laborers? There never was a tyrant in the history of the world but who found some judge to clothe in judicial form the tyranny exercised and the cruelty imposed on the people." When Brandeis told Gompers he was being emotional, the leader of the AFL replied, "It is true that I am emotional but I am also emphatic."[40]

Curiously, one person keenly interested in these questions was Attorney General Richard Olney, the official who had orchestrated the Cleveland administration's assault on Debs and the ARU during the Pullman affair. In the months after Pullman, Olney had been criticized by the press for his transparent loyalty to the very railroad interests he'd served in the private sphere; there had been at least one petition demanding his impeachment. Said to be personally insulted by the outcry, Olney was chastened enough to sever some of his financial ties to the railways. He was also candid in his regret for the immense financial harm that had come to the railroads—$5 million in lost revenue and damage—notwithstanding the success in dethroning "King Debs."

Olney eventually adopted the view that unions and strikes were not inherently bad and that the growing power of the corporation probably demanded the parallel development of strong labor unions.[41] "The time is passed when the individual workman is called upon to pit his feeble single strength against the might of organized capital," he wrote in an amicus curiae brief in a case involving the Reading Railroad. "Organized labor now confronts organized capital . . . and the burning question of modern times is how shall the ever-recurring controversies between them be adjusted and terminated."[42] He accepted, as did Theodore Roosevelt, the Progressive notion that organized labor could be a potentially conservative factor in society, valuable in tamping down strike disruptions and disarming the need for more radical solutions. Likely under the sway of the conclusions of the Cleveland administration's inquiry into Pullman, Olney urged the need to maintain some means of federal strike arbitration. He also advocated the far more contentious idea that, in cases of absolute stalemate in labor disputes involving necessary industries such as coal or railroads, the government should supplant the disagreeing parties.

Some of Olney's suggestions would become enshrined in the Erdman Act of 1898, which acknowledged railroad unions' right to exist, offered contending sides in a labor dispute the option of federal arbitration, and banished yellow-dog contracts—agreements new hires were sometimes made to sign that forbade them from joining a union. Four years later an Industrial Commission set up by President McKinley before his death delivered its recommendations—a retreat from the use of injunctions in labor disputes, the regulation of child labor, maximum-hour laws, and a general recognition that labor unions were not devious "combinations" in restraint of trade or in any other way criminal. Echoing Erdman, it also denounced the hated yellow dogs.[43]

Then the judicial rollback began. The most definitive anti-labor ruling of the era was to be *Lochner v. New York* (1905), which dealt with attempted state regulation of the baking industry. The New York state legislature, at the urging of reformer Edward Marshall, had in 1895 passed the Bakeshop Act, regulating the hours of bakery workers. Many bakeries were situated in substandard, poorly ventilated environments such as tenement basements, where workers were forced to combat cockroaches and rodents and inhale flour dust for as many as one hundred hours per week. Reformers like Marshall were concerned not only about the workers' health, but the safety of food products made in such environs.

The underlying issue in *Lochner* was what was viewed as an employer's "contract rights," the "liberty" or "freedom of contract" that some jurists held existed between an employer and his workers. This was a controversial area of judicial reasoning that involved the interpretation of the due process clause of the Fourteenth Amendment, adopted in 1868, which guarantees that no state shall "deprive any person of life, liberty, or property, without due process of law." On its face it appears to offer procedural safeguards to each citizen's life, freedom, and belongings, much as the due process clause of the Fifth Amendment makes the same guarantees at the federal level. But beginning with the infamous Dred Scott case of 1857 (*Scott v. Sandford*), in which the Supreme Court ruled that the Constitution protected the status of slaves as private property, there had arisen an enlarged understanding of the guarantee of due process. This view held that what the Constitution was providing was a more basic promise that certain rights were inviolate and could not be denied or legislated against at all. This trend of legalistic thought, which in the twentieth century would come to be known as "substantive due process," had also been glimpsed in the *Slaughterhouse Cases* of 1873, wherein the high court had suggested that the liberty safeguarded by the Fourteenth Amendment included "the right to pursue an ordinary trade or calling." As historian Paul Kens has written, "With subsequent decisions expanding the idea, it became the means by which the judicial supervision envisioned by proponents of substantive due process could be applied to laws regulating the employer-employee relationship." The result was the idea that employers and their workers were to negotiate and manage their relationship without government intrusion or regulation.[44]

The Lochner dispute began when Joseph Lochner, owner of a bakery in Utica, violated the law created by New York State's Bakeshop Act limiting the hours a baker could work to no more than ten hours a day or sixty in a week. Convicted and fined on two separate occasions, he appealed the second conviction on the grounds that the state regulation interfered with his private right to set working arrangements with his employees, citing previous court rulings that defined legislated restrictions as acts of government intrusion and usurpations of individual freedom. Even these rulings, however, had made an exception where conditions of public health and safety were so abject they necessitated the use of police powers. In *Lochner* the argument was over that exception. Attorney Henry Weismann, who argued *Lochner* for the plaintiff, decried that the individual freedom of contract might be forfeited to a dubious claim of police power, when the "average bakery of the present day is well-ventilated, comfortable both summer and winter, and always sweet-smelling."

Weismann's imagery was apparently effective, for the court in *Lochner* swept away the police powers exception, interpreting the due process clause broadly enough to mean that the government had no right whatsoever to interfere with a business's liberty of contract. It defined both employer and employee as free agents capable of negotiating a work contract without government intrusion, and refused to allow New York State to intervene even where there was an issue of public health the state wished to ameliorate through its police powers. Justice Rufus W. Peckham, writing the 5–4 majority opinion, characterized laws "limiting the hours in which grown and intelligent men may labor" as "meddlesome interferences with the rights of the individual." The idealization of individual free will has always been a central tenet of American life; what appeared to particularly trouble Peckham and other conservatives on the court was the fear that legislative bodies would enact—in the form of the Bakeshop Act and similar efforts—"class legislation," laws that were aimed at enabling one class of people over another, in this case giving workers undemocratic authority over their employers.

The venerable Justice John Marshall Harlan, known as "The Great Dissenter" for his seminal opinions in *Civil Rights Cases* (1883) and *Plessy v. Ferguson* (1896), suggested in dissent that there were significant health risks related to professional baking, and that it *was* the job of state legislatures, not the Supreme Court, to investigate and make laws over such issues of workers' health and safety. Harlan was a great believer in the sanctity of the Fourteenth Amendment; he had argued in both *Civil Rights Cases* and *Plessy* for a reading of the amendment he believed its framers had intended, as a safeguard for the individual rights of citizens. He also believed that while corporations were valuable social and economic entities, the impact of their business on society was too vast to go unregulated, and thus did not deserve extra-judicial protection from the court. Justice Oliver W. Holmes joined Harlan in dissent in *Lochner*, questioning whether the Fourteenth Amendment should be used to "enact Mr. Herbert Spencer's Social Statics." Spencer was one of the key promoters in America of the creed of Social Darwinism, so what Holmes was criticizing was the formula by which ordinary people were left to struggle for survival because the court had endowed corporations with the rights of individuals, thus denying efforts by the people's government to assist the people themselves. The economist Herbert Croly captured the matter succinctly in warning that

> a simple and poor society can exist as a democracy on a basis of sheer individualism. But a rich and complex industrial society cannot so exist; for some individuals, and especially those artificial individuals called corporations, become so very big that the ordinary individual . . . cannot deal with them on terms of equality. It therefore becomes necessary for these ordinary individuals to combine in their turn, first in order to act in their collective capacity through that biggest of all combinations called the government, and second, to act also in their own self-defense, through private combinations, such as farmers' associations and trade unions.[45]

A ruling such as was handed down in *Lochner* was what Samuel Gompers had in mind when he had urged, in his testimony before the Pullman Strike commission, that the Constitution, conceived and written in a preindustrial age, was being misused to impede the flow of needed reforms in labor relations. At the time of the Constitutional Convention in 1787, Gompers said,

> men knew scarcely anything of the existence of the power of steam; they knew nothing at all of electricity; they had no suspicion even in the days of Adam Smith of the steam engine and the electric motor or the telegraph, the telephone, the application of steam and electricity to industry; and yet the laws that had been made in the period . . . are sought to be applied to modern industry and modern commerce. . . . I submit that industry and commerce cannot go back to conform to old thoughts, old theories, and old crusty customs of law, but that the law, sooner, must be changed to conform to the changed industrial and commercial conditions. It was revolution that saved France, it was reform that saved England, it is a question what will save America.[46]

The Supreme Court would follow *Lochner* with other decisions made in the spirit of substantive due process, protecting employers from the regulatory power of legislatures to the extent that the decade after 1905 became known as "the *Lochner* era." In *Adair v. United States* (1908), the Supreme Court struck down as unconstitutional that part of the Erdman Act banning yellow-dog contracts. The case originated when railroad official William Adair took exception to worker O. B. Coppage's membership in a union and, in violation of Erdman, fired him. When the case came before the high court, the justices ruled that Congress had no authority to govern trade union membership or the employer's right to contract for labor.[47] Olney termed the *Adair* ruling "archaic," objecting to its extension of due process rights to large business enterprises and noting that it represented "a long step back into the past—to conceive of and deal with the relations between the employer . . . and the employee as if the parties were individuals."[48] State statutes against yellow-dog contracts were overturned also in *Coppage v. Kansas* in 1915 and against minimum wage laws in *Adkins v. Children's Hospital* in 1923.[49]

Labor's tactic of mounting consumer boycotts also came under attack by the courts. The AFL, because of its large membership, had made effective use of this strategy, pressuring manufacturers by advising AFL members (and their families and friends) to refrain from purchasing certain goods. In retaliation, manufacturers started the American Anti-Boycott Association and sought injunctions against the practice. A determinative legal contest over boycotting, known as the Danbury Hatters Case, was fought tooth and nail in the lower courts before finally arriving at the Supreme Court in 1908. The saga had begun in 1902, when the United Hatters of North America attempted to unionize D. E. Loewe & Company of Danbury, Connecticut. The firm's owner, Dietrich Loewe, refused to acknowledge or meet with union representatives, and the United Hatters struck. Loewe responded by hiring scabs to continue the manufacture of hats, while the union retaliated by obtaining a list of Loewe's regular retail outlets and appealing to them not to carry Loewe's products. The hatters also asked the AFL to put Loewe's name on the "We Don't Patronize" list, which ran in the AFL's journal, the *American Federationist*. In *Loewe v. Lawlor* (1908), the Supreme Court ruled that the AFL's boycott constituted a restraint of trade under the Sherman Act—a powerful ruling with dire meaning for labor, since neither the strike nor the boycott had physically interfered with Loewe's business. The potential interpretation of the decision was that any work stoppage by employees could be held to have disrupted commerce, dangerously close to characterizing the routine functions of any labor union as illegal. Labor advocates were outraged that the court appeared willing to twist the intent of the Sherman Act in new and devious ways.

As disappointing as was the ruling, further claims by the plaintiff led to a lower court agreeing that, under the terms of Sherman, Loewe was entitled to collect triple financial damages from the members of the United Hatters local, to the point of attaching their individual bank accounts and threatening to foreclose on more than two hundred of the workers' homes. This decision was upheld by the Supreme Court in 1915. The AFL, stunned and incredulous, agreed to pay the hatters' fines, raising the money in two nationwide "Hatters Days" among AFL-affiliated unions, in which individual workers each donated an hour's pay. The show of solidarity was reassuring, but the Danbury rulings were a crushing setback for labor in that they portended an era in which unions could not only lose the right to orchestrate boycotts but be made to pay dearly for using them, even to the point of bankruptcy.[50]

The AFL was also on the receiving end of a highly detrimental court decision in *Gompers v. Buck's Stove and Range Co.* (1911). The case originated in 1906, when metal polishers at the St. Louis–based Buck's Stove and Range Company went out on strike over the firm's reneging on a nine-hour day that had been instituted in 1904. After the *American Federationist* instructed members not to buy Buck's products, sales of the company's wares fell sharply. Company president J. W. Van Cleave, who was active in two national pro-business groups, joined with the American Anti-Boycott Association to secure a court injunction against the boycott, one so broadly worded it prohibited the AFL from even publicizing the strike. When the AFL, which planned an appeal, did not act swiftly enough to remove Buck's name from its published lists of boycotted products, the firm pursued a criminal contempt citation, which carried a potential punishment of a twelve-month jail sentence against Samuel Gompers and lesser sentences against John Mitchell (now an AFL vice president) and AFL secretary Frank Morrison. The Court of Appeals of the District of Columbia found the defendants guilty as charged.

Gompers, mortified by the possibility he could be sent to prison, demanded that Congress amend the Sherman Act so that it was no longer used against labor unions. Mitchell took a different tack, vowing noncooperation and declaring it "the duty of all patriotic and law-abiding citizens to resist, or at least to disregard, the injunction." Rather than submit to such arbitrary misuse of the law, he said, "it is better that half the workingmen of the country remain constantly in jail."[51] Attorneys for the AFL contended that the First Amendment protected the boycott as a form of free speech, an argument that failed to gain traction with the court, although the criminal aspect of the case was eventually dropped, partly due to the statute of limitations. Neither Gompers nor any other AFL leader came close to a jailhouse door, but the highest court in the land had recognized that the property rights of business were to be safeguarded from product boycotts; this, and the fact that one of the most respected moderates in American labor had been threatened with a punishment usually reserved for radicals, sent a decided chill through the leadership of the nation's unions.

To workers and reformers, all of these judicial roadblocks, as well as the ever-present threat of court injunction, had the cumulative effect of suggesting that something remained terribly wrong in capitalist society. "Outside the walls of the private enterprise," writes historian Nelson Lichtenstein, "American political culture celebrated a Jeffersonian world of free speech, democratic participation, and masterless autonomy. But within the corporate world . . . autocracy, obedience, and social deference were the order of the day, bolstered by a century of legal precedent and legal practice." In efforts to confront management on anything approaching equal terms, workers found themselves thwarted, with no rights of free speech or petition. The judiciary, by clinging "to an imaginary world of 'free labor' in which individual workers freely and equitably negotiated their pay and perks with those who hired them," had created a striking inequity.[52] The challenge to American workers, as Walter Reuther, a leader of the nation's autoworkers beginning in the 1930s, would astutely observe, was "to save truly free enterprise from death at the hands of its self-appointed champions."[53]

DESPITE THE ANTI-LABOR TREND of the judiciary in the period between Pullman and the First World War, state legislatures and Congress did manage to advance labor reforms. One issue that received legislative attention, no doubt because it so glaringly required regulation, was child labor, a cause hammered into the conscience of America by one of labor's most colorfully outspoken characters, "Mother" Jones. In

1867 Mary Jones (née Harris) was living in Memphis with her husband, George Jones, a factory worker and member of William Sylvis's International Iron Molders' Union, when a yellow fever epidemic struck, taking the lives of George and all four of their children. After the molders' union helped her bury her family, Jones went to Chicago, where she worked as a dressmaker and, with a partner, ran a small clothing business that was destroyed in the Chicago Fire of 1871. Remaining in her adopted city as it rebuilt, she became caught up in the fervor of the numerous labor crises of the next two decades—the railroad strike of 1877, the campaign for the eight-hour day, the Haymarket bombing and trial—and eventually joined the Knights of Labor. "Those were the days of sacrifice for the cause of labor," she later said of the era. "Those were the days when we had no hall, when there were no high salaried officers, no feasting with the enemies of labor. Those were the days of the martyrs and the saints."[54] In 1894 she joined Coxey's Army, traveling with a band of men from Denver heading toward St. Louis en route to Washington. Here Jones came fully into her own—raising money, rallying morale, admonishing "her boys" to demand what they deserved and not be "cringing serfs." She did not make it to Washington, but by the adventure's end she had become a full-time itinerant labor agitator, and never had a permanent home again. "My address is like my shoes. It travels with me," she once replied to a congressional committeeman who asked where she lived. "I abide where there is a fight against wrong."[55]

One seemingly clear-cut fight against wrong grew out of her concern for the lack of federal child labor laws. "Breaker boys" as young as six and seven sat all day at the mouths of coal mines sorting anthracite from shale; little girls tended spools in textile mills. They were paid a pittance and denied an education. Such facts prompted her in 1903 to lead a group of striking underage textile workers from Pennsylvania to the Oyster Bay, Long Island, home of President Theodore Roosevelt.[56] The Liberty Bell from Independence Hall in Philadelphia was at the time on a cross-country rail tour, drawing huge crowds, and Jones, noting that "these little children were striking for some of the freedom that childhood ought to have," decided they, too, should go before the public, for "these little toilers, deformed, dwarfed in body, soul, and morality," had "nothing but toil before them and no chance for schooling."[57] At seventy-three years of age, no more than five feet tall, adorned always in black with a starched white blouse and a small flower in her hat, Jones was irresistible fodder for the press, whom she rewarded with such outlandish antics as placing working children in the cages of Frank Bostock's animal show at Coney Island. "Fifty years ago there was a cry against slavery and men gave their lives to stop the selling of black children on the block," she said. "Today the white child is sold for two dollars a week to the manufacturer." The coverage intensified as Jones and the children marched east toward their objective, holding aloft signs that read PROSPERITY IS HERE, WHERE IS OURS? and WE WANT TIME TO PLAY. The public also responded, offering sympathy, box lunches, and overnight accommodations.

The effort's immediate goal proved fruitless—Roosevelt refused to meet with the children or their leader, and his personal secretary later replied to a letter from Jones only to remind her that the states, not Washington, regulated children's working conditions. But she had succeeded at publicizing the uncomfortable reality that boys and girls were daily sent to work in mines and mills, and denied the pleasures and enrichment of childhood; it was, recalls an historian, "an early moment in a long change of consciousness that led to the abolition of child labor in America."[58] The documentary photographer Lewis Wickes Hine followed Jones, traveling the course of industrial America beginning in 1907 on behalf of the National Child Labor Committee to capture images of the very young engaged in a life of deadening mine and factory work. Many of Hine's photographs were published in *The Survey*, a reformist magazine; Americans also came to know the lines written by poet Sarah Norcliffe Cleghorn:

The golf links lie so near the mills,
That almost every day,
The laboring children can look out,
And see the men at play.[59]

By 1912, thirty-eight states had adopted child labor laws and in 1916 Congress passed the Keating-Owen Child Labor Act, although not until 1941, with the Supreme Court's upholding of the Fair Labor Standards Act of 1938, would the employment of children younger than sixteen become formally proscribed nationwide.

Keating-Owen was one of many gains for working people achieved during the administration of President Woodrow Wilson. The AFL in particular felt some pride of ownership in Wilson's agenda. In 1906, determined to make itself heard in Washington, it had submitted a labor "Bill of Grievances" to Congress, and in the presidential election year of 1908 Gompers personally traveled to both parties' conventions in an attempt to influence them to include workers' rights in their respective platforms; only the Democrats had agreed to do so. Four years later Wilson was not initially labor's choice for the White House, but as a candidate he wisely responded favorably to labor's overtures, partly at the urging of Louis Brandeis, vowing to oversee a new federal initiative on workers' interests. He entered office with Democrats in control of both houses of Congress and, after his inaugural in 1913, began reaching out to labor as no chief executive ever had, meeting with labor officials to seek their advice and becoming the first chief executive to address an AFL convention. "If securing justice to those who earn their bread in the sweat of their faces constitutes partisanship," Wilson declared in 1914, "then count me as a partisan of labor."[60]

Wilson honored an idea first proposed by William Sylvis and created the Department of Labor, and in alliance with Samuel Gompers brought legislation before Congress that became the Clayton Antitrust Act of 1914, which at long last granted unions relief from abusive injunctions under Sherman, a goal the AFL had pursued doggedly, especially since the unkind setback of *Loewe v. Lawlor*. Gompers hailed the Clayton Act as labor's "Magna Carta," although his enthusiasm proved premature as the law held out several exemptions under which injunctions still could be used, and these were soon exploited. In 1921, the Clayton Act's attempted insulation of labor unions from Sherman was gutted by the Supreme

Court in *Duplex Printing Press Co. v. Deering*, in which the Court upheld the notion that boycotts were a restraint of trade and were subject to injunctive relief.[61]

The Wilson years also saw passage of the Kern-McGillicuddy Act (1916), which established workers' compensation rights, and release of the recommendations of the U.S. Commission on Industrial Relations, a bipartisan panel formed in the waning days of the Taft administration to review the nation's turbulent labor history and offer recommendations. Wilson assigned Frank P. Walsh, a Midwestern labor lawyer and advocate, to lead the commission's extensive hearings; its report, published in July 1915, brought robust cheers from labor (and charges of bias from corporate interests), as the document was highly critical of both large capital and the imbalance of wealth in America. Described by labor scholar Melvyn Dubofsky as "perhaps the most radical document ever released by a federal commission," the report suggested tax reforms and both old-age and unemployment insurance.[62] Citing labor unions favorably as democratic checks on "industrial autocracy," it recommended the federal protection of unions' rights to organize and bargain collectively. Because many of these proposals would be enacted into law by Congress a generation later, historians often refer to the Wilson commission's suggestions as a kind of blueprint for the New Deal. This compliment might be paid to the Progressive Era generally for its confidence that the legitimate rights of workers were integral to the survival and integrity of free market capitalism.

ONE OF THE MORE PROMINENT TESTS for "industrial democracy" came in New York City, where the years 1909–1911 brought a series of challenging labor-related crises. The flowering of the International Ladies' Garment Workers Union (ILGWU) led to a spirited strike by young, mostly female garment workers that became celebrated as "the Uprising of the 20,000," while a horrific fire at the Triangle Shirtwaist Company outraged the nation, awakening it to the desperate need for workplace safety and resulting in the creation of the New York State Factory Investigating Commission. The period would be characterized by stunning displays of union militancy, innovative third-party attempts at collective bargaining, and a determined push-back against the stranglehold of *Lochner*, which had denied legislatures and government agencies a role in labor reform.

The ILGWU, founded in 1900, had both male and female members; in New York the men were skilled fabric cutters and tailors who belonged to Local 10, the women shirtwaist (or blouse) makers were members of Local 25. The factories that employed these workers varied greatly in size, from large enterprises with hundreds on the payroll to small three- and four-person businesses. Given the seasonal nature of fashion retailing and the modest overhead needed to manufacture clothes, many garment businesses consisted of little more than a few sewing machines and a pile of fabric occupying part of a tenement apartment. The industry itself was highly specialized and competitive to the point of being cutthroat. A factory might be charged with manufacturing a single accessory, such as a zipper or a collar, for a particular garment; the smaller enterprises often subcontracted work from larger mechanized factories; thus a manufacturing entity might spring into existence solely to meet the demands of a particular fashion season.

It was the jury-rigged pay system and Byzantine subcontracting practices within the shops that accounted for the name by which these places were known: "sweatshops." The term was not a reference to the temperature in the workplace (although in summer that may have been appropriate), but rather the management practice of "sweating" labor, assigning specific jobs on lots of garments to ever-smaller shops or units within the same factory. Manufacturing costs were "sweated" downward as at each lower level small shop owners, floor supervisors, and the workers themselves negotiated and renegotiated wages and production deadlines. This system pertained throughout the New York garment industry, leaving many workers vulnerable in regard to wages and, due to the fluctuations in demand, with little job security.

Conditions, even in the larger factories, were far from ideal. Hours of work were typically 8 a.m. to 6:30 p.m., with a half hour for lunch, and possibly a half day on Saturday. Salaries ranged from $8 to $13 per week, with the smaller shops often paying on a piece-rate system that had the effect of pressuring employees to work fast and stay late. Workers were routinely charged for the needles and thread they used, and for electricity; some shops expected them to provide their own sewing machine. Seamstresses were crowded in so tightly they worked literally back-to-back, the work areas were poorly heated and ventilated, bathroom breaks were discouraged or forbidden, and there were myriad rules and a system of fines for tardiness, absenteeism, and other infractions, such as smoking or excessive talking. Verbal and physical abuse was not uncommon. Workers also complained of routine condescension, sexual touching, and harassment. There was no grievance system, and complaining about unfair practices could get one not only fired from one firm but blacklisted from the trade completely. No wonder the women, as had their forebears in the textile mills of New England, referred to their situation as "slavery."

About 50 percent of the workers were Russian Jews, another 35 percent Italian. The Lower East Side, where most of the garment business was concentrated, was by 1905 both the most crowded residential area in the United States and the world's largest center of Jewish population; it was, not surprisingly, also a stewpot of intellectual and activist thought.[63] For these immigrants—many of whom had some familiar connection with political or labor agitation in the Old World—the nascent labor movement in the garment industry was a vehicle for assimilation in their adopted land. "The trade union became to the Jews," one historian has said, "what urban politics had long been for the Irish."[64]

In the warm summer of 1909 the young seamstresses, grown impatient with their subjugation in the garment shops, finally rebelled. The strike originated at Rosen Brothers, a company that "sweated" labor by hiring contractors to manufacture its clothes based on the firm's designs and patterns. The contractors worked inside the factory, paying and supervising their own hires. This arrangement allowed Rosen Brothers to not only cut labor costs to the bone but distance themselves from those who sewed and stitched on their premises. The trouble started when negotiations soured on the basic piece rate between Rosen Brothers and its inside contractors, who had little difficulty convincing the workers that a declining piece rate was not in their interest either; both contractors and workers then walked out together. The ILGWU led a five-week stoppage that forced Rosen Brothers to recognize the union, establish a shop floor grievance committee, and grant a 20 percent rate increase. Encouraged by what had occurred, workers struck two of the city's other large clothing factories, the Triangle Shirtwaist Company and Leiserson's.

Triangle employees were upset because the firm had recently created a company union, or "association," to thwart independent union organizing, and the association had been seen to play favorites with its distribution of bonuses to "worthy" employees. When a group of workers met off-premises after work to discuss their grievances, Triangle supervisors discovered who they were and fired many of them, using the excuse that fewer workers were needed as the result of a seasonal work shortage. But when it became known that the firm was making new hires to replace those who had been dismissed, the former workers declared they were being locked out and in late September announced a strike.

As almost all the garment factories shared to an extent the problems that had appeared at Rosen Brothers and at Triangle Shirtwaist, interest in a larger strike became widespread throughout the fall of 1909. Many small operators, having witnessed the ILGWU's resolve in breaking Rosen Brothers, settled almost at once; but Triangle was able to resist by shipping some of its work to its operations in Philadelphia and Westchester County, or farming it out to some of the smaller shops that had settled with the union.

The ILGWU had a critical ally in the Women's Trade Union League (WTUL), a group of middle- and upper-class reformers that *Collier's* magazine described as "a foster mother to women's unions."[65] Founded in 1903 under the auspices of the AFL by William English Walling, Jane Addams, and Mary Kenny (individuals also involved in the 1909 founding of the National Association for the Advancement of Colored People [NAACP]), the mission of the WTUL was to assist the organizing activities of female workers, especially by fund-raising, and to link labor activism to broader women's issues such as suffrage, public education, and temperance. The alliance between the WTUL and the ILGWU united a diverse array of New Yorkers—immigrant garment workers, "uptown" Progressives, settlement house movement reformers like Addams, as well as college students from Barnard and Vassar who volunteered to stand with workers on picket lines outside garment factories.

Picketing was made difficult by the neighborhood pugilists and down-on-their-luck streetwalkers hired by the companies to "protect" replacement workers. Strikers and their allies were often shoved, kicked, and intimidated, although the policy backfired on the factory owners once readers of the daily newspapers began seeing accounts of teen-aged seamstresses being harassed by "gangs of men" who "used their fists against girl strikers," or, in one instance, "hurled a picket to the ground and then stamped on her."[66]

The WTUL tactic of placing college students and women of means on the picket line was intended to grant the strikers some protection; if arrests were made, the WTUL women could witness the workers' treatment by police or perhaps intervene on their behalf in court. But it proved hard to remain above the fray. On November 4, Mary Dreier, president of the WTUL and "a wealthy champion of laboring women in this city," was herself arrested on an assault charge after arguing with a policeman and a female scab named Anna Walla in front of the Triangle Shirtwaist building on Washington Street. Dreier explained that when she informed Walla, "There's a strike in the Triangle," Walla had struck her with her fist. To Dreier's surprise, Walla then complained to policeman Joseph De Cantillon, who placed Dreier under arrest and took her to the Mercer Street station house, where Walla told a magistrate that Dreier had said, "I will split your head open if you try to go to work." Dreier, who was released once authorities realized who she was, told a reporter that the police's preferential treatment of the scabs made her suspect the cops had been "sugared" by the factory owners.[67]

While the police denied Dreier's accusation,[68] detectives hired by the WTUL confirmed that the "roughs and toughs" were being provided by the employers to menace the strikers. Employers defended the practice, complaining that replacement workers were suffering abuse. Max Blanck, co-owner of Triangle Shirtwaist, invited reporters into the plant to meet several young replacements who claimed harassment at the hands of ILGWU pickets. One of the women told the newsmen that a male picketer "had thrown a potato which struck her . . . leaving a bruise that could still be seen if necessary."[69]

At the time, picketing was a fairly new labor tactic, and the WTUL and other sympathizers were pressed to defend its legality. It was in their eyes protected free speech, not trespassing, although employers insisted the strikers' presence before their place of work was aggressive. "You are on strike against God!" one magistrate frustrated by the vagueness of the law bellowed at a young demonstrator hauled before his bench. But the newspapers continued to write sympathetically of the picket lines.[70]

O N NOVEMBER 22, MEMBERS OF THE ILGWU and the WTUL and other city unionists gathered at Cooper Union to consider a broader garment industry strike. As the speechmaking wore on, Clara Lemlich, a young Socialist from the Ukraine and a member of Local 25 of the ILGWU who had helped lead the walkout at the large Leiserson's factory, grew weary of the meeting's "bureaucratic drone." Suddenly she leaped onto the stage and exclaimed in Yiddish:

> I am a working girl, one of those who are on strike against
> intolerable conditions. I have listened to all the speakers, and I
> have no further patience for talk. I am one who feels and suffers
> from the things pictured. What we are here for is to decide
> whether we shall or shall not strike. I offer a resolution that a
> general strike be declared—*now.*

The young woman's dramatic rush to the stage and her bold words had an electrifying effect. The hall rose to its feet, waving hats and handkerchiefs. A seconding motion was quickly passed, to more cheers. Meeting chairman B. Feigenbaum then asked if those present would take "the old Jewish oath," and he intoned in a stern voice, as the assembly repeated each word, "If I forget thee oh Jerusalem, may my right hand wither, may my tongue forget speech." The next morning fifteen thousand garment workers walked off their jobs in a crippling industry-wide strike,[71] an uprising, according to the *New York Times*, "such as never [had] been known since woman entered the Garden of Eden."[72]

Now the street violence intensified. On November 26 "a cyclonic time" was observed before the J. M. Cohen & Co. factory at 189 Greene Street, as female pickets and female scabs tangled; a crowd of onlookers gathered as the girls pushed, tore, and scratched at one another. When police arrived to disperse "the Amazonian attack," they had to rescue the sole male participant, picket organizer Morris Parillo, whose clothes were in a state of disarray and who, according to press accounts, was relieved to have been arrested. Sixteen other people were taken into custody and brought to the Jefferson Market Court.[73] By Christmas 1909 nearly eight hundred arrests had been made, including two teenage girls caught attacking a factory owner with their hatpins; nineteen young women were dispatched to the city workhouse on Blackwell's Island.

These measures against the strikers led the WTUL to coordinate a public meeting at Carnegie Hall on January 2 that turned into a giant pageant, with hundreds of girls who had been arrested and released appearing onstage adorned in white sashes bearing the words ARRESTED or WORKHOUSE PRISONER. When ten-year-old Rosa Perr stood center stage to tell the audience about the police brutality she had seen, sobbing was heard in the audience. Such ILGWU-WTUL gatherings were full of passion and drama, but the alliance was not without some cultural tensions. The WTUL's more socially prominent members, sometimes referred to as "the Mink Brigade" by the young immigrants, tended to see the workers' problems through a feminist or suffragist lens, while the workers themselves remained focused on pay and conditions of work. No one could say the WTUL had failed to garner wider attention for the ILGWU's cause, but some events, such as a lunch at the fashionable Colony Club at which sweatshop girls were brought to speak before society matrons, or a motorcade in large fancy touring cars down Fifth Avenue organized by Alva Belmont, could feel a bit incongruous. Mrs. Belmont, an abundantly wealthy widow who had once been married to William K. Vanderbilt, often came off as surprisingly radical, as when she publicly advocated a general strike in New York of all women workers to support the shirtwaist strikers, an idea that was swiftly squelched by the city's thirteen thousand female teachers.[74] The occasional tensions between the WTUL and the ILGWU were universal, in a sense, the same kinds of cultural differences that have historically hindered awkward reform alliances, but at the heart of the struggle the solidarity of the strikers remained intact. "I have observed many a Jewish girl with her arm around an Italian girl's neck, not able to speak one to the other," one contemporary reported, "but both understanding they are fighting the same fight for each other's interest."[75]

The day after the Carnegie Hall gathering a spirited rally was held at Lipkin's Theater on Bowery and Rivington, after which suffragettes joined garment workers in a march to city hall, a "monster indignation parade" led by the WTUL's Mary Dreier, Helen Marot, and Rose Schneiderman, a former garment worker. Banners bobbed over the marchers' heads declaring PEACEFUL PICKETING IS THE RIGHT OF EVERY WOMAN. While there remained some doubt among the ILGWU unionists as to the efficacy of the ballot, they were open to the pleadings of the suffragists, who argued that all female workers, unionized or not, would benefit when American women obtained the vote. "Our cause is your cause, and your cause is our cause," Anna Shaw assured the workers. "You can't strike a blow with one finger or two fingers, but when you want to strike you put all your fingers together, clinch them hard, and then let drive."[76] The march received extensive news coverage, as did the foray of a five-member committee into city hall for an audience with Mayor George B. McClellan Jr., son of the Civil War general. The women handed McClellan a petition protesting the police department's "flagrant discrimination . . . in favor of the employers," and demanded an immediate halt to the "insults, intimidations, and abuses," to which lawful picketers had been subjected. The mayor listened and vowed an inquiry.

Meanwhile, the roughing-up of young women textile workers continued to pay huge public relations dividends, for while the intricacies of the sweatshop system might remain obscure to the news-reading public, "word portraits" of eighteen-year-old girls manhandled by ex-convicts and police rarely failed to hit home.[77]

Since December, the National Civic Federation had been offering to broker a resolution to the strike. NCF members Marcus M. Marks and John Mitchell suggested a board of arbitration with six members, two from each side as well as two members of the public to be selected by the other four. Additional pressure on the owners to settle came when Local 25 persuaded workers in Philadelphia garment shops to also go out on strike, thus boxing in the New York shirtwaist firms that were using out-of-town factories to avoid bargaining with the ILGWU. Negotiations commenced but broke down ultimately over the issue of union recognition. Both sides cited the cause of *freedom*. The seamstresses saw recognition of the ILGWU as key to their freedom to bargain with employers; the factory owners cited their fear of the closed shop as an undemocratic impingement on their right to freely conduct their business. Eventually the owners agreed to a fifty-two-hour workweek, some paid holidays, shop committees to help set rates and wages, and an end to employee charges for supplies. Because union recognition was not offered, however, the ILGWU turned the deal aside.

But by late January, with their resources drying up, women began returning to work as individual shops cobbled together agreements, and on February 13 the ILGWU officially terminated the strike. Not all objectives had been obtained, but some of the most offensive employer practices had been curtailed and the workers' stature improved overall.

THE ILGWU, WHOSE MEMBERSHIP had grown from five hundred to twenty thousand in only six months,[78] had successfully utilized public opinion, outside reformers, and the linking of workers' rights with issues such as suffrage and urban poverty. But already there was talk of a second strike—one destined to introduce a far more intricate and groundbreaking form of industrial democracy. It would build on the alliances and experiences gained in the 1909 strike, yet prohibit workers from agreeing on separate contracts with smaller shops and insist upon industry-wide recognition of the ILGWU. This massive work stoppage, led by the ILGWU Cloak Makers, began on the morning of July 7, 1910, when seventy-five thousand clothing workers walked off their jobs, not only in New York City, but in upstate New York towns and large manufacturing centers such as Philadelphia and Cleveland.

Filene's Department Store in Boston was not threatened by the strike except indirectly as a purveyor of men's and women's clothes, but brothers Abraham Lincoln Filene and Edward Albert Filene, who had taken over operation of the store from their father, William, in 1901, were intrigued by the tenets of industrial democracy. They had often seemed as interested in the rights of their eight hundred employees as in running a successful business. Indeed, they saw the two objectives as one; only the year before the store had introduced its "Automatic Bargain Basement," a revolutionary concept that would make Filene's a retail legend, while workers at Filene's enjoyed participatory innovations such as an arbitration board in which employees reviewed grievances filed by and against fellow employees, worker control of the lunchroom, and direction of relief and entertainment funds. When the 1910 stoppage in the garment industry occurred, Lincoln Filene reached out to the NCF and various reformers and Boston friends, including attorney Louis Brandeis, who had done some labor management work for the store, in the hope of influencing settlement talks with the New York factory owners.

Brandeis, a Boston native who had attained the highest grades in the history of Harvard Law School, belonged to an emerging breed of lawyers who saw themselves not solely as advocates for their business clients but rather as advising counsel; it made better sense and was more cost-effective to keep companies free of potentially harmful legal problems rather than fight such matters out in court. When in 1910 Brandeis found himself and his family comfortable enough that he could give up paid legal work, he began devoting himself to causes that appealed to his sense of social justice and in which he could be not so much an effective litigant but "counsel to the situation," as he put it, an honest broker between conflicting interests. He had tremendous faith in the idea that there was nothing that could not be resolved in open and constructive dialogue. "Nine-tenths of the serious controversies which arise in life," he once said, "result from misunderstanding, result from one man not knowing the facts which to the other man seem important, or otherwise failing to appreciate his point of view."[79] An article Brandeis would publish in 1911 about industrial democracy bore the apt title "The Spirit of Get-Together."[80]

Brandeis's interest in labor issues dated to the 1892 Homestead strike. At the time he had been preparing lectures for a course he was to lead in business law at the Massachusetts Institute of Technology. Studying the news accounts of Homestead, he recalled, "I saw at once that the common law, built up under simpler conditions of living, gave an inadequate basis for the adjustment of the complex relations of the modern factory system. I threw away my notes and approached my theme from new angles."[81] For the next decade Brandeis's thinking was guided by the concern that law would need to find ways "to keep pace with the new phenomenon of highly concentrated capital—at least if it was to be truly moral."[82] In 1905 he told an assembly of Filene's employees:

> The civilized world today believes that we must adhere to the
> system we have known as the monarchial system, the system
> of master and servant, or, as [they] now [are] politely called,
> employer and employee. It rests with this century and perhaps
> with America to prove that as we have in the political world
> shown what self-government can do, we are to pursue the same
> lines in the industrial world.[83]

An early adherent of the "scientific management" movement, which he had named, Brandeis believed along with its founder, Frederick Taylor, that "prosperity for the employer cannot exist through a long term of years unless it is accompanied by prosperity for the employee."[84]

In 1908, Brandeis had made legal history in a labor-related case before the Supreme Court, *Muller v. Oregon*.[85] Muller, owner of a laundry, had been fined $10 by the state of Oregon for making a female employee work more than the ten-hour day allowed under state law; he appealed the case all the way to the nation's highest court, which affirmed his conviction. In direct contradiction of *Lochner*'s prohibition of the issuance of state regulations regarding the workplace, *Muller* decreed that women's maternal responsibilities made long hours of work potentially injurious and that, as the bearers of children, women workers' physical well-being *was* a matter of public interest, and could be state-regulated. Brandeis's contribution was to file a brief with the Court that included extensive data on the abuse of women workers generally, the first time social science and factual data had been joined to advance a legal argument. The "Brandeis Brief," as it was known, would serve as a model for similar forms of legal advocacy in the twentieth century, most notably in the 1954 school desegregation case, *Brown v. Board of Education*.

Brandeis was eager to help his friend Lincoln Filene in resolving the 1910 cloak makers' strike, but warned that he did not believe in the closed shop the ILGWU was demanding, as he feared such a policy would only tip the balance of power too greatly in favor of labor unions. He made two trips to New York before the ILGWU agreed not to insist on it. Of German-Jewish heritage, Brandeis had expected to find the more recently arrived immigrant Jews from Russia and Eastern Europe timid, easily dominated people. Instead he was awed by the garment workers he met, self-possessed young men and women who managed to be articulate despite their struggles with a new language and who appeared unintimidated by their shop superiors.

To appease those rank-and-file garment workers most loyal to the closed shop concept, Brandeis invited their representatives to join the group of twenty factory owners and ILGWU leaders whom he convened. He suggested that easier matters of disagreement between labor and management be dealt with first, in order to create a sense of collaboration among the participants. When the closed shop topic was finally raised the owners cried foul, for they had thought it was to be off-limits; some union men, dissatisfied with what seemed Brandeis's moderate agenda, also seemed ready to bolt the meeting, but he presented a creative middle position—not an open or closed shop but what he called a "preferential shop," one in which owners would give preference to hiring union men where qualified union hires were available. The owners were willing to accept this, but the ILGWU, caught off guard by the new proposal, abruptly ended the conference. In adjourning, Brandeis asked that the parties maintain those agreements that they had managed to reach in order to have a starting point for a future conclave.

Back home in Boston, Brandeis persisted at tooling with the language of the "preferential shop" to make it more palatable to the ILGWU, even as the union continued to resist the concept. However, pressure on the stalled negotiations grew in early August when the owners announced their intention to start importing replacement workers, who would work under the protection of "special detectives." Fights and confrontations along picket lines had already become a fixture of the strike, and there had been numerous arrests. Unlike the strike of 1909, this time there were no vulnerable young women being harassed, so the ILGWU did not benefit from similar public outrage; instead the media began to criticize the union's obstinacy. The one bright spot was that there was a new mayor in New York, William Jay Gaynor, who was less tolerant of rough police tactics than his predecessor, McClellan. "The world does not grow better by force or by the policeman's club," Gaynor had once said, and he promptly ordered the police to stay away from the strike demonstrations, insisting that peaceful picketing was a protected right.

While the ILGWU cheered Gaynor's stand, the owners reacted by obtaining a temporary court injunction against the ILGWU, complaining that their business premises were at risk from gangs of strikers; the injunction threatened to shatter the pursuit of any agreement. With rank-and-file unionists giving no sign of relinquishing their demand for a closed shop, Brandeis contacted several influential New Yorkers who did extensive business with the garment manufacturers, including banker Jacob Schiff; Louis Marshall, a corporate lawyer and chief of the American Jewish Committee; Herbert Lehman of Lehman Brothers; and banker Felix Warburg. They agreed to at least help get the owners and union men back to the bargaining table.

Once reseated, the group returned to Brandeis's preferential shop idea. It was subjected to extensive comment and retooling before a final, painstakingly worded version won agreement from both sides:

> The manufacturers agree that as between union men and non-union men of equal ability to do the job, they will employ the union men . . . the preferential union shop is a shop in which union standards prevail and the union man is entitled to the preference. This preference shall consist in giving employment to union men as long as they are obtainable.[86]

The union could go away feeling it had won a closed shop, since it was confident it would always be able to supply union workers. But the owners also got what they wanted—an arrangement that was *not* a closed shop and mandated no formal recognition of the ILGWU. When some rank and file continued to resist the agreement and refused to return to work, the judge who had ruled on the injunction declared the strike illegal and banned picketing under its terms. His hand forced by the law, Mayor Gaynor then instructed his police to arrest pickets, which they did as soon as the strikers tested the ban. The ILGWU itself also acted to suppress its more intractable members, taking the strike vote away from the rank and file and instead having two hundred shop stewards cast votes on the Brandeis compromise. On the evening of September 2, the ILGWU voted to approve the preferential shop, which had now been joined to the other agreements Brandeis had obtained in the earlier meetings and which was being called the "Protocol of Peace." In addition to the preferential shop, the protocol set hours and wages superior to what garment workers had previously enjoyed, did away with charges to workers for supplies and electricity, established committees of owners and workers to monitor working conditions and hear grievances, and banned strikes and lockouts for the duration of the contract.

Between the strike settlement of February 1910 and the signing of the "Protocol of Peace" that fall, New York garment workers had managed to make headlong strides within the context of the new paradigm of industrial relations. Their example of solidarity, nonviolence, and use of the conference system had helped stabilize the American workplace; unions, workers, and businesses everywhere would benefit as a result. In early 1911, however, an unimaginable disaster would vanquish the New York garment trade and reveal why Brandeis's accomplishment, and the willingness of labor and capital to bargain cooperatively toward realizable goals, was little more than a promising beginning.

THE TRIANGLE SHIRTWAIST COMPANY was adamant in its resistance to industrial democracy. Staving off the ILGWU through both the 1909 and the 1910 strikes, it had managed to keep its order books filled and its sewing benches manned by young workers, many recent immigrant arrivals. By spring 1911, with the previous two years' labor unrest quieted and business returning to normal, the firm, located in the top three floors of the Asch Building at Greene Street and Washington Place, was operating at full capacity. Because it was nonunion, the shop observed no weekly limits on hours, nor did it grant a half day on Saturdays. So it was that on Saturday, March 25, there were between six hundred and seven hundred employees present in the Triangle factory and its offices when, at 4:40 p.m., a fire, likely the result of a discarded cigarette, started in the corner of an eighth-floor workroom where scraps of unused fabric were collected.

At first the blaze appeared containable. Five precious minutes passed as workers tried to smother the flames before someone called in an alarm, but by then it was too late for an orderly evacuation. Panic ensued as workers tried to flee amid upended sewing machines and tangled electrical wires. The door to the stairway had been locked from the outside, so most attempted to escape by means of the one functioning elevator. The employees in the executive offices on the tenth floor, notified by phone from the eighth, were able to exit from the roof to a New York University law school building next door. Those on the ninth floor were less fortunate. They had the least warning and no way to get out as the fire rapidly engulfed the building's upper floors.

The Triangle's practice of locking the exit doors to the stairway from the outside to deter workers from leaving early, taking unapproved breaks, or stealing fabric was a crucial element in the disaster. The sole elevator, crowded with those trying to flee the eighth floor, never made it to the ninth, where hundreds were stranded. As the fire roared upward through the building, thirty women from the ninth floor, seeing that the elevator was not going to reach them, jumped down on top of the car, where their burned, crushed remains were later found. A lone flimsy interior fire escape proved woefully inadequate, a fire marshal later noting it would have taken three hours to empty the factory's hundreds of employees by that method.[87]

It was several minutes before passersby outside noticed the conflagration high overhead. A policeman, one of the first on the scene, saw a bundle fall to the street and assumed someone in the factory was trying to save valuable cloth from a fire; it took several moments, and the arrival of more "bundles," before he realized they were human bodies. "Oh! They are jumping! They are jumping!" exclaimed two distraught young women who encountered the WTUL's Rose Schneiderman on nearby lower Fifth Avenue.[88] Schneiderman raced to the Triangle in time to see firemen and their machines roar into Washington Place; however, because neither their ladders nor their water hoses reached beyond the sixth floor, the men could only watch helplessly, along with an awed crowd that had gathered, as the people stranded high above climbed out onto the window ledges. Shouted instructions from the firemen were ignored, and would have been futile in any case. Alone, or in small groups, some holding hands, the workers leaped, smoke and flames licking at their clothes from the windows behind them. A few tried without success to grasp the extended fire ladders. So great was the force of the victims' descent that tarpaulins, horse blankets, and other impromptu efforts by firemen below to catch the jumpers had no effect; they fell and lay broken upon the pavement.

"I looked upon the heap of dead bodies and I remembered these were the shirtwaist makers," a reporter lamented. "I remembered their great strike of last year in which these same girls had demanded more sanitary conditions and more safety precautions in the shops. These dead bodies were their answer."[89]

As hellish as were the scenes of carnage on the street, the devastation awaiting police and would-be rescuers inside the factory was overwhelming. Dozens of victims, burned beyond any hope of recognition, were huddled together near the elevator door and by the locked stairway; several had attempted to hide from the fire in a closet. Coins were strewn about the floor, for the young women had received their weekly pay minutes before the fire broke out; some could only be identified by the names written on their pay envelopes. One hundred forty-six people, mostly young women garment workers whose average age was nineteen, had perished.

The next day stunned relatives and survivors mutely examined the lists of the dead and missing. There were numerous Tessies. There was a Gussy, a Fannie, two Yettas, and a Sophie. Julia Aberstein died holding her pay packet, which contained $7.50; a Mrs. Rosen had $352 tied around her ankle inside a stocking; Becky Nerberger, nineteen, of Clinton Street, had leaped from a window, lived a few hours with severe burns and a broken leg, and died in New York Hospital. An unidentified man known as "Number 4" was described as twenty-five years old, smooth shaven, with black hair, a brown striped coat, and black patent leather shoes. "Number 11" was a woman, five feet two inches tall, wearing white bead earrings, white underwear, and a signet ring with the initials T.L. Finally, there were those never to be known, their remains so grossly charred and disfigured, they offered no hope of identification. Relatives crowded the makeshift morgue set up on a pier on East Twenty-sixth Street, where the overtaxed police had been forced to enlist an army of derelicts to help carry in the dead.

The city reeled for days, all other news pushed aside by the disaster, but grief changed to anger as details filtered out about exits that had been locked and inadequate safety measures. The terrible loss of life had been avoidable. "Two of our demands were for adequate fire escapes and for open doors from the factories to the streets," Rose Sabran, a survivor, said of the company's resistance to the strike agreements. "But the bosses defeated us and we didn't get the open doors or better fire escapes. So our friends are dead."[90]

At mass protest meetings the outrage was palpable. "There was a time when a woman worked in the home with her weaving, her sewing, her candle making," declared suffragist Anna Shaw at Cooper Union. "All that has been changed. Now she can no longer regulate her own conditions, her own hours of labor. She has been driven into the market with no voice in the laws and powerless to defend herself."[91]

On April 2 an audience of thirty-five hundred packed the Metropolitan Opera House, rented by the WTUL to memorialize the victims. "I would be a traitor to those poor burned bodies if I were to come here to talk good-fellowship," warned Rose Schneiderman in the day's most forceful remarks. Memorable for her shock of red hair and diminutive height (she stood under five feet), Schneiderman was destined to become the voice of the Triangle Fire's dead. She told the good men and women at the Opera House:

> We have tried you, citizens! We are trying you now and you have a couple of dollars for the sorrowing mothers and brothers and sisters by way of a charity gift. But every time the workers come out in the only way they know to protest against conditions which are unbearable, the strong hand of the law is allowed to press down heavily upon us. . . . I can't talk fellowship to you who are gathered here. Too much blood has been spilled. I know from experience it is up to working people to save themselves.[92]

Better prepared to "save themselves," at least in the short term, were the two owners of the Triangle factory, Isaac Harris and Max Blanck.

Their trial in December 1912 on charges of first- and second-degree manslaughter took place amid still-volatile public sentiment: that the two villains be found guilty and harshly punished was a prospect awaited eagerly by virtually all New Yorkers. Families of the dead were especially riled that Harris and Blanck, in the eighteen months since the fire, had been allowed to carry on with their shirtwaist business, using a building on University Place not far from the Asch Building; they had hardly missed a production deadline.

The most damning charge against the partners was that they had locked the stairway doors in violation of existing safety codes, trapping the victims. Their defense attorney, Max D. Steuer, however, was successful at diminishing the impact of eyewitness testimony in a series of tough cross-examinations, chiefly by suggesting that young immigrant girls were not reliable in their recollections of what had occurred as a result of their sheer panic during the event and their severe emotional distress afterward. Steuer also managed to create sufficient doubt as to whether either Harris or Blanck had known that the stairway doors were locked at the time of the fire.

To universal disappointment both men were acquitted. As one juror, echoing the defense's argument, told a reporter, "I cannot see that anyone was responsible for the disaster. It seems to me to have been an act of the Almighty. . . . I think the girls who worked there were not as intelligent as those in other walks of life and were therefore the more susceptible to panic."[93] In 1915 civil suits against the owners were settled, with the surviving families receiving $75 per victim, although about $100,000 in private donations had also made its way to them.[94]

The catastrophe at Triangle Shirtwaist was one of a number of horrific big-city fires in the early years of the new century—Chicago's Iroquois Theater Fire of 1903; the burning of the excursion boat *General Slocum* in New York's East River in 1904—all characterized by a callous disregard for fire safety and the deaths of hundreds of innocent people. These incidents inevitably prompted speeches and editorials decrying the greed and callousness that permitted such disasters, accompanied by vows of reform that went unfulfilled. Triangle Shirtwaist was destined to be the exception. The cataclysm had demonstrated in ghastly terms the absurd cruelty of the judicial sensibility that had shaped *Lochner*. By shaming business's tired argument that it had the right to police itself, the Triangle Fire became the impetus for one of labor's signature achievements in the Progressive Era, a crusade to enact enforceable laws to curb industrial negligence.

O N M A R C H 2 4 , 1 9 1 1 , coincidentally the day before the Triangle Fire, the New York Court of Appeals had quashed the state's workers' compensation law in the case of *Ives v. South Buffalo Railway Co.*, terming it "plainly revolutionary" for its attempt to place liability on employers in cases of industrial accidents. Anger over the *Ives* ruling was of course intensified by the glaring employer misconduct at Triangle Shirtwaist.

The question at the heart of *Ives*—who bore the responsibility for illness or injury workers received on the job—was as old as the republic. Early-nineteenth-century law governing the relationship between employer and employee had been colored by the ideology of free labor: a hiring was an agreement between independent entities. Employees took the risk of injury as part of this "contract," while employers accepted blame only in instances of extreme company negligence, and then usually with paltry restitution to victims or their survivors. Lemuel Shaw, the New England jurist who in *Commonwealth v. Hunt* in 1842 ruled that labor unions were not illegal conspiracies, decided that same year in *Farwell v. Boston and Worcester Railroad Corporation* that employment contracts clearly left the risk and responsibility for workplace health and safety to employees. This arrangement, Shaw suggested, would help motivate workers to remain alert to workplace dangers. When a job did pose heightened risk, as in mines or on the railroads, he reasoned, the degree of peril would be reflected in higher wages, thus compensating the worker for chancing the hazard. Shaw's views mirrored the contemporary view that the possibility of injury was the understandable danger a free individual accepted in taking a job.[95]

Injured workers might be cared for in union hospitals or compensated by brotherhood funds, or even by irregular funds kept for such purposes by employers, but lawsuits seeking substantial awards had the challenge of proving employer negligence. This was extremely difficult, as potential witnesses to an accident were usually themselves employees and were often intimidated by the prospect of testifying against those who paid their wages. In addition, many injuries occurred due to reasons of worker fatigue or inadequate safety precautions on the shop floor; while this might indict management for maintaining excessive work schedules or allowing unsafe conditions, it often did not meet the higher standard of negligence.

As a result of the revolution in Progressive thinking about the limits of an individual's ability to ward off misfortune, workers' compensation came more fully into its own in the early years of the twentieth century. American social scientists had gone on a fact-finding mission to Europe to investigate national workers' compensation models already in use there, primarily one introduced in Prussia in 1884 by Prince Otto von Bismarck; back home, a 1907–1908 study in Allegheny County, Pennsylvania, funded by the Russell Sage Foundation, known as "The Pittsburgh Survey" and published initially in *Collier's*, examined the whole scope of industrial workplace accidents, focusing on their short- and long-term impact on families. It concluded that most injuries could be linked to some environmental factor within the workplace caused by employer disregard, and even where employers responded sympathetically to the plight of injured workers, it was the survivors and their families who suffered the lasting emotional and financial burdens. President Roosevelt had echoed reformers in urging the passage of state workers' compensation laws, and eventually industry had lent its support as well, attracted by the idea that such programs would allow it to manage its liability as a cost of doing business, minimizing individual injury lawsuits that could be both expensive and ruinous to a business's reputation.[96] Led by Wisconsin, twenty-five states enacted such laws between 1911 and 1921, although labor frowned on the condition that employees covered by the laws had to forfeit their right to sue for damages, and expressed concern that the system, by allowing employers to amortize the financial risks of worker injuries, would not be motivated to improve factory safety. This drawback would be addressed only in the 1930s, when states adopted "experience rating" for workers' compensation insurance, meaning an employer's insurance tab would rise with every accident.

The toll of workplace suffering has always been something of a hidden detail of the American work experience, but never more so than in the years 1880–1910, when as many as ten thousand to fifteen thousand American workers a year perished in on-site accidents, with thousands more injured or sickened, mostly in connection with mine and railroad work. Rail travel today is the nation's safest mode of transportation, but in the nineteenth century, before the coming of uniform codes regarding track gauges, switches, and the introduction of the Westinghouse air brake, it was highly dangerous to both passenger and workman alike. Derailments, collisions, trestle fires, and boiler explosions all contributed to a staggering death toll. In 1889 alone, 8,500 U.S. trainmen were killed on the job; in 1895, 6,450; in 1901, 7,350. Mining accidents—everything from explosions and cave-ins to flash underground fires and poison fumes— claimed almost six thousand men per year between 1890 and 1894, and an average of sixty-six hundred each year between 1900 and 1904. Pittsburgh steel mills also proved dangerous, with as many as three hundred workers killed and two thousand hurt on the job annually during the 1890s.[97]

The first minimal efforts toward worker safety had come in 1867 in Massachusetts, where factory inspections were mandated by law. A decade later the state passed the nation's first specific workplace safety regulations, insisting that guards be installed on textile mill spinning devices to keep women's and children's hands and hair from getting entangled. Several other states followed suit, although enforcement was shoddy, mostly due to the failure of legislatures to provide funding to support the policing of the regulations. Manufacturers, meanwhile, often found ways to bar inspectors from entering their premises, while business-friendly legislators hindered progress by warning that if safety enforcement was too draconian, it would drive free enterprise into neighboring states that had fewer rules.

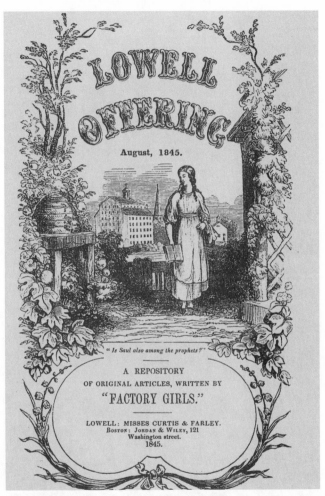

LOWELL OFFERING

August, 1845.

"*Is Saul also among the prophets?*"

A REPOSITORY
OF ORIGINAL ARTICLES, WRITTEN BY
"FACTORY GIRLS."

LOWELL: MISSES CURTIS & FARLEY.
BOSTON: JORDAN & WILEY, 121
Washington street.
1845.

Published by female textile mill operatives, the *Lowell Offering* was hailed internationally as an example of the superior virtues of American industry; but the journal soon expressed concerns about the harshness of workers' lives.

(LEFT) Power-loom weaving on a factory scale as practiced in Lowell and elsewhere in the Northeast in the mid-nineteenth century.

(BELOW) AMERICAN LADIES WILL NOT BE SLAVES: GIVE US A FAIR COMPENSATION AND WE WILL LABOUR CHEERFULLY, read one prominent banner as eight hundred women marched through falling snow in the Lynn shoemakers strike of 1860, at the time the largest organized work stoppage in the country's history.

FRANK LESLIE'S ILLUSTRATED NEWSPAPER

NEW YORK, AUGUST 11, 1877.

(LEFT) "It is Here!" declared a Chicago newspaper of the 1877 railroad upheaval. Vicious street fighting characterized encounters between authorities and strike supporters.

(BELOW) Scene at the Martinsburg, West Virginia, roundhouse, where angry Baltimore & Ohio employees began halting trains on July 16, 1877, precipitating a nationwide strike.

HARPER'S WEEKLY.
JOURNAL OF CIVILIZATION

Vol. XXI—No. 1076.]   NEW YORK, SATURDAY, AUGUST 11, 1877.   [WITH A SUPPLEMENT. PRICE TEN CENTS.

Entered according to Act of Congress, in the Year 1877, by Harper & Brothers, in the Office of the Librarian of Congress, at Washington.

(LEFT) The Maryland militia's Sixth Regiment came under mob assault as it marched to the Baltimore depot in the rail strike of 1877; cursed and spat upon, bombarded with stones and bricks, its troops opened fire, killing ten people.

(BELOW) William H. Sylvis believed that if workers understood the vast power of capital arrayed against them, they would surely join a union. America's first national labor leader, he worked tirelessly to build the Iron Molders International as well as the country's first workers' federation, the National Labor Union.

(LEFT) Terence Powderly found his calling at the Avondale mine disaster of 1869, and went on to become the controversial Grand Master Workman of the Knights of Labor.

(BELOW AND NEXT PAGE) "To arms, we call you, to arms!" The fateful anarchist notices of a meeting to be held in Chicago's Haymarket Square on May 4, 1886, to protest police shootings of workers at the McCormick Reaper plant.

Attention Workingmen!

GREAT

MASS-MEETING

TO-NIGHT, at 7.30 o'clock,

AT THE

HAYMARKET, Randolph St., Bet. Desplaines and Halsted.

Good Speakers will be present to denounce the latest atrocious act of the police, the shooting of our fellow-workmen yesterday afternoon.

Workingmen Arm Yourselves and Appear in Full Force!

THE EXECUTIVE COMMITTEE.

REVENGE!

Workingmen, to Arms!!!

Your masters sent out their bloodhounds — the police —; they killed six of your brothers at McCormicks this afternoon. They killed the poor wretches, because they, like you, had the courage to disobey the supreme will of your bosses. They killed them, because they dared ask for the shortening of the hours of toil. They killed them to show you, 'Free American Citizens', that you must be satisfied and contended with whatever your bosses condescend to allow you, or you will get killed!

You have for years endured the most abject humiliations; you have for years suffered unmeasurable iniquities; you have worked yourself to death; you have endured the pangs of want and hunger; your Children you have sacrificed to the factory-lords — in short: You have been miserable and obedient slave all these years: Why? To satisfy the insatiable greed, to fill the coffers of your lazy thieving master? When you ask them now to lessen your burden, he sends his bloodhounds out to shoot you, kill you!

If you ar men, if you are the sons of your grand sires, who have shed their blood to free you, then you will rise i your might, Hercules, and destroy the hideous monster that seeks to destroy you. To arms we call you, to arms!

Your Brothers.

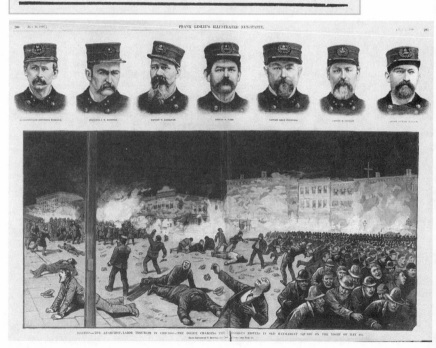

The seven police fatalities of the Haymarket bombing and a sketch of the tragedy's immediate aftermath appeared in *Frank Leslie's Illustrated Newspaper*.

(LEFT TOP) "We *are* peaceable," Samuel Fielden, the last speaker in the Haymarket, tried to assure the police.

(LEFT MIDDLE) "We are called Communists, or Socialists, or Anarchists," said Haymarket defendant Albert Parsons. "We accept all three of the terms."

(LEFT BOTTOM) His death on the gallows moments away, August Spies cried out, "The time will come when our silence will be more powerful than the voices you strangle today."

(RIGHT TOP) Lucy Parsons was an effective radical in her own right, and a tireless advocate for her husband's innocence.

(RIGHT BOTTOM) Hostile anarchist defendant Louis Lingg defied the Haymarket court's verdict of execution by conspiring to take his own life in his jail cell.

(LEFT) Johann Most's urging of revolutionary violence and the use of dynamite led the press to use him for what became the standard illustrated caricature of the bomb-hurling anarchist—full-bearded, crazed, and dangerous.

(BELOW) Daughter of a prominent Chicago family, Nina van Zandt grew convinced of the defendants' innocence, and of her love for August Spies.

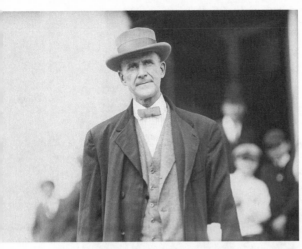

(LEFT) Eugene Debs, leader of the Pullman Strike of 1894 and one of America's best-loved labor leaders. "While there is a lower class I am in it; while there is a criminal element I am of it; while there is a soul in prison I am not free," he said.

(BELOW) "King Debs" caricatured at the height of the Pullman Strike as a petulant man-child thwarting the nation's railways and commerce.

HARPER'S WEEKLY

JOURNAL OF CIVILIZATION

Vol. XXXVIII.—No. 1960.

NEW YORK, SATURDAY, JULY 14, 1894.

TEN CENTS A COPY.
FOUR DOLLARS A YEAR.

(TOP) In July 1892 steelworkers and their families at Homestead, Pennsylvania, stunned America with a brutal, sustained assault against the three hundred Pinkerton agents sent by Carnegie Steel.

(BOTTOM) After the workers' violent rejection of the company's hired Pinkertons, Pennsylvania state militia march into Homestead to restore order.

(LEFT) "Study your union card, Sam," a mentor advised cigar maker Samuel Gompers, later the head of the American Federation of Labor, "and if the idea does not square with that, it ain't true."

(BELOW) Gompers began work as a boy in an urban cigar-making factory similar to the one pictured here.

COPYRIGHTED 1892

"The removal of a tyrant is not merely justifiable; it is the highest duty of every true revolutionist," mused anarchist Alexander Berkman (LEFT), as he headed toward his confrontation with Carnegie Steel's authoritarian Henry Clay Frick (BELOW).

(ABOVE) Striking New York City messenger boys posed on the corner of Sixth Avenue and Thirty-second Street in 1900.

(LEFT) The irrepressible Emma Goldman—intellectual, writer, and revolutionary.

(TOP) Coxey's Army, the so-called "petition in boots" led by the visionary reformer Jacob S. Coxey, en route from Ohio to Washington in 1894.

(BOTTOM) Industrialist George M. Pullman, workers' antagonist in the Pullman Strike of 1894.

(LEFT) "By God, if I decide that these men are innocent I will pardon them if I never hold office for another day," stated Illinois governor John Peter Altgeld in 1893, reconsidering the verdicts of the three living defendants in the controversial Haymarket trial.

(BELOW) "I despise the law and I am not a law-abiding citizen," warned Big Bill Haywood of the IWW, which formed in 1905. "We are the Revolution!" Having lost his right eye in a childhood accident, he made it a practice always to turn his left profile to the camera.

(LEFT) "I don't want to be an actress," proclaimed youthful soapboxer Elizabeth Gurley Flynn. "I'm in the labor movement and I speak my own piece."

(BELOW) Attorney Clarence Darrow, defending Bill Haywood and two others in the 1907 Steunenberg murder trial, assured the jury, "Don't be so blind in your madness as to believe that if you make three fresh, new graves you will kill the labor movement of the world."

Another, more nuanced, management reaction was to co-opt the issue of safety. In 1913 employers, following the lead of U.S. Steel president Elbert Gary, whose industry had been criticized for lax safety standards, founded the National Safety Council (NSC). Its self-appointed mission was to educate workers and the public on workplace (and later home and traffic) safety, but the chief effect of its efforts was to ensure that the onus for job safety and health issues remained with the employee. No representatives of labor were consulted by the NSC or included on its boards. This "blame the victim" approach used posters and brochures to emphasize the risks of worker carelessness, such as putting one's hands inside machinery or leaving buckets where they might be tripped over. The subtext of these NSC campaigns was that employers could maintain a safe factory by reminding workers to be careful and regulating their behavior, making actual government regulations unnecessary.[98]

NEW YORK STATE HAD BEEN UNABLE to prove criminal neglect on the part of the owners of Triangle Shirtwaist, but it was clear even before the acquittals of Harris and Blanck that the real culprit had been the absence of enforceable factory safety measures. The consensus for immediate action to reform factory safety rose at once, and as often occurs after tragedies of such magnitude, objections to reform suddenly appeared trivial and small-minded, even heartless. Signing on to the effort were leading New York City reformers and labor activists, including a petite, outspoken New Englander named Frances Perkins, who ran the New York office of the National Consumers League and had witnessed Triangle's devastation firsthand. Visiting a friend for tea in nearby Washington Square the afternoon of the fire, she had suddenly seen through a window a black plume of smoke rise above the trees of the square, and raced to the scene as victims were beginning to leap from the high ledges of the Asch Building. Perkins was also in the audience at the Metropolitan Opera House on April 2 to hear the "little red-headed girl . . . [with] blazing eyes and pretty too," Rose Schneiderman,[99] dismiss as inadequate the pieties of liberal reformers. Schneiderman had called on the masses to challenge the sweatshop system and its dangers; Perkins's experience,

however, told her it was up to government to transform the modern factory. From her work with the Consumers League, she knew that unions
and employers were almost intrinsically incapable of resolving matters
related to health and safety.

Perkins was a veteran of the settlement house movement, having
worked at Hull House in Chicago, one of the first of approximately four
hundred settlement houses that opened in America by the early years of
the twentieth century. She went on to serve as general secretary of a Philadelphia organization that sought to disrupt prostitution rings in that
city, educating and protecting the vulnerable young women on whom
the rings preyed, before moving in 1909 to New York's Greenwich Village.
There she befriended the writers John Reed and Sinclair Lewis as well as
a young, ambitious city official named Robert Moses, and became active
in the suffrage movement, briefly joining that issue's corps of soapbox
orators.

She soon found a calling and a role model in Florence Kelley, the
dynamic Quaker attorney and reformer who had written the legislation
that in 1893 created the Illinois State Factory Inspection agency, one of
the nation's first. Illinois's early devotion to industrial health and safety
stemmed from its strong tradition of urban reform as embodied in its
governors John Peter Altgeld and Charles S. Deneen, the presence of a
militant core of Progressives in Chicago, and the city's status as a major
rail crossroads and hub of the nation's food distribution system. It was
after touring the Chicago packinghouses that muckraker Upton Sinclair
had published his novel *The Jungle*, shocking American readers with an
account of the industry's unsanitary practices and prompting the passage of the Federal Pure Food and Drug Act of 1906. Like Upton Sinclair,
Florence Kelley was an "impatient crusader"—settlement house worker,
factory inspector, consumer advocate, cofounder of the NAACP, and later
a leading pacifist. When Perkins encountered her in 1902, Kelley was the
executive secretary of the National Consumers League, which she had
founded. The idea of the league, its origins linked symbolically with the
historic refusal of abolitionists to use sugar or wear garments made of

cotton produced by slave labor, was that middle-class purchasers of goods could exercise reformist influence through their buying habits. In the early 1900s, the league targeted child labor and the tenement "factories" where workers suffered from diphtheria, typhoid, and tuberculosis (conditions not good for workers or the consumers who purchased the items they made). The group also provided labels of approval that industries practicing good hygiene were allowed to affix to their merchandise. Kelley had reacted angrily to Harris and Blanck's escape from accountability for the Triangle Fire, wondering

> whether our statistics of the deaths of working people . . . would not move rapidly toward zero if we stopped extending Christian forgiveness to those who . . . lock their doors for fear lest a cheap shirtwaist be stolen, and themselves steal 146 young lives, if we went back to the old Jewish law, which gave an eye for an eye, a tooth for a tooth, a life for a life. If we should apply that law . . . let us see just what lives would be called for if the working class really sent in their bill.[100]

Out of the Opera House meeting devoted to Triangle had come a resolution to carry the demand for immediate action on factory safety to the seat of state government in Albany. A committee was elected, with Perkins as chief lobbyist, to urge the creation of a New York State factory inspection force.

At the legislature in Albany, Perkins went to work converting two young dynamic New York City politicians—Assemblyman Al Smith and Senator Robert Wagner, known by the newspapers as "The Tammany Twins" for their affiliation with Tammany Hall, the city's all-powerful Democratic political machine. Smith, who represented the Lower East Side, had been born on South Street, and as a child had watched the construction of the Brooklyn Bridge; by age fourteen he had left school to don an apron in the nearby Fulton Fish Market. Wagner had grown up in the heavily German Upper East Side neighborhood of Yorkville, the son of a janitor. Along with Smith, he had been tutored in politics by the sachem of Tammany, Charles F. Murphy, although unlike the charming but unlettered Al Smith, Wagner, with the help of his family, had managed to attend law school. Both men were known in Albany for their legislative acumen in doing Tammany's bidding and for their ability to find civil service jobs for Tammany faithful. The families of those killed at Triangle, and the thousands of other New Yorkers who poured into the streets for their emotional public funeral, were largely Tammany constituents.

Perkins, toughened by her experience among Philadelphia street-walkers (she'd occasionally had to personally face down their pimps), understood the rough underside of urban politics and saw the Tammany machine for what it was—a corrupt enterprise, but one that nonetheless served and held sway with New York's immigrant working class. She set out to help awaken its youngest lieutenants to the dire need for workplace safety legislation. "We used to make it our business," recalled Perkins, "to take Al Smith . . . to see the women, thousands of them, coming off the ten-hour nightshift. . . . We made sure Robert Wagner personally crawled through the tiny hole in the wall that gave exit to a step ladder covered with ice and ending twelve feet from the ground, which was euphemistically labeled 'Fire Escape.' "[101] Smith in particular required little convincing. He had made the rounds of the Lower East Side in the days after the Triangle Fire, consoling victims' relatives; he had even toured the morgue where the charred remnants of the deceased lay, an experience he never forgot.

With the able leadership of her new allies and the wind of public outrage at their backs, Perkins and her colleagues pushed through the legislation creating the New York State Factory Investigating Commission (FIC), Governor John Alden Dix putting his signature to it on June 30, 1911, only three months after the Triangle Fire. Mary Dreier was to sit on the commission, the sole woman, while Rose Schneiderman, Frances Perkins, and Clara Lemlich were hired to serve as field investigators under the guidance of Dr. George Price, a well-regarded sanitation and public health authority. Abram Elkus, attorney to the commission, suggested that sanitation and industrial disease would also be examined. Endowed with the authority to subpoena witnesses, demand documents, and hire outside consultants, the FIC quickly became a Tammany vehicle over which Smith and Wagner exercised extensive control; it in turn enhanced their reputations as liberal, moral men willing to use the power of the state to right social wrongs.

With Tammany providing the political juice as well as its star players, the FIC's work garnered approving notices from the press. While the New York FIC was not the nation's first state factory safety endeavor, it became the most prominent and sweeping in its efforts; its determined use of the state apparatus to regulate workplace conditions was seen as the "answer" to Triangle as well as the corrective to *Lochner*, in the very state where the bakeshop laws of the Lochner case had been discounted. There was no denying the commission was impressive in its accomplishments. In 1911 alone it investigated nearly two thousand factories, held public hearings in numerous cities including New York City, Syracuse, Buffalo, and Rochester, and grilled more than two hundred witnesses, creating almost thirty-five hundred pages of testimony. Fifteen new laws were suggested based on the commission's work in just the first year, eight of which were enacted by the legislature.[102]

Understandably, its signature issue was fire safety. FIC investigators found extensive manufacturing taking place in tenement buildings, brick structures with wooden interiors that offered little in the way of fire protection or evacuation measures. Even in more modern sites that housed factories, such as the Asch Building, the FIC discovered that owners tended to be made complacent by a false confidence that their premises, fitted with elevators and constructed of fireproof materials, required fewer precautions. Smith and Wagner pushed through the legislature a passel of fire regulations that mandated automatic sprinklers in tall buildings, the regular removal of flammable rubbish and other materials, doors that remained unlocked and opened outward, regulations governing employee smoking and the use of gas illumination, routine fire inspections and fire drills in firms with more than twenty-five employees, as well as new restrictions on manufacturing in tenement apartments.

The FIC was also active in investigating the "dangerous trades"—

industrial processes that used substances whose effects on workers could be deleterious, such as lead, arsenic, phosphorus, benzene, coal tar, turpentine, and mercury. The commission looked at 359 chemical facilities and found that protection for workers from dust and fumes was virtually nonexistent. Few factories had proper lighting or ventilation. Workers, uninformed about the risks to which they were exposed, toted chemicals in open containers up stairs and through narrow passages with little thought to safety. Non-English-speaking immigrants were often given the most at-risk tasks and had the least understanding of the dangers involved, while employers entertained convenient prejudices—that immigrants from Southern Europe succumbed to contamination because they bathed infrequently, or that Mexican fieldworkers were so childlike and careless it did no good to tell them about the dangers of insecticides.

Here the FIC benefited from the pioneering work of Alice Hamilton, a community and industrial health expert who, like Kelley and Perkins, had apprenticed in Chicago's settlement house movement. Hamilton, inspired by English reformer Thomas Oliver's book about occupational diseases in Britain, *Dangerous Trades*, was among the first Americans to insist that workplace safety went beyond preventing mine cave-ins or hands mangled in power looms but must include a concern for the less obvious risks of industrial poisons, contamination, and disease. Afflictions relating to industrial chemicals were quiet killers, for their effects were often years in developing. In 1908 Hamilton published the first article in America on industrial disease, inspiring Illinois governor Deneen to create a commission to study the problem of trades that used lead, brass, arsenic, and other suspect materials. Hamilton served the commission by investigating such problems in the Chicago area.

"When I talked to my medical friends about the strange silence on this subject in [America]," Hamilton later recalled, "I gained the impression that here was a subject tainted with Socialism or with feminine sentimentality for the poor. The American Medical Association had never had a meeting devoted to this subject."[103] She became recognized for her inquiries into the dangers of lead poisoning and of neurological problems afflicting workers in the hat-making industry due to exposure to high levels of mercury, which was the source of the expression "mad as a hatter."

Hamilton, who ultimately became the first woman on the faculty of the Harvard Medical School, tended to be nonconfrontational toward employers, at least in the early years of her career. She was willing to believe that it was ignorance rather than negligence that kept factory owners from correcting health and safety issues, and that businessmen *were* capable of being educated and would respond conscientiously if given convincing information—a faith she had largely abandoned by the early 1920s when she took on the DuPont Corporation and Standard Oil of New Jersey over the deadly effects on workers of the leaded additive used in ethyl gasoline.

Frances Perkins and the New York Factory Commission's George Price, along with Pauline Goldmark of the Consumers League, also returned to the issues that had been at the heart of *Lochner*. That 1905 Supreme Court decision had rejected the idea that New York State could police sanitation and other conditions in bakeries, but Price and Gold-mark shrewdly transferred the focus from the workers to the consumer, uncovering compelling evidence that urban bakeries, frequently located in basements, were horribly unclean and so foul as to be infested with bugs and vermin. One could only imagine the condition of the bread and other baked goods produced in such environs. The public reacted with strong concern to this type of exposé, much as it had to Upton Sinclair's eye-opening critique of the meat business a few years earlier. So did the business sector, which argued that any new restrictions in the name of bakery sanitation would raise the price of bread, thus destroying the profit margins of small businesses. Still, the FIC won legislation that set minimum standards for the health, safety, and cleanliness of baking facil-ities, including provisions for washup sinks, clean bathrooms, and safe drinking water. Later the FIC turned to issues of child labor, the mini-mum wage, and work performed in the home.

Perkins once observed that the New Deal originated with the victims of the fire at Triangle Shirtwaist. There's no doubt the tragedy was a source of lasting feeling, an emotional touchstone for the labor movement and liberals generally. The memory of the disaster—a city's utter helplessness as teenage working girls fell from the sky to their deaths—would haunt a generation of activists and politicians; many, including Perkins and Robert Wagner, were destined to join fellow New Yorker Franklin Delano Roosevelt in devising the century's greatest agenda of worker reforms.[104]

★ CHAPTER SIX ★

WE SHALL BE ALL

IT WAS LABOR STRUGGLE THAT HELPED KILL off the fable of the Old West. As bloody conflict in Idaho's Coeur d'Alene in 1892 and the uprising of armies of unemployed in 1894 had demonstrated, western workers, despite the region's storied reputation as a place of limitless possibility, where a person might rise on his or her own ability, shared fully the desperation of industrial labor in the cities of the East. Pacific Northwest lumberjacks, harvest migrants in California, Rocky Mountain coal and hard-rock miners, all struggled no less, and almost always in greater isolation, than their toiling brethren in the mills and factories of New England or New York. On June 27, 1905, the two factions—eastern and western labor, 186 delegates representing thirty-four labor unions—came together in the middle of the country in the hope of unifying their cause; in a multiday meeting at a Chicago union hall they founded the Industrial Workers of the World (IWW).

"Big" Bill Haywood, a legendary miner, saloon-brawler, and Western Federation of Miners (WFM) organizer out of Denver, termed the gathering "the

Continental Congress of the Working Class," and surely an observer seeking to confirm the diversity of America's laboring men and women could have summoned no more convincing a scene. Roughhewn types in kerchiefs and cowboy boots from the rambunctious WFM mingled with bookish eastern Socialists and radicals; Eugene Debs of the Socialist Party greeted Mother Jones; Haywood introduced himself to tiny Lucy Parsons, the widow of Haymarket martyr Albert Parsons and now a Chicago labor activist in her own right. Daniel DeLeon, head of the Socialist Labor Party, was in attendance, as were Vincent St. John, a much-admired WFM leader of Colorado miners known as "The Saint," and the Southwest's fighting labor priest, Father Thomas J. Hagerty.

The group made an emotional pilgrimage to the Haymarket martyrs' memorial in Waldheim Cemetery, before returning to the hall to begin work. The goal the participants had set for themselves was nothing less than the reimagining of the American labor movement, offsetting the power of ever-bigger corporations with "One Big Union" that would unite the concentrated yet vulnerable workers in eastern industries with the dockworkers, fruit pickers, miners, and "timber-beasts" of the West. Unlike the AFL, which was a federation of trade unions, or the ARU, which had been an industrial union of rail trades, the IWW was to be a syndicate representing all trades and industries; it would be open to skilled and unskilled workers regardless of race, gender, or nationality; the unemployed would also be welcomed. The movement would wear proudly its class consciousness. "The working class and the employing class have nothing in common," declared the preamble to the IWW's constitution. "There can be no peace so long as hunger and want are found among millions of working people and the few, who make up the employing class, have all the good things in life."[1]

The IWW's embrace of unskilled workers offered a sharp departure from the policy of the AFL, a group the founders of the IWW did not hesitate to rebuke. "The American *Separation* of Labor," they called it, a "coffin society" obsessed with illness and death benefits rather than real change for workers. The AFL, Debs joked, sought "to chloroform the working class while the capitalist class goes through its pockets."[2] Haywood, who had once watched Sam Gompers in action at a WFM conclave, thought it "amusing to see the big broad-shouldered men of the West taking the measure of this undersized individual that called itself the leader of labor."[3]

The AFL didn't hesitate to return fire. Gompers dismissed the IWW's Chicago gathering in the pages of the *American Federationist* as simply the latest futile effort by radical Socialists to "divert, pervert, and disrupt" the American labor movement.[4] "The mountain labored and brought forth a mouse," Gompers quipped of the IWW's emergence, "and a very silly little mouse at that."[5]

The IWW's gadfly delight in tweaking the labor establishment would match its taste for heated rhetoric as it vowed a class struggle that would dramatically transform American society. "I despise the law and I am not a law-abiding citizen," Haywood warned. "We are the Revolution!"[6] The organization's eventual membership, never more than sixty thousand, was slight compared to the AFL's 3 million, but because the Wobblies, as the group became known, favored high-profile, at times theatrical methods, it quickly came to enjoy an outsize reputation. "There was something about the Wobs that made stars sparkle and beam," member Len De Caux recalled, "that raised one's eyes to the heavens."[7] (The precise origin of the term "Wobblies" is uncertain, although it was likely inspired by the two *W*s in the group's name and possibly denoted the IWW's freewheeling style of labor advocacy, which, especially to outsiders, could appear erratic.)

While the IWW was convincing in its stated aim to disturb and unsettle the complacent, it was less precise about what the "cooperative commonwealth" or "industrial commonwealth" it spoke of achieving would actually be like, other than to propose that a syndicate of industrial unions would provide a superior organizing basis for society. This would not be attained by "dropping pieces of paper into a hole in a box,"[8] as the IWW held no faith in the electoral process, nor was the group drawn to notions of industrial democracy or the conference system. Power would be won by "a series of strikes, leading to a general strike which would force the capitalists to capitulate," explains historian Patrick Renshaw. The IWW would be "the embryo of the new society" as well as "the revolutionary instrument for achieving it,"[9] an idea captured in the IWW's version of "The Internationale":

> Arise, ye prisoners of starvation!
> Arise, ye wretched of the earth!
> For justice thunders condemnation.
> A better world's in birth.

> No more tradition's chains shall bind us;
> Arise, ye slaves! No more in thrall!
> The earth shall stand on new foundations;
> We have been naught—We shall be All!

> 'Tis the final conflict!
> Let each stand in his place.
> The Industrial Union.
> Shall be the Human Race.[10]

"You never heard anybody sing the way those guys sang," author James Jones said of the IWW. "Nobody sings like that unless it's for religion." Nor was it possible to entirely dismiss the visions of cataclysmic social change that occupied them, for an actual workers' revolution was at that moment occurring in Europe. The founding of the IWW took place only six months after Bloody Sunday—January 22, 1905—when a peaceful march to petition Tsar Nicholas II for national representation had ended in bloodshed as soldiers opened fire on the protestors outside the Winter Palace in St. Petersburg, killing and wounding hundreds. Infuriated Russian workers staged a national general strike, and sailors mutinied aboard the battleship *Potemkin*, among other disruptions. In an attempt to restore calm, Tsar Nicholas was forced to relinquish some of his authority to an elected parliament and establish civil rights and other reforms. The IWW looked to the possibility that, in America, too, sweeping change might be inspired by the chaos that could ensue through the withholding of labor. Indeed, many of the western veterans of the WFM could identify wholly with the Russian people who had thrown off tsarist rule; they believed that in recent labor fights in the West they had glimpsed the face of capitalism in its most ruthless guise, and that it was as oppressive and inhumane as any Old World regime.

Some crises in American labor history were particularly formative—Haymarket, Pullman, Homestead. In the West a seminal event had been the harsh defeat handed striking miners in Idaho's Coeur d'Alene region in 1892. A Mine Owners Protective Association (MOA) had cut wages and increased hours, and when the Coeur d'Alene Miners Union struck, several mines reopened using scab labor. A Pinkerton agent, Charles A. Siringo, who called himself "the Cowboy Detective," had, under the name C. Leon Allison, obtained work at the Gem mine and infiltrated the miners' union so convincingly he was made its recording secretary. He fed the MOA the kind of sensational intelligence it most wished to hear—that there were anarchists in the union and a plan to destroy the Gem's company store.

In early July news came of the battle waged by the workers at Homestead against the Pinkerton barges; at the same time, internal union information mysteriously turned up in the owners' newspaper, the *Coeur d'Alene Barbarian*, leading to the exposure of Siringo as a Pinkerton spy. The revelation that they'd been duped by one of the breed of villains who had caused the horrors at Homestead infuriated the miners, and their rage was compounded when he managed to escape by hiding under the floor of a boardinghouse. On July 11 the enraged union men attacked the Frisco mine, set off dynamite charges, and took sixty mine guards prisoner; they then turned on the Gem and Bunker Hill mines, "arresting" 130 scabs and forcing them to board a train leaving the state. In response, Governor Norman B. Willey, who had declined earlier MOA appeals for troops, declared martial law and sent to Coeur d'Alene both the state National Guard and federal soldiers obtained by order of President Benjamin Harrison. Willey's attorney general, in his telegram to Washington about the need for U.S. troops, explained that "the mob must be crushed by overwhelming force" and sought "Gatling guns and small howitzers," for "the woods may have to be shelled."

With so massive a military show of force, the mines were soon reclaimed by their owners and scabs allowed back to work under the troops' protection. In vicious reprisals carried out under the martial law decree, whole villages of strikers were rounded up, along with lawyers, bar owners, shopkeepers, even judges—anyone believed to have sympathized with the miners' union. Six hundred were incarcerated in wooden stockades known as "bull pens," lumber stockades with no sanitary facilities, where many spent the rest of the summer in squalid conditions and on a meager diet of inferior rations. Several men were driven to commit suicide. Although the union was ultimately vindicated in a series of court rulings, organized labor was basically decimated for good in the Coeur d'Alene, a formal ban put in place on worker organizing at area mines.

This setback, and the brutal treatment the miners had received in the bull pens, gave rise to the founding of the WFM in 1893. Like Eugene Debs's ARU, the WFM was an industrial union, open to all mine and smelter workers skilled and unskilled. It made provision for the use of full-time organizers to bolster membership and to reach out to miners in even far-flung locales, factors that contributed to the federation's rapid growth. It fought its first hard battle at Cripple Creek, Colorado, in 1894, in a strike in which the MOA tried to overwhelm the newborn WFM with thirteen hundred armed deputies; fortunately for the miners the populist governor, David Hanson Waite, took the unusual step of calling in the militia to roust the deputies from their entrenched positions. In 1896 Ed Boyce, a survivor of the Coeur d'Alene bull pens, took over the federation's leadership, overseeing growth to two hundred locals, making the WFM not only the West's most potent union but America's largest industrial union. The WFM briefly affiliated with the AFL, but departed by 1898 when it became apparent that the larger organization was not going to provide financial assistance.[11]

A more recent example of employer-government overkill in the West had come in renewed violence at Cripple Creek in 1903–1904, when a WFM strike against copper mine owners erupted into a violent turf struggle between miners and scabs. On June 6, 1904, as a train arrived in the local depot to pick up replacement workers, a bomb exploded, killing fourteen scabs and injuring dozens more. Governor James H. Peabody blamed the explosion on the WFM and used the incident as an excuse to declare martial law. The miners professed innocence, accusing the authorities or their spies of having set off the bomb. The militia nonetheless descended on Cripple Creek to arrest large numbers of WFM men as vagrants, while a local vigilante group shut down the local WFM union hall and sacked several cooperative stores the WFM had helped create; at one point the militia leader, General Sherman Bell, arrested the entire staff of a newspaper. The vigilantes then joined with the militia to force the arrested miners out of Colorado.

Confronted by such overwhelming odds in a semifeudal place where corporations controlled state government, the WFM never had the luxury of developing an interest in industrial peace, as had the United Mine Workers under John Mitchell in 1902. The western miners had come to have little faith in the state or the vote, and had been essentially denied the ordinary "niceties" of labor advocacy, whether it went by the name industrial democracy, mediation, or collective bargaining. The answer for such bitter veterans was the action-oriented IWW, which took from the WFM not only its all-embracing membership policy but also its insurrectionary spirit.

"Tell the people who sent you here that I have a brace of Colts and can hit a dime at twenty paces," Father Hagerty had once told a group of harassing railroad enforcers in Arizona.[12] The men and women who departed the historic 1905 Chicago founding of the IWW became fond of quoting Hagerty's quaint warning, for they were determined to emulate his kind of bravado in their own words and deeds.

O N JANUARY 1, 1906, a stranger who had been living in a downtown hotel in Caldwell, Idaho, under the pretense of being a sheep buyer, was taken into police custody and accused of murdering the state's former governor, Frank Steunenberg. The governor had been mortally wounded on a wintry evening a few days earlier when a bomb rigged to the gate of his home exploded. To interrogate the arrested man, who gave his name as Harry Orchard, authorities called in James McParland, the Pinkerton agent who had gone undercover to expose the Molly Maguires in Pennsylvania in the 1870s, and who now ran the agency's Denver office. (He had, in the years since his well-known exploits in coal country, added a *D* to his surname.) Subjected to three days of interrogation by the Pinkerton, Orchard confessed to the assassination, explaining that he had been angry with Steunenberg for having interfered with his effort to secure the fractional ownership of a mine. But Orchard, who was acquainted with the Denver officials of the Western Federation of Miners, had much more to say. At McParland's urging he went on to name a cadre of WFM leaders—including Big Bill Haywood—as having conspired with him in the plot to kill Steunenberg.

The slain governor, a former union printer, had enjoyed a decent record on labor relations until 1899, when he had asked President McKinley for federal troops to help restore order in a local strike dispute. Idahoans might have forgiven Steunenberg for the soldiers' presence, but Washington had dispatched an African American regiment, whose duty consisted in part of guarding arrested miners, who were white. The spectacle of black soldiers "lording it over" white prisoners inflamed local sensibilities, and the governor was held responsible for facilitating such an outrage. But while Steunenberg's gaffe might have irritated some western labor elements, there was no evidence beyond Orchard's allegations that the WFM had anything to do with his assassination.[13] Yet, in a nighttime extradition of dubious legality, Big Bill Haywood, along with WFM president Charles Moyer and George Pettibone, a former miner and businessman who worked for the union, were seized by authorities in Denver (Haywood, according to legend, was surprised at a brothel), hustled aboard a train, and carried across the state line to Boise to face murder charges. The young IWW had thrived in the six months since its founding, establishing no fewer than 384 locals across the country; however, the arrest of its principal organizer in an assassination conspiracy could hardly bode well for the organization's future.

To his admirers, Big Bill seemed to have stepped from the pages of a western dime novel. He was born in Salt Lake City in 1869, the same year the driving of the Golden Spike outside the nearby town of Promontory linked America's railroads. His father, a former Pony Express rider, died when Bill was three, and his mother, who had come west in an ox-drawn wagon, remarried and relocated the family to Ophir, a rough-and-tumble Utah mining camp. At age seven the boy permanently blinded himself in one eye while carving a slingshot (the adult Haywood always turned in profile before photographers so as to hide the deformity); two years later he left school and went to work in an Ophir silver mine. He married young, homesteaded, but was made to forfeit his land when the government reclaimed it to create an Indian reservation. This sent Haywood back to the mines, where, in 1893, he joined the WFM. A year later he fell in with one of the "industrials" of Coxey's Army, although his contingent did not make it east of the Mississippi. A person of keen native sensitivity, he had been deeply troubled by the Haymarket affair, especially the executions of November 1887, and a decade later he watched, inspired, as Eugene Debs's "big union" of the nation's rail workers brought the country to a halt in the Pullman Strike—at least until the courts and troops intervened. As head of his WFM local and a member of the organization's national executive board, Haywood journeyed throughout the western mine regions, conducting union meetings, stealthily evading militia and vigilantes, and going armed to secret midnight conclaves of miners too frightened to greet a WFM organizer by daylight. At the same time he honed his political thought as editor of the federation's journal.[14]

Never a shouting type of agitator, Haywood nonetheless made a convincing impression on the soapbox, especially before an audience of immigrant workers, using his compelling physical presence and a knack for well-chosen words. "Surrounded by a dense crowd of short, dark-faced men, [he] towered in the center of the room," the author John Reed wrote. "His big hand made simple gestures as he explained something to them. His massive, rugged face, seamed and scarred like a mountain, and as calm, radiated strength."[15] To show a crowd of non-English speakers the difference between the AFL and the IWW, Haywood would spread his fingers as wide as he could. "The AFL organizes like this," he would say; then drawing his huge hand into a powerful-looking fist held above his head he would exclaim: "The IWW organizes like *this!*"[16] Big Bill Haywood "believes in men," wrote *Outlook* magazine in vouching for his enigmatic appeal, "not as you and I believe in them, but fervently, uncompromisingly, with an obstinate faith in the universal goodwill and constancy of the workers worthy of a great religious leader. That is what makes him supremely dangerous."[17]

Arriving in Chicago for the founding meeting of the IWW in June 1905, Haywood was already something of a movement legend. He had lived rough in the bracing air of the West, had his land stolen, and used his fists when circumstances demanded; there was a rumor he had once hurled an adversary through a plate glass window. Haywood knew the effect this reputation had on suit-and-tie Progressives, and hardly minded if people thought him ragged around the edges. In an age smitten by President Teddy Roosevelt's celebrated ruggedness and love of the West, "Big" Bill, the one-eyed miner and actual western brawler, seemed more the genuine article than the occupant of the White House.

By the time the Steunenberg trial began in May 1907, Haywood, Moyer, and Pettibone had been held behind bars for a year, while their fate attracted almost daily commentary from the nation's press. "The Molly Maguires of the West," the "radical" trio was termed by one conservative sheet, and even Roosevelt weighed in, denouncing them as "undesirable citizens," an insult to which Haywood publicly objected, insisting he and the others were innocent until proven guilty and that the president of the United States, of all people, should know as much.[18] When Roosevelt refused to apologize and instead heaped more insults on the defendants and, for good measure, upon Eugene Debs, it was the hero of

Pullman who took umbrage, accusing the president of showing "the cruel malevolence of a barbarian" and privately scorning the "Rough Rider" as "a cowboy in imitation." IWW supporters donned I AM AN UNDESIRABLE CITIZEN buttons mocking Roosevelt's remarks, while sympathizers across the country decried the case as political persecution and raised a quarter of a million dollars for the defense, which was to be led by Clarence Darrow.[19] But despite the rallying of support and a widespread faith in their innocence, the stakes for the defendants could not have been greater: if convicted, they would face execution as surely as had the real Molly Maguires and the martyrs of Haymarket.

The first trial was to be that of Haywood, the others to follow. In court, Darrow argued that Harry Orchard had killed Steunenberg as a personal vendetta. He conceded that Haywood had telegraphed WFM lawyers out of concern for Orchard's arrest immediately after the murder, but insisted McParland had worked up Orchard's confession and testimony to incriminate Haywood and the others.[20] Thus the case soon came to hinge on Orchard's credibility, which faded fast as he made a number of dubious claims—that he had blown up mills in the Coeur d'Alene, owned part of several mines, and had burned a cheese factory to the ground—all of which, under scrutiny, appeared to be tall tales. Darrow labeled him "the most monumental liar that ever existed."[21] Even his identity was successfully challenged, as it appeared his real name was Albert E. Horsley and that he had also used the alias Thomas Hogan. After Orchard's lengthy but unconvincing testimony, the prosecution seemed itself to lose faith in its star witness, and, borrowing a page from Haymarket, lapsed into the strategy of reading from left-wing labor papers (including twenty-year-old issues of the *Alarm*) in an attempt to soil the defendants' characters with the repeated recitation of terms like "anarchist," "bomb," and "revolution."[22]

"I don't claim that this man is an angel," Darrow said of Haywood in the defense's summation:

> The Western Federation of Miners could not afford to put an
> angel at their head. Do you want to hire an angel to fight the Mine

Owners Association and the Pinkerton detectives and the power
of great wealth? Oh, no, gentlemen, you'd better get a first-class
fighting man who has physical courage, who has mental courage,
who has strong devotion, who loves the poor, who loves the weak,
who hates inequity and hates it more when it is with the powerful
and the great.[23]

Darrow assured the jury:

Don't be so blind in your madness as to believe that if you make
three fresh, new graves you will kill the labor movement of the
world . . . a million men will take up the banner of labor at the
open grave where Haywood lays it down, and in spite of prisons
or scaffolds or fire, in spite of prosecution by jury, these men of
willing hands will carry it on to victory in the end.[24]

Haywood was acquitted, as was Pettibone; charges against Moyer
were dropped, while Orchard alone took the rap for Steunenberg's killing
and drew a life sentence. The image of the IWW as a dangerous radical
group was, however, now more or less fixed in the public consciousness.

The year of incarceration, the threat of the gallows, then the trial's
daily nip and tuck, had been an ordeal, but Big Bill came out of the
Steunenberg case a famous man, the brash westerner who put working
people's rights above all and who'd now added beating a murder conviction to his résumé. Emma Goldman found the adulation he inspired
among "well-educated literary writers" amusing, noting, "They follow
Haywood much as a bunch of giggling girls go wild over the physical
prowess of a quarterback."[25] (Although his fans supported his innocence, many seemed to cherish the idea that somehow Haywood actually *had* killed Steunenberg.) Turning aside lucrative offers to take to the
vaudeville stage for fear "my prestige would be lessened every day," he
nonetheless toured widely, giving speeches, playing up his reputation as
a "roughneck," and cementing his role as the nation's leading Wobbly.[26]

In Chicago, Milwaukee, and elsewhere he drew rallies only Eugene Debs could rival—twenty thousand, thirty-five thousand loyal listeners quieting to a churchlike hush to hear Big Bill's words.

Despite Haywood's celebrity, the alliance of disparate forces that had convened at Chicago in 1905 to create the IWW did not long adhere. The WFM fell away, much as Haywood himself broke with many old western friends. Debs would play very little part in the IWW, focusing his energies instead on his own Socialist Party, which was hardly idle in the Wobbly era. After abandoning the idea of founding a utopian "socialist territory" in the western United States, the party embarked on an ambitious crusade—sending speakers across the land, running candidates for state and local offices, and reaching immigrant readers through a range of publications such as the *Jewish Daily Forward* and the *Appeal to Reason*.[27] Daniel DeLeon had also departed the IWW, intent on nurturing his Socialist Labor Party.

New members, however, continued to flood into the IWW, and its organizing efforts, characterized by the skillful harnessing of the unified power of immigrant workers, the use of strike reinforcements, and innovative mass actions such as the sit-down strike, scored several key victories. In its negotiations with employers the IWW eschewed the AFL policy of agreeing to no-strike pacts; the Wobblies protected the strike threat, which they saw as a valuable tool in boosting employee morale and keeping management honest.[28] The IWW sit-down strike in December 1906 at a General Electric plant in Schenectady was probably the first in the country's history, while that same year a Wobbly contingent in Portland, Oregon, won a nine-hour day and a wage hike for sawmill employees. In 1907 the IWW realized an impressive $4.50 minimum daily wage for all trades at Goldfield, Nevada, and summer 1909 found the Wobblies assisting eight thousand steelworkers at McKees Rocks, Pennsylvania, in a bloody eleven-week war against the Pressed Steel Car Company, state police, and professional strikebreakers, which eventually succeeded in winning employer concessions.

———

WHAT THE PRESSED STEEL CAR COMPANY and other firms found unsettling in these early IWW struggles was the group's ability to reconfigure the dynamics that usually governed labor-capital confrontation; the Wobblies, instead of becoming worn down and losing focus as a labor fight was protracted, only seemed to gather strength. The organization's national leadership didn't simply monitor the progress of localized strikes, it championed and publicized specific conflicts until they became national campaigns, drawing IWW members from afar to aid a troubled strike—marching, protesting, submitting to arrest. To a dedicated Wob, his IWW dues card good for free passage on almost any moving freight manned by sympathetic trainmen, a labor fight anywhere—on the Minnesota Iron Range or in a California picking field—was the front line. In the dozen years between its founding and America's entry into the First World War, the IWW would display similar grit and adaptability in a number of turf battles in western farm and mining towns, campaigns that began as efforts to expose corrupt labor agents or win improved conditions for workers, but rapidly morphed into hard-fought challenges to restrictions on free speech. The very presence of labor radicals in these communities was often sufficient to spark determined resistance, and not entirely without design, the conflicts proved excellent rallying and recruiting opportunities for the Wobblies.

In Missoula, Montana, in fall 1909 the IWW discovered that predatory employment agencies regularly conned itinerant workers by setting them up with jobs, then arranging with foremen to fire the workers as soon as they earned the fee they owed the agency, thus creating job openings so the deception could be repeated on other unsuspecting workers. Wobblies who spoke out in public against these so-called labor "sharks" were arrested. Missoula authorities, however, were caught off guard by the arrival of one of the IWW's star soapboxers, Elizabeth Gurley Flynn, a teenage prodigy from New York City. Slim, attractive, with sparkling blue eyes and red hair (she was known as "the Red Flame" for both her politics and Irish good looks), Flynn took to the streets of Missoula to rally the depleted Wobbly ranks. With others she devised a strategy to break the town—filling the jails with Wobblies who broke the law by making speeches in public, thus draining the municipality's coffers and overwhelming its administrative resources. As Flynn later recalled, most of the men were more fearful of having to get up and make a speech than they were of being put behind bars, and some had to be prodded to the podium.

The plan was effective. The town fathers were forced to convert the local firehouse into a jail in order to house and feed the growing number of people in custody, and, as envisioned, the community quickly tired of the bother and expense. Missoula agreed to abandon the prosecutions and release the prisoners, saying the Wobblies could make all the radical speeches they cared to give. Some of the released men had the audacity to return to the lockups at night seeking a meal and a place to sleep after a day of organizing; at one point they pounded on the doors to be let in. It was said ranchers from the surrounding area came on buckboards and mules to witness the spectacle of men who wanted to get into jail.[29]

If it was possible to be born a Wobbly, no one personified that ideal more than young Elizabeth Flynn. Reared in an Irish American Socialist family "with its own hagiography, its own radical saints, its own fairy tales of the Haymarket martyrs and the Molly Maguires,"[30] she had "lived" the last hours of Spies and Parsons, memorized the words of Debs, and knew the haunting tale of the condemned Molly Maguire whose handprint, decades after his execution, remained visible on the death-house wall. She devoured Upton Sinclair's *The Jungle* as well as the words of Marx and Engels. Once, at a Mother Jones rally, she became so swept up in Jones's passionate account of labor injustice that she keeled over in a dead faint. ("Get the poor child some water!" barked Jones.)[31] Soon, with her parents' approval, she began giving curbside orations of her own.

At sixteen she was arrested along with her father for lecturing and displaying a red flag in Times Square. The arrest and its resulting publicity—"Mere Child Talks Bitterly of Life"—were more thrill than embarrassment to the girl, and she elected to leave high school to devote her time fully to the cause. Vivid in a simple black skirt, white shirtwaist, and red tie, perched above a crowd on Broadway, she was a phenomenon, preaching the imminent downfall of capitalism. "We gesticulated, we paced the platform, we appealed to the emotions," she later said. "We provoked arguments and questions. We spoke loudly, passionately, swiftly."[32]

In *Broadway Magazine* the author Theodore Dreiser dubbed her "An East Side Joan of Arc," a youngster "as sweet a sixteen as ever bloomed, with a sensitive, flower-like face," but who, "mentally . . . is one of the most remarkable girls that the city has ever seen."[33] Theatrical producer David Belasco was also smitten, proposing to star her in a "labor play." Flynn spurned the offer. "I don't want to be an actress. I want to speak my own words and not say over and over again what somebody else has written. I'm in the labor movement and I speak my own piece." An amused Belasco reflected, "She's the only girl I've ever met who did not want to be an actress."[34]

An early convert to the IWW, Flynn was excited to meet some of the very movement personalities she had long admired—Lucy Parsons and Oscar Neebe of Haymarket fame; Emma Goldman ("a . . . rather stout woman, with mild blue eyes . . . wearing a funny little flat hat and a flower cocked on one side of it"); as well as Alexander Berkman and the Czech revolutionist Hippolyte Havel, who flirted so shamelessly with her over dinner at Luchow's that Berkman had to kick his colleague under the table.[35] A precocious and attractive young woman with the ability to draw crowds (not to mention the press), she was an automatic reproach to critics who would dismiss the Wobblies as bums or anarchists. Known in the IWW ranks as "Gurley," she was accorded near-reverential treatment, it being understood by even the roughest male "Wob" or western "timber-beast" that she be respected and that her personal reputation remain unassailable.

A larger version of the Missoula campaign Flynn had helped resolve played out soon after in Spokane, Washington, where employers' agents routinely hired lumberjacks and produce pickers and dispatched men across the Idaho border to the silver and copper concerns in the Coeur d'Alenes. When the local IWW attacked rigged employment agencies in March 1909 the city council immediately banned the group's speakers. The Wobblies were strong in Spokane, with about fifteen hundred local members, but summer was not a good time for labor organizing in the region because migratory workers tended to be on the move. The union decided to heed the ban and resume the campaign in the fall. Mass arrests began near the end of October, cops infamously pulling one Wobbly off the speakers' platform as he read the Declaration of Independence. Within days almost four hundred Wobblies were jailed, and on November 3 police stormed the local IWW hall, indicting the union organizers they captured for "criminal conspiracy." The Wobblies tried all the methods that had driven the jailers mad in Missoula—singing, banging in unison on the bars of their cells, demanding food—but the Spokane authorities responded with only greater brutality, cramming the prisoners into tighter cells or casting them into unheated rooms without beds or blankets. Many were forced to seek medical treatment during their four months of captivity.

Flynn arrived in spring 1910, determined to break the town the same way she'd humbled Missoula. She was nineteen years old and pregnant. Jailed almost immediately for violating the speech ban, she demonstrated a flair for creative activism by informing the press that female inmates in the city lockup were being forced into prostitution by their jailers. This scandalous allegation, made by an expectant young mother who was herself incarcerated, chastened the city and, at least momentarily, made the IWW appear morally superior. When Flynn came to trial the jury balked at the very notion of convicting her, its foreman assuring the district attorney, "If you think this jury, or any jury, is goin' to send that pretty Irish girl to jail merely for bein' bighearted and idealistic, to mix with all those whores and crooks down at the pen, you've got another guess comin'."[36] Worn down by the expense of arresting, trying, and jailing Wobblies, its spirit drained by the Flynn fiasco, Spokane finally struck a deal with the IWW. The union hall could be reopened, free speech would be allowed, and the employment sharks would be regulated, authorities acting at once to shutter some of the more flagrant operations—an undeniable Wobbly victory.[37]

As Spokane was winding down, another free speech struggle opened in Fresno. The town had long served as the labor source for the surrounding San Joaquin Valley, and ranchers and railroad operators were outraged when an IWW local under the guidance of the renowned western activist Frank Little, who described himself as "half Indian, half white man, all IWW," began organizing workers. After one contractor had difficulty hiring for an irrigation dam project and complained to police, the town denied the IWW a permit to stage public gatherings and warned it would arrest for vagrancy anyone not gainfully employed. Basing their tactics on the success in Spokane, the IWW focused on filling the jails in order to bust the town's resources. Wobblies flooded in from all over the country, bumming rides on freight trains, walking over mountains, trooping along rural byways singing Wobbly songs—or at least so went the legend within the ranks of an increasingly confident IWW. In February 1911, Fresno—like Spokane before it—agreed to meet the union's terms.

These victories, however, appeared to gird reactionary defenses at San Diego, where the next free speech battle was to be waged. All of Southern California was then on edge over radical speech-making due to a notorious case involving a deadly terrorist attack against the *Los Angeles Times*. On October 1, 1910, a mysterious explosion and fire had destroyed much of the *Times* building, killing twenty-one people, several of whom had been found buried beneath rubble at the rear of the partially collapsed structure. The paper's owner was Harrison Gray Otis, a virulent anti-labor man and proud Civil War veteran who had named his own home "The Bivouac" and had designed the newspaper's headquarters to resemble a medieval fortress. At the time of the assault, Otis and his newspaper were leading the fight against a closed shop movement among Los Angeles trade unions. Its first headline upon resuming publication after the fire read "Unionist Bombs Wreck the Times."[38]

The labor movement had come rushing to the defense of the men charged with the heinous crime, brothers John and James McNamara. Eugene Debs, who suspected another frame-up like the Steunenberg case, demanded that "the villainous plot shall not be consummated!"[39] McNamara Defense Leagues sprang up all over the country. Even Sam Gompers extended support to the accused siblings, traveling to California and having his picture taken with them in their jail cell. Defenders of the brothers pointed out that prior to October 1 *Times* employees had complained of a gas leak in the building; some suggested the brothers were being set up so that the paper could evade responsibility for the gas explosion and subsequent loss of life, with the good name of labor to be sullied in the bargain.

The supporters of such theories, and of the McNamara brothers themselves, were to be sorely disappointed. When the trial opened in October 1911 a man named Ortie McManigal, who claimed to be the brothers' accomplice, agreed to testify for the state. James McNamara then admitted to planting the bomb, explaining that his intention was only to terrorize the newspaper owner and editors for their open shop advocacy; he had not foreseen that the bomb would ignite a fire, which may or may not have had something to do with the gas leak. "Well, if I swing, I'll swing for a principle," James conceded philosophically,[40] but defense attorney Clarence Darrow dug in for the fight with his usual diligence, aided by muckraker and California native Lincoln Steffens. Their objective, once James admitted his guilt, was to save the brothers from a death sentence. Los Angeles and the state of California were also keen on not turning the McNamaras into martyrs, fearing that executions would exacerbate already fractious local labor relations. Steffens and Darrow arranged a compromise with the court wherein, in exchange for the men's lives, they would provide full confessions; the McNamaras would admit that, as laboring men, they had been driven to violence by the oppressive nature of capitalism. James McNamara was sentenced to life in prison, John to fifteen years at hard labor.

There was across the country a sense of a trust betrayed. The labor movement had united behind the brothers, pitying their plight and rallying in their defense. The sense of embarrassment was especially acute among those who had sworn publicly to the duo's innocence and raised cash for their defense. And both Darrow and Steffens came in for criticism for having brokered a deal that left the state appearing triumphant over the murderous forces of labor radicalism.

The IWW had been fully in the McNamaras' corner, support that now looked ill-conceived, and this vulnerability likely emboldened the vicious reaction that met the Wobblies in San Diego. Authorities there had in December 1911 prohibited public speaking on a stretch of a downtown street traditionally designated for that purpose, and three months later put an even more comprehensive anti-soapboxing law into effect. For their mutual defense, the IWW and other leftists formed a two-thousand-member local Free Speech League, while the reactionary *San Diego Tribune*, setting the tone for the war that was to come, recommended that "all demonstrators should be shot down or hanged."[41]

First came a brutal nighttime ambush of IWWers riding the rails into San Diego by a small army of vigilantes; then the editor of the *San Diego Herald*, who had written sympathetically of the free speech cause, was abducted, driven out of town, and beaten within an inch of his life. As if local tensions weren't sufficient, Emma Goldman and her business manager, Ben Reitman, arrived in May on a lecture tour. Goldman was by now a notorious radical celebrity, beloved by those sympathetic to her various causes, which included anarchy and birth control, but virulently despised by the rest of the country, partly due to the allegation that she had been an accomplice to Leon Czolgosz, the 1901 assassin of President McKinley.[42]

Goldman was accustomed to drawing crowds, but there was no adulation intended by the mob that greeted Reitman and her at the train depot. "Give us that anarchist," a vigilante mob demanded. "We will strip her naked; we will tear out her guts." Goldman escaped harm with the help of local sympathizers and police, but Reitman was abducted from their hotel that night, stuffed in the back of a car, and taken to an isolated clearing in the woods where he was stripped, tortured with hot tar, and had his body branded with the letters *IWW*.[43]

Not content to merely let some of its residents exact frontier justice on the IWW and other visiting "troublemakers," the city of San Diego appealed to the federal government for help, making the absurd claim that the Wobblies were conspiring to take over Southern California. To appease the city's concerns, President William Howard Taft publicly denounced the IWW but refused to involve the federal government in suppressing the group. Instead, local police allowed the vigilantes to continue and intensify their terrorist assaults; within weeks most of the IWW members had been jailed or chased away.

At San Diego the Wobblies learned a hard lesson: violence trumped even the cleverest radicalism. It was possible to outfox authorities where the rule of law prevailed, where established powers-that-be could be made to appear inadequate and forced to countenance their own hypocrisy; but where vigilantism went unchecked and police were inclined to look the other way or even collaborate, the odds became insurmountable.

THE FREE SPEECH CAMPAIGNS were a dramatic rite of passage for the IWW, but their disadvantage was that the larger goal of labor organizing often receded into the background as members' attention was drawn to defense of the First Amendment and the legal plight of arrested colleagues.[44] The resulting perception—that the Wobblies were scrappy but lacked follow-through—may explain America's rather stunned reaction to the IWW's next act: the successful coordination in 1912 at Lawrence, Massachusetts, of the famous "Bread and Roses" textile strike (named after a poem written the year before by James Oppenheim), one of the more disciplined labor actions in the nation's history. In retrospect, probably no one but the Wobblies could have managed the feat.[45]

Built in the mid-nineteenth century as a model manufacturing town, its numerous large mills hugging both sides of the Merrimack River, Lawrence by 1912 offered a kind of snapshot of urban industrial America. With almost 90 percent of the workers and residents immigrant Italians, Slavs, Belgians, Portuguese, Germans, or French Canadians, the city was a "melting pot," a term that had only recently entered the American vernacular. The strike was triggered by an announcement from the town's largest employer, the American Woolen Company (AWC), that in response to a new state law shortening the workweek from fifty-six to fifty-four hours, all laborers would be forced to accept a weekly pay cut.

Textile work already ranked among the lowest paid in the country. Mill employees at Lawrence earned between $3 and $6 a week; by comparison, steelworkers in Pennsylvania earned almost $14 and even Lawrence's garbage men received $12.[46] Still, the AWC defended the reduction as necessary. Since textile factories in other states were not affected by the new law, the company insisted, "the iron law of competition" meant that without the cut the Lawrence mills would be unfairly disadvantaged. But many workers recalled that a similar law, passed in 1909, had shortened hours *without* reducing pay. Concerned over American Woolen's stance, a small Wobbly local in Lawrence began organizing outside the mills and asked for help from the IWW's national office.

The strike's initial moments were characterized by outrage and anger. On the morning of Friday, January 12, the day when the first pay envelopes reflected the salary cut, workers marched out of the AWC's Washington Mill, crying "short pay." With "the most ungodly yelling and howling and blowing of horns," they then headed to other mills nearby shouting "Strike!" and demanding that other workers "come out."[47] Some of the demonstrators stormed into mills to roust their fellow workers, then roamed the shop floors harming looms and other equipment. At the Wood Mill, one of the city's largest, guards responded to the invasion by shutting off the power; someone then activated the emergency sprinklers, sending water down onto the untended machines. In front of the nearby Duck Mill, the massing strikers cheered impromptu speeches of defiance made by fellow workers, then hurled rocks, chunks of coal, and even their dinner pails at the mill's windows.[48]

The terrorizing of American Woolen's machines and property reflected the workers' long-simmering contempt for its president, William "Billy" Wood, who lived with his family in a mansion in a neighboring town. One of Wood's innovations at Lawrence was a bonus system that paid employees extra for realizing manufacturing quotas. This increased production—the Wood Mill alone processed a million pounds of wool per week into fabric (forcing AWC to build a new facility across the street, the Ayer Mill, to assist with the Wood Mill's output)— but such gains involved stricter rules for workers and the speeding up of the looms. The AWC also had a public relations problem with its own employees, for it was an article of faith among the mill hands that American Woolen had advertised in Europe with posters and even a short film, urging emigration to Lawrence—a place where "no one goes hungry, all can work"—and showing contented workers with satchels of money.[49] The existence of such propaganda has never been substantiated, but the workers of Lawrence believed in it, and so they viewed the treatment they received at the hands of Billy Wood as a promise broken. Their opinion of the Lawrence town fathers was not much higher: in what was touted as a model industrial city, they subsisted in rickety wooden tenements, slums so crowded that on some blocks there were as many as six hundred people to an acre, enduring poor sanitation and lethal rates of diseases such as dysentery, measles, and scarlet fever among their children.[50]

A philanthropic investigation of living conditions conducted just before the 1912 strike mourned the disappearance of the long-ago corporate paternalism that had attended the incorporation of Lawrence in the nineteenth century:

> The mill owners [who] founded the town . . . planned pain-
> stakingly for it and its welfare. . . . The industrial revolution
> had at that time . . . not yet spoiled the feelings of the employers.
> Boarding-houses were maintained or controlled by the
> companies at a low profit . . . for the purpose of preserving a
> proper supervision over the operatives. The attempt was made to
> safeguard not only the physical welfare of the tenants, but their
> moral and religious life . . . [but this] surveillance . . . proved too
> troublesome.[51]

The town had been conceived in the same exemplary spirit as Lowell, but Lawrence's vaunted mutual regard between employer and worker was by 1912 little more than historical legend. The disconnect between the town's boosterish self-image and the reality as lived by the workers extended to Billy Wood, who chose to take his employees' rebellion as a personal betrayal. Sounding, as historian Bruce Watson notes, "more like a jilted lover than a textile tycoon," Wood notified the strikers:

> Last Friday many of you left our mills and have since remained away. This action was wholly a surprise to me. You sent me no notice of what you were intending to do and you stated no grievances and made no demands. I learned from the papers that the reason for your staying away is that the company paid you for only fifty-four hours work.

He did not respond to the workers' demands for a 15 percent pay increase, double pay for overtime, an end to the premium pay for sped-up production, and a promise that no strikers would be terminated for their actions.[52]

Meanwhile, the call from Lawrence's IWW had brought New York–based organizer Joseph Ettor to town. Ettor had visited Lawrence the year before, and was familiar with the basic issues separating workers from the mill owners; he duly arrived prepared for a lengthy stay, lugging his personal effects and a suitcase full of IWW literature. Like Elizabeth Gurley Flynn, Ettor, twenty-six, was something of a Wobbly natural, raised on radical lore. His father had been wounded in the Haymarket bombing, and the boy knew intimately the catechism of history's labor martyrs. "While other children grew up on *Alice in Wonderland* or *Little Lord Fauntleroy*," notes Watson, "Ettor's father told his son bedtime tales from the triumvirate of infamous American strikes in the late nineteenth century—Haymarket, Homestead, and Pullman."[53] Soon Joe displayed his own rebellious nature, abandoning school to join the itinerant world of the bindle stiffs, migrant workers who traveled with their own bedding on their backs. Traversing the West, he toiled on railroads, in steel plants, and in lumber mills before becoming a full-time organizer for the IWW.

Known as "Smiling Joe" for his round pleasant face, Ettor soon had the Lawrence textile workers in hand, his ease with language well suited to the multiethnic town. "His attire," a colleague noted, "with his big soft hat worn jauntily on one side and his big flowing Windsor tie and natty blue suit is suggestive of the pompous bourgeoisie or the artistic Bohemian, although Ettor is neither of these, being sound and substantial in all aspects."[54] These sartorial flashes seemed to be his sole extravagance; as an organizer he was no-nonsense, carefully delegating authority and hearing out strikers' grievances, maintaining detailed lists and charts, and even carrying his own gavel in an attaché case so as to be ready, at a moment's notice, to hammer a meeting to order. In contrast to the brawling and vandalism that had characterized the strike's first days, Ettor counseled discipline and nonviolence; simply staying out of work was the best weapon, he advised, particularly after militia arrived to guard the mills. "I want you all to understand that the cause cannot be won by spilling blood," he told the workers. "Peaceful persuasion is the only weapon advocated from this platform."[55] Ettor saw that the mills exploited the workers' ethnic divisions, so one of his first tasks was to assemble relief committees with representatives from all the city's ethnic groups in order to keep strikers and their families fed.

As Ettor worked, the authorities had also been busy—in ways that were bound to challenge his call for "peaceful persuasion" by the strikers. Massachusetts governor Eugene Foss had sent in the state militia almost at once, and soldiers and strikers faced off daily, often at a canal that separated the business district from the mills. When mounted troops swung their horses close in to the lines in an attempt to intimidate the protestors, one animal appeared reluctant. "You see," an immigrant striker told a mounted soldier, "*horse* IWW."[56] But the confrontation was far from jocular on the freezing morning of January 15 outside the Prospect Mill when militiamen turned a powerful fire hose on a crowd of thinly clad demonstrators; the strikers were furious at the tactic, one they believed was intended not to disperse them but to drench them and make them deathly ill.[57] Later some soldiers jabbed at striking women and children with their bayonets.

Governor Foss suggested strike negotiations and a monthlong labor truce, an idea the mill owners favored as it would at least get the looms moving again, but the IWW rejected the offer, fearing a loss of momentum. "We want no honeyed talk,"[58] cautioned Ettor, although he agreed to sit for a brief chat with Billy Wood, which proved nonproductive. Lawrence mayor Michael Scanlon also tried to intervene. Newly elected on a reform ticket, Scanlon, while an alderman, had helped expose corruption involving his immediate mayoral predecessor, William White, and the town had recently adopted a leaner commission-style government that created several new oversight positions, including a Commissioner of Public Health and Charities to help deal with the poverty endured by the mill workers. For all his Progressive ideas, however, Scanlon was outflanked by Ettor, whose worldview was radical by contrast and more in sync with that of the textile workers. When, in one meeting, Scanlon accused Ettor of stirring up local antagonisms, the Wobbly replied, "I am not responsible for what men do when they have been downtrodden, when their faces have been ground into the dirt so that they no longer resemble human beings." Scanlon conceded the workers deserved better treatment, but asked for less militancy and confrontation. "We have had strikes," the mayor explained, "but we never had to call the police to suppress disorder, let alone send for the people of other cities to help us and employ the militia." At one point he implored Ettor to "take the first train back to New York where you came from," to which Ettor replied, "I shall stay here and do what I can for these people,"[59] a sentiment echoed in a broadside issued by the strikers that declared:

> Our enemies are making an effort to blind the issue by making a cry of "foreigners," "rioters," to which we may reply we were not considered foreigners when we meekly consented to being robbed of our labors and opportunities; we were considered good citizens as long as we were traitors to our best interests.[60]

Ettor also brushed away rumors that the IWW would resort to the use of dynamite to win the strike. "Tell the people not to believe them till they hear the explosion," he said.[61] But the town elders were hardly reassured. They, like most Americans, equated the IWW with violence and the anarchist philosophy of bombing and assassination—the deadly assault on the *Los Angeles Times* was recent news—and on January 20 Lawrence police swept into the city's tenements and seized three stashes of dynamite, together with various fuses and percussion caps. One was found in an Italian's "cobbler shop"; another turned up in a house in the Syrian neighborhood; a third had been left out in plain view at a local cemetery. Several suspicious persons were arrested, including shoemaker Urbano da Prato; Faris Murad, a Syrian tailor prominent in the strike; and Trinidad Bushon, described as a "Porto Rican Negro." Upon the sensational discovery of the explosives, new, frightful rumors spread. "Professional" dynamiters were said to be on the loose, intent on blowing up mills, the police station, the armory, even Billy Wood's house. Rather than be alarmed by the dynamite scare, the striking workers savored the effect the threat had on the city and the mill owners; it was gratifying for once to see the authorities unnerved.

The sense of gathering momentum, the idea that the strike might actually be won, crested on January 24 when Big Bill Haywood arrived in Lawrence. The strikers and their families turned out in droves, lining the streets around the railroad depot in what one newspaper termed "probably the greatest demonstration ever accorded to a visitor to Lawrence." The crowd raised a din at the first glimpse of Haywood,[62] and as a band boomed out spirited tunes, the people swept up Big Bill and carried him through the narrow streets to the speakers' stand in Lawrence Common. There, Haywood looked out over the crowd of expectant immigrant faces—men, women, and children of two dozen ethnicities, backgrounds, and dialects—and to a roar of approval from this new America, exclaimed, "There is no foreigner here except the capitalists."[63]

ITHIN A WEEK THE LAWRENCE STRIKE was transformed by tragedy. The trouble began in the early morning hours of January 29, when workers used ice and rocks to smash windows on streetcars carrying scabs to the mills along Essex Street, the town's main drag. Later that afternoon, as day turned to winter dusk, strikers renewed their protesting, engaging in a verbal scrimmage with police in the vicinity of the Everett Mill. Some workers began hurling snowballs, icicles, and chunks of coal toward the officers, who suddenly rushed the mob. In the tumult a gunshot was heard and Anna LoPizzo, a thirty-three-year-old mill worker, fell to the street dead, shot through the chest.

That same night John Breen, an undertaker who was an ex-alderman and the son of a popular former Irish mayor, was arrested, accused of planting the dynamite found days earlier in what now, it was evident, had been an attempt to frame the strikers and the IWW. It appeared Breen had wrapped one of the stashes of dynamite in a funeral trade magazine from which he had neglected to remove the mailing label for his own business.[64]

The next day, January 30, an eighteen-year-old Syrian named John Rami and his friends threw ice at a group of militiamen, who gave chase; one of the troops poked Rami with his bayonet, attempting only to halt the boy's flight, but the wound proved fatal. When residents demanded the militiaman be detained by police, the city marshal was incredulous. "Arrest him? Why, you can't arrest a soldier for doing his duty."[65]

That evening Ettor was in his room at the Needham Hotel when police burst in, accusing him of involvement in the death of Anna LoPizzo. A short time later they also arrested, on the same charge, Arturo Giovannitti, a Socialist poet and editor of an Italian-language workers' newspaper, *Il Proletario*. Although neither man had been present when LoPizzo was killed, both were held as "accessories before the fact" for having incited the demonstrators. Giovannitti, a former schoolteacher who had studied briefly at the Union Theological Seminary in New York, had joined the strike effort at Ettor's behest only a few days earlier in order to assist with relief operations. A slender, classically handsome man, and an immigrant himself, Giovannitti had been an immediate hit with the town's Italian strikers, speaking a calm and beautiful Italian from the podium and occasionally reading his poems. "Capitalism is the same here as in the Old Country," he told the Lawrence workers. "Nobody cares for you. You are considered mere machines—less than machines. If any effort is made to improve your lot and to raise you to the dignity of manhood and womanhood that effort must come from yourselves alone."[66] A mill worker named Joseph Caruso was also soon taken into custody and charged with being part of the murder conspiracy, even as the police conceded it was unclear who had shot LoPizzo.

For Ettor, a man steeped in the Haymarket case, his and Giovannitti's arrests offered a close parallel to the allegations made against Parsons and Spies et al in 1886, including the detail that the person suspected of committing the crime was unknown and nowhere to be found. The IWW lost no time in denouncing the arrests, which were an obvious attempt to remove Ettor from the strike leadership and keep Giovannitti from replacing him. For two days the town's workers publicly mourned Anna LoPizzo and John Rami. As the two victims were laid to rest, one phase of the strike ended, with a pall over the struggle and its leaders sitting in the Essex County jail. Ettor, in a note smuggled out, consoled his followers that Bill Haywood would return soon to guide the strike.

Haywood, before leaving New York, had a chance to see firsthand the effect news stories out of Lawrence were having on labor sympathizers. He had stopped by unannounced at Carnegie Hall, where a public debate was under way between Emma Goldman and Sol Fieldman. Fieldman, a Socialist who favored engagement in electoral politics, cited the assassination of President McKinley as a troubling result of Goldman's brand of anarchism. Despite the allegation linking Goldman to assassin Leon Czolgosz (which Goldman had always denied and had never been proven), the audience largely seemed to be in Goldman's corner. "Scores of finely dressed women," it was reported, "were every whit as enthusiastic as were the poorer people . . . in their applause" of Goldman's "anarchistic utterances." The program was halted so that Big Bill could speak, and no sooner had he uttered the words, "I am here tonight representing 22,000 textile workers who are on strike in Lawrence, Massachusetts," than the hall erupted in cheers. "The men and women of Lawrence are fighting for their right to live," he added. "They are the persons who clothe you and yet they are the persons who are naked." Buckets were passed for strike donations, and when Haywood implored, "I don't want a man or woman in this audience to go out of this place with more than carfare in his or her pocket," a shower of additional coins and bills rained down onto the stage, Fieldman and Goldman stepping out from behind their podiums to help gather the money. Haywood then left to catch his train, bearing $750 in contributions for the Lawrence strikers.[67]

By the next day he had moved into Ettor's room at the Needham Hotel and assumed many of "Smiling Joe's" duties—meeting with strikers and urging them to avoid violence by keeping "their hands in their pockets." Their strength of numbers alone, he promised, would suffice to win the struggle with the mills. At the same time, some Italian workers came forward with an interesting suggestion. In Italy, they explained, workers engaged in lengthy standoffs with employers had sometimes sent their children to another location in order to lessen the economic burden on their families. None of the Lawrence organizers were aware of this ever having been done in America, but they saw at once its potential usefulness; not only would a "children's exodus" lighten the load on the striking mill workers, many of whom had four or five extra mouths to feed, it would command headlines, calling greater national attention to their plight. The power of children to garner sympathy for labor had been convincingly demonstrated in 1903 by Mother Jones.

When notices appeared in several East Coast cities asking for households that would receive a child from Lawrence for the duration of the strike, the response was overwhelming. Homes were available in Boston, New York, and as far away as Philadelphia. On Saturday, February 10, the first train departed Lawrence for New York bearing 119 children between the ages of two and twelve, chaperoned by Elizabeth Gurley Flynn and Margaret Sanger, the Socialist reformer and birth-control advocate, among others. (Sanger had become impressed with Flynn after seeing her lead a laundry workers' strike in New York in 1911; Flynn had developed an interest in birth control due to the hardships of poor, overly large working families she saw at places like Lawrence.) A directive released by a New York–based committee coordinating the February 10 exodus explained, "The children arriving today come from a city held in the grip of an armed terror. These children have seen the gleam of edged weapons on the streets. . . . [They] are fresh from the battlefield stained with the blood of your fellow-workers."

Five thousand supporters turned up at Grand Central Station to make the Lawrence youngsters welcome. "At 6:50 the searchlight of the electric engine that pulled the train from Highbridge was sighted coming into the train shed," it was reported. "Then the excitement started in earnest. Slowly the hum of 'La Marseillaise' started, gradually gathering in volume. It ended when the train came to a stop and then ensued a series of frantic shouts and yells in a dozen languages. . . . The children were formed in columns of twos, and at a signal from a young man . . . they announced their arrival with a yell:

Who are we, who are we, who are we!
Yes we are, yes we are, yes we are,
Strikers, strikers, strikers."[68]

Sanger later told a congressional committee investigating the Lawrence strike that of the 119 children who arrived on February 10, many were sick and emaciated, only 20 had coats, no more than 4 wore underwear, and very few had hats, most having to protect their ears from the cold by wrapping a scarf around their heads. Volunteer doctors in New York declared many malnourished, noting that in some instances children of seven or eight years of age were so "under-grown" as to appear to be only four.

The youngsters were escorted out of the station to a union hall, where a warm meal awaited. "The hungry children did not need any instructions about disposing of that meal. They ate and ate until they couldn't eat any more," noted the *Times*,[69] which also related:

They have never had so many warm, comfortable clothes. One hundred and twenty pairs of small hands have been covered with as many pairs of warm black mittens . . . and all the children who needed them have been given sweaters. . . . A four-year-old girl from a French family in Lawrence was particularly charming to her New York hosts, throwing her arms eagerly around the neck of anyone she met, declaring "I love you."[70]

The IWW announced from Lawrence that an additional one thousand "strike waifs" were waiting to be sent away, but the exodus was already the subject of criticism from Lawrence's elders, who were furious at the attention the children's crusade was receiving and its implied insult to their town. They challenged the notion that it was really necessary to deport the young people and accused the IWW of using them to gain publicity. A local paper published an article headlined "Spineless," quoting a militia leader to the effect that the Lawrence police had been lax in allowing the children to depart in the first place. All this belated concern for the mill workers' children was hypocritical, of course. "When children quit school to work in the mills, no city official or local employer cried neglect," historian Melvyn Dubofsky points out. "But now that the IWW sent these same children out of Lawrence to good homes with the guarantee of ample food, medical care, and supervision, the owners and the officials screamed neglect."[71]

The printed rebuke of the police, however, had hit home. On the morning of Saturday, February 24, a group of forty-six children was assembled at the railroad depot to board the 7:11 a.m. train to Boston, from where they were to go on to Philadelphia. Town Marshal John J. Sullivan had insisted the previous day that no more children were to be sent from Lawrence, citing an order issued by the city government. The legality of the city's edict was dubious, and the IWW had made sure to obtain the parents' written permission for the children who'd be departing. Some parents had come along to the station, where they learned that Bill Haywood himself would be among the chaperones. As the train arrived, however, police suddenly filled the platform and attempted to corral the children. "When one of these big burleys would lay his hand on a child, of course it would scream," Haywood recalled, "and its mother would fly to the rescue of her captive young."[72] The mothers tried to push the police away. "The hysterical screams of the crazed women and the piteous cries of the frightened children resounded through the train shed," reported the *Lawrence Evening Tribune*. Several women were taken into custody, and were loaded with their children onto a truck for transport to jail. No children were allowed to board the train.

Word of the incident spread instantly, and a crowd swarmed to the jail. The scene there was manic, as children cried, mothers with babes in arms were led behind bars, and angry bystanders shouted at the police. Some who tried to intervene were put down with police truncheons. The officers appeared satisfied to have at last shown their mettle, and the hometown papers were duly impressed. "There were two companies of militia on hand to act if necessary but the police proved themselves equal to the task of handling the situation and the soldier boys were not needed," crowed one afternoon edition.[73]

The Lawrence police had shown they were not "spineless," but as public relations the arrest of little children and their mothers proved disastrous. The *New York Tribune* termed the cops' interference "as chuckle-headed an exhibition of incompetence to deal with a strike situation as it is possible to recall,"[74] while the *New York Sun* worried at the precedent of authority placing "an embargo on the movements of residents of an American community."[75] President Taft was moved to order the Justice Department to make inquiries, while Congressman Victor Berger of Wisconsin called for a congressional hearing and the Metropolitan Opera star Enrico Caruso announced a benefit concert for the Lawrence families.

With the strike about to enter its third month, and the negative publicity connected with the children's exodus tilting public opinion decidedly in favor of the Lawrence mill workers, American Woolen agreed on March 12 to negotiate. Improvements in hours and benefits were granted, and wages were raised by between 5 and 25 percent. New adjustments were agreed to for overtime, and the mills consented to rehire the workers who had gone out. Immediately many other textile mills in Massachusetts, Rhode Island, and New Hampshire, eager to head off labor trouble and nervous about what had just played out in Lawrence, fell in line with AWC's realignments.

The actions of the Lawrence strikers had, it was estimated, won millions of dollars in concessions for their fellow textile mill workers throughout New England. As Haywood assured a festive crowd on Lawrence Common:

> You, the strikers of Lawrence, have won the most signal victory
> of any body of organized working men in the world. You have
> won the strike for yourselves. . . . You are the heart and soul of the
> working class. . . . You have won over the opposed power of the
> city, state, and national administrations, against the opposition
> of the combined forces of capitalism.[76]

The workers deserved Haywood's praise, but so did the IWW, which now claimed sixteen thousand grateful members in Lawrence alone. The strike and relief efforts had been intelligently run and the participants had remained militantly devoted to their objective, a remarkable achievement given that the strikers were not a tight band of skilled trade unionists but tens of thousands of unskilled immigrants from diverse ethnic groups who barely shared a common language. As one mill hand assured a reporter who'd asked his nationality, "I have no country. I am IWW."[77]

CONSERVATIVE ELEMENTS IN LAWRENCE were as alarmed over what had happened in their town as the workers and IWW were exuberant, fearful that the victory over American Woolen by "the off-scourings of Southern Europe" would only embolden those who "will not be assimilated and have no sympathy for our institutions."[78] The Lawrence Citizens' Association, organized during the strike, left no doubt as to its views with an explicitly titled pamphlet, *Lawrence as It Really*

Is: Not as Syndicalists, Anarchists, Socialists, Suffragists, Pseudo Philanthro-pists, and Muckraking Yellow Journalists Have Painted It. The community had been invaded, the association said, by "The Sob Squad"—judgmental New York reformers predisposed to find fault wherever they went.

The *Atlantic Monthly*'s postmortem on the strike scolded the mill owners for their mishandling of the situation, but suggested the real problem was the immigrants themselves, who "collect in such compact masses as to make it impossible to . . . teach them American principles." The growth of such dense foreign populations "in our industrial centers," the magazine warned, "is preparing a very dark problem for the future."[79] The *New York Tribune* likewise voiced concern over "the ease with which an American city . . . may be seized by a gang of outside agitators,"[80] while Winthrop L. Marvin, secretary of the National Association of Wool Man-ufacturers, worried that with the influx of immigrants to America, "there are just enough of these excitable races to furnish the material for . . . mob law, carefully organized in the supposed interest of advanced socialism."[81] The *Atlantic* article ascribed dangerous motives to the Wobblies and com-pared them unfavorably with the AFL, "a responsible body."[82]

Perhaps it was not surprising that the AFL-affiliated United Textile Workers of America (UTW) had been displeased with the IWW's pres-ence in Lawrence, for UTW chief John Golden had once entertained notions of organizing Lawrence's skilled workers. The IWW had pitched a much larger and more inclusive tent, of course, leaving the UTW lead-ership outside; Golden, rather than walk away gracefully, had harassed the IWW throughout the strike, belittling the Wobblies' tactics and even urging skilled workers to remain on the job. *The Textile Worker*, a UTW magazine, had gone so far as to publish a derogatory article titled "Straw-berries and Spaghetti" that listed a number of IWW abuses, including the allegation that Ettor and Giovannitti had lived like royalty while the workers starved, even partaking of a lavish $42 dinner at a Lawrence restaurant.[83]

Nothing damaged the IWW's standing in Lawrence, however, as much as a gaffe committed by its own organizers. During a Labor Day parade in September 1912, months after the strike's conclusion, a contingent of anarchist marchers had raised a banner that read ARISE! SLAVES OF THE WORLD! NO GOD! NO MASTER! ONE FOR ALL AND ALL FOR ONE. Immigrant workers, many of whom were devout, objected to the words "No God! No Master!" (the phrase dated from the French Revolution), but far more troubling was the swiftness with which local conservatives seized upon the offensive display and used it as leverage to destroy the IWW's credibility. As Elizabeth Gurley Flynn observed, "That banner was worth a million dollars to the employers."[84]

The appearance of the slogan was traced to Flynn's lover at the time, Carlo Tresca, an Italian-language journalist who had already managed to irritate local authorities by leading processions each Sunday to visit the grave of Anna LoPizzo. ("You can't have a funeral every Sunday for that woman," the chief of police had complained.[85]) There probably was no more provocative Wobbly than Tresca, whom Max Eastman of *The Masses* described as "the most pugnaciously hell-raising male rebel I could find in the United States." With a speaking voice that "took possession of all outdoors as an organ does of a church,"[86] Tresca aroused powerful sentiment among Italian American workers.[87] But his personal recklessness worried his colleagues; fiercely anticlerical, he had once written letters to Catholic Church leaders in Philadelphia threatening to expose the sexual indiscretions of local priests, even though he'd been jailed in that city for misconduct involving an underage girl.

The "No God! No Master!" uproar had handed the elders of Lawrence the opportunity to win back the allegiance of the town's residents. Local minister James O'Reilly lost no time in organizing a "For God, For Country" parade on Columbus Day that drew fifty thousand people, including most of the community's Italian population. For the event, Mayor Scanlon oversaw the free distribution of thirty thousand American flags and encouraged citizens to affix flag pins to their lapels. Father O'Reilly arranged for a banner to hang across Essex Street above the line of march, reading:

FOR GOD AND COUNTRY
THE STARS AND STRIPES FOREVER. THE RED FLAG NEVER!

A PROTEST AGAINST THE IWW,
ITS PRINCIPLES AND METHODS.[88]

While the massive turnout certainly didn't undo the IWW's achievement in Lawrence, the sense that the Wobblies had shown their true colors as godless agitators had allowed the town to regain some of its former equilibrium. The police, the city, the mill owners, all those who'd come off poorly in the lengthy strike, were able to manipulate the public display of faith and patriotism to reassume their positions as the community's arbiters of law and morality.

At around the same time that Tresca was offending religious sensibilities in Lawrence, the fate of IWW leaders Joseph Ettor and Arturo Giovannitti, along with mill hand Joseph Caruso, was set to be decided in nearby Salem. There, on September 30, 1912, the three went on trial for conspiracy in the murder of Anna LoPizzo. The state had never discovered who had fired the fatal shot, nor had it recovered a murder weapon, but it was convinced the accused men had created the volatile atmosphere in which the shooting had occurred. This of course was the prosecutorial strategy honed at the Haymarket trial; here it was if anything less valid, for neither Ettor nor Giovannitti had used rhetoric as heated as that spoken in Chicago in 1886. More inappropriate was the authorities' insistence on keeping the defendants shackled in an iron cage in the center of the courtroom, an excessive measure the IWW vehemently protested.

There was much that was absurd about the defendants' situation, but the case had to be taken seriously and the IWW accordingly raised a large defense fund. The trial was taking place in a country yet unnerved by the assassination of President McKinley at the hands of an anarchist and the lethal bombing of the *Los Angeles Times*, among other acts of terrorism; the likelihood that radical words might be linked to conspiracy and murder did not seem far-fetched. Many states had been moved by McKinley's death to pass criminal anarchy laws intended in part to muzzle incendiary speech, and courts had shown themselves willing to mete out convictions and harsh punishments in such cases.[89]

Fortunately for Ettor and his codefendants, the holes in the prosecution's case were substantial. The defense was able to establish that the state had used detectives to spy on the IWW, and in cross-examination exposed the fact that one of these detectives, a key prosecution witness, was unable to translate the most basic Italian, even though he had quoted Giovannitti, who barely spoke English, as having made threatening statements. In stark contrast, the defense witnesses—men, women, and even teenage mill hands who testified in a variety of accents—reported that far from urging destruction, Ettor and Giovannitti had consistently admonished the strikers to "keep your hands in your pockets," and assured them their best hope for winning the strike lay in remaining nonviolent. It was also shown that Billy Wood, after meeting Ettor, had praised the Wobbly for advocating a peaceful strike.

Caruso's defense was the most prosaic, his wife, Rosa, displaying a handful of beans to the jury to bolster her testimony that her husband had been at home eating his dinner at the time of the LoPizzo shooting. Others corroborated Caruso's alibi. Several witnesses said it had been a policeman, not a protestor, who had actually fired the shot that claimed LoPizzo's life. Ettor and Giovannitti proved effective witnesses when they took the stand in their own defense. They cited specific events and even the exact words spoken at strike meetings, facts that tended to exonerate them and that could be corroborated by reporters present at the trial.

After the defense rested, Ettor made a Darrow-like speech to the jury, appealing to local pride by recalling Massachusetts's stirring example in the American Revolution and in the cause of abolition. Here again, in 1912, he insisted, decent men were being pilloried for a noble idea that was ahead of its time, one not yet accepted by society—the principle that workers should be treated fairly and were entitled to a fair portion of the profits of their labor. "As I have gone along I have raised my voice on behalf of men, women and children who work in the factories of this country, who daily offer their labor and their blood and even their lives in order to make the prosperity of this country. I have carried the flag along . . . I carry it here today, gentlemen; the flag of liberty is here."[90]

On November 26, after fifty-six days of testimony, all three defendants were acquitted. Onlookers wept and applauded as a court officer returned to Caruso the simple cap taken from his head at the time of his arrest and the relieved mill worker rushed into his wife's arms. Ettor and Giovannitti were whisked outside to meet a crowd of cheering supporters who had nervously awaited the verdict. "There were constant ebullitions of emotion," noted the *Boston Globe* of the celebration that ensued. "Never was there so much male kissing."[91]

News that the three men had been freed received a somewhat more subdued reaction in Lawrence. By now, after nearly a year of strikes, militia, parades, and counterdemonstrations, the town seemed to desire nothing more than an end to the turmoil and a return to daily life conducted out of the nation's headlines. Over the coming decades it would be not the "bread and roses" version of the events of 1912 that the town necessarily recalled—the unity of men, women, and children of diverse immigrant backgrounds organized around basic human needs by a benevolent IWW—but the violence and disruption the Wobblies had brought. When, a few years after the strike, Joe Ettor returned to Lawrence on a visit, he was intercepted by cops and made to board the next outbound train, the community raising not a whimper of protest. Not until the time of the nation's bicentennial in 1976 did younger town residents, curious about the community's history, begin asking the few living survivors of the strike to tell of its meaning.

L EAVING LAWRENCE AND ITS GRUMBLING Citizens' Association behind, the IWW came out of New England after the Ettor-Giovannitti acquittals confident and much admired; in early 1913 it set its sights on replicating the Massachusetts victory in its aid to a strike by immigrant silk workers at Paterson, New Jersey.

Built around the powerful, seventy-seven-foot-high Great Falls of the Passaic River, Paterson was—perhaps with Lowell—the most historic mill town in America, having been designated a planned industrial village, or "national manufactory," by Secretary of the Treasury Alexander Hamilton in 1792. Hamilton and his colleague Tench Coxe wanted the Paterson model, which was to be designed by Pierre L'Enfant, to serve as an example of how manufacturing could be integrated into American life without falling prey to the dehumanizing evils of the English factory system.[92] Although the model town was never built, Hamilton's sense that Paterson's location made it an ideal site for industrial development proved correct. Textiles, milled paper, revolvers, and locomotives were among the products that flowed from the factories along the banks of the Passaic. Paterson was also an early center of organized labor; a strike of women and children textile workers there in 1828 had so distressed manufacturers throughout the Northeast that the expression "New Jersey feelings" became a euphemism for labor unrest. By the late nineteenth century it had even developed its own anarchist subculture; one of its native sons, Gaetano Bresci, after years of shooting empty beer bottles in his Paterson backyard, sailed to Europe and on July 29, 1900, assassinated Italy's King Humbert I.[93]

In 1913 the local silk industry employed nearly a quarter of the town's 120,000 residents. Skilled mill workers were then receiving less than $12 per week, the unskilled about $7, and wages appeared at risk of being driven downward. More women and children (who could be paid less) were joining the workforce; some firms had decamped for Pennsylvania, diminishing the number of available jobs; and new loom technology had been introduced that called upon workers to manage more equipment for the same pay. Eight hundred workers walked out of the Doherty Mills on January 27 after their entire grievance committee was fired for protesting the attempted change from two looms to a three- and four-loom system. Management, arguing that the multiple loom setup was easier to operate, refused to abandon the plan. Walkouts continued, and by March 3 as many as twenty-five thousand were out, affecting three hundred mills. The workers demanded, in addition to modifications to their workload, an eight-hour day and $12 minimum weekly pay, as well as extra wages for overtime.

The IWW joined the struggle. "We were very welcome to the [Paterson] workers," Elizabeth Gurley Flynn remembered. "But we were set upon by the city authorities with vicious fury."[94] Much as San Diego had determined in 1911 to halt the IWW's free speech movement at any cost after it had racked up impressive victories elsewhere in the West, Paterson officials in spring 1913 appeared ready to do whatever was necessary to keep their city from becoming another Lawrence. And unfortunately Flynn and the Wobblies were not functioning at full strength, coming off a smaller labor campaign that had gone sour in New York City just that winter.

It involved an International Hotel Workers Union local, which had broken away from the AFL and appealed to the IWW to lead them. The restraint and good sense the Wobblies had brought to Lawrence, however, seemed nowhere in evidence in New York, beginning with the usually cautious Joseph Ettor advising hotel restaurant workers to sabotage their employers by adulterating the food they served. "If you are compelled to go back to work," he suggested to the waiters and chefs, "go back with the determination to stick together and with your minds made up it is the un-safest proposition in the world for the capitalists to eat food prepared by the members of your union."[95] He then departed, leaving IWW colleagues Flynn and Carlo Tresca to explain away his reckless comment. Flynn, whom the *New York World* cited as "The Girl Captain Who Is Leading a Host of Men in a Great Strike," soon made an equally bizarre gaffe, announcing that the health standards at most hotel restaurants were already so lax, union members needn't poison anybody; they could simply report on the establishments' ordinary kitchen practices, which were unsanitary. Tresca, rather than urge nonviolence, as the IWW had in New England, directed marches of as many as two thousand striking waiters, busboys, and bellboys through the Broadway theater district in which the protestors heckled customers and threw projectiles, often at the doors and windows of their regular places of employ. All these aggressive methods proved detrimental, as outlandish remarks and hooliganism only legitimized police suppression and allowed employers to appear righteous in refusing to countenance workers' demands. The only saving grace from the IWW's perspective was that Tresca usually spoke in Italian, thus hindering reporters from quoting his harsher utterances.[96]

On January 24, 1913, Tresca and Flynn were caught in a police riot that flared suddenly on a sidewalk in front of an IWW strike meeting at

Bryant Hall, just off Times Square. Two police spies had been detected in the audience and Tresca, witnesses claimed, had shouted, "Kill the cops!" Outside a waiting squad of police fell on the strikers as they tried to leave the hall; both Flynn and Tresca were struck with police batons, and Tresca was taken into custody. Angered by his arrest, as many as three thousand strikers then swarmed through Times Square, shattering Delmonico's plate glass window with umbrellas and besieging the Ritz-Carlton Hotel, which, unfortunately for the protestors, turned out to be the residence of Police Commissioner Rhinelander Waldo. Adding embarrassment to injury, during his scuffle with the cops Tresca had dropped a book of poems by Elizabeth Barrett Browning—a recent gift from Flynn in which she had written an affectionate note that read "I love you, Carlo. Thine, Elizabeth"—and she was red-faced the next morning to find a newspaper had reproduced the inscription.[97]

The hotel strike soon was given up as lost. Vague threats about poisoning customers and the smashing of lobby and restaurant windows alienated rather than won public sympathy, and most of the strikers drifted back to work having won no concessions once it became apparent hotel workers who'd remained on the job were simply covering their shifts.

Paterson chief of police John Bimson had followed the saga of the hotel work stoppage in the New York papers and chose to emulate Commissioner Waldo's no-nonsense approach, unleashing his police and raiding strike offices; he placed under arrest not only Wobbly organizers and troublesome mill workers but also reporters and other "anarchist" busybodies who came poking around. No warrants were necessary. "We may be compelled to do things which we would not have legal grounds for doing in normal times," he declared, prompting a number of New Jersey newspapers to cheer that at last Paterson had in authority a man "who has not a cowardly hair in his head." When accused by an irate Elizabeth Flynn of abusing the law, Bimson assured her, "You may have the rights, but we have the power."[98]

Journalist John Reed ventured across the Hudson from his home in Greenwich Village to cover the strike and was almost immediately seized by one of Bimson's cops. He spent four days in lockup, where he encountered Big Bill Haywood, who urged the many imprisoned strikers there to entrust Reed with their stories. Reed then wrote about the experience, and at his behest other Village denizens went to Paterson, including the *Masses* editor Max Eastman, Margaret Sanger, newspaper columnist Walter Lippmann, and saloniste Mabel Dodge (who drove picketers around Paterson in her luxury automobile). Here the engagement of New York artists and intellectuals with the struggles of the immigrant working masses, evident in the Lawrence campaign, came fully into fruition. Because the Paterson silk workers were, as historian Christine Stansell writes, "the bearers of revolutionary purpose," involvement in their cause offered a "kind of politics very different from the slow, methodical efforts of progressives, devoted to changing laws and policies."[99] Assisting the downtrodden workers was inherently meaningful, the workers' strivings complementing the bohemians' crystallizing ideas about the liberation of social relationships and expanded artistic expression.[100] The prosaic features of the strikers' lives—their simplicity, lack of affectation, and extreme poverty—combined with the nobility of their aspirations to create an authenticity so intense it became, with some effort of perception, avant garde.

Chief Bimson refused to issue parade permits to the IWW and the silk strikers, so each Sunday afternoon they held their rallies in the adjacent, more welcoming town of Haledon, which had a Socialist mayor, William Brueckmann, himself a former Paterson silk worker. At Haledon, from the balcony of a farmhouse owned by strike sympathizer Pietro Botto overlooking a large meadow, "a natural platform and amphitheatre," Tresca, Flynn, Haywood, and others preached the gospel of the IWW to as many as twenty thousand workers and their families, who picnicked on the "grassy slopes, eating bread and cheese and drinking wine."[101] Even after Chief Bimson's cops provoked an incident at the Botto house and detained Mayor Brueckmann for "malfeasance and unlawful assembly," the outdoor gatherings continued.

Paterson's mayor, Andrew F. McBride, was having problems of his own with Elizabeth Gurley Flynn. Taking a page from the Lawrence strike, she had complained publicly that the silk strikers' children were going without meals and that they would need to be sent away for better care. Indignant, McBride insisted his city could look after its own, demanding, "Where are your hungry children? Bring them here." Historian Anne Huber Tripp suggests the IWW dropped the plan to stage a children's exodus when Paterson threatened to send the children to the almshouse, but the *American Mercury*, in a flattering profile of Flynn, reported that she did call McBride's bluff, marching three hundred youngsters to the courthouse only to discover the mayor had been forewarned and left town.[102] Whatever actually occurred, Paterson authorities managed to defeat the IWW's goal of gaining publicity from the plight of strikers' children by avoiding Lawrence's mistake of having the police interfere. Some Paterson children were bundled off to sympathetic homes out of town, but with none of the uproar that had attended the process in Lawrence.

The city's mill owners tried two strategic efforts of their own in mid-March. The first was to issue a joint statement calling workers to return to their jobs. It blamed the strike on "professional agitators," suggested the adoption of an eight-hour day would "destroy Paterson industrially," unless adopted nationwide, and defended the three- and four-loom system, warning that "no fight against improved machinery has ever been successful."[103] The other came as a response to a remark by Haywood that one day all the world's flags would be red, "the color of the working man's blood." The owners and the Paterson town fathers responded by declaring March 17 Flag Day, flying the American flag from atop every mill. This attempt to offer their own patriotism as the antithesis of the Wobblies' alien radicalism, and possibly divorce native from immigrant strikers, had been used successfully by employers at McKees Rocks and at Lawrence; in Paterson, however, it backfired, the strikers staging a dramatic march through town carrying their own stars and stripes as well as a banner that read:

WE WEAVE THE FLAG.
WE LIVE UNDER THE FLAG.

WE DIE UNDER THE FLAG.

BUT DAM'D IF WE'LL STARVE UNDER THE FLAG.[104]

As much as local authorities wished to avoid Paterson becoming another Lawrence, an incident on April 19 offered a regrettable parallel. During a stone-throwing fracas between mill detectives and strikers, Valentino Modestino, a husband and father who was not a silk worker and was not involved in the strike, was struck by a bullet and killed. At the moment of his death Valentino had been in the act of shepherding his young daughter off the front porch of their home and out of harm's way. Flynn, who went to the house to assure his family that the IWW would pay for the funeral, found Valentino's grieving widow, in the late stages of pregnancy, lying distraught on a bed in the same room with her husband's open casket.[105]

"I spoke at the funerals of men and women shot down on the picket line and the iron entered my soul," Flynn later wrote. "I became and remain a mortal enemy of capitalism. I will never rest contented until I see it replaced by a government of the people, led by the working class."[106]

I T IS THE CURIOUS FATE of the Paterson Silk Strike to most often be remembered not as an actual struggle for workers' rights, but as a staged representation of one. The idea for what would become known as the Paterson Strike Pageant originated in spring 1913 among the clique of friends that included Mabel Dodge, John Reed, and Big Bill Haywood. Dodge, a wealthy American who had lived in Europe, was a patron of modern art who enjoyed cultivating stimulating friendships. Admitting her own ignorance about radical politics and referring to herself as a "student" of her numerous crusading and literary acquaintances, she hosted "evenings" in her lower Fifth Avenue apartment that brought together Village artists, writers, radicals, and intellectuals including Emma Goldman, Margaret Sanger, Lincoln Steffens, Walter Lippmann, Max Eastman, and Hutchins Hapgood. Dodge "collected people and arranged them like flowers," notes author Christopher Lasch. "She loved to combine people in startling new juxtapositions."[107] The ever-class-conscious Tresca took a harsher view, recalling Dodge as one of those "gentle, restless, well-intentioned, good-for-nothing ladies of the upper class."[108] Many of those, like Dodge, who were working for the silk strikers' cause, were also involved in arrangements for the seminal Armory Show of 1913, which, with its thirteen hundred impressionist, postimpressionist, and cubist works, introduced modern art to America.

As with the Women's Trade Union League and the youthful immigrant seamstresses of the 1909 garment strike, there was always a current of tension accompanying the granting of money, food, and other acts of benevolence to those engaged in the more gritty realities of the labor struggle. The colorful characters Dodge attracted to her home didn't always mix as well as their hostess might have liked. One soiree imploded when Haywood, who was briefly Dodge's lover, became too drunk to explain what syndicalism was; on another occasion he offended the artists present by suggesting that in the "workers' future" *everyone* would have the leisure to try their hand at painting. But it appears to have been Big Bill who asked what might be done to generate wider interest in the strike at Paterson, and Dodge who suggested the answer might be a "strike pageant," although no one disputes it was Reed who was most taken with the idea and proceeded to act on it.

A short time before, John Reed had undergone a moment of personal transformation at the Botto house in Haledon, when during one Sunday afternoon gathering Big Bill cajoled him out onto the speakers' balcony. The former Harvard football cheerleader froze for a moment before the assembled workers and their families below; he was a journalist who covered other people's speeches, not made them himself; but then, on impulse, he began singing, and the people joined in, first "La Marseillaise" and then "The Internationale," as Haywood and others laughed approvingly. The director of the Paterson Strike Pageant had been born.

The pageant idea had not emerged entirely out of the blue. Pageants—public spectacles usually based on historical motifs—were a popular form of mass participatory entertainment in the decade before the First World War. Pointedly democratic, they used citizen-actors rather than professionals, and featured processions or reenactments involving large numbers of men, women, and children in period dress. The trend was British in origin, but notable pageants had been staged recently in Philadelphia and Saratoga, prompting the *New York Times* society pages to declare that "America, Like England, Has Become Pageant Mad."[109] Reed grasped intuitively that the pageant idea fit perfectly into the cross-fertilization of art and proletariat revolution then in vogue among his artistic friends; it would be used by the Wobblies not as an act of civic remembrance but as a vehicle for social justice, in this case the rights of the Paterson silk workers.

The entire enterprise came together in three weeks' time. Reed enlisted John Sloan, artist and illustrator from *The Masses*, to paint the scenery, and other Village supporters to build sets, arrange publicity, and sell tickets; Mabel Dodge helped with fund-raising; planning sessions were held at Margaret Sanger's apartment. Reed wrote the script and imagined the staging, commuting back and forth to Paterson to rehearse the "actors," real silk workers who would portray themselves in the pageant along with selected IWW leaders.

On June 7, Haywood and Tresca led twelve hundred strikers across the Hudson River by ferry to Madison Square Garden. After a buffet of coffee and sandwiches they were put through a hurried dress rehearsal, Reed in shirtsleeves yelling instructions through a bullhorn from atop a stepladder. Outside, at nightfall, electric lights spelled out "IWW" on all four sides of the Garden tower, as a crowd of fifteen thousand filed in to see the once-only performance.

As the lights dimmed, viewers saw the Paterson looms at work, the strikers emerging from the mills singing "The Internationale." Then came the strikers booing a scab, fights between cops and pickets, the death of Valentino Modestino, and the sending of some of the Paterson children to New York–based "strike mothers." The audience was on its feet from the opening and remained standing throughout the show, joining in a reconstituted "May Day parade," cheering the speeches of Haywood, Tresca, and Flynn, and witnessing the re-created funeral of Modestino, with members of his actual family seated front and center to reenact their grief. Four strikers carried the coffin, which was then opened so workers could file past to deposit red carnations, "the red badge of blood-brotherhood." Sobbing was heard in the auditorium as IWW leaders repeated, word for word, the speeches they had given at Modestino's graveside.

Despite some favorable press reviews—"a poignant realism that no man . . . will ever forget"—and the faith among participants that the triumphant zeal of the show might be transferred to the strike itself, the bad news arrived with the financial accounting.[110] After an initial rumor circulated that the event had earned $6,000, it was learned that the night's actual take was only $348. In fact the show had lost $2,000, as many of the tickets had been sold cheaply or given away, and the high rent of the space prohibited the possibility of adding shows to generate income. The expenses had also been formidable; a special train to move the striker/actors to the embarkation point in New Jersey alone had drained the pageant's funds of almost $700.[111]

The silk workers were understandably disappointed. Likely with the encouragement of the IWW, they had allowed themselves to imagine that profits from the show would help carry their families through the summer while they remained out of the mills. Some New Jersey papers immediately compounded the letdown by suggesting that the pageant had indeed made money, but that the earnings had been fleeced by the Wobblies. The accusations were untrue but damning nonetheless; the IWW did look irresponsible as the strike itself lost momentum, its energy seemingly sucked dry by the massive distraction of the pageant's promotion and staging. Elizabeth Flynn was correct in hailing the pageant as "a unique form of proletarian art," probably the first dramatization anywhere of a labor struggle,[112] but even her enthusiasm was dimmed by the messy aftermath. On top of the financial untidiness and charges of corruption, many strikers were upset that they had been left out of the pageant; most had not even had the chance to attend.[113]

"That pageant did it!" exclaimed a Paterson policeman to a reporter.

"After that measly $348 that was handed in for the strike relief fund, watch for a stampede back to the mills."[114] The officer's words were prophetic. By late summer 1913 many of the twenty-five thousand silk workers who had defied the mills and Chief Bimson's police for five months returned to work; having attained none of their demands, they resigned themselves to accommodating the new multiloom system.

The nation's conservative press alighted with talons extended, ripping the IWW as dreamy revolutionaries good at propaganda but incapable of providing the real leadership sought by the poor workers they professed to esteem. Largely unremarked upon at the time was the likelihood that the planners of the pageant had known full well that the event would be lucky to break even, but had plunged ahead anyway because they had become devoted to it as an artistic endeavor. For radicals relegated most often to speech-making and organizing on behalf of others, the pageant was a singular opportunity to invest themselves and their talents in the labor struggle directly.[115] Mounting the pageant, however, meant that the IWW, no different from other elements in society, could appear to savor radicalism as theater and tabloid sensation, with the added potential for disgrace if, as had now occurred, the actual objective of aiding the silk workers was somehow fumbled and lost.

Extensive finger-pointing ensued within the IWW. Flynn seemed to feel the Village artists and intellectuals had hijacked the strike with their pageant, while Sanger thought the IWW itself had been uncharacteristically timid, hiding from Chief Bimson in the safe haven of Haledon when it should have been fighting it out with his minions on the streets of Paterson and filling its jails if necessary.[116] "We are to the labor movement what the high diver is to the circus," wrote another disaffected Wobbly, Ben Williams. "A sensation, marvelous and ever thrilling, we attract the crowds. We give them thrills; we do hair-raising stunts . . . [but] as far as making Industrial Unionism fit the everyday life of the workers we have failed miserably."[117] *Il Proletario*, the Italian workers' sheet, perhaps achieved the wisest overview, suggesting that "the Paterson strike . . . teaches one lesson . . . that there is no 'cocksure' method yet devised or devisable under the present system by which a strike can be won, when the workers are confronted by capitalists of unlimited wealth and viciousness."[118]

John Reed, the event's driving force, writes a biographer, "eventually did come to understand that the battle of an industrial union to win recognition was too immense a problem to be solved by a theatrical performance."[119] For the moment, however, he simply felt unwell, and it was reported he intended to depart New York in order to convalesce.[120] On June 19 he boarded a liner for Europe in the company of Mabel Dodge, with whom he was to spend the summer in Florence, Italy. Big Bill Haywood left soon after for Provincetown to recuperate from an ulcer, and then also went on to Europe. The appearance of a hasty exit by both men from the dissatisfying experience of Paterson was perhaps unavoidable, and would be remarked upon by many, including the silk workers now left to their own fate.

T HE LABOR WAR AT PATERSON and the pageant had been waged under the full gaze of the big-city press. But there were other workers' battles being fought far from the nation's view, in places where even the most dogged news reporter rarely went in search of a story. One such locale was the remote, underpopulated southeast corner of Colorado, where John D. Rockefeller Jr. operated the Colorado Fuel and Iron Company (CFI). Before 1913–1914 few if any outsiders let alone journalists came here, no one to notice the extent to which the CFI and several smaller mine owners—Rocky Mountain Fuel, Victor-American Fuel, and Primrose Coal, among others—exerted complete feudal control over the region's coal miners, its communities, and its laws. This sense of a fiefdom-in-isolation had once prompted the WFM's Charles Moyer to ask on the front page of a labor newspaper, "Is Colorado in America?" But the state and its hard-scrabble mining towns were about to lose their long-preserved anonymity.

The United Mine Workers had dispatched organizers in 1913 to offer a "river of friendship" and support for the miners in southeast Colorado, most of whom were recent immigrants.[121] The workers' goals were straightforward—better wages and working conditions, regular payment of wages, the fair weighing of the coal they dug, and the right to buy dry goods where they chose rather than at the company store. What they and the UMW found frustrating was that the state of Colorado had mine reform laws on the books mandating an eight-hour day, semimonthly wages, and a prohibition against the use of company scrip, rules routinely ignored by the mine owners, who defended the policy of doling out miners' pay as they saw fit as a means of keeping the workers from squandering the money in saloons and brothels. It was this total control exercised by the company over their lives that grated most on the miners and their families. John Reed, who toured the area in 1914, found no sweeping revolutionary dogma at work:

> [The strikers] do not want to . . . destroy the wage system;
> industrial democracy means nothing to them. . . . They had
> come to America eager for the things that the Statue of Liberty
> in New York harbor seemed to promise. . . . They wanted to obey
> the laws. But the first thing they discovered was that the boss, in
> whom they trusted, insolently broke the laws.[122]

Rockefeller remained unbending in the attitude that he could ignore the UMW, couching his position as a defense of the open shop. He threatened to shutter the mine operations and "lose all the millions invested" before he would allow "American workmen [to] be deprived of their right, under the Constitution, to work for whom they please."[123] The only son of financier John D. Rockefeller, he had taken on the CFI assignment as a matter of family trust, and had never visited the site of the company's Colorado operations. Knowing little about coal mining or labor-management issues, he was completely reliant for guidance on the executives stationed there, President L. M. Bowers and Superintendent E. H. Weizel, both firm antiunion men. Rockefeller's allusion to the U.S. Constitution in the context of CFI was curious, insomuch as Colorado governor Elias M. Ammons had acknowledged publicly that that revered document was considered not to be in force in CFI's mining domain, as

CFI "owned all [the] houses, schools, saloons, churches and stores; hired all [the] teachers, doctors and ministers; [and] picked all [the] judges, coroners, sheriffs and marshals."[124] Corporate control in CFI territory went literally right to the lip of the grave, for the local coroner, who was in the employ of the mine owners, was also the undertaker, and the "coroner's juries" he convened to examine on-the-job deaths were appointed by the companies. In five years of deadly cave-ins, explosions, and other mine catastrophes, he had in only one instance rendered a verdict casting blame on a mine operator.[125]

As the UMW continued to build a presence in the region, the mining companies reaffirmed their alliance with Rockefeller, who stood by his vow to forfeit his investment in the coal region before he would recognize any miners' union. There would be no negotiation. The CFI and other employers also began importing crates of rifles, machine guns, and ammunition, and hired company guards, some of whom worked for the Baldwin-Felts Detective Agency, to intimidate union workers and serve as potential "scab-herders," guarding any nonunion replacement workers who might be needed in case of a strike. The Baldwin-Felts men, who were infamous back east for antiunion "enforcement," brought with them a heinous contraption known as "The Death Special," an armored vehicle able to transport several detectives and customized with a searchlight and a mounted machine gun.[126] These men, whom a Colorado state inquiry would later term "imported assassins,"[127] were despised on sight by the workers, and indeed had been savaged in a poem titled "Mine Guard" by the Wobbly writer Ralph Chaplin:

> You psychopathic coward with a gun:
> The worms would scorn your carcass in the mud;
> A bitch would blush to hail you as a son—
> You loathsome outcast, red with fresh-spilled blood.[128]

The UMW had done some hiring of its own, arranging for several organizers—Louis Tikas, known as "Louis the Greek"; Mike Livoda, of

Eastern European heritage; and an Italian named Gerald Lippiatt—to work with the miners' various ethnic constituencies. Tikas, who had once operated a coffeehouse in Denver, stood out among the miners for his natural leadership abilities; it was said he'd attended a university in Europe. Many of his Greek fellow-workers had been soldiers in the Greek army in the First Balkan War, and were recognized for their martial background and familiarity with weapons and military tactics.[129]

Blood was first spilled on August 16, 1913, when Gerald Lippiatt was slain by Baldwin-Felts detectives in a shoot-out in the town of Trinidad. Enraged miners retaliated by assassinating George Belcher, a Baldwin-Felts man suspected in the Lippiatt murder, and Bob Lee, an arrogant mine guard who claimed to have ridden with the outlaws Frank and Jesse James.

The miners had set a September 23 deadline to receive the companies' response to their demands, and when no word from CFI was forthcoming, they gathered in the Trinidad Opera House for a prestrike rally. Mother Jones, "The Miners' Angel," was there, her tiny gray head adorned as ever by a small bonnet with a flower attached. "For God's sake, strike—strike until you win,"[130] she told the assembly. "Don't be afraid, boys; fear is the greatest curse we have. I was never anywhere yet that I feared anybody. I would rather be shot fighting for you than live in any palace in America."[131] Eleven thousand miners soon walked off the job, but as they and their families resided in company housing, they were immediately evicted and took up residence in a dozen tent colonies provided by the UMW on land the union had purchased, the colonies situated so that the strikers could keep an eye on the roads by which scabs might be brought in. The largest was near the village of Ludlow and held about thirteen hundred men, women, and children in rows of white canvas tents, which residents dubbed "The White City," an allusion to the Chicago World's Fair of 1893.[132] Harassment from the mine guards and Baldwin-Felts agents began almost at once, the guards scanning the tent colonies at night with powerful searchlights and occasionally shooting machine-gun bursts into the air.

Governor Ammons initially ignored the coal companies' request for the Colorado National Guard; it was expensive for the state to maintain the Guard in the field, and Ammons owed his election in part to the backing of organized labor. But by late October he bowed to the wishes of the mine owners.[133] At first the twelve hundred arriving militiamen were greeted warmly by the strikers, who assumed the militia would offer protection from the hated mine guards. The strikers challenged the soldiers to a game of baseball, and later organized a dance for the visitors. But the mine owners grew impatient with such camaraderie; they wanted the troops' presence to discomfort the strikers and nudge them back to work. Because they had begun subsidizing the upkeep of the militia, the owners were in a position to urge Ammons to order the soldiers to assist the company guards in protecting scabs, a move certain to alienate the miners.[134]

The soldiers' actions on behalf of the scabs did prove infuriating, and as Reed reported, "the attitude of the militia [toward the tent colonists] suddenly changed." Militia incursions into the colonies began on the pretext of finding guns; in some instances soldiers beat or arrested uncooperative strikers; one old miner was so roughly handled he was unable to walk back to his tent and instead had to crawl on his hands and knees. The only encouraging sign was that some of the scabs rebelled, claiming to have been lured to Colorado under false pretenses. These mutineers quietly took leave of their compound at night to seek refuge in the miners' tent colonies.[135]

Mother Jones, meanwhile, was beginning to grate on the nerves of Governor Ammons. In an age when reformers were commonly maligned as "agitators," the octogenarian Jones wore the title proudly. In a West Virginia strike the year before, she had mobilized miners' wives to join her with "mops, brooms, and dishpans" to chase after scabs, and had driven mine owners to distraction with her small army of "wild women." She firmly believed the rightful place for strikers' wives was at the barricades. Greedy capitalists created "ladies," Jones liked to say, "but God Almighty made women."[136] During a streetcar strike in New York City, she'd once so thoroughly roused a female audience that the women, upon exiting the hall, attacked the first "scab" streetcar to come by, smashing its windows, assaulting the crew, and fighting with arresting police.

Ammons moved to ban Jones from the southeast part of the state, although she made several attempts to defy his edict and was eventually jailed—first in the convent-run San Rafael Hospital outside Trinidad, later in a courthouse cellar. "The soldiers have the bayonets," Jones complained, "and I have nothing but the Constitution."[137] On January 22, 1914, Brigadier General John Chase of the Colorado militia was the antagonist in the so-called Mother Jones Riot, which broke out in the town when Chase's mounted troops confronted two hundred miners' wives who were marching to support the imprisoned Jones. At one point Chase lost his grip on his horse's pommel and fell to the ground; believing the women were laughing at him, he quickly remounted and in a rage ordered, "Ride them down! Ride them down!" The troops surged their horses forward and, amid screams of protest, attacked the fleeing women, prodding them with their sabers and bringing numerous complaints of injury, including a victim who claimed a part of her ear had been severed.[138]

B Y SPRING 1914 THE STRIKE WAS more than half a year old, and the ranks of the National Guard, due to state budget constraints, were drawn down to two hundred men. Meanwhile the militia's leaders heard rumors that more guns were coming into the miners' possession, and became newly vigilant. On the morning of April 20 a woman informed the troops that her husband was being held in the Ludlow tent colony against his will. The task of confronting the strikers over the woman's husband—and possibly the secret stockpiling of guns—fell to two National Guard officers, Major Patrick C. Hamrock, a Denver saloon keeper and former Indian fighter; and Lieutenant Karl E. Linderfelt, who called the miners "wops" and had a reputation as a petty tyrant even among his own troops. Linderfelt had once struck a miner's young son who had failed to respond to an order, screeching, "I am Jesus Christ, and all these men on horses are Jesus Christ, and we have got to be obeyed."[139]

Linderfelt and Hamrock sent word to the Ludlow colony that the missing man would have to be turned over, but when soldiers entered the colony Louis Tikas assured them he was not there. They warned Tikas that if the miners didn't produce him soon, they would return in greater numbers and search more thoroughly. A short time later Major Hamrock contacted Tikas by telephone and ordered him to appear at the militia's camp. Tikas suggested they meet halfway, at a small rail depot, which was agreeable to Hamrock. There Tikas spoke with Hamrock and Linderfelt. It was a few minutes before ten o'clock.

As the group was talking, gunfire was heard from the direction of the colony, followed by a loud explosion. It has never been entirely clear what happened; either some of the miners were positioning themselves in anticipation of an attack, and the soldiers perceived their movements as aggressive, or the soldiers simply opened fire. Tikas immediately raced back to the colony, waving a white handkerchief as he urged men to return to their tents, while Hamrock telephoned his headquarters, saying, "Put the baby in the buggy and bring it along," an order to move a machine gun onto the firing line.[140] The shooting, once commenced, proved difficult to halt. The Guard, holding the high ground at a place called Water Tank Hill, forced the miners to retreat; the troops then descended among the tents, looting their contents and setting many afire. The miners had dug pits beneath some as hiding places, and in one, eleven women and children were discovered, dead from smoke inhalation. A total of twenty-two people died in the assault.

Tikas, taken captive, was brought again before Lieutenant Linderfelt. They argued over whose actions had triggered the day's bloodshed and Linderfelt, in a rage, struck Tikas over the head with the stock of his rifle, opening a vicious wound. Linderfelt later testified that Tikas "called me a name any man with red blood in his veins will not stand."[141] The lieutenant then left him in the custody of a militia sergeant and several soldiers. According to the militiamen, Tikas and another prisoner named James Fyler tried to escape, prompting them to open fire, killing both. The soldiers bent over Tikas's corpse and shook its hand, mockingly "wishing him well in the next world." An autopsy revealed that Tikas's "scalp had been laid open by a blunt instrument" (the blow from Linderfelt) and that he'd been shot three times in the back.[142]

News of a massacre—the multiple deaths of innocent women and children in the Ludlow tent colony as well as the assassination of Louis Tikas—rippled through the nation's headlines. UMW president John P. White was livid. "The State of Colorado," he said, "has spent nearly a million dollars to aid the coal companies to drive the miners back to the mines and a vacillating governor has directed the use of the militia in such a manner and way as to bring discredit and disgrace upon the state. Scores of men, women and children have been murdered."[143] Even the conservative press was stunned, the *Denver Express* mourning the "mothers and babies crucified on the cross of human liberty" as "a burnt offering laid on the altar of Rockefeller's Great God Greed."[144]

The Colorado Senate also reeled over the affair, its Progressive members blaming the coal operators who had waved away possible arbitration, the governor for taking money from the coal corporations for support of the militia, and the militia itself for being trigger-happy. State Senator W. C. Robinson offered a resolution finding Governor Ammons "incompetent to run the state government" and urging his immediate resignation. In a speech supporting his resolution he referred to Ammons as "The Great Squaw Catcher" for detaining Mother Jones, and suggested he take the name as his formal title upon leaving office.[145] The Colorado Women's Peace League, a group of Denver society women who sent a committee to view the carnage at Ludlow, insisted to Ammons that "Rockefeller gunmen and thugs" be "purged" at once from the militia and demanded the state take over the operation of the mines until a labor agreement could be obtained.[146] The Socialist *Appeal to Reason* lampooned Rockefeller and his famous family's supposed devotion to Christian ideals and institutions:

> . . . *as long as he has the cash to spend, it's easy the people to fool,*
> *As long as he builds a cottage or two and teaches Sunday School.*

The toadies fawn, and the lickspittles kneel,
He's worshipped by all the freaks,
While the bodies of little children are burned 'neath Colorado's peaks.
And this skulking, sanctimonious ass, this breeder of crime and hate,
With the greed of a jackal and a heart of brass,
Whines, "Nothing to arbitrate."[147]

John Reed and Max Eastman traveled to Ludlow shortly after the massacre, toured the devastated tent colony, and moved on to observe the shooting war that had erupted between miners and militia. A published "call to arms" had gone out, a message of vengeance for the Ludlow deaths, urging striking miners "to protect the people of Colorado against the murder and cremation of men, women, and children by armed assassins employed by the coal corporations."[148] For days, gunfire echoed in the hills and canyons surrounding remote mining villages around Ludlow. Along a 250-mile front, three thousand miners were under arms. They were soon joined by others. Passions were so heated and the impact of the strike on local commerce so extensive that after the burning of the Ludlow colony all manner of men—teachers, bankers, drivers—sought weapons and took to the hills, creating "one of the nearest approaches to civil war and revolution ever known in this country in connection with an industrial conflict."[149] Several mines were destroyed and seventy-five people perished during ten days of fighting. No doubt the only thing that kept the actual dimensions of this bitter struggle largely from public view (and memory) is that it occurred in such an out-of-the-way place.

Governor Ammons vowed that his militia would put down the insurrection; however, the Colorado Women's Peace League had other ideas. Leading a march by a thousand Denver women on the state capitol, they took up positions inside the building and vowed not to move until the governor alerted the White House. President Woodrow Wilson had followed news of the strike since the previous fall, when he had judged that "the situation was unraveling because the operators [had] tried to force tenth-century despotism onto a twentieth-century industrial situation."

He had urged the owners to accept the involvement of outside media-tors.[150] Now he hesitated to send federal troops to Colorado, wanting the state to resolve the crisis on its own; but the descriptions of the deaths at Ludlow and the advocacy of the Women's Peace League had combined to force his hand, and he ordered seventeen hundred soldiers into the state. Concerned that Ammons was not taking seriously the responsibility to restore order, the president warned that "my constitutional obligations with regard to the maintenance of order in Colorado are not to be indefi-nitely continued by the inaction of the state legislature."[151]

Despite a coroner's inquiry, a National Guard commission hearing, and a court-martial concerning the tent killings of the miners' families and the murder of Louis Tikas, no one was ever successfully prosecuted for any of the violence at Ludlow. That the inquiries produced this result may have partly had to do with the fact that not a single striker's tes-timony was heard in the latter two venues, their representatives having refused to take part in the proceedings because they were not open to the public. The most damning evidence at the coroner's hearing came from a Colorado & Southern Railroad train crew, which witnessed the militiamen torching the miners' tents and firing at a group of women and children who were attempting to use the passing train as cover so they could escape the militia assault. At the court-martial, Guard officers who testified offered a number of reasons for the attack on the colony and the deadly conflagration, all difficult to prove or disprove—that they had been responding to shooting by miners; that a strong wind had caused the tents to catch fire; that some soldiers had acted excessively, but only after finding a fallen comrade whose body had been mutilated by the strikers. A Guard corporal named Mills, implicated in the killing of Louis Tikas, did not appear at the hearing because he was said to have fled to Mexico, fearful that Tikas's friends were looking to even the score; Lieutenant Linderfelt also complained to the court that he was a hunted man. Although neither Major Hamrock, who was allowed to sit at the defendants' table wearing his six-shooter, nor Linderfelt was punished, the tribunal concluded that Hamrock had erred in ordering a machine gun used against the strikers' colony, that it had been soldiers who had set the tents on fire, and that Lieutenant Linderfelt had failed to keep them from doing so. The court also adjudged him guilty of striking Tikas over the head with a rifle, but elected to attach no criminal motive to it.[152]

THE SUFFERING OF THE Ludlow families resonated that spring in distant New York City, where there was labor agitation of a different kind. An estimated three hundred thousand jobless men had taken to roaming the streets, standing for hours on breadlines or besieging relief agencies and church missions. Labor reformers had embraced the crisis, waging a kind of low-scale guerrilla war on behalf of those out of work. When city and charitable efforts proved inadequate, this Revolt of the Unemployed, as it was named, invaded the sanctuary of churches and synagogues while services were under way, desperately seeking to make their plight known. "I asked for permission to go into the church with the boys and the priest would not give me that permission," Frank Tannenbaum, a youthful leader of the revolt, later testified. "I then asked for food which was refused, and then for money which was also refused. Then I said to the priest, 'So this is your Christian gospel?' And he said, 'Never mind about that. I will not allow you to talk to me in that way.'"[153]

The city's newspapers uniformly denounced those who would interrupt a place of worship, but Emma Goldman and Alexander Berkman's magazine *Mother Earth* roundly applauded such activism; what could be more fitting than that the "well-fed, pharisaical clergymen and their smug, self-righteous congregations [be] rudely awakened from their fatuous dreams of seventeenth century theology by hordes of angry men demanding food and shelter." When the churches hired guards to keep the masses away, the "ragged, starving men" bearing "the Black Flag of Hunger" invaded the city's better neighborhoods, reported *Mother Earth*, home to "the world's industrial potentates."[154]

The police grew frustrated by their inability to defeat the roving bands and, when they did manage to corner the wanderers, fell on them with vicious glee, clubbing and sometimes arresting the vagrants. A visit by Lincoln Steffens to police headquarters helped end the worst forms of brutality, although the authorities threw the book at Tannenbaum, the young idealist, a court convicting him of inciting to riot and sending him to Blackwell's Island for a year, as well as fining him $500. "There is no instance in the world's history where the efforts of the slave class to free themselves have been considered legal," Tannenbaum assured the judge in a final statement. "I belong to the slave class."[155] Goldman and Berkman tried to carry on in Tannenbaum's absence, on March 21 leading protestors from Union Square in a march uptown that produced the headlines "Emma Goldman Tells Mob to Storm Churches and Shops," "Reds Go up Fifth Avenue Cursing the Rich," and "Marchers Drive All Well-Dressed Persons to Seek Refuge in Doorways."[156]

Soon local resentment came to fix on the news of the Ludlow Massacre and the apparent indifference of the man responsible, New York's own John D. Rockefeller Jr. In protests coordinated by muckraker Upton Sinclair, Rockefeller's offices at 26 Broadway were picketed by demonstrators wearing black armbands in memory of the tent colony victims. The irrepressible Sinclair also helped engineer a cross-country fund-raising and consciousness-raising tour led by a prominent Denver Progressive, Judge Benjamin Barr Lindsey, featuring women and children survivors of the Ludlow disaster. Judge Lindsey was no friend to the Colorado coal operators—he had recently published data showing that between 1910 and 1913, 622 children had been left fatherless by coal mining accidents in the state—nor did the hometown Denver press look approvingly on his national mission to publicize the horrors of Ludlow. In retaliation it began trafficking in rumors that his eastbound delegation was in fact an avant garde sexual caravan in which the lecherous judge took advantage of the now-husbandless Ludlow widows.[157] Of course the reality could not have been more different; one of the women, Mary Petrucci, who had lost three of her children in the blaze, had been turned mute by the tragedy and, utterly inconsolable, seemed to scarcely know where she was.[158] The Lindsey group reached Washington and was welcomed at the White House by President Wilson, who held one of the surviving Ludlow babies in his arms as he listened to the victims' accounts.

In New York, meanwhile, students from the Socialist Rand School decided to use one of the tactics from the "Revolt of the Unemployed," and crashed the services at Rockefeller's church, Calvary Baptist on West Fifty-seventh Street. Rockefeller and his family were not in the congregation that day, but a young man named Charles Morrison confronted the pastor, the Reverend Cornelius Woelfkin, to demand to know if "as a preacher and of the word of God, do you think that Jesus would uphold John D. Rockefeller in his attitude toward the Colorado strikers?" Morrison asked the question four times without receiving a response from the clergyman, who turned and walked away as Morrison was escorted forcibly from the building. The Reverend Woelfkin shared with a reporter his belief that "it is only these people who have no responsibility who go about making trouble. If these people had some responsibility we would hear very little from them."[159]

Rockefeller, it appeared, had slipped out of Manhattan to his country estate at Tarrytown. The protestors followed, and in the quaint little Hudson River community just north of New York City they contended for the right to make speeches denouncing the coal baron in the village square. Rockefeller himself was said to be confined indoors, having caught cold playing golf in the rain. Upton Sinclair arrived, demanding that local officials allow a public meeting where the Colorado situation could be discussed, but a permit for such a gathering was refused. On May 30 a dozen protestors returned to Tarrytown and, not bothering to seek official approval, initiated a series of speeches in the square. They were arrested, charged with blocking traffic, disorderly conduct, and endangering the public health. The next day Alexander Berkman led another group from the city to make speeches in Tarrytown, and all were likewise taken into custody. That very night twenty more speakers arrived and were promptly detained; many complained of rude treatment by the village police, whose ranks had been augmented by detectives from Rockefeller's private security forces and members of a local patriots' group.[160]

Nursing his cold, looking out from the broad windows of his estate, Rockefeller surely recognized that the situation was untenable. The Colorado fiasco—or "Rockefeller's War," as some insisted on calling it—was having a dreadful impact on his and his family's reputation, as well as their personal safety. Congress's inquiry into the situation had concluded that Rockefeller had been negligent and arrogant about the management of labor relations for refusing to meet with the miners and rejecting outside proposals of mediation. "The statement that a man or company of men who put their money in a business have a right to operate it as they see fit, without regard to the public interest, belongs to days long since passed away," the congressional report asserted. "Every individual who invests his capital ... is entitled to the protection of the law ... but he owes something to society."[161]

Rockefeller, to his credit, was by now questioning his long-standing faith in the guidance of the western managers of the CFI, and to doubt their consistent claims that all the violence during the strike had been caused by the miners. His reaction was twofold; he hired Canadian industrial reformer Mackenzie King, who had been that country's deputy minister of labor, to head up a fact-finding inquiry into the Colorado situation, and also launched a public relations effort to counter the negative publicity he was receiving. In one inadvertently revealing action, the Rockefeller forces formally announced that CFI was now prepared to concede certain improvements to the Colorado miners, only to learn that many of these "privileges" were already the law in Colorado, that they had long been stifled by the company, and that their denial had been among the strikers' major grievances. Ivy L. Lee, a former spokesman for the Pennsylvania Railroad whom Rockefeller hired as a publicist, began editing weekly reports from the Colorado coal operators and publishing them as *Facts Concerning the Struggle in Colorado for Industrial Freedom*. Lee's tracts praised the militia, rehashed unflattering rumors about Mother Jones, noted how many miners had remained loyal to the operators, and editorialized against the "bloodthirsty agitators" who had fomented all the trouble in the first place. So extensive were Lee's distortions that the radical press dubbed him "Poison Ivy."

Rockefeller had better luck satisfying his critics when, after the strike was formally terminated by the UMW in December 1914, he fired the CFI managerial personnel he now suspected of having fed him inaccurate and biased information about the strike, and personally visited the Colorado coal region. There he mingled with miners and their families, descended into the mines, inspected living quarters and schools, gave impromptu talks, and vowed to henceforth give his workers' needs a greater share of his attention. According to reports Rockefeller's personal charm and diplomacy did have a favorable impact on those he met, suggesting that all along it was his style of "absentee capitalism" that was part of the problem. With the assistance of King, he drew up a Colorado Industrial Plan, also known as "The Rockefeller Plan," that aimed to correct many of the underlying issues of feudalistic paternalism that had brought on the difficulties of 1913–1914, although one aspect, a company union, which Sam Gompers dismissed as "a pseudo union," failed predictably to impress labor and government observers.[162]

However much Rockefeller wished to deter outsiders from linking the Ludlow disaster to his personal or family life, his Tarrytown abode was thrust back into the news on July 4, when a bomb believed to be meant for the mansion detonated prematurely at an anarchist bomb factory in New York City. All three men killed in the explosion at an East Side tenement—Arthur Caron, Charles Berg, and Carl Hanson—were anarchists who had been involved in the free speech effort at Tarrytown. "So great was the force of the explosion," it was reported, "that articles of furniture were blown hundreds of feet into the air, some of the wreckage landing on the tops of houses more than a block away."[163]

Alexander Berkman was greatly moved by the incident. Like him, Caron, Berg, and Hanson had embarked on a noble *attentat* to exact revenge upon a living monster of greed and capital, and, like him, had been unable to realize their objective. Under the circumstances Berkman could do little but transfer his concern over Ludlow and his grief to the pages of *Mother Earth*, where he produced an issue largely dedicated to the Colorado troubles; it reprinted several speeches from a well-attended Union Square memorial gathering that had been held for the bomb factory victims, where a consoling banner near the speakers' stand had proclaimed, THOSE WHO DIE FOR A CAUSE NEVER DIE—THEIR SPIRIT WALKS ABROAD.[164]

I F THERE EVER WAS A MAN remembered for having lived and died for a cause, it was the Wobbly songwriter who went by the name Joe Hill, perhaps the most beloved and celebrated labor movement martyr of all. The final chapter of his life—his 1914 murder trial and the worldwide crusade to stay his execution—took place during the intense phase of the American labor struggle that coincided with Lawrence, Paterson, Ludlow, and the coming of the First World War. Hill's story is thus something of a coda to the early romantic phase of the IWW, which may explain why his martyrdom has long been embraced as among the purest and most meaningful.

A merchant marine and itinerant laborer who came to the United States from Sweden in 1901, Hill (whose original name was Joel Häggland) was a self-taught writer and musician who scribbled his impressions of the country's labor struggle as he traveled the West in the first decade of the century. He worked in a rope factory, shoveled coal, and served as a common seaman. In 1910 he joined the IWW, participated in the Fresno and San Diego free speech campaigns, at least once apparently getting knocked around by cops and vigilantes, and spent thirty days in jail in San Pedro, California, on a "vagrancy" charge after serving on a dockworkers' strike committee. He became a prolific writer of labor songs such as "Workers of the World, Awaken," "There Is Power in a Union," "Union Maid," and "The Preacher and the Slave," by taking well-known tunes and setting new words to them, the idea being that immigrant workers would be more likely to sing along if the tune was familiar. Hill's songs were printed frequently in IWW publications, bringing him a degree of renown, his words always emphasizing the tremendous confidence that buoyed the labor struggle. "If the workers took a notion, they could stop all speeding trains," Hill sang, "every ship upon the ocean, they can tie with mighty chains."[165] "There Is Power in a

Union," one of Hill's best-remembered efforts, was set to a church hymn and admonished workers:

> *There is pow'r, there is pow'r*
> *In a band of workingmen.*
> *When they stand, hand in hand.*
> *That's a pow'r, that's a pow'r*
> *That must rule in every land—*
> *One Industrial Union Grand.*

For "Workers of the World Awaken," he provided both original words and music:

> *Workers of the world, awaken!*
> *Break your chains, demand your rights.*
> *All the wealth you make is taken*
> *By exploiting parasites.*
> *Shall you kneel in deep submission*
> *From your cradles to your graves?*
> *Is the height of your ambition*
> *To be good and willing slaves?*[166]

Joe Hill might have remained one of many respected "hobo folk composers" attached to the IWW, such as Ralph Chaplin and Richard Brazier, had not his life been altered fatefully on January 10, 1914, in Salt Lake City. A butcher named John G. Morrison, a former policeman, and his seventeen-year-old son, Arling, were shot dead in what at first appeared to be a botched robbery. The sole witness was another son, Merlin, thirteen, who claimed the killers had shouted at his father, "We've got you now!"—suggesting the shooting was an act of retribution by criminals against Morrison; no money or goods were taken in the crime, nor was a murder weapon found. Arling, however, had managed to return fire, hitting one of the holdup men before he himself was mortally wounded.

Later that night Joe Hill went to a hospital seeking treatment for a gun-shot wound. He told police he had been shot in a quarrel over a woman whose name, as a matter of honor, he would not reveal, and proceeded to make his situation more precarious by initially refusing legal counsel.

Given the paucity of evidence, he might under ordinary circum-stances have gone free. There was no discernible motive to be ascribed to Hill and the prosecution was technically unable to prove his guilt beyond a reasonable doubt. But the atmosphere surrounding the trial was biased against an itinerant workman who belonged to the IWW in a case in which a former lawman and his son had been slaughtered. The legal bur-den wrongly shifted to whether Hill could prove his innocence, which in court he appeared unable or unwilling to do. He did, however, protest in a letter to the *Salt Lake City Telegram*:

> I never killed Morrison and do not know a thing about it. He was,
> as the records plainly show, killed by some enemy for the sake
> of revenge, and I have not been in this city long enough to make
> an enemy. Shortly before my arrest I came down from Park City,
> where I was working in the mines. Owing to the prominence
> of Mr. Morrison, there had to be a "goat," and the undersigned
> being, as they thought, a friendless tramp, a Swede, and, worst of
> all, an IWW, had no right to live anyway.[167]

Although Hill was pilloried at trial for being a Wobbly, he tried to keep the IWW out of the case, insisting the accusation against him did not involve the organization; he even attempted (unsuccessfully) to dis-suade the IWW from raising funds or depleting its treasury in his behalf. Once he was convicted and sentenced to death by firing squad, his plight came to wider attention, prompting a crusade for clemency or a pardon. Letters and petitions flooded into the office of Utah governor William Spry, with influential people including Samuel Gompers and the Swedish ambassador to the United States asking that Hill's case be given further review. Hill himself wrote an article for *Appeal to Reason* professing his innocence[168]; however, he remained mute about the details of the alleged crime, even when given a last chance to reveal the truth before a specially convened Board of Pardons. He explained to Elizabeth Gurley Flynn, with whom he corresponded throughout the ordeal:

> I have no desire to be one of them what-ye-call-em martyrs. On the square I'll tell you that all this notoriety stuff is making me dizzy in the head and I am afraid I'm getting more glory than I really am entitled to. I put in most of the later years among the wharf rats on the Pacific coast and I am not there with the limelight stuff at all.[169]

As the date of his execution neared, Flynn appealed directly to President Wilson, who, at the additional urging of the AFL, telegraphed to Governor Spry requesting another look at Hill's case and a stay of the death sentence. Wilson in fact attempted twice to convince Spry to halt the execution. But time had run out, and Joe Hill went before a firing squad on November 19, 1915. In one of his last letters he told Big Bill Haywood, "Good-bye, Bill. I will die like a true blue rebel. Don't waste any time in mourning. Organize!" His only request was that his body be removed from the state of Utah before it was cremated. Hill's final words—"Don't waste any time in mourning. Organize!"—became a popular IWW slogan, one frequently invoked by Wobblies headed for incarceration.

CHAPTER SEVEN

DYNAMITE

THE MEN AND WOMEN OF THE IWW BELIEVED that wars were waged for the benefit of monarchies, dying nations, and captains of industry, and turned workers against one another. The real struggle, in their view, remained the one they and millions of other "brothers and sisters of toil" fought every day—the war between labor and capital. Thus, when war overcame Europe in 1914, the Wobblies rejected talk of American involvement, Big Bill Haywood reminding members, "It is better to be a traitor to your country, than a traitor to your class."[1] Addressing a workers' rally from the stage of Carnegie Hall, he threatened to lead a general strike if the United States allowed itself to be lured into the conflict.[2]

When America did enter the war in April 1917, however, nine out of ten draft-eligible Wobblies registered with the Selective Service, and most of those called to arms reported for duty, more or less on par with members of the AFL, which had remained loyal to the government's foreign policy. Given the great popular support for the war, Big Bill also found it wise to adjust his position, cautioning IWW locals against voicing strident opposition rhetoric, as it would only draw government scrutiny. His change of tone came too late, however; the IWW had already made too many noisy objections, and the nation had embraced the war so fully as to make even a hint of skepticism repugnant. The paranoia that was the by-product of this jingoistic ardor fell hard on the Wobblies, as it did on anyone perceived to be a radical, draft resister, or naysayer.

The irony was that since 1912 or so, with its efforts in Lawrence and Paterson, the IWW had behaved more as a traditional labor union than a movement of revolutionary change. Even its free speech campaigns of earlier years could be perceived as expressions of faith in the Bill of Rights. But it was unable to shed its reputation for promoting class upheaval, and after the Bolsheviks in Russia, whom the Wobblies supported, ousted the moderate government of Alexander Kerensky in October 1917 and brokered a treaty with the Germans (Brest-Litovsk), the IWW was accused of being in cahoots with the enemy and tarred by the fierce anti-German sentiment sweeping the United States. In towns big and small, German-sounding surnames and place-names were changed, sauerkraut became "Liberty Cabbage," and anyone persisting in their German ways or "other-ness" was deemed alien or suspect. Victor Reuther, an official of the United Auto Workers, recalled that during a patriotic parade through his hometown of Wheeling, West Virginia, "one of the oldest music houses in town threw all of its recordings of German classics and German folk songs out into the street as the crowd marched by."[3] In this atmosphere, radical labor organizations sympathetic to revolutionary ideas from Europe, such as the IWW, had little chance. "May God have mercy on them," pronounced U.S. attorney general Thomas W. Gregory, "for they need expect none from an outraged people or an avenging government."[4] West Coast labor activists Tom Mooney and Warren Billings were made an early example, convicted and given substantial prison time for allegedly planting a deadly terrorist bomb that exploded at a Preparedness Day parade in San Francisco in July 1916.

Of course, once the United States was in the war, domestic labor union activity appeared in a new context, as the country looked to workers and industry to maintain high production levels of copper, coal, steel, and other essentials. Laboring men in these key industries took seriously the government and military's needs, but saw the situation also as an opportunity to attain deserved improvements in pay and work conditions; unfortunately, when such demands originated with groups like the IWW they readily became conflated with radicalism or were criticized as unpatriotic. American troops had barely reached Europe when one such altercation broke out in Jerome, Arizona, in early summer 1917. The IWW, which was assisting copper miners who had struck for improved pay and conditions, was confronted by the Jerome Loyalty League, an enforcer organization backed by mine owners and local men of commerce; the league's armed members stood ready to punish anyone who impeded mine production or harassed replacement workers. On July 10, these vigilantes, braced with guns and pick handles, seized the IWW strike leaders and drove them from the town. When the IWW cabled Washington to complain of so blatant a violation, the Justice Department replied by offering to prosecute the Wobblies.

Heartened by the ease with which the Jerome town fathers had acted, authorities in Bisbee, Arizona, made a similar assault on the IWW. Even before the onset of American involvement in the First World War and its related demand for copper, Bisbee—its Copper Queen mine the richest source of copper in the country—had become a desert boomtown controlled by Phelps, Dodge & Company; by 1908 it had eight thousand residents, new schools, hospitals, churches, a YMCA, and a well-stocked library. European immigrants, mostly Slavs and Finns, as well as Mexican workers, arrived in droves. Bisbee's development had been guided by the paternalistic corporate welfare philosophy of Dr. James Douglas of Phelps Dodge. In 1911, however, Douglas's son Walter had assumed control as general manager. Strongly suspicious of labor, he not only toughened conditions for Phelps Dodge miners but dedicated his efforts to speaking out against mine unionization generally. In part his views were a reaction to the state's adoption of a number of union-friendly policies written when Arizona attained statehood in 1912, measures that put Phelps Dodge on the defensive. Like John D. Rockefeller Jr. at Colorado Fuel,

Walter Douglas vowed to shutter the Copper Queen before he'd allow a union in, saying, "We will not compromise with rattlesnakes."[5]

In late June 1917 the Bisbee local of the International Union of Mine, Mill and Smelter Workers, many of whom were also members of the IWW, struck for increased wages of $6 a day, for more men assigned to operate mechanical equipment, and reform of the system by which Phelps Dodge deducted from the miners' weekly paychecks for water and electricity and the rental of worker housing. Another demand was that the company's sham physical examinations, by which able-bodied men were frequently excluded from work because of their political convictions, be stopped. By all accounts the strike was peaceful, but the presence of "labor radicals" worried local authorities, and white sensibilities were inflamed after Mexican men affiliated with the IWW transgressed local custom by approaching American women employed in a laundry, ostensibly to see if they would join the union. The Wobblies, with their ambitions for "one big union" inclusive of all races and both genders, clearly posed an unacceptable threat.

Adding to local tensions was the conviction held by Sheriff Harry Wheeler and other Cochise County authorities that strikes which hindered war-related production were both unpatriotic and dangerous. "At a time when our country needs her every resource," read a public proclamation issued by Wheeler, "these strangers persist in keeping from her the precious metal production of this entire district. . . . We cannot longer stand nor tolerate such conditions. This is no labor trouble. We are sure of that. But it is a direct attempt to embarrass the government of the United States."[6] He also had reason to worry about border security. Only five months earlier Germany had sent the infamous Zimmerman telegram, offering to restore Texas, Arizona, and New Mexico to the Mexican government if Mexico would attack the United States, and there had been fears along the border for years of encroachments by Mexican armies associated with the revolutionary Pancho Villa. President Wilson, it was widely believed, had not done enough to protect American citizens from the possibility of such incursions.

Wheeler, along with a two-thousand-member vigilante organization calling itself the Citizens' Protective League, launched a campaign to oust the Wobblies and any strikers who would not agree to return to work. At dawn on July 12, Wheeler—with the help of Phelps Dodge officers—cut off all phone, telegraph, and rail service to Bisbee; he then deputized and distributed weapons to those League members who had none, and set the white-armbanded legions to scour the town "until the last IWW is run out."[7] It was reported that "armed men went through lodging houses and restaurants questioning everyone. Two men, a League member and a miner, were killed in a shoot-out when the miner fired at those who had come to apprehend him. Those who did not answer satisfactorily to questioning were marched between lines of citizens to the park."[8] At this baseball field in the adjacent town of Warren, nearly thirteen hundred Wobblies and IWW-loyal miners (and three women sympathizers) were collected and informed of their imminent deportation from the state. An automobile fitted with a machine gun and manned by Wheeler's men stood by, visible to the captives.

Despite their protests that their wives and families were in Bisbee, that they owned property, had bank accounts, and had lived in the town for as long as fifteen years, the men were herded into twenty-four boxcars of a waiting freight train. William B. Cleary, a local attorney who sided with the strikers, dispatched an urgent telegram to a federal mediator—"Two thousand miners being deported this morning by corporation gunmen from Warren district; stop that train!"—but Cleary himself was soon collared and forced into a boxcar.[9] At some point Arizona's assistant attorney general, Louis Whitney, got wind of what was taking place and demanded of Sheriff Wheeler by telegraph, "State by what authority of law you are acting. State fully what violations, if any, took place prior to decision to deport strikers"; however, it is not certain if or when Wheeler received Whitney's message.[10]

For those crammed aboard the train a trip of several hours through the day's heat ensued—automobiles filled with armed Protective League members driving alongside—until the deportees reached Hermanas, New

Mexico, 180 miles away. Stranded without food or water, they were told they would be killed if they attempted to return to Bisbee. The men were eventually given refuge at a U.S. army camp at Columbus, New Mexico.

The IWW, as it had at Jerome, protested to Washington, Big Bill Haywood terming the Bisbee affair "an outrage," while denying emphatically "that German money, German influence, or wartime motives are behind the western copper strikes . . . [they] are simply an effort to get living wages and just working conditions for our miners."[11] An editorial in the *New York Times* conceded Haywood's point, but insisted that "if [the IWW's] passion for mischief is not fomented and paid for by German agents, at any rate its fruits are for German benefit." Sheriff Wheeler "was on the right track," the paper noted, to arrest IWW members as vagrants, for the disaffected workers, "tramps and all sorts of yahoos [and] summer roamers," the Wobblies attracted had become "pilgrims of disturbance" in the West. The editorial did chastise the sheriff for taking the law into his own hands,[12] as did President Wilson, who reminded Arizona governor Thomas E. Campbell, "Bisbee had the right to defend itself against violence, not to do violence."[13]

Many Americans were disturbed by the "kidnapping" of the Bisbee workers, organized labor railing the loudest at the prospect that capital had now added forcible deportation to its methods of countering legitimate worker grievances. The IWW threatened a general strike and/or the "retaking" of Bisbee by armed force; it also suggested that the cure for the likes of Sheriff Wheeler and Phelps Dodge's feudalistic control lay in the nationalization of the copper mines. But so much huffing and puffing was of little avail. Although a federal inquiry into the Bisbee deportation led by Labor Secretary William B. Wilson found the actions of Sheriff Wheeler and the vigilantes "wholly illegal," and some mining officials and deputies were placed under arrest, a federal court ultimately dismissed the case.[14] Indeed, the lesson President Wilson appeared to take from the Bisbee fiasco was that the IWW was treacherous, would potentially hinder war manufacturing, and would need to be closely watched. As for the stranded Bisbee men, most lingered on as guests of the army at Columbus until September, then scattered, only about 6 percent daring to return to their homes in Bisbee.

Bisbee signaled the beginning of a disheartening season of confrontation for the IWW, as the ruthless nature of the Jerome and Bisbee affairs was soon replicated in distant Butte, Montana, a tough antiunion town that had chased the WFM out in 1914 and where the IWW was active on behalf of striking copper workers of the Metal Mine Workers Union. Bill Haywood called Butte "the city with the copper soul"—a place where "the people . . . breathed copper, ate copper, wore copper, and were thoroughly saturated with copper." Work-related disease and injuries were so numerous it was said there were as many miners in the local cemeteries as there were toiling in the mines.[15] The summer of 1917 had gotten off to a particularly gruesome start, when on June 8 an electrical cable that powered underground pumps at the Speculator mine outside Butte broke, filling the lower levels of the mine with smoke and gas, claiming 164 workers' lives. By mid-July word had arrived of the massive deportation at Bisbee, and nervous Butte strikers appealed to Montana congresswoman Jeannette Rankin, a pacifist and the first woman to serve in the House of Representatives, to safeguard their rights and block any similar action by local mine owners. These efforts were of no avail, for at month's end the Montana copper bosses, reading closely from the Bisbee playbook, gathered a vigilante force that with the assistance of helpful U.S. soldiers seized and deported Butte's IWW leaders.

One of the high-profile targets of the sweep was Frank Little, the by-now legendary Wobbly organizer known to describe himself as "half Indian, half white man, all IWW." Little had been in the thick of several nasty IWW scrapes out west and was known for putting his body on the line. He had the bruises to show for it, and was walking with the aid of a pair of crutches when he arrived in Butte to aid the strike. He lost no time calling attention to himself, mounting a soapbox and disparaging the war in Europe as capitalist slaughter, while referring to U.S. troops serving there as "Uncle Sam's scabs in uniform."[16]

Late on the night of July 31 six masked men entered Little's boardinghouse room as he slept, abducted him in his underclothes, and dragged him out to a waiting car. After driving around for a couple of hours and subjecting him to occasional beatings and torture—at one point they pulled him by a rope from the automobile's rear fender—they arrived at a desolate railroad trestle on the outskirts of town and hanged him from one of the crossties. A note found pinned to his corpse the next day read: "First and Last Warning," followed by the numbers "3–7–77," an allusion to the state of Montana's required dimensions for a grave: three feet wide, seven feet long, and seventy-seven inches deep.[17] Among the dead man's scant personal effects at the boardinghouse friends found a small envelope with some curious residue inside; upon it were written the words "Ashes of Joe Hill."[18]

GIVEN THE COUNTRY'S MOOD, the lynching of Frank Little was horrific but predictable—the murder of an outspoken IWW radical by vigilantes consumed with righteous patriotism. What the Wobblies were beginning to understand as they buried their comrade, however, was that it wasn't only mobs of angry citizens they had to fear; the federal government also had drawn a bull's-eye on the IWW.[19] Its labor activism at Bisbee, Butte, and other copper mining towns had convinced President Wilson that the IWW intended to use the war to bleed concessions from industry, a threat that would potentially interfere with war manufactures; Wilson decided to order a full investigation of the group to be led by Judge J. Harry Covington, a distinguished law professor and former congressman from Maryland.

The creation of the Covington inquiry was only one of many steps Washington took in response to the war and the intensified concern about disloyalty at home. In 1917 Congress passed the Espionage Act to criminalize the relating of "false reports or false statements" that had the potential to interfere with the U.S. military, or any acts that aimed to cause insubordination among military personnel or obstruct military enlistment or recruitment. It also banned any interference with war manufacturing. The Sedition Act of 1918 made it a crime to "utter, print, write, or publish any disloyal, profane, scurrilous, or abusive language" about the government, the Constitution, or the military, or to "encourage resistance to the

United States, or to promote the cause of its enemies." The Immigration Act of 1918, expanding on the Anarchist Exclusion Act of 1903, which had been crafted in response to the murder of President McKinley, decreed that aliens who were anarchists or believed in the overthrow of the federal government or the assassination of government officials could be barred from America, and those already here could be deported. An immigrant's membership in an anarchist group was sufficient for deportation; there was no requirement he or she be proven guilty of wrongdoing.

These three acts were so sweeping and so broadly written that numerous cases arose of labor organizers, immigrants, and other individuals being arrested who had done little more than speak, write, or express an interest in the Wobblies, anarchism, or the political situation in Russia. Many were held incommunicado and detained indefinitely, and it often proved impossible to reverse the gears of "justice" once an individual, particularly one not native-born, became ensnared. Another way in which radicals found themselves in the government's sights was for violation of the Conscription Act, which had become law in May 1917; all aliens were required to register with the draft, and any who had begun naturalization proceedings could be called up for military service.

Made aware of Judge Covington's assignment, Big Bill tried a preemptive maneuver—offering the IWW's full cooperation, including the opening of the group's files, to the government. Instead, apparently hoping to obtain incriminating information before the Wobblies could cover their tracks, Department of Justice raiders struck on September 5, 1917, invading forty-eight IWW halls across the country and bagging five tons of documents. "The books in which were recorded the transactions of the organization, the literature, the furniture, typewriters, mimeograph machines, pictures from the wall and spittoons from the floor were seized as evidence," Haywood recalled.[20] Three weeks later, on September 28, a federal court in Chicago indicted 165 Wobblies, largely on charges involving violation of the Espionage Act; many were incarcerated at the Cook County jail, some in the very cells once occupied by the martyrs of Haymarket.[21]

The issuing of the indictments brought dissension within the IWW into the open when Elizabeth Gurley Flynn, Carlo Tresca, Joe Ettor, and

Arturo Giovannitti insisted that their cases be severed from the rest. Flynn contended this was the best means of thwarting the prosecution, since demanding that the government show specific evidence of individual wrongdoing would hinder the kind of guilt-by-association argument used in the Haymarket tribunal and at Ettor and Giovannitti's trial in Massachusetts. Haywood and other leading Wobblies disagreed; the IWW lacked the funds to combat individual cases and, most important, the organization saw the trial as a matter of conscience in which the accused should stand and fall together. What Haywood was not aware of was that Flynn had written a rather obsequious letter to President Wilson, offering mild apologies for her radical past and dissociating herself from the IWW. She was fortunate that its contents were not then known by others.

Tensions already existed between Haywood and Flynn stemming from the IWW's organizing work a few years before in the iron ore mines of the Mesabi Range of northern Minnesota. In 1916 Tresca had been charged there as an accessory to murder in the death of a sheriff's deputy. Flynn, against Haywood's wishes, urged four miners also accused in the case to plead guilty and accept a reduced sentence, a move that went against IWW policy and was seen as an expedient to get Tresca, who might have been deported if convicted, out of legal jeopardy. Flynn herself later insisted that her falling-out with Haywood had more to do with her criticism of his handling of the flow of strike and relief monies for Mesabi from the Chicago IWW office. In any event, the move by Flynn and the others to challenge the government by isolating their cases turned out to have been correct, as charges were ultimately dropped against all four.

On April 1, 1918, the trial of 101 Wobblies commenced in Chicago, while other proceedings against scattered cells of IWW members ensued in Omaha, Wichita, and Sacramento. John Reed rendered a romantic description of the Chicago defendants as those "who believe the wealth of the world belongs to him who creates it . . . the boys who do the strong work of the world,"[22] but the trial judge, veteran jurist Kenesaw Mountain Landis, was unimpressed by the scruffy radicals who filed into his courtroom. Known for his no-nonsense attitude toward activists or moral transgressors, he had helped ban black heavyweight boxing champion Jack Johnson from the sport after Johnson's indictment for violation of the Mann Act, and had sentenced Victor Berger, a Socialist congressman from Wisconsin, to twenty years in prison simply for publishing an antiwar editorial in a Milwaukee newspaper. Reed, perhaps ungenerously, described the judge, who was in his early fifties, as "a wasted man with untidy white hair, an emaciated face in which two burning eyes are set like jewels, parchment skin split by a crack for a mouth; the face of Andrew Jackson three years dead."[23]

While the charges against the Wobblies centered on the Espionage Act, each defendant was accused of over one hundred specific crimes as part of what prosecutors depicted as a substantial IWW conspiracy; these included opposing the draft, urging other IWW members to refuse induction, encouraging insubordination in the army, and taking part in strikes aimed at crippling the war effort. "How we one hundred and one defendants had conspired together to arrange such a conspiracy we never knew," Richard Brazier, one of the defendants, later said. "For most of us had never met prior to our arrests."[24]

The prosecution was formally led by Charles F. Clyne, the U.S. attorney for northern Illinois, although the actual lead lawyer was Frank K. Nebeker, a veteran legal representative for western mine owners. The IWW defendants had as their lead attorney George Vanderveer, known as the "Counsel for the Damned" for his willingness to defend hard-luck Wobblies in several western courtroom fights. In advance of the trial, Vanderveer tried several times to get the case dismissed, arguing that the arrests and the seizure of evidence violated the First and Fourth amendments, and that the treatment of those detained and even their friends and family who attempted to visit them had been abhorrent. One of the examples most talked about involved a young California woman named Theodora Pollok, who had gone to the Sacramento jail to bail out IWW acquaintances; police immediately placed Pollok herself under arrest, impounded all the cash she'd brought along, then subjected her to a thorough body examination that included a vaginal probe.

When Vanderveer's tactics proved fruitless, he warned Landis that bringing such a spurious case against the IWW would agitate working people everywhere and cause even greater industrial strife. The government shrugged off the attorney's caution; it had already moved to limit the IWW's ability to retaliate by raiding the group's Chicago office a second time and making additional arrests, thereby disrupting efforts to raise a defense fund. At the same time, Congress was considering several bills in spring 1918 that would declare the IWW an illegal organization. While none were passed, the surrounding headlines did little to improve the Wobblies' already teetering public image.

By any rational measure the prosecution's case was weak, blaming the alleged Wobbly "conspiracy" on the "seditious and disloyal character and teachings of the organization." To such a broad insinuation the defense's most effective reply was the plainspoken testimony of individual Wobblies, one of whom inquired:

> If you were a bum without a blanket, if you had left your wife and
> kids when you went West for a job and never located them since;
> if your job never kept you long enough in one place to vote; if you
> slept in a lousy bunkhouse and ate rotten food; if every person
> who represented law and order beat you up . . . how in hell do you
> expect a man to be patriotic?

One allegation the IWW found harder to disown was that of industrial sabotage, as the organization had at times encouraged it. A term of Belgian origin, *sabotage* referred to the act of working with deliberate slowness, as in the manner of a peasant who wore the clunky wooden shoes known as sabots, or, in some definitions, of placing said footwear into the gears of a machine. Flynn had once published a booklet in praise of the practice, and the IWW had used a related symbol—the "Sab-Cat"—as part of an organizational logo since 1910.[25] However, the offenses ticked off in court—Wobblies were alleged to have placed objects in gearboxes, driven copper nails into fruit trees, destroyed threshing machines, and even to have shoved a company horse down a well—seemed purely anecdotal, and were unsupported by any credible proof.[26]

The prosecution fell back on reading to the court, and trying to shock the jury, with incriminating statements of radical philosophy culled from confiscated IWW publications and correspondence.[27] This was the reprise of Haymarket that had been expected (no source of comfort to the defendants, given that affair's tragic outcome). In an effort at exoneration the defense turned to published material of its own choosing, including a recent report from the president's Commission on Industrial Relations, which concluded that American workers by and large had made great sacrifices for their country during the war, and that of more than five hundred strikes called after the U.S. entry into the conflict in 1917, only three had involved the IWW. Vanderveer pivoted on the commission findings to insist that the IWW sought merely to better the nation's social equity, not to interfere with or threaten the government. Judge Landis, however, ruled off-limits the commission material, as well as other data the defense wished to introduce that detailed the challenging conditions American workers faced. Some of this information did get into the record through the testimony of various Wobblies, although the prosecution retaliated by reminding the jury that as much as those testifying looked like ordinary workingmen, they were in fact dangerous radicals.

Haywood declared under oath, however, that "the aim and purpose of the [IWW] literature . . . was to disseminate the idea of industrial unionism, not to destroy but to build, to construct." As to whether the IWW sought to impede the nation's war effort, he stated:

> I am very much opposed to war, and would have the war stopped today if it were in my power to do it. I believe that there are other methods by which human beings should settle any existing difficulty. It is not only the murdering of the men, it is the suffering of the wives and children. And it is what this war means to society after this war is over. . . . Nothing to follow but war cripples, war widows, war orphans, war stories, war pictures and war everything. . . . I hope . . . that every man that is imbued with the spirit of war will fight long enough to drive the spirit of hate

and war out of his breast . . . that this may be the last war that the world will ever know.[28]

Vanderveer inquired of Haywood about the charge of conspiracy. "We *are* conspiring," Big Bill affirmed.

We are conspiring to prevent the making of profits on labor power in any industry. We are conspiring against the dividend makers. We are conspiring against rent and interest. We want to establish a new society, where people can live without profit, without dividends, without rent and without interest if it is possible; and it is possible, if people will live normally, live like human beings should live. I would say that if that is a conspiracy, we are conspiring.[29]

After four months of testimony and the examination of hundreds of exhibits and forty thousand pages of IWW records, the jury required only a single hour's deliberation to bring in a verdict of guilty. On August 31, 1918, Judge Landis sentenced thirty-five of the men to five years in prison, thirty-three men to ten years, and fifteen men, including Haywood, to a term of twenty years. Benjamin Fletcher of Philadelphia, the only black Wobbly among the defendants, quipped as he was taken away, "Judge Landis is using poor English today. His sentences are too long."[30]

It had been obvious all along that the trial of the IWW was not truly about espionage or sabotage or any of the fantastical allegations heard in Landis's courtroom; the aim was to cripple a union whose style was aggressive, its members militant, its philosophy so revolutionary it could only be alien, and which, in its inclusion of men, women, blacks, whites, skilled, and unskilled, stood as a rebuke not only to the nation but to the rest of the labor movement. Another cause of the discomfort the IWW provoked was that, despite its Bolshevik sympathies and the twisted allegation of its traitorous collaboration with Germany, it was, in reality, *too American*. Certainly it had its Tresca and Giovannitti, who could be dismissed as alien political romantics, or the easily red-tainted George Andreytchine or Vladimir Lossief; but it was Bill Haywood, Elizabeth Flynn, Vincent St. John, and Frank Little who were the more unnerving for their clearly native provenance, a quality shared by a majority of those convicted in Judge Landis's court, men named Glen Roberts, Fred Nelson, George Hardy, "Third-Rail Red" Doran, Charles McWhirt, "Tex" Fraser, Clyde Huff, Archie Sinclair, and so on.

Due to the chill atmosphere of wartime domestic repression in which the trial had been held, and disdain within the general labor movement for the Wobblies, nary a rallying cry emerged from the rest of U.S. labor and the left, as it had for Ettor and Giovannitti, the McNamara brothers or Joe Hill. The government's conduct at trial, Landis's rulings, the sweeping verdicts and sentences—none elicited much comment from the usual bastions of support. As Dubofsky suggests, Americans had been bothered by the drumhead deportations at Bisbee and the mob murder of Frank Little, but it may have appeared less prudent to object openly to what appeared the normal functioning of due process, in this instance the legal persecution of the IWW.[31]

THE ARMISTICE OF NOVEMBER 1918 brought relief and happiness as well as signs of irrevocable change. In Europe governments had fallen; others were under siege from forces within. Communist insurrections had occurred in Hungary and Bavaria, civil violence was rife in Germany; Italian workers occupied their factories, and England's emerging Labour Party vowed to reform the British economy along socialistic lines. Most disturbing to Western observers, the Bolsheviks remained in control in Russia. In America the mood of intolerance lingered, particularly the hatred of Germans and the fear of Bolshevism,[32] while isolationism was stimulated by the war's devastation and the continuing upheaval in Europe. The big foreign policy idea of the day, the League of Nations, a part of the Treaty of Versailles that ended the war and which President Wilson had helped negotiate in Paris, received an ambivalent public reception and was viewed skeptically by Congress. "The American people, who but a few years before had so enthusiastically embraced the reform spirit of Progressivism and then had projected themselves with great zeal into the lofty idealism of the war, were weary of any further experimentation either domestically or internationally," notes historian Robert K. Murray. "They were far less concerned with making the world safe for democracy than with making America safe for themselves."[33]

President Wilson, showing signs of exhaustion, and in defiance of his doctor's advice, embarked on a cross-country speaking tour in early September 1919 in an attempt to resuscitate domestic support for the League of Nations by speaking directly to the American people. At Pueblo, Colorado, he suffered a nervous breakdown and on October 2 a paralytic stroke; the tour canceled, he was immediately brought home to Washington, where he would spend the remaining seventeen months of his presidency a semi-invalid. The next month Congress formally rejected U.S. membership in the league. Wilson was awarded the 1920 Nobel Peace Prize for his efforts.

"Every reform we have won will be lost if we go into this war," the president had told Secretary of the Navy Josephus Daniels in 1917. "The people we have unhorsed will inevitably come into control of the country for we shall be dependent upon the steel, ore and financial magnates. They will run the nation."[34] Wilson's caution was borne out by subsequent events. Just as the war had transformed the president, the laws, and the country, so had it affected industry. On the defensive for many years from forces of reform, industry had attained a position of dominance with the production mandates of the American entry into Europe. It had responded loyally and it had done well, and by 1919 was ready to flex its new confidence and strength.

Labor also strove to realign itself as the peacetime economy slowed production and caused layoffs. In March 1919 there were 175 major strikes; in April, 248; in June, 303; in July, 360; in August, 373. A great number involved unemployed war veterans—a development troubling in numerous ways. There was a sense that men who had sacrificed for their country *should* have jobs. In their absence African Americans had stepped into the

industrial workforce as never before, and the intensified racial compo-
nent in job competition had sparked deadly riots in East St. Louis in 1917
and Chicago in 1919, among other places. Finally, there was a factor many
Americans would have been loath to openly admit—an anxiety about the
returning soldiers, who, scarred by their experiences in a horrific war and
hungry for work, might act out in bold, desperate ways, falling in with
radicals or even fomenting domestic revolution.[35] For all these reasons,
and often with the help of excitable public officials and a sensationalist
press, strikes in the war's immediate aftermath appeared to a nation on
edge unduly portentous; one in particular, the 1919 general strike in the
city of Seattle, assumed the scale of a mass uprising.

The strike crisis began in late 1918 in Seattle's government-run shipyards, where shipbuilders' unions organized as the Metal Trades Council
sought improved wages for unskilled workers. Supervisors tried to break
the unions' solidarity by offering higher pay for skilled laborers only, but
the cause remained intact. Seattle's mayor, Ole Hanson, was determined
to resist labor's demands. A successful real estate speculator who, legend
had it, had come west as a young man from his native Minnesota in a
wagon, Hanson had barnstormed the state of Washington in 1914 as the
Progressive candidate for the U.S. Senate, visiting every town and speaking to audiences from the front seat of an open car; he had initially held
pacifistic views about the United States getting into the war, but once
American troops sailed for Europe he became a super-patriot. He was
known to leave his desk at city hall some afternoons to drop by the shipyards, volunteering to labor beside the ironworkers as a show of support
for the war effort.

Seattle was at war's end a vibrant union town, with active AFL and
IWW locals as well as longshoremen and shipbuilders' unions; even
though employment had been ample in the government-run shipyards
during the war, many unionists had become politicized over the use of the
port as an embarkation point for war matériel to anti-Bolshevik forces in
Russia, who were being assisted by eighty-five hundred U.S. troops. Pamphlets about the revolution in Russia had circulated in the seafront city,

encouraging "workers' power" and discussing the inevitability that trade unions would someday take over industry. The left-leaning Central Labor Council hosted meetings at which speakers recently returned from Moscow described the Revolution's success; a local crowd had in December 1917 welcomed the *Shilka*, the first Soviet vessel to reach Seattle; and local longshoremen several times refused to load vessels carrying munitions to support the anti-Bolshevik fighters.

These disputed munitions were the cause of street violence on January 12, 1919, when police attacked a downtown rally protesting the shipments, clubbing participants and making numerous arrests. So angry were workers at this mistreatment that they gathered a few days later, on January 16, only to once again be set upon by police. With labor issues now merged fully with resentment of official heavy-handedness, on January 21 as many as thirty-five thousand skilled and unskilled shipyard workers walked off the docks. The local Labor Council immediately offered to conduct a general strike to aid the action, with the AFL and IWW locals signing onto the idea. Although newspapers cried alarm over labor's capitulation to Bolshevism, on February 6 an estimated sixty thousand Seattle laborers representing 110 of the city's 130 labor unions halted work, closing a wide array of businesses and services. The city shut down so completely, it was said, even the elevators stopped running.

The general strike was not a familiar labor tactic in America; it had surfaced fleetingly in St. Louis in 1877 and again in New Orleans in 1892. Such disciplined actions were always viewed as alien, carrying a whiff of European-style revolution, and in the politically charged atmosphere of Seattle in 1919 it raised a palpable fear of Bolshevik influence, even anxiety that actual Bolsheviks had insinuated themselves into the town's working masses.[36] Joe Tumulty, an adviser to President Wilson, termed what was occurring in Seattle "the first appearance of the Soviet in this country."[37] But if revolution had come to Seattle it had a willing nemesis in Mayor Hanson. "His ability to guess what the other fellow is going to do amounts to genius," noted one admiring contemporary, "and methods do not disturb him greatly. His rule of fighting is to hit his opponent with everything except perhaps the water bucket."[38] He personally led the arrival of federal troops into the city, riding in a large sedan emblazoned with an American flag. To augment the nearly one thousand soldiers from nearby Fort Lewis, who were reported to have brought with them "a machine gun company and 200 hand grenades," Hanson swore in more than two thousand special deputies, including students from the University of Washington. "Any man who attempts to take over control of municipal government functions here will be shot on sight," Hanson warned.[39] Selected "radical" offices in the city were raided, leading to the arrests of thirty-nine Wobblies, who were denounced as "ringleaders of anarchy."[40]

Local laborites sometimes joked that Hanson suffered from a case of "the Wobbly Horrors," the exaggerated perception that the IWW represented evil incarnate, but the Wobblies had no choice but to take Mayor Hanson's harassment seriously, even as privately they derided him as a "crazy clown."[41] In spring 1918 an IWW stenographer named Louise Olivereau was jailed under the Espionage Act for sending letters urging young men to rethink compliance with the draft, while two AFL leaders, Hulet Wells and Sam Sadler, were also arrested, charged with publishing an antidraft pamphlet. Wells and Sadler had a nightmarish time in prison, Wells at one point being trussed up and suspended by his hands. Anger over the arrest of Olivereau and the abuse of Wells and Sadler spilled over into large protest meetings and street rallies, a surge broad enough to unite even the usually disparate IWW and AFL.

Although in principle a group like the IWW, dedicated to the downfall of capitalism, and the more conservative AFL had little in common, the Lawrence strike as well as the IWW's work with the Marine Transport Workers' Industrial Union on the Philadelphia waterfront had showed the Wobblies capable of organizing around such ordinary union aims as wage increases, overtime pay, and employer recognition of workers' committees. As for the moderate AFL, its locals were capable at times of sharp-elbowed militancy. Clearly the willingness to stop work extended through the leadership and rank and file of these two union causes,[42] and the Seattle AFL, having bettered its members' affairs in the war-production buildup, had a great deal to fight for in resisting assaults on any local labor entity, including the Wobblies.

As revolutions went, the Seattle general strike proved relatively tame. The participants did not attempt to confiscate any private property, nor did they try to seize the reins of city government; they made no effort to commandeer military installations, nor were they themselves armed or organized into fighting units. In addition, a strike committee was designated to ensure that basic municipal services such as trash collection and the provision of milk and coal were maintained. The strike committee approached the city with an offer to call off the general strike if the mayor's aides would press the shipping authorities to accept the demands of the Metal Trades Council, but the city replied that nothing would be discussed until the dockworkers reported to their jobs. These mitigating details, however, were ignored in the flurry of articles and editorials that applauded Hanson's flag-waving and his vow to crush the strike, and that cheered his rejection of the "Bolshevik experiment" on American soil.

Hanson's grandstanding was, if nothing else, timely. Across the country in Washington, a subcommittee of the Senate Judiciary Committee chaired by Senator Lee Slater Overman had been investigating pro-Germanism in America; with the peace in late 1918 and then the outbreak of the Seattle strike a few months later, the subcommittee quickly pivoted, obtaining new directions from Congress to look into domestic radicalism. The Overman panel convened for a month beginning in mid-February, hearing witnesses ranging from John Reed and his wife, journalist Louise Bryant (both of whom had traveled to Moscow), to the conservative New York attorney Archibald E. Stevenson, a former intelligence officer and one of America's leading hysterics on the Soviet menace. Soon it had heard enough to conclude that Communism represented a true global threat, one against which the wide Atlantic and Pacific oceans were no safeguard. In this same season of fear and outrage Eugene Debs was convicted under the Espionage Act for a speech he'd made in Canton, Ohio, denouncing the war, and in March 1919 New York's legislature, apparently grown self-conscious that the Empire State was home to tens of thousands of aliens and real or potential radicals, created its own anti-sedition task force. The Lusk Committee, named for State Senator Clayton R. Lusk, launched immediate inquiries to discover if radicals were plotting—through labor activism, bombings, and the spread of propaganda—to establish a "Dictatorship of the Proletariat."[43]

Watching these developments with mounting alarm, the AFL and other national labor groups recommended that the Seattle workers end their general strike. The Seattle Central Labor Council agreed, and after five days the effort was called off. But the fact that labor had essentially policed itself—had itself judged it wise to tamp down a volatile crisis—received little notice or praise in the nation's press. Instead, the country's acclaim went to Ole Hanson, "a man who has brought himself up by his own efforts to wealth and power," sang a *New York Times* tribute. "[He] was strong enough and brave enough to stand up against the insolent alien efforts to reproduce here the horrible disorders that have ruined Russia. Unconsciously and instinctively Ole Hanson defended and represented the inbred, undying, ineradicable American spirit of ordered freedom."[44]

So enamored was Hanson of his new status that he resigned as mayor and immediately departed eastward on a national speaking tour. At $500 an event he addressed church groups, American Legion posts, ladies' auxiliaries, and businessmen's luncheons, denouncing Bolshevism and vying to fight its menace single-handedly if need be. "If the government doesn't clean them up, *I will*," he swore, a line he repeated at each appearance to predictable audience frenzy. Full of sass and seemingly unstoppable, he urged the federal government to "hang or incarcerate for life all the anarchists." When an aging Samuel Gompers challenged disparaging remarks Hanson had made about the patriotism of the AFL, the Seattle upstart was full enough of himself to dismissively inform the lion of American labor, "I realize that you are old and feeble, and as the body weakens, so does the mind."[45] Over the next seven months Hanson earned the tidy fortune of $40,000 from his lectures, and when asked about his political plans for 1920 and its upcoming presidential election, chose not to discourage speculation.

O LE HANSON REMAINED IN THE NEWS, although not entirely for his political aspirations; on April 28, 1919, a package arrived in the mail at his Seattle office containing a bomb. He was not present, and the contents were harmlessly disposed of, but the incident marked the beginning of an ominous trend. The very next day a mysterious parcel was delivered to the Atlanta home of former U.S. senator Thomas W. Hardwick, who had co-sponsored the Immigration Act of 1918; upon being opened by his maid, Ethel Williams, it exploded, blowing the woman's hands off and injuring the senator's wife, who was standing nearby. A day or two later New York City post office employee Charles Kaplan happened to read in the newspaper about the Hanson and Hardwick bombs, and recognized that their description fit a large number of curious packages he had recently set aside for lack of postage. He immediately notified police, who on investigation discovered that each of the sixteen packages Kaplan had quarantined, all roughly seven inches by three inches, contained a wooden tube loaded with explosives and an acid detonator. Each bore a return address from Gimbels Department Store and was marked NOVELTY—A SAMPLE. Eighteen similar bombs were soon discovered at other post offices across the country, targeting a total of thirty-six people, including J. P. Morgan, John D. Rockefeller Jr., U.S. attorney general A. Mitchell Palmer, Judge Kenesaw Mountain Landis, Supreme Court Associate Justice Oliver Wendell Holmes, and Frederick C. Howe, the immigration chief at Ellis Island. Many of the bombs (which were later found to have come from an Italian anarchist cell centered around Luigi Galleani, publisher of the anarchist periodical *Cronaca Sovversiva*) were accompanied by notes declaring, "There will have to be bloodshed. . . . We will kill, we will destroy to rid the world of your tyrannical institutions," and similar sentiments.

The list of targets was somewhat haphazard, but it was assumed that "Reds" were responsible and on May 1, 1919, extensive police raids went forth against left-leaning offices and newspapers in Boston and New York, while in Cleveland wholesale violence and arrests resulted when war veterans broke up a May Day parade and later joined in ransacking a local Socialist Party office. A new rash of bomb attacks began on June 2, targeting the mayor of Cleveland, a federal judge in New York, and a silk manufacturer in Paterson, among others. The most daring was made on the Washington home of Attorney General Palmer. He and his wife were about to turn in for the night at about 11:15 p.m. when a powerful bomb detonated on the front steps of the house, killing the man who had been apparently about to leave it, an anarchist named Carlo Valdinoci, but so obliterating his features he was not immediately identified; based on the body parts investigators gathered, they at first assumed that two men had been involved in planting the device and had been killed. No one else was injured, but there was extensive damage to the Palmer dwelling and neighboring homes had their windows blown out, including the home of Franklin Delano Roosevelt, then the assistant secretary of the navy, who lived directly across the street. "I had just placed my automobile in the garage and walked home when the explosion took place," Roosevelt told a reporter later that same night by telephone, mentioning that he was standing on broken glass as he spoke. Palmer, raised in a Quaker family, was so shaken that he addressed Roosevelt as "thee" numerous times as the two men surveyed the destruction to the attorney general's house. Roosevelt found a fragment of the bomber's body on his own doorstep, and other neighbors discovered similarly grisly items both inside and outside their damaged homes. The area for blocks around was strewn with leftist pamphlets the bomber or bombers had apparently been carrying and which had been flung far and wide by the blast. Roosevelt referred to them as "Black Hand" leaflets.[46]

As in the case of the bombs sent in late April, no evidence was discovered linking the June 2 bombs to a particular source, let alone a radical clique. But if anything, the police failure to expose those responsible for the bombings only fanned anxiety that the conspiracy at work must be particularly diabolical, consisting of "alien enemies . . . human snakes that are crawling and working their way into the very citadels of our prosperity," according to the *Manufacturers Record*.[47] Soon the *Literary Digest* was reporting the existence of "50,000 aliens in the United States who are openly or secretly working for a Bolshevist form of government," a plot abetted by the "3,000 foreign-language newspapers published here [and] the 8,500,000 residents of this country who are unable to read and write the American language."[48]

While the Progressive press warned against an overreaction and even hinted at a possible frame-up, Palmer's Justice Department set about establishing the means to confront this new and serious threat, the attorney general's efforts invigorated by the attempt on his own life and the lives of his family. Palmer named William J. Flynn, former head of the Secret Service, to lead "the most determined war on anarchy the federal government has ever undertaken,"[49] and Congress stepped up to aid the endeavor with a generous half-million-dollar earmark. Since 1908 the department had had a Bureau of Investigation, the forerunner to the modern FBI; on August 1, 1919, Palmer created a new entity within the bureau that he called the Radical Division (later known as the General Intelligence Division) with the exclusive assignment of ferreting out radicals. The attorney general drew up plans for a campaign that would be comprehensive and leave no stone unturned, placing at its head an officious twenty-four-year-old department attorney, J. Edgar Hoover.

AT THE END OF THE SUMMER OF 1919, the toxic mixture of political paranoia over Bolsheviks and labor unions struggling to manage the postwar economic reconversion erupted in crisis in Boston. City policemen upset over wages and working conditions had founded their own union and sought affiliation with the AFL. The idea of municipal police unions was not new—there were thirty-seven across the country that were part of the AFL, and the Boston Fire Department had an AFL-affiliated union—but in the fearful climate of 1919 a strike threat by society's most essential public servants in so large and important an American city stirred considerable unease.

Work stoppages by municipal employees, in 1919 as throughout U.S. labor history, are roundly disliked not only because they deprive citizens of services integral to the public's safety and well-being, but because government workers are compensated by tax dollars. Public sympathy quickly turns against government employees in such circumstances, and becomes hostile if a strike proves of long duration.

The Boston policemen's grievances included pay not commensurate with postwar inflation—they earned $1,100 per annum and were responsible in their first year of employ for $300 worth of uniforms and equipment—and lengthy twelve-hour shifts that often forced them to stay overnight in police stations without pay. Most of the station houses were inadequate as dormitories; some were unsanitary; one had a single bathtub and only four toilets for the use of 135 officers. "The vermin are so numerous in that station," reported Boston Policemen's Union president John F. McInnes, "that the leather is eaten off the helmets of the men." Patrolmen complained of being used by their superiors as errand boys for purposes of casual graft, such as visiting restaurants to pick up free meals, and were prohibited on their one day off each week from leaving the city limits on the chance they might be recalled to duty. "The Policemen's Union," stated McInnes, "was formed for the sole purpose of breaking these shackles."[50]

Police commissioner Edwin Upton Curtis reacted to the strike murmurings and the union's interest in AFL affiliation by ordering that the Boston police could not join any outside organization, with the exception of war veterans' groups or the American Legion. Lawyers for the commissioner cited the U.S. Supreme Court rulings in *Adair v. United States* (1908) and *Coppage v. Kansas* (1915) as precedents that had established that liberty of contract protected an employer's right to deny employees labor union affiliations with national unions and to discharge employees for union membership. The policemen ignored the commissioner's edict, and on August 11 obtained a formal charter from the AFL, prompting an enraged Curtis to arrest nineteen of the union's leaders for insubordination, including John McInnes. Curtis offered to suspend their sentences if the AFL affiliation was dropped, and set a deadline of September 4 for McInnes and the others to choose their fate.

Boston at that moment was already distracted with multiple labor issues, including the darkening of most of the city's theaters by a work stoppage involving actors, stagehands, and musicians upset with the lack of a grievance process and a policy of nonpayment for rehearsals. Pictures of striking chorus girls ran on the front page of the *Boston Globe* juxtaposed with news of a local Labor Day parade that saw eight thousand workers march in disciplined procession through the city, carrying signs reminding spectators of labor's contribution to the recent war effort.[51]

Mayor Andrew J. Peters attempted to intervene in the threatened police strike, charging a committee of prominent local men led by banker James J. Storrow to find some compromise, perhaps the establishment of a union acceptable to the police that would *not* affiliate with the AFL. Commissioner Curtis, however, backed by Governor Calvin Coolidge and Boston's business elite, spurned any such deal-making. He did not want his police empowered by affiliation with a national labor union, nor did he believe that policemen, firemen, and other essential municipal employees had a right to strike. Representatives of the mayor's committee, the Boston Policemen's Union, and lawyers for the commissioner huddled for five days at the Parker House in late August and early September with no break in the impasse. The standoff gained national attention on September 2, when George T. Page, president of the American Bar Association (which by coincidence was meeting in Boston), denounced the police-AFL affiliation in his annual address. "Men who by the nature of their employment are pledged to the duty of maintaining public health and peace, which depend on the unbroken performance of their duty, now join themselves with an organization whose weapon is the strike," Page lamented. "It is as true as when Christ walked by Galilee that 'ye cannot serve two masters.' "[52]

The Boston police were unfazed by such noble admonitions. Many were former Teamsters or members of the Carmen's or Longshoremen's unions; they were no strangers to labor conflicts and strikes, and most were secure in the knowledge they could return to work in their former fields if necessary. "As far as I am concerned," one confided to a reporter, "I would go back to my old trade, and there are hundreds that feel just as I do." This confidence among the rank and file was reinforced by the stature of the police union's president, the stalwart John McInnes, whose regular duties included directing traffic but was "no ordinary citizen and no ordinary private of the police force. His life history," wrote the *Globe*, "reads like a chapter of a book of adventure." An army veteran, McInnes had been wounded in the Indian Wars, and often told the story of having been present at the death of Sitting Bull; he had also served in the Spanish-American War and fought in the Battle of San Juan. Having learned Italian during a minor army diplomatic posting in Rome, he returned to Boston in the early years of the new century to become a police investigator in a series of Black Hand murders, and was highly regarded both inside and outside the department.[53]

Commissioner Curtis had already set about enlisting a volunteer force of citizens to replace the police in case of a strike, mostly students, war veterans, and members of the American Legion. Several of the enlistees were well-known former Harvard athletes, such as Huntington R. "Tack" Hardwick of Harvard's football and baseball squads; John Richardson Jr., captain of a championship Crimson rowing club; Morrill Wiggin, also a renowned Harvard oarsman; Bartlett Hayes, pitcher on the Harvard nine of 1898; and Thomas G. Cabot, described by one news account as "a husky from the class of '19." At the urging of President A. Lawrence Lowell of Harvard, about 150 current Harvard students also volunteered. "Harvard Organizing Force for Police Duty in Boston," read a headline in the *Globe*. The paper ran display ads offering "Riot, Strike, and Civil Commotion Insurance" to storefront businesses, which were expected to be the targets of looting and vandalism if the police vanished from the city's streets.[54] Curtis had his volunteer recruits put through rudimentary drills at the Irvington Street Armory, and each was issued a pistol, a badge, and a baton.

The situation worsened on September 8, a day before the union's announced strike deadline, when Curtis suspended McInnes and the eighteen others arrested earlier. By now it was evident that the commissioner was only aggravating the situation, and the state AFL and other observers began clamoring for his removal; Governor Coolidge, however, vowed to stand by him, and the city braced for the worst as police officers, fed up with Curtis and his mistreatment of union leaders, voted to strike by an overwhelming margin of 1,134–2.

When, as threatened, most of the force's fifteen hundred police officers walked off their posts at 5:45 p.m. on September 9 (the only exceptions being those officers nearing retirement, who feared endangering their pensions), criminal gangs, gamblers, and juvenile troublemakers began to roam free. As Bostonians cringed behind locked doors, windows were smashed and stores looted along Washington Street, the main shopping thoroughfare; shoe stores were especially hard hit, looters removing their acquisitions to the curb so they could try them on. Muggings were rampant, while players of craps and other outlawed dice games took over Boston Common. "Boston has never seen such a night," observed the *Globe*. "Utterly without police, in the hands of wanton hoodlums, a proud city has fallen into pointless, meaningless disorder."[55] The police stand-ins did their best but proved largely inadequate. Boston authorities may have allowed some of this "crime wave" for its sensational effect, the better to blacken the image of the striking police; if so, it produced the desired result.

Curtis was all for combating the rowdies tooth and nail, while Mayor Peters, chastening Curtis for provoking the crisis in the first place, again proposed some sort of mediation. Governor Coolidge joined Curtis in refusing any compromise with the traitorous strikers. As shop owners boarded up their windows or sat before their premises armed with shotgun and pistol through a second night of rioting and vandalism, Peters called on five thousand members of the state militia to patrol Boston's streets.

The Boston Central Labor Union briefly entertained talk of a general strike in support of the police, but the recent example of Seattle argued against such a move. It was also readily apparent—in the Boston papers as well as in commentary from across the country—that press and public disapproved of the police going on strike, condemning the action in grandiose terms much as it had the Seattle walkout. The *Philadelphia*

Public Ledger decried the "fact" that "Bolshevism in the United States is no longer a specter; Boston in chaos reveals its sinister substance."[56] Even President Wilson was moved to comment, labeling the strike "a crime against civilization."[57]

The introduction of the militia brought tragic results in a number of "rumpuses" across town. In Scollay Square soldiers fired into what was perceived to be an unruly mob, killing several people; on Boston Common, an eighteen-year-old merchant marine was shot to death after he tried to interfere with the arrest of craps players. Dozens of people were injured. "If you stop to watch a crowd you become in an instant part of it," warned the newspapers in a special bold print notice. "There is no such thing now as 'an innocent bystander.' "[58]

The AFL's Samuel Gompers, just back from a labor conference in Europe and quickly taking stock of the situation, advised the police to return to their jobs and seek the judgment of a board of mediation. There were conflicting reports that the police were willing to be reinstated, although they refused under any circumstances to surrender their union affiliation. Unfortunately the bias against the strikers, even without Commissioner Curtis's animosity, had now gone too far to be reversed, and in any case Curtis was backed by Coolidge in rejecting the possibility of reinstatement. "It is manifest that the places in the police force of Boston, formerly held by the men who deserted their posts of duty, have by this action been rendered vacant," Curtis announced.[59]

Gompers publicly warned Curtis that he would be held accountable for his decision. "The situation in which the policemen found themselves today was provoked and practically forced upon them by the autocratic action of Police Commissioner Curtis," Gompers said, "who at any time might have honorably settled the dispute by such action as is naturally expected of a public official in his responsible position."[60] Governor Coolidge then famously replied to Gompers, "Your assertion that the commissioner was wrong cannot justify the wrong of leaving the city unguarded. . . . *There is no right to strike against the public safety by anybody, anywhere, any time.*"[61]

Coolidge's defiant utterance was reprinted in almost every paper in the country, and thousands of approving letters flooded Beacon Hill. Like Seattle's Ole Hanson, the Massachusetts governor was catapulted overnight to national fame. "Thank God for Governor Coolidge and the hard-headed people of Massachusetts," raved the *St. Paul Pioneer Press*, while the *Philadelphia Record* saw the Boston police fight as one of "Americanism vs. Anarchy," and cheered that "Americanism was overwhelmingly victorious." Other papers noted the significance of Coolidge's stand for the stricter handling of labor unions generally, one proposing that it should "stiffen the heart and backbone of every executive in the land."[62]

As threatened, Curtis moved quickly to permanently refill the police ranks, which proved an easy task given the large number of unemployed war veterans in the city. Hundreds of locked-out cops then sued to demand reinstatement, and a boisterous rally was held in their behalf, but the effort was effectively denied. Similarly, an attempt to restore the nineteen union leaders to their jobs was quashed by the courts.

The policemen's modest desire to belong to a national labor union, a conservative one at that, which would help them secure more equitable pay and working conditions, had been interpreted as "crazy Bolshevism" and as an assault on America itself. It was about this time that "Americanism," in the hands of entities such as the American Legion, became a term connoting not the country's purported values of openness and democracy, but rather the worst spirit of reaction. Sadly, this trend of thought affected not only organized labor. Strikers were lacking in "Americanism" for their selfish demands and willingness to cause disruption and inconvenience, but myriad other people, those who did "brain work," such as teachers, writers, and sociologists, or in some way sympathized with labor's cause—the "parlor Reds" and high-society bleeding hearts—all could be stigmatized as untrustworthy, and all warranted scrutiny.

A MERICA'S STEELWORKERS in the difficult summer of 1919 felt much aggrieved, as the wartime improvements in wages and working conditions enjoyed by other industries had largely passed them by. Many still turned in ten- and twelve-hour days, six and even seven days per week, with no benefits, sick time, or vacation—this despite the fact that war had been very good to the industry; profits at U.S. Steel reached $500 million in 1919, a staggering leap from $135 million in 1914. As the old Amalgamated Association of Iron, Steel, and Tin Workers had largely been suppressed in the years since Homestead, it wasn't until 1918 that a consortium of two dozen smaller unions, calling itself the National Committee for Organizing Iron and Steel Workers, joined together to bring steelworkers meaningful union representation. "One mighty drive to organize the steel plants of America," was how William Z. Foster, an IWW veteran, general organizer of the Railway Carmen's Union, and leader of the newly united steel unions, described the workers' ambition.[63] Foster and steel's rank and file demanded a wage increase, an eight-hour day, a system of collective bargaining, and union recognition.

The prospects were good, or so it seemed, because the Wilson years had brought labor several key advances—the Clayton Act, the creation of the Department of Labor, the Industrial Commission Report of 1915— and unions had come out dependably for the president's reelection in 1916. The following year, 1917, saw the president again extend a helping hand to his labor friends by appointing a President's Mediation Commission to address workers' issues related to the war. The panel examined copper mining, Chicago packinghouses, and the telephone and lumber businesses, and in January 1918 determined that what was needed was a government-recognized policy of collective bargaining between workers and management, employer-established grievance mechanisms, and the eight-hour day. Like the Industrial Commission Report, these wartime recommendations are now recognized as a kind of rough draft of the New Deal, and at the time, labor was not shy in its enthusiasm. "Messiah is arriving," Sidney Hillman of the Almalgamated Clothing Workers exulted. "He may be with us any minute—one can hear the footsteps of the Deliverer—if only he listens intently. Labor will rule and the world will be free."[64] Foster, like Hillman and many others, was emboldened by the board's findings to believe it a propitious time for progress in steelworkers' rights. "The gods were indeed fighting on the side of labor," echoes Dubofsky. "It was an opportunity to organize the [steel] industry as might never again occur."[65]

U.S. Steel chairman Judge Elbert H. Gary, however, refused to negotiate with the National Committee for Organizing Iron and Steel Workers, and President Wilson appeared reluctant to intervene. Foster and other union leaders warned that strike talk was too prevalent among the workers to hold back what was about to occur, and on September 22, 1919, as the White House remained mute, 350,000 steelworkers from nine different states walked off the job. It appeared that in the year and a half since the Mediation Commission's labor-friendly pronouncements of early 1918, much had changed. The war, and the collaborative mood based around manufacturing production, had ended, and both the Justice Department and Congress had fallen under the spell of anti-Communism. The strike also occurred as Wilson was preoccupied with promoting the League of Nations to the country, and after suffering a stroke on October 2 he was, for all intents and purposes, a convalescent.

The truth was that there had always been more than met the eye in the generally favorable relationship between Wilson and labor. His presidential commissions and boards released bold prescriptions for meaningful reforms, but the administration rarely followed up on their recommendations; industry, meanwhile, was pleased to deny unionism its basic rights as long as Wilson's attorney general, Palmer, was determined to flex his department's might in the full-time business of busting "labor radicals." "No American president had ever before succeeded in so humbugging the people as Woodrow Wilson," a disappointed Emma Goldman later said. "[He] wrote and talked democracy, acted despotically, privately and officially, and yet managed to keep up the myth that he was championing humanity and freedom."[66] Laborites could only watch in despair as a moment of opportunity passed by, and recall that only eighteen months before, as one historian writes, "The steel worker was made to feel that he was mightily helping to win the war [and] the American worker read in the newspaper that he was an important person, that President Wilson, General Pershing and other great men were relying on him."[67]

In rejecting the possibility of strike talks, Judge Gary said he accepted the right of workers to unionize, but feared unionization meant a closed shop that would allow a small number of workers to bend others to their will. "If such a minority were to control the industries of the country," he exclaimed, "it would mean national decay and defeat in the trade competition with other countries."[68] Observers recognized a familiar impasse, no different from that which had afflicted the Colorado coalfields five years before, in that big steel's owners and stockholders were using misleading terms like "freedom of choice" and "liberty of contract" to refuse labor the very power of combination the corporations themselves enjoyed, thus denying workers the ability to bargain in any meaningful way. As the AFL helpfully pointed out to Judge Gary, "When trade unionism enters an industry that industry ceases to be despotism, because the union workers have a voice."[69]

Curiously, one of the critics of Gary's stance was none other than John D. Rockefeller Jr., the scourge of Ludlow. At the urging of his labor guru, Mackenzie King, and through his greater involvement with the operations of his Colorado coal interests, Rockefeller had become a convert to the idea that, as King had said, "this is a period of transition in which organized labor is bound to come in for an ever increasing measure of recognition." Called to Washington by President Wilson in 1919 to join a conference that focused in part on the impending steel strike, Rockefeller met with Judge Gary as well as Henry Clay Frick of Homestead notoriety. Both men rebuffed Rockefeller's advocacy for fair worker representation and collective bargaining, Gary going so far as to suggest to Rockefeller that he was showing disloyalty to the very concepts that sustained large industry. Rockefeller stood his ground, urging Gary to modernize his views in order to avert a dangerous steel strike. "Surely," said Rockefeller, "it is not consistent for us as Americans to demand democracy in government and to practice autocracy in industry."[70]

At the steel mills three months of picketing and fierce recriminations ensued, as law enforcement at every level of government joined with large numbers of scabs, spies, and deputized enforcers to confront striking steelworkers and stir up dissent within union ranks. Martial law was declared in various steel towns, and eighteen strikers were killed. At Gary, Indiana, both the National Guard and federal troops were called in to occupy the community. A particularly gruesome murder, that of UMW organizer Fannie Sellins, occurred at West Natrona, Pennsylvania. Sellins, who had been cautioned by a local magistrate "not to emulate Mother Jones," was on her way to file a complaint with authorities about a special deputy who had killed a miner when she and a colleague, Joseph Starzelski, were set upon by a posse of deputies and shot dead. Despite arrests in the case, the killings were ruled "justifiable homicide" and no one was ever prosecuted. A photograph of the murdered woman's face was made into a button worn in protest by steelworkers.[71]

The willingness of the federal government to side with the corporations, as it did in dispatching troops to Gary, was a grave disappointment to the nation's steelworkers, although equally hurtful to the strike's chances was the refusal of the railroad unions to honor the strike with sympathy stoppages that would have had a crippling effect on big steel, and the willingness of tens of thousands of black workers to step in as replacements for the striking men. Even more devastating was the campaign of red-baiting embarked upon by the mills, successfully shifting the battle from a labor-management dispute over wages and conditions to one that invoked the alleged radicalism of "Bolsheviks" and Wobblies. The idea that the steel strike represented any kind of conspiracy, Bolshevik or otherwise, was ludicrous, since, as one commentator quipped, "A strike movement of 300,000 men in a dozen states is about as secret as a presidential campaign."[72] Indeed, as a follow-up study by the Interchurch World Movement noted, the steel strike's leaders made every effort to avoid the charge of radicalism by handling the work stoppage in a straightforward manner more common to traditional trade unionism.[73] But the propaganda spewed by the steelmakers was as effective as it was relentless, finding ready outlets in daily newspapers.

These efforts were abetted by the steel industry's discovery of a book William Foster had written years earlier in which he'd condemned the wage system as a "brazen and gigantic robbery" and demanded that "the thieves at present in control of the industries must be stripped of their booty."[74] Foster dismissed the work as juvenilia; it had been out of print for many years and no steel striker was found to be carrying a copy, but a facsimile edition was printed by the steel owners and distributed to churches, government agencies, and members of the press. Foster's youthful anticapitalist thoughts, recycled by Big Steel, played into the assumption that the strikers, for their willingness to halt one of the nation's essential industries, were un-American.

Making little headway, the unions sought help from outsiders who had offered to mediate, but Judge Gary, sensing victory and continuing to dismiss Foster's emissaries and the strikers at large as "Soviets," remained firm in his refusal to negotiate. In the bitter cold of January 1920, the strike committee surrendered to U.S. Steel's far greater strength and resources, and most workers—excepting those ostracized for strike activities—went back to the mills, having failed to attain even a hearing for their demands. It was estimated that more than $100 million in wages had been lost during the work stoppage.

The strike's collapse represented a lost opportunity for a labor movement whose hopes had risen with the shared patriotism of the war, and for American labor-industrial relations generally. A disciplined strike leadership making reasonable demands, and a deserving workforce that had performed heroically during the war, had been given the cold shoulder by a powerful corporation disdainful of democratic processes. U.S. Steel had refused to share influence, even proportionately, with unionized workers, while a president and administration often sympathetic to the cause of unionism had failed to intervene. As the Interchurch study found, U.S. Steel had from the start been largely and willfully ignorant of its workers' grievances, and had remained throughout the crisis basically incurious about the strike's motivations. Their goal instead had been to paint the strikers as something they were not, and it had worked. Laborites could only watch as a potential moment for reform ebbed away, a keenly felt disappointment.

THE OWNERS OF THE NATION'S COAL MINES proved as steadfast as the steel bosses in rejecting negotiation when, on November 1, 1919, the United Mine Workers struck for a postwar adjustment on wages and hours. The public understandably grew apprehensive as, with winter coming, half a million coal miners switched off their headlamps and set down their tools. The *Memphis Commercial Appeal* urged a swift resolution, noting that while miners and mine owners deserved respect, "the rights of 110,000,000 American freemen are superior to those of a few hundred operators or 500,000 miners." Publisher William Randolph Hearst suggested that "the mines must be worked even if the government itself has to work them."[75]

During the war the cessation of coal production would have been not only unpatriotic but illegal, and although the war had technically ended, a federal court in Indianapolis, with a nod from President Wilson, went ahead and issued an injunction against the strike. The return of the hated injunction, which labor had hoped it had seen the last of with the passage of the Clayton Act of 1914, infuriated unions; the AFL denounced the court's action in no uncertain terms and urged the miners to stand firm. But UMW chief John L. Lewis knew well that the public had a very short patience for coal strikes, and having studied how devastating injunctions had been in the past, particularly against Debs and the ARU in 1894, he ordered the UMW rank and file back to work. "We are Americans. We cannot fight our government," he told reporters.[76] Lewis's loyal words didn't save him from a contempt citation, however, when some UMW miners wildcatted and refused his order to resume work. A continuation of the crisis was averted only when the government suggested a 14-cent wage increase as a stopgap, and established an arbitration council to look into the miners' claims of being underpaid.

While the miners fared better than their brethren in the steel mills, in that they did obtain some concession for their trouble, it was distressing that a federal injunction had once again been effectively deployed to break a strike, and that the public had been led to resent labor for its "radical" intentions. The *Seattle Times* arrogantly termed the rejection of labor's demands "the natural outcome" of a war fought for democracy, and applauded the fact that "before the force of that righteous, American 'solidarity,' the bogus 'solidarity' preached by the IWW . . . has crumbled and is crumbling everywhere."[77]

At the moment, these two "solidarities" were on a collision course in the town of Centralia, Washington, about sixty-five miles south of Seattle. Situated in lumber country, the town had a strong IWW presence, but was also home to several reactionary organizations—the Employers Association of Washington, the Citizens' Protective League, as well as chapters of both the Elks and the American Legion. Local police were in sympathy with these groups and had made no attempt to intervene on Memorial Day 1918 when "patriots" stormed the Centralia IWW office, carried boxes of the group's records, literature, and furniture into the street and fed the entire haul to a giant bonfire; even the local's typewriter was sacrificed. A handful of Wobblies were arrested, while a blind news dealer who faithfully sold the IWW's *Industrial Worker* was kidnapped, taken by car to a neighboring county, and shoved into a ditch.[78]

By November 1919 the IWW had managed to open a new hall in a former hotel. Hearing rumors that members of the American Legion were planning to use the distraction of an upcoming Armistice Day parade to launch another assault, the Wobblies issued a leaflet reassuring locals that rumors of Bolshevism and radicalism in the community were exaggerated. "Our only crime is solidarity, loyalty to the working class and justice to the oppressed," the appeal explained.[79] They braced for the expected attack, arming men within their headquarters on the day of the parade and positioning others across the street and on an adjacent hillside. "I fought for democracy in France," vowed one Wobbly, "and I'm going to fight for it here."[80] When the parade passed by as scheduled, a squad of Legionnaires led by Post Commander Warren Grimm, a former football All-American at the University of Washington who went by his gridiron nickname, "Wedge," broke off from the procession and charged the IWW hall. The well-positioned Wobbly guns opened fire, cutting Grimm down, but the Legion had superior numbers and could not be repulsed for long; they successfully scattered the Wobblies, some of whom hid in an old meat locker until arrested while others escaped out a back door and fled.[81]

Wesley Everest, an IWW lumberjack and decorated war veteran, had donned his uniform that morning in honor of the holiday. He had fired at the attackers from the IWW hall, then dropped his rifle and sprinted for safety as the Legion men came crashing in. He made it as far as a river just outside the town before he was overtaken. Wheeling around and holding his pursuers at bay with a pistol, he cried, "Stand back! If there are 'bulls' in the crowd, I'll submit to arrest. Otherwise lay off me."[82] When Dale Hubbard, nephew of the president of the Employers Association, ignored Everest's warning and advanced, Everest fired, killing Hubbard on the spot. Everest was then swarmed by Legion men, who, furious over the deaths of "Wedge" and Hubbard, beat him mercilessly before marching him to jail and leaving him in a bloodied heap on the floor of the lockup. That night the streetlights were doused long enough for a lynch mob to enter the jail. As he was dragged toward the door Everest shouted to his cellmates, "Tell the boys I died for my class."[83]

E ACH DAY, IT SEEMED, there were new threats to consider, new reports of radical mischief reaching the desk of Attorney General A. Mitchell Palmer. In March 1919 the Third International meeting in Moscow had confidently embraced a policy of world revolution. The left wing of the Socialist Party, favoring the shift in direction shown by the Third International, did well in party elections in the United States that spring. In response the party ruptured, the more staid executive committee expelling forty thousand members, two-thirds of its body, for trying to turn the party into a revolutionary cause. In August this left wing departed formally, itself splitting into two factions—the aliens forming the Communist Party, with about sixty thousand members; the Americans, led by John Reed, forming the Communist Labor Party, with ten thousand. The old Socialist Party was left in the hands of Eugene Debs and Morris Hillquit.

Palmer had no sooner been confronted with the fact that two separate Communist parties had formed in the United States than muckraker Lincoln Steffens emerged after a brief visit to Moscow to make the spirited pronouncement, "I have seen the future, and it works."[84] Given the simultaneous rise in the number of strikes in America, the attorney general perhaps could not be blamed for imagining Communist and anarchist plotters in every darkened doorway. The increase in labor stoppages alone was disturbing—up from twelve hundred in 1914 to about thirty-five hundred each in the years 1918 and 1919, a trend accompanied by a soaring rate of new union membership, from 2.7 million at the beginning of the war to 4.2 million shortly after the armistice. President Wilson, meanwhile, distracted by his advocacy for the League of Nations and convalescing from the stroke he had suffered, was out of touch, not convening a single cabinet meeting between August 1919 and April 1920. In lieu of any calming words from the White House, and with increased action and rhetoric on the radical and labor fronts, the public outcry about dangerous "reds" grew in volume. Congress was moved in October 1919 to pass a resolution, aimed at the attorney general, demanding greater strides in the effort to rid the country of subversives.[85]

The apparent lameness of the White House in the crisis was a reminder that 1600 Pennsylvania Avenue would soon have a vacancy, and there was no discounting Palmer's political ambition as he strategized how best to put down domestic radicalism. Two provincial figures, Ole Hanson and Calvin Coolidge, men far less connected to federal authority than he, had been transformed overnight into American icons for their sturdy displays of patriotism in the face of local labor troubles allegedly fomented by radicals. Surely leading the Justice Department's crusade in that same battle on a national scale would be an even more impressive accomplishment, and a fitting enhancement to Palmer's résumé if the Democratic Party wished to consider him as their standard-bearer.

The expectation of such an opportunity was not unrealistic. His life thus far had been more or less a steady, unimpeded march toward ever-grander attainments and rewards. Declared an intellectual prodigy as a child, he had graduated from Swarthmore at age nineteen in 1891 with the highest honors in the college's history; in 1893 he passed the bar and worked in private practice for a decade before winning election to two terms in Congress from northeastern Pennsylvania. As vice chairman of the Democratic National Committee in 1912, he had helped deliver Pennsylvania to Woodrow Wilson, who in gratitude offered Palmer the position of secretary of war, which Palmer graciously turned down on account of his Quaker faith. He did accept from Wilson a series of key judicial assignments, including the influential post of alien property custodian, overseeing the wartime seizure of German patents and their sale to U.S. interests on the open market; the president named him attorney general in early 1919 over the objections of Thomas W. Gregory, the man retiring from the position, who distrusted Palmer as a smooth-handed political operator.

While Palmer worried about anarchists and possible Soviet influence in the United States, the outlook of his special deputy, J. Edgar Hoover, was somewhat more complex. Hoover's dedication to ferreting out radicals appears to have been motivated not solely by concern for their politics, but by contempt for what he perceived as their hatred of authority, their disrespecting of religion, and their expressions of sexual freedom. As one historian of the era notes, to Hoover, a character such as Emma Goldman, for her long-standing belief in free love, atheism, and political assassination, "must have appeared a witch and a whore all wrapped in one."[86] Having worked initially for the Library of Congress, Hoover proved adroit at cataloging and managing vast reams of information, and he had quickly become the Justice Department's leading expert on U.S.-based radicals, keeping tabs on no fewer than sixty thousand suspects.[87] He also maintained a scrapbook of "anti-American" articles published by the radical press, soon to be joined by a second scrapbook of press notices about his and Palmer's activities.

Because of their adoption of the revolutionary creed of the Third International, both of the new domestic Communist parties were now, in Hoover's view, vulnerable to the Immigration Act of 1918, in that they were pursuing an alien ideology to seek the overthrow of the U.S. government. On November 7, 1919, his and Palmer's agents responded, staging raids against the Union of Russian Workers, a New York–based labor organization founded in 1907 with four thousand members nationwide. The raids—timed to coincide with the second anniversary of the Bolshevik Revolution—were carried out in a dozen cities, although the main focus was on the group's lower Manhattan headquarters at Fifteenth Street off of Union Square, where two hundred men and women were captured along with numerous boxes of "radical propaganda." A *New York Times* account suggests a scene that would be repeated dozens of times in cities across the country in the coming months:

> The raid was executed swiftly. Automobiles filled with detectives, uniformed police, and federal agents drove up quietly one by one and parked on side streets. Those within had not the slightest idea of what was coming and the police had penetrated the Russian People's House from top to bottom before any alarm was given.
>
> Some of the women [were] especially vociferous in their demands to know the meaning of the raid. The harsh command to "Shut up, there, you, if you know what's good for you," brought silence, and those in the building were hustled into waiting automobiles and driven away.
>
> A number of those in the building were badly beaten by the police during the raid, their heads wrapped in bandages testifying to the rough manner in which they had been handled. . . . Doors were taken off, desks were ripped open, and even the few carpets were torn up to find possible hiding places for documents.[88]

The November 7 raids were roundly applauded. "A fine looking bunch they are," Buffalo's chief of police said of fifty arrested radicals in his city. "It's too bad we can't line them up against a wall and shoot them."[89] The mayor of Davenport, Iowa, was even more explicit: "Load up the riot guns for immediate use and give them a reception with hot lead. We don't want any Reds here and we will go to the limit to keep them out."[90] Humane by comparison was Tennessee senator K. D. McKellar's suggestion that America erect a penal colony on Guam for the nation's political undesirables.[91]

Despite public and official applause for the Justice Department's actions, the raids had scored little in the way of actual radicals. Most of the Union of Russian Workers' upper echelon had repatriated to Russia following the Bolshevik Revolution, and the members who had stayed in the United States were chiefly engaged in nonpolitical work such as reading circles, musical events, and English-language classes. As historian Richard Gid Powers details, "Of the 650 arrested in New York [there was] evidence to hold only 39 after their initial interrogation."[92]

There remained considerable pressure on Palmer from Congress, however, to carry through with the deportation of more then two hundred radicals seized in recent months and held at New York's Ellis Island, particularly after November 25, when a supposed "bomb factory" was discovered in New York City and linked by investigators to the Union of Russian Workers. Deportations required the complicity of the U.S. Department of Labor, which governed issues related to immigration, and soon, with the coordination of the Labor and Justice departments, the first of what was assumed would be many large deportations was scheduled. Hoover had found the vessel necessary for the job in an aging troop transport, the *Buford*, bought by the United States from Britain in 1898 to ferry military personnel home from the Spanish-American War.

On December 20, after a last supper on American soil of frankfurters, cabbage, rice pudding, apple sauce, and coffee, the 249 deportees at Ellis Island were told to ready themselves for departure. The three best-known were Emma Goldman, Alexander Berkman, and Peter J. Bianki, general secretary of the Union of Russian Workers. "Lugging their grips and old-fashioned, foreign-looking portmanteaus," it was reported,

the Reds trooped into . . . the brilliantly lighted [waiting] room. They put their belongings down in heaps and squatted down on them. Some sat with hands under chin, elbows on knees; some read books; others glanced through tattered copies of newspapers. Groups talked noisily in Russian. Here and there a man strummed the melancholy strains of Russian peasant songs upon a battered banjo, guitar, or mandolin.[93]

Goldman and Berkman had been arrested at the *Mother Earth* offices on June 15, 1917, and charged with conspiracy to interfere with the draft; both were sentenced to two years in federal custody. Berkman was dispatched to a penitentiary in Atlanta, and Goldman to a facility in Jefferson City, Missouri; *Mother Earth* and a paper Berkman edited, the *Blast*, had been shut down. Despite their arrests on antidraft efforts, Hoover had managed to steer both of their cases into immigration violations, claiming Goldman's long-ago naturalization to have been irregular and citing her "advocation of violence" for having published remarks in *Mother Earth* sympathetic to the three bomb-makers killed in the July 4, 1914, explosion in New York.[94]

"I do not consider it a punishment to be sent to Soviet Russia," Goldman, who was dressed entirely in black, informed a reporter covering the *Buford*'s departure. "On the contrary I consider it an honor to be the first political agitator deported from the United States. The Czar of Russia never resorted to such autocratic methods as the government of the United States has in dealing with Russians. . . . This practice of deportation means the beginning of the end of the United States government."[95] Peter Bianki told the same newsman, "Damn the country . . . glad to go!" Ascending the gangplank of the ship, Bianki turned one last time and with a gesture toward shore shouted, "Long live the revolution in America!"[96]

The *Buford* hoisted anchor at dawn on December 21. "Shortly after 6 o'clock, splashing and rasping in the silence of the empty bay, the *Buford*'s prow swung lazily eastward," it was recorded. "A patch of foam slipped from under the stern, and 249 persons who didn't like America left it."[97] A security detail of 250 soldiers rode along on what the newspapers had dubbed "the Soviet Ark." "It is hoped and expected that other vessels, larger, more commodious, carrying similar cargoes, will follow in her wake," suggested the *Cleveland Plain Dealer*.[98] Press coverage of the sailing was ample and mostly positive, providing Hoover with many new articles to add to his scrapbook, as well as the limerick:

> *I saw fair Emma leave our shores,*
> *And crepe was festooned on her lid;*
> *She sailed with many other bores who talked too much,*
> *As Emma did.*[99]

Two weeks after the boat's departure, on January 2, 1920, Palmer's agents struck again, as raids in thirty-three cities nabbed four thousand people. On January 6 the exercise was repeated, bringing the total number of suspects detained to almost ten thousand.

Lost in all the excitement of the raids, however, was the fact that somewhere at the bottom of all this activity there was supposed to be a conspiracy actively trying to overthrow the government of the United States. Thus far only four bombs, small iron balls actually, had been discovered in a single Communist Party meeting place. These had been removed under great care to a U.S. attorney's office and for precaution submerged in a large pail of water, where they were duly exhibited to curious reporters, who transmitted word of their seizure far and wide. This damning evidence of a planned revolution, however, one critic of the raids later noted, "must have melted in the pail of water, for they were never heard of again."[100]

Q UIET MISGIVINGS ABOUT THE MANNER in which the campaign to rid America of "undesirables" was being carried out had begun to be shared among some jurists, journalists, and reformers. Raids, deportations, and the holding of suspects incommunicado as a means of battling un-Americanism had itself begun to feel un-American. Was the threat truly so great that it merited the disregard of civil liberties and—in the case of New York's legislature, which in April 1920 expelled five duly-elected Socialists—the notion of democratically elected government?

The five Socialists—Charles Solomon, Louis Waldman, Samuel Orr, August Claessens, and Samuel DeWitt—had been called before the Assembly Speaker and accused of "seeking seats in the Assembly after having been elected on a platform that is absolutely inimical to the best interests of the State of New York and the United States." In an all-night session at which the ouster was discussed, State Senator Clayton R. Lusk, who led the effort, insisted the Socialists represented revolutionary elements and declared that "any man who says the country is not in danger is uninformed, unintelligent or disloyal."[101] The Socialists' defenders included Senator William Copeland Dodge, who countered that expulsion would contradict the Bill of Rights,[102] as well as Assemblyman Theodore Roosevelt Jr., son of the former president, who warned that despite the body's abhorrence of the principles of the Socialist Party, neither the accusations of disloyalty during the war nor intent to overthrow the U.S. government had been proven; to expel men duly elected to office would be "a crime against representative government."[103] After extensive and rancorous debate the Assembly voted 140–6 to suspend the five.

This bizarre act was instantly denounced. "Even the Czar of Russia," pointed out the *Schenectady Citizen*, "permitted Socialists to sit in the Duma," adding that about fifty thousand New York residents would be effectively without representation in the state Assembly with the expulsion of the men they had elected to office.[104] There was also increasing doubt about the excessive actions of the legislature's Lusk Committee, which had authorized raids on several left-leaning entities, chiefly in New York City. While some of the individuals captured in the Lusk raids had been aboard the *Buford*, most of the raids had produced rather comical results—Russian musicians captured during a rehearsal and packed off to jail with their instrument cases; "thirty-eight merrymaking youths" arrested while dancing at a party in Brooklyn; and several elderly men who seemed, upon reflection, as likely a threat to the United States as the pigeons in Herald Square.

Above all, it was the *Buford* deportations that had begun to haunt the nation's conscience, gathering doubt about the sailing's propriety best captured in a cartoon in Max Eastman's *Liberator* showing the smoke from the departing vessel's funnel obliterating the face of the Statue of Liberty.[105] Labor Secretary William B. Wilson reported that the original intention had been to not deport anyone with family in the United States until arrangements could be made for all to travel together, but that officials at Ellis Island had taken matters into their own hands. Authorities there later professed to have been unaware that married men were among the deportees, a claim that was hardly credible since a group of wives and children had staged a noisy, heartrending demonstration in a futile attempt to see their husbands and fathers as the *Buford* prepared to leave.[106]

It was more troubling that the deportees had been treated with scant regard for their civil rights. Palmer and Hoover had exploited the fact that deportation issues were under the jurisdiction of the Labor Department, whose inquiries were pursued as an administrative matter under the Immigration Act of 1918 and were not subject to the legal constraints of criminal law or due process. As the deportations were technically not punishment, none of the accused was represented by counsel, nor did a judge or jury evaluate any of the "verdicts." The *Buford*'s passengers, categorized by the press as "the un-holiest cargo that ever left our shores,"[107] were for the most part only "guilty" of being aliens who harbored left-leaning thoughts. Alexander Berkman had tweaked Hoover about this just before the ship left, slyly pointing out that most of the "passengers" were not yet anarchists, but that he (Berkman) would make them so by the time they'd crossed the Atlantic.

A discernible shift in opinion was also taking place on the Supreme Court, evident in strong dissenting opinions in the case of *Abrams v. United States*. During the war a Russian immigrant and anarchist named Jacob Abrams and six others had printed and distributed five thousand pamphlets criticizing President Wilson's interventionist policy toward Russia and advising American workers that a general strike in the United States might be an effective means of protesting it. In October 1918 five of the defendants, all Russian aliens, were convicted under the Sedition Act and sentenced to prison for from three to twenty years. On November 10, 1919, the Supreme Court heard *Abrams* on appeal and affirmed the convictions. In dissent were justices Louis Brandeis and Oliver Wendell Holmes.

This represented a turnabout for Holmes, who earlier that year had voted with the court's unanimous ruling in the case *Schenck v. United States*, in which Schenck, a Socialist, had been arrested under the Espionage Act for distributing antidraft pamphlets. At issue was whether strong political opinions were protected by the First Amendment or could be deemed dangerous by Congress. "The question in every [such] case," Holmes had written, "is whether the words used are used in such a nature as to create a clear and present danger that they will bring about the substantive evils that Congress has a right to prevent."[108]

By November, however, when the *Abrams* appeal came before the court, Holmes's thinking had evolved; now in his dissent he emphasized that the "clear and present danger" standard he had proposed in *Schenck* must relate to some very specific plot or act. "When men have realized that time has upset many fighting faiths," he wrote, "they may come to believe . . . that the ultimate good desired is better reached by free trade in ideas [and that] the best test of truth is the power of the thought to get itself accepted in the competition of the market. We should be eternally vigilant against attempts to check the expressions of opinions we loathe."[109]

Perhaps the most effective assault on the Red Scare mentality rose from within the federal government itself. Louis Post, the assistant secretary of labor, was a veteran journalist and attorney whose scope of experience included assisting the federal Reconstruction-era suppression of the Ku Klux Klan in South Carolina. In March of 1920 Labor Secretary Wilson fell ill, and Post became acting secretary. Never entirely comfortable with the hysterical tone of the hunt for radicals, he acted quickly to undo the arrangement wherein confessions wrought from hastily rounded-up suspects, without benefit of counsel, were used against them in Labor Department deportation hearings. He began canceling deportations and releasing from custody those who appeared innocent. "Very few, if any,"

Post later said, "were the kind of aliens that Congress could in all reasonable probability have intended to comprehend in its anti-alien legislation."[110]

As he acquainted himself further with Palmer's and Hoover's methods, Post grew outraged at the extensive use the government had made of spies and agents provocateurs to entrap suspects. In one scenario, suspected Detroit subversives were sent notices that a package was being held for them at an American Express office. Federal agents had stuffed the packages with Communist literature the government had recently confiscated, and when the victims came to pick up the packages they were arrested. A more blatant and unfair form of entrapment the seventy-one-year-old Post could not remember.[111]

Given the character of his inquiries, Post would not have been surprised to learn that Hoover was in the process of investigating *him*, in the hope of connecting Post to the IWW or some other radical cult. Post had in fact defended men and women persecuted in free speech fights during the First World War, and he and his wife had once entertained Emma Goldman in their home.[112] But when Attorney General Palmer asked a House Rules subcommittee to consider impeaching Post, Congress stated it saw no reason to do so. Post, however, cleverly seized the opportunity to testify, using the platform to turn the tables on Palmer by publicly voicing his conclusions of the wrongs inherent in the Justice Department raids. In a book he wrote about the era, *The Deportations Delirium of 1920*, Post accused the department of reviving "the revolting secret-police operations of Germany and Russia before the World War had abolished Kaisers and czars."[113] Considering the thousands of people Palmer had "charged with [a] deportable offense," there were in the end, according to Post, hardly "more than a canoe load of deportees."[114]

Post's apostasy was echoed in June 1920 in a Massachusetts court ruling that membership in neither the Communist Party nor the Communist Labor Party was adequate grounds for deportation. Judge George W. Anderson, in handing down his decision, scolded the federal government and its agents for the slipshod, unconstitutional methods they had employed in their raids in November 1919 and January 1920. In *Colyer v. Skeffington*, Anderson characterized the extensive use Hoover's agency made of spies and agents provocateurs as un-American. Through these secret agents' infiltrations, Anderson posited, the U.S. Justice Department actually "operates some part of the Communist Party in this country." Such a damning accusation from the bench infuriated Hoover,[115] who immediately ordered a stealth inquiry into Anderson's background and beliefs. Then a minor bombshell struck: a letter surfaced written by a Hoover surrogate instructing Justice Department agents to have informers arrange "radical" meetings for the night of January 2, 1920, in order to facilitate the second round of the Palmer raids. Congress and much of the press recoiled at such barefaced evidence of entrapment. "In the light of what is now known," the *Christian Science Monitor* observed, "it seems clear that what appeared to be an excess of radicalism on the one hand was certainly met with something like an excess of suppression."[116]

Attorney General Palmer had probably played the fear card for the last time in any case. In late April 1920 he had warned of a radical uprising likely to be staged on May 1, the traditional "radicals' holiday," and urged sharp vigilance. Dutifully, many state and city governments called out militias and placed guards at official buildings and monuments. Police ringed the New York Public Library, Pennsylvania Station, the main post office, and other civic structures, while prominent judges, politicians, and the notably wealthy received extra protection. "City Under Guard Against Red Plot Threatened Today," blared the *New York Times*, which warned that authorities would "strike swiftly in the event of Red hostility."[117] But when not a single incident or disturbance was reported anywhere in the country, the press, so long complicit in the antiradical fever, finally turned on Palmer, one paper suggesting that the May Day scare had been "a mare's nest hatched in the attorney general's brain," and calling on Palmer to get over his obsession with Reds and let the country move on.[118] Palmer and his associates tried to defuse the criticism by saying it had been the government's astute warnings that had prevented trouble, but few appeared willing to accept such a claim.

Finally there came a most sweeping indictment. On May 28 a group of some of the country's most prominent judges, including Felix Frankfurter, Roscoe Pound, Swinburne Hale, and Frank Walsh, published, with the help of the American Civil Liberties Union, an explosive pamphlet titled *A Report Upon the Illegal Practices of the United States Department of Justice.* Calling Palmer's brand of intolerance "the most alarming manifestation in America today," it gave a detailed account of his methods,[119] citing that

> the office of the Attorney General, acting by its local agents throughout the country, and giving express instructions from Washington, has committed illegal acts. . . . Wholesale arrests both of aliens and citizens have been made without warrant or any process of law; men and women have been jailed and held incommunicado without access of friend or counsel . . . agents of the Department of Justice have been introduced into radical organizations for the purpose of informing upon their members or inciting them to activities.[120]

The report reprinted numerous affidavits in which arrested radicals complained of being served inedible food, placed for punishment in "sweat rooms," threatened with death, and denied exercise or reading material as well as access to medical assistance.

Hoover, having been tipped off about the publication, had immediately ordered a thorough secret inquiry into the lives of the book's authors in hopes of discrediting them. The idea of a young self-important Washington bureaucrat like Hoover seeking ways to besmirch the reputations of the nation's most eminent jurists, including four Harvard Law School professors, most of whom he had never heard of, was laughable, although it anticipated the paranoia and underhandedness for which Hoover would be known in his long tenure as director of the FBI.

Palmer and Hoover themselves proved uncooperative witnesses when brought before a Senate hearing into the Justice Department's tactics in spring 1921. Convened by Montana's Thomas J. Walsh, who had led President Wilson's Industrial Commission inquiry, the hearings confirmed much of what had appeared in the *Report Upon the Illegal Practices*. Of Hoover's letter instructing agents to get radical suspects to hold a meeting at a specific time in order to better enable arrests, Walsh remarked, "It is difficult to conceive how one bred in the law could ever have promulgated such an order."[121] In his own turn in the witness chair, Palmer appeared willing to fob off responsibility for the department's excesses on Hoover, saying his young associate had been the person "who was in charge of this matter."[122]

In fairness to the attorney general, his investigations had been demanded by Congress and by an anxious press and citizenry, and some sort of radical violent conspiracy did actually appear manifest in the various bombing and attempted letter-bomb attacks of 1919–1920, including the traumatic assault on Palmer himself. That he and Hoover had misjudged the scope and sophistication of the threat, however, and had proceeded against it in ways both reckless and excessive, there was by spring 1920 little doubt.

This much-publicized failing helped neutralize Palmer's hopes for the 1920 Democratic presidential nomination. However, Governor Calvin Coolidge, hero of the Boston Police Strike, fared better, receiving the nomination for vice president on the ultimately victorious Republican ticket behind Warren Harding. When Harding died in office on August 2, 1923, Coolidge, who had won America's heart with the words, "There is no right to strike against the public safety by anybody, anywhere, any time," became the thirtieth president of the United States.

AND SO THE PEOPLE came eventually to recognize something wayward, un-American even, in what their own fears had produced. One clear measure of the rapidly declining influence of anti-red fever was the nation's reaction to what proved to be the actual worst terrorist event of the era, a horrific bombing on Wall Street in New York City on September 16, 1920. The powerful bomb, secreted in a parked horse cart near the offices of J. P. Morgan and Company and set to detonate at noon, when lunchtime crowds would fill the street, killed forty people and wounded two hundred; it harmed only a handful of the leading Wall Street financiers assumed to have been its targets, none seriously, instead maiming and snuffing out the lives of clerks, messengers, and secretaries. While Palmer lost no time in declaring it a radical plot, a call that would have found vengeful support just a year earlier, now the cry of "Anarchist!" or "Bolshevik!" fell on mostly skeptical, or at least apathetic, ears. (Police, suspecting that Carlo Tresca might be involved, rushed immediately to his office, where they grew alarmed by a bulge in his suit coat pocket that turned out to be a sandwich.)[123] The case was investigated by the New York police and the Federal Bureau of Investigation but never formally solved, although in all likelihood the bomber was Mario Buda, a New England anarchist who was part of the loose-knit group that gravitated around Luigi Galleani, publisher of the anarchist periodical *Cronaca Sovversiva*. Buda, historians believe, was angry over the Palmer era's persecution of his anarchist colleagues, particularly his friends Nicola Sacco and Bartolomeo Vanzetti, who several months earlier had been indicted for killing a South Braintree, Massachusetts, shoe company paymaster and a guard. Buda, who sailed to Italy, was never apprehended.[124]

The easing up of the great radical scare even lightened the mood toward the IWW. By July 1920 the *Atlantic Monthly* was lampooning the endless legal crucifixion of the Wobblies:

Pietro is a laborer from Milan. He is standing on a street corner in Chicago. A cop tells him to move on. Pietro does not understand English and remains where he is. The cop thinks he is insolent and hits him with his club. Pietro makes wild gesticulations, which the cop interprets as violations of law and order; so be beats Pietro up and takes him to jail. Next morning Pietro is sentenced to a ten-dollar fine for resisting an officer. He hasn't the money and works out the fine by ten days in the stone-quarry. By the time he is released, Pietro firmly believes that the government of the United States is brutal, unjust, and tyrannical. He finds an IWW pamphlet, or hears a soapboxer, and a "Red" radical has been manufactured.[125]

But such journalistic empathy for the IWW came too late. Bloodied by vigilantes, cops, and government prosecutors, its leadership rent by the kind of small internecine turf wars that appear eventually in any cash-starved movement, the IWW was in a weakened condition. Certainly, its rhetoric of societal transformation already felt outmoded. The idea that capitalism was to be overthrown simply did not persuade a substantial number of American workers, nor did many adhere long to a belief in some vague millennial revolution that would create a workers' society. In addition, the ranks of once-reliable IWW foot soldiers, such as harvest migrants and itinerant lumbermen, were diminished by the coming of the automobile and the arrival of greater mechanization in agriculture that reduced the need for field labor. The two Communist parties lured away many Wobblies, while others simply wandered off or did not rejoin the IWW after the upheavals associated with the First World War and the Red Scare.

The "One Big Union" also increasingly found itself cut off philosophically from innovative trends in industrial labor relations such as government commissions of inquiry, corporate welfare programs, and the Protocolism of the 1909–1910 garment workers strikes. William Z. Foster delineated the ways in which the Wobblies and other groups had fallen out of step, writing, "For many years radicals in this country have almost universally maintained that the trade unions are fundamentally non-revolutionary; that they have no real quarrel with capitalism, but are seeking merely to modify its harshness through a policy of mild reform." But, Foster emphasized, the efforts of the trade unions *had* proven effective, their brand of struggle "evolutionary" rather than utopian. "How long are American progressives going to continue deceiving themselves with the words of high-sounding preambles?" he asked. "When are they going to quit chasing rainbows and settle down to real work?"[126]

Of course one very authentic reason for the IWW's problems was that the Chicago trial of 1918 had impounded the organization's leadership cadre. Rather than pursuing the agenda of a vital labor organization, those members who remained free on the outside found their time and effort largely consumed by the need to raise funds and mount clemency campaigns on behalf of those stuck in prison. "Remember you're outside for us, and we're inside for you," went the words to one IWW song—a touching sentiment, but not altogether useful as the operational basis for a functioning labor organization.[127]

Even among the incarcerated Wobblies differences arose. Some demanded a principled approach of noncooperation, agitation, and perhaps even the staging of a "strike" against prison work assignments. Others endorsed cooperating with prison authorities in the hopes of speeding their release, and to lessen the burden on those fighting on the outside.[128]

In August 1919 the IWW managed to raise enough cash to pay bond for a number of the jailed Wobblies, who were released pending an appeal of their case. Forty-six men, including Big Bill Haywood, who was in poor health, walked out of prison, then embarked almost immediately on a nationwide speaking tour to raise additional defense money. With the war over, there were hopes that sympathy might be shown men convicted under the Espionage Act. But neither President Wilson, who continued to revile the Wobblies, nor Attorney General Palmer showed any inclination to offer commutation of the original sentences, and the Supreme Court ultimately refused to hear the IWW's appeal.

With the Court's ruling, thirty-seven of the forty-six released men turned themselves in to be reimprisoned. Several jumped bail, most sensationally Haywood, who discreetly boarded a ship bound for Russia, never to return. While his flight can be judged a flagrant insult to the Wobbly faithful, a refusal "to be martyred for the cause he personified,"[129] he was by 1919 not the same combative, inspiring man who had gaveled the "Continental Congress of the working class" into existence in 1905. Worn down as he was by years of imprisonment, suffering from various physical ailments, his use to the IWW had probably become limited in any case, and given the government's unwillingness to extend forgiveness, a return to the penitentiary had come to look very much like a death sentence.[130]

DESPITE THE EFFECTIVENESS of Louis Post and respected jurists like Felix Frankfurter and Roscoe Pound in exposing the shameful methods of the Red Scare, it is impossible to disregard the large impact the Palmer raids had on America. They not only pasted the badge of radicalism and un-Americanism ever more firmly on the labor movement, they helped reinvigorate the gospel of "liberty of contract" and the open shop. More than 240 open shop advocacy groups appeared in forty-four states during the early 1920s, joining influential civic and business organizations such as the Chamber of Commerce, the National Association of Manufacturers, and the National Grange that championed the open shop as a fundamental freedom, a vital redoubt against labor collectivism. Unions and labor supporters resisted and often tried to puncture the open shop propaganda, but business had latched on to a campaign linked to core American values, and knew it had a winner.

The Communist Party, forever stigmatized, saw its membership decline from between sixty and eighty-eight thousand in 1919 to less than six thousand at the end of 1920.[131] Among conservatives, the fervent dedication to the theme of "Americanism" continued to find righteous spokesmen in the American Legion and in a revived Ku Klux Klan, which in the 1920s became a quasi-religious business association, complete with a ladies' auxiliary, devoted to the suppression of aliens, Jews, blacks, Catholics, and social transgressions it deemed immoral, such as drinking, adultery, and spousal abuse.

While the fervor and hysteria of the Palmer era had been reined in, the impulse to suppress radicals and anarchists lived on most famously in the celebrated case of Sacco and Vanzetti, veteran anarchists connected to the proudly violent Galleani group and involved in immigrant labor efforts in southern New England. Both had come to America as young men: Nicola Sacco becoming a skilled shoemaker, and Bartolomeo Vanzetti making his way through several unskilled jobs, his only preference being that the work was out of doors. Vanzetti had once helped lead a successful strike at a rope factory, and had been subsequently blacklisted by management; at the time of his arrest he was living in Plymouth, Massachusetts, supporting himself as a fish peddler. Sacco had been active in efforts to assist the Lawrence strikers and their families, and had been a spectator at the trial of Joseph Ettor and Arturo Giovannitti in Salem in 1912.

On May 3, 1920, Vanzetti learned that an anarchist friend, a printer named Andrea Salsedo, had mysteriously wound up dead on the pavement fourteen floors below the Department of Justice offices in New York City, where he'd been held incommunicado for eight weeks as a suspect in the string of bombings that included the assault on Attorney General Palmer's home. Vanzetti had made an unsuccessful trip to New York earlier that spring to see if he could learn anything about Salsedo's detention. Stunned by the strange circumstances of their friend's "suicide," Vanzetti and Sacco were in the process of organizing a meeting to be held in Brockton on May 9 to protest Salsedo's death when, on May 5, they were both arrested and charged with the South Braintree robbery and shootings of April 15. Vanzetti was also charged with taking part in a failed payroll holdup in Bridgewater, Massachusetts, on December 19. Regarding the Bridgewater allegation against Vanzetti, Judge Webster Thayer remarked, "This man, although he may not have actually committed the crime attributed to him, is nevertheless morally culpable, because he is the enemy of our existing institutions."[132] Vanzetti assured Elizabeth Gurley Flynn that he was hardly surprised he had been fingered as a threatening anarchist capable of murder. "I have [known] many good individuals among the American people—more good in them than I would have dreamt, but I have a too big pair of moustache, and the Americans do not know if I am a bear or a man, and consequently, feel unsure at my presence."[133]

Worldwide protest over the Sacco-Vanzetti case and convictions became the 1920s' reigning liberal crusade, and helped stave off their executions for six years. But after the court denied a retrial and Governor Alvan T. Fuller of Massachusetts ordered a committee to review the convictions, the sentences were carried out on August 22, 1927. There was near-universal revulsion at the men's deaths, "the never-ending wrong," as author Katherine Anne Porter called it, a gross injustice on par with the Haymarket executions. Upton Sinclair considered what had occurred "the most shocking crime that has been committed in American history since the assassination of Lincoln," and warned it would "empoison our public life for a generation."[134]

In death, Sacco and Vanzetti were enshrined as martyrs to the cause of justice and tolerance.[135] As Vanzetti reflected a few months before he and Sacco went to the electric chair:

> If it not been for this case, I might have lived out my life, talking on street corners to scornful men. I might have died unmarked, unknown, a failure. . . . Now we are not a failure. This is our career and our triumph. . . . Our words—our lives—our pains— nothing! The taking of our lives—lives of a good shoemaker and a poor fish-peddler—all! The last moment belongs to us.[136]

It was the sole consolation America had to offer.

CHAPTER EIGHT

LET US HAVE PEACE AND MAKE CARS

WE IN AMERICA ARE NEARER TO THE FINAL triumph over poverty than ever before in the history of any land," presidential candidate Herbert Hoover declared in 1928, speaking of the phenomenal business expansion and worker contentment that characterized the 1920s.[1] The decade following the First World War had indeed been an era of transformation—a boom time of accelerating profits, rising wages, and, most noticeably, the arrival of new consumer products available to the working class, such as refrigerators, cars, radios, phonographs, as well as, in some rural areas, the first electrification and indoor plumbing. Industrial workers enjoyed shorter hours, increased leisure time, and new levels of corporate generosity in the form of benefits and employee programs.

Finding work itself was easier in part because immigration had ebbed, due initially to the disruption of the war and later to a quota system that restricted the coming of workers from Southern and Eastern Europe. Immigrant arrivals fell from 5 million per annum before the war to about 150,000 afterward.

In these years of peace, many employers returned

to the Taylorism of the Progressive Era, exploring ways to improve efficiency and productivity, and also showed an increasing willingness, in conjunction with these aims, to bear in mind the aspirations and anxieties of workers. There appeared new methods focused on worker pacing and task variety on the job, as well as greater appreciation of the value of worker retention, developments that reflected a trend away from the harsh industrial-labor relations of the past, as well as from the cutthroat competition among businesses that had typified American enterprise in the nineteenth century. "Even the most skeptical devotees of the old dog-eat-dog theory," observed one Chamber of Commerce leader, "are being gradually persuaded from the sheer, cold pressure of the facts that . . . war doesn't pay in this complicated world of ours."[2] A well-run plant depended "more and more upon the management of men than upon the organization of machines."[3]

Manufacturers came out of the war convinced that worker output increased when production goals were linked to patriotism. The possibilities inherent in this discovery were advanced through research done between 1924 and 1932 at the Hawthorne Telephone Company outside Chicago. There, a team led by the Australian sociologist and "organizational theorist" G. Elton Mayo found that production improved each time the lights were turned up or down in consideration of worker comfort. Mayo's conclusion was that employees responded positively to being noticed and having something done on their behalf. Certain factors such as praise from their superiors, simple job perks, the feeling of camaraderie with coworkers, actually appeared to outweigh wages as integers of overall worker happiness. From Mayo's writings emerged "the Hawthorne effect," a reaffirmation of the anecdotal Progressive Era experiences at Filene's, National Cash Register, and elsewhere that improved on-the-job human relations and employee programs could be useful dynamics in binding a worker to the employer and reducing the friction and frustration that brought on labor disputes.[4]

The beauty for employers in such discoveries was that they diminished the need for workers to form unions, and fit nicely with the postwar resurgence of the open shop concept, which sought to deny unions the power of collective bargaining under the guise of safeguarding individual Americans' liberty and freedom of choice. The "open shop" drive, first articulated in the years before the First World War, rose on the wartime mood of national pride and distrust of the "alien" notion of collective unionism; so identified was it with homegrown virtues, its boosters came to refer to it as the "American plan." Enhancing the open shop concept was a compelling program of welfare capitalism, the provision of paid vacations, bonuses, pension plans, picnics, and sporting events. Chairman Elbert Gary of U.S. Steel, which spent $10 million a year on employee benefits in the 1920s, summed up the philosophy neatly with the observation that such costs were worthwhile "because it is the way men ought to be treated, and . . . because it pays to treat men in that way."[5] As for that perennial favorite of employers, the company union, created to give workers a sense of having a democratic voice and perhaps a grievance process, there were by 1926 about four hundred company unions nationwide (about half the total number of independent trade unions affiliated with the AFL), boasting memberships of 1,370,000.[6]

Benefits programs and company-managed employee representation, and the accompanying notion that working cooperatively with management was the most secure way to promotion and better wages, augured poorly for traditional labor organizing. Just before the stock market crash of 1929 there were about 3.5 million workers in noncompany unions and by 1933 only about 2 million, not even 6 percent of the total of U.S. workers, as compared to 12 percent in 1920.[7] A committee of the Amalgamated Clothing Workers (ACW) compared the impact of welfare capitalism on the labor movement to "Delilah's method of robbing Samson of his power. It destroys the self-respecting manhood and womanhood in the American citizen." ACW head Sidney Hillman cautioned that "the difficulty with most plans of industrial democracy is that they are granted by employers, and what the employers grant they can take away." Real industrial democracy, he predicted, would require a more "genuine and definite transfer of power."[8] As for George J. Anderson, managing director of a printing employers' group, told John D. Rockefeller Jr., whom he served as a consultant:

> There is a psychological appeal in labor unionism which has not yet been analyzed. It seems to give the men a sense not only of power but of dignity and self-respect. They feel that only through labor unions can they deal with employers on an equal plane. They seem to regard the [company-sponsored] representation plan as a sort of counterfeit, largely perhaps, because the machinery of such plans is too often managed by the employers. They want something which they themselves have created and not something which is handed down to them by those who pay their wages.[9]

But the lulling effect of corporate largesse perhaps suited the times. By 1920 and the end of the Red Scare, the reformist spirit of the prewar years had abated. "The nation was tired of public crisis," notes Arthur Schlesinger Jr. "It was tired of discipline and sacrifice. It was tired of abstract and intangible objectives. It could gird itself no longer for heroic moral or intellectual effort. Its instinct for idealism was spent."[10] With the cry of "Bolsheviki" heard less often these days and the bugles of patriotism muted, business found new ways to assault the legitimacy of unions, such as alleging that labor organizations were corrupt. Some firms turned to stealth tactics such as spies and informers to keep tabs on unionizing efforts and disrupt them where possible.

Organized labor also lost ground on the legal front. The Clayton Act of 1914, which had attempted to free unions from the threat of antitrust actions and to permit standard labor practices such as peaceful strikes, picketing, and secondary boycotts, was gutted in 1921 by unfavorable Supreme Court decisions in *Duplex Printing Press Co. v. Deering* and *Truax v. Corrigan*. Among other things, the Clayton Act's critical provisions against yellow-dog contracts were disallowed and the hated injunction came back into play. The 1920s saw several hundred antiunion injunctions granted by state or federal courts. Also, in 1923 the court ruled in *Adkins v. Children's Hospital* against a 1918 federal law establishing a minimum wage for women workers in the District of Columbia. In its 5–3 decision, the court acknowledged that workers, in this case nurses, had a right to a living wage, but found that the employer, Children's Hospital, was under no obligation to offer one and that the wage could not be mandated by law, citing "liberty of contract," which was proving to be a very durable legal concept. Indeed it appeared somewhat too robust for Justice Oliver Wendell Holmes, who in his dissent criticized the overuse of so blind an application of the constitutional right to make contractual arrangements without government interference or regulation.

Thus the decade overall lifted the American worker upward, out of the poverty of the muckraker era to a new consumer status that approached middle class. But if consumerism and welfare capitalism were a success, they also were, as Sidney Hillman had said, something of a delusion. For beneath it all remained the stubborn dynamic in which management held all the authority and workers lacked an effective right to collective bargaining. The long puppet strings of corporate control always dangled in plain sight, especially where company unions were involved. Another weakness of the system, soon to be exposed, was that a business's generosity toward its personnel did not exist independent of the results printed in its annual report; a company would play the role of caring parent only as long as it could afford to do so.

Most labor historians have treated the era of welfare capitalism as a kind of stopgap, a makeshift philosophy designed to stave off unionization and destined to fail because it denied the natural tendency of workers to organize. Alternatively, labor scholar David Brody suggests that it was killed off only by the monumental economic devastation of the 1930s, and that it may well have been, as its boosters then claimed, the emerging dynamic of American industrial-labor relations. Certainly recent experience has shown that generous corporate benefits and profit-sharing can be persuasive factors in diminishing employee interest in labor unionism.[11]

When the economy entered its severe downturn in 1930, of course, all the fears about managerial largesse came real: employee benefits dried up, perks vanished, and the company unions proved toothless, unable to protect workers. As consumer demand plummeted and production and hiring fell, many firms tried to honor a request by President Hoover against wage-cutting, and to the credit of some corporations there were efforts to reduce hours across the board so as to limit layoffs, as well as severances and other arrangements made for hard-hit workers. But not even large entities such as the Ford Motor Company and U.S. Steel could avoid "the inexorable law of the balance sheet."[12] Worse, many unions had become dulled by inactivity during the years of rising wages and corporate munificence, leaving the labor movement standing but vulnerable in the path of the oncoming Great Depression.

T HE NATION'S PREEMINENT ISSUE, Franklin Delano Roosevelt said on assuming the presidency in early 1933, is "our economic condition—a Depression so deep that it is without precedent in modern history."[13] Roosevelt had used the expression "a new deal for the American people" at the 1932 Democratic Convention, where he was chosen as his party's candidate and pledged that "the federal government has always had and still has a continuing responsibility for the broader public welfare."[14] That responsibility would be tested at once, for the day he took office, between one-third and one-half of American workers lacked a job. Tens of thousands of homes and farms were in foreclosure, banks had failed, and in the cities the traditional civic and church-based charities had run out of resources to help the indigent. "The country needs and, unless I mistake its temper, the country demands bold, persistent experimentation," Roosevelt declared. "It is common sense to take a method and try it: if it fails, admit it frankly and try another. But above all, try something."[15] As other nations met the global economic crisis with totalitarian programs of Far Right or Left, the president urged the United States to resort to its own best instincts of pragmatism, rational experimentation, and collective initiative.[16]

Roosevelt might not at first glance have seemed the person best suited to guide the country in its hour of need. The scion of a wealthy Hudson River Valley family, he had grown up the only child in an insular world of privilege, and remained close even as an adult to his strong-willed mother, Sara Delano. He attended Groton and Harvard, married a distant cousin, Eleanor Roosevelt, became a New York State senator, and was assistant secretary of the navy during the Wilson administration. He then experienced two setbacks. He was defeated as a candidate for vice president on the Democratic ticket with James M. Cox in 1920, and the next year contracted polio, probably during a day's visit to a Boy Scout camp in upstate New York. Partially paralyzed thereafter, Roosevelt was said by those who knew him to grow in his depth of empathy and compassion for others. He had never known economic hardship, nor been a laborer or run a business, but by the time he entered the White House, after serving two terms as governor of New York, he had come to possess qualities of resolve, reasonableness, and calm before adversity that proved a tonic to a suffering nation.

What marked Roosevelt's New Deal from the start was its willingness to challenge the moneyed interests, "the economic royalists," as the president called them, and to put the U.S. government to work solving the problems of everyday people. Rejecting the Social Darwinism of the late nineteenth century, Roosevelt recognized that the level to which men and women ascend is often due not to their nature or even their own efforts, but to social and economic factors beyond their individual control. Progressivism had articulated this view as it exposed society's inequities, although it was the unique predicament thrust upon the nation by the Depression that made reform essential. No one doubted capital's ability to drive markets, spark innovation, and provide jobs, but the notion that it could function freely, as though its actions did not impact or concern the public interest, would have to be met and conquered. "The power of the few to manage the economic life of the nation," Roosevelt would tell Congress, "must be diffused among the many or be transferred to the public and its democratically responsible government."[17]

Despite this concern, Roosevelt was not out to revive the antitrust antagonisms of prior decades. His objective was to obtain results. He would work with the corporations, with the big-city political machines, and with workers and their unions. All able hands would be needed. The crisis was immense, a "national emergency" as it was described in the preamble to the National Industrial Recovery Act (NIRA) soon rolled out by Congress, "productive of widespread unemployment and disorganization of industry, which burdens interstate commerce, affects the public welfare and undermines the standards of living of the American people."

The NIRA created an enforcement agency in the National Recovery Administration (NRA), which was to frame a working partnership between business and government to get the nation's economy back on track. It arranged for corporations, working with government, to design codes of fair competition to regulate prices and wages; its goal was to restore consistent profits so that jobs might be saved and wages elevated.

An encouraging step toward setting organized capital and organized labor on a more equal footing had already been taken in March 1932 with the passage of the Norris–La Guardia Act, which abolished yellow-dog contracts and restricted injunctions in labor crises to only a very few special circumstances. Norris–La Guardia was a seminal piece of legislation in that it removed the federal courts from labor disputes, and with the courts went the threat of intrusion by militia or U.S. soldiers sent to enforce injunctions. Taking the suspended weight of injunction from above labor's head, it opened the way for unions to strike, boycott, and maneuver more spontaneously. But this was just a start. Except for railroad workers, whose rights to union membership were safeguarded by the Railway Labor Act of 1926, most employees could still be dismissed for union affiliation or forced into company unions, and the right of collective bargaining had yet to be secured.

Initially, Roosevelt and Labor Secretary Frances Perkins, his colleague from the New York legislature in the era of that state's Factory Investigating Commission (FIC), did not necessarily perceive a need for workers' representation or collective bargaining elements in the New Deal. Labor unions were generally weak, and it appeared the government could do more for workers directly than by empowering unions. "I'd much rather get a law than organize a union," Perkins later recalled, "and I think it's more important."[18] While the president did not shy away from strong rhetoric regarding corporate arrogance—"No business which depends for existence on paying less than living wages to its workers has any right to continue in this country," he'd said upon signing the NIRA into law—he was also cautious about ceding too much authority to workers' organizations. Perkins tended to place high value on the Progressive efforts she'd seen effective in New York, such as the National Consumers League, the Women's Trade Union League, Louis Brandeis's "Protocols for Peace," or government regulatory action in the manner of the FIC.[19]

Winning and enforcing safety regulations in New York through the FIC had given Perkins a special appreciation of the reforming power of the law, and she had come to believe that some form of national labor regulation was essential. It must be a federal effort, for state-by-state laws would always remain piecemeal and ineffective in that capital would likely exploit the availability of those locations where workers had the fewest protections. She expected national labor reforms would not come easily; they would be questioned by Congress, challenged by employers, and subjected by the courts to tests of their constitutionality.

Perkins had an experience in 1933 while touring the steelmaking facilities at Homestead, Pennsylvania, that helped galvanize her feelings about both the need for federal authority and the resilience of laboring Americans. The mayor of Homestead, who was accompanying her, had stopped her from speaking to a group of steelworkers gathered at the city hall. Perkins then suggested they move to a nearby park, only to be informed by the same official that local laws forbade meetings in city parks. Growing irritated with her companion, and spying a U.S. post office, Perkins asserted that as the secretary of labor, she had the right to address an assembly of citizens anywhere an American flag flew above a federal building. To the chagrin of the mayor and other local authorities, she proceeded to convene her meeting with the workers in the lobby of the post office, standing on a chair to speak to them and hear their concerns. "We ended the meeting with hand-shaking and expressions of rejoicing that the New Deal wasn't afraid of the steel trust," Perkins recalled,[20] and announced soon after the incident, "I have come to the conclusion that the Department of Labor should be the Department FOR Labor, and that we should render service to the working people, just as the Agriculture Department renders service to the farmers."[21]

The first woman cabinet member in the country's history, Perkins received special scrutiny from the press, not all of it kind—it was said her clothes looked "as though they had been designed by the Bureau of Standards"—but her Progressive roots were unimpeachable, and she enjoyed the president's full confidence.[22] Fiercely loyal to Roosevelt—she was his oldest friend in the administration—Perkins had contributed to his positioning for the 1932 election against the incumbent Herbert Hoover by publicly questioning Hoover's misleading statements about the unemployment rate in the United States. Never starry-eyed about labor's leadership (she personally distrusted or had low expectations of many of its "big men"), she nonetheless proved a staunch advocate for unions, particularly as she became impressed by their response to the organizing opportunities afforded by the New Deal.

Senator Robert Wagner of New York and the UMW's John L. Lewis also contributed to the discussion of the administration's labor strategy. Wagner believed that finding a way out of the Depression required kick-starting industry by increasing consumer purchasing power, which could only be done by turning workers once again into buyers. Reducing unemployment meant stabilizing the workforce, a function both men thought organized labor could provide. The government's role would be to guarantee workers the right to organize and bargain collectively and to set standards for hours and wages. Hopefully, with such a secure means of redress in place, labor unions would gain confidence and their leaders would not be driven to prove their mettle through strikes or the threat of strikes. And as labor developed new habits of restraint and enjoyed reasonable expectations of fair contract negotiations, so, too, would management grow less paranoid and cease trying to disrupt worker organizing.

On February 17, 1933, Lewis went before the Senate Finance Committee to suggest emergency powers for the government to safeguard collective bargaining and oversee national economic strategy. His words had considerable sway, for he was at the moment labor's most recognizable national figure, a flamboyant character with a shock of unkempt hair, prominent bushy eyebrows, and "the majestic presence of a veteran ham actor."[23] Born in Iowa in 1880, he had gone to work in the mines at age twelve, detoured briefly as a young adult into a life in regional theater, then became immersed in labor issues and ascended through a number of posts to become UMW president. He had initially graced the national labor stage (and been credited as a man of substance) in 1919 when he had refused his own rank and file's demand for a coal strike against the wishes of the Wilson administration, saying, "We are Americans. We cannot fight our government."[24]

Now he wanted the government to fight for Americans. He defended the granting of the authority he sought for Washington by recalling that similar emergency measures had been deemed appropriate in the First World War, "when the enemy was three thousand miles from our shore. Today the enemy is within the boundaries of the nation, and is stalking every community and every home." In late March, Lewis and other UMW leaders convened with the president, as well as Perkins and Interior Secretary Harold Ickes; in these strategy sessions the Roosevelt administration listened closely to Lewis's ideas for revitalizing the economy.[25] UMW economist W. Jett Lauck, an adviser and speechwriter for Lewis, worked with Perkins, Senator Wagner, and Wagner's aide, Simon Rifkind, among others, to devise the NIRA's Section 7(a). This heroic segment of the legislation guaranteed to workers "the right to organize and bargain collectively through representatives of their own choosing," free of employer interference or coercion.

With the labor movement having been some years at low ebb, and industry focused most intently on the bill's implications for business recovery, the full consequences of Section 7(a) were likely at first not immediately evident.[26] Business groups such as the Chamber of Commerce and elements in Congress did challenge it, although the law's proponents had firm union backing as well as Roosevelt's support. Section 7(a) was nothing short of a "charter of industrial freedom," in the admiring words of AFL president William Green, who had assumed the federation's leadership upon the death of Samuel Gompers in 1924, and who had lobbied for the collective bargaining clause in the act.[27] Lewis concurred, certain that "from the standpoint of human welfare and economic freedom . . . there has been no legal instrument comparable with it since [the] Emancipation Proclamation."[28]

Lewis's most famous response to the passage of Section 7(a) was to instruct the country's workers, "President Roosevelt wants you to join the union!" The wide dissemination of this message on posters and lapel buttons was said to annoy the president, since it put words in his mouth he had not said, but its meaning was not lost on those who began to fill union ranks. One and a half million new members joined the AFL between June and October 1933, and 3,537 new locals were created, bringing total federation membership to 4 million, an increase so dramatic Green was moved to predict a future membership of 25 million.[29] Other organizations witnessed comparable growth, including the UMW. "It was the most remarkable thing I ever saw," labor reporter Louis Stark told Frances Perkins of the surge in mine union membership. "Those miners came out of those towns . . . like an army moving out of the mountains. They signed up by the thousands, which showed that they always did really want to belong to a union."[30]

SOME OF THIS WILLINGNESS by America's workers to act and to organize can be attributed to efforts by the Communist Party USA, which had busied itself not only on behalf of labor but also for the rights of the unemployed. Since the late 1920s the party had viewed the rapidly growing U.S. economy as ripe for crisis or collapse and possibly some form of workers' upheaval. The economic disaster of October 1929, when it came, surpassed even the party's expectations: wages fell precipitously in Alabama textile mills as they did in the major industries of Pennsylvania, Ohio, and Michigan; tens of thousands of jobs were lost; and for those fortunate to have work, the available days and hours of employment were reduced. In Detroit the Ford Motor Company laid off 90,000 of its 130,000 workers between March 1929 and August 1931; elsewhere in that city the Briggs Manufacturing Company cut most of its employees to half days, for which men earned 10 cents an hour and women 4 cents.[31] The Communists, seeing desperation as well as opportunity in such widely shared pain, launched the Trade Union Unity League (TUUL), dispatching organizers to assist restive agricultural workers in Southern California and miners in Pennsylvania and West Virginia, as well as Northern autoworkers. Although the TUUL focused on everyday goals such as improved wages and conditions, employers, the local press, and patriot organizations reacted with special animosity to the Communist interlopers; management frequently used their presence as an excuse to void any chance of reasonable negotiation or settlement with workers. Several of these struggles turned violent. In Gastonia, North Carolina, in 1929, the local police chief and a young union songwriter named Ella May Wiggins were killed when a Communist-led union took on textile mill interests and vigilantes; dozens of people were wounded, and eleven workers were sent to prison. Communist labor organizers were also jailed in California when they came to the aid of unionized lettuce pickers and cannery workers.[32]

More significantly, the party led a campaign to turn legions of newly unemployed workers into an organized protest movement, the Unemployed Councils. Outside of Coxey's Army, the New York church-invasion crusade led by Frank Tannenbaum, and other scattered efforts, this had never been attempted before on a large scale; but the vast number of people out of work—15 million by March 1933, up from 500,000 in spring 1929—and the paucity of available public and private relief greatly enabled recruitment.[33] The looting of bread trucks and other food sources by the homeless and unemployed had become an ugly feature of the Depression's early years, and the councils introduced a degree of purpose and even civility to these individuals' urgent, fundamental needs. They staged rent strikes and helped tenants avoid eviction; showed poor residents how to turn their gas back on when it was shut off by a public utility; raised money through such traditional means as raffles, dances, and bingo parties; and led marches on relief agencies. Men and women who on their own had been ignored or refused by bureaucrats found their demands taken more seriously when they returned in the company of an Unemployed Council delegation. While the usual tactic was to present a show of numbers and, if necessary, occupy agency offices and refuse to leave, there were occasional reports of more aggressive invasions, such as the demonstration in Harlem in June 1932 in which members of a local council were arrested after smashing down a relief agency's doors and destroying its furniture.[34]

The organization generally focused less on Communist ideology than on people's everyday problems, although as labor writer Len De Caux observed:

> In hundreds of jobless meetings, I heard no objections to
> the points the Communists made.... Sometimes, I'd hear a
> Communist speaker say something so bitter and extreme I'd
> feel embarrassed. Then I'd look around at the unemployed
> audience—shabby clothes, expressions worried and sour. Faces
> would start to glow, heads to nod, hands to clap.[35]

The Council movement gained wide attention with massive public demonstrations on March 6, 1930, which it dubbed International Unemployment Day. San Francisco and Chicago saw large parades and demonstrations; cops in Washington needed tear gas to chase a crowd away from the White House; and in Los Angeles a bizarre confrontation occurred when baton-wielding cops encountered Japanese American Communists trained in martial arts combat. Similar confrontations brought vicious street fighting to Detroit, Boston, Milwaukee, and Cleveland, while in New York a fracas ensued when activists including William Z. Foster defied police orders and tried to lead some thirty-five thousand protestors down Broadway after a rally in Union Square.

> Hundreds of policemen and detectives, swinging nightsticks,
> blackjacks and bare fists, rushed into the crowd, hitting out at

all with whom they came into contact, chasing many across the
street and into adjacent thoroughfares and rushing hundreds
off their feet. . . . From all parts of the scene of battle came the
screams of women and the cries of men, with bloody heads
and faces. A score of men were sprawled over the square with
policemen pummeling them. The pounding continued as the
men, and some women, sought refuge in flight.[36]

Foster and other leaders were jailed, although the city was moved by
the disturbance to begin gathering contributions for those without jobs.
Overall the day's organizers were pleased enough with the nationwide
turnout—the CPUSA claimed 1 million participants—that the council declared itself a national entity, convening in Chicago in July 1930 to
found the Unemployed Council of the United States. It followed up in
February 1931 by sending a delegation to Washington to lobby Congress.

The council's work differed from earlier efforts on behalf of the
unemployed in that now the jobless were more closely aligned through
the TUUL with the labor movement, and their plea for help had become
not so much a call for immediate relief, although that was important,
as a demand for lasting government reforms—federally administered
unemployment insurance and public works programs. The efforts of the
Unemployed Council and other attempts to aid the destitute had made
it abundantly clear that the existing system of relief based on local public and private methods, some permanent, many ad hoc, were designed
for small numbers of the needy and were totally inadequate for dealing
with a countrywide emergency. When Congress rebuffed the delegation
the council had sent in February 1931, the organization planned and carried out a hunger march on Washington on December 6 of that year,
parading in phalanx down Pennsylvania Avenue and ringing the Capitol;
after serenading officials inside with "The Internationale," they attempted
to enter both Congress and the White House before being pushed back
by authorities. These protests anticipated a related effort in spring 1932,
when twenty thousand veterans of the First World War, forming what

became known as the Bonus Army, descended on Washington for four months, encamping in makeshift tents and lean-tos, to demand payment of a disputed $50 or $100 cash bonus due them retroactively for their military service. In a lamentable climax, the ex-soldiers and their supporters were ultimately driven from the city by federal troops under the command of General Douglas MacArthur, with several veterans killed and numerous others hurt in the process. The Unemployed Council's own "army" returned to the capital in December 1932, after Roosevelt's election, to remind the incoming president of the persisting crisis for those without work.

These highly visible demands by impoverished, forgotten Americans for respect and inclusion in American society helped inspire a parallel cultural development—a surge of national feeling for old-stream patriotism and curiosity about the lives of common people. Rocked by unprecedented internal economic chaos and eyeing warily the surge of Fascism abroad, America seemed to find reassurance in historic reminders of the country's basic decency, fairness, and collaborative spirit. "The American 'people,' declared obsolete by [Walter] Lippmann in the 1920s and viewed by many intellectuals in that decade as a repository of mean-spirited fundamentalism and crass commercialism," writes historian Eric Foner, "was suddenly rediscovered as the embodiment of democratic virtue."[37] This vigorous interest included a new veneration for mainstays of freedom such as the Declaration of Independence and the Bill of Rights, the Liberty Bell, and Revolutionary figures like Paul Revere, and was displayed in an array of artistic works, from Work Projects Administration murals to the Hollywood films of William Wellman and Preston Sturges. It surfaced in the photographs of Dorothea Lange and in James Agee and Walker Evans's compelling *Let Us Now Praise Famous Men,* an innovative prose and photographic essay about three Alabama sharecropping families; the works of playwright Clifford Odets; the collecting of slave narratives by members of the Federal Writers Project; and an appreciation of African American music and art. As literature it found its greatest resonance in the novels of John Steinbeck, particularly *The Grapes of Wrath* (1939), which

told of the Joad family's trek from Dust Bowl Oklahoma to the harvesting fields of California in search of home, work, and security—the 1930s'
ultimate quest vividly brought to the page. This latter preoccupation lay
at the heart of the Unemployed Council's renewed push in early 1934 for
legislation guaranteeing relief for the unemployed, following Minnesota
congressman Ernest Lundeen's introduction of the first unemployment
insurance bill in the nation's history.

The Communist Party USA's emphasis on democracy and New Deal
reforms in America anticipated a formal recognition from the Seventh
World Congress of the Communist International, which met in Moscow
in summer 1935, of the party's failure to adequately see the rise of Fascism as the moment's most severe threat to the working class. From the
world congress was heard the call for what became known as the Popular
Front, an anti-Fascist alliance of Socialists, Communists, and Progressive forces in the United States, including the labor movement. Seizing
at last the opportunity to testify before a House Subcommittee on Labor,
CPUSA general secretary Earl Browder and other Communists described
the plight of the unemployed in stark terms. Browder reassured Congress
that a federal legislative cure granting security to the jobless was fundamentally American, "the front-line trench today in the battle for preserving a measure of life, liberty and the pursuit of happiness in this country.
It is the essential foundation for preservation of a measure of civil liberties, for resistance to fascism and war. It is a fight for all those good things
in life, which the masses of the people, as distinguished from the professional patriots, mean when they speak of 'Americanism.' "[38] Browder's
words epitomized one of the Communists' most significant contributions to the New Deal, the belief that the remedy for the unfavorable circumstances that befell a worker or any citizen in America did not lie with
him or her alone, but could and should be alleviated with the help of the
national government.

EMPLOYERS HAD THEIR OWN REASONS to welcome the passage
of the NIRA, although they were less enchanted by the reports

of the massive union membership growth the document had inspired. Where they could, some began to exploit the vagueness of the new law. Questions that Section 7(a) left unresolved included the job status of older workers, how employees' representatives were to be chosen, and whether a union elected by workers had to be recognized by an employer. The company union, or "employee representation plan," proved a nifty subterfuge, a means to frustrate Section 7(a) by appearing to meet its mandate for collective bargaining, yet without actually offering true bargaining power to the employees. As the NIRA allowed for proportional representation in any collective bargaining scenario, a company union could still be heard from even if a legitimate union had enrolled a majority of workers, hopelessly complicating the negotiating process.

A National Labor Board created by the administration to sort out disputes under the NIRA and urge employer compliance with the law proved inadequate to deal with the numerous employer challenges; when some employers turned to the courts to challenge the board's right to oversee union representation elections, Roosevelt was forced to issue an executive order guaranteeing that right. But the board remained weak and ineffectual against employers' mounting resentment; it possessed no actual powers of enforcement beyond punishing uncooperative firms by referring incidents to a Compliance Board that could remove a company's Blue Eagle insignia, a symbol of its participation in the NRA economic recovery campaign, or in more serious instances recommending an inquiry by the Justice Department. Employers knew that these chastisements were largely meaningless.

Starting in 1934, misunderstandings over the government's underdefined labor reforms were blamed for labor violence in several U.S. cities, leaving the administration no choice but to rethink how to enshrine labor's basic rights in law. Major strikes erupted in three cities—Toledo, Minneapolis, and San Francisco—that throughout the 1920s had enjoyed relatively calm labor-industrial relations. In Minneapolis and San Francisco this was largely due to the presence of patriotic business alliances that had effectively suppressed union activity. Unfortunately, but predictably, this employer domination left local industry and labor with no functioning tradition of engagement or communication when serious problems arose.

Toledo's Electric Auto-Lite was one of the nation's largest makers of automobile parts in a city that was home to many independent parts suppliers. These firms mass-produced items for pennies less than could the Detroit automakers; fiercely competitive with one another and with their own bottom line, they were always desperate to trim costs in order to realize marginal profits. As a result of the Depression and the attendant drop-off in automobile manufacturing, the Toledo factories had entered a steep retrenchment, bringing layoffs and a cutback in hours and wages for those who did retain their jobs. When an AFL union struck Electric Auto-Lite in April 1934 over union recognition and unsatisfactory wages, no more than half the plant's workers stopped work, allowing the company to continue operation with its loyal employees and some replacement workers. In sympathy, employees at two neighboring factories—the Logan Gear Company and the Bingham Stamping Company—had joined the strike, but the real boost along the picket line came from the Lucas County Unemployed League, a counterpart to the CPUSA's Unemployed Councils.

The Lucas League was affiliated with the Marxist-leaning American Workers Party (AWP) led by A. J. Muste, a Christian pacifist minister who had founded the Unemployed League in Seattle in 1931.[39] Less ideological than the Communist councils, the league chapters served initially as self-help groups focused on survival tactics for the out-of-work, but as the hardships of the Depression deepened, their efforts expanded into rent strikes, "bread marches," and other demonstrations seeking jobs or relief. Based on the AWP philosophy that employed and unemployed workers' interests were one and the same, indeed that everyone, employed or not, was part of the labor struggle, the Unemployed Leaguers fought courageously on behalf of striking workers; this had the dual benefit of giving labor a veritable army of ready protestors while denying employers a source of replacement workers.

Electric Auto-Lite had obtained an injunction to restrict picketing, but with the help of the Unemployed League the strike was able to put as many as six thousand protestors before the plant's gates, rendering impossible any attempt to enforce the court's order, especially since many local police were sympathetic to the strikers. In fear of the crowd and to protect the scabs it had brought in, the company arranged for special deputies to be sworn in by the county sheriff. When one of the deputies beat an elderly man to the ground in view of the crowd of protestors, thousands of angry strikers and their unemployed allies surged toward the plant, threatening the fifteen hundred scabs inside. The untrained deputies fell back as the protestors, who had maneuvered a wagonload of bricks into position so as to have a steady supply of ammunition, smashed the plant's windows and caused other damage. A federal labor mediator who'd arrived at the site was seen running for safety. Three times the crowd stormed the factory grounds, fighting hand to hand with the deputies, as cars were overturned and set afire and random gunshots were heard. Hundreds of Ohio National Guardsmen were rushed to the scene, but although they were able to free the scabs trapped in the plant, they themselves were then surrounded and stoned by the protestors. The Guardsmen tried to escape using their bayonets, and when that failed they opened fire, killing two protestors.

The operators of Electric Auto-Lite, in the wake of more than two days of carnage, made the judicious decision to simply shutter the plant until tensions abated. When it eventually reopened, management had agreed to recognize the AFL local as the employees' collective bargaining agent, introduced a slight wage hike, and rehired most of those who had gone out with the strikers.

Local employers and authorities were stunned by what had taken place: here was a new fighting spirit and determination among the working class—striking workers allied with militant unemployed—winning with strategy, bravado, and sheer strength of numbers. They had defied the entire arsenal of weapons that had historically ensured employer domination in such disputes—the courts, police, hired thugs, the militia, even the use of tear gas and bayonets.

A similarly bold labor campaign was soon under way in San Francisco. The ranks of the International Longshoremen's Association (ILA) had grown substantially since summer and fall 1933 in response to the passage of Section 7(a), a spurt that alarmed the local Industrial Association, created by businessmen in the 1920s to rid the town of labor radicals. The waterfront workers were tired of the employers' use of the "shape-up," the early morning hiring call in which foremen picked that day's workers, a method prone to bribery and corruption. The system fostered nasty competition among individual longshoremen and inhibited their willingness to complain for fear of falling out of favor with those who ruled the daily selections. In addition, of course, it denied dockhands steady employment and reliable wages.

The ILA leadership was hesitant at first to challenge so long-standing an institution as the shape-up, but a breakaway group of rank-and-file members, many of whom were Communists, fell in behind an enigmatic Australian organizer named Harry Bridges; they demanded that the shape-up be replaced with a hiring hall to be operated by the union. In late spring 1934, after attempts at negotiation proved useless, and a last-ditch effort by ILA president Joseph P. Ryan produced a lackluster management offer that was spurned by the ILA members, longshoremen went out from Seattle to San Diego, hitting dozens of West Coast shipping interests. When ship and warehouse owners in San Francisco, the strike's epicenter, attempted to import scabs, the local Teamsters, siding with the ILA, refused to haul any goods to and from the docks. Several thousand crewmen from cargo ships also voluntarily went idle in support of the longshoremen.

In early July San Francisco's Industrial Association, working with local police, tried to reopen the docks using guarded convoys of trucks. A daylong battle broke out, as strikers overpowered police escorts, seized trucks, and dumped cargo into the streets. Cops fired tear gas and drenched strikers with fire hoses, to which the rioters replied with bricks, stones, and railroad spikes; these latter objects, six inches long and weighing about a pound, were handy projectiles and did maximum harm when making contact with a policeman's head. But the police had a unique new tool of their own—vomiting gas, which was designed to sicken its victims and incapacitate them for as long as forty-eight hours; one official described it as "the most effective non-fatal gas known to military science."[40]

At a time when participants on both sides recalled the use of gas as a weapon in the First World War, its appearance here was disturbing; some strikers duly arrived at the "front" wearing the gas masks the army had issued them in 1917. The street fighting did resemble lethal warfare—"the Embarcadero ran blood," reported the *New York Times*—as two strikers were killed and dozens of men wounded on both sides before National Guard troops arrived to restore calm, the first time the militia had been called into the streets of San Francisco since the great earthquake of 1906. Vowed a determined Colonel R. E. Mittelstaedt, who led the mobilization of troops to the waterfront, "We have 4,000 additional men to back us up if necessary, and if that is not enough we will call the national army, the navy and the Marine Corps."[41]

Taking Mittelstaedt at his word, Bridges cautioned his followers against further combat with the authorities, be they police or soldiers. He did, however, announce a general strike. The Teamsters spread their sympathy stoppage from the docks to the whole city, and other unions joined as well, creating by mid-July the first general strike since the 1919 Seattle shutdown. This coordinated action by an estimated 125,000 workers essentially closed the city of San Francisco, bringing vicious reprisals by local vigilantes and calls for federal troops to resolve what West Coast papers termed a "civil war" and a "Communist-led insurrection."

With President Roosevelt away at sea aboard a naval vessel, Attorney General Homer Cummings and Secretary of State Cordell Hull were inclined to honor the request by California officials for U.S. forces, but Labor Secretary Perkins said she believed the cries of distress from the state were overwrought. "There was quite a tie-up in San Francisco," she later recalled, "but it never had a generalized purpose, plan, or leadership, and could not, therefore, be regarded as a general strike.... I thought it unwise to begin the Roosevelt administration by shooting it out with working people who were only exercising their rights . . . to organize and demand collective bargaining."[42] When Cummings said he thought Perkins was not taking the situation seriously enough, she replied:

> Mr. Cummings, I think I do see it seriously. I see the military moving in there from the Presidio. . . . It will create the most terrible resentment and all the trade unions who are not out now will go out. . . . They'll gather in crowds to hoot and jeer at the soldiers driving a bakery wagon through the streets. You know what will happen. The soldiers will fire. Somebody will get hurt. The mob will attack . . . and a lot of people will drop in the streets. I call THAT very serious.[43]

Roosevelt, when apprised of the situation, concurred with the need for restraint. Perkins's decision may have been influenced in part by her having met Harry Bridges once before, "a small, thin, somewhat haggard man in a much-worn overcoat"; as she remembered him, self-effacing in manner and appearance, "just an inexplicable man who had appeared from the mist." She later learned that he was married with one child, had been with the same shipping line for a dozen years, and for relaxation after work liked to strum on a mandolin. Rather than a rabble-rouser or fierce ideologue, she chose to see him as primarily a person with natural leadership qualities, inspired by the possibilities of the NIRA, whose style compelled his fellow workers.[44]

Her judgments about Bridges and his movement proved correct: the San Francisco general strike collapsed after four days, and the ILA and the employers agreed to arbitration. The longshoremen were forced to give up their demand for union-run hiring halls and accept a system of employer-operated halls that retained some of the original weaknesses of the shape-up, but the dockside straw boss selections were done away with. Bridges actually argued against the settlement but was overruled; the Teamsters also voted to return to work. The ILA, ironically, which had been dragged into the strike against its will, emerged a more respected voice in West Coast labor precisely for its rank and file's show of militancy and fighting spirit. For years afterward, the empowered veterans of the general strike continued to keep local shipping concerns honest with spontaneous, small, but costly work stoppages.

A HEADSTRONG LOCAL BUCKING a union's national leadership was also the key to a major confrontation in late spring and summer 1934 in Minneapolis, where a daring Teamsters local took on unified employers, a powerful business association, vigilantes, and the police. Teamsters Local 574 leadership—the brothers Vincent, Grant, Ray, and Miles Dunne, along with Farrell Dobbs and Carl Skoglund—were Trotskyists, Communists who identified with the Russian revolutionary Leon Trotsky, expelled from the Soviet Union in 1929 for criticizing Stalinist Russia's loss of political fervency. Their first act of rebellion was to ignore the attempts at restraint by International Brotherhood of Teamsters president Daniel J. Tobin. An Irish immigrant and Boston coal-wagon driver who had helped found the Teamsters in 1907, Tobin was a tough old-time union leader, a favorite of President Roosevelt's, who demanded and usually received deference from his rank and file.

In fact, the Teamsters' demands were hardly radical. Local 574 asked Minneapolis employers to abide by the NIRA Section 7(a)'s collective bargaining guarantee and honor worker seniority in hiring and layoffs; they sought the creation of an arbitration board to resolve disputes between drivers and management, and insisted there be no employer discrimination against union members. But employers stated in a prominent newspaper advertisement that

> the real issue involved in this strike is the closed union shop—
> complete unionization of all truck drivers in Minneapolis. . . . A
> great many of our employees do not now belong to [574] and
> have expressed themselves as being unwilling to join. It is our
> intention to protect these employees in their right to exercise
> freedom of choice, as provided in Section 7(a) of the National
> Industrial Recovery Act.[45]

Here of course was one of the key weaknesses of Section 7(a)—it was open to "interpretation" by employers fearful of the closed shop.

Also taking aim at the Teamsters was the Citizens Alliance, a national employers association whose Minneapolis chapter had been particularly effective at quashing local unionism. Formed in 1908, it had come into its own during a 1917–1918 trolley car strike and had held considerable sway ever since. Led by retailer George Dayton and industrialists O. P. Briggs and A. W. "Bert" Strong, the Citizens Alliance was one of "Constitutional" opposition to the "un-American" closed shop mixed with warmed-over Social Darwinist rhetoric about each man being allowed to make his own way free of the restricting influence of workers' organizations. The alliance had for almost two decades broken every major strike in the city, making Minneapolis, in Arthur Schlesinger Jr.'s phrase, "a citadel of the open shop."[46] At its most benign the alliance served as an employment agency for local workers, but its activities also included secret surveillance of union meetings and boycotts of businesses sympathetic to organized labor.[47] Local 574's determination to unionize the city's truckers appeared to the alliance an effort to take control of the flow of commerce in and out of Minneapolis, and thus nothing short of a declaration of war. The alliance established a strike headquarters on Hennepin Avenue, the city's main artery, and put out the call for citizens to form an antistrike army to neutralize the Teamsters' pickets.

The strike commenced on May 12 in the sprawling produce market area located in the narrow cobblestone blocks north of Minneapolis's downtown. One of 574's best strategic decisions was to immediately grant local unemployed workers' union membership; as in Toledo, their addition to the strikers' ranks greatly bolstered the union's ability to put troops on the street. The local and its supporters had established a strike headquarters of their own, a converted garage on Chicago Avenue, where many in the Teamsters leadership took up more or less permanent residence. The large structure held a makeshift auditorium for speeches and rallies, a car bay where the union's "fleet" of vehicles could be serviced, and a dining area offering food almost any hour of the day.

"The Dunne Brothers . . . organized the strike as none had been organized before in American labor history," remembered Eric Sevareid, who covered it for the *Minneapolis Star*. "They had patrol cars of their own . . . a daily strike newspaper, loud-speaker broadcasts, a commissary, and medical and ambulance services for their wounded."[48] For its precision, the 1934 Minneapolis Teamsters strike would long be viewed, and studied, as a model of urban labor organizing. The leaders regularly submitted strike decisions for members' consideration, a feature of Local 574's makeup that would prove critical when its chieftains disappeared into the custody of raiding police.

Receiving up-to-the-minute intelligence by telephone from spotters manning watch stations on roads leading into town, the Teamsters effectively stopped all unwanted truck traffic in and out of the city using "the flying squadron," a mode of rapid response in which strikers at headquarters stood by, ready to flock to any spot where employers were seen attempting to move goods. Local 574 also devised a clever strategy of sending legions of strikers into a specific area in staggered waves, thus frustrating the police department's efforts to gauge the enemy's strength. Sympathy stoppages were carried out by twenty-five thousand unionized workers throughout the city, especially carpenters, bricklayers, and electricians from the local building trades. The Teamsters won the backing of the state's farmers by permitting them to enter the city and deliver produce, although the union did force many gasoline stations to close. Unable to restock perishable goods, restaurants and grocery stores were shuttered; bakeries closed because they could not deliver their bread. When taxi drivers joined the strike and stopped picking up fares, hotels had to improvise ways to get stranded guests to the train depot. The city staggered under the effective assault on its commercial lifelines.

The first several days of the strike were relatively peaceful, but the tone changed sharply after an incident in which an agent provocateur who had ingratiated himself with the union, and who was soon revealed to be an alliance member, used a phony pretext to dispatch a group of male and female pickets into a police ambush in an alley behind the

Minneapolis Tribune building. Their vehicles hemmed in by police cars, the unarmed strikers were easy prey for cops and vigilantes, who beat them with fists and nightsticks. At strike headquarters, where the union's ambulance corps brought the victims, volunteers worked hastily to aid the bloodied pickets; several women had to be revived. "When the strikers saw them lying around with the nurses working over them, they got hold of clubs and swore they'd go down and wipe up the police and deputies," Carl Skoglund recalled. "We told them no, the [*Tribune*] Alley was a trap. We'll prepare for a real battle, and we'll pick our own battleground next time. That night, all next day, and the next night, fellows began to collect clubs. They'd gone unarmed before that. Now they got sticks, hose, and pipe."[49]

The anger over the ambush no doubt inspired the brutality the strikers showed the "special deputies." The police might be contemptible, but they were simply doing a job; the deputies, who had volunteered for the assignment, were alliance members and other conservatives who "had expected a little picnic with a mad rabble," recalled Farrell Dobbs. Some had come to the picket lines wearing football helmets for protection; one, Al Lindley, a former Yale athlete, wore a padded polo helmet. "Like the rest of his ilk," said Dobbs, "he anticipated having a bit of a lark as he went about the business of clubbing down working-class sheep."[50] On May 21 the strikers strategically isolated the deputies from their police allies in the market. Using baseball bats and other weapons, the strikers chased the "socialites" into the nooks and crannies of the old produce stalls and warehouse buildings, beating them mercilessly even after many threw down their own clubs and made signs of surrender. The strikers had a score to settle with the cops as well, but were mindful that the police wore guns. In order to deny the officers the use of their weapons, the Teamsters sent a truck directly into police lines. Union fighters then leaped out and engaged the cops hand to hand, suspecting the police would not fire at close range for fear of hitting fellow officers. The day's action appeared to have been won by the Teamsters, who bloodied the deputies badly and sent two dozen police to the hospital.

The next day, despite the police having assigned officers to remain with the alliance deputies to protect them and keep them from retreating, the strikers again overwhelmed the vigilantes, not only beating them soundly but chasing many out of the market area entirely. A truck carrying twenty-five deputies that had the poor timing to enter the district at the height of the melee was at once surrounded by strikers, who pulled the surprised volunteers from the truck and whacked them with baseball bats and homemade saps. Police who tried to intervene were themselves routed. One cop was seen hiding under a car, as strikers poked at him with their clubs. The deputies' extensive casualties included the death of the prominent C. Arthur Lyman, counsel for the Citizens Alliance and the father of five. Lyman had been seeking refuge in a grocery store when his skull was fractured by a blow to the head; he died later at the city's General Hospital.[51] Another deputy, Peter Erath, was also killed.

Watching these events with deepening concern from the state capital in neighboring St. Paul was Floyd B. Olson, the popular Democratic Farmer–Labor governor and dedicated New Dealer. A kind of Scandinavian American version of New York City's Fiorello La Guardia, Olson was popular with Minneapolis's diverse ethnic constituency of Swedes, Poles, Jews, and Norwegians (he spoke several languages), and was, according to historian Irving Bernstein, "the farthest left of any man in high station in America."[52] He had personally given $500 to the Teamsters strike fund, and was said to appreciate the opportunity the strike presented to once and for all end the Citizens Alliance's stranglehold on the city. Nonetheless he abhorred the lethal violence occurring in the market and had little choice but to mobilize the National Guard, although he resisted giving the order that would send troops into the streets.

The prospect of imminent intervention by the militia, however, and exhaustion on both sides at the strenuous combat already endured, helped create a temporary lull in the strike. On May 25 a concord was reached between Local 574 and the employers, allowing for recognition of the Teamsters and no blacklisting of men who had been active as strikers. But after a few weeks of peace the agreement unraveled. The employers insisted the deal would exclude "inside workers," those Teamsters who worked as warehouse employees and did not drive vehicles. The union balked, and as of July 17 the strike was back on.

The Local 574 strikers had obtained the vengeance they sought for the ambush in Newspaper Alley, but the police harbored their own grudge over the bloody May 21 and 22 battles in the market. Graphic news photographs of the street fighting had run in the nation's newspapers, mostly showing strikers taking the fight to the police and the alliance deputies. On July 20, police gave themselves the chance to erase that humiliation. By clever design they escorted a produce convoy into the market as if attempting to make deliveries; when, as anticipated, the lead vehicle was blocked by a truck carrying union pickets, police armed with shotguns suddenly emerged "as if from everywhere." This time there was no hesitation about using firearms at close quarters, and strikers in the truck as well as pickets on the street had no chance as the police guns blazed; within moments seventy people were wounded, two mortally.

"The cops had gone berserk," Farrell Dobbs explained. "They were shooting in all directions, hitting most of their victims in the back as they tried to escape."[53] Henry Ness, one of the strikers mowed down, clung to life for three days in a local hospital as his family and Teamsters brethren stood vigil. "Tell the boys not to fail me now," he admonished those keeping watch at his bedside. The city came to a standstill the day of his funeral, as tens of thousands of union rank and file from the area heard Ness eulogized as a hero.

Governor Olson, fearful of further reprisals in the wake of the July 20 bloodbath, determined to put an end to the carnage. "If it is necessary to assume military control, I will make the city of Minneapolis as quiet as a Sunday school," he announced, threatening martial law.[54] He did send National Guardsmen to disperse a protest march at city hall, where demonstrators furious about the police shootings were clamoring for the heads of Mayor A. G. Bainbridge and Chief of Police Mike Johannes. When strikers vowed to defy any martial law edict, Olson on August 1 ordered a surprise 4 a.m. raid on Teamsters headquarters, taking dozens of people into custody, including most of the strike managers, and imprisoning them in a stockade at the state fairgrounds in St. Paul. The union vowed to carry on with the strike even if shorn of its leadership.

Olson then made a series of shrewd moves aimed at calming the waters. He released those Teamsters held at the fairgrounds and allowed them to resume use of their strike hall; at the same time he ordered a raid on the Citizens Alliance headquarters, something that would have been unthinkable a year before. After consulting with President Roosevelt, Olson also softened the alliance's influence by bringing pressure on two leading local financial institutions, First Bank and Norwest Banco; both helped finance the local alliance chapter and both were in debt to the federal government on account of Reconstruction Finance Corporation (RFC) loans. Olson communicated to their executives diplomatically but directly that Washington desired their cooperation.

As in many protracted strikes, sheer fatigue was probably accountable for nudging both sides toward resolution, aided by the leverage Olson had brought against the alliance's backers. Like the coal strike of 1902 and the New York garment workers' uprising of 1909–1910, the outcome of the Minneapolis labor crisis came to rely in part on the willingness of wealthy stakeholders who, while remaining out of the thick of the fight, nevertheless had substantial motivation to avoid permanent disruption to commerce. In August, Local 574 and the employers agreed that workers at each trucking firm would vote as to whether the Teamsters would represent them; at almost all the large local trucking firms the union attained victory in these elections.

As in San Francisco, a disciplined local had ignored the guidance of its national union and won a tough labor ground war against determined and unscrupulous foes. The omniscient authority of the Citizens Alliance had been ended; Minneapolis was no longer "a citadel of the open shop."[55] As for the Teamsters, the local's success at defending, as part of its fight, the rights of broader categories of warehouse workers marked the beginning of the union's expansion. Over the next generation the IBT's outreach, sometimes guided by Farrell Dobbs himself, would come to include over-the-road truckers, dock loaders, and various other ancillary occupations, making the Teamsters an ever more formidable labor force.

THE RESURGENCE OF UNION ACTIVITY brought new focus to such basic questions as how organized labor would confront racial disparity within its ranks, and whether trade or industrial unions offered the best means of flexing workers' power. The Communist Party had made the organizing of black workers a priority early on, much as it had the unemployed. Perceiving African Americans as a nation within a nation, the most abused sufferers of class prejudice who, when liberated, would help spur society's transformation, Communist organizers reached out to black locals in Northern industrial cities such as Detroit but also ventured bravely into the Deep South, a region historically inimical to labor organizing. They formed Unemployed Councils and staged protests in Birmingham, Chattanooga, Atlanta, and other cities and towns, in addition to publishing a regional party news sheet called *The Southern Worker*. Biracial demonstrations initiated by the party in the heart of the former Confederacy were almost suicidal in their audacity, angering local whites and bringing about numerous attacks on labor organizers—at least two were killed in Florida—as well as an overnight resurgence of the Ku Klux Klan. Meanwhile the Communist-allied International Labor Defense distinguished itself by taking on a number of high-profile legal lynching cases including, most famously, the defense of the Scottsboro Boys, a group of young black men wrongly accused of raping two white women aboard a freight train in Alabama in 1931. In 1935 the party was instrumental in the creation of the National Negro Congress, which sought the easing of the effects of unemployment and an end to Jim Crow segregation.

One of the great stories of black labor advance during this era was that of A. Philip Randolph and the Brotherhood of Sleeping Car Porters. Pullman porters were among the best-paid black workers in America; the job's mobility, the company's reputation for quality service, even the impressive Pullman uniform, granted men fortunate to have such jobs an envied status. But work conditions were rigorous. Many employees were on duty as many as eighty to one hundred hours per week, yet there was no ladder of promotion to better-compensated positions such as conductor, which was reserved for whites; nor were the porters paid for overnight off-train layovers, during which they were left to absorb the costs of meals and lodging. And because the porters relied on tips for the lion's share of their income, they had no choice but to endure the routine condescension of white passengers and the indignity of being addressed as "George," an allusion to the company's founder, George M. Pullman. Employees who became disgruntled or attempted unionization were banned from service.

When five hundred porters gathered in 1925 to found the brotherhood, they elected Randolph, a Socialist writer, editor, and labor organizer, as their leader precisely "because he was not a porter [and] the company could not discipline him, fire him, nor find his car untidy." Pullman counterpunched by forming a company union, even though the Railway Labor Act of 1926 theoretically prohibited such company-rigged employee organizations. For almost a dozen years the porters waged two significant battles—to eliminate the company union and win recognition from the AFL. Finally, in 1935, the Brotherhood of Sleeping Car Porters won a federally mediated election over the company union, and in 1937 struck a collective bargaining pact with the Pullman Company, the first such achievement between a black union and a major corporation. The victory was a particularly meaningful effort because New Deal labor reforms largely excluded jobs in which blacks were prominent, such as farmwork and domestic labor, a denial so egregious that black newspapers had taken to calling the NRA the "Negro Removal Act."[56] After several years in which AFL president William Green moved forward, then back, then dithered some more on the matter, the porters also eventually won federation standing and affiliation.

Having come reluctantly to at least a partial accommodation on race, the AFL was soon confronted by another difficult question—whether federation workers were best served by being organized in trade unions or along industrial lines. Trade organizations were in effect the descendants of the guild and apprentice-journeyman systems of labor tradition, and were represented by mostly skilled workers organized around a specific expertise. Industrial unions were those organized by an entire industry, an early example being Eugene Debs's American Railway Union, which gathered together the unified might of all rail brotherhoods.

The leaders of industrial unions such as Sidney Hillman of the Amalgamated Clothing Workers and John L. Lewis of the UMW had begun to resist the hegemony of the established AFL trade unions. The rise of mass production industries, which tended to make craft traditions obsolete, suggested a larger role for industry-wide unions, a view supported by statistics: craft unions within the AFL had grown little, about 10 percent annually, in recent years, whereas new industrial unions were coming on line at a rate of 130 percent. Industrial organizing, Lewis argued, would better keep step with management's growing clout. "Great combinations of capital have assembled to themselves tremendous power and influence," he remarked. "If you go in there with your craft unions [the bosses] will mow you down like the Italian machine guns will mow down Ethiopians in the war now going on in that country."[57]

Rapid adaptation to new conditions had never been a hallmark of the AFL. Many older AFL members, if anything, saw the growth and mechanization of industry as more reason to adhere to the fixed AFL structure, not change it. President William Green insisted trade unions would always enjoy an advantage in bargaining with employers, and be better suited to ward off the vagaries of the economy or government interference. But Lewis grew impatient with such views, believing the AFL's practice of lumping unskilled workers into preexisting craft unions left workers in large industries less unified, with less ability to leverage against management. He reminded Green and others that labor's "fundamental obligation is to organize people."[58]

Vows were made at a San Francisco AFL gathering in 1934 to take steps toward industrial organizing. But the lack of follow-up led Lewis, at an AFL convention in Atlantic City the next year, to accuse the leadership of reneging on "the promissory note that this Federation held out [at San

Francisco] to the millions of workers in the mass-production industry."[59] Lewis counted among his supporters for a new direction Hillman of the ACW, Charles P. Howard of the Typographical Union, David Dubinsky of the ILGWU, and Philip Murray, Lewis's right-hand man at the UMW.

Lewis, pivoting on the AFL's broken promises from San Francisco, waged a strident campaign at the Atlantic City convention, demanding in soaring words that the AFL deacons "heed this cry" that "comes from the hearts of men," to "organize the unorganized and in doing so make the American Federation of Labor the greatest instrument that has ever been forged in the history of modern civilization to befriend the cause of humanity." On the AFL's response, he warned, rested the organization's fate.[60] In a convention-wide vote, however, the old craft ways held firm against industrial unionism by a substantial margin. As the Lewis forces continued to try to raise the issue for debate, William L. Hutcheson of the carpenters' union (whom the journalist I. F. Stone once described as "a six-foot oaf") moved to suppress further discussion.[61] Lewis challenged the parliamentary maneuver. Hutcheson then called Lewis a "bastard," prompting Lewis to jump over a row of chairs and punch Hutcheson in the side of the head, knocking him against a table. The carpenters' chief was led away by friends to wash the blood from his face while Lewis, according to a witness, "casually adjusted his tie and collar, relit his cigar, and sauntered slowly through the crowded aisles to the rostrum." The rift tearing apart the AFL could not have been better illustrated; the sound of Lewis's punch, it was said, "resonated through the working class."[62]

A split in the AFL now appeared inevitable. The next day those favoring organizing along industrial lines—Lewis, Hillman, Dubinsky, joined by a half-dozen others—caucused and established a Committee for Industrial Organization; soon after, on November 23, 1935, Lewis resigned his office as AFL vice president. The announcement was covered extensively by the press, Lewis taking advantage of the limelight to expound on his theory that only unionism that addressed current realities would allow America to recover from the Depression without recourse to the extremes of Fascism or other forms of dictatorship.

In January 1936 the nascent CIO made one last appeal to the AFL to charter industrial unions. Far from responding favorably, the AFL demanded that the CIO, still formally a committee of the AFL, disband at once. Lewis informed the members of the AFL executive council that he would see them "wearing asbestos suits in hell" before he would surrender his breakaway group.[63] The matter simmered for several months until late summer 1936, when the AFL suspended the ten unions that had affiliated with the CIO; in March 1937 they were formally expelled.

It was Lewis and his CIO, however, who had read the trends most astutely, for the appeal of the industrial approach, if anything, had only gained in strength. Previously nonunionized workers flooded into the CIO, while Lewis emerged as perhaps America's best-known labor leader. His public appearances across the nation's industrial heartland drew on his theatrical background. "In places like Detroit and Akron," recounts labor lawyer Thomas Geoghegan, "he would speak with his own thunder, at huge open-air rallies of workers, roaring like Lear into the wind and rain, and denouncing Wall Street and the AFL, both of them, with Bible-type blasts, in the cadence of King James, and bringing to it all the grandeur and majesty of the English stage."[64] Such was the enthusiasm for Lewis that those who could not gain admittance to his appearances frequently waited outside as he spoke; one group at a labor convention was so smitten it followed him into a men's room and stood by while he urinated.[65]

In leading the cause of industrial unionism out of the AFL, Lewis had fired the aspirations of working people in ways even he probably didn't expect, for he had not only offered a superior means to confront capital but had attacked big labor as well, and in championing industrial organization he won the support of the Communists, then perhaps the best organizers in the country; after some hesitation, Communist-led unions departed the AFL to join the CIO. At the same time Lewis's close working relationship with Roosevelt positioned him as a father of the New Deal, saving capitalism and democracy, as well as adjusting the nation's economy so as to benefit workers. The importance of his multifaceted role was not lost on his admirers. It is difficult today to imagine Lewis's popularity during the Depression and war years; radio addresses by the so-called President of the Workingman drew tens of millions of listeners; his observations, and his advice or criticism of the AFL, Congress, or the White House, were avidly read. As aide Lee Pressman later said, when Lewis pronounced the words "United Mine Workers of America," he somehow made it sound more important that if he had said "United States of America."[66] It seemed in no way incongruous when Lewis had the insignia on his UMW stationery designed to resemble that of the presidential seal.

Within months the CIO's 3.7 million members surpassed the AFL's 3.4 million. Such figures have long suggested to labor historians the significant opportunity for American labor that had been lost in the AFL-CIO split. Had the groups managed to forge an alliance, the resulting organization would have stood as a truly national labor contingent of almost limitless authority. In retrospect, the AFL's inability to adapt to and embrace the industrial organizing around which the CIO was founded appears pointlessly shortsighted, particularly because, unlike previous union movements accepting of unskilled workers, such as the Knights of Labor or the IWW, the CIO was for the most part faithful to the AFL's basic creed. It was neither utopian nor an advocate of revolutionary change, but sought only enhanced conditions for the nation's laborers; its greater idealism showed in its inclusiveness toward blacks, women, Communists, and immigrants, but it was fundamentally a hardheaded labor organization focused, as the AFL had long been, on improving workers' lives through practical means.

THE TOLEDO, SAN FRANCISCO, and Minneapolis actions offered convincing proof that labor was keen to organize along the lines suggested by the NIRA's Section 7(a), and that it was capable of mounting massive, disciplined strike actions. But there was clearly more work for the federal government to do. Unions were stymied in many instances by employers' skill at thwarting the rights entailed in the law. One of the more outlandish examples appeared in the textile strike of 1934. Inspired by the enactment of the NIRA, membership in the United Textile Workers had exploded between September 1933 and August 1934—increasing from 40,000 to 270,000. This had come as a surprise and delight to Northern labor New Dealers, for the South—through state "right to work laws," racial exclusion in trade unions, and a rigidly unified regional culture—had long suppressed union organizing. But textile mill owners were not going to concede easily, nor buckle under to the fair labor practices codes of the National Recovery Administration (NRA). They ignored the NRA strictures by "code chiseling"—manipulating the regulations so as to force greater production from workers, or setting production standards so high that they were then freed to terminate older workers and women who couldn't meet their quotas. In response to such sleight of hand, and also in reaction to the Southern mills' disregard for minimum wage and collective bargaining reforms, the UTW called a strike for September 3, 1934, demanding union recognition, humane production levels, and a thirty-hour week.

Beginning with a walkout by employees at Spindale, North Carolina, and facilitated by "flying squadrons" of strikers in pickup trucks and jalopy automobiles who tore through back roads to outlying mill sites to urge on the revolt, 376,000 textile workers abandoned their machines at mills extending up the East Coast as far as Maine; it stood, at the time, as the largest strike in U.S. history. The years of pent-up frustration and suffering were evident as men, women, and children took to the streets of long-sleepy villages to march, picket, and threaten the bosses, as well as the store owners and property owners who had long deprived them of their meager pay. At Honea Path, South Carolina, heavily armed and trigger-happy "deputies" fought back, killing seven strikers. In neighboring Georgia Governor Eugene Talmadge declared martial law, terming the strike the worst trouble to hit the region since Reconstruction.

The mill hands believed they had a powerful ally in the NRA and the president, one worker terming Roosevelt "the first man in the White House to understand that my boss is a son of a bitch." It was to their great disappointment then that the Roosevelt administration reacted hesitantly, seemingly fearful of alienating the Southern congressmen whose support was essential for New Deal legislation.[67] The president asked the strikers to return to their jobs and vowed the appointment of a mediation board to examine their grievances, but this body did little more than request further study of the issues. By September 22, their worksites hemmed in by soldiers and police, most of the strikers had obeyed Roosevelt's request. They not only were left to resume their jobs with none of their demands realized, many were forced to sign no-strike pledges. The defeat of the strike and the sense of abandonment by the federal government inhibited labor organizing in the South for decades.

At the same time, companies everywhere were finding some of the more than seven hundred NRA rules governing all aspects of their businesses unwieldy; the codes had begun to be challenged in courtrooms across the country. Eventually, in May 1935, the question of their constitutionality came before the U.S. Supreme Court in *Schechter Poultry Corp. v. United States.* The case involved the A. L. A. Schechter Poultry Corporation, a Brooklyn chicken slaughtering and retailing concern run by several brothers. The Schechters had appealed a lower court verdict that found them guilty of violating the wage and hour restrictions of the NRA code governing their employees, as well as rules about how wholesale customers selected the birds they wished to purchase. Among the charges, the brothers were accused of selling a chicken whose condition violated public health restrictions, causing the court action to become known as the "sick chicken case." The appellants argued that while the chickens they sold came from another state, they had bought them from a middleman in New York and thus were engaged solely in *intrastate*, not interstate, commerce; hence the operation of their business was not subject to federal regulation.[68] This line of attack sought to void the NIRA's basic premise—that Congress, based on the Constitution's commerce clause, possessed the authority to adjust and reform features of the nation's economic, trade, and labor policies. The underlying issue, of course, was whether the Roosevelt administration, even given the extraordinary circumstances of the Depression, had the right to dictate how and in what manner an individual operated his or her business.

By unanimous vote, the Court in *Schechter* declared the NIRA, including Section 7(a), unconstitutional. The ruling was clearly a conservative interpretation, an expression of the judiciary's weariness with the codes and the many complaints they had prompted; it was a severe setback for the New Deal, for it implied that the administration lacked the right to address the ailing economy through acts of Congress. Roosevelt was furious at what he called the Court's "horse and buggy" interpretation of the Constitution. To the president and his policy makers it was an article of faith that the interconnectedness of American life and commerce was what made sweeping reforms necessary; "a nation-wide problem demands a nation-wide remedy," he had said.[69]

Riding to the rescue was Senator Wagner. An alien-born citizen, the New Yorker could not aspire to advance in politics beyond the U.S. Senate, unlike his former Tammany colleague Al Smith, who had run for president in 1928. Instead, Wagner had taken on a role as the New Deal's driving force in Congress, helping to parent the Social Security Act, the Works Progress Administration, and the Civilian Conservation Corps. Certainly the New Deal had other paladins on Capitol Hill, such as Senator Robert La Follette Jr. of Wisconsin and Congressman George W. Norris of Nebraska, but Wagner, as I. F. Stone wrote, "knew what it was to live in a slum basement, to eat stale rolls, to sell papers on icy street corners." While similarly gifted men sought affluence or privilege (or in Smith's case, questioned the New Deal), Wagner remained "the champion of the underprivileged," dedicated to "one task . . . that is to raise the living standards of the lower-income groups in our society."[70] As he told the Senate Finance Committee in early 1933, "We are not in a mere business recession. We are in a life and death struggle with the forces of social and economic dissolution."[71] So great was his fervor that at times it seemed not so much a case of Wagner falling in line with the New Deal, as the New Deal coming to resemble Wagner.

He had been irritated by the devices employers came up with to evade the meaning of Section 7(a), and by the *Schechter* ruling, but as it had long been expected that the NIRA would be assaulted in court, Wagner and his aides had already developed legislation to clarify and buttress the New

Deal's pro-labor provisions. Working with Leon Keyserling, his economic adviser; William Leiserson of Columbia University; and Sidney Hillman's garment-industry colleague Isador Lubin, Wagner in 1934 introduced a new bill to clarify the government's powers of enforcement, chiefly by requiring employers to bargain with the labor representatives chosen by workers and to streamline the methods of the federal government in safeguarding those choices. "Section 7(a) was written by Congress to protect the weak who could not protect themselves, and it was intended for universal application, not universal modification," Wagner told the Senate.[72] He took special aim at company unions, saying, "Collective bargaining becomes a mockery when the spokesman of the employee is the marionette of the employer." While not endorsing the closed shop outright, he allowed as to how it might be warranted in particular situations; above all he insisted that the right to collective bargaining must be free of trickery or restraint:

> Business men are being allowed to pool their information
> and experience in vast trade associations in order to make a
> concerted drive against the evil features of modern industrialism.
> If employees are denied similar privileges, they not only are
> unable to uphold their end of the labor bargain but, in addition,
> they cannot cope with any issues that transcend the boundaries
> of a single business. And under modern industrial conditions
> problems of wages and hours are regional or even national in
> scope.[73]

What Wagner grasped more fully than some of his colleagues was that the New Deal attainment of "collective bargaining" was code for much more than the right to negotiate with an employer; it was the fulfillment of the Progressive ideal of industrial democracy, allowing the Constitution at last to enter the workplace. "The responsibilities and expectations of American citizens—due process, free speech, the right of assembly and petition," suggests historian Nelson Lichtenstein, "would now find their place in factory, mill, and office. A civil society would be constructed within the very womb of the privately held enterprise."[74]

The legislation Wagner brought before Congress, soon to be known as the National Labor Relations Act or simply the Wagner Act, sought to put teeth in the New Deal's guarantees to labor. It forbade employer interference with union organizing, banned employer-supported company unions, prohibited any firing of men for union membership, and insisted that employers enter into collective bargaining with the representatives of the union backed by a majority of a company's workers as demonstrated by their votes. The bill also endowed an administrative government board—soon to be known as the National Labor Relations Board—that would determine union legitimacy through on-site elections, thus enabling employers to know they were dealing with a union supported by a majority of workers; at the same time the provision meant employers would not be able to delay bargaining by claiming instead of denying that a particular labor organization did not truly represent employees.

The bill had some influential friends, such as Lincoln Filene, the Boston retailer and industrial relations reformer whose Twentieth Century Fund had issued a report proposing some of the same solutions. Filene used his status as a prominent employer to speak directly to those of his business peers who had dragged their heels on 7(a). Infuriated by "the average cupidity and narrow-mindedness of his fellow businessmen," writes historian Steven Fraser, Filene "began delivering scathingly sarcastic tirades against their anachronistic fondness for the ethos of frugality, their inability to formulate anything but the most immediately selfish policies, and a provincialism he warned would lead to revolution, a grim prospect to be avoided only by encouraging industrial unionism on a nationwide scale."[75]

Despite Filene's strong words to his business cohorts and Wagner's strenuous advocacy, both President Roosevelt and Labor Secretary Perkins had reservations about the legislation. Perkins worried, as the fate of the NRA codes in the run-up to *Schechter* suggested, that legislation designed to force employers to behave a certain way would not be effective; she had begun to think of changing capital's attitude toward labor's rights as an "educational process" that might take years. Wagner, on the other hand, felt duty-bound to go to bat for workers but also for those employers who had willingly accepted 7(a), who had been "good citizens" and had tried to work with unions; to abandon the effort now would be to reward those very firms that had stalled and been the least helpful.[76] Perkins did come to see that unions and labor leaders such as the AFL's William Green were willing to give Wagner's legislation their support, which surprised her. She had "felt sure labor would object [to it], for

> the recognition of a union under the [Act] would depend upon the counting of noses. A labor union would have to prove it had the backing of a majority of workers in a plant. This was certainly new doctrine in 1934. It had not been AFL policy in the past to count noses before a committee went in to see the boss to demand better wages, hours, working conditions. No labor union had ever asked a government board to tell it whether they could represent [employees]. That was the union leader's judgment. Closed shops had been gained by bold methods at times. This bill would make that impossible."[77]

Roosevelt, like Perkins, was not committed at first to the legislation; for one thing, the bill seemed "remedial," addressing the shortcomings in Section 7(a); it fell short of the far more comprehensive ethical code of labor-industrial relations the White House had once imagined as its goal. The president also feared the Wagner legislation would meet a fate identical to 7(a), and arouse fresh hostility from business. In any case, with Wagner himself having donned full armor to force a path for his bill, Perkins and the president had the luxury of watching intently from the sidelines as the Senate took up the matter in spring 1935. Roosevelt became more supportive of the measure once it became clear the Supreme Court would invalidate the NIRA in *Schecter*.[78]

The debate over the bill in Congress was involved, for like seminal disputes about labor's status dating back to *Commonwealth v. Hunt*, it asked the fundamental question of who a worker was to be in America's industrial society—a cog, a partner, an investor—and how much power he should be given. Advocates of the Wagner bill emphasized that only collective bargaining and the right to organize would secure working people a place in a democratic society; allowing them a protected means for the expression of their discontent was the kind of policy that distinguished America from societies that suppressed such freedom, and would pay back the nation in dividends of labor peace. Business, through its traditional defenders in Congress, saw the rights embedded in Wagner as representing an unpalatable intrusion into the nation's capitalist system, granting far too much say to those who were neither businessmen nor stockholders.

The Senate Labor Committee reported favorably on the bill on May 2; on May 15 Wagner delivered a powerful address in the Senate, reassuring his colleagues that "the pending bill is designed merely to apply to industry generally the benefits of our rich American experience. While it has been branded radical by some and ultraconservative by others, every one of its principles has been sanctioned by a long train of laws of Congress," an allusion to the Clayton, Norris–La Guardia, and National Industrial Recovery acts. "[It] is responsive to the ominous industrial disturbances of last summer, when blood ran freely in the streets and martial law was in the offing, [and] appeals to the conscience and intelligence of all those who know the history of our country and are imbued with its high ideals."[79] Wagner continued to coax votes and the next day—with the measure appearing to be riding "on greased skids"—the bill passed by a count of 62–12.[80]

There were several reasons for the speed with which the legislation won approval, beginning with the fact that Senator Wagner by then was associated with a number of successful New Deal programs and enjoyed considerable sway in the Senate. With the NIRA having just been dispensed with, and the lack of any agreement to extend its protections, there was also no doubt a sense among many senators that a vote for the Wagner Act was required to soothe voter anxiety or resentment. Another factor was that members of Congress opposed to Roosevelt's reforms were eager for the current, mostly conservative Supreme Court to have a chance to sit in judgment of the Wagner Act and other disputed New Deal programs before the president liberalized its bench with his own appointments. Thus it was in their interest to "put no particular legislative obstacles" in the way. "Several members of the court are old men," noted the *New York Times*, "and the next few months may bring great changes. If those changes come, the majority mind of the court inevitably will turn more sympathetically to the objectives of the administration."[81] It was precisely this eventuality that the congressional conservatives wished to avoid. The bill passed the House, the president signing it into law on July 5, 1935.

THE NEW DEAL DREW organized labor in from the fringes. Not every program worked, business continued to fuss and grumble, but the era's sustained attitude of government concern had the effect of enshrining the concepts of labor organization and workers' rights as integral to the maintenance of democracy. Particularly against the frightening rise of European Fascism and the ever-present fear of totalitarian Communism, the homegrown American labor organization appeared to have won some semblance of a place in society and to have shed the historic stigma of radical "otherness." Labor, historically wary of entanglements with major party politics, adjusted to its new status by becoming more politically involved, for it now had compelling reasons to do so.

The romance bloomed fully in the election year of 1936. Labor was determined to safeguard advances already delivered and those yet to be attained. The administration and the Democratic Party wanted to win reelection convincingly in order to validate the New Deal, as many of the president's policies remained under fire from conservative forces. All allies, all who had benefited from the Roosevelt program, were urged to pitch in, labor's involvement replacing, to an extent, the former influence of the big-city political machines, whose power had begun to wane.[82] As the election neared—Roosevelt's opponent was Republican Alf Landon, governor of Kansas—the incumbent became more confident of victory, but feared winning by so narrow a margin that his program of reforms would be handicapped by the lack of an overriding mandate.

Senator Wagner again played a key role, giving a series of nationally broadcast radio talks that hailed the accomplishments of the New Deal; he also supervised the writing of the Democratic platform, which itself was an eloquent restating of the administration's vision. The preamble echoed the Declaration of Independence, setting forth "self-evident truths" regarding a modern government's "obligations to its citizens," including the importance of home and family, the creation of "a democracy of opportunity" for all citizens, and the need to assist those "overtaken by disaster." It vowed that the Democratic Party would "continue to use the powers of government to end the activities of the malefactors of great wealth who defraud and exploit the people," while reminding readers that the party had "given the army of America's industrial workers something more substantial than the Republicans' dinner pail full of promises.

"The worker has been returned to the road to freedom and prosperity," the platform vowed. "We will keep him on that road."[83] The document took care to flatter both labor and capital by suggesting that their respective wisdom and restraint would ultimately limit the need for government interference.

John L. Lewis and Sidney Hillman contributed to the campaign by creating the Non-Partisan League, a labor entity designed to aid Roosevelt's reelection yet not formally affiliated with the Democratic Party. They were also involved in a New York–based splinter group, the American Labor Party, which worked to bring Socialist and independent voters in line behind the president. "American labor will keep faith with the president next November as the president has kept faith with American labor," Hillman assured.[84] Lewis, always unpredictable and reserving the right to criticize, nonetheless offered Roosevelt his and the UMW's hearty endorsement. The UMW also gave the reelection effort a $500,000 donation, while the CIO chipped in with loans, contributions, and other in-kind support.

ROOSEVELT WAS REELECTED with the help of a massive voter turnout from organized labor, and began 1937 with the mandate he'd sought from the American people as well as Democratic control of both houses of Congress. One of his first acts brimmed with the superior confidence gained from so heartening a victory: on February 5, 1937, he set out to conquer the last obstacle to his administration's economic program: the United States Supreme Court. The high court had thwarted him not only in *Schechter*, which had voided the NIRA, but also in *United States v. Butler*, which had declared unconstitutional the Agricultural Readjustment Act of 1933, an effort to manage the nation's farm economy by reimbursing farmers to limit crop production. Roosevelt seethed that the needs of the American people, and the ability of the president to regulate commerce, were being undermined by "the private, social philosophy" of the majestic, and unfortunately traditionalist, figures who sat with lifetime appointments on the Supreme Court.[85] His hubristic proposal to address this annoyance, the Judiciary Reorganization Bill, or as it was known by critics, "Roosevelt's court-packing plan," was to expand the Court's membership in order to alter its present unadventurous majority. Using the rationale that the justices were too few and too old to keep up with the obligations of their docket, the president proposed that a new justice be added to the Court for each existing justice who had served ten years and did not resign or retire within six months of reaching seventy years of age.

Conservatives pounced on so transparent a scheme. Even many Democrats were dubious about the idea, including the stalwart Senator Wagner, himself a former judge who cherished the ideal of the bench's independence from politics. Press and public alike also seemed uneasy, concerned that the plot was overbearing, even dictatorial. No less a personage than Chief Justice Charles Evans Hughes publicly contradicted Roosevelt's claim that the Court was overwhelmed by its docket.

Roosevelt's Court-restructuring bill died in the Senate Judiciary

Committee in July, and a House version also failed to advance, the defeat suggesting the limits of an otherwise popular president's influence; the Court, however, did soon show itself to be more accommodating of the administration's wishes, a turnabout that came just in time to preserve the constitutional justification for the Wagner Act.

In *Schechter* the Court had drawn a narrow interpretation of the scope of the Constitution's commerce clause, ruling that the NIRA and its Section 7(a) could not be applied broadly as it only affected businesses literally engaged in interstate commerce. Employers had cherished the hope that the Wagner Act would be dismissed on similar grounds. But on April 12, 1937, the Wagner Act was found constitutional in a series of rulings, especially *National Labor Relations Board v. Jones & Laughlin Steel Corp.* The Court reversed itself on two main points formerly invoked to thwart pro-labor legislation—that labor disputes were a private matter because of the liberty of contract protection of the due process clause of the Fifth and Fourteenth amendments, and the objection that such matters could not be legislated by Congress under the commerce clause. Regarding the question of liberty of contract—whether the Wagner Act's empowerment of workers' organizing power constituted an unfair restraint on business—the Court ruled that workers "have as clear a right to organize and select their representatives for law purposes as the [employer] has to organize its business and select its own officers and agents."[86] The Court was also willing to cede that labor union battles were not merely local affairs, as it had previously, but that their ramifications impacted the national economy, and thus Congress had the right to address them with appropriate legislation. The key to the Court's reversal in the narrow 5–4 vote in *National Labor Relations Board v. Jones* was the changed opinions of Chief Justice Hughes and Justice Owen Roberts, a shift some observers attributed to the effect of Roosevelt's threatened restructuring.

Supreme Court Justice Robert Jackson later said that he thought the real reason behind the Court's change of heart on the Roosevelt administration's economic program may have been tied to the president's overwhelming reelection in 1936, which some of the justices, like Roosevelt himself, were willing to see as an affirming national referendum on the New Deal:

> I think that the Court in the early days had felt that the New Deal was a sporadic and passing thing; that the people of the country hadn't really in 1932 given a mandate for it. I think that when the 1936 election came about, [justices] felt that such measures were a real-felt necessity on the part of the people of the country and that the Court ought not to strive to support objections to it.[87]

Whatever the Court's motivations, the successful validation of the Wagner Act became one of numerous second-term New Deal victories for Roosevelt. An important corollary to the Wagner Act was the administration's effort to tackle the era's staggering unemployment by creating jobs through the Civil Works Administration and the Federal Emergency Relief Administration. These programs represented a significant political as well as cultural turnabout, overthrowing the long-reigning sentiment that inhibited government from helping provide people in need a means of making a living. Insomuch as the president and his aides grappled with this ethical readjustment, they did so by inverting the long-fixed dynamic of rugged individualism without negating the sacred matter of self-reliance. Such a value was *so* central to individual Americans, they pointed out, the nation would never fully recover until workers regained their self-respect. This would result from their having meaningful work, fairly paid. They must be given a chance to stand again on their own two feet.

Reengineering the government's relationship with America's working people remained a priority. The movement for some kind of government-assured old-age pension had been around since the Progressive era, and Frances Perkins, while industrial commissioner of New York State, had advocated the idea in 1930 to then-governor Roosevelt along with the need for unemployment insurance. The state of Wisconsin had in 1932 enacted unemployment and retirement compensation, and the former muckraker Upton Sinclair ran a surprisingly popular campaign for governor of California in 1934 championing a $50-per-month old-age pension. From the California community of Long Beach emerged the unique grassroots phenomenon known as Townsend Clubs, named for physician Francis Townsend, a crusade that convened in religious revival-style gatherings across the nation, urging a federal stipend of $200 per month to senior citizens.

Perkins had traveled to England to study that nation's unemployment compensation methods and returned speaking well of them, although she suggested that any such programs in America be automated, avoiding the mountainous paperwork created by the British system. To counter the expected constitutional challenges to unemployment insurance and old-age pensions, she acted on a suggestion made by Supreme Court Justice Louis Brandeis that the unemployment provision be supported not by direct taxation but rather by employee and employer contributions to state reserves designated for this purpose.[88] The Social Security Act, an "epochal development in the history of a nation so long wedded to *laissez-faire* concepts of the role of government in economic and social matters,"[89] was signed into law in August 1935, providing a system of insurance for workers once they had attained age sixty-five, and benefits to support surviving children and spouses of workers who died at a younger age.

While the Wagner Act had addressed the need for unions to be able to organize and bargain collectively, the administration also sought more directly to affect the questions of wages and working conditions. The Walsh-Healey Public Contracts Act of 1936 standardized the forty-hour week and minimum wages for employees of government contractors, and prohibited the employment of children. The idea behind the act, which was strongly supported by Perkins, was that reduced hours would motivate employers to hire more workers, while increased wages would give workers more consumer power. But when the administration sought to expand the Walsh-Healey standards to all American workplaces, there were warnings that the Supreme Court would block it on constitutional grounds.[90] Congress was slow in moving on the legislation, so the president called the body into special session, stressing the need to enlarge the spending power of the average worker by giving him a fair consistent wage and rational hours of work that did not sap his lifeblood. The Fair Labor Standards Act passed in May–June 1938, creating a 25-cent-per-hour minimum wage (which would be increased to 40 cents per hour within seven years), a forty-four-hour workweek that would decrease to a forty-hour week within three years, and a ban on the employment of children under the age of sixteen. By now the complexion of the Court had changed somewhat, with two justices voluntarily retiring (perhaps in response to newly passed legislation guaranteeing their pensions), and the act was upheld as constitutional in the Supreme Court's unanimous ruling in *United States v. Darby Lumber Co.* in 1941. A number of other forthcoming rulings by the high court also benefited labor, such as *Thornhill v. Alabama* (1940), in which the right of peaceful picketing was upheld as an expression of free speech.

I N LATE 1936 THE UNITED AUTO WORKERS, which had departed the AFL for the more militant CIO, sought recognition from the Big Three automakers—General Motors, Chrysler, and Ford. Of the three, GM, whose main plants were in Flint, Michigan, was the biggest; indeed, it was the most profitable company in America and the dominant force in automobiles, employing 262,000 of the 400,000 workers in the industry. Its fifty-seven plants scattered across North America manufactured over 2 million cars and trucks each year.[91]

The UAW found GM's response to its quest disappointing—an assurance from GM vice president William S. Knudson that, in lieu of an exclusive collective bargaining agreement with the union, individual GM plant managers would be glad to deal with outstanding employee grievances. The UAW president was Homer S. Martin, an ordained Baptist minister known for his passionate speeches on behalf of autoworkers' rights but little respected as a labor negotiator. Martin's well-known nickname, "The Leaping Parson," an allusion to the National Hop, Step, and Jump championship he had won as a young man, doubtless contributed to the difficulty Martin had being taken seriously at the negotiating table, along with his penchant for wandering off to take in a movie when the pressures of his job grew too strenuous.

CIO chief Lewis, suspecting that Martin would not be able to deal effectively with GM, asked for a national conference between GM and the UAW, but GM president Alfred Sloan adhered to the terms of Knudson's offer, refusing to recognize the UAW, although he did discuss the matter with Labor Secretary Perkins. Sloan drew some of his confidence that GM could hold out against any UAW labor action because Flint had long been a company town—its workers, elected officials, and even its daily press loyal to the town's majority employer. As a disturbing sign of the uphill battle the UAW faced, some Flint autoworkers had gone so far as to join the Black Legion, a right-wing paramilitary group that resisted the influence of unions generally and was known to target immigrants and blacks who competed for "American jobs" or seemed otherwise intrusive.[92] Against this conservative intransigence the UAW did benefit from the presence among the Flint movement's leaders of veteran Communist organizers, bringing a degree of militancy to the operation both within and outside the walls of GM's plants

Sloan was very pre–Wagner Act in his outlook, a member of the pioneering generation of tinkering automotive engineers such as his good friend Charles Kettering, GM's head of research, who had electrified the automobile. He may not have fully grasped the extent to which the individuals who manned the assembly lines in the big auto plants had grown frustrated by increasing levels of automation and the speedups that disregarded their needs as human beings. "You have to run to the toilet and run back," a worker in a Buick plant complained of the most basic human inconvenience. "If you had to . . . take a crap, if there wasn't anybody there to relieve you, you had to run away and tie the line up, and if you tied the line up you got hell for it."[93] One wife of an auto assembly-line worker said that after a long shift "the children don't dare go near him, he's so nervous and his temper's bad. And then at night in bed he shakes, his whole body, he shakes." Another woman complained, "They're not men anymore, if you know what I mean. They're not men.

My husband is only thirty, but to look at him you'd think he was fifty and all played out."[94]

On December 30, 1936, workers at two GM Fisher Body plants in Flint learned that management, fearing a UAW work stoppage just before a busy production season, was preparing to ship materials and dies used by the factory to other GM locations. The employees decided that the Fisher plants should be immediately shut down, but instead of walking out remained at their posts: they simply stopped working.

The work-stoppage technique known as the sit-down, used initially in 1906 by the IWW at a General Electric facility in Schenectady, had resurfaced in February–March 1936 at a Goodyear rubber facility in Akron. As journalist Ruth McKenney reported, the shutting down of an assembly line by the workers who were its slaves was an emotional experience. "The whole room lay in perfect silence," she reported of the first incredible moments after a line was turned off.

> The tire-builders stood in long lines, touching each other, perfectly motionless, deafened by the silence. A moment ago there had been the weaving hands, the revolving wheels, the clanking belt, the moving hooks, the flashing tire tools. Now there was absolute stillness, no motion anywhere, no sound. . . . "We done it! We stopped the belt! By God we done it!" And men began to cheer hysterically, to shout and howl in the fresh silence. Men wrapped long sinewy arms around their neighbors' shoulders, screaming, "We done it! We done it!"[95]

The Fisher strike would be the first large-scale use of the sit-down, a tactic to which automobile assembly lines were especially vulnerable because manufacturing in the auto industry was based on the continuous flow of production, and the cessation of work by even a handful of men in one department could bring an entire plant to a halt. The sit-down had other advantages. Strikers operated on defensive territory, the inside of the factory, whose physical qualities they knew better than anyone. And workers remaining by their machines stymied any employer ideas about scabbing and put management in a position where, if it chose to retake its plant by force, a rush by police and any worker resistance would likely damage the premises. Management was even kept from turning off the heat on the strikers because insurance companies feared the men inside the building would then start fires to stay warm.

Sit-downs also enjoyed a certain philosophical purity. For one thing, they were nonviolent. Rather than besieging a place of work from outside, as in most strikes, a sit-in was a protest in which the participants retained possession of that which they considered rightfully theirs. "Just sitting on our jobs," was the expression the workers used. To maintain the strike's integrity and deny employers any excuse to send in police or soldiers, those occupying the plant allowed no vandalism to the machinery or the building itself.

It appeared the sit-downers might even have the law on their side. A Detroit prosecutor informed GM that, as the workers had entered the factory at the employers' "invitation," they could not be accused of trespassing; and because such a strike was not forbidden by statute, there was no basis for police to oust those inside.[96]

GM nonetheless insisted that the strikers vacate the premises they occupied in Fisher Body plant No. 2 before any negotiations could occur. The strikers agreed to leave if GM recognized the union, leading GM's Knudsen to complain to Homer Martin, "Collective bargaining cannot be justified if one party, having seized the plant, holds a gun to the other party's head."[97] But John L. Lewis had seen enough of high-stakes labor disputes to know that corporations ceded nothing voluntarily; only through the interference with a company's production and profits would labor win concessions from an uncooperative player like GM, and the Fisher plant strikers, with their effective sit-in, had the firm nicely cornered. The CIO thus backed the UAW wholeheartedly, Lewis emphasizing that as collective bargaining was now "the law of the land," thanks to the Wagner Act, GM, not the strikers, was in defiance of that law.[98]

When Secretary of Labor Perkins queried President Roosevelt about the matter, she found his views rather relaxed. "Well, it's illegal, but what law are they breaking?" the president said. "The law of trespass, and that is about the only law that could be invoked."

> And what do you do when a man trespasses on your property? Sure, you order him off. But shooting it out and killing a lot of people because they have violated the law of trespass somehow offends me. . . . There must be another way. Why can't these fellows in General Motors meet with the committee of workers? Talk it all out. They would get a settlement. It wouldn't be so terrible.[99]

Roosevelt and Perkins, while formally voicing concern about the sit-down, took a wait-and-see approach; neither was inclined to endorse the use of force to oust the UAW men.

Such was the standoff when, on January 2, GM obtained an injunction from Judge Edward D. Black ordering the strikers out of the plant. Quick-thinking UAW aides, however, discovered that Black owned 3,365 shares of GM stock valued at $219,000. The UAW immediately shared this information with the press, forcing GM to back off the injunction, its judge clearly compromised. GM then demanded that the militia be called in to dislodge the strikers, but Michigan governor Frank Murphy, along with Perkins and Roosevelt, thought that a poor idea. Murphy, a former judge and mayor of Detroit known for his determination to aid the unemployed and for his restraint of the police, had been swept into the governor's chair as part of Roosevelt's landslide win in 1936. As mayor he had acted on the faith that unions were a potential means of stabilizing industrial society, actively encouraging the city's workers to seek expanded rights, including unemployment insurance and an end to court injunctions aimed at labor activity.[100] Murphy believed the UAW was in the right to force GM to honor the terms of the Wagner Act.

With the government appearing to side with the union, the strike soon spread to dozens of other GM plants across the country, seriously curtailing production of GM's Chevrolet and Cadillac lines. Significantly, the other major carmakers—Ford, Chrysler, Nash, and Packard—far from showing solidarity with GM, continued manufacturing, thus compounding GM's predicament.

Ten days into the standoff GM decided it had had enough. Shortly after nine o'clock in the evening of January 11 police approached Fisher Body plant No. 2 and ordered the strikers out, then, moments later, smashed windows at the entrance and began firing tear-gas canisters inside. The strikers, who had anticipated such an incursion, drove the invaders back with "coffee mugs, pop bottles, iron bolts, and heavy automobile door hinges."[101] Local UAW leader Victor Reuther, who was outside in a "union sound car" with amplification equipment and a rooftop speaker, began shouting advice and encouragement to the men inside the building. "We wanted peace!" he shouted. "General Motors chose war. Give it to them!" Workers had made makeshift slingshots by stretching inner tubes across iron pipes, and from the plant's roof "let loose a barrage of pound-and-a-half hinges," Reuther recalled.[102]

Driven back once, the cops tried a second assault with the tear gas, although the wind blew much of it back in their faces. At the same time, strikers activated the building's fire hoses, spraying the cops with water in the frigid air. Their retreat was hindered by UAW pickets stationed outside the plant, who pelted the fleeing officers with snowballs and pieces of asphalt pried from the parking lot; at one point they surrounded a sheriff's squad car and rocked it back and forth with him inside it. Infuriated at their failure to take back the factory, some officers drew revolvers and fired into the crowd, prompting a female picketer to grab the microphone in Reuther's car and shout, "Cowards! Cowards! Shooting unarmed and defenseless men!"[103] Thirteen pickets were wounded in the fray, and nine policemen suffered injuries, mostly from being struck on the head by objects hurled from the building. The strikers, stunned but pleased to have beaten back not one but two police assaults, hurriedly erected a stronger barrier of cars before the entrance.[104]

However much observers might privately enjoy the news that "unarmed" strikers, using whatever weapons came to hand, had successfully resisted the attempt to roust them, such violence against uniformed officials could not be condoned. Governor Murphy had no choice but to order National Guardsmen into Flint, although he stopped short of authorizing them to do anything beyond keeping order on the streets. He did induce UAW and GM to meet for talks, which produced a truce proposal that involved the workers exiting the premises and GM agreeing not to bargain with anyone but the UAW. This arrangement, however, scheduled to start January 17, stalled when UAW representatives learned that GM meant to include in the negotiations the head of a GM company union called the Flint Alliance; suspecting "a double-cross was in the offing," the workers continued to occupy the plant.[105]

On January 31 GM requested a new court order to clear the premises, this time being careful to seek out a judge with no financial interests in GM. But the strikers were also busy. On February 1, in a diversionary maneuver, they provoked fighting with police guards in front of a ball-bearing factory known as Chevrolet No. 9. When cops from the surrounding area rushed to the scene, a second group of strikers invaded Chevrolet No. 4, an engine-making plant that had remained open during the strike. After chasing floor bosses and nonunion workers out of the building, the strikers began a sit-down in No. 4, occupying a facility even more central to GM's production system, for the engines for Chevrolet cars, the corporation's best seller, were built there.

The next day GM obtained the injunction it wanted, which gave the strikers until three o'clock on the afternoon of February 3 to depart the GM buildings and carried a potential fine of $15 million to the UAW if the injunction was disregarded. This placed the matter back in the governor's office, since militia would be required to enforce the injunction. Murphy got little help from CIO chief Lewis, who with his usual flair for melodrama told him that if troops stormed Chevrolet No. 4, "I shall then walk up to the largest window in the plant, open it, divest myself of my outer raiment, remove my shirt and bare my bosom. Then, when you order your troops to fire, mine will be the first breast that those bullets will strike."[106]

Murphy heard from the strikers, as well, who in a telegram reminded him that their sit-down was peaceful and designed to force GM to "obey the law and engage in collective bargaining." They further vowed that they would resist again with force if assaulted. "The police of the city of Flint belong to GM," the UAW workers wrote. "The sheriff of Genesee County belongs to GM. The judges of Genesee County belong to GM. . . . It remains to be seen whether the governor of the state also belongs to GM."[107]

Murphy wrestled with the decision. As governor he could not ignore a court injunction, but as a labor-friendly politician with aspirations to national office he could hardly side with GM against strikers who largely had the public's sympathy and with whom he essentially agreed. He chose to resist calls to order the state militia to enforce the injunction. "I'm not going down in history as 'Bloody Murphy,'" he averred. "If I sent those soldiers right in on the men there'd be no telling how many would be killed. It would be inconsistent with everything I have ever stood for in my whole political life."[108]

To buy time, Murphy brought GM's Knudson together with John L. Lewis, a move backed by President Roosevelt, who strongly urged Knudson and Lewis to find a solution. Knudson had as GM's strongest bargaining chip the fact that the strikers were defying a court injunction; Lewis felt secure in the knowledge that Governor Murphy would not likely order the militia to enforce it and that Roosevelt desired an outcome in which GM conceded collective bargaining rights to the autoworkers. On February 11, after forty-four days of the sit-down, a four-page agreement emerged: the workers would exit the plants; for a six-month period GM would bargain only with the UAW; it would not interfere with workers seeking to join the UAW or blacklist workers who had struck; the firm would also call off the court injunction and address employee grievances. Lewis credited Governor Murphy with creating the negotiation that led to the settlement, while an exhausted Knudsen told reporters simply, "Let us have peace and make cars."[109]

The UAW failed to win the eight-hour day or the thirty-hour week it had sought, but had set in motion the process that would ultimately unionize the U.S. auto industry, and the workers who finally departed

GM property to their supporters' cheers and applause seemed to know they had done something valorous and possibly historic. The pact with the nation's largest corporation had made collective bargaining rights inevitable everywhere. "When the boys came out, I never saw a night like that and perhaps may never see it again," recalled one witness. "I liken it to some description of a country experiencing independence."[110]

THE UAW VICTORY GREATLY ENHANCED the CIO's reputation, while popularizing the sit-down. In the immediate aftermath of Flint it was this last result that most worried Main Street, for suddenly sit-down strikes were everywhere—in textile mills, glass factories, breweries, even Woolworth Five and Dimes—and wherever they appeared they continued to attract headlines and public support. In Gillespie, Illinois, 450 coal miners staged their own version—a "stay-down," in which they occupied part of a mine 360 feet belowground and refused to leave pending new restrictions on the introduction of machines into the mine works.[111] Sit-downs were also taken up by groups with grievances against government, such as those protesting evictions or demanding greater public relief. Even members of a National Guard unit that had been on duty at Flint sat down when their pay was not forthcoming. Nine hundred sit-downs were recorded between 1935 and 1937, *Time* magazine suggesting that "sitting down has replaced baseball as [the] national pastime."[112]

The CIO also won a crucial breakthrough in steel. Beginning in 1936 the Steel Workers Organizing Committee (SWOC), chaired by CIO vice president Philip Murray, had tackled the difficult challenge of organizing the steel industry, which for the half century since Homestead had successfully resisted outside unionization. The aim was to get the nation's largest steel producer, U.S. Steel, to agree to recognize SWOC, with the idea that other steel companies would then also fall into line. U.S. Steel maintained large company unions that had actually shown signs lately of resisting management, an insurrectionary trend that allowed CIO members to infiltrate these unions and sway members to align with SWOC.

CIO president Lewis, meanwhile, played an essential role. Riding high on the Wagner Act, Lewis was convinced that only "a madman or a fool" would try to deny the industrial organizing of workers, "this river of human sentiment," as he called it, which could no longer "be dammed or impounded by the erection of arbitrary barriers of restraint."[113] On January 9, 1937, he encountered Myron C. Taylor, chairman and CEO of U.S. Steel, in the dining room of the Mayflower Hotel in Washington; a brief discussion led to several additional meetings over the next few days in which Lewis set out to persuade Taylor that unionization would bring stability to the steel industry.

Taylor was a successful financial wizard brought in to help guide U.S. Steel through the Depression, and as a result he did not possess the ingrained contempt for unions that often characterized major industrialists. The passage of the Wagner Act had certainly suggested to Taylor the shifting landscape of U.S. industrial relations. Roosevelt's aims for an expanded government guardianship of working people had been endorsed at the polls, Lewis pointed out, and New Deal reforms were having a salutary impact on growth and production; it was time for capital to afford labor an enlarged stake. But however vigorous Lewis's arguments, Taylor was likely most influenced by the hopeful financial news coming from Wall Street: the economy was beginning to rebound; and with U.S. Steel's profits increasing for the first time in years, this was hardly the moment for a crippling strike, which, it had been rumored, might take place as soon as April.

By the time the two men met again in mid-February, word had arrived of the UAW's win in the protracted sit-down strike against General Motors. The CIO's handling of the auto strike, in which Lewis had been much involved, and the helpful attitude taken by President Roosevelt and Michigan governor Frank Murphy, helped convince Taylor that it made sense for U.S. Steel to also seek a meaningful employee pact. On March 2, U.S. Steel, the descendant of the mighty Carnegie conglomerate that had, after Homestead, clobbered unionized steelworkers, formally recognized the SWOC, announced a 5 percent wage hike, and accepted the eight-hour day and the forty-hour week. In what became known as "the Myron Taylor Labor formula," the company also agreed to respect its employees' right to bargain collectively "through representatives freely chosen by them without dictation, coercion or intimidation in any form or from any source."

The breakthrough was a signal achievement for the CIO and for the labor movement generally, reversing almost five decades of antiunion fervor by the large steel interests. By offering a firm handshake across the labor-capital divide, the steel industry indicated its acceptance of the profound changes in workers' status in American life.[114] Several other large firms followed U.S. Steel's conciliatory lead.

Resistance to the Taylor formula, unfortunately, cropped up at smaller steel companies such as Republic Steel, Youngstown Sheet and Tube, Inland Steel, and Bethlehem Steel, entities known collectively as "Little Steel." As a result, in May 1937, seventy-five thousand workers walked off their jobs. Led by Republic's tough antiunion negotiator, Tom Girdler, Little Steel owners at first tried a clever subterfuge, offering to make verbal but not written pacts with unions, since the Wagner Act did not specifically require written collective bargaining agreements. They also reacted to the strike with more time-tested measures such as hired enforcers, intimidation of union leaders, and police to protect replacement workers.

On the south side of Chicago on the warm Sunday afternoon of May 30, several hundred strikers, their families and supporters, had gathered at a former dance hall adjacent to a Republic Steel plant to hear a series of speeches from SWOC leaders. Leaving the rally, they began a spirited march toward the gates of the plant, chanting "C.I.O.! C.I.O.! C.I.O.!" Two young men led the way holding aloft American flags. Many were oblivious to the squad of city police waiting just ahead, and the protestors may have pressed in uncomfortably close to the cops; police claimed that rocks were thrown. Witnesses, however, agreed the shooting began before the full contingent of marchers had even reached the plant's gates—a sudden pop, then another, then another—suggesting it was the police who instigated the assault. The lead marchers turned around to flee, stumbling into their comrades still headed toward the gates; those who hadn't heard the gunshots did not understand at first the reason for the sudden retreat. The cops gave chase, shooting at the protestors as they attempted to run across a "prairie-like field." Many people threw themselves on the ground; others who turned to fend off the police were savagely beaten down with truncheons. When it was over, ten marchers lay dead or dying in the grass, and more than one hundred were wounded, including two children.

"The people cried and hollered like sheep and they scattered in all directions," worker Peter Mrkonjich recalled of the police charge. "Women, children, and men were running and falling and screaming like madmen. I turned and ran, too, but when I went just a few feet a bullet hit me in the arm."[115]

Wounded striker Joseph Hickey told a reporter from his hospital bed:

I went out with the rest of them and started to walk over to the plant. I was about 100 yards behind the head of the line when the uproar began. They were like trapped rats, panic-stricken, terrified. I saw a woman fall as she was being clubbed by the policeman. She was bleeding and looked like she was dying. I ran over to help her and leaned down to pick her up, when the police hit me over the head. I was out after that.[116]

Conservative Chicago papers sought to convince readers that the marchers had been the aggressors. A "Mexican" in the crowd had fired the first shot, said one police officer. Another claimed to have fired his gun only in self-defense after the crowd knocked him to the ground and kicked him.[117] But graphic news photos refuted all such falsehoods. It had been a police riot, frenzied cops clubbing and shooting unarmed men and women, then chasing them down as in a massacre to inflict more damage where they lay. The images captured that day remain among the most iconic in American labor history.

The violence at Republic Steel and the making of yet more labor martyrs did not prove cathartic or ease the way to peace in the Little Steel strike. Little Steel proved as intractable as Big Steel had been accommodating, and the strike eventually petered out without attaining the desired concessions. It was a setback for the CIO, but only a momentary one.

WITH THE WAGNER ACT'S VALIDITY AFFIRMED by the Supreme Court and the CIO riding high after victories in automobiles and steel, it was understandable that most Americans saw John L. Lewis and President Roosevelt as partners in the effort to ameliorate economic injustice. This widely held perception made the ensuing break between the two men especially disappointing.

The signs of a rupture had been visible as early as 1933 when Lewis, to Roosevelt's chagrin, channeled the enthusiasm surrounding the NIRA's Section 7(a) into the much-publicized admonishment to laborers, "The president wants you to join the union!" Trumpeting the president's support for labor by putting words in his mouth was not merely rude, it left Roosevelt on the spot, since he wasn't about to disown the claim Lewis had made for him. And this was not an isolated incident. Lewis on numerous occasions seemed to push Roosevelt to identify with expressions of policy that would have been more carefully nuanced had they originated with the president himself. A characteristic ruse was pulled by Lewis in January 1937 when he met with Edward McGrady, assistant secretary of labor, at the Willard Hotel in Washington to discuss the Flint sit-down strike. Unbeknownst to McGrady, Lewis had tipped off the press about their meeting, so that a group of reporters was waiting when Lewis and a startled McGrady emerged from the hotel lobby; neither had any progress to report, but Lewis, in staging the scene, had succeeded at broadcasting that the president had dispatched a high-level representative to huddle with the CIO.[118] The president, by now familiar with such methods, cautioned Michigan's Governor Murphy at one point to "disregard whatever Mr. Lewis tells you." Lewis somehow learned of the comment and was furious. "It was during the winter of 1937, when we were gripped in fatal conflict with [GM]," he later said, "that I discovered the depths of deceit, the rank dishonesty, and the double-crossing character of Franklin Delano Roosevelt."[119]

The president seemed almost determined to get Lewis's goat that spring, when the CIO was in its fight with Little Steel. Having grown impatient with what he termed "extremists on both sides of the controversy," Roosevelt observed to reporters that the whole country would likely conclude of the CIO–Little Steel impasse, "A plague on both your houses." The remark appeared in the *New York Times* under the headline "Roosevelt Quotes Shakespeare," a not-so-subtle dig at Lewis, the former thespian who was well known for doing so.[120] Lewis used a nationwide Labor Day radio address on September 3, 1937, to hit back. After accusing Roosevelt of showing ingratitude for labor's massive support in the 1936 election, he turned his attention to the "plague on both your houses" quip. "It ill behooves one who has supped at labor's table and who has been sheltered in labor's house," Lewis said, "to curse with equal fervor and fine impartiality both labor and its adversaries when they become locked in deadly embrace.... [Labor] feels that its cause is just and that its friends should not view its struggles with neutral detachment or intone constant criticism of its activities."[121]

According to Saul Alinsky, the Chicago community organizer and theorist who wrote a biography of the UMW chief, Lewis saw Roosevelt as "an aristocrat with an intellectual sympathy for labor but [one] incapable, by virtue of his background, of grasping the real needs, feelings, and the solidarity of labor, born of common travail."[122] On a deeper level, of course, Lewis struggled as any close ally might with the inability to compete with the aura of the presidency. Although he received abundant recognition for his efforts, he was too much of an egoist not to resent the degree to which many Americans, working people in particular, had come to worship Roosevelt, and the fact that labor's fortunes, and his own, had become so utterly entwined with this deity. For his part, Roosevelt saw Lewis as a wild card, but also as a brilliant, headstrong man who was, for all his arrogance, the most powerful labor leader in the country. He had revived organized labor with his creation of the CIO, secured a role for industrial unions, grappled successfully with automotives and steel, and had influenced New Deal legislation and the nation's energy policy. "He was not a nice man, no Eugene Debs," writes Thomas Geoghegan, "but in a more complicated way, Lewis was also on the side of Good."[123] The president had made special efforts to bring Lewis into his confidence, meeting with him privately at the White House in June 1936 to read him parts of the Democratic platform, with its lofty words of commitment to the cause of organized labor and the significance of labor's role in bolstering American democracy.

Frances Perkins claimed that the source of the final Lewis-Roosevelt split involved Lewis offering himself as a running mate on the 1940 ticket, an offer that Roosevelt rejected out of hand. Lewis aide Lee Pressman also remembered the scene, recounting that Lewis told Roosevelt, "Mr. President, I think if you run for a third term, you may be defeated, unless you have a representative of labor on the ticket, and unless that representative is myself," to which the president was said to have replied, "That's very interesting, John, but which place on the ticket are you reserving for me?" The Rooseveltian gibe sounds authentic, but the story itself is dubious; as scholar Melvyn Dubofsky points out, by 1940 the rift between the two men was fairly substantial, and it seems improbable Lewis would leave himself vulnerable by approaching Roosevelt with a proposal so likely to be spurned.[124]

A more nagging bother, from Lewis's perspective, was Roosevelt's friendship with Sidney Hillman. The president, without consulting Lewis, had named Hillman as labor's representative to an advisory group on war production needs. Hillman told Lewis how flattered he was by the honor, how much it meant to him as an immigrant to this country to be invited to the White House and have the president address him by his first name. According to Frances Perkins, Lewis likely had somewhat anti-Semitic feelings toward Hillman, as well as contempt for his link with the Chicago settlement house movement and the genteel Progressive Era thinking associated with it. The "cerebral-looking rabbi of industrial concord,"[125] as one writer has described Hillman, remained in Lewis's eyes "Hilkie," a Yiddish-speaking arriviste so pleased and impressed to be included in Roosevelt's inner circle, Lewis feared he might prostrate himself and labor's cause to ensure his continued acceptability.[126] Mary Dreier of the WTUL had early in Hillman's career dubbed him "one of the leading labor statesmen of this generation." To the vexation of Hillman's critics the moniker stuck,[127] and was even immortalized in 1939 with the publication of the highly flattering *Sidney Hillman: Labor Statesman* by George Soule. The title alone was enough to give John Lewis fits.[128] Lewis was convinced that industry, once stuffed with fat defense contracts and charged with stepped-up war production, would find ways to run roughshod over labor unions; a tough, independent-minded laborite—like John L. Lewis—was the man needed on the high councils of war and peace, not Sidney Hillman.

Soon more substantive issues roiled the Roosevelt-Lewis relationship. Lewis was an ardent isolationist, who "remembered World War I [as] a time when a reform president, Woodrow Wilson, had misled the nation into an unnecessary foreign war and then allowed reactionary businessmen and politicians to repress labor and persecute radicals in the guise of national security."[129] He thought he saw Roosevelt headed down the same path in response to the war brewing in Europe, and feared that U.S. involvement would not only subject Americans to great horror and carnage, but make America into an imperialist nation, strengthening the powers of the large money interests. "Europe is on the brink of disaster and it must be our care that she does not drag us into the abyss after her," Lewis warned Jewish trade unionists at an anti-Nazi rally in Madison Square Garden in 1937; two years later, as German troops were invading Poland, he assured the nation in his annual Labor Day radio talk, "Labor in America wants no war nor any part of war. Labor wants the right to work and live—not the privilege of dying by gunshot or poison gas to sustain the mental errors of current statesmen."[130]

Lewis's eagerness to distance himself from the war may well have been an expression of his anxiety about the closeness that labor had developed with the Roosevelt administration, the New Deal, and the Democratic

Party in general since the election of 1936. Because there was no Labor Party in America, unions historically had learned to steer clear of fixed associations with political parties, no matter how attractive their platforms appeared in the near term, wishing to preserve their independence of thought and action. Becoming overly confident that one set of politicians or policies would consistently deliver for labor was naive, a reliance that could only rob the movement of initiative and leave it vulnerable. If such fears darkened Lewis's outlook, they were prescient.

Roosevelt and his advisers tried to patch things up with Lewis as the 1940 fall election loomed, but a meeting between the two men at the White House on October 17 went sour almost from the start. The president tried to strike a cordial, relaxed tone; Lewis went on the attack, accusing Roosevelt of having ordered the FBI to spy on him and listen in on his telephone conversations—an allegation Roosevelt didn't confirm or deny.[131] A week later Lewis lowered the boom, lambasting Roosevelt's eagerness for war in a live radio address over all three networks that was heard by as many as 30 million Americans. He accused the president of aspiring to lead an all-powerful, imperial presidency. "America wants no royal family," Lewis warned, adding that the country could no longer afford at its head "the economic and political experiments of an amateur, ill-equipped practitioner in the realm of political science." Lewis's remarks became more outlandish throughout the broadcast, culminating when he endorsed Roosevelt's Republican opponent, Wendell Willkie. "I think the re-election of President Roosevelt for a third term would be a national evil of the first magnitude," he averred. "He no longer hears the cries of the people." Finally, he offered the nation a bizarre wager, vowing that were America's workingmen and -women to go against his advice and grant Roosevelt a third term, it would signal that they had tired of his (Lewis's) leadership, and he would immediately resign as head of the CIO. "Through the years of struggle, you have been content that I should be in the forefront of your battles," Lewis told his listeners. "I am still the same man. Sustain me now, or repudiate me."[132]

What was America to make of such a performance, and of such a request? Was Lewis worried on labor's behalf about the deepening Democratic-labor partnership? Had he really detected shallowness and poor judgment in his old ally? Did the president's thinking suggest "a mind in full intellectual retreat," as Lewis alleged?[133] Or were his strange words the result of some more personal belligerence?

Labor, respecting John L. Lewis mightily, nonetheless did not choose to honor his grudge against the occupant of the White House. "The personal spite or the hatred of one man will not switch labor's votes from Mr. Roosevelt," observed the UAW's Walter Reuther. "American labor will take Roosevelt!"[134] Labor did as Reuther, not Lewis, predicted, and voted overwhelmingly for the president, helping to sweep him to an historic third term. Lewis in turn honored the ultimatum he had issued, and forfeited his leadership of the CIO.

While his melodramatic self-destruction may have suggested to some an imminent break in labor's alliance with the Democratic Party, what more truly rankled Lewis was the opposite: that no such division was likely. "The Party of Roosevelt" had become "the political expression of America's working class." The president's popularity with workers, and with much of the American public, was by now thoroughly associated with the New Deal's restorative gift to the nation—the legislation and relief efforts, certainly, but moreover a buoyancy and optimism, a sense of collective recovery managed by a caring government.[135]

T WO MONTHS AFTER the Flint sit-down conflict had been resolved, in April 1937, a small airplane appeared in the sky above the Ford Motor Company's massive River Rouge plant in Detroit, the largest industrial complex in the world, covering twelve hundred acres and employing more than eighty thousand workers. Inside the cockpit Victor and Walter Reuther of the UAW held a microphone and shouted a message of UAW solidarity down to the employees below, who were in the midst of a shift change, their words amplified by loudspeakers the brothers had strapped to the underside of the airplane's wings. The flight, while remembered as one of the more dramatic efforts at union organizing in American labor history, was technically a flop, as the plane could not fly low or slow enough for its occupants' voices to be heard on the ground. What the Reuthers' mission had demonstrated, however, was the UAW's powerful resolve to unionize Ford autoworkers.

Under the autocratic leadership of founder Henry Ford, the company had been a pioneer of automobile mass production as well as a leader in the field of welfare capitalism. For years Ford's sprawling operation in Detroit offered steady wages and benefits, and retained a relatively stable workforce; it also made inroads into the hiring of black workers. But the flip side of Henry Ford's benevolence was his adamant refusal to surrender control of any aspect of his vast operation to labor unions. To help keep busybodies like the Reuthers at bay, Ford had hired former boxer Harry Bennett to oversee the euphemistically named Ford "Service Department," a collection of toughs and ex-hoodlums loyal only to Bennett, who in turn was devoted to Mr. Ford. "A combination of Dracula and J. Edgar Hoover," one Ford executive would later describe Bennett,[136] whose private army and extensive spy network allowed him to track virtually everything that went on in the plant. So omniscient were his powers and so total the trust placed in him by Henry Ford, Bennett and his men were feared equally by assembly-line workers and senior management.

As Henry Ford's health began to decline in the late 1930s with a series of mild strokes, he ceded ever greater authority to Bennett, appointing him manager of the employment office at the Rouge. Ford biographer Steven Watts suggests that Bennett, a seemingly uncomplicated man's man, served as a kind of surrogate son to Ford, whose relationship with his own son, Edsel, was fraught with unrealized expectations. Nominally the president of the Ford Motor Company after 1919, Edsel had helped supervise construction of the Rouge, but in everyday decisions he was often overruled by his father and, like other company executives, found he was rarely able to challenge Bennett's authority.

Henry Ford eyed warily the UAW's successful sit-down strike against GM, and its other advances in the automobile business, including the attainment of union recognition at Chrysler, Studebaker, Nash, and Packard. With the Depression having taken a toll on Ford Motor Company fortunes, he knew his business was vulnerable to labor unrest. Still, floor bosses only drove workers all the harder as conditions toughened. Speed-ups increased the pace of the assembly lines and new rules restricted everything from lunch hours to bathroom breaks.[137]

Ford's resistance to unions was strategic, but also intrinsic to his worldview. Friend and colleague to a generation of shed inventors like Thomas Edison, Charles Goodyear, and the Wright Brothers, he sub-scribed fully to the ethos of self-reliance; he distrusted unions for their collectivism, among other things, and believed they dampened individual ambition and encouraged class resentments. While he admitted to hav-ing qualms about the impact on men of mass production work, he had long ago reconciled those concerns with the faith that the assembly line offered the modern industrial worker the best means of sharing in the abundance of the new consumer age, the unprecedented bounty that his own factories helped make a reality, a philosophy that had come to be called Fordism.

Ford likely felt ample justification for insisting that he knew what was best for his workers, for he'd often been lauded as a visionary in the field of industrial relations. In 1914 he had introduced the Ford Five-Dollar Day, $5 for a day's work, an innovation that overnight doubled the salary of most Ford employees and made them the highest-paid autoworkers in the nation. It was a breakthrough in the simmering war between capital and labor over the adjustment to mass production, a demonstration that at least one capitalist was willing to recognize and reward labor's con-tribution to profits. Even journalist John Reed approved, as did Eugene Debs and muckrakers Upton Sinclair and Ida Tarbell. "[Ford] is a power-ful industrial baron who is interested in human beings instead of stocks and bonds," Reed concluded in *Metropolitan Magazine*.[138] Reed's research into the impact of Ford's munificence on Ford workers discovered that living conditions for most workers had improved measurably thanks to the "Flivver King's" generosity and Progressive outlook.[139]

But like many self-made millionaires, Ford's weak spot was that he had come to assume the infallibility of his own judgment. He believed whole-heartedly in Henry Ford the folk hero, the innovative industrialist with world-shaping ideas—not only about car-making but about all manner of things, including politics, foreign policy, and worker relations. As some-one who had contributed so enormously to defining what work was in the twentieth century, it was only natural for him to believe he also knew what workers needed, and Harry Bennett's "Service Department" had done a superb job of seeing to it that what they didn't need was a union.

Time and economics, however, had caught up even with Henry Ford, and pressure from the UAW to organize America's last nonunionized automaker became irresistible; by spring 1937 the tensions were fully out in the open. With Bennett serving as chief labor negotiator, Ford Motor took the position that unions were unwanted by a majority of contented Ford employees and that the UAW itself was an alien, likely Commu-nist entity. In response the UAW launched an informational campaign designed to entice Ford workers, distributing a leaflet outside the Rouge, titled *Unionism, Not Fordism*, that urged, "Now is the time to organize! The Wagner Bill is behind you! Now get behind yourselves!"

The afternoon of May 26, 1937, saw a group of UAW representatives, including Walter Reuther, who at that time headed a UAW local, and Richard Frankensteen, a former University of Dayton football player and head of all UAW Detroit organizing, lead several labor sympathizers, cler-gymen, and reporters across an overpass approaching the Rouge's busy Gate Four. The Ford Company had built the overpass—employees used it to reach the streetcar stop across Miller Road—but it had been leased to the streetcar commission for the use of the general public and was not considered private property. Reuther, just to be safe, had obtained a city permit to distribute the UAW flyers, and women volunteers of a UAW auxiliary group had been delegated to actually hand the flyers to depart-ing employees during a Ford shift change in order to minimize the pos-sibility of confrontation.[140]

Suddenly a contingent of Bennett's men appeared to challenge the UAW group's presence "on Ford property." Words were barely exchanged before several thugs jumped Reuther and Frankensteen and proceeded to attack them in full view of news photographers. Frankensteen was pummeled as his assailants immobilized him by pinning his suit coat over his head. Reuther was chased and kicked down a flight of stairs. Nearly twenty people in the union group were injured, including four women who complained the Ford toughs had shoved and kicked them. The enforcers also turned on members of the press, snatching cameras and yanking out film, but shots of Frankensteen being assaulted were snapped by a photographer who did manage to escape, and his pictures were widely circulated.[141]

Published photographs of what newsmen dubbed the "Battle of the Overpass" upset many Americans and did irreparable harm to Ford's image. Where was the benign inventor Henry Ford the country had come to know and love in these images of bullies ganging up on a lone labor organizer? When the company's effort to blame the UAW and the press for an "attack [on] a peaceable body of Ford workmen" proved ineffectual,[142] Henry Ford angrily withdrew the firm's advertising from the nation's leading magazines—*Time, Life,* and *Fortune*—for carrying news of the incident.[143] The city of Dearborn, where the Rouge was located, reacted (on Ford's behalf) by banning the distribution of leaflets in "congested areas," leading to the arrest of almost a thousand UAW volunteers during summer 1937 for attempting to give away union brochures in the vicinity of the plant.[144]

It so happened that at this very time spying and belly-bumping operations like Ford's "Service Department" were receiving long-overdue scrutiny from Congress. Wisconsin senator Robert M. La Follette Jr. and Senator Elbert D. Thomas of Utah, prompted by the NLRB's difficulties in enforcing the Wagner Act, had in 1936 launched an inquiry into corporate anti-labor abuses such as espionage, provocation, and terrorism used to disrupt union organizing. The La Follette Civil Liberties Committee based its inquiries on the principle that workers' fundamental right to organize was being violated by these irregularities. "Prior to the Wagner Act anti-labor practices had presented ethical rather than legal problems," one history recounts. "After 1935, however, these practices were no longer merely unethical but also illegal." The extent of the abuses uncovered proved staggering.[145]

Released in December 1937, the committee's report cited labor spying "to be a common, almost universal practice in American industry," and listed no fewer than twenty-five hundred U.S. corporations engaged in antiunion espionage and trickery. Nearly four thousand spies and detectives, some from the Pinkerton Detective Agency, had been involved, at an estimated aggregate cost to business, and hence consumers, of almost $10 million in the years 1933 to 1936. The extent of the spying alone was considerable, with as many as ninety-three unions having been infiltrated. General Motors was the Pinkertons' largest manufacturing client and the most flagrant offender, spending $800,000 on espionage during the four-year period, and said to possess "the most super-system of spies yet devised in any American corporation."[146] Pinkerton agents testified that even Edward F. McGrady, the assistant secretary of labor, had been spied on while meeting with GM.

GM was so invested in workplace espionage, the report indicated, that when the firm grew concerned that some of its spies might be stealing company trade secrets, it hired additional spies to report on them; soon it felt compelled to employ yet a third tier of spies to keep tabs on the previous two. "Here is the essence of spy stuff," Senator La Follette wrote. "So ineradicable is the spy habit that when faced with the evils it produces it has only one answer—more spies. Spies beget spies, lies beget lies, distrust begets distrust—until faith in all is gone. . . . Industry cannot survive this endless dependence upon unreliable knowledge which begets fear of all things and of all men."

The big auto titan was one of many corporate heavyweights exposed in the report. Bethlehem Steel and the Pennsylvania Railroad, as well as the far less likely Warner Bros. Studios, Walgreen's Drugstores, and the Brooklyn Jewish Hospital, were also found to have employed labor spies. While those involved gave various reasons for their behavior—a fear of Communism, the potential loss of trade secrets, the improvement of efficiency, the guarding against theft and sabotage—the La Follette Committee was absolute in its conclusion that "the real motive in all cases was resistance by employers to the organization of their employees for collective bargaining." And the spies' actions were far more treacherous than simply reporting what they saw and heard; they themselves often posed as labor organizers in order to entrap those workers who responded to the spies' bogus anti-employer rhetoric. One spy had managed to become a union's national vice president.

In response to the publication of the La Follette report, the Pinkerton and Baldwin-Felts agencies announced their intention to quit the labor espionage business; at Ford, however, Harry Bennett's troops and company management simply dug in deeper against UAW encroachment. While some Ford executives, including Edsel Ford, warned of the inevitability of unionism, Henry Ford continued to resist, his sturdy companion Bennett also vowing to fight the union nail and claw. Their position, however, became increasingly anachronistic and hard to maintain; by 1940, Ford's once-golden reputation for industrial relations had deteriorated so badly that there was outrage from the press and public when the federal government handed the firm lucrative defense contracts to produce airplane engines. President Roosevelt justified the awarding of the contracts by saying that he hoped that Ford, by taking the federal work, would be more inclined to accept unionization,[147] but even Eleanor Roosevelt, herself a unionized member of the Newspaper Guild because she wrote a syndicated column, joined the chorus of disapproving voices, among which *The Nation* cited Ford Motor as "the country's foremost violator of the Wagner Act."[148] The following year, in a sign that concern about Ford's rejection of collective bargaining had come to rest in Washington, an otherwise competitive defense-related bid submitted by the company was denied.

Perceiving Ford's vulnerability, the UAW launched a new organizing campaign at River Rouge in spring 1941, sponsored in part by a $100,000 grant from the CIO. On April 1, prompted by the firing of eleven night shift workers linked to the UAW, a strike was called. The huge Ford labor force split over the matter, and unfortunate scenes took place outside the plant, where strikers fought with colleagues who had remained on the job. Many of the "loyal" Ford men were African American employees, who accounted for 20 percent of Rouge workers. Shunned histori-cally by major labor unions, black workers couldn't help but appreciate businessmen such as Henry Ford who made it a point to hire them. Taking no chances the Rouge's black workers would forget their debt to Mr. Ford, the company had "wooed" black ministers in the city over the years "to make sure they disseminated the views of the Ford Company from their pulpits."[149] Now it was largely black workers who resisted the UAW strike efforts, occupying a part of the Rouge premises, engaging in hand-to-hand combat with UAW picketers, and at one point hurl-ing heavy metal buckets from the roof onto a throng of marchers below. The potentially explosive situation—a violent labor dispute with racial overtones—was monitored with deep concern at the White House.

The standoff at River Rouge was eventually broken with the help of NAACP executive secretary Walter White, at the time one of the most respected African American leaders in America and a friend of both Franklin and Eleanor Roosevelt. With the president's blessing, White came to the Rouge plant and addressed the black workers from a sound car, convincing them to stop serving as strikebreakers and to side with the UAW. The willingness of the black employees to abide by White's counsel and cross over to the UAW, rejecting their longtime allegiance to Ford, helped turned the tide in the strike.[150]

Ten, even five years earlier, Henry Ford's resistance to such a con-centrated union campaign might have proven insurmountable. But his health had faded again recently, and for perhaps the first time in their relationship his son Edsel, who accepted unions as an element of modern industrial relations, was able to withstand the influence of both his father and Harry Bennett. Edsel, along with Michigan governor Murray D. Van Wagoner, arranged to settle the dispute by allowing the NLRB to conduct an election among the eighty thousand Ford workers in the River Rouge and nearby Lincoln plants to determine the unionization issue. The ballot offered workers the choice of representation by the UAW-CIO, the AFL, or no union at all.

The May 21 vote went overwhelmingly to the UAW, with fewer than 3 percent favoring no unionization. One UAW official characterized the vote as "the end of an era in American industry. Fordism has been repudiated by the men who know it best, by the Ford workers." He vowed that the UAW was eager to "erase all bitterness" and move immediately to negotiation of a fair contract.[151] Even Harry Bennett, while carping that the outcome represented "a great victory for the Communist Party, Governor Murray D. Van Wagoner, and the National Labor Relations Board," conceded publicly that the UAW had carried the day. "The law provides that we must live with them," he said, "and we never violate the law."[152]

Henry Ford, however, stubborn to the end and unlike Bennett not yet willing to hoist the white flag, refused to sign the UAW contracts drawn up after the election. He threatened to shut down the company before he would share his long-held authority with an outside union. Warned by aides that his noncooperation would likely bring government intervention, Ford famously replied, "Well, if the government steps in, it will be in the motorcar business and it won't be me."[153]

Ford was by now seen, even by company loyalists, as a tired, unwell old man, but his power was still legend and his obstinacy resolute. Thus his sudden change of heart on the matter caught even close colleagues by surprise. The very day after his line-in-the-sand remark about the government taking over the motorcar business, he reversed himself, agreeing to the UAW's provisions and guaranteeing full cooperation with the automakers' union on wages, work conditions, and the collection of union dues by withholding money from workers' paychecks.

He may have decided that it would be unbearable to watch the government meddle in his affairs, or worried that he would lose market advantage to other unionized carmakers through further noncooperation. Veteran Ford aide Charles E. Sorensen suggests a more homespun resolution. When he asked Ford what had made him change his mind, the company's founder reported that his wife, Clara, perhaps the one person in the world who could get away with scolding the aged inventor, had lectured him in no uncertain terms about the "riots and bloodshed" his further recalcitrance would surely create. "She did not want to be around here and see me responsible for such trouble," Ford said. "What could I do?"[154]

(ABOVE) "I remembered their great strike of last year in which these same girls had demanded more sanitary conditions and more safety precautions in the shops," noted a reporter of the Triangle Shirtwaist Fire of 1911. "These dead bodies were their answer."

(RIGHT) Spirited New York City garment workers gather at a May Day celebration.

(BELOW) Seamstresses of the International Ladies' Garment Workers Union (ILGWU) picket in support of the huge 1910 walkout.

(TOP) Mother Jones with President Calvin Coolidge at the White House. "My address is like my shoes. It travels with me," Jones replied when Congress asked where she lived. "I abide where there is a fight against wrong."

(BOTTOM) (Left to right) Joseph Caruso, Joseph Ettor, and Arturo Giovannitti, IWW defendants and leaders of the 1912 Bread and Roses strike in Lawrence, Massachusetts, shackled together at their trial for the alleged murder of mill worker Anna LoPizzo.

(TOP) In the strike of 1912, textile workers and Massachusetts state militia faced off almost daily in front of the Lawrence mills.

(BOTTOM) Before Lawrence police halted the exodus, children of the town's striking mill workers prepare to depart for temporary shelter in New York, Boston, and Philadelphia. The IWW effort was meant to aid stricken workers' families, but also proved effective publicity for the Lawrence strike.

MISS E.G. FLYNN I.W.W. SPEAKER ADDRESSING PATERSON STIKERS JUNE 1913.

(TOP) "We gesticulated, we paced the platform, we appealed to the emotions," Elizabeth Gurley Flynn said of the Wobblies' style of orating. Here she addresses striking Paterson silk workers in 1913.

(BOTTOM) A group of IWW supporters is joined by Big Bill Haywood (center) and Elizabeth Gurley Flynn (far right).

(TOP) The winter of 1914 brought hardship to southeastern Colorado's striking coal miners, who sought refuge with their families in union tent colonies. An assault on one workers' enclave by militia resulted in the notorious Ludlow Massacre, and stirred nationwide outrage at the rigid anti-union policies of coal baron John D. Rockefeller Jr.

(BOTTOM LEFT) The defiant IWW songwriter Joe Hill went before a Utah prison firing squad in 1915 for a murder he probably didn't commit. "Don't waste any time in mourning," he wrote Big Bill Haywood. "Organize!"

(BOTTOM RIGHT) Veteran western activist Frank Little, "half Indian, half white man, all IWW," enraged authorities and patriots' groups from California to Montana, and earned the limp and scars to show for it.

FELLOW WORKERS:

Remember!

WE ARE IN HERE FOR YOU; YOU ARE OUT THERE FOR US

(LEFT) The desperate need for activism to win the freedom of Wobblies held in the Cook County jail at the time of the 1918 IWW Espionage Act trial inspired this sticker by one of the imprisoned men, poet and artist Ralph Chaplin.

(BELOW) "We will not compromise with rattlesnakes," the Bisbee, Arizona, copper magnates said of the IWW in the early summer of 1917. On July 12, at the order of Sheriff Harry Wheeler, vigilantes herded more than a thousand striking miners and other "undesirables" into cattle cars for deportation to New Mexico.

(TOP) At the urging of Congress and the press, Attorney General A. Mitchell Palmer targeted suspected Bolshevik sympathizers and labor radicals across the country, an effort that became personal after his own Washington home was bombed by anarchists.

(BOTTOM) The young J. Edgar Hoover was the Justice Department's leading expert on U.S.-based radicals, keeping tabs on no fewer than sixty thousand suspects.

(ABOVE) A "radical" office searched and demolished by raiding federal agents—a not unusual scene during the era of the Palmer and Lusk Committee raids.

(LEFT) "The most pugnaciously hell-raising male rebel I could find in the United States," was how Max Eastman of *The Masses* described Carlo Tresca, who played a prominent role in IWW-led strikes in Lawrence, New York, and Paterson in 1912–1913. Fortunately, Tresca often spoke to striking workers in Italian, leaving police spies unsure exactly what he had said.

MADE IN ALABAMA
PRODUCTS WE BOAST
LUMBER, COTTON GOODS, IRON & STEEL and OTHERS
$145,000,000 A Year
PRODUCTS WE IGNORE
THESE YOUNG WORKERS

USHER　　DEP'T STORE GIRL　　WAGON BOY　　SODA FOUNTAIN

COTTON MILL WORKERS

MINE BOY

OYSTER SHUCKING

ERRAND BOY

ILL-EQUIPPED SCHOOL　　OLD AGE AT 47　　ILLITERATE FAMILY

SUCH INDUSTRIAL MORTGAGES
BRING EARLY FORECLOSURE

(LEFT) A poster created by documentarian Lewis Hine for the National Child Labor Committee, a reform group that advocated for a federal child labor law in the early years of the twentieth century.

(BELOW) Coal mine "breaker boys," appearing here in a Hine photograph from Pennsylvania, sifted rocks and debris from the coal as it arrived at the mine's surface. Most were adolescents, but some began work as young as age seven.

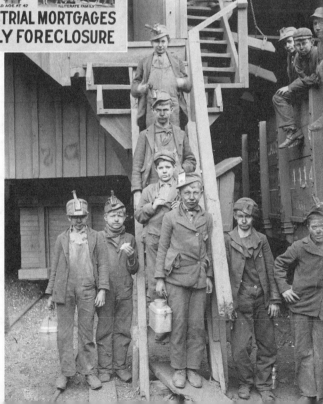

(TOP) "C.I.O.! C.I.O.! C.I.O.!" chanted strikers as they marched to a Republic Steel facility in Chicago on Memorial Day, 1937. Authorities attempted to blame demonstrators for the ensuing violence, which left ten dead, but news photos revealed the police were at fault.

(BOTTOM) Mild and unassuming in manner and appearance, the successful West Coast dockworkers' organizer Harry Bridges, here attending a 1937 meeting in Washington, gained the trust and admiration of Labor Secretary Frances Perkins.

(TOP) The "stormy petrel of American labor," United Mine Workers chief John L. Lewis (left), confers with fellow Washington labor insider Sidney Hillman of the Amalgamated Clothing Workers of America.

(BOTTOM) Labor Secretary Frances Perkins, the first woman cabinet member in U.S. history, knew President Franklin D. Roosevelt well from his early political career in the New York legislature, when she had been a factory safety reformer; during the New Deal she was one of his closest advisers on labor and social welfare issues.

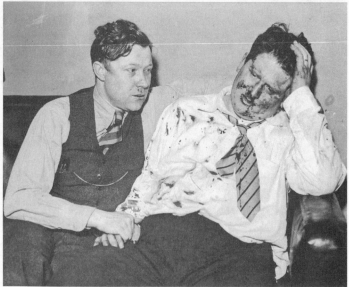

(TOP) In the notorious Battle of the Overpass, UAW official Richard Frankensteen is attacked by members of the Ford Motor Company's "Service Department" outside the River Rouge plant on May 26, 1937.

(BOTTOM) Walter Reuther comforting a bloodied Frankensteen after the assault.

(TOP) In the protracted Flint sit-down strike of 1937, workers successfully held the General Motors facilities against court injunctions, a police assault, and the threat of militia. The strike set in motion the process that would ultimately unionize the U.S. auto industry.

(ABOVE) Autoworkers making creative use of the workplace to wait out strike developments.

(RIGHT) The 1941 UAW-CIO strike against the Ford Motor Company finally succeeded in organizing America's last non-union automaker.

STRIKE CALL!
To FORD ROUGE WORKERS:

Effective today, Wednesday, April 2nd, a strike is in effect at the Rouge plant of the Ford Motor Company.

The Demands of The Strikers Are:

Immediate reinstatement of all workers discharged for union activities.

A general wage increase. A seniority system.

Abolition of Ford spy system and service department.

Recognition of the UAW-CIO as the spokesmen of the Rouge workers and negotiation of a contract covering wages, hours, overtime, grievances, speed-up and other matters of importance to the Ford workers.

ALL WORKERS REPORT FOR PICKET DUTY. All picketing must be peaceful and disciplined.

By keeping our ranks UNITED, VICTORY WILL BE OURS!

United Automobile Workers of America, CIO.
R. J. THOMAS, President
GEORGE F. ADDES, Secretary-Treasurer
MICHAEL F. WIDMAN, Jr., Director,
Ford Division.

CIO IS BEHIND YOU
ONWARD TO VICTORY!

(LEFT) Stoop labor in a cotton field photographed by the Farm Security Administration's Dorothea Lange during the Great Depression.

(BELOW) An organizer addresses a night rally for striking California cannery workers in 1938.

(BOTTOM LEFT) Jimmy Hoffa's appearance on the cover of *Life* signaled his emergence as a troubling and divisive national figure. Tough workers' advocate to some, most Americans perceived in him the ugly influence of corruption on the country's union movement.

(ABOVE) Martin Luther King Jr., recognizing that the struggle for equal rights was meaningless if not joined with a crusade for workers' rights and economic justice, lent his support to the plight of low-paid Memphis sanitation workers in the spring of 1968.

(LEFT) "The picket line is a beautiful thing," observed César Chávez, leader of the United Farm Workers, "because it does something to a human being."

(TOP) United Farm Workers and their supporters protest the sale of Gallo wines on Long Island during the nationwide UFW grape boycott of the 1970s.

(BOTTOM) "Dammit, the law is the law, and the law says they cannot strike. If they strike, they quit their jobs," President Ronald Reagan warned the air traffic controllers union in 1981. PATCO's decimation, and the administration's quick hiring of replacement workers, came to epitomize the loss of organized labor's stature in the 1980s.

CHAPTER NINE

SPIES, CROOKS, AND CONGRESSMEN

WITHIN WEEKS OF THE U.S. DECLARATION
of war against Japan and Germany in December 1941, President Roosevelt gathered labor and
business leaders to discuss wartime production and
to obtain mutual pledges that there would be no
strikes or lockouts for the war's duration. Labor disputes were to be resolved through a newly created War
Labor Board manned by representatives of industry,
organized labor, and the public.

Strikes diminished in response to the president's
initiative, but they did not disappear. By early 1943
union leaders from the AFL's William Green to John L.
Lewis of the UMW had concluded that while industry
appeared to be profiting from the war, labor was not;
workers were helping to meet accelerated production schedules, but their wages were failing to keep
up with inflation. Hearing labor's grumbling, the War
Labor Board devised a means of compromise known
as the Little Steel formula, based on a wartime wage
adjustment worked out in the steel industry. Instead
of meeting worker demands for higher wages based
on the current fast rate of inflation, it used as a measure the pace of inflation during the more stable eco-

nomic period of January 1941 through May 1942. Workers resented this approach, for the rate of adjustment never topped 15 percent, and they believed manufacturers were seeing far better returns. "When the mine workers' children cry for bread, they cannot be satisfied with a 'Little Steel Formula,'" Lewis warned. "When illness strikes the mine workers' families, they cannot be cured with an anti-inflation dissertation. The facts of life in the mining homes of America cannot be pushed aside by the flamboyant theories of an idealistic economic philosophy."[1]

The truth was that neither side was completely happy. Labor thought there was too much adherence to the Little Steel formula, thus denying workers fair cost-of-living raises, while industry disliked the board's solution of "sweetening" the restrictions of the formula by substituting non-wage inducements to workers such as expanded benefits. Nonetheless, the board fulfilled its mandate to keep labor peace during the war, providing settlements in 17,650 disputes and approving 415,000 voluntary wage adjustments.

Labor's response to these inflationary wage issues took place in circumstances much changed since the Depression. Almost 8 million Americans had been unemployed in December 1940, but by December 1943 the number of jobless stood at only 1 million. Compared to the 1.5 million people who had held jobs in the defense industries in 1940, 20 million people—including 5 million women—had joined the industrialized war effort by 1943.[2] Unions reacted with patriotism and loyalty to the increased production quotas created by war, and largely adhered to the no-strike pledge. The spirit of partnership with government only solidified labor's connection to the ruling Democratic Party, a bonding Republicans increasingly resented. This cozy political relationship, labor's ever-present power to cause havoc for management, as well as too-frequent outbursts from John L. Lewis, prompted reactionary elements in Congress to seek ways to undermine the rights handed labor by the New Deal.

"My stock in trade is being the ogre. That's how I make my way," Lewis once confided to an associate,[3] and conservatives were only too glad to bestow upon Lewis the monstrous caricature of big labor over-endowed with influence and privilege. After the declaration of war, the UMW boss had suspended his opposition to U.S. military involvement and toned down his antagonism for the president. In late 1942, however, he returned to form, angrily voicing his miners' resentment at having to shoulder the war's crushing demand for coal. Due to his peculiar and very public disavowal of Roosevelt in the election of 1940, Lewis was now viewed skeptically by many Americans, which was unfortunate, in that his perception that miners had been dealt a bad hand was not entirely off base. Expanded production meant that miners worked longer, often punishing schedules; as a result, the rate of workplace deaths and injuries multiplied. Miners stricken in war production, Lewis believed, were no different from soldiers wounded at the front.

Building on rank-and-file resentment evident in a series of coalfield wildcat strikes that began in January 1943, Lewis announced his willingness to fight. When in April 1943 the contract between the UMW and coal operators came up for renewal, Lewis sought a $2-per-day increase for miners plus an added form of compensation, known as portal-to-portal pay, to cover the time miners spent getting to the mine face underground. Calling no formal strike (in observation of the no-strike pledge), Lewis nonetheless shunned the meetings called by the War Labor Board to examine the situation and announced that UMW miners would not enter coal owners' property in the absence of a contract. On May 2, Roosevelt ordered a government takeover of the mines and went on radio to ask the miners to go back to work for the nation's good. Representative William M. Colmer of Mississippi, echoing the president's concern, declared, "Without coal you cannot make steel and without steel you cannot make ships and planes and tanks and guns."[4] While newspapers and even government were probably exaggerating the likelihood that the nation would run out of coal, the administration's more genuine fear was that Lewis's antics and his defiance of the no-strike pledge would leach over into other defense industries.[5]

The situation infuriated the coal operators, who were stuck with the government's possession of their mines even as no coal was being extracted from the ground. Eventually Lewis agreed to a six-month wait-and-see period and ordered miners back to work, although some rebellious UMW members continued to stage walkouts. In the end, Lewis won for the miners a $1.50-per-day wage increase, higher than the Little Steel formula allowed. Thus the strike ended, but with considerable bad publicity for Lewis, the UMW, and the labor movement generally. The *New Republic* excoriated "Lewis the Dictator," while other publications labeled him a racketeer, a Nazi sympathizer, and a defeatist, recalling his earlier dissent regarding the war.[6]

Lewis's experience of being shredded in the press for appearing unhelpful to the dire needs of the war was a problem all organized labor shared. The war's reigning spirit of public cooperation and sacrifice, its Victory Gardens and rubber and metal drives, made many ordinary union activities, especially strikes and "strike talk," appear selfish, a form of labor "blackmail." Soldiers in their foxholes did not go on strike; sailors at sea did not mutiny; pilots did not ground their planes. Who were coal miners, then, to hold up *their* part of the vital war effort, and for money? A legislative solution proposed by Texas representative Hatton Sumners, who "would not hesitate one split second to enact legislation to send [strikers] to the electric chair," hinted at the depth of the resentment.[7] The bill submitted by Sumners and like-minded forces on Capitol Hill, soon known as the Smith-Connally Act, authorized the president to seize operation of a factory where a strike threatened national security. It mandated a thirty-day cooling-off period before any work stoppage, put criminal penalties in place against those who persisted in urging or leading a strike, and forbade union contributions to political campaigns. This last condition was particularly offensive to labor, as it had used its political muscle to support the New Deal (an example being the UMW's $500,000 contribution to Roosevelt's reelection in 1936), and enjoyed "calling in" that debt when useful. Labor also resented, quite understandably, the idea of establishing criminal offenses for strike activities.

Smith-Connally was rightly seen by many editorial pages as drastic legislation designed to punish one man, John L. Lewis, the "stormy petrel of labor."[8] But the bill's congressional advocates had public opinion on their side. Even Senator Claude Pepper, one of Congress's staunchest labor allies, had castigated Lewis as "an unscrupulous and sinister figure," and joined the chorus that sought to curtail what was perceived as Washington's indulgence of Lewis and other influential union men.[9] "For the last decade the government and its agencies have in effect become organizers of unions," the *New York Times* concurred, "building them up in size, strength and immunities to the point where they can successfully defy the government itself."[10] The expression of such sentiments signaled a harmful trend of thought—the idea that the excessive generosity of the New Deal was to blame for the current wartime problems with organized labor.

Lewis, it seemed, had handed reactionary forces in Congress a weapon with which they might now deny not only the positive results of wartime production cooperation, which were in fact considerable, but the New Deal's good works as well. Just as government had acted to empower labor in the 1930s, the momentum could swing the other way, with Smith-Connally hailed as the needed fix, "the first regulatory bill that has breached the bulwark of union resistance in a decade."[11] Union executives, seeing the legislation for what it was, were quick to speak out. The AFL's William Green cautioned the Roosevelt administration that labor would respond at the polls if the act became law, and along with characterizing the pending bill as "a fascist measure pointed like a revolver at the heart of labor," reminded reporters that fewer than one-half of one percent of American industrial workers had taken part in a strike since the war's no-strike pledge had been adopted. Daniel J. Tobin of the Teamsters similarly warned both parties that any "crucifying" of the trade union movement would reverberate loudly in the election of 1944.[12]

Smith-Connally passed, but Roosevelt had heard labor's cries and vetoed it. He thought it punitive toward labor unions and not aimed strictly enough at the immediate need to maintain war production.

But his counterproposal, that Congress raise the age limit for noncombat military service from forty-five to sixty-five years of age so that workers in vital industries could be drafted, thus voiding the entire worker-union-management system, was widely denounced as unpatriotic: it would turn the honor of wearing the uniform of the nation's military into a badge of slave labor, even dishonor. In any case, his veto of Smith-Connally was overridden by Congress, and by late June 1943 the War Labor Disputes Act, as the legislation was formally known, had become law.

Within a month labor moved to make real its threats regarding the passage of such deviant legislation. The CIO formed the Political Action Committee (PAC) to energize and focus the labor vote in the elections of 1944. The PAC, led by Sidney Hillman, distributed literature linking the goal of victory in war with the aim of postwar labor policies that would ensure a continuation of New Deal concern for labor's rights. Hillman's insight was that labor's battles were no longer going to be fought strictly at the factory gates or police barricades, but within the nation's corridors of power. In lieu of an independent labor party, the PAC could serve as a counterbalance to the ever more polished lobbying efforts by nationally powerful corporations and their front groups like the National Association of Manufacturers and the Chamber of Commerce. "Workers can no longer work out even their most immediate day to day problems through negotiations with their employers," Hillman explained. "Wages, hours, and working conditions have become increasingly dependent upon policies adopted by Congress and the [government]. . . . Labor must bring its full influence to bear in shaping these decisions."[13]

The PAC's agenda was not simply to see Roosevelt elected to a fourth term, although that was important; it included broader reforms for the postwar era, including investment in public works and public housing, assistance for returning GIs, and publicly subsidized medical insurance. The action group proved surprisingly effective at the grassroots level, managing a strong get-out-the-vote drive directed at women and minorities that was unprecedented for its time. In the Southern primaries it unhorsed several congressional representatives with records of voting against working people's interests. Perhaps the highest tribute to Hillman's effort was the reaction it spurred. *Time* derided the PAC's campaign material as "the slickest political propaganda produced in the United States in a generation,"[14] while others denounced the PAC as part of a plan "to dominate our government with radical and communistic schemes."[15] As ever, it was left to a representative of the state of Mississippi to make the most outrageous charge, Congressman John L. Rankin asserting that Hillman was "a Russian-born racketeer" despised by his fellow Jews, who "wants to be the Hitler of America."[16]

The specter of labor or even Jewish "domination" of the president reappeared in the allegation that Roosevelt had granted Hillman say-so over the Democratic Party's vice presidential pick for the fall 1944 election. When the *New York Times*'s Arthur Krock wrote that Roosevelt had instructed an aide to "Clear it with Sidney"[17] regarding the vice presidential choice, the phrase proved electric, signaling to conservatives the undue authority "alien" labor elements had gained over the nation. "It's Your Country—Why Let Sidney Hillman Run It?" asked a Republican Party billboard.[18] But even if the "Clear it with Sidney" rumor was valid, historian Steven Fraser points out, what Hillman's purported clout should have suggested was not that labor had become a powerful alien influence at Roosevelt's shoulder but the exact opposite—that its views were becoming inseparable from those of the political mainstream.[19] In the end Roosevelt chose as his running mate the pro-labor but relatively unknown Harry S. Truman, U.S. senator from Missouri, whose career in government had begun in the Depression when Frances Perkins named him to head a public works employment agency.[20]

L ABOR JOINED THE REST OF THE COUNTRY in cheering the war's end in 1945, sharing fully in the quite palpable relief and rush of national pride that was recalled by one witness as "the greatest moment of collective inebriation in American history."[21] The reconversion to a peacetime economy, however, was a challenge the nation would have to face without the man who had guided it through the Depression and the war, for President Roosevelt had died that April while at his summer home in Warm Springs, Georgia.

American workers had suffered badly from the loss of jobs, overtime wages, and bonus pay following the armistice that ended World War I, and the related sharp reduction in full-capacity production. The result had been the widespread labor strife of 1919. Organized labor was determined that no such collapse recur, although it was unclear how the spirit of progress that had governed industrial relations since 1933 would carry over into the postwar era, especially with troubling indicators of reaction such as Smith-Connally already visible. There was much to mourn in Roosevelt's passing, but from labor's perspective nothing would be missed more than his fundamental understanding of workers' value to society, his belief that they deserved an "industrial citizenship" that guaranteed work, security, and democracy, specifically the rights to organize and petition for reforms. He held so great a faith in such a doctrine that he sought to give it permanence in a Second Bill of Rights, which he proposed in his State of the Union address of 1944 and would not live to pursue.

Eyes turned to Harry Truman, Roosevelt's successor. "Wage increases are imperative to cushion the shock to our workers, to sustain adequate purchasing power and to raise national income," the new president said of the reconversion. Industry's handsome wartime profits, he believed, would contribute to what he hoped would be a gradual transition. But the Rooseveltian concern for the nation's wage earners had become a harder sell. FDR had done his work in the midst of severe economic crisis; labor's considerable gains had been linked to the urgency of national recovery. Now the situation had changed: American industry, having responded heroically to the demands of wartime production, was ready to flex its power. Labor had had its moment—it had been rewarded amply by the New Deal; now, with the crises of economic trial and global conflict receding, its loyal contribution to the war effort was often overlooked; better remembered were the prominent episodes of wartime strike mischief.[22]

In November 1945, in an attempt to appease nervousness on either side of the industrial relations divide, Truman followed the example of President Wilson at the conclusion of the First World War and convened a national labor-management conference in Washington. The meeting was looked to for its potential to "lay the groundwork for peace and justice on the home front," as one senator phrased the objective, much as the recent United Nations gathering in San Francisco had established a foundation "for external peace and justice."[23] Truman greeted the attendees by thanking both sides for their wartime cooperation, but reminded his listeners that in the absence of wartime governmental controls, the future of peaceful labor-management relations, "the whole system of private enterprise and individual opportunity," now rested on their shoulders.[24]

Well-dressed executives departing the conclave arm in arm with their scruffier labor counterparts would have made a pleasing news photo, but the response to Truman's remarks was, on the whole, somewhat listless, and from the round of meetings emerged only statements of goodwill and vague promises to respect collective bargaining. No actual procedures were agreed upon to make labor-management relations function smoothly once wartime restrictions expired. Hearing criticism that he had not shown sufficient initiative in the matter, Truman reacted by asking Congress to consider new legislation based on the Railway Labor Act of 1926, which had outlawed yellow-dog contracts and safeguarded rail and airline workers' right to form or join a union. Capitol Hill, however, appeared more intent on correcting, not expanding upon, the government's existing labor policies.

With the irrefutable economics of reconversion at work, and absent any new labor-management protocols or conferences, unrest in America's workplace was probably inevitable. Strikes became rampant throughout late 1945 and early 1946—in Stamford, Rochester, Pittsburgh, and Oakland—while a nationwide steel walkout in 1946 took four hundred thousand workers off the job, at the time the largest coordinated work stoppage in American history. Not to be left out, the conservatives' favorite nuisance, John L. Lewis, was soon at it again, seeking wage increases for the UMW as well as the creation of a miners' welfare fund to which coal operators would contribute. The operators refused Lewis's entreaties, and on April 1, 1946, tens of thousands of miners abandoned their jobs. Truman had the government seize the mines on May 21, citing coal as an essential resource and claiming the strike had created a national emergency. When the miners refused to work in government-controlled mines, the administration obtained an injunction against the strike; Lewis, citing the supposedly injunction-limiting protections of the Norris–La Guardia Act, openly defied it, and was charged with contempt. This high-stakes standoff wound up before the Supreme Court, which in *United States v. United Mine Workers* ruled that the protections of Norris–La Guardia had been superseded by the terms of Smith-Connally, and that the government was entitled to seek an injunction where a strike endangered national security.[25]

Lewis had no choice but to back down, and the miners returned to work, although when Smith-Connally, as a war measure, expired in 1947, the UMW boss renewed his demand for an operator-funded welfare fund and succeeded in obtaining it. The court's ruling on Smith-Connally, how-ever, was clear encouragement to Congress to move on more restrictive antiunion legislation, *Newsweek* describing the determination to bring organized labor into line as "an anger that burned across the nation."[26]

Even Truman's patience had begun to wear thin. When in May 1946 three hundred thousand Railroad Trainmen and Locomotive Engineers struck, rejecting a government-sponsored settlement, the president responded by threatening to have the government run the railroads and to deploy soldiers to defend replacement workers. He also reprised Roo-sevelt's idea of drafting recalcitrant workers into the armed forces. Secre-tary of War Robert Patterson advised Truman that Congress could amend the Selective Service Act, raising the upper age limit of draftees from thirty to forty-five in order to snare more railroad men able to run the trains. As in Roosevelt's time, however, the threat of drafting strikers was denounced as excessive, as well as potentially demeaning to the military.

Not to be intimidated, Truman went before Congress in a mood far from conciliatory, warning that he would seek injunctions against indi-vidual rail union leaders, assign federal arbitrators to set wages, and put any profits earned by government operation of the railways into the U.S. Treasury. (He meant his remarks also for the ears of the National Maritime Union, which had scheduled a strike for June 15.) The rail unions balked, calling off their strike even as Truman was at the podium issuing his strong remarks. Word of the capitulation filtered into the Capitol, gratifying Congress, although the even better news for conservative representatives was that the president appeared to have at last seen the light. The moment had come, Truman said, to "adopt a comprehensive labor policy which will tend to reduce the number of stoppages of work and other acts which injure labor, capital, and the whole population."[27]

Representative Francis Case of South Dakota sought to act on the White House's shifting sympathies by proposing a bill that would establish a Federal Mediation Board, a sixty-day prestrike cooling-off period, and, significantly, the surrender of workers' Wagner Act rights for violating the cooling-off restriction. It also banned secondary boycotts and allowed for injunctions against certain forms of picketing. The *New Republic* termed Case's suggested legislation "an unashamed and hateful attempt to emasculate organized labor,"[28] and organized labor itself lost no time in crying foul. An angry Sidney Hillman attributed Truman's weakening before anti-labor forces to "a moment of national hysteria deliberately provoked by the reactionary forces of big business." The CIO gathered a million signatures on a petition urging the president to veto the Case bill "before it is too late and we embark on the road to fascism."[29] Even the *New York Times*, which thought Case would "begin the long-needed . . . job of revisiting existing federal legislation for the purpose of curbing a present monopoly of industrial labor," deemed the legislation imperfect.[30] Truman, heeding the concerns of labor and the advice of his attorney general, Tom Clark, vetoed the bill.

Its conservative sponsors, however, merely bided their time. Republicans had not controlled both houses of Congress since 1930, but the upcoming fall 1946 midterm elections were expected to bring the historic Roosevelt era on Capitol Hill to an end. As anticipated, large margins of victory in numerous congressional races that November gave them enough new seats in both houses of Congress to achieve a veto-proof majority, as well as the ability to claim overwhelming public support. The time had arrived for conservative America's own "new deal."

THEIR EFFORT COALESCED AROUND a series of proposed amendments to the National Labor Relations Act of 1935 (the Wagner Act) that would become known as the Taft-Hartley Bill, after its Republican sponsors, Ohio senator Robert A. Taft, chairman of the Senate Labor Committee, and his House counterpart, Congressman Fred A. Hartley Jr. of New Jersey. Taft, the eldest son of President William Howard Taft, was the star of this drama and wouldn't have had it any other way. "Mr. Republican," as he was sometimes known, had made no secret of his intention to "cast out a great many chapters of the New Deal, if not the whole book."[31] The legislative fix he envisioned for Wagner would begin a far more sweeping campaign to reset the nation's course along conservative lines, an effort that would require his close guidance and might well guide him into the White House. Taft's war dance made liberals anxious, but they believed that Social Security and unemployment insurance at least were safe, as these programs had proven so popular with voters they were embraced even by the Republican Party platform; labor laws enacted by Congress at the height of the Roosevelt era, however, were a different matter. "It took 14 years to rid this country of prohibition," said Alfred Sloan, CEO of General Motors. "It is going to take a good while to rid the country of the New Deal, but sooner or later the ax falls and we get a change."[32] Taft's partner Fred Hartley was less ardent an advocate of sweeping reform; he was close to retirement and some observers speculated he had joined Taft's initiative in order to link his name with a major and potentially historic legislative undertaking.[33]

The bill, introduced first in the House, was a comprehensive denial of the rights labor had won over the past generation. It would give management greater control of how union representation elections were conducted and allow individual states to pass anti-labor restrictions of their own, most significantly "right to work" laws stipulating that union membership could not be required as a condition of employment, in effect an undermining of the closed shop. It forbade industry-wide collective bargaining. Employers could sue unions over secondary boycotts. Unions would have to notify management of any intention to challenge or change a contract, and could be sued in federal court for breaching one; they were prohibited from giving money to political campaigns or using funds from union treasuries to aid candidates, and union officers were required to sign statements that they were not members of the Communist Party. Finally, it expanded presidential authority to obtain injunctions against strikes thought to be endangering national health or safety.

Critics of the bill in Congress immediately pointed out that it had been written by corporate lawyers working at the behest of the National Association of Manufacturers and the Chamber of Commerce. As evidence, Democratic congressman John Blatnik of Minnesota circulated a list of legislative recommendations drawn up by NAM in 1946 and distributed as part of a booklet titled *Now . . . Let's Build America*; it showed a clear similarity to the House version of Taft-Hartley.[34] Although these charges were aired in the House, debate on the bill itself was limited.

In the Senate the conversation was more extended, conservatives proposing the Wagner Act be viewed as a kind of experiment, one crafted with good intentions, but that had proven extreme in some of its effects, and now sorely needed repair. Wagner's defenders argued that New Deal labor legislation had largely been a success and that gutting it would set back industrial relations half a century. They pointed to the health and vitality of organized labor compared with the 1920s—the large numbers of railway, mining, and manufacturing workers who were now unionized, with more unions winning NLRB elections every year. Such a degree of organization among American workers, they insisted, had a stabilizing effect on the economy, indeed on all of society.

The NAM, if it listened to these arguments at all, hesitated not a minute in launching a well-oiled public relations effort to rebut criticism and smooth the bill's passage. Labor returned fire with what were becoming familiar words of outrage, the ILGWU's David Dubinsky terming Taft-Hartley "a monstrous piece of legislation" and "a body blow to our democracy." In retrospect labor's response may have focused too heavily on its adversaries in Washington without fully acknowledging the extent to which public opinion itself had shifted; it was no longer 1935. The ominous details of Taft-Hartley could be challenged, but harder to defeat was the sense that it was conservatives who were prepared to do the nation's "new business" while labor unions and their faithful remained entrenched in the old.[35] Understandably, labor became distracted by the bill's requirement of an anti-Communist oath. Many union officials, led by John L. Lewis, decried as insulting the idea that government would infantilize union officials by this stipulation; indeed, such an imposition seemed to validate Lewis's long-held fear of what might come of labor's bonding so tightly with the Democratic Party, the New Deal, and government "control" of labor unions through the National Labor Relations Act. Other labor leaders, including Walter Reuther of the UAW, agreed to sign the affidavits and chastised fellow UAW leaders reluctant to do so. The AFL also fell into line, Secretary-Treasurer George Meany urging colleagues that little would be lost to principle by anyone's swearing a public oath against a political philosophy so universally despised.

The House bill had been intentionally designed as stringent so that Bob Taft and his forces, who would take it up in the Senate, might appear conciliatory. The goal was to bring a sufficient number of Democrats on board and convince President Truman that the final bill sent to his desk contained enough compromise to be veto-proof. Even in its supposedly milder form the bill, which swept through both houses by substantial margins (308–107 in the House, and 68–24 Senate), offered a potent anti-labor restructuring of the country's industrial relations. Lewis described the conservatives' handiwork as "the first ugly, savage thrust of Fascism in America"; others termed it a "slave-labor law." But these were sounds of helpless rage as labor was shoved over a cliff. Politically, given the bond between labor and the Democratic administration, President Truman had no choice but to veto the bill, noting as he did so that Taft-Hartley held "seeds of discord which would plague this nation for years to come" and would "reverse the basic direction of our national labor policy."[36] With such substantial vote totals in Congress, however, even the president knew resistance was futile. His veto was overridden and in June 1947 the Taft-Hartley Act became law.

DESPITE THE HOPES of its chief author, the law's passage did not prompt Congress to forge ahead with a more substantive rollback of the New Deal. Nor did it prove as effective at quelling union activity as labor had feared. Indeed, a seminal victory for labor followed close on the heels of Taft-Hartley. In fall 1949, the United Steelworkers threatened to strike over the issue of whether employers should bear the entire cost of employee benefits such as pensions and health insurance, or whether employees should contribute to such costs.

Two recent federal court rulings had allowed that, under the Wagner Act, workers could bargain for retirement and health benefits with employers. After Truman persuaded the union three times to delay strike action, the steelworkers ran out of patience, and on October 1 a half-million employees walked off the job. Steel companies and their subsidiaries were affected from New Jersey to the iron ore mines of Minnesota's Mesabi Range.

Industry executives balked at the notion of shouldering all the costs of the disputed benefits, partly out of contempt for what management saw as the lingering New Deal's ethos of "something for nothing." It was important to industry that they not assume quasi-governmental responsibilities, providing for workers' welfare independent of any initiative on the part of the individual worker. The Steelworkers, led by CIO president Philip Murray, countered that employers taking just such responsibility for workers' health and retirement needs would help "safeguard the democratic way of life against totalitarian onslaughts from left or right." A fact-finding board established by President Truman appeared to concur with Murray, concluding "that depreciation of 'the human machine' should be as much a charge against industry as care of plant equipment"; it pointed out that the steel industry had long provided comprehensive noncontributory benefits of the sort desired by the union to its own top executives. The board proposed that industry contribute 10 cents per hour per worker toward benefits, which the steel employers agreed to, with the stipulation that employees pay an additional amount from their weekly salary. The union, however, believed there was no need for any extra employee contribution since the 10 cents per hour paid by industry for employee benefits was itself a kind of wage—one that went toward the worker's needs but not into his pocket. The union also contended that such coverage should be automatic and in no way voluntary, thus ensuring that all workers would be covered.[37]

Truman was in a difficult spot, because his own board had recommended the 10-cent cost to industry; as far as the union was concerned, that was the matter to be acted upon; but industry reminded the president that both sides had agreed the board's advice would be nonbinding, and thus the companies felt their demand for a employee contribution remained valid. The other complicating factor was that since the union had already postponed its strike at the request of the White House for seventy-seven days, three days short of what Truman could have demanded under Taft-Hartley, it would now be grossly unfair for the White House to invoke Taft-Hartley and seek an eighty-day injunction. A critical sidebar to the steel imbroglio was that 380,000 mine workers had also gone out on strike in September, raising the specter of a near-total shutdown of the nation's industry if both steel and coal workers stayed away from their jobs, since so many other types of businesses—automotive, manufacturing—relied on them. In the UMW's case, Truman was free to invoke the national emergency provisions of Taft-Hartley and obtain an eighty-day injunction, but such a move against one industry (coal) and not the other (steel) would appear inappropriate. His options in lieu of Taft-Hartley, which he had vetoed and was known to dislike, would be to invoke the Selective Service Act of 1948, which allowed for the government to compel the production of coal for use by the armed forces; use the "inherent powers" of the presidency to act in the public interest as defined in the 1895 Supreme Court ruling *In re Debs*; or attempt to win emergency legislation in Congress. None were politically appealing.[38]

Eleven days into the steel strike its impact was already being felt nationwide. Railroads had less to transport, and steel-reliant businesses were forced to step down production and even lay off workers. The Big Three automakers notified the White House that their production would slow dramatically within weeks for want of a steady supply of steel. A few days later Commerce Secretary Charles Sawyer stoked further anxiety by warning that if the stoppage in steel and coal continued until November 1, as many as 2 million American workers would be unemployed, and were it to go as far as December 1, the number of those out of work would rise to 5 million. Indeed, it was inevitable, he advised, that some smaller businesses whose production was sidelined would not have the capital or capacity to recover, and would cease to exist along with the jobs they provided.[39] Within days newspapers were caught up in the dire images Sawyer had suggested, warning of school and hospital closings and a remorseful Christmas for the nation's children.

In such news Philip Murray saw a potential win for the steelworkers. Speaking before enthusiastic CIO rallies and by radio he vowed "no retreat," praising the Truman board's 10-cent recommendation and holding up as ridiculous the notion that steel companies couldn't afford the benefits arrangement the union requested. Murray stood firm against criticisms that organized labor was using the greater public welfare as a bargaining chip; when his AFL counterpart, President William Green, questioned the holdout in steel, Murray dismissed him as "an old faddy-doodle . . . who has never rendered a public service in his life."[40]

The break in the standoff came on October 31, when Bethlehem Steel Corporation, the nation's second-largest steelmaker, agreed to provide pensions that would be noncontributory for individual employees. Bethlehem workers reaching sixty-five years of age with twenty-five years on the job would be eligible for pensions of $100 per month and upward, while those with fewer years of employ would receive lesser amounts. The agreement included a life insurance provision and a comprehensive Blue Cross health plan with coverage for workers and their dependents, the health insurance to be paid for by a 50–50 contribution of 2½ cents an hour from Bethlehem and the same from each of the firm's seventy-seven thousand employees.

Murray hailed the agreement as "a vindication of the union's position that there is a social responsibility in industry to take care of the aged and their families." The Bethlehem compromise was copied not only by other steelmakers, but served as a model for employer-based pension and health benefits in hundreds of U.S. companies, helping to ground a philosophy of corporate benefits and pension administration that would pertain for much of the next half century.[41]

L ABOR WOULD NOT ALWAYS BE so successful at managing a victory around the new restrictions imposed by Taft-Hartley; in fact the detrimental effects of the law would prove both powerful and enduring. Even the atmosphere of reaction associated with the act could prove toxic, as organizers affiliated with the CIO's ambitious Operation Dixie discovered in the late 1940s when they spread out across the South in the hope of unionizing textile mills. This was an historic undertaking. The insular South, with its rigid folkways and its legacy of slavery, sharecropping, convict labor, and states' rights, had rejected labor unionization as doggedly as it defended racial segregation. Efforts to bring reform in either area had encountered fierce resistance since Reconstruction following the Civil War; indeed one of Reconstruction's chief legacies was the idea, shamelessly sold by the South, that its society was unique and not easily understood by outsiders, and that it must be left to handle its own affairs. But because by the 1940s Northeast textile firms were beginning to head for the region in pursuit of cheaper, nonunion labor, the CIO had nobly felt compelled to follow. Organizing the Southern mills would have two benefits: it would bring Southern workers into the fold of organized labor, and possibly, by equalizing wages between North and South, stymie the exodus from New England mills.

As ambitious as the plan was, the CIO could rightfully claim to have exerted influence on a large demographic scale before; its organizing of the Midwestern industrial belt in the 1930s along with the efforts of the

Communist Trade Union Unity League (TUUL) had helped open the doors of Northern industry to blacks, who in large cities such as Chicago, Detroit, and Philadelphia had subsequently become a significant voting bloc, chiefly Democratic. This significant development had made possible the success of the March on Washington Movement of 1941, led by A. Philip Randolph, president of the Brotherhood of Sleeping Car Porters, which demanded an end to racial discrimination in the defense industries accompanied by the threat of a massive labor demonstration that would bring one hundred thousand protesting black workers to the nation's capital. In response, President Roosevelt had issued an executive order banning such discrimination and created an enforcement agency, the Fair Employment Practices Commission (FEPC).

The timing of the launch of Operation Dixie, spring 1946, appeared in some ways fortuitous. America remained buoyed by a mood of postwar pride related to its role in the world's triumph over Fascism overseas, and everywhere—in schools, churches, Congress, in the public discourse—the nation's core values of tolerance and democracy were extolled and celebrated. Some of the nation's founding documents—the Declaration of Independence, the Bill of Rights, and the Emancipation Proclamation—were taken on a whistle-stop tour of the country aboard a "Freedom Train," to tremendous popular reception. There was a corresponding sense of incremental progress in race relations. President Truman, following up on Roosevelt's 1941 executive order desegregating defense work, in 1948 issued one of his own, ending segregation in the armed forces. He also established the U.S. Commission on Civil Rights, took the unprecedented step of demanding the federal investigation and prosecution of a multiple lynching in Georgia, and became the first president to address a gathering of the NAACP. At the same time John L. Lewis, along with NAACP executive secretary Walter White and legal adviser Thurgood Marshall, began work to address many of the long-simmering problems of black labor—emphasizing the advantages of worker solidarity across racial lines and counseling blacks not to serve as scabs. White, who had been influential in convincing black Ford workers to side with the UAW at River Rouge in 1941, had in the postwar years launched an effort to swing the votes of black labor behind Democratic candidates. Meanwhile, in 1947 the Congress of Racial Equality (CORE), a biracial civil rights organization that had proved its mettle with public accommodations sit-ins in the Chicago area during the war, sponsored a series of integrated interstate bus rides into the South known as the Journey of Reconciliation.

Still, this was also the era of the Dixiecrat rebellion, the walkout led by white supremacist Senator Strom Thurmond of South Carolina from the 1948 Democratic National Convention, in protest over the party's civil rights plank, and it was a very real question whether the genial postwar spirit of reconciliation and "freedom trains" would extend to the sleepy textile mill villages of Appalachia. The CIO's operation was run out of its Southern Organizing Committee office in Atlanta and headed by Van A. Bittner, a UMW organizer, and George Baldanzi, a veteran official of the Textile Workers Union of America. Many of the frontline organizers had been chosen because they were Southerners and were thought to thus have a better chance of promoting trust among workers, given the region's customary suspicion of outsiders. It was critical to the operation's success that organizers establish a core of workers in each plant to carry on the actual in-factory organizing around union objectives, the goal being the building of enough interest to warrant NLRB-supervised certification elections. In retrospect, however, the operation was inadequately staffed. While the CIO's successful 1937 GM autoworkers' sit-down had strategically targeted a single employer, the CIO in the South—with about twenty organizers per state—was spread thinly across the region from the Carolina Piedmont to the Texas Gulf Coast. Only here and there could the union hope to bring concentrated force to bear against a specific firm.

Logistics aside, much of the South retained the region's entrenched system of caste as well as its reactionary, think-alike institutions of press, pulpit, business, and police. Here, labor advocates would not merely encounter the resistance of a single manufacturer or town, but animosity on a pervasive regional scale, a uniform reaction to what was perceived quite literally as an "invasion" of labor agitators. To puzzled white South-erners, the likelihood that the CIO effort was driven by some powerful ideology, probably "Communist," served as the only possible explanation for why outsiders would be as foolish as to defy local custom by attempt-ing to unionize black and white workers. Even the name "Operation Dixie" was unfortunate in its suggestion of a military undertaking, in a region with fabled memories of federal occupation.

It certainly didn't help that the labor movement itself in the postwar years was not above occasional red-baiting. George Meany of the AFL called the CIO leadership "the devoted followers of Moscow" and charac-terized it generally as "an organization that has openly followed the com-munist line and is following that line today."[42] The phobia slowly pervaded the CIO itself. Having welcomed Communists as members in the late 1930s (John L. Lewis had then insisted, "I do not turn my organizers and CIO members upside down and shake them to see what kind of literature falls out of their pockets"), the CIO now bent over backward to reassure the public that Communists would not be active within its ranks.[43] The United Electrical Workers and the Farm Equipment Workers had departed the CIO after the dustup over the anti-Communist oath requirement in Taft-Hartley, and at its 1949 convention the CIO went so far as to rule that individual Communists would not be allowed to hold executive union jobs. The following year the CIO expelled nine left-leaning unions, many of which had committed the wayward sin of bucking the CIO endorse-ment of Harry Truman for reelection in 1948 and had instead supported Progressive Party candidate Henry Wallace.[44] While such housecleaning may have buffed the CIO's image, in a practical sense cutting loose the Communists meant chasing away some of the CIO's most experienced organizers as well as whole unions with solid records of core activism, such as the Food, Tobacco, Agricultural and Allied Workers, which had won eighteen recent certification elections with integrated locals and was known for promoting black union leadership.

Of course, Operation Dixie represented more than just an affront to local racial custom—it threatened the South's ability to offer the low-priced and durable labor status quo vital to attracting commercial and industrial investment. Here there was something of an unhappy precedent as far as labor was concerned: the United Textile Workers strike of 1934, which had ended with Southern mill owners discharging leading union activists from their jobs and even evicting many of them and their families from company towns. In a double blow to Southern organizing, the loss of the 1934 strike had exiled a generation of potential local union leaders while thoroughly inhibiting anyone inclined to follow in their footsteps. Fifteen years after the failure of the big UTW walkout, Southern employers could still feel confident in the extreme economic vulnerability of local workers, the federal government's reluctance to act on civic disorder in the South, and the remoteness of the campaign from crusading big-city newspapers.

Of course, for Operation Dixie staff there were myriad everyday challenges. Many Southern mill hands were working their first salaried, non-agricultural job. To such workers, who came from dire poverty and the company-store tradition of sharecropping, a job in a textile plant that paid real wages represented a significant step forward. "These people had just come off of . . . red clay country farms," observed one CIO organizer. "They figured these were the best jobs they had ever had," and were understandably hesitant to align with a Northern-based labor organization.[45] Race was also a considerable barrier, since any biracial gathering, especially one based around labor organizing by outsiders, was seen as a transgression of local mores, if not the law. Churches were no refuge, as the textile mills routinely sugared local churches with donations as a way of softening ministers on local plant policies. Nor could organizers count on local police or officials for assistance. CIO organizers, forced to stay in whites-only motels, could not use the rooms of those establishments for holding meetings, and were frequently left little choice but to gather interested workers under bridges, by railroad sidings, and in other out-of-the-way places.

Operation Dixie had some initial success in tobacco, pulp and paper, lumber and woodworking factories; its first major test in textiles came in

August 1946. Three CIO-induced union elections were to be held in North Carolina—at the Sidney Blumenthal Company in Caramount and at two factories in Rockingham, the Pee Dee Manufacturing Company and Hannah Pickett Mills. The CIO lost narrowly in Caramount, but was defeated by substantial margins at both plants in Rockingham. A subsequent election at the Avondale Mills in Alabama also went to the nonunion forces.

Meanwhile, police and employer harassment of Operation Dixie organizers was being stepped up across the region. Textile employers and local authorities tapped CIO organizers' telephones, jotted down license plate numbers of vehicles at union gatherings, and started bonfires near to where CIO literature was handed out as a not-so-subtle hint that there existed a handy place to discard it. One South Carolina police chief crafted his own solution by grabbing a CIO organizer off the street and driving the man around town in a squad car; the organizer was innocent of any wrongdoing and was soon set free, but not before everyone in town knew he'd been in police custody. Elsewhere police found they could intimidate workers by simply standing nearby when organizers set up outside a plant. Such conditions made it almost impossible to convince a mill worker he or she would be safe if they joined a union.

Operation Dixie, which sputtered to an end in 1953, was a demoralizing loss for labor, and one that augured badly for the future. The UAW in particular paid a price for the campaign's failure, as foreign carmakers such as Nissan, Honda, BMW, Volkswagen, and Mercedes-Benz ultimately took advantage of the region's persistent low wages and antiunion resiliency to open plants that were more cost-effective than the Big Three manufacturing centers in Michigan. Automakers in Tennessee, Alabama, and other Southern states could operate at considerably lower expense by using nonunionized labor and avoiding the ample wage and benefit obligations that burdened Detroit. In one sense the grand effort to transform the textile mills of the South wound up having a far greater impact on the organization behind the plan, for the experience soured the CIO on further civil rights activism and even on its own internal efforts to attain wage equality among members.

Some historians have pondered whether, with more national support, Operation Dixie might have served as the opening salvo of the modern civil rights movement. It seems unlikely. There was not yet a movement of black Southerners in towns like Montgomery or Atlanta, or on college campuses in North Carolina, willing to march, protest, and be arrested to secure a good job at a textile mill, as there would be a decade later over segregation on buses, at lunch counters, and in reaction to voting injustices. Nor was there yet adequate commitment from the Justice Department, the courts, or the federal government. Not until 1954 in *Brown v. Board of Education* would the Supreme Court remove the legal underpinning for Jim Crow segregation; and it would take the subsequent desegregation of Central High School in Little Rock, Arkansas, in 1957 to move a U.S. president, Dwight D. Eisenhower, to send troops to quell racial difficulties in the South, the first time this had occurred in more than eight decades. From a labor perspective, success by Operation Dixie would have likely transformed not only the country's union movement but possibly the political history of the United States in the latter half of the twentieth century, for as labor attorney Thomas Geoghegan writes, the CIO's ability to organize the South would have made labor "a truly national force, and not a regional one, [that remained] trapped in the Northeast and Midwest."[46] On either score, if Operation Dixie was convincing of anything, it was that any future commitment to change in the South would need to be overwhelming, and draw upon support from a wider proportion of American society.

AFTER THE PASSING of a generation, the differences over trade unionization that had caused the rupture of the AFL and the breakaway of the CIO in the 1930s had begun to ebb. Industrial unionism's appropriateness was now apparent; large-membership locals of unskilled industrial workers could not be kept subordinate to old-time craft unions. With the CIO at 6 million members and the AFL at 9 million (the railway brotherhoods had about 2.5 million members), it was not difficult to perceive the potential in reuniting the country's two major workers' organizations, especially in an era so inimical to labor's gains. Personal antagonisms on the part of some of the unions' elders had long impeded any movement toward reconciliation, but in November 1952, by coincidence, both William Green of the AFL and Philip Murray of the CIO died, creating a power vacuum that could be filled by men far less tainted by the groups' contentious history. The case for maximum labor unity was urged by another factor that same month—the election of Republican Dwight D. Eisenhower to the White House over liberal Democrat Adlai Stevenson.

Replacing Murray as CIO president was Walter Reuther, who in 1935 had been one of the founders of the UAW. Originally a Ford tool-and-die craftsman, he had earned his union stripes in the Flint struggle of early 1937 along with his two brothers, Roy and Victor, who were also UAW officers, and later that year at the Battle of the Overpass, where he had been among those assaulted by the Ford "Service Department" men. By 1946 he had won out over his fellow Overpass sufferer Richard Frankensteen to assume the UAW presidency.

Reuther's was possibly the friendliest face ever to emerge from the leadership ranks of the U.S. labor movement. Likable and gregarious, he possessed a quality of genuineness and an irrepressible energy that endeared him to his followers and the American public. These very attributes, and his popularity, often grated on the sensibilities of tougher, more no-nonsense union men—George Meany considered him soft and John L. Lewis once called him "a pseudo-intellectual nitwit"[47]—but to most Americans Walter Reuther was the labor leader one might want as a next-door neighbor. Throughout his long career he was also perhaps the union movement's most prominent exponent of the idea that organized labor should serve as a vehicle for promoting expanded human rights and democracy, if for nothing else than as a means of safeguarding the future of a free working people. "The smart, dancing-eyed Reuther," wrote *Harper's* during the war, "is something special among labor leaders, a person who moves in a world of ideas that includes a concept of the general welfare as distinct from short-term labor welfare."[48]

One of Reuther's cherished recollections was of the time he and his younger brother Victor had been taken by their father, Valentine Reuther, the Socialist leader of a brewers' union, to visit Eugene Debs when he was incarcerated at the Moundsville Penitentiary in West Virginia.[49] "Tell my comrades that I entered the prison doors a flaming revolutionist, my head erect, my spirit untamed and my soul unconquerable," Debs had declared upon his arrival at Moundsville. Reuther, then eleven years old, never forgot the convict's calm, saintly presence, or how, when leaving the cellblock, his father had begun to cry, asking, "How can they imprison so kind and gentle a man?"[50]

Walter was by 1922 a skilled tool-and-die worker at the Ford Motor plant at River Rouge. Laid off in the early days of the Depression, in 1933 he and Victor, having saved $450 each, embarked together on a three-year working trip in Europe. They bicycled across the Continent and toured the ruins of the recently burned Reichstag in Berlin before going on to Russia. There they joined other foreign technicians hired in an arrangement between the Ford Motor Company and the Soviet state to help adapt Ford manufacturing methods to Soviet automobile production. The two-year work experience at the Gorki plant would come to haunt both Reuthers once the dread fear of Stalinist Russia became a deep-seated anxiety in America. In 1938 Walter was one of three hundred CIO members called before Congress's Dies Committee (a forerunner of the House Un-American Activities Committee [HUAC]), led by Congressman Martin Dies of Texas. Reuther fended off allegations that he was a Communist, explaining that he and Victor, while initially enthusiastic about working at the Russian factory, had become disillusioned by the Communist Party hierarchy and the ways it mistreated workers and interfered with shop operations. The Reuthers' final split with Moscow came the following year when Russia and Nazi Germany signed the Molotov-Ribbentrop nonaggression pact. Walter Reuther, disgusted with the Soviets' cynical appeasement of Hitler, also turned against leftist influence in the UAW.

Reuther was famously known as an ideas man, a scribbler of thoughts on notepads and scraps of paper, and in 1940 he came forward with an interesting proposal. The war in Europe had begun and Reuther, having been in Germany as Hitler came to power as well as in Japan on his way home from Russia, was, unlike many Americans, under no illusion that the United States could remain on the sidelines. He suggested that some of the nation's automobile manufacturing facilities be refitted to produce airplanes, using the mass production techniques of auto-making as opposed to the time-consuming craft methods then used for building airplanes one at a time. Five hundred planes could be built in a day, Reuther predicted, writing, "England's battles, it used to be said, were won on the playing fields of Eton. This plan is put forward in the belief that America's can be won on the assembly lines of Detroit."[51] The CIO's Philip Murray and R. J. Thomas, then chief of the UAW, passed Reuther's idea on to President Roosevelt, who thanked labor for its efforts and shared the concept with his war production team. William Knudson and Charles Kettering of GM were among those who raised technical questions as to whether Reuther's proposal was realistic. The airplane-making business itself, through its Aeronautical Chamber of Commerce, also balked at the notion.

Knudson's concerns were the most critical, as he sat on the board of the Office of Production Management (OPM). He and Reuther had crossed swords a few years earlier during the Flint sit-down strike, when the GM boss had been sufficiently impressed with Walter's negotiating skills to confide, "Young man, I wish you were selling used cars for me."

"Used cars?" asked Reuther.

"Yes, used cars. Anyone can sell new cars."[52]

It was decidedly a "new car" that Reuther was selling this time, with his talk of five hundred airplanes a day, but Knudson wasn't buying. Reuther nonetheless took the GM executive's brush-off as a challenge. In Detroit, he gathered a task force of UAW men and others who served the various carmakers and conducted a lengthy technical inquiry to test his own hypothesis. The consensus opinion after a thorough review was that the scheme was feasible. But there were larger nontechnical issues inhibiting industry enthusiasm. Reuther's conversion plan would require the nation's automobile companies to pool their equipment, manpower, and brain trust into one collective enterprise—a vision that was off-putting to car company executives. Equally troubling was Reuther's assumption that, due to the urgency of the conversion, labor would be involved as a partner in management and production decisions. He had proposed a joint oversight board with three committees—technical, labor supply, and subcontracting—all of which would be coordinated by representatives of industry, government, and labor.

"This was not labor standing by the edge of the desk, hat in hand, gratefully accepting the opportunity to make a suggestion here and there," historian Bruce Catton recalled. "This was labor declaring that it had just as much responsibility for winning the war as management had and asserting that, on the whole, it possibly had just about as much to contribute. It was a revolutionary proposal—not Fascism, not Communism, nothing that could be put in any of the familiar pigeonholes, but something breathtakingly new."[53]

To Reuther the practical tool-and-die man, this was all just common sense. If, in the interest of winning the war, the way industry functioned had to be suspended or changed, so be it. But the prospect remained distasteful to company heads. What if the CIO attempted to adapt the plan to other essential wartime industries, such as copper mining? And how could executives be sure such realignments of authority would disappear when peace returned? In the end, the devastation of Pearl Harbor stunned even the most hardened war skeptics into action; the conversion of the auto and other industries to the production of wartime matériel did occur, although not with the unique labor-industry-government coalition Reuther had envisioned.[54]

Following the passing of Philip Murray and William Green, Reuther's counterpart at the AFL was newly elected president George Meany, an official at the New York City Plumbers Union who had come up within AFL leadership ranks. Intimidating to look at—he was commonly described as "a cross between a bulldog and a bull"—Meany was a dominating character, one of the few labor leaders brazen enough to scold John L. Lewis for balking at the anti-Communist oath required by Taft-Hartley. Reuther and Meany were markedly different personalities, but they shared the experience of representing the first generation of American labor leaders who were union professionals, that is, men who spent far more time at union headquarters or with government officials and corporate leaders than mixing with their own rank and file. Although with his signature stogie clamped in his teeth Meany looked like a rabble-rouser, he had expensive tastes in food and travel and liked to brag he had never walked a picket line; Reuther had more the manner of a well-heeled businessman than someone who'd ever worked in an automobile factory, let alone one in Russia. "If anyone can bring about a merger, Reuther is the man," the AFL's Green had once said. "We can get along with him better than anybody else in the CIO." This was partly due to Reuther's anti-Communism, which made him one of the few CIO upper echelon types palatable to the super-patriotic Meany.[55]

The cautious first steps toward AFL-CIO reunification began in 1953 with a "no raiding" agreement aimed at reducing conflict between rival AFL and CIO unions; a Joint Unity Committee was then established, working in secret to perfect the terms of the merger, which took place formally in February 1955. The new AFL-CIO, it was agreed, would focus on membership growth and the suppression of union-related corruption and Communist infiltration. The spirit of cooperation was nowhere better illustrated than in Reuther's offer to forfeit the top job in the combined organization. Meany would be president of the AFL-CIO, with Reuther serving as vice president in charge of industrial unions.[56]

The press and public's comfortable acceptance of the joined AFL-CIO was itself a measure of the extent to which unions, by the 1950s, had come to be seen as conservative features of American life—securing decent wages and working conditions and supporting the decade's high standard of living. It was in fact in 1956, the year following the merger, that the peak of labor union membership in the United States was attained, with 17.5 million people in unions, representing 33.4 percent of the non-farm workforce.[57]

It was at this very juncture, however, that organized labor began to suffer a bit from its own success. Many large employers had by now embraced the welfare capitalist philosophy that valued worker retention and a satisfied, productive workforce; most offered competitive pay and benefits, regular hours with compensated overtime, paid vacations, sick days, and other perks. With such nurturing from employers and a strong economy at their backs, workers began to identify increasingly with their place of work or regard themselves as independent entities in little need of employee solidarity. In a consumer society where workers could afford their own homes, two cars, and household appliances, and look forward to sending their children to college, the old fighting spirit of American unionism—that of Homestead, Lawrence, Toledo, or Flint—was becoming something of a relic.

This curious "accomplishment" resulted from more than simply the rising tide of living standards and the flood of affordable consumer goods. Blue-collar workers in mining, transportation, and heavy industry, long the bulk of unionized workers, were declining in number, while the number of white-collar workers in service positions, retail, and municipal and federal government jobs continued to grow. As new technology displaced industrial workers, new "soft jobs" were created—in insurance, real estate, financial services. Although some service-industry jobs, such as retail sales, did come to be unionized, they had nowhere near the clout or energy of the major craft and industrial unions of yore—the miners, railway men, and steelworkers.

Mobility was also a factor: unionism generally was associated with industrial jobs fixed by location—a steel center like Pittsburgh or the automobile-making nexus of Flint and Detroit. But most white-collar positions came with the promise of possible transfer to new cities or branch offices, movement that paralleled the increased transience of American life generally. The Sunbelting of America—made possible by the advent of air-conditioning and the building of the interstate highway system—opened whole areas of the country for relocation, such as Houston, Atlanta, Phoenix, and Southern California. Automobiles carried workers away to new opportunities in faraway states, or took them home at night from the plant or the office to their own backyard patios in the suburbs. With workers commuting to their jobs each day by car, a workforce no longer needed to reside within the shadow of the mill or plant, nor did men congregate in union halls or gather over beers each night to swap workplace grievances; increasingly they perceived their lives and their aspirations as things separate from their means of earning a paycheck. They no longer saw themselves as rooted in one occupation or at one plant, nor did they accept that they might devote years of labor to a particular employer.

Finally, while common wisdom held that the merger of the AFL and CIO would create a more powerful, dynamic super-union, the irony was that union membership had hit its historic high during the 1950s partly *because* of the intense organizing competition between the AFL and the CIO. With the merger, fewer resources and man-hours were expended to lengthen the membership rolls, and the determined "passion for growth" within the groups gently began to recede.[58]

HOUNDED FOR DECADES by aspersions of radicalism, many U.S. labor organizations had developed by the postwar years what amounted to almost a fright mechanism about anything that resembled or reeked of Communist influence, an anxiety reflected in society generally. But in what would become one of organized labor's least admirable endeavors the AFL, and later the CIO and the combined AFL-CIO, motivated by anti-Communism, embarked in the late 1940s on a protracted misadventure of covert intervention in the affairs of foreign labor groups, ultimately acting in concert with the Central Intelligence Agency (CIA) to undermine left-leaning unions abroad.

This interference was rationalized as necessary to protect the democracy and high standard of living of American workers against potential encroachments of the Communist system. Given the liberal resentment of conservatives' success at painting U.S. labor as "radical," however, there was something disturbing about a policy that saw American labor foster the conservative suppression of foreign workers' organizations.

In spring 1945, just before the Second World War ended, hundreds of trade union representatives from the Allied nations had met in London to discuss ways to coordinate the postwar revitalization of European, British, and Soviet trade unions. At a follow-up convention in October representatives from fifty-six nations founded the World Federation of Trade Unions (WFTU). Sidney Hillman, one of the leaders of the American delegation, had been strongly influenced by a speech Vice President Henry Wallace gave in 1942 titled "The Century of the Common Man," in which Wallace called for a "global New Deal" that would raise standards of living, end colonial regimes, rebuild infrastructure, and promote free trade. Having been active during the war funneling aid to Progressive labor unions in Europe and China, Hillman agreed with Wallace that the emerging postwar corporate economy would require a globally connected labor movement. Walter Reuther also thought the effort to cooperate with British and Russian trade unions meritorious, and shortly after the WFTU's founding the CIO began lobbying for the WFTU to receive delegate status at the United Nations.

The AFL, however, refused to participate in the effort, feeling the WFTU embraced too many unions that were under Communist influence. George Meany insisted that *real* trade unions were impossible under the Soviet system. Speaking at one of the early postwar international labor forums, Meany called the Russian organizations "pseudo trade unions . . . instruments of the state . . . official branches of the government and of its ruling dictatorial political party," remarks that were perceived by many in attendance as undiplomatic.[59] But the U.S. State Department sided with Meany and the AFL, while Labor Secretary Perkins, who discussed the matter with Hillman, came away concluding that the former Roosevelt confidant was too trusting of the Soviets. Washington urged the AFL to create an alternative international labor body, the International Confederation of Free Trade Unions (ICFTU), and eventually the CIO and many European unions also abandoned the WFTU.[60]

The AFL's leadership in foreign affairs dated at least from 1910, when Samuel Gompers sought to limit the entry of immigrants he suspected might be used as strikebreakers. He subsequently aligned the AFL with Woodrow Wilson's decision to enter the First World War, and was among the U.S. labor officials selected by Wilson to confer with their British and European counterparts after the armistice. Gompers encouraged European labor organizations to resist Bolshevism and Socialism and to emulate America's democratic trade union tradition. He was one of the founders of the International Labor Organization (ILO), affiliated with the League of Nations, which united representatives of labor, industry, and government to stand up against communistic union activity in Europe; one of his Italian contacts was an apostate Socialist named Benito Mussolini.[61]

By the time of the Second World War the AFL had its own International Affairs Department, headed by Jay Lovestone, a former American Communist who had been exiled from the party in 1929 and had in turn become rabid in his contempt for the Soviet Union. "A shrewd, brilliant Jew with an overwhelming ambition to be one of the big shots," one contemporary called him.[62] Lovestone, who had arrived in America as a Polish immigrant in 1907 and was raised on the Lower East Side, had attained the position of general secretary of the CPUSA in the 1920s before being repudiated by Stalin at a congress in Moscow for his "deviationist" views. Back in New York Lovestone joined the ILGWU's David Dubinsky in chasing followers of Stalin out of the garment unions, and Lovestone carried out similar expulsions for the UAW. Meany, along with Dubinsky, who was dismissive of his garment industry cohort Sidney Hillman's dovish outlook toward the Soviets, in 1944 tapped Lovestone to lead the Free Trade Union Committee (FTUC), a covert program to destabilize leftist labor movements in postwar Europe. FTUC was funded by a grant of $35,000 per year from the AFL, with Matthew Woll of the Photo Engravers as chairman, Dubinsky as treasurer, and Meany serving as liaison between FTUC and the main AFL leadership. FTUC's public face was that of publisher of the *Free Trade Union News*, which in various languages was circulated worldwide, but its actual operations were secret and known to only the few principals.[63]

Meany's and Dubinsky's fears of Communist infringement on European labor were not entirely unrealistic: there was good reason to assume that Continental trade unions, still smarting from their unhappy experience with free enterprise and Fascism in the 1930s, would naturally drift leftward, and that this inclination would be encouraged and co-opted by the Soviets. Indeed, within a year of the war's end, it was apparent that Russian "social engineers" were active in Germany, if not elsewhere in Europe, trying to win favorable public opinion for eastern occupiers, while the Western nations were making no comparable effort.[64] The Russians had lost little time in creating puppet governments in the small nations of Eastern Europe. In January 1946 they took over Poland, in May 1947 Hungary came under Soviet domination, and in February 1948 Communist-led labor unions aided in a pro-Soviet coup in Czechoslovakia. The Soviets also expedited their development of an atomic bomb, which they detonated successfully in a test in 1948.

As a former Communist, Lovestone knew better than anyone that the party considered labor unions a vital stepping-stone to political authority, and he assumed that the Russians would employ all manner of subterfuge in order to secure that access in Europe. The West would have to fight hard, matching if not surpassing Soviet determination. "Lovestone had an utterly Manichean view of the world," recalls Victor Reuther.[65] Living alone in Manhattan, working out of a modest office in the Garment District, Lovestone maintained an extensive network of contacts throughout Europe and North Africa, wrote much of the *Free Trade Union News*, and gained the confidence of numerous diplomats and foreign ministers with his insider's grasp of leftist labor activities on the world stage. Whether providing raw intelligence to union heads or ghostwriting articles for Dubinsky, Meany, and others that ran in U.S. newspapers and magazines, Lovestone transformed selected American labor leaders into fierce Cold Warriors.

In France, Lovestone's trusted agent was Irving Brown, who had established a beachhead in Paris in November 1945. While Brown covered Europe, FTUC representative Richard Deverall ran operations first in India and later in Japan. Harry Goldberg organized Indonesia. Willard Etter financed the Free China Labor League from Formosa. All answered to Lovestone. Brown crafted a model for AFL involvement in Europe by conspiring against the democratically elected Confédération Générale du Travail (CGT), an AFL-like but Communist-influenced workers' federation with 5.4 million members. Using laundered funds from the United States to stir dissent about Communist influence within CGT's leadership ranks, Brown splintered defectors off into a white-collar union, the Force Ouvrière (FO), headed by former resistance fighter Robert Bethereau and Socialist Léon Jouhaux. Dubinsky took the lead on sustaining a flow of money to the FO in $5,000, $10,000, and $15,000 donations, even as the FO denied the CGT's accusations of American sponsorship.[66]

One of Lovestone's most successful endeavors in undermining the appeal of Communism to European workers was his publication of a detailed booklet, *The Survey of Forced Labor and Measures for Its Abolition*, which revealed the location of Soviet gulags where slave labor was enforced and reproduced survivors' harrowing accounts. The publication, which was widely disseminated, did grave injury to the image of the Soviet Union as any kind of "workers' paradise." Lovestone published *The Survey* in no fewer than eleven languages and had its findings presented to the United Nations. The Soviets confiscated the work wherever it surfaced in Eastern Europe.[67]

The broader significance of the struggle Meany, Dubinsky, and their representatives were waging was not lost on President Truman, who in 1947 was persuaded to establish the CIA to replace the wartime Office of Strategic Services (OSS). Soon after the newly formed agency entered the picture in Europe, it began utilizing the infrastructure Brown and Lovestone had put in place. Beginning in early 1949 CIA funds were funneled to FTUC and soon far outstripped all labor union donations; nonetheless it was the AFL operatives who had anticipated U.S. policy, and were the old hands at the game of checking Soviet influence in postwar Europe. At times, muses historian Ted Morgan, "it seemed that American foreign policy was an instrument of the AFL."[68] Indeed, Lovestone often bridled at the arrangement, dismissing the operatives the CIA dispatched to the field as "Fizz Kids," bright products of Ivy League colleges who lacked both a feel for how labor unions functioned and an intimate understanding of working people.

What made the CIA-AFL intrusion especially hypocritical was that the Lovestone-guided actions were in themselves examples of the dark influence of government on trade unions the American efforts were nominally designed to halt. And in their obsession with blunting Soviet manipulation, the AFL often wound up in bed with ultraconservative political actors of dubious character. "The chief weakness of American foreign policy is the predilection of our State Department for dealing with anybody who will promise to hate Communists," Walter Reuther wrote in 1948.[69] The unwanted backlash from this policy became manifest when the French federation CGT attempted to use strikes to disrupt the unloading of U.S. goods in Marseilles under the Marshall Plan. The five-year $17 billion U.S. aid program named for Secretary of State George C. Marshall aimed to revive the economies of Europe along the lines of free enterprise—a program the Soviet Union characterized as "a direct threat to the sovereignty of Europe."[70] To block CGT's interference on the Marseilles docks, Irving Brown hired the notorious labor racketeer Pierre Ferri-Pisani and his Corsican followers, the Comité Méditerranée, to act as strikebreakers. They successfully counteracted the CGT's strike efforts; however, rather than disband after its assignment was complete, the Comité Méditerranée hung around for years, terrorizing labor relations in the South of France and elsewhere and even ultimately shaking down Brown and the CIA.

THE AFL'S INTERFERENCE in Europe in the 1950s had an early critic in a young CIA officer named Paul Sakwa, who began advising higher-ups in Washington of the harm Lovestone's and Brown's efforts were doing to the very labor unions they were propping up. "Elections were influenced if not purchased outright, union dues remained uncollected, organizing activities ceased," Sakwa wrote. "What began as an effort to promote and defend democracy evolved into operations designed to thwart real, incipient, or imagined Communist threats at the expense of democracy itself." As a U.S. labor attaché, Sakwa was once assigned to accompany George Meany and his wife to a dinner function in Brussels; Sakwa took the opportunity to share his concerns about Lovestone. When Mrs. Meany expressed interest in Sakwa's words her husband lost his temper and ordered them both out of the car, then went on to the dinner alone.[71]

The paranoia of the Red Scare era in Washington associated with the investigations of Senator Joseph McCarthy was extensive enough to cause worry at the CIA over the ceding of so much power to Lovestone and the other FTUC representatives. It was not overlooked that Lovestone, as well as some of his closest colleagues, all of whom were taking CIA money, had themselves once been ardent Communists. Of particular concern was a man named Carmel Offie, a veteran Foreign Service officer known as "Mr. Fixit" for his numerous contacts throughout Russia and Western Europe. Offie was close friends with the Kennedy family, had been a favorite bridge partner of Mrs. Wallis Simpson, and seemed to know anyone worth knowing in the transatlantic diplomatic sphere. He served as chief liaison between FTUC and the CIA, although his sympathies came to rest more with FTUC; for this he was regarded with increasing distrust by the CIA, and soon had the FBI and Senator McCarthy investigating his homosexuality and political background. To add to FTUC's image problems, Lovestone and Brown were soon targeted by the conservative columnist Westbrook Pegler, who alleged they were Communists who had wormed their way into guiding U.S. government actions in Europe. Similar suspicions were voiced in 1954 by Assistant Secretary of Labor Spencer Miller, who testified about Lovestone and his ring of operatives before HUAC.[72]

After the merger of the AFL and CIO in 1955, the AFL chaffed at the possibility it would be required to share CIA funding with the CIO. But the merger, by making the CIO complicit in the AFL's foreign entanglements, presented other, more ideological, problems.[73] Walter and Victor Reuther, as critics were eager to point out, had themselves once transferred $50,000 in U.S. funds to a German labor union, but generally the brothers Reuther disapproved of FTUC's cloak-and-dagger subversion of trade unions abroad and of anti-red bashing generally; Walter termed it "a destructive monomania."[74] Reuther-Meany antagonism over this issue became public in December 1955 when Meany derided the Indian prime minister, Jawaharlal Nehru, as a Communist sympathizer, angering Indian trade unionists. Reuther, at the request of U.S. ambassador to India John Sherman Cooper, embarked in spring 1956 on a goodwill journey to make amends, giving speeches to Indian labor groups and praising Nehru publicly as a respected statesman and world leader. A few years later Reuther again turned diplomat when, in 1959, Russian premier Nikita Khrushchev toured the United States. Meany adamantly refused to meet with the Soviet leader, while Reuther and other labor officials hosted a "workers' dinner" for the visitor and his entourage in San Francisco.

Meany dismissed Reuther's criticisms of the AFL's international skullduggery as those of a weak-kneed liberal, although it's likely that what partly annoyed the AFL-CIO chief was the consistently favorable reception Reuther received abroad. No doubt Meany was also aware that Reuther disapproved of the AFL leader's professional habits and decorum. If Reuther "represented the afterglow of the labor idealism of the thirties," as historian Arthur Schlesinger Jr. suggests, Meany was every inch the national union executive, embracing all the trappings of high office.[75] Meany dined in elegant restaurants, smoked expensive cigars, and convened the AFL-CIO winter council meeting each year at a beachfront hotel in Miami. Reuther earned a third of Meany's salary, carefully monitored his official expenditures, and donated proceeds from his speeches to a college fund for workers' children. An abstainer of both tobacco and alcohol, he disliked wearing a tuxedo and believed labor leaders should live like the workers they represented; he let it be known he thought that holding meetings for union big shots in sunny Florida was an affront to most rank and file, who spent their winters in Northern industrial cities. A favorite story around UAW headquarters told how the famously proper Reuther, upset that male visitors to his office invariably stared at his secretary's legs, demanded a front panel be installed on her desk.[76]

The American interference in the labor movements of other nations was not limited to Europe, but extended to Israel, China, and increasingly Latin America. A characteristic endeavor was the American Institute for Free Labor Development (AIFLD), created in 1962 and led by George Meany and J. Peter Grace, CEO of W. R. Grace & Co. Funded by the federal government, the AFL-CIO, and contributions from U.S. corporations, the AIFLD operated in the guise of an educational program to inculcate principles of democratic unionism (and a dread of Communism) among Latin American labor leaders. Victor Reuther, a critic of the program, scoffed at its absurdity—the very U.S. corporations that had frequently exploited Latin American workers presuming to instruct them about the importance of democracy. The AIFLD staged local symposia and training programs for as many as two hundred thousand Latin American unionists and cultivated some eleven hundred for special training at an AIFLD facility in Front Royal, Virginia, known as "the Little Anti-Red Schoolhouse."[77]

The AIFLD's fingerprints were later found on a number of U.S. covert incursions in Latin America—including the toppling in 1954 of the labor-supported Guatemalan government of Jacobo Arbenz, whose land reforms were opposed by the United Fruit Company, the CIA, and the AFL-CIO. Arbenz had won the presidency of the small Central American nation in 1950 by taking on the vested interests of wealthy landowners and major American agricultural concerns. He had installed in his government some Communists who had backed his election, and in 1953 announced his intention to reclaim lands controlled by United Fruit in the name of the Guatemalan people. Working with Serafino Romualdi, a veteran Italian anti-Communist and CIA operative whom Arbenz had sent into exile, AIFLD abetted a Guatemalan uprising led by the CIA-backed military "liberator" Colonel Carlos Castillo Armas. The collapse of Arbenz's government was cheered in America, but Colonel Armas soon revealed himself to be a right-wing dictator intent on murdering his political opponents and eradicating the country's trade unions.

The CIA went on to use an AFL-CIO supported union in British Guiana in 1961 to undermine the duly elected government of Prime Minister Cheddi Jagan, and AIFLD and AFL-CIO staff were involved in the overthrow of labor-friendly governments in the Dominican Republic in 1965 and in Chile in 1973. "We have permitted our unions to become perverted by the dogma of anti-Communism to the point where we support clearly fascist governments," wrote investigative reporter Fred Hirsch in the wake of the CIA-engineered toppling of Chilean president Salvador Allende. "Now workers in other countries find it impossible to know the difference between the AFL-CIO and the CIA, and the term 'AFL-CIA' has become a standard joke that is never funny."[78]

The U.S. meddling in the affairs of foreign labor unions remained a secret for many years, revelations first surfacing by accident in the mid-1960s during hearings into tax-exempt philanthropic foundations by Democratic congressman Wright Patman of Texas. Patman, whose Small Business subcommittee was looking for tax abuses, stumbled onto evidence that various real and dummy U.S. philanthropic foundations were used by the CIA as a "secret conduit" to direct U.S. funds to covert operations like Jay Lovestone's. American unions also appeared to be involved, as the treasuries of the Oil, Chemical and Atomic Workers (OCAW) as well as the American Newspaper Guild were among those used to pass through large cash payments. One item that caught Patman's eye was an unusually large grant of $395,000 from the J. M. Kaplan Fund, a philanthropy that supported civic improvements in New York City, to the Institute of International Labor Research, a group operated by Sacha Volman, a Romanian refugee "who has long been identified with anti-communist causes in Europe and Latin America."[79] Angered when his queries about the money trail were stonewalled, Patman went public, causing an article about the mysterious CIA funds to appear in the *New York Times* on September 1, 1964. "I feel I have been trifled with," Patman complained, citing the failure of anyone to offer an explanation for what he'd uncovered.[80]

The article, headlined "Patman Attacks 'Secret' CIA Link," astonished many readers, for at the time the American public knew little about the CIA aside from the fact that some of its operatives had been involved in the failed Bay of Pigs invasion of April 1961. Meany issued at once what would become a stock denial of any AFL-CIO involvement with other countries' labor unions, while Patman, who had obviously been tapped firmly on the shoulder by sources high in the government, immediately tried to backpedal, telling reporters in a statement that the CIA did not belong in his committee's investigation of private foundations.

But it was too late. Critics pounced on the revelations, including the report that the foundations were distributing the laundered U.S. dollars to conservative research groups and individual scholars both in America and on foreign soil. It appeared the integrity of all American research- ers or fieldworkers abroad would be compromised. Of course for the moment the extent of Lovestone's actions, the reality that they went well beyond intelligence gathering, was not known; the only thing that for years saved the AFL-CIO from total embarrassment in the matter was the fact that Lovestone's network of global labor espionage was so Byz- antine and secretive as to be incomprehensible to an outsider. Even when Congress finally got around to formally investigating him in the 1970s, it proved difficult for any inquiry to establish what he had done or even exactly who he was.[81]

W HILE ELEMENTS WITHIN THE U.S. labor movement were focused on checking the advance of Communism elsewhere in the world, at home it found itself on the defensive—not from allega- tions of radicalism, but rather of corruption. There had long been labor union–related crime, especially in trades that were transient in nature or time-sensitive, such as trucking, dock-loading, and the construction trades. Payoffs were made for preferential treatment in shape-ups, kickbacks were provided to labor agents, and protection money extorted from immigrant garment workers. No product or service was completely immune. What did appear to be a relatively new and growing phenomenon in the post– World War II era was that of large unions organized along business lines tolerating extensive corruption and abuse from within their own leader- ship, as well as attracting full-time criminals from without.

Part of the problem was that with the rise in memberships the amount of money gathering in union treasuries, strike funds, and pension funds had grown so large it could not but have a transformative organizational effect. Controlling millions of dollars changed the "character of the union leader's job," labor writer A. H. Raskin suggested in 1959, and "often his character as well."

> The union builder, once able to get by on an elixir of idealism, energy, and personal magnetism, is forced to convert himself into an administrator, more engulfed in intricate questions of law, banking, corporate structure, trade prospects, insurance procedure, office management, public relations and policies than in the day-to-day concerns of his union rank and file.[82]

A related trend was the dimming of the guiding light of labor Progressivism characteristic of the 1910s and 1930s. "The real sickness lies in the decline of unionism as a moral vocation," *Fortune* magazine reported in 1953. "Where there has not been outright spoliation, one finds among union leaders an appalling arrogance and high-handedness in their relation to the rank and file, which derives from the corruption of power."[83] Huge pots of money inspired temptation, and many unions were structured in such a way that autocratic leadership was rarely called upon to explain financial decisions. Due to the tremendous pressures on union leaders to excel for their rank and file, and the vicious power struggles that often went on among the upper echelon, leaders who did manage to win control tended to rule in the spirit of divine right. And because most unions were themselves often under assault from the outside world—from employers, the government, the courts, and the press—members as well as loyal lieutenants were inclined to cede vast power to a central paternal figure.

Observers who analyzed the phenomenon found that members, even when they suspected a union's management of illegal or unethical shortcuts, were disinclined to voice concern. There might well be evidence of questionable practices, payoffs, and graft in the leadership ranks but so long as leaders delivered on basic needs and stood up for workers, an acceptable level of corruption would be tolerated. Most union crooks—the abusers of pension funds, the bribe-takers, the doers of special favors—tended to be greedy amateurs unable to keep their hands out of the cookie jar. Far more worrisome, as historian John Hutchinson suggests, was the other kind of labor criminal, the professional hoodlum with utter disdain for the law, the thug, enforcer, racketeer, collector of protection money, "whose justice could be swift, terminal, and unrequited." No wonder the average worker's focus was on coming home with a paycheck. What gain was there in speaking out? Denouncing hoodlums through a congressional hearing or an editorial was one thing, doing so down by the docks after quitting time quite another.[84]

It was corruption on the New York waterfront that dramatically reminded America of its problem with labor-related crime. Longshoremen had always been among the country's most rugged workers, dozens of times a day "carrying everything from two-hundred-pound sacks of potatoes to five-hundred-pound slabs of bacon" up rickety gangplanks and depositing them in a ship's hold.[85] Such jobs attracted unskilled workers with more brawn than brains, while the pressure of unforgiving sailing schedules and the presence of myriad customs and other officials made wildcat strikes, payoffs, and the pilfering of goods common.

This was the world brought to light when *New York Sun* reporter Malcolm Johnson was sent in 1947 to the West Side piers to cover the murder of a Cunard Line hiring boss. Johnson investigated and wrote up his story but, intrigued, remained on the waterfront for the better part of a year, documenting an "outlaw frontier" of "unchecked thievery . . . smuggling, shakedowns, kickbacks, bribery, extortion, and murder." His twenty-four-part exposé in the pages of the *Sun* revealed the existence of what Johnson called "an underworld syndicate," one whose reach extended throughout America and even the world. "I know it sounds fantastic, but it's true," a lawman told Johnson. "The syndicate is like a big trade association in crime. It began back in Prohibition, and it is still strong today. It has big interests in New York, of course, and in Hollywood, Miami, Chicago, Detroit, and other key cities." The heart of this enterprise was a labor union, the International Longshoremen's Association, through which, Johnson wrote, "mobsters are able to control all key jobs on the piers and rackets operate without interference."[86]

Johnson's *Sun* series, which won a Pulitzer Prize in 1949, helped inspire an even more public exposé in 1950–1951, when Tennessee senator Estes Kefauver led nationally televised hearings into the "underworld syndicate" that featured the testimony of real-life criminals. Since Prohibition the American public had known of the sensationalized activities of gangsters, and the 1940 prosecutions of Murder Inc. had revealed the existence of a nationally coordinated Jewish and Italian mob execution squad.[87] But the idea that the underworld was organized on a national or even international basis was slower to gain recognition. Partly this was due to the fixation on Communism by such leading crime fighters as FBI chief J. Edgar Hoover and the reluctance to concede that a vast criminal enterprise existed, although Harry Anslinger of the U.S. Bureau of Narcotics, who had been following the efforts by Charles "Lucky" Luciano, Meyer Lansky, and others to develop an offshore criminal haven in Cuba, had as early as 1946 understood that the "syndicate" was far-reaching in scope. Anslinger had long advocated the need for a congressional inquiry, the very kind Kefauver now proposed to lead.[88]

Known formally as the Senate Special Committee to Investigate Organized Crime in Interstate Commerce, the Kefauver panels convened in seven cities, including New York, Washington, and Los Angeles; the hearings were televised. The inquiry was notable for popularizing the term "Mafia," and for eliciting finally from Hoover the admission that a large organized crime syndicate did indeed exist. This syndicate, the public learned, was a criminal "phantom government [that] enforces its own laws, carries out its own executions, and not only ignores but abhors the democratic processes of justice which are held to be the safeguards of the American citizen." The report that emerged from the hearings was very much of its time, imagining labor corruption—not unlike

Communism—to be a "secret government of crimesters" capable of subverting the country from within.[89]

The Kefauver hearings helped usher in an era in which televised inquiries into Communism, organized crime, or other threats to society were to become a popular novelty, their potential underscored by phenomenal viewer ratings and simultaneous, often sensationalized, press coverage. Viewed on one's home screen, these events offered vivid realism as well as "leading men" like Senator Kefauver or later the handsome young congressional counsel Robert Kennedy, juxtaposing them with underworld figures straight from central casting named "Machine Gun," "Tony Cheese," or "Crazy" Joey Gallo, the latter a New York labor enforcer who told Kennedy the rug in his Washington office "would be nice for a crap game."[90] No doubt to a nation grown weary of the pursuit of Communists, the more straightforward struggle of Good versus Evil in the form of members of Congress questioning criminals and corrupt union bosses came as something of a relief; executives of the new medium of television were delighted to find that such civic-minded programming garnered high ratings, as 20 million Americans were believed to have watched some of the Kefauver extravaganza. Only one in five American households had televisions, but those who did not were found gathered on the sidewalks outside stores where owners had placed television sets in the windows. The hearings' dramatic high point came when Frank Costello, a ranking New York mobster closely affiliated with Lucky Luciano and Meyer Lansky, refused to testify before television cameras; a compromise was worked out by which the camera would show only Costello's hands as he spoke, but the effect was, if anything, more chilling. "The result was both sinister and mesmerizing," writes historian T. J. English. "Millions of people in cities large and small became addicted to Costello's testimony, which on television consisted of a voice and hands."[91]

The link between organized crime and the longshoremen's union of New York was central to both Malcolm Johnson's and Estes Kefauver's work, and of course raised uncomfortable questions about organized labor generally. It was Robert Kennedy who would investigate this connection more closely. The inquiry he led, known as the McClellan Committee after its chairman, Senator John L. McClellan of Arkansas, was sparked by an incident in New York City on the evening of April 5, 1956, when *New York Post* labor columnist Victor Riesel, who had just left Lindy's Steak House, was attacked by a group of men who tossed acid in his face. The assault came only a few days after Riesel had published a column criticizing New York's trucking and clothing industries for alleged connections to organized crime; Riesel had named John Dioguardi, known as Johnny Dio, a union officer and racketeer in the garment business who'd already done a stint at Sing Sing, as one of the more prominent culprits in the scheme.

Convinced that Dio had hired the hoodlums who had attacked him, Riesel appeared on the network television program *Meet the Press* wearing sunglasses to protect his injured eyes from the studio lights, and bravely related what had happened to him on the sidewalk outside Lindy's. Alluding to the protracted inquiry by Senator Joseph McCarthy into alleged Communist influence in America, Riesel asked why it was that a government committee could investigate a foreign threat such as Communism and not a serious homegrown one like labor racketeering. The vicious attack he described on national television stirred anger, prompting public figures including Vice President Richard Nixon and New York attorney general Jacob Javits to denounce the criminal underworld responsible for it. Talk spread in Congress of an inquiry into labor corruption and legislation to curtail it, while President Eisenhower appealed to the AFL-CIO to make necessary reforms.

George Meany was quick to respond, vowing that "just as we have defeated the enemies without, who tried so desperately to destroy the labor movement, so will we defeat the enemies from within whose wrongdoing can undermine the effectiveness of everything we are trying to accomplish."[92] The AFL-CIO's Ethical Practices Committee was ordered to expand its staff to confront the dilemma, as others braced to deal with what loomed as a major public image crisis for the federation and all organized labor.

It was Clark Mollenhoff, a lawyer and investigative reporter for the *Des Moines Register-Tribune*, who approached Robert Kennedy about the possibility of following up on Riesel's suggestion for a formal inquiry into labor racketeering.[93] Kennedy was then serving as counsel to the Senate Permanent Committee on Investigations, which had been recently looking into corruption on the part of suppliers and low-level government officials in the clothing-procurement system of the armed forces. The clothing inquiry had already revealed the participation of gangsters in the making and shipping of military uniforms, and Mollenhoff suggested to Kennedy that it might be possible to redirect the committee's efforts to labor-related corruption.

Mollenhoff outlined for Kennedy the legal rationale for such a probe. By law, labor unions were required to submit annual financial accounts to the secretary of labor; but the reporting was very hit-or-miss and often incomplete; the Labor Department lacked the will and the manpower to scrutinize these submissions in any detail. All information the reports held was considered confidential, unavailable to the public. Mollenhoff suggested, however, that as union financial holdings were tax-exempt funds, any potential inconsistencies could be viewed as questionable dealings of interest to the government, and that an inquiry into the administration of these funds would be well within the purview of the committee since its mandate was to investigate government waste and malfeasance.

Kennedy was intrigued by the idea. He had been a key aide and Senate staff investigator for the long-running anti-Communist probe headed by Senator McCarthy. While he admired McCarthy as a person, he had, along with the rest of the country, become disenchanted with McCarthy's methods, and in any case by summer 1956 the zeal for hunting real or imaginary Communists in the federal government appeared to have exhausted itself. With McCarthy it had never been clear if he was sincere in his demands for reform, or simply attracted by the oversized megaphone his investigative powers gave him. With Kennedy there was no such question. A devout Catholic and ardent patriot who believed the country had a duty not to look away from its own lapses in judgment or conduct, the young congressional counsel was as close as Washington came to a bona fide moral crusader. He agreed to turn his scrutiny toward organized labor.

His first step was to visit several cities where labor corruption had been reported; accompanying him was former FBI agent and accounting expert Carmine Bellino. Kennedy and Bellino, on Mollenhoff's advice (and benefiting from the advice of tipster Eddie Cheyfitz, a disgruntled former Teamsters' publicity agent), focused primarily on the International Brotherhood of Teamsters, with 1.6 million members the nation's largest trade union, and on meeting journalists and police knowledgeable about its activities. In the course of their travels, Kennedy heard enough tales of extortion, thievery, and violence to more than confirm the claims he'd heard; indeed he was shocked. According to historian Thaddeus Russell, Kennedy saw the evidence of corruption touching the labor movement as so extensive as to represent "a crisis of both manhood and spirituality in American society." Organized labor, "a movement of the righteous poor," Kennedy realized, had been thoroughly infiltrated "by men who were degraded and emasculated by the sin of covetousness."[94]

More important than Kennedy's outrage at this early stage of the inquiry were the unique skills of his traveling companion. For Bellino, a table full of canceled checks, ledgers, and scraps of paper offered a forensic key to Teamsters wrongdoing, and the accountant confirmed to Kennedy that deceit and phony transactions appeared to abound. However, as a veteran of several federal investigations into large companies or organizations that cooked their books, he knew it could be difficult to tie the suspicious financial data to specific individuals, or to get such persons to incriminate themselves or others in the limited prosecutorial atmosphere of a congressional hearing. "Unless you are prepared to go all the way, don't start it," Bellino cautioned as the men flew home to Washington. "We're going all the way," Kennedy replied.[95]

THE FIRST TARGET OF the probe was Teamsters president Dave Beck, the former head of the union's Western Conference who had taken over the IBT in 1952 from the union's aging founder, Daniel J. Tobin. The legendary "Old Danny Boy" having held office for forty-five years, Beck found plenty of room for innovation; he introduced new management methods, pumped up membership rolls, and offered a personal style far different from his venerable predecessor, becoming, as New York columnist Murray Kempton observed, "the first national labor leader who unashamedly talks the language of a Chamber of Commerce secretary."[96] With $5 million from the Teamsters treasury, Beck oversaw construction of an impressive new five-story union headquarters in Washington with a five-hundred-seat theater, extra-large meeting rooms, and an office for its top executive that struck Kennedy, upon his initial visit, as being "as big as it possibly could have been without being an auditorium."[97] Not for nothing, it appeared, had Beck become known to Teamsters rank and file as "His Majesty, the Wheel."

Kennedy and Bellino suspected Beck of playing fast and loose with union funds, making questionable purchases, often by siphoning money through a Chicago labor relations intermediary named Nathan W. Shefferman, a longtime union-buster for Sears, Roebuck and Company. Beck had spent union money on everything from home appliances to boats, as well as lavish renovations to his family's house in Seattle; one set of receipts indicated he had dipped into Teamsters' coffers to pay for kneesocks and a bow tie. In another instance he had looted money from a memorial fund that had been established to support the widow of a close colleague. The only explanation for such wanton abuse of trust, Kennedy concluded, was that Beck was "motivated by uncontrollable greed."[98]

Instead of using the standing Senate Permanent Committee on Investigations to examine abuses in organized labor, the Senate had created a new panel, the Senate Select Committee on Improper Activities in the Labor or Management Field, to be chaired by John L. McClellan of Arkansas and endowed with an appropriation of $350,000. Kennedy was chief counsel. In addition to McClellan, the other Democrats on board were Sam Ervin, Patrick McNamara, and John F. Kennedy, who joined reluctantly but at his brother's insistence in order to keep Strom Thurmond, "noted then, as later, for regressive views on all questions," off the committee.[99] Republicans included Irving Ives, Karl Mundt, Barry Goldwater, and Joseph McCarthy. It was Robert Kennedy, however, who was expected to lead the inquiry, which would be televised.

In early 1957, after Kennedy issued a subpoena for Beck to appear before the panel, the Teamsters president conveniently left the country to spend several weeks in the Caribbean—he claimed the extended vacation was for his wife's health—and when he finally presented himself in Washington it was only to refuse cooperation with the inquiry by invoking his Fifth Amendment right against self-incrimination. George Meany, with the concurrence of Walter Reuther, had warned that any union official taking the Fifth in order to evade the committee's questions would be expelled from the AFL-CIO, but Beck, by his stonewalling, seemed willing to incur Meany's disapproval. One day he invoked the amendment from the witness chair no fewer than sixty-five times. AFL-CIO executives were unamused, assuring reporter A. H. Raskin that "Beck will wish he were back before Senator McClellan by the time Meany finishes with him at the next council meeting."[100] What neither Beck nor his lawyers likely could have known, in that relatively innocent age of emerging mass media, was the extent to which invoking the Fifth Amendment repeatedly on television, before millions of viewers, amounted to a plea of guilty. Forced to resign his Teamsters' post, "His Majesty, the Wheel" was later convicted of grand larceny and tax evasion and sentenced to five years in a federal penitentiary.[101]

Beck would prove something of a mild tune-up for Kennedy and the McClellan Committee, for waiting in the wings—both to assume Beck's job and to sit in the Senate panel's witness chair—was James "Jimmy" Hoffa, one of the scrappiest characters in organized labor. The son of an Indiana coal miner who died when James was four, he and his family relocated to Detroit, where the young man left school after the seventh grade to work on the loading dock of a grocery warehouse. He led his first strike at age nineteen and ultimately brought his three-hundred-man union into Teamsters Local 299. Eventually heading that local, Hoffa ascended rapidly in the Teamsters hierarchy, becoming a protégé of Farrell Dobbs, one of the leaders of the Minneapolis Teamsters strike of 1934 who, as a national IBT official, had been instrumental in extending Teamsters membership to long-haul truck drivers. In an era when long-distance freight transport was leaving the railroads for trucking, this policy had added tens of thousands of members to the Teamsters' ranks even as it displeased Dan Tobin, who considered the Dobbs-led expansion as little more than "chartering the riffraff." Dobbs's efforts were in step with the all-inclusive mood of 1930s industrial unionism, however, and he had the support of younger colleagues such as Hoffa.

The expansion gave the Teamsters enormous organizing strength, because by controlling over-the-road trucking as well as local delivery-men and warehousemen, they could essentially bring local, regional, or even national commerce to a halt. "I don't care what kind of strike you've got," Hoffa once remarked. "Once you organize the road, the city, the warehouses, nobody can whip the Teamsters, nobody."[102] Hoffa had been investigated in the 1940s for strong-arm operations involving Detroit milk truck drivers, jukebox businesses, and vending machine firms, but that had barely slowed him down. His and Dobbs's efforts to grow the Teamsters had led to such expansive membership growth, the IBT's welfare and pension funds grew to almost $250 million, making the Teamsters the largest, wealthiest union in America.

Hoffa was also no stranger to Capitol Hill, having recently been the subject of a House investigation led by Representatives Clare Hoffman of Michigan and Wint Smith of Kansas into the misuse of some of those vast IBT resources. It was alleged that Hoffa, in a bid to gain entrée to Chicago's powerful criminal underworld, had handed management of a Teamsters Health and Welfare Fund to a start-up insurance agency run by Allen and Rose Dorfman, relations of Paul "Red" Dorfman, a suspected organized crime figure who headed a large Chicago trash haulers' union. The Dorfmans, who prior to receiving the Teamsters fund had no experience in insurance, reaped as much as $3 million in fees and commissions from the fund, half of which came from overbilling and excessive fees.

The Hoffman-Smith inquiry was mysteriously terminated before it could complete its work, probably under pressure from the Republican Party, which was eager to win IBT support for an upcoming election in Michigan, but it succeeded in creating the distinct impression that there was something unwholesome about the Teamsters. The exposure also introduced Jimmy Hoffa to the nation as a tough-talking, probably corrupt urban unionist. But what differentiated him from other compromised labor leaders was his style and popularity. No allegation of wrongdoing seemed capable of diminishing his star, particularly as far as the Teamsters rank and file was concerned. Unlike the aristocratic and remote Dave Beck, or the irreproachable "founding father," Daniel Tobin, Hoffa was a mid-twentieth-century workingman's workingman, at home in the company of the most road-hardened drivers; his brashness, and the fact that his success had been self-made, endeared him to his followers. The grueling legal problems he encountered, even as they exposed his abuse of his membership's trust, seemed to only inspire greater devotion.

Hoffa came up for scrutiny by the McClellan Committee due to his connection to Johnny Dio, the New York garment business racketeer suspected of ordering the assault on Victor Riesel. Dio was believed to have helped Hoffa maintain paper locals in New York City—local unions with no actual members that were used to swing control of union elections. When Dio himself arrived at the Capitol to testify, he managed to make headlines before uttering a word. Irritated when news photographers came too close to snap his picture, he erupted in anger, striking one of them and demanding, "Don't you know I have a family?" A photograph of Dio, arm cocked, cigarette hanging from his lips, looking cruelly arrogant and abundantly more gangster than labor leader, ran in the nation's newspapers the next day. It was an exceedingly poor advertisement for the image of organized labor.[103]

Hoffa, in contrast to the excitable Dio, exuded confidence as he took the witness stand to face Kennedy's questions. He knew the committee had limited authority and that, like the Hoffman-Smith investigation, its findings would either be marginalized by backroom political maneuvering or it would simply run out of steam. Television cameras notwithstanding, most of America, Hoffa believed, would not have any sustained interest in the bookkeeping practices of a truckers' union.

I N 1951, IN AN ATTEMPT TO CAPITALIZE on the popularity of the televised Kefauver hearings, Movietone News wove together some of the more sensational excerpts from the hearings and released a fifty-two-minute theatrical film titled *The Kefauver Crime Investigation*. Box office results were unimpressive, an early lesson for movie executives of television's superior ability to capture live reality. Hollywood, however, would have the final say, for a film version of the New York longshoremen's corruption saga Malcolm Johnson had uncovered, *On the Waterfront* (1954), directed by Elia Kazan and starring Marlon Brando, became one of the decade's most acclaimed and successful movie releases. In telling a story taken from the day's headlines, screenwriter Budd Schulberg crafted a vivid morality play about an imperfect but decent workingman, dockworker Terry Malloy (Brando), struggling against a union leadership turned to greed and brutality. Loyal to his friends among the longshoremen but bitter about the heavy-handed tactics of union boss Johnny Friendly, played by Lee J. Cobb and based on the character of Johnny Dio, Malloy ultimately shuns the corrupt waterfront and testifies to a government commission.

Using the piers and factories of Hoboken, New Jersey, as his backdrop, Kazan captured the grit and moral precariousness of the longshoremen's world, one of kickbacks, shakedowns, pilferage, and racketeering, where violence and intimidation upheld a frontier hierarchy. Yet *On the Waterfront* suggests an essential purity to workingmen and organized labor, and offers a parable of redemption. Malloy eventually works up the courage to confront Friendly, cleansing himself of the evil that has insinuated itself in the union; he takes a brutal beating from Friendly's goons, but then, in a Christlike allegory, manages to stand and walk haltingly, but resolutely, toward his job, leading his fellow workers.

The film was a popular and especially a critical success, winning no fewer than eight Academy Awards and compelling further attention to the need to root out the cancer destroying American labor unions. One fan of the film was Robert Kennedy, who likely identified with the film's moralizing priest, Father Barry (Karl Malden), who seeks to guide the confused Terry Malloy.[104]

A less acclaimed film in a similar vein was the noir feature *Slaughter on Tenth Avenue* (1957), in which a young district attorney, William Keating (Richard Egan), who bore a distinct physical resemblance to Bobby Kennedy, attempts to penetrate the secret world of waterfront labor racketeers. The story was based on the 1947 killing of stevedore Andy Hintz by racketeer John "Cockeye" Dunn, who went to the electric chair for the crime. Keating—whose name was that of an actual New York district attorney helpful to Malcolm Johnson's reportage—attempts to prosecute the murder of Solly Pitts (Mickey Shaughnessy), a respected dock leader who had dared defy the hoodlums preying on his labor union. Venturing onto the troubled docks, Keating doesn't hesitate to use his fists to advance the cause of justice; his greater struggle is to convince Pitts's widow and his own supervisors to find the courage to stand up against the influence of the waterfront gangs and testify against them in court. The more profound danger to America is not criminal racketeers and weak labor unions, *Slaughter on Tenth Avenue* teaches, but society's apathy and fear.

Like the heroes of these labor corruption films, Robert Kennedy found himself in a fierce struggle with an intractable union boss, a man who seemed to operate with few morals beyond tribal fealty and who used the power he had attained to game and misuse the system. "[Hoffa] plainly regarded capitalism as a racket that the strong manipulated to their own advantage," Kennedy's biographer, Arthur Schlesinger Jr., suggests, "a system in which everyone was on the take, morality was bullshit and no holds were barred."[105] Hoffa returned Kennedy's deep enmity in full, referring to him as a friendless person, a bully, "a spoiled brat," someone who "never had to work, wouldn't know how to work,"[106] a "curly-headed smart-aleck."[107]

Hoffa was ordinarily too slick an operator to be caught red-handed, but his curiosity about just what information Kennedy had on him led him to make a fateful stumble. In early 1957 he approached John C. Cheasty, a former member of the Secret Service, and offered him a "salary" of $2,000 per month if he could obtain a job with the McClellan Committee in order to tip Hoffa off about what witnesses the government had lined up, and to feed Kennedy information that would help doom Dave Beck, whom Hoffa was eager to succeed as Teamsters boss. Cheasty, whose character Hoffa had obviously misjudged, promptly reported the proposal to Kennedy. The FBI then managed to photograph Hoffa on March 13, 1957, appearing to hand a payoff to Cheasty in Washington's Dupont Circle, leading to Hoffa's arrest on bribery and conspiracy charges.

When the case came to trial, Hoffa claimed that he thought he was paying Cheasty for legal services, not a bribe. Recognizing the vulnerability of that argument, Hoffa's defense team pursued a bold secondary strategy—targeting the jury, which was two-thirds African American, by importing boxing legend Joe Louis, who knew Hoffa from Detroit, to show support for the defendant; they also added to the defense table Martha Jefferson, a black attorney. Hoffa already had substantial support in the African American community, as he was known for having opposed segregation in the IBT. In a flip, overconfident moment during the trial, Kennedy had told reporters that he would "jump off the Capitol" if Hoffa was acquitted. When the jury voted to do just that, Joe Louis, asked by an intermediary to give an autograph for one of Kennedy's sons, replied, "I'll give it to you for his son, but not for him. Tell him to go take a jump off the Empire State Building."[108]

In the McClellan Committee hearings it proved difficult to get Hoffa to admit to anything, as he feigned a lack of recall—what Senator Ives termed "the most convenient forgettery"—or made long, time-consuming responses that led nowhere and that were evidently meant to get television viewers to switch the channel. As in Dave Beck's appearance, however, Kennedy's airing of the government's many suspicions about Hoffa on television was sufficient to raise questions about the union boss, the

Teamsters, and organized labor as a whole. It didn't hurt that Kennedy's television presence contrasted favorably to Hoffa's.[109]

Of particular embarrassment for the leading Teamster was the interrogation's exposure of his apparent use of union funds to back a crooked land development scheme in Florida, one that purported to benefit rank-and-file retirees. In the mid-1950s, Hoffa and other Teamster executives had pitched to members the prospect of buying plots of land in a retirement village known as Sun Valley outside Orlando. As part of what became an increasingly shady arrangement, Hoffa took half a million dollars from a Detroit IBT local and used it for collateral on a Florida bank loan to the "developer," a Teamsters official named Henry Lower, who had had earlier entanglements with the law. In exchange, Lower, who had affixed the honorific "Colonel" to his own name, was to make almost half of the plots available to Hoffa privately at a steep discount.

Brochures were created touting Sun Valley as the "Teamsters' Model City of Tomorrow," where union members and their families might retire in dignity and among friends. But Colonel Lower frittered the loan away without actually making Sun Valley habitable. Sewers, electricity, and other infrastructure were nonexistent; some lots remained submerged underwater. "Nothing had been done to put the property in shape," reported a developer who saw the half-finished project. "There were a few houses built there, and a short road of about 2,000 feet. But there was no possibility for the purchasers to get to their property. There was nothing there."[110] Hoffa had delved into real estate speculation with funds not his own, cutting himself in for a handsome share of the profits; but when the developer proved inept and the deal went bad, the Florida bank kept the collateral, which was money that had belonged to the union members. The McClellan Committee's condemnation of this subterfuge could not have been more sweeping, warning that "if Hoffa is unchecked he will successfully destroy the decent labor movement in the United States."[111]

Yet, even as the scrutiny of Hoffa and his "Hoodlum Empire" intensified, his personal popularity among the Teamsters swelled. In a speech to the membership, Hoffa compared himself to Samuel Gompers, William

Green, and Philip Murray, leaders of workingmen who had also been denigrated by forces hostile to labor, but had never surrendered. Whether his listeners accepted such wayward comparisons, or simply admired their leader's cocky spirit, most were satisfied with Hoffa and rallied around him. "He speaks the Teamsters language," labor consultant Nathan Shefferman later recalled, explaining Hoffa's unique stature:

> At Teamsters' assemblies he moves about, throwing a stinging
> blow to the biceps of one, wrestling a headlock on another. . . . I
> think he would take a collect call from any rank and filer in
> the land. . . . John L. Lewis firmly believed that playing the
> role of craggy, lonely giant on the mountaintop was an asset.
> Dave Beck . . . was shy and ill at ease with other than intimates.
> Dan Tobin's bellowing raised a storm in which he was nearly
> inaccessible. Walter Reuther is the cool intellectual. . . . Jimmy
> Hoffa is the single leader who appears to enjoy the mass as
> individuals.[112]

As Hoffa assured his followers, "I have given 25 years of my life to fighting for this union. I have fought for what I believe is right and good against forces more vicious than you can imagine. I propose to continue that fight as long as I live."[113]

HOFFA'S BLUSTER HARDLY TYPIFIED the union movement's overall reaction to the McClellan Committee's revelations. Allegations of criminal behavior magnified by television and print media, hearings that spread over three years and 1,526 witnesses, and created 46,510 pages of testimony—this was a public besmirching that went well beyond the innuendo and even the arrests and deportations of the Red Scare years. Congress's discoveries had been so extensive—rampant corruption, racketeering, bossism in union leadership, violence, alliances with known gangsters, as well as examples of pure theft like Hoffa's Sun Valley fiasco—that even without the cooperation of many subpoenaed witnesses, the McClellan Committee hearings had rung down on the head of U.S. labor a most searing, and time would prove enduring, public arraignment.

Robert Kennedy had managed to make the unholy nexus of organized crime and labor corruption loom very large, and he had been adamant about sharing his concern with the public. "Either we are going to be successful, or they are going to have the country,"[114] he had warned in no uncertain terms, echoing the McClellan Committee's own estimation that "because of the tremendous economic power of the Teamsters . . . the underworld [will be] in a position to dominate American economic life."[115] Both in his role as chief counsel to the Senate labor investigation, and later as attorney general, Kennedy would take the lead in not only pursuing organized crime but in framing the perception of it as a major danger akin to Communism. "The gangsters of today work in a highly organized fashion and are far more powerful now than at any time in the history of the country," he wrote in *The Enemy Within*, his memoir of the era. "They control political figures and threaten whole communities. They have stretched their tentacles of corruption and fear into industries both large and small. They grow stronger every day."[116]

The negative image that had long haunted labor was that it was radical or socialistic; now, ironically, even as the movement had struggled to defeat such impressions by publicly denuding itself of Communist influence, and striking at its manifestations elsewhere, it had been blindsided by attacks that linked it with something tawdrier, a sin even more offensive. Radicalism, after all, for all its perceived menace, was an external, alien threat; it involved foreign concepts of social and economic organization that idealistic labor activists at times might be foolish enough to embrace. The idea of corruption in labor unions, however, cut deeper because it was a homegrown failure, a violation of democracy and of Americans' own virtuous self-image.

Somewhat lost in all the statements of righteous denunciation about labor's having lost its way was the fact that, despite the glaring examples of bad behavior, the labor movement as a whole was *not* corrupt. But the revelations of the McClellan Committee, perhaps because they had not disappointed Americans so much as confirmed what they already suspected about labor unions, were devastating to public opinion. Would people forgive, or instead lose faith altogether in organized labor? Certainly some forces would not hesitate to press for that conclusion. "American labor had better roll up its sleeves," Walter Reuther advised.

> It had better get the stiffest broom and brush it can find, and the strongest disinfectant, and it had better take on the job of cleaning its own house from top to bottom and drive out every crook and gangster and racketeer we find. Because if we don't clean our own house, then the reactionaries will clean it for us. They won't use a broom, they'll use an axe.[117]

No one resisted the staining of labor's reputation more fiercely than George Meany, who led his executive council in 1957 in booting the Teamsters out of the AFL-CIO along with two other suspect unions, the Bakery and Confectionery Workers and the Laundry Workers. Chasing the IBT, with its huge membership, out of the federation, was an enormous step; but there were political ramifications as well. The cooperation between Meany and Walter Reuther during the McClellan hearings, and their like response in pursuing corrective actions, served to bond both men to Robert Kennedy, thus deepening labor's entrenchment with the Democratic Party and swinging its support behind John F. Kennedy's run for president in 1960. The Teamsters would align with the Republican candidate, Vice President Richard Nixon.

As a gesture to the Republican-faithful Teamsters, conservatives on the McClellan Committee set out to score some petty political points against Walter Reuther and the Kennedy brothers before the panel wrapped up its business. They had watched helplessly as Bobby Kennedy flayed Jimmy Hoffa's reputation (the Teamsters leader would ultimately go to prison in 1967 on jury tampering and pension fraud convictions); now they sought a turn at sullying the name of the country's leading labor do-gooder; they would make Walter Reuther *their Hoffa*. Hoffa himself assisted this effort by passing along potentially damaging information about the UAW, involving allegations that the autoworkers' union had used underhanded tactics in a strike at Kohler, a plumbing supply manufacturer in Sheboygan, Wisconsin. Republican senator Barry Goldwater of the committee, who had assured a Republican dinner in 1958 that "Walter Reuther and the UAW-CIO are a more dangerous menace than Sputnik,"[118] was so pleased by the chance to "get" the Kennedys by exposing Reuther, he declared himself "as happy as a squirrel in a little cage."[119] Reuther, bracing for Goldwater's inquiry, fired a preemptive shot by describing the Arizona conservative as America's "number one political fanatic, its number one anti-labor baiter, its number one peddler of class hatred."[120]

When the McClellan Committee looked into the Kohler situation, it found a company with a long history of labor abuses and violence dating back to the 1930s, a poor record of plant safety, and a tradition of executive opposition to worker organization. In 1954, UAW pickets had closed the Sheboygan plant for two months, at which point the owner obtained an injunction under Taft-Hartley and imported scabs. The strike dragged on amid charges that scabs were being harassed by workers, and vice versa. The most serious accusation leveled against Reuther was that two auto unionists from Detroit had traveled to Wisconsin and, on instructions from the UAW local, had assaulted two replacement workers as well as the elderly father of one of them who attempted to intervene on his son's behalf. The attacks were particularly savage; both scabs required hospitalization and the older man subsequently died.

Reuther condemned the violence unequivocally and assured the committee the attacks had not been authorized or ordered by the UAW, nor could anyone produce evidence that they had. Goldwater and his allies then turned to red-baiting Reuther and his brother Victor, producing a letter sent home from Russia in 1934 by the youthful pair that only a zealous conservative like Goldwater could construe as urging the spread of Communism in America. It was a thin reed on which to indict the reputation of so popular a man as Walter Reuther.

Content to have inflicted at least some damage by innuendo, and recognizing that their effort to besmirch Reuther had probably gone as far as it could, the Republicans moved quickly to pull the plug on the inquiry, but Robert Kennedy insisted Reuther be allowed to testify in order to clear his name. Reuther ably defended the UAW's efforts in the protracted strike at Kohler, and at one point made the inquiring senator from Arizona look sheepish by reversing the questioning in such a way as to reveal Goldwater's faulty comprehension of the Taft-Hartley Act. Kennedy's investigator Carmine Bellino, having examined several years' worth of Reuther's income tax returns, then testified that the UAW boss was one of the most squeaky-clean senior executives in the country, meticulously managing his business expenses so that no personal costs were applied to his union and regularly contributing his speaking honoraria to charity.[121] In the end the attempted ambush of Reuther fell flat; Kohler was chastised by the NLRB for unfair labor practices; while the McClellan Committee, as well as the American viewing public, was left with the only possible conclusion: "The Hoffas, who supported the business system, were, alas, crooked," notes Schlesinger. "The Reuthers, who criticized it, were, alas, honest."[122]

Of course conservatives hardly came away empty-handed. The McClellan hearings had stirred a groundswell of support on Capitol Hill and in the mainstream press for new legislation to stem union corruption, especially the abuse of welfare and pension funds. Given what the country had seen and heard over the past three years, labor leaders had no choice but to sign on to the need for such legislation, while conservatives crowed at being presented a new mandate to restrict unions' sphere of activity. Senator John F. Kennedy led Democrats in proposing a bill aimed at limiting the autocracy of union officers by standardizing the elections that placed them in power. Senator McClellan added provisions by which union members could, in cases of apparent operating malfeasance, sue union brass.

But Goldwater demanded more. Eventually the milder Kennedy legislation was shunted aside in favor of a bill sponsored by Democrat Philip Landrum of Georgia and Republican Robert Griffin of Michigan, soon known as the Landrum-Griffin Act. It retained many features of the Kennedy proposal but included stronger safeguards for democratic procedures within unions and for the management of union treasuries, held out criminal prosecution for union officials who abused employee health and pension funds, and decreed that anyone leaving prison could not be a union official for five years. Landrum-Griffin also placed new restrictions on secondary boycotts and picketing—specifically, it closed a loophole in Taft-Hartley that had allowed the Teamsters to corner recalcitrant employers by refusing to carry their freight—and permitted some local labor disputes to be resolved by the states, not the NLRB. Warnings from labor-sympathetic newspapers that union rights and the ability to strike were at risk of being legislated away proved futile, for it was this tougher version of the bill that sailed to passage in Congress and went to the desk of President Eisenhower. As for organized labor, having been publicly examined, poked, probed, and diagnosed as ailing, it could, with the signing of the Landrum-Griffin Act in September 1959, do little but swallow its medicine.[123]

CHAPTER TEN

IF AMERICA'S SOUL
BECOMES POISONED

THE 1960S SUBJECTED NEARLY EVERY INSTI-
tution and all that was conventional in American life to scrutiny and reevaluation; the labor
movement was no exception. In the decade between
the first Southern civil rights lunch-counter sit-in in
1960 to the defeat of peace candidate George McGovern in the election of 1972, the traditional workingman's query—"Which side are you on?"—came to
apply to more than the inevitable struggle between
labor and capital, but to divisive issues of social justice, racism, patriotism, and foreign policy. Was organized labor a forward-looking movement anymore?
Did it still stand with the forces of social change? And
if not, what was it, and what was it to become?

Unions could certainly take pride in what they
had achieved, in having made a difference in the way
all Americans lived. Yet along the way, particularly
after the troublesome big coal, steel, and rail strikes
of the late 1940s and early 1950s, and the congressional corruption inquiries, organized labor had begun
to appear less a movement of workers agitating from
below than another privileged interest maneuvering

for advantage. The emergent civil rights movement, by setting a high bar for those who would consider themselves true spokesmen for the underrepresented, tacitly challenged the position of unions as the leading agents of social change. Workingmen and -women still filed through factory gates each morning, punched their time cards at stores, restaurants, and loading docks, or gathered in union meeting halls, but increasingly when people thought of organized labor, what came to mind were men in business suits who controlled vast sums of money and spent their days among other powerful elites. Perhaps the problem was that America's workers weren't "hungry" anymore; for decades they "fought for bread," activist Saul Alinsky observed, but now "they too sat down and ate cake."[1] The perception was that unions had settled on protecting what they already had, and no longer pushed for the amelioration of broader social inequities. Such impressions were not entirely accurate or fair, but were reflected in public opinion polling. A Gallup Poll in February 1957 had found that 76 percent of Americans had positive feelings about labor unions; by the mid-1960s, the approval rate had fallen to 50 percent, an integer that would continue to decline in the coming years.[2]

The loss in the perceived importance of unions was due in part to worker complacency made possible by a strong postwar economy. Technology had also played a role, diminishing the number of industrial jobs around which labor organizing was traditionally centered, and creating new white-collar occupations more associated with management than with labor. Taft-Hartley had excluded foremen and supervisors from labor-law coverage, which made workplace unity more difficult because fewer new jobs were blue-collar in character and more positions in the emerging service fields were designated as supervisory, meaning that a wide array of employees from bank tellers, insurance agents, and finance brokers to café managers and college professors were denied the right to unionize.[3] Of the approximately 22 million white-collar workers in America in 1965, only 10 percent belonged to unions. The impact of automation on the blue-collar workplace was likewise significant: long-unionized industries, such as mining, railroads, steel, and the large automakers, had all managed to lay off workers in the generation since the war without sacrificing productivity, a trend that was expected to grow. In 1964 President Lyndon Johnson predicted that by 1975 the nation would be capable of maintaining its present levels of production with 20 million fewer workers.[4]

Despite its obvious benefits, technology had historically been the bane of the American worker. Industrialization made the craft tradition virtually obsolete; then came multiple-loom systems and factory speed-ups; the mid-nineteenth century introduced interchangeable parts, and the early twentieth the assembly line. No wonder the legend grew of the mythic black railroader John Henry, who, in a bid to save his and his coworkers' jobs, challenged the boss's new steam-powered drill to a race. Henry beat the drill, only to collapse and die "with his hammer in his hand."[5] Millions of "John Henrys" would fall as the pace of technological change accelerated, as the age of steam and the coming of electricity gave way to electronics and atomic energy. Large corporations such as General Motors, DuPont, and General Electric opened research divisions in the early twentieth century whose main purpose was to create new innovations that drove production and advanced corporate profitability, but inevitably wreaked havoc with employees' lives and livelihoods.

Like other Americans, workers welcomed progress, sharing in the considerable national pride attached to innovations such as communications satellites, improved devices for treating and detecting disease, nuclear power, computers, and the competition for supremacy in outer space. And many joined their fellow countrymen in looking forward to new, laborsaving methods, or anticipated the opportunity to learn new skills. But for older workers and the unskilled in a time of rapid technological change, the fear of being replaced by a machine was all too real; while in some communities, businesses prepared to abandon older-technology plants altogether, in order to reconfigure with new automation elsewhere. Such pressures were often hard to deflect with traditional union negotiating, for automation came with the imprimatur of Progress; it was difficult to make the argument that an employer should eschew efficiency and decreased production costs in the interest of sustaining jobs that had become obsolete.

Not that people didn't try. The job of locomotive fireman was a position once integral to the operation of steam locomotives, but it had been superseded with the introduction of diesel locomotives beginning in the 1930s. As diesel replaced steam over the next two decades, many firemen were lost to attrition, yet in 1958 there were still thirty-two thousand locomotive firemen working at an estimated annual cost to the railroads of $200 million. Employers moved to reclassify and/or phase out the fireman's job, in some instances accusing those who held the position of featherbedding, the maintaining of a union-protected job that was unnecessary and required little or no effort. The firemen's brotherhood countered that his role was still essential, as he served as a critical extra pair of eyes and ears for the engineer, helping to avert derailments and collisions. This was important, the brotherhood pointed out, because railroads now ran fewer but longer trains, adding to safety concerns.[6] Management allowed that having a second pair of eyes and ears on passenger trains was valid as a safety measure, but that the advent of radio communication and innovations in locomotive design that allowed an engine to be controlled from either side meant two men were no longer required to drive a freight train or assemble trains in a yard. From the standpoint of publicity the union's fight for the firemen came off poorly, as it appeared in asking for the job's retention to be demanding special exemption from a modernizing, more efficient world.

A panel created by Congress to resolve the issue proposed that 90 percent of firemen's positions be phased out, but not without retaining longtime workers or offering comparable work and/or generous severance packages. When the rail unions balked, challenging the elimination of nineteen thousand jobs and the power of Congress to order compulsory resolution of the dispute, the case went to the Supreme Court, which upheld the commission's ruling. In reaction, a walkout was threatened by the nation's five railway unions. Only the direct involvement of President Johnson broke the logjam, the rail unions accepting in principle the end of the fireman's position in exchange for improved working conditions and the promise that the transition would be phased in gradually. A similar agreement took shape in the newspaper business, where linotype operators whose jobs were made obsolete by the introduction of computerized typesetting were guaranteed job and retirement security in exchange for unions agreeing to accept other changes in the workplace.[7]

As these kinds of negotiations suggested, the era of the 1950s and early 1960s differed from earlier periods of rapid technological transition in that anxiety about technology as a job-killer was more widely shared. Strike activity in the early 1960s was as low as during the era of the no-strike pledge of the Second World War, but when strikes did occur, as they did in the printing trades, among butchers, in aviation and aerospace, and in marine-related work, they tended to involve issues of displacement due to automation, retraining programs, job security, severance packages, and bonuses for early retirement.

Large firms such as General Electric and the Armour Meat Packing Company tried to preempt the difficulty with extensive worker retraining programs, and various states made similar efforts. The federal government had begun addressing the crisis in 1954 with the formation of the Office of Manpower Administration, an effort that carried over into the New Frontier era, culminating in the Manpower Development and Training Act of 1962, which assigned $35 million to assist technology-displaced workers. The attention to so sensitive a labor issue would bolster support from organized labor for both the Kennedy and the Johnson administrations.

While the labor movement may have lost a good deal of its fervency for reform, it identified with and embraced Johnson's major domestic initiatives, particularly his plans for what he termed the Great Society, aimed at improving basic living conditions for all Americans—in health care, housing, civil rights, and employment. The Great Society program mirrored a growing liberal concern for the widening gulf between rich and poor that had informed one of the era's most seminal books, Michael Harrington's *The Other America,* published in 1962. Harrington's account of the extensive poverty and need in America that lay hidden from view aroused indignation, much as had Jacob Riis's 1890 exposé of slum conditions, *How the Other Half Lives*. Readers closed Harrington's book with the conviction that the most affluent nation on earth could not walk into the future while substantial numbers of its population remained uneducated, unemployed, hungry, and desperate for decent housing.

The Voting Rights Act and Medicare, both enacted in 1965, and the Fair Housing Act of 1968 were aligned closely with labor's own historic concern for the fundamental economic and social vitality of working people. Especially meaningful was the breakthrough Equal Employment Opportunity Act, part of the Civil Rights Act of 1964, which laid assault to discrimination in the workplace and made $1 billion available specifically to develop young people's work skills for jobs created by new technology. A distinguishing feature of Johnson's social agenda was that, unlike the New Deal, which created large government programs to alleviate economic suffering, the Great Society aimed at empowering individuals through education, job training, and community programs and giving them options that they themselves would be required to act upon. Surely the most emotionally compelling part of Johnson's program was his "War on Poverty," which sought to address directly the crisis outlined by Harrington, that amid the tremendous affluence of American life at mid-century, pockets of extreme poverty still existed, a neglected subpopulation Harrington called "the invisible poor."

A S FAR AWAY FROM WASHINGTON as one could travel in the United States, in the fertile agricultural valleys of California, migrant Latino farmworkers were among those Americans struggling fiercely to become less "invisible." Historically among the country's most neglected laborers, the farmworkers sought to win the right to organize and bargain collectively from the state's powerful growers, who had long ignored or easily rebuffed such demands. This time the workers expected things to go differently; in addition to the Great Society reforms emanating from Washington, they could look to the dramatic inspiration of the Southern civil rights movement, and to the quiet determination of their own charismatic spokesman, César Chávez.

Seasonal fruit and vegetable picking—stoop labor, as it was known—had not been included in the collective bargaining regime of the New Deal because Southerners in Congress had influenced the legislation creating both the Wagner Act and Social Security to exclude agricultural and domestic labor, which at the time employed half of all African American workers. Three decades later pay and conditions for migrant workers remained abysmal; they had no guarantee of a job and benefited from no protective laws; even child labor was unregulated. The work itself—picking fruit or vegetables under a warm California sun—was backbreaking. "The workers hunch under the vines like ducks," reported journalist John Gregory Dunne. "There is no air, making the intense heat all but unbearable. Gnats and bugs swarm out from under the leaves. Some workers wear face masks; others, handkerchiefs knotted around their heads to catch the sweat."[8] The workers' camps adjacent to these "factories in the fields"—whether provided by the growers or improvised by the migrants themselves—had poor sanitation, inadequate toilets and showers, and often little provision for shelter or safe drinking water.[9]

For the better part of a century, regional crop and vineyard growers had successfully repulsed attempts at worker organization. Part of their clout came from the sheer size of their estates, some as large as three hundred thousand acres. Unlike large agricultural property elsewhere in America that often consisted of many former small family farms sewn together, California's extensive farm holdings were created by Mexican and Spanish land grants that predated the U.S. possession of California, as well as Gilded Age railroad landgrabs that carved parts of the state into vast estates. These large enterprises, which often remained intact over several generations, harvested tremendous annual tonnages of produce and required a steady supply of cheap labor—successive waves of Chinese, Japanese, South Asians, Mexicans, and Filipinos who toiled in the fields. The results of this kind of agricultural organization were insular fiefdoms that controlled the lives of the people who lived and worked on them and dominated local politics as well as the courts, sheriffs' offices, clergy, and the press—a civic culture with no parallel in the United States outside the plantation South or the Colorado coalfields of the early 1900s.

The repression the workers suffered was licensed in part by a useful caricature of them as carefree nomads who required such an authoritarian structure. "There was nothing you could do about these insouciant and lighthearted boys," wrote one historian of the early days in the fields. "You couldn't pay them a decent wage for they would drink it up right away. As for providing them with shelter or a bed—why, they loved the open air and would rather die than take a bath."[10] When the workers dared defy this stereotype, growers never hesitated to use the law and the threat of official or vigilante violence to maintain control. There was an intense local dislike of unionism, rooted in Southern California's history of being overrun by immigrant and transient job-seekers; while the Wobbly free speech battles, the 1910 *Los Angeles Times* bombing, the assault on a 1916 Preparedness Day parade in San Francisco, and the 1934 longshoremen's strike had conditioned public anxiety toward "radical" labor. In the case of the farmworkers there were also economic reasons to denigrate unionization, for although the work they performed was menial, its seasonal nature and the importance of bringing in each harvest in a timely manner made any disruption potentially ruinous; stoop labor was best kept "cheap and unorganized" in the Golden State.

An often-cited cause for vigilance was the state's experience with the IWW, which more than any other labor organization had succeeded at adapting to the migrants' own lifestyle. The Wobblies were held responsible for one of the deadliest outbreaks of farm labor violence in the state's history, a riot in the town of Wheatland in August 1913. The owner of the Durst Ranch, seeking to drive down wages, had intentionally advertised for far more pickers than he actually needed. Three thousand men, women, and children descended on the site, eager for work. Finding they'd been lied to, but believing some work might actually materialize, many remained—camping without adequate food, water, or sanitary facilities. Whole families were left to sleep on the open ground.

When Wobbly "agitators" organized a rally to protest the situation, the sheriff, his deputies, and the local district attorney arrived by car, accompanied by a legion of armed enforcers hired by the growers. Someone—it was never established who—fired a shot into the air, triggering a massive brawl as the workers, furious at their mistreatment, lashed out against the officials and vigilantes with knives, sticks, and fists. The "Wheatland Riot" ended with the district attorney, a deputy, and two workers killed, and dozens wounded on both sides. Hundreds of migrants were rounded up by police, and two men deemed to have been the insurrection's leaders and alleged to be IWW, Blackie Ford and Herman Suhr, were convicted of murder and sent to prison for life.[11] As a California newspaper had opined of the IWW, "Hanging is much too good for them. They are the waste material of creation and should be drained off into the sewer of oblivion, there to rot in cold obstruction like any other excrement."[12]

The fact that the newly settled Roosevelt administration in Washington was moving toward labor reforms in the early 1930s offered a glimmer of hope for the farmworkers. One small victory came in 1933 when Labor Secretary Frances Perkins dispatched her own representative, retired army general Pelham Glassford, to California. Glassford visited the small towns and fields, met with both growers and workers, and concluded that the underlying problem was that wages were too low. Acting on his own and with questionable legal authority, he presented to the growers what "the U.S. government" believed fair wages for farmworkers should be, and posted the information on broadsides pinned to walls and trees throughout the region. The "Glassford Wage," as it became known, was denounced by California conservatives including the reactionary governor James Rolph and largely ignored, but it did offer one of the first objective conclusions that workers were underpaid and put the growers on notice that the federal government was paying at least a modicum of attention to what went on in their hidden kingdom.[13]

A Communist-affiliated union allied with the CIO, the United Cannery, Agricultural, Packing, and Allied Workers of America, arrived in the harvest fields in the late 1930s to find the growers willing to use every weapon in their arsenal to stymie the union's progress, from scabs to court injunctions. A series of strikes brought vicious reprisals from a vigilante group calling itself the Associated Farmers of California who, concealing their identities behind masks, kidnapped strike leaders, subjected some to torture, and drove others out of the area at threat of death. Despite the use of such Ku Klux Klan–like tactics, investigating state authorities blamed the violence on United Cannery and arrested several of its leaders, squelching any further efforts at unionization. In 1940 the Associated Farmers would be heard from again, condemning the publication of John Steinbeck's revealing account of life in the harvest fields, *The Grapes of Wrath*.

During the Second World War, growers found themselves desperately short of labor as manpower was drawn out of the picking fields to defense work or the military, and thousands of Japanese harvesters were sent to internment camps. This led in 1942 to an informal pact between the United States and Mexico to allow seasonal non-American guest workers, known as braceros, to be recruited and transported across the border to assist with the harvest. The agreement stressed that braceros were to work at an arranged location and not remain in the United States in the off-season, restrictions often ignored by the growers, as was the pay scale assigned by the pact. Amid complaints from braceros of unpaid wages and inhuman treatment, growers began importing illegal laborers who were far less likely to complain and who, unlike the braceros, could be shifted from one picking assignment to another.

The availability of relatively cheap braceros and numerous illegal workers continued after the war, undermining union organizing. Not until 1954 did Washington address the problem, with President Eisenhower's creation of Operation Wetback, a military effort to locate undocumented Mexicans for deportation. A few years later the AFL-sponsored Agricultural Workers Organizing Committee (AWOC) asked Congress to insist that "the approximation of slave labor conditions which [the growers] have perpetuated will no longer be tolerated by this nation," and in 1964 the bracero program itself was formally terminated with further agitation from the AFL-CIO and other liberal reform elements.[14] That same year another blow was dealt the hegemony of the growers when the U.S. Supreme Court in *Reapportionment Cases* ruled that state legislative representation would be based on voting population as opposed to acreage, diminishing the power of rural counties in state assemblies. In California this meant that the burgeoning suburbs of Southern California would now gain electoral precedence over the rural agricultural regions, weakening the growers' traditional political clout.[15]

ONE REFORM GROUP AT WORK in the California harvest lands beginning in the early 1950s was the Community Service Organization (CSO), whose focus was on creating people power through voter registration efforts. The group took its inspiration from community organizer Saul Alinsky's theory that the poor and disenfranchised, if mobilized in significant numbers, could become a potent political force. In his *Reveille for Radicals*, a primer on grassroots organizing published in 1946 and used by a generation of activists, Alinsky warned that "if [people] continue inarticulate, apathetic, disinterested, forlorn and alone in their abysmal anonymity, then democracy is ended."[16] One young Mexican American drawn to the CSO's work was César Chávez, a migrant worker who had been born in Arizona in 1927. Chávez and his family had lost their land in the Depression and gone west to join the armies of migrant farmworkers working California's Imperial and San Joaquin valleys, picking greens, carrots, tomatoes, grapes, prunes, and cotton in a seasonal loop from Delano—about a half hour's drive north of Bakersfield—to San Jose, Sacramento, Fresno, and back again. The family eventually settled in a section of San Jose known as *Sal si Puedes* ("get out if you can"). César, the eldest son, helped his mother keep the family intact after his father was hurt in the fields and could no longer work. He joined the navy toward the end of World War II, returning to California to marry and raise a family.

In 1952 Chávez and his wife, Linda (they eventually had eight children), were living in a Mexican American neighborhood in Delano. A CSO staffer named Fred Ross sought out César, having heard he enjoyed a reputation as an informal community counselor, a man whose judgment was respected by his neighbors. Chávez was initially suspicious of the outsider—Anglo college students and social workers had flitted in and out of the local scene before—but he was impressed to learn that Ross had advocated for Mexican prisoners beaten by Los Angeles police in an infamous 1951 case known as "Bloody Christmas," in which the cops themselves were ultimately indicted. For his part, Ross was struck by Chávez's "kind of burning interest" in voter registration as a means of social change. "[César] made the connection very quickly between the civic weakness of [his Mexican American neighbors] and the social neglect of the barrio," Ross recalled, noting in his diary at the time, "I think I've found the guy I'm looking for."[17]

Chávez served CSO for a decade, becoming a paid staff member and eventually the organization's general director. In 1962, however, when he and a Latina colleague, Dolores "Lola" Huerta, expressed an interest in forming a farmworkers' union, the CSO informed them that labor organizing was outside the scope of the group's mission. Venturing off on their own, Chávez and Huerta launched the National Farm Workers Association (NFWA).

Chávez's organizing style was appropriately low-key. Favoring farm-workers' attire, never a business suit, he spoke plainly, without rhetorical flourishes, telling the workers their exploitation at the hands of the growers was their problem, and that only they could end it. He balanced intimate house meetings, where people would be free to talk, with occasional larger gatherings designed to make the attendees feel empowered by their numbers. The fledgling union made it a point to charge dues to inculcate a sense of ownership among members; and in order to demonstrate that the NFWA could deliver something of value, it offered numerous social services. A direct labor action was not planned, for Chávez and Huerta believed several years would be needed to build and fortify their union before confronting the growers. But events intruded on September 7, 1965, when an AWOC local of Filipino farmworkers staged a walkout against Delano grape growers over dismal wages. The local, led by Larry Itliong, turned to the NFWA for support. There was a history of ill will between Filipino and Mexican workers, and Chávez doubted his untested union was ready for a strike, but there was considerable pressure from his supporters to join the AWOC action. At issue were demands for a wage increase from $1.25 to $1.40 an hour and recognition of AWOC and the NFWA. At a meeting on September 20 Chávez submitted the question to the rank and file, who voted unanimously to join the struggle.

Rapidly gaining strength, the walkout soon involved five thousand workers on agricultural lands covering more than four hundred square miles; as it was increasingly a Mexican American strike, the NFWA and Itliong's AWOC chapter merged the following year into the United Farm Workers Organizing Committee (UFWOC), with Chávez as its leader.

Picketing agricultural concerns presented a unique challenge to strikers because the targeted farms were spread over so wide an area. One advantage they held, however, was that grapes required harvesting at a particular moment, so a strategically timed strike could inflict maximum damage; and because a grape crop required the attention of semiskilled workers ten months out of the year, the field hands tended to be more experienced, less migratory, and hence less replaceable. Nonetheless, the growers gave no sign of interest in working things out peacefully. They used tractors to kick up dust that would gag the picketers, fired guns over the strikers' heads, and, on one occasion, crop-dusted them from a low-flying airplane. They also utilized the local courts, obtaining an injunction so explicitly worded it forbade the picketers from shouting the word "Huelga!"—Spanish for "strike."

"The growers were giving us the knee and elbow," recalled Chávez, who was himself attacked by growers' thugs, "knocking us down and throwing us down. But we remained nonviolent. We weren't afraid of them. We just got up and continued picketing."[18] He had worried that his fellow strikers might turn and run before the growers' violent tactics, but the workers only seemed emboldened by the challenge, driven in their purpose by deeply felt grievances held too long in check. "The picket line is a beautiful thing," Chávez concluded, "because it does something to a human being."[19]

Another of Chávez's insights was to take a page from the Southern civil rights movement and counter the unified local opposition by appealing to forces outside the harvesting regions. He turned to the nation's most experienced protestors, the youthful members of the Student Nonviolent Coordinating Committee (SNCC) and Students for a Democratic Society (SDS), who had recently emerged from the cauldron of civil rights activism in the Deep South, as well as the Berkeley Free Speech movement. He traveled personally to the campuses of nearby Berkeley and Stanford to enlist the student activists, some of whom came to the picking regions to conduct workshops in nonviolent civil disobedience for the farmworkers.

Chávez, a devout Catholic, also benefited from the consistent interest of the Church, specifically its philosophy of liberation theology, the belief (only recently sanctioned by the Vatican) that priests and other church members had a duty to assist the poor in their struggle for economic and social justice. A migrant worker all his life, Chávez had something of an uneven education, but with the guidance of a local priest, Father Donald McDonnell, he devoured books about and by Mohandas Gandhi and Martin Luther King Jr. From his reading he took away the idea of framing the farmworkers' cause not as a mere labor dispute, but as a broad-based civil rights crusade, one that would include all the elements of a Gandhian campaign, such as marches, consumer boycotts, even fasting. McDonnell also shared with Chávez portions of the transcripts of the La Follette Committee Hearings held in Los Angeles in the 1930s, which revealed the underhanded techniques regional growers had used to ravage earlier farmworkers' movements. The consumer boycott would become a favored advocacy technique of the farmworkers, as the logistical difficulties of protesting in the fields and the too-ready availability of replacement workers made a traditional strike difficult.

In adopting satyagraha, or Gandhian nonviolence, Chávez was staking out new terrain for organized labor in the United States. Picketing, strike rallies, and sit-downs were in essence nonviolent means of protest, but American workers had at times instigated violence or, more often, reacted to it in kind. What was revolutionary about Chávez's approach—as it had been for Gandhi, King, and others—was that it was absolute. There was to be no violence, even in reaction to that fomented by others. While some practitioners of the method embraced nonviolence as a spiritual philosophy, others simply valued it as a useful tactic; what had been proven in the civil rights movement was that it could be a very effective strategy, compelling public interest, sympathy, and support. Another advantage was that it was not easily linked to Communism. Conservatives certainly didn't give up trying—Chávez was red-baited much as King had been—but the accusation of Communist influence simply proved impossible to make stick given the plainly indigenous character of the farmworkers and their cause.

Impressed by the exemplary nature of the campaign, both Walter Reuther of the UAW and Robert Kennedy, now a U.S. senator from New York, were drawn to California. Local growers watched this development with curiosity bordering on outrage. It was incomprehensible to them that a local movement of scruffy migrants had managed to enlist national political figures in their crusade. The growers knew Chávez as a perennial troublemaker; some still derided him as "that dumb Mex." Never had they expected he would be transformed into a Pied Piper to thousands of local farmworkers and attract powerful friends from Washington, as well as growing legions of volunteers and well-wishers from across the country. "You are making history here," Reuther assured a boisterous rally in Delano, announcing that the farm strike had the formal support of the AFL-CIO. "We will march here together, we will fight here together, and we will win here together."[20] Kennedy, who impaneled a hearing of the Senate Subcommittee on Migratory Labor while in town in order to hear local testimony, vowed that if America could dream of putting a man on the moon, it could manage to improve the lives of California farmworkers.

THE ALLIANCE BETWEEN ORGANIZED LABOR and the Democratic Party, forged in the decades since the Wilson administration and solidified by the New Deal and the Great Society, was about to face a critical test. It would arrive in the form of a tragedy in the sphere of foreign policy—Washington's decision to commit vast resources and the U.S. military to prop up the unstable government of South Vietnam, and to defend it as a bastion against the spread of Communism. President John F. Kennedy dispatched as many as fifteen thousand military advisers to guide and train the country's fledgling army; his successor, Lyndon Johnson, ultimately sent a half million American combat troops and ordered the aerial bombing of North Vietnam.

Supremely loyal to President Johnson was George Meany, leader of the AFL-CIO and for all intents and purposes the U.S. labor movement. He had been personally devastated by the death of President Kennedy, and had been deeply touched when President Johnson made it a point to reach out to him for help in guiding the reforms of the Great Society. Like other labor representatives, Meany welcomed those reforms as a "reincarnation of the verve and excitement of the New Deal,"[21] and was also pleased with Johnson's 1964 vice presidential choice, Hubert Humphrey, who possessed one of the most stellar pro-labor voting records in Congress. He concurred as well with Johnson's Vietnam policy, having been hawkish on the subject long before most Americans had heard of the distant country.

Johnson's escalation of the war, however, contained an inherent conflict for organized labor. Even as the war drained resources from Johnson's domestic programs, military-related spending boosted domestic manufacturing and created jobs. No one had forgotten that it had been the production buildup of the Second World War that had really ended the Great Depression, and a similar positive impact had been seen during the Korean War. Business spawned by the growing war in Vietnam was most visible on the West Coast, where numerous defense contractors were located and where shipping concerns and warehouses serviced what was known as the Vietnam Run, the busy trade lanes to U.S. military depots in Hawaii, the Philippines, and Southeast Asia. "Billions poured into war industries meant millions of jobs," notes historian Philip Foner. For organized labor, "the war was far away and jobs were a reality."[22]

Meany, who quickly emerged as Johnson's leading defender among

U.S. union heads, wanted to believe that the nation could afford both the war and the Great Society, a view that was tested when the White House cited escalating war costs in opposing a hike in the minimum wage from $1.25 to $1.60 per hour. Walter Reuther also backed the president's war, although he rejected the idea that job security at home in any way validated armed conflict. "What good is the General Motors pension plan," he asked, "if the whole world is engulfed in nuclear or catastrophic war?"[23] To see young men sacrificed in the rice paddies and mountains of remote Vietnam no doubt also grated on Reuther's fundamental optimism about the potential of America's youth. As early as 1956 he had suggested the organization that would, under President Kennedy, become the Peace Corps, saying, "The more young Americans are sent to the places in the world where people are hungry, and sent with slide rules and textbooks and medical kits . . . the fewer of our sons we will have to send with guns to fight Communism on the battlefields of the world."[24]

The initial anxiety that the North Vietnamese insurgency represented a bid to spread Communist rule throughout the region was soon compounded by the equally specious concern that the United States could not walk away from the conflict once it had become a proxy war for clashing East-West ideologies, a test of American will. Meanwhile, the choice of Vietnamese partners seemed characterized by the same arrogance and lack of scrutiny that had haunted previous foreign entanglements such as the 1954 American-engineered coup in Guatemala. The quagmire that Vietnam soon became was, in a sense, the bill that had come due for decades of reckless tinkering with the world in the name of anti-Communism. Perhaps Jay Lovestone and the CIA had always made it look too easy.

At home, slowly at first, there came a loosening of tongues. Elements within the labor movement were among the first to voice concern that the war in Vietnam had been hastily entered into and was a mistake. On February 24, 1965, Local 1199 of the Drug and Hospital Employees Union, which had a long history of challenging racial discrimination and other injustices, sent telegrams to President Johnson and New York senators Robert Kennedy and Jacob Javits, urging a peaceful settlement of "a war no one can win." Other unions came on board in the coming months—the Negro American Labor Council, the Missouri Teamsters, District 65 of the AFL-CIO, and members of the UAW. "Tell the president we don't like to be lied to," Emil Mazey, secretary-treasurer of the UAW, urged a student antiwar rally. "We were lied to by Ike on the U-2 over the Soviet Union, lied to by the Kennedy administration on the Bay of Pigs, and now LBJ says we are in Vietnam to defend democracy."[25]

Students also began to speak out. On March 24, 1965, the first antiwar teach-in, sponsored by SDS, was held at the University of Michigan at Ann Arbor, involving three thousand students and faculty; it lasted all night and culminated in an antiwar demonstration in the morning. Forty other colleges copied the format, and on May 15 a national teach-in was held over television and radio, with 110 colleges in thirty-five states participating. Of greater concern to the Johnson administration were the large public antiwar rallies, such as the SDS-led March on Washington to End the War on April 17 that brought fifteen thousand students, faculty, veteran civil rights protestors, and clergy to protest outside the White House. "I feel that the president responds to public opinion—look what he did on civil rights," observed a nineteen-year-old marcher, "and I want him to know that public opinion is behind him if he sees the possibility for negotiations."[26] On August 6, in commemoration of the twentieth anniversary of the dropping of the atomic bomb on Hiroshima, one thousand protestors, including folksinger Joan Baez and A. J. Muste, the eighty-year-old pacifist and labor militant, arrived in Washington. Calling themselves the Assembly of Unrepresented People, the group carried a petition calling on Americans of draft age to conscientiously refuse service in the military and to request a discharge if they were already in uniform.

Local 1199's opposition remained steadfast. In November 1965 it purchased an ad in the *New York Times* demanding a cease-fire in Vietnam, an end to the bombings of North Vietnam, and an effort to negotiate a settlement. By early 1966 it was joined by the Amalgamated Clothing Workers of America in condemning a war that, due to college draft deferments, was being fought largely by soldiers drawn from the working class, with blacks a proportionately high percentage. The jungles of Vietnam, it was said, had become "a poor man's graveyard."[27]

This latter issue was one that might have galvanized broad labor resistance to the war, but despite the activism of selected unions like 1199, the movement at large chose to step delicately. Anyone within labor's leadership ranks who criticized the war risked excommunication at the hands of Meany, who defended the conflict as necessary "for freedom to survive" and dismissed protestors as "academic do-gooders" and "apostles of appeasement." He cautioned AFL-CIO members that the White House foreign policy varied not an iota from that of the federation's executive council.[28] The debate came fully into the open at a December 1965 AFL-CIO gathering in San Francisco. Speeches in support of the war were heard from Meany, Vice President Hubert Humphrey, and Secretary of State Dean Rusk (who was loudly booed by college students in the balcony), as well as an official from the American Legion. The students, who were attending as observers from Berkeley and San Francisco State College, grew restless when it became apparent the convention leadership was intentionally avoiding an actual discussion of the war. They began to yell at the delegates below, calling them "Labor fakers" and admonishing them to "Get out of Vietnam." Some on the floor heckled back, shouting "Get a haircut!" or "Go to Russia and debate!" while Meany slammed the gavel, demanding, "Will the sergeant of arms clear these kookies out of the gallery."[29] Mazey, the UAW's outspoken secretary-treasurer who had emerged as his union's leading dissident voice on the war, used his turn at the podium to challenge the convention to rethink labor's position. Offering a quick summary of U.S. policy toward Vietnam since the Second World War, he pointed out that America, like earlier French occupiers, was exhibiting a reckless imperialism, and insisted that the rampart against Communism it had chosen to back in Vietnam was a flawed and corrupt puppet dictatorship. He demanded the AFL-CIO reverse course at once and come out for peace negotiations "so that we can bring this unhappy conflict to an end."[30] Meany immediately countered Mazey, insisting that while the French had been a colonial presence in Vietnam, the United States was there as a force of liberation, and that the "unhappy conflict" would end when the Communists stopped trying to take over Southeast Asia.[31]

For many who had been present it was the exchange of shouts and heckling that stood out, evidence of the widening gap between organized labor and student activists over Vietnam. It didn't help that most of the big trade unions' senior labor executive councils were truly *senior*—white men in their seventies or eighties, many of whom had retired or been relieved of their day-to-day union duties yet hung on as esteemed elders. Meany was a particular embarrassment, his cold war paranoia and dismissal of those who challenged him as "jitterbugs," "kookies," or "woo-woos" appearing outdated and even childish. Liberals and intellectuals who felt a sincere connection to the labor movement and labor history could not help but feel alienated. Of course the dynamic also functioned the other way: older union members, even those who disapproved of the war, could not countenance the more outlandish forms of activism the young people favored, which went so far as to disrespect the president and the country.

O N MARCH 7, 1966, 150 MEN AND WOMEN, mostly Mexican Americans but also some black and Anglo volunteers, along with a handful of nuns and priests, embarked with César Chávez on a three-hundred-mile march from Delano to the state capital in Sacramento. The marchers carried their own sleeping bags and held aloft an embroidered silk tapestry of Our Lady of Guadalupe, traditional defender of the poor, as well as American and Mexican flags and a wooden sign painted with the word the growers had forbidden, *"Huelga."* They also hoisted banners emblazoned with the thunderbird, "the NFWA's splendidly barbaric coat of arms," which was known among those hostile to the movement as "Chávez's Trotsky flag."[32] Despite a march of striking farmworkers across California being unprecedented, the event had a relaxed feel, less protest than religious pilgrimage—a *peregrinación*,

Chávez termed it—with some participants strumming guitars or playing accordions as they walked. The ultimate destination was the capital steps, where a rally would be held in hope of gaining the attention of California governor Edmund G. "Pat" Brown, who had thus far largely kept his distance from the workers' plight.

As the growers' arguments—that migrant workers were by nature carefree, did not want to be unionized, or were led by Communists—each failed in turn, their barbs had become increasingly hostile. "Chavez and his cohorts have imported the long-haired kooks, professional loafers, winos and dregs of society to carry their *Huelga* banners," one conservative leaflet asserted, suggesting the march was being stage-managed by outsiders.[33] A local newspaper accused the pickers of following blindly the teachings of big-city radicals. "Most of these people don't know who [Saul] Alinsky is," the article complained. "All they know is he's got a name like a bomb thrower."[34] At times the vehement resistance appeared motivated less by the NFWA's specific demands than by the sense among growers that their honor was at stake. "What Chavez was challenging was a way of life," Dunne notes. "A heady history of casually breaking farm strikes had given the owners an emotional investment in not yielding to this one."[35]

Meanwhile, Chávez's *peregrinación* snaked north through the fertile San Joaquin Valley, through vineyards and cotton fields, losing but also gaining people along the way. After many miles Chávez could walk no longer, and was obliged to ride along in a car. At every stop a NFWA member named Luis Valdez read the official resolution the marchers had written: "Our sweat and our blood have fallen on this land to make other men rich. . . . We are poor, we are humble, and our only choice is to strike. . . . We want to be equal with all the working men in the nation. . . . We Shall Overcome."[36]

Upon the group's arrival in Sacramento on Easter Sunday, the fifty-seven *originales*, those who had walked the entire distance, were swept up in triumph onto a stage festooned with Mexican and American flags. The celebration was particularly appropriate, for during the final days of the march the first grower had capitulated. On April 7, 1966, the

Schenley Corporation, which owned the Dubonnet Wine Corporation and regularly employed about 450 farmworkers, had signed a contract with the NFWA. The company's surrender may have had to do with a rumor its own attorney had heard, and passed along to Schenley's management, that a Los Angeles bartenders' union was considering a boycott of Schenley products in sympathy with Chávez. Such a boycott would be devastating, as the Schenley brand was well known. Whatever the company's reasons, the moment was historic, the first instance of a California grower agreeing to formally recognize a union of fieldworkers.[37] "Farm workers . . . are excluded from virtually all the laws Congress has passed to protect industrial workers, including the statutes governing collective bargaining and minimum wages," the *New York Times* applauded. "The ability of the California grape strikers to make themselves heard despite this absence of legal safeguards is attributable to the fervor with which they have fought for emancipation."[38]

Chávez followed up on the breakthrough at Schenley by targeting DiGiorgio, a larger corporation that controlled several hundred thousand acres in California and employed as many as fifteen hundred pickers. Founded in the early twentieth century by Joseph DiGiorgio, a Sicilian immigrant, the firm had broken farmworker strikes in 1939, 1947, and 1960. The current president, Robert DiGiorgio, the founder's nephew, was a prominent businessman who sat on the board of the Bank of America. To defeat DiGiorgio, with its family tradition of strikebreaking and its connections to California's financial powers, Chávez used a controversial strategy, insisting that the company's available workforce be reduced by sending undocumented Mexican workers home. This came at a time when the idea of Chicano rights was dawning, especially among the farmworkers and their supporters, and many were displeased with the notion of urging the expulsion of migrants. There had in fact been talk of the NFWA unionizing workers on both sides of the border. But Chávez defended it as necessary to break DiGiorgio.

A more serious complication was that the Teamsters, who had aided the NFWA in defeating Schenley by refusing to cross NFWA picket lines, now maneuvered so as to be able to participate in any possible contract resolution with DiGiorgio. Chávez was furious. "Those bastards," he said of the Teamsters. "We shook the tree and now they're trying to pick up the fruit. That's how they operate. And if they get away with it this time, we'll never get them off our back. Just when we get a grower softened up, they'll come in and try to make a deal with him. That's the way they do it, through the bosses."[39]

It was a strange power struggle. The Teamsters were a business union, the farmworkers more akin to a social movement, and Teamsters head Jimmy Hoffa was said to vehemently oppose getting involved with fruit pickers. But Hoffa was mired in legal problems, and it was believed that Einar Mohn, director of the Western Conference of Teamsters and a competitor for Hoffa's office, perceived the Teamsters' entry into the vineyards as a means of raising his own status within the union, especially were Hoffa to go to jail. (He would soon begin serving a thirteen-year sentence for jury tampering and pension fund fraud.) Mohn and his supporters dismissed that allegation, insisting that the actual motivation was that the Teamsters already had one hundred thousand members in various farm-related jobs in California, working in transport and canneries, and could not allow the farmworkers to gain control over so substantial a part of the industry, since theoretically any NFWA strike would impact the numerous Teamsters locals reliant on agribusiness. DiGiorgio by now also seemed to acknowledge that some unionization of pickers was inevitable, and preferred the prospect of dealing with the Teamsters, not least because it would irritate Chávez and the NFWA. Robert DiGiorgio demanded a union representation election that the Teamsters easily won, further angering Chávez, who believed the balloting had been sham, and who in desperation turned again for help to Governor Brown.

The governor had been noticeably absent from the capital on Easter Sunday when the farmworkers had arrived at his doorstep, but since then he had begun feeling more vulnerable about his chances of winning reelection in the fall. At Chávez's suggestion, and recognizing he could not afford to look unconcerned about the state's labor unrest, Brown ordered a state inquiry into the recent DiGiorgio representation voting; when the inquiry substantiated Chávez's suspicion of improprieties, Brown arranged for a new election to be held under state authority. Chávez and his forces received additional new support when the AFL-CIO agreed to charter the NFWA, on condition it merge with AWOC. In August 1966, as a result of the merger, Chávez's movement became known as the United Farm Workers of California (UFW). That same year Congress amended the Fair Labor Standards Act of 1938 to include farmworkers in minimum wage protection.

The fight leading up to the DiGiorgio election was intensely ideological. The UFW cited the Teamsters' alleged links with organized crime, distributing excerpts in English and Spanish of Robert Kennedy's book *The Enemy Within*, which recounted sordid details about the Teamsters from the McClellan Committee inquiry. Tainting the Teamsters, or any old-line union, as more organized *crime* than organized *labor*, had become easy sport of late. Hoffa's legal battles had by now dominated headlines for so long that the Teamsters' reputation for shadiness was more or less fixed in the public mind.

The Teamsters fought back by red-baiting the UFW, at one point referring to the farmworkers as "the Vietcong." But the UFW handily won the election—Chávez by now simply had superior control of the ground forces—and in April 1967 the union signed a contract with DiGiorgio providing for a union shop, a $1.65 per hour minimum wage, paid vacations, and an agreement that pickers would receive four hours' pay for showing up for work even if none was available. In July peace was made between the Teamsters and the UFW. In negotiations with the Perelli-Minetti vineyards, it was agreed that the UFW would have control of the fields and the Teamsters would represent workers in canneries, processing facilities, and warehouses.

With the Teamsters dispute settled, the UFW shifted some of its focus to promoting a national boycott on table grapes in order to bring other growers in line. Taking to the road, UFW members staged demonstrations and fasts in league with college and church groups, and appeared before labor, civil liberties, and civil rights organizations, urging American consumers not to buy grapes. Supermarket chains like A&P and Safeway were ubiquitous targets in what proved a highly effective secondary boycott, and grapes proved the ideal item for an enduring boycott since they were hardly an essential grocery item. Eighty-five percent of the nation's grape growers, including Gallo and several in the Napa Valley, eventually capitulated, agreeing in 1970 to recognize the UFW and sign durable contracts that governed wages, benefits, working conditions, and the use of pesticides, and allowed the union to play a larger role in hiring. The victory was the largest labor-related consumer boycott in history and further confirmation of the Chávez movement's skill at identifying likely forms of contemporary grassroots activism, then using them to mobilize and nationalize a cause. Because of the large profile it attained, the farmworkers' movement became a beacon for not only workers' rights but a more general recognition of Mexican American culture, the movement for Chicano rights that would soon emerge on college campuses across the country. Although it was not immediately evident, Chávez and the farmworkers had also set an inspiring example for what would become a dominant labor movement trend in the final decades of the twentieth century—the successful unionization of long-neglected, traditionally unorganized workers such as nurses, home attendants, janitors, sanitation workers, and domestic workers.

WALTER REUTHER, head of the historically activist UAW and a man of humane, socialistic views suggestive of his hero Eugene Debs, was often considered the conscience of the labor movement; it was appropriate then that his personal struggle came to embody labor's difficult response to President Johnson's unpopular war. Reuther remained devoted to the president and the agenda of the Great Society even as he quietly began to share the disillusionment with Vietnam. In 1965 he recommended that peace negotiations be initiated under the auspices of the United Nations, and two years later he supported a halt in the U.S. bombing of North Vietnam. But his views were consistently less strident than those of his UAW cohorts such as Emil Mazey, whom he disappointed in 1967 by endorsing another term for the man in the White House. At the same time Reuther tried, with little success, to get Mazey and others of the louder critics of the war to tone down their rhetoric and, at Johnson's personal request, appealed for patience to Martin Luther King Jr., who in spring 1967 issued an eloquent demand for an end to the conflict.[40]

Victor Reuther, also of the UAW, was far less constrained by the loyalties that seemed to bind his brother. In 1964 he characterized "the Cold War view of the world" as "distorted" and "over-simplified," and at a 1966 UAW gathering openly accused Meany and Jay Lovestone of using the AFL-CIO as a cover for CIA covert operations in the Dominican Republic in 1965 and elsewhere, thus contributing to the foreign relations boondoggle that Vietnam had become.[41] He was said to have piqued Meany's resentment in particular by alleging that the federation had committed an egregious foul by allowing a rogue element like Lovestone to roam free.[42] Ironically, even as Victor Reuther spoke, the old Meany-Lovestone axis was at work in Vietnam, propping up the Confederation of Vietnamese Labor (CVT) in order to keep U.S. supplies flowing into the port of Saigon without hassle from longshoremen or other harbor workers. The AFL-CIO also used money from the U.S. Agency for International Development to create the Asian American Free Labor Institute in Vietnam, with the aim of guiding and training CVT officials and other moderate labor leaders. It gave in-kind support to CVT offices across Vietnam, supplying buses, mimeograph machines, public address systems, and office equipment.

The differences between the two Reuther brothers highlighted questions of tremendous relevance to the labor movement overall. Could labor criticize the war even as it maintained its support of the administration's domestic reforms? To what extent would antiwar opinions endanger its alliance with the Democratic Party? Had the movement's hesitation on the subject already rendered it toothless as a credible force for social change?

The argument made increasingly by SDS and others on the left was that organized labor, "because it is closely tied to established political and corporate interests and committed to working with them," was no longer a viable source of meaningful social advocacy.[43] While this might have been true of the major unions' faithfulness to the president's Vietnam policy, one could point to the farmworkers' crusade in California as an example of supportive engagement by the AFL-CIO, the UAW, and other union entities; the big labor groups had also siphoned money and support to the civil rights struggle in the South; indeed the origins of SDS itself lay in an industrial democracy league founded in the 1930s, while its own mission statement had been drafted at a UAW summer camp in Michigan in 1962. Still, the left's frustration with labor was understandable, as expressed in Alinsky's witticism that "the fault with the American radical is not that he chose to make his bed in the labor movement, but that he fell *asleep* in it."[44]

Through it all Walter Reuther agonized. After the 1966 midterm elections a kind of turning point was reached in the nation's political discourse: the Great Society, so dear to Reuther, would henceforth be little spoken of, while maximum attention seemed to shift more or less permanently to the crisis of Vietnam.[45] As the war consumed more of the nation's energy and antiwar fervor intensified, he began to question whether his words on the subject even mattered, for from atop the AFL-CIO Meany continued resolutely to tamp down critical dissent. It was the protesting students who owned the moment and held center stage, increasingly with emerging allies such as movements of black liberation, Chicano activists, and returning war veterans. While student antiwar signs and literature often alluded to a labor-student alliance, such unity largely remained chimerical; it was far more likely that a protesting student would find herself marching alongside a disaffected GI from Vietnam, still in his fatigues, or the concerned mother of a soldier, than a contingent of workers. It was the students who had gotten this one right, and the unkind fate of time and history that Reuther and those of his generation had let slip their place of prominence as the nation's moral and ethical guardians. No doubt this was always how it was; even the most righteous causes settled ultimately with reality. For participants there lingered memories of days aflame with purpose, but also regret—for compromises made, or all that had been left undone.

George Meany, of course, suffered no such attack of conscience. In his speeches, many ghostwritten by Lovestone, he continued to vow that the AFL-CIO would stand behind President Johnson and the war. It was Meany, or most likely his muse, who unknowingly coined one of the era's most notorious refrains when, at a 1967 federation convention, he asserted that the labor movement's support of the war "spoke for the vast, *silent majority* in the nation." This phrase—the "silent majority"—was recycled in 1970 by Johnson's successor, Richard Nixon, who like Meany defended the war as necessary and insisted it enjoyed the backing of most ordinary Americans, those who did not criticize their country, protest, burn draft cards, or occupy college administration buildings. These "silent" Americans, writes Philip Foner, were those "children of the Depression" who

> had had no chance to get a college education, yet they saw
> draft-deferred college students . . . wasting their time in
> demonstrations. . . . Their sons and relatives were fighting
> and dying in Vietnam, and they were told it was all for
> nothing. . . . They had been taught in school and church to
> venerate the flag, yet they saw youthful demonstrators spitting
> at and burning it. In short, the world they believed in was
> disintegrating before their eyes.[46]

"The silent majority" would eventually be understood to refer to those who not only stood behind the war but working-class white people generally, especially those alarmed by the sudden changes that seemed to have overtaken society—the loosening of sexual mores, outlandish styles of dress and public behavior, the widespread use of drugs, and the rise of black militancy. The era's most televised domestic crisis, and a depressing counterpart to the nonviolent civil rights movement in the South, was the eruption of lethal race riots in many Northern U.S. cities—Harlem and Bedford-Stuyvesant in 1964; the Watts riots in Los Angeles in August 1965; Chicago and Cleveland in 1966; Newark in 1967. The violence in Watts lasted four days, killed thirty-four people, and injured one thousand, with damages estimated at $50 million. By 1967 Cincinnati, Buffalo, Boston, Atlanta, Dayton, and even unlikely places such as Waterloo, Iowa, had been struck by similar outbreaks, attended by looting and mass arrests. Americans who tuned to nightly television news in late July saw the city of Detroit descend into what looked like an urban war zone, with National Guard tanks and armored personnel carriers rumbling through the streets; whole blocks were reduced to smoldering rubble, as police reported thirty-six deaths and twenty-five hundred arrests. So vivid a breakdown in public order spawned soul-searching editorials and sermons across the country, while government panels formed to try to make sense of the chaos.

At times conservative reaction became manifest. Pro-war unionists had their say in May 1967 at a "Support the Boys" labor march in New York City, led by members of the International Longshoremen's Association. The dockworkers, joined by rank and file from the Teamsters and the Maritime Union, as well as members of the John Birch Society and the American Legion, streamed down New York's Fifth Avenue shoving and arguing with young antiwar protestors. They chanted "Burn Hanoi, not our flag!" and hoisted a sign that read DROP THE H-BOMB ON HANOI.

While to the antiwar movement the "Support the Boys" march was out of step with reality, even harebrained, the hand-wringing of labor moderates like Walter Reuther, as well as the continued sniping among union officials over the war, had come to feel equally pointless. At times George Meany's tether to the real world seemed to have slipped entirely. Angered by a labor peace gathering in Chicago in May 1967 that demanded the AFL-CIO drop its backing of the war, Meany made the absurd allegation that the meeting had been planned in Hanoi and its resolutions printed earlier in a Communist newspaper. Emil Mazey responded by calling Meany "a senile old man" and questioned his fitness to "lead the American labor movement."[47] But Mazey then also turned his criticism on the antiwar crowd, denouncing the tactics of overt confrontation on display at a Pentagon demonstration in October 1967, which ended with protestors being driven from the building by troops using tear gas.

By now the young people had run out of patience. They saw, according to Philip Foner, "no distinction among labor leaders. . . . Mazey, Victor Reuther [and others] were no different than Meany. The fact that these leaders had broken with Meany over Vietnam and had begun to mobilize against the Meany-Lovestone forces made not the slightest difference. . . . Many among them . . . had long since written off the labor movement as a meaningful ally."[48] As Robert Kennedy concluded before a dinner hosted by the Americans for Democratic Action that year, "Labor has been in the forefront of many a great battle. But youth looks with other eyes, and their view is very different: they think of labor as grown sleek and bureaucratic with power, sometimes frankly discriminatory, occasionally even corrupt and exploitative; a force not for change but for the status quo."[49] The students hardly noticed or cared when in December of that year, at an AFL-CIO conclave in Miami, the executive council reaffirmed its support of the war and the convention's honored guest, a beaming President Johnson, strode to the podium amid a clamorous ovation.

T HE CIVIL RIGHTS MOVEMENT had by 1967 attained many of its initial objectives, at least formally, in terms of federal legislation guaranteeing equal treatment in public accommodations (the Civil Rights Act of 1964) and voting rights (the Voting Rights Act of 1965). In doing so, however, it had lost some of the faith of younger activists who, worn down by the years of foot soldiering in the most resistant pockets of the Deep South, had grown cynical about the pace of actual change. Many of the black students who'd led the original Southern movement had chafed at the Mississippi Freedom Summer, which in 1964 brought one thousand Northern white college students into the state to teach in rural schools and serve in voter registration drives, but had then become dominated by news of the investigation into the June 21, 1964, Ku Klux

Klan/police murders of an integrated team of civil rights workers, James Chaney, Andrew Goodman, and Mickey Schwerner. Later that summer at the Democratic National Convention in Atlantic City, a faction of black and white Mississippi delegates excluded by the state's racist power structure, the Mississippi Freedom Democratic Party (MFDP), demanded to be seated instead of the all-white delegation, leading party authorities at the direction of President Johnson to shut down the attempt. After all that they had accomplished in bringing expanded voter's rights to wayward Mississippi, MFDP members and their supporters felt betrayed by the collusion of party bigwigs and even some otherwise supportive moderates in keeping their delegates out. Walter Reuther and Hubert Humphrey had been among those running interference on the president's behalf. The weary activists returned to Mississippi embittered by the experience.

Martin Luther King Jr. perceived, as did the younger activists, that America's racial problems were linked to intractable challenges that no federal legislation could necessarily touch, and he shared their frustration. His ideas about possible solutions were programmatic, including the determination to tackle head-on the poverty that was to blame for urban race riots. His Southern Christian Leadership Conference's (SCLC) Operation Breadbasket, begun in Atlanta in 1962 and then launched more fully in 1966 in Cleveland and Chicago (where the SCLC also had led marches for open housing), sought to address the core economic tensions that created such violence by using consumer boycotts to demand equal hiring and investment in black neighborhoods by businesses that profited there. "As long as people are devoid of jobs they will find themselves in moments of despair that could lead to continuation of these disorders," King stated in summer 1967.[50] But despite some breakthroughs—in Chicago a successful rent strike and an agreement by two national grocery chains to begin stocking products made by black-owned firms; in Cleveland a product boycott—not much had really been won for all the exertion and trouble, and violent white reaction had greeted some of the Chicago efforts.

Veteran civil rights leaders like King and his SCLC colleagues knew better than to allow their forces to bog down in protracted local campaigns that produced minimal results. By early 1968 a variation on Breadbasket had evolved that sought a far greater and more immediate national impact—a Poor People's Campaign that would bring an encampment of representative poor from various parts of the South and urban North to Washington. Putting the nation's highest decision-makers under siege, the campaign would dispatch movement spokesmen to Congress and federal agencies urging immediate action on economic issues, while participants trained in nonviolent protest methods staged demonstrations. The campaign, slated for late spring or early summer 1968, engaged members of labor's peace wing in its planning phase, as unemployment, job discrimination, and the wasteful use of resources in the war were all issues the Poor People's Campaign intended to address.

The preparations for the crusade, however, soon became fraught with disagreement over tactics and objectives, as well as more pragmatic questions about funding. Historically, efforts to amass the jobless, the needy, or the resentful in Washington—from Coxey's Army in 1894 to the Bonus March of stipend-seeking First World War veterans in 1932—had not ended well,[51] and many people—white officials as well as some blacks—worried that the Poor People's Campaign could not help but appear provocative. The prospect of an "army" of the poor and dispossessed descending on the capital, at a time when urban violence had begun to feel endemic, seemed to many irresponsible and dangerous, creating a situation that even Dr. King, for all his good works and intentions, would not be able to manage.

Expressions of racial frustration such as Black Power and riots offered convincing evidence that King had lost the ability to control the movement he had done so much to create, even as he reinvented himself as a crusader for the jobless and the working poor. The dominant images of the civil rights movement were of orderly nonviolence—sit-ins, peaceful picketing, the inspiring tableaux of thousands assembled at the 1963 March on Washington. But these had given way to far different pictures—graphic scenes of bloodied American citizens in U.S. cities and soldiers, fearful of snipers, crouching for cover behind burned-out vehicles. King himself remained resolute, but many moderate whites who had been receptive to his message of nonviolent healing were frightened by the riots and the younger, newly minted black spokesmen of outrage; they could follow King no longer, especially now that he had turned his persuasive voice to the harder issues of economic racism and, increasingly, to criticism of Vietnam.

King's first major address on the war came on April 4, 1967, at New York's Riverside Church, where he asserted that it lacked moral and strategic validity, evaporating resources needed at home to rectify social and economic crises, and that it sent predominantly poor and minority young men to fight and die. He asked for an end to the bombing, an immediate cease-fire leading to peace negotiations, and the setting of a fixed date for a U.S. military exit. In some of the address's strongest language, he termed the United States "the greatest purveyor of violence in the world today" and compared the use of sophisticated weapons on the peasants of Vietnam to the Nazis' methods of testing "new medicines and new tortures" in European concentration camps. "If America's soul becomes poisoned," he warned, "part of the autopsy must read 'Vietnam.' "[52] He endorsed the need to channel the moral fervor of the civil rights cause into the antiwar movement, and even proposed a "Vietnam Summer," inspired by the civil rights Freedom Summer of 1964, in which young activists would enter American communities to awaken public awareness about the war's detrimental impact.

King did not single-handedly move the moral indignation of the civil rights cause to the antiwar front—that groundwork had to a great extent been accomplished by former civil rights workers from SDS and SNCC—but his public pronouncement, his coming out against the war, could not help but seem a national turning point. And as he was at least two years ahead of the mainstream media and the general public in souring on Vietnam, he paid a considerable price for his courage. Indeed, so shocked were many at what he had said, the initial response was a stunned silence, even fellow civil rights leaders refusing at first to comment upon his words. Baseball legend Jackie Robinson stated that he respectfully disagreed with Dr. King. The Jewish War Veterans of the United States of America took him to task for comparing the U.S. military to the Nazis. Civil rights colleague Whitney Young of the Urban League worried that King had drifted out of his proper sphere of advocacy.

An especially hurtful blow came from popular black columnist Carl Rowan, who assailed King in the pages of *Reader's Digest*, a periodical with a readership of several million. Accusing him of having developed an inflated idea of his own influence, the writer scolded King for having abandoned the humble methods and philosophy of social change that had characterized his Montgomery Bus Boycott and other civil rights victories. And Rowan went further, suggesting that communistic influence had led to King's "tragic decision" to oppose the war. In these failings, the columnist alleged, King had done himself and the nation a double disservice by forfeiting his rapport with the White House and weakening the moral authority of the fight for equal rights.

King replied by reminding Rowan that in America speaking out even in unpopular terms did not signify disloyalty, and he branded the allegation about Communism as tired red-baiting. King was right on these points, of course, no matter what one thought of his views on Vietnam, but Rowan's harshly worded chastisement had struck a nerve.[53]

By February 1968 King and the SCLC had refined plans for the Poor People's Campaign. Approximately three thousand demonstrators would come to Washington from the cities of the East and Midwest as well as rural areas of Mississippi and West Virginia, and there take up residence in a "shanty town"—actual sharecroppers' shacks from Mississippi transported and set up on the Mall. From there they would initiate a ninety-day effort of advocacy before Congress as well as agencies such as the Department of Housing and Urban Development. Were the powers-that-be to give the campaign's "economic bill of rights" short shrift, a plea would go out for more protestors to come to Washington. "Waves of the nation's poor and disinherited" would join the encampment already in place, and remain there "until America responds" with needed programs of assistance for the indigent and unemployed, for those without homes or equal opportunity.[54]

While critics continued to scorn these plans, the campaign gained some much-needed legitimacy in early spring 1968 when the Kerner Commission, a board of inquiry appointed by President Johnson in reaction to the 1967 riots and headed by Governor Otto Kerner of Illinois, released its findings.[55] The commission explained the recent upheaval as the result of the migration of blacks to large cities and the accompanying exodus of whites, compounded by the discrimination blacks encountered in work and housing. This had created ghetto slums of little opportunity, isolated from and at odds with the larger municipality in which they were situated, neighborhoods that were tinderboxes liable to be sparked into violence by the slightest provocation, such as hostile encounters with white police. The panel, which found the riots to have been spontaneous outbursts, not organized or controlled by any person or group, called for special training for police who worked in inner-city areas, the recruitment of more black journalists (the media was slighted for having exaggerated the violence in certain areas, such as the claims about "black snipers"), the development of more affordable housing, and job programs for the hardcore unemployed. It suggested the immediate creation of 2 million jobs by the federal government and the private sector, the establishment of a guaranteed minimum income, and a larger federal contribution to state welfare budgets. The Kerner report's most quoted admonition warned that "our nation is moving toward two societies, one white, one black, separate but unequal."[56]

The Poor People's Campaign was centered on demands not radically different from those agreed upon by the Kerner Commission (King at one point offered to call off the campaign if the government agreed to honor the Kerner recommendations), although the SCLC's program remained unpopular for being confrontational. One very practical criticism was that, even if the crusade made its case admirably and without trouble, Congress was unlikely to now craft additional civil rights laws, having just done so; the view from Washington was that the attainments of the civil rights era had been rewarded with major legislation, and that it must be given time to prove its effect.

WHILE PLANS FOR the Poor People's Campaign went forward, two developments—one national in scope, another highly localized—engaged King's attention. From the antiwar front had emerged a Dump Johnson movement, coordinated by gadfly New York congressman Allard K. Lowenstein, to remove the erstwhile leader of the Great Society, now an obstinate war president, from office. The movement's candidate was Senator Eugene McCarthy of Minnesota, whose entry into the Democratic primaries at first appeared as quixotic as the Dump Johnson campaign itself; then, at the end of January 1968, the Vietcong and North Vietnamese army launched the Tet Offensive, an assault on the cities of South Vietnam that was so effective it saw enemy soldiers briefly occupy the U.S. embassy in Saigon. Although the offensive was repelled, its daring and magnitude served to newly worry many Americans about the war's being winnable. McCarthy's campaign quickly gained ground, and in March he won an impressive 42.2 percent of the vote against Johnson's 49.4 in the New Hampshire primary.

Robert Kennedy had been reluctant to join the primary race, believing the president held an insurmountable lead, but in opinion surveys of New Hampshire voters he had scored almost as high as Johnson without having even been on the ballot. On March 12, noting "a deep division within the party [which] clearly indicates that a sizable group of Democrats are concerned about the direction in which the country is going," Kennedy formally announced his candidacy.[57] The entry of the popular younger man was a setback for the less prominent McCarthy, although it excited expectations that the sitting president might actually be unseated by his own party, that Johnson could indeed be "dumped." Labor unions took sides, some leaders, such as Walter Reuther and George Meany, staying loyal to Johnson; Meany screened for his close AFL-CIO colleagues a film of the president vowing the war would not reduce his commitments to labor's social and democratic objectives, and on March 29 warned that the Dump Johnson movement would wind up electing a Republican president. But then came Johnson's stunning announcement of March 31, when he declared on live television that he would not seek, and would not accept, the nomination of his party for another term as president, an apparent admission that he had led the nation into a cul-de-sac in Vietnam and hadn't the wherewithal to extricate it. Meany, as surprised as the entire nation, reacted swiftly, throwing the AFL-CIO's support behind Vice President Humphrey as a successor to Johnson without even consulting the federation's executive council.

In this same period King had been drawn to a labor dispute with civil rights overtones in Memphis. On February 12 sanitation workers of Memphis Local 1733 of the American Federation of State, County and Municipal Employees (AFSCME) staged a wildcat strike as the result of mounting grievances, including a recent accident in which two workers had been crushed to death by defective machinery. The local had thirteen hundred members, all but five of whom were black, and had long endured pay and promotion disparities and other slights, even as the city for five years had staved off the union's demand for recognition. "The mayor of that city [Henry Loeb], who was living in the eighteenth century," explained Walter Reuther, "was arguing ... that it should take a worker five years to get the going rate of $1.80 an hour because, he said, it takes five years to learn the skill to empty a garbage can."[58] The men were so poorly compensated, with no overtime or vacation pay, many were forced to rely on welfare and food stamps.

The city, eager to get the workers back on the job, agreed to some of the local's demands, including a more just system of promotion, improved health and retirement benefits, and a streamlined grievance procedure. But it shunned union recognition and a pay hike, and Mayor Loeb, already unpopular with Memphis's substantial black community, refused to negotiate further until the men returned to their jobs; he threatened to fire any who stayed away. An injunction the city had obtained against a sanitation strike in 1966 was still in effect, and could be wielded against the local.

Work stoppages by public employees anywhere tend to rapidly

become politicized because the withdrawal of their labor involves a direct threat to residents, businesses, and municipal treasuries.[59] Memphis was no exception. The strike had quickly awakened long-simmering tensions in the racially polarized city, yet the sanitation workers were energized by the news that their counterparts, New York City's sanitation crews, had recently won concessions as the result of a walkout. While the Memphis NAACP and several black ministers, including civil rights veteran James Lawson, a former King lieutenant, made efforts along with some white labor leaders to negotiate further with city officials, the mayor was adamant that Memphis would not sign a contract with a municipal workers' union. Loeb, whom *Newsweek* described as "a native Memphian who got his wealth from his family's laundry business and his segregationist politics from the white plantation paternalism that still permeates Memphis at every level," was (like many other white Southern politicians of his generation) inclined to believe he understood black people and had their best interests at heart, even though he had received only 2 percent of their votes. In his mind he was doing them a service by keeping a union from meddling in the relationship the workers enjoyed with their city.[60]

When Loeb authorized the hiring of scabs to man the garbage trucks with police officers riding shotgun, tensions mounted, exacerbated by both local newspapers; one, the *Commercial Appeal*, had compared the strikers to the Vietcong.[61] The union, defying a new court injunction against picketing and demonstrating, conducted protests along Main Street, the workers and their supporters carrying signs that read I AM A MAN, clearly articulating the strike's larger meaning as a demand for dignity. Simultaneously the black community launched a boycott of downtown white businesses. There were a number of incidents: white officers sprayed Mace on black youths who pounded their fists on a passing squad car; police cleared people from the streets and made arrests without cause; even Local 1733's president, T. O. Jones, was taken into custody, accused of disorderly conduct and inciting to riot.

After a boisterous crowd of nine thousand filled a church on March 14 to hear visiting civil rights leaders Bayard Rustin and Roy Wilkins voice their support for the strike, local ministers and the AFSCME began to perceive in the standoff with Mayor Loeb the possibility of a major civil rights/labor protest. As Birmingham police commissioner Eugene "Bull" Connor had shown the world in 1963 during the SCLC's campaign in that city, successful civil rights campaigns often thrived on a prickly antagonist, which the difficult Mayor Loeb promised to be. Memphis, in the context of civil rights activism, had been relatively quiet, but Lawson and the others concluded that feelings about the sanitation strike were so strong, Martin Luther King Jr. might inspire and lead a meaningful campaign in the city. After communications with King and his aides, a nonviolent march to be led by King was scheduled for Thursday, March 28. While engagement in the Memphis strike would be a distraction from King's planning for Washington, surely the temptation was great to use the struggle in Memphis for workers' rights as an example of the movement's new direction.

One precarious difference between King's entry into the Memphis strike and the Southern civil rights campaigns he and his core SCLC staff had personally led was that here King was flying somewhat blind, entering into a local struggle whose outlines were familiar but whose specifics he and his closest aides had not had the opportunity to fully examine. Some information not shared with King and his entourage was that a group of local black teenagers calling themselves the Invaders rejected nonviolence, and that Lawson and other leaders had not adequately engaged with them or heard them out.

King's lack of intelligence on what was transpiring in Memphis was compounded on the day of the march itself, when his plane was delayed and he arrived at the Clayborn Temple AME Church, where six thousand marchers awaited him, two hours late. Neither he nor his aides were told that earlier that morning black high school students trying to leave school to join the march had clashed with police, hurling rocks and empty soda bottles. Finally under way along Beale Street, the procession with King at its head had traversed only three blocks when young marchers at the rear began taunting cops and smashing shop windows. Police, edgy from the earlier battle at the high school, surged into the crowd, flailing with riot sticks and eventually deploying both Mace and tear gas. At the sound of the disruption the entire march stopped, then splintered, as adult participants dropped their placards and retreated in confusion to their homes or back to the Clayborn Temple. King was quickly hustled into a commandeered car and driven away.

With the march in disarray, street fighting escalated. Amid reports of looting, a black teenager, sixteen-year-old Larry Payne, was shot and killed by police who said he'd attacked them with a butcher knife. By the time order was restored, fifty people required medical attention and more than a hundred had been arrested. The local press denounced King and declared the chaos he'd brought to Memphis a "riot," while Mayor Loeb called out four thousand National Guardsmen.

The city's response was an overreaction, no doubt based on the prevalent anxiety regarding urban racial violence. Loeb, it was reported, had called for the militia only minutes after the first window was broken, and some of the soldiers came equipped with rifles fitted with telescopic sights in order to combat the fictional threat of "Negro snipers."[62] The looting, it turned out, had been rather minimal, and some of the reports of fires lit by arsonists were found to have been people burning their own garbage because the city was no longer picking it up. The rapid deterioration of a peaceful march led by Dr. King into street violence, however, was nonetheless an embarrassment; it sent the worst possible message about the wisdom of conflating civil rights movement tactics with a labor conflict, and King was personally singled out for criticism for fleeing the scene, rather than doing something to halt the rioting. "The whole incident underscores the general national edginess," averred the *New York Times*, reminding King that Gandhi had seen fit to suspend his followers' street protests when violence had occurred, and that King would do well to "appreciate the consequences for the civil rights movement and the nation of an April explosion in Washington."[63]

King was distraught over the death of Larry Payne, and angered by his staff's failure to gather adequate intelligence about the Memphis strike. He was also discomfited by the murmurings from old allies like the NAACP's Roy Wilkins, who suggested the Poor People's Campaign be reconsidered since it appeared King no longer possessed the ability to manage large-scale demonstrations. Some Southern members of Congress were already recommending that King's protestors be banned from entering Washington altogether. Senator Robert Byrd of West Virginia thought a court order should be obtained for that purpose. "If this self-seeking rabble-rouser is allowed to go through with his plans here," warned Byrd, "Washington may well be treated to the same kind of violence, destruction, looting and bloodshed" that had occurred in Memphis. Congress already had a bill under consideration that would make it a crime to cross state lines to take part in urban violence—a measure aimed at militants and perhaps broad enough to include the leaders of the SCLC.[64]

To King, however, the plight of the black sanitation workers in Memphis illustrated precisely how the issues of economics and race intertwined, and he announced that another march would be held in Memphis, this time organized by his own staff. He sought out and met with the representatives of the teenage Invaders, and was upset when he learned what Lawson and others had largely kept from him: that the youth had felt excluded from the earlier community protests and were irritated that their input had been spurned. King recognized that it was important to take the young men seriously. Rather than scold them, he listened to their complaints and seemed to succeed, through the force of his celebrity, at convincing them to mend their ways for the rescheduled march, which was to take place on Friday, April 5. The city had obtained a federal court injunction against the event, which, despite the pleading of the U.S. attorney and city officials, King insisted he would defy. However, he agreed to postpone the protest until Monday, April 8, in order to allow national labor delegations time to make it to town to participate.

The night of Wednesday, April 3, Memphis was deluged by heavy rains, and King—assuming the weather would diminish attendance at a scheduled church rally for the striking sanitation workers—sent his chief lieutenant, Reverend Ralph Abernathy, to speak in his stead. Soon Abernathy was on the phone to King's room at the Lorraine Motel to report that the turnout at the church was both sizable and spirited, despite the bad weather, and that his presence was earnestly desired. Abernathy no doubt thought it would be beneficial for King, who was still upset by recent events, to bask in the adulation of a sympathetic audience in the familiar setting of a black church. When King arrived at the gathering he went to the pulpit and, seemingly wanting to clear his troubled mind, launched into a prophetic rumination. "Well, I don't know what will happen now," he told the expectant audience,

> But it really doesn't matter with me now. Because I've been to the mountain top. . . . Like anybody, I would like to live a long life. Longevity has its place. But I'm not concerned about that now. I just want to do God's will. And He's allowed me to go up to the mountain. And I've looked over, and I've seen the Promised Land. I may not get there with you, but I want you to know tonight that we as a people will get to the Promised Land. So I'm happy tonight. I'm not worried about anything. I'm not fearing any man. "Mine eyes have seen the glory of the coming of the Lord."[65]

If Abernathy believed the outing would be therapeutic for King, he was right: the emotional words King had spoken and the profuse adulation of his listeners seemed to restore the leader's equilibrium, granting a momentary tranquillity after all the tension of the past several days. By the following evening, Thursday, April 4, even the skies above Memphis had cleared, and as day turned to dusk he and his aides dressed for dinner at the home of a local supporter. At a few minutes before six, from a perch across the street, assassin James Earl Ray looked up from his rifle to see a man wearing a crisp black suit, white shirt, and tie emerge from a second-floor room and come to stand alone by the railing of the motel balcony. "If you are cut down in a movement that is designed to save the soul of a nation," King had said not long before, "then no other death could be more redemptive."[66]

AS THE DIVERGENT REACTION within the labor movement to the war in Vietnam became harder to ignore, some sort of split began to seem inevitable. One of the most fragile potential breaking points was the Meany-Reuther partnership at the helm of the AFL-CIO. Their relationship had never been rock solid. Reuther in the mid-1950s had denounced the Lovestonian cold war meddling that Meany fathered, and while relations improved when the two leaders joined to respond to the McClellan Committee's indictment of labor, that thaw ended in 1963 when Meany refused AFL-CIO endorsement of the March on Washington, which Reuther and the UAW wholeheartedly supported. Most recently Reuther had donated $50,000 from the UAW to the Memphis sanitation strike, only to then be informed that Southern UAW members had refused to lower flags to half-mast after King's murder on April 4. Reuther was truly a man in the middle—unable to separate himself from the outdated leadership cadre around Meany, irritated by reactionary members of his own union, and getting little if any sympathy from UAW doves who were irked by his hesitation to criticize the war.

Reuther characteristically responded to his dilemma by making forward-looking plans. He launched an effort to build education centers aimed at reviving labor's conscience and developing young talent in the labor field, the facilities also being available as recreational retreats for union members and their families. He sought to reestablish the movement's ties to liberals and intellectuals. He called for more direct aid to farmworkers and intensified efforts to organize the nation's public service employees, and spoke of finding ways for the UAW to play a larger role in combating racism. With great prescience he warned of the need to develop common bargaining goals for autoworkers in all auto-producing nations as a means of counteracting global wage competition, and recommended the country turn its attention to repairing bridges, roads, and other infrastructures.

He did not believe the AFL-CIO was up to these challenges. "As the parent body of the American labor movement, [it] suffers from a sense of complacency and adherence to the status quo, and is not fulfilling the basic aims and purposes which prompted the merger of the AFL and CIO" in the first place, Reuther remarked in December 1967. "[It] lacks the social vision, the dynamic thrust, the crusading spirit that should characterize the progressive, modern labor movement which it can and must be if it is to be equal to the new challenges and the opportunities of our twentieth century technological society."[67] The AFL-CIO, he said, had come to have "little to do with America today. It has much to do with yesterday."[68]

Meany brushed off Reuther's criticism. "We resent being called tottering old men who do not know what we are doing!" he argued, but he consented to a special meeting Reuther requested to describe the UAW's plans and air the automakers' frustrations with the federation. However, when Meany insisted the meeting be held with the understanding that the UAW would accept its conclusions no matter what, Reuther replied that his organization was not about to "give anybody a loyalty oath," and the gathering was canceled.[69] In early 1968 the UAW began withholding its AFL-CIO dues of $90,000 per month, and in May of that year, following an exchange of threats and warnings between the two leaders, the UAW was dropped from the AFL-CIO for nonpayment of dues. On July 1, 1968, it announced its formal separation.[70]

The departure of the UAW from the nation's mainstream labor coalition was only one more item of adverse news in what had become a troubling, dismal season. After the funeral for Martin Luther King Jr., the SCLC, groping its way forward without its leader, had gone through with the Poor People's Campaign in Washington, part sheer determination, part memorial for King; although violence was averted, the crusade was halfhearted and its results negligible. Once the participants departed Washington and the campaign's tent city was razed by the government, it was almost as if it had never happened. In the meantime the promising Bobby Kennedy, his eloquence and antiwar position carrying him toward the Democratic nomination for president, was assassinated in Los Angeles in early June, moments after being declared the winner of the California primary.

Reuther had known and admired both King and Kennedy. With President Johnson having abdicated, Reuther now turned his efforts toward helping Vice President Humphrey's candidacy. But nothing seemed to work as it once had for the Democrats. The party's convention in Chicago self-destructed, as the forces that had been gnawing at American society erupted in full view of the world. Rallies by antiwar protestors brought fierce assaults from Mayor Richard Daley's police, the chaos—as well as the tear gas—spilling into the convention itself as Daley's minions intimidated delegates, reporters, and supporters of the remaining antiwar candidate, Eugene McCarthy. Humphrey appeared small and ineffectual against the backdrop of lawlessness as he tried to bridge the antiwar cause and yet remain loyal to the Johnson administration's policies; only in the convention's last hours did he offer to halt the U.S. bombing of Vietnam if elected. With the Democrats in turmoil, Richard Nixon, the former vice president who had narrowly lost to John F. Kennedy in 1960 and appeared to have exited politics after losing a bid to become governor of California, staged an impressive comeback, winning the 1968 election by vowing to bring peace with honor to the conflict in Vietnam and to stand for law and order at home.

O NCE HE WAS IN OFFICE, Nixon also appeared to have no immediate solution for the war, and domestic impatience deepened over the summer of 1969, fed in part by news of a shocking war crime perpetrated by U.S. soldiers. It was revealed that in March 1968 an American infantry brigade had entered the Vietnamese village of Song My and its six hamlets, named My Lai, and killed more than five hundred Vietnamese civilians.[71] This disclosure, supported by graphic images of the bloodied victims piled in a ditch, served to finally push many previously undecided citizens toward opposition to the war. "Americans must face up frankly to what has become a severe test of conscience," possibly "one of this nation's most ignoble hours," the *New York Times* told its readers.[72] The atrocity helped usher in a new phase of antiwar concern; the protracted engagement in Vietnam was no longer simply an act of disputed foreign policy, a course to be rectified, but something horrific and sickening. After My Lai, observed Tony Mazzocchi, a veteran labor organizer with the Oil, Chemical and Atomic Workers (OCAW), "a lot of people came out of the closet."[73]

It was a surprisingly broad spectrum of society that turned out on October 15, 1969, when a national one-day moratorium against the war left no doubt that antiwar sentiment had crossed over fully into the mainstream. A near "general strike" atmosphere seized the country, as at midday huge marches and observances took place involving students, teachers, businessmen, and many labor unions, including the UAW. It was in response to this overwhelming display of antiwar fervor that President Nixon took to the airwaves on November 3 to invoke "the great silent majority" of Americans who, he contended, still supported the war.

Mazzocchi, a New York native who was a combat veteran of the Second World War, was disappointed with the lack of consistent major labor union backing for the antiwar cause. Believing that labor had a moral obligation to demand the troops return home, he began organizing public meetings featuring speakers like Senators George McGovern and Alan Cranston as well as the UAW's Victor Reuther, and urged that labor back an antiwar amendment sponsored by McGovern and Senator Mark Hatfield that, in lieu of Congress issuing a formal declaration of war, would cease all funding of the Vietnam conflict except what was required to withdraw U.S. troops. Mazzocchi also coordinated one of labor's most prominent antiwar efforts—a full-page advertisement that ran in the *Washington Post* on February 25, 1970, signed by 110 individuals from the American Federation of Teachers, the UAW, the Teamsters, and the AFL-CIO. Headlined "A Rich Man's War and a Poor Man's Fight," the ad listed the war's costs to life and limb, its moral failings, and its harm to the U.S. society and economy ("Vietnam Eats Up Workers' Wages"; "Vietnam Causes Inflation") while demanding the immediate withdrawal of American forces. By May 1970, Washington Labor for Peace, the ad hoc group founded to place the *Post* advertisement, joined Business Executives Move for Vietnam Peace to hold a four-hundred-person public fast in Lafayette Square across from the White House.

That business executives should be found clasping hands with union members and other protestors in joint opposition to the war was in itself a remarkable acknowledgment of how far antiwar opposition had come, but the provocation for the unique event at Lafayette Square, a prime-time presidential address broadcast on April 29, had in fact unified protest nationwide. In his talk, Nixon revealed that he had ordered U.S. troops into Cambodia, an incursion he defended as necessary to attack Vietcong who were using Cambodia as a safe bastion from which to launch sorties against U.S. soldiers. "We will not allow American men by the thousands to be killed by an enemy from privileged sanctuary," the president said. He also announced that he was stepping up the bombing of North Vietnam, and then shared his justification for defying the intensity of antiwar sentiment at home. "If when the chips are down the world's most powerful nation . . . acts like a pitiful, helpless giant," Nixon averred, "the forces of totalitarianism and anarchy will threaten free nations and free institutions throughout the world." He offered to stake his own political future on staying the course, vowing, "I would rather be a one-term president and do what I believe was right than to be a two-term president at the cost of seeing America become a second-rate power and to see this nation accept the first defeat in its proud 190-year history."[74]

These two new strategic actions escalating the war, and Nixon's strongly worded defense of his policy, confirmed the antiwar movement's worst fears. The war would go on, and on. The sense of outrage was tragically compounded on May 4 when Ohio National Guardsmen fired on a group of student protestors at Kent State University, killing four and wounding eleven. Additional shootings of young people and students occurred in Augusta, Georgia, and at Jackson State in Mississippi, triggering massive protests as numerous colleges across the country were closed by student strikes. Several unions—from the left-leaning Local 1199 to the conservative Teamsters—sent telegrams to the White House demanding the president reverse course. "We've Had It!" declared an ad signed by 451 West Coast trade union leaders that ran in San Francisco papers. "You have created a credibility gap of incredible proportions. You have pledged to the American people that we will be out of Cambodia by June 30. In the light of [your] record, all we can say is—we don't believe you!"[75]

While it was not given particular notice amid the storm of protest, another significant chastisement came from Walter Reuther, who demanded the country's immediate withdrawal of its forces. On May 6 he issued a statement reprimanding Nixon for expanding a war that was based on a bankrupt policy, reminding him, "It is your responsibility to lead us out of the Southeast Asian War—to peace at home and abroad." Tragically, it would be Reuther's last public utterance. On the night of May 9 he and his wife, May, and four others flew in a chartered jet to the town of Pellston in northern Michigan, 260 miles north of Detroit, to inspect a UAW Family Education Center being built nearby on Black Lake. While attempting to land in fog and rain the plane descended short of the runway, clipped a number of trees, then crashed and burned a mile and a half southwest of the airport. There were no survivors.[76]

In a bizarre juxtaposition, reports of the sudden loss of one of labor's great men adjoined the extensive news accounts of one of the more shameful incidents in labor movement history—the assault on May 8 by hundreds of New York building trades workers on a lunchtime student antiwar protest in lower Manhattan. The students, from New York University, Hunter College, and area high schools, had rallied peacefully all morning at the corner of Wall and Broad streets; the construction workers had wandered over from their jobs on the World Trade Center site. "You brought down one president and you'll bring down another," a speaker had just assured the students, to loud applause, when the construction workers rammed their way to the front of the assembly and began using their yellow safety hard hats as bludgeons to attack the young people, as well as adult passersby who attempted to intervene. Yelling "Love it or leave it!" and "Kill the Commie bastards!" the attackers pursued their victims through the corridors of the city's financial district, knocking them down, kicking and stomping them, before heading en masse to nearby city hall, where liberal Republican mayor John Lindsay had ordered the American flag flown at half-staff to honor the students killed at Kent State.

Blue-collar New York had long had its doubts about Lindsay, beginning with the mayor's first day in office, January 1, 1966, when he'd been greeted by a paralyzing Transport Workers Union (TWU) strike. In the fourteen-day strike, which sidelined thirty-three thousand workers, the patrician, Yale-educated Lindsay met an implacable foe in TWU leader Mike Quill, an Irish immigrant and former Communist. City transit jobs, traditionally a bastion of working-class Irish, were increasingly being taken by blacks and Hispanics, and Quill was under pressure to close the gap between the less-than-$3-an-hour wage paid to minority cleaners and token booth clerks and the higher wage of $4 an hour he sought to accommodate the old-guard skilled Irish motormen. The new mayor had little experience dealing with labor issues, and for a New York politician he was singularly ill-prepared to tussle with a roughhewn character like Mike Quill, who gruffly dismissed one city offer as "a package of peanuts" and to his face told Lindsay (whose name he delighted in mispronouncing "Lindsley"), "You are nothing but a juvenile, a lightweight, and a pipsqueak. You have to grow up. You don't know anything about the working class. You don't know anything about labor unions."[77] When Quill was served an injunction for violating a state no-strike order governing the transit workers, he tore up the court's papers, defiance that led to his being jailed for contempt along with eight other union leaders. The TWU leader, who suffered from a heart condition, was sent to the prison ward at Bellevue Hospital.[78]

It was New York City that was in critical condition, however, losing millions of dollars a day in business and tax revenue. Bitter, unproductive strike negotiations ensued amid news reports of stranded commuters sleeping on armory cots, offices and stores unable to function, and tourists canceling their plans to visit the city. At a raucous TWU demonstration in City Hall Park, Lindsay was burned in effigy. Eventually the city capitulated, increasing wages and throwing in a special pension bonus. (Quill had scant time to savor his victory; he died of heart failure two days after being released from the hospital.)

Working-class resentment of the new administration, however, did not abate. This restive group saw its income depreciating, its streets and neighborhoods declining, while hippies and other elites acted out and elected officials appeared to bend over backward to assist minorities and the inner city. "What the hell does Lindsay care about me?" a New York ironworker complained to journalist Pete Hamill in 1969. "He doesn't care whether my kid has shoes, whether my boy gets a new suit for Easter, whether I got any money in the bank. None of them politicians give a good goddam. All they worry about is the niggers."[79] The mayor came in for a special bruising on February 9, 1969, when an unpredicted blizzard dumped fifteen inches of snow on New York City, closing streets and parkways for three days as the city struggled to locate snow-clearing equipment; the outer boroughs of Queens, Brooklyn, and the Bronx were largely ignored in the hasty cleanup effort. When the mayor traveled to Queens to walk the streets and reassure residents, he was greeted by boos and insults. "Get away, you bum!" one woman snapped as he tried to say hello, a reproach that might have been spoken by an increasing number of the city's 8 million residents toward a mayor who seemed more intent on grooming his image for a possible run at national office than seeing that the city delivered needed services to regular working people.[80]

Thus, at the time of the "hard hat" assaults of May 1970, Lindsay's decision to honor the martyred antiwar protestors of Kent State by flying the U.S. and city flags at half-staff struck many as further evidence of his clueless detachment. Demanding the banner above city hall be restored at once to its full height, the mob of construction workers easily intimidated the small police unit on hand, who quickly arranged for the flag to be raised. Moments later, however, a mayoral aide named Sid Davidoff re-lowered it, prompting the outraged workers to leap over barricades and charge to the front doors of city hall, where they threatened to storm inside if the flag was not immediately placed again in its rightful position. When this had been done, the men removed their helmets and sang the national anthem. Before leaving the area, some crossed the street to the campus of Pace University and proceeded to smash the school's ground-floor windows, which were covered in antiwar banners, then roughed up more students. That evening, television news reports showed scenes the likes of which America had never seen, as the burly "hard hats," seemingly unhampered by police, mobbed and beat terrified young men and women, many of whom were shown cowering defensively on the ground.[81]

Peter J. Brennan, head of the Building and Construction Trades Council of Greater New York, explained that the incident had not been orchestrated by union higher-ups—a claim exposed as false by subsequent press investigation. The office of Congressman Lowenstein had learned the night before of shop stewards telling construction workers they should take time off "to go and knock the heads of the kids who are protesting the Nixon-Kent thing," and had notified New York City police.[82] Brennan was no doubt more honest when he suggested the hard hat violence was deserved payback for the "violence" of the student demonstrators, "those who spat at the American flag and desecrated it," a view that, to the embarrassment of organized labor, was then echoed by George Meany. (There is no evidence the demonstrators had burned a flag, as Brennan and others contended.)[83]

Mayor Lindsay's wrath came to bear on the city's police brass, which he summoned to city hall and dressed down in private for three hours, demanding a review of police methods for controlling public protest. In response to these chastisements, on May 11 an even larger crowd of construction workers, estimated at two thousand, swarmed the same streets of lower Manhattan, chanting "Lindsay Is a Bum!" and carrying signs that read IMPEACH THE RED MAYOR! Approaching Pace University, the workers held signs intended for the eyes of students watching from the safety of upstairs windows: DON'T WORRY, THEY DON'T DRAFT FAGGOTS.[84]

In the wake of the hard hat spectacle, and in gratitude for Meany's support of the incursion into Cambodia, Nixon on May 12 received the AFL-CIO executive council, offering its members an exclusive briefing on reports from the war front. Clearly pleased to have found a core of blue-collar labor support, living proof of his "silent majority," the president also welcomed a group of building trades unionists to the White

House, where one presented him with an orange hard hat with NIXON written on it. May 20 brought the crowning of the New York construction workers' triumph, a massive, largely peaceful pro-war rally at city hall that aimed "to demonstrate that love of country and love and respect for our country's flag are not as old-fashioned and as out of date as the 'know-it-all's' would have us believe." Police estimated the gathering at one hundred thousand people.[85] Not to be outdone, the next day an antiwar crowd of about the same number convened in the same location. Calling itself the Labor-Student Coalition for Peace and hoisting signs that declared PEACE NOW, AVENGE KENT STATE, and MEANY DOESN'T SPEAK FOR ME, the rally sought to show that the hard hats did not represent organized labor and could not deter the antiwar solidarity of students and workers—a camaraderie that was largely still more wishful than fact.

While most Americans were repulsed by the scenes of bullies assaulting peaceful protestors, others expressed a sense of gratitude and relief that at last someone had stood up to the radical demonstrators. Such reaction bespoke a resentment for the perceived excesses of the antiwar movement and youth generally—the teach-ins and endless protests, the insults to the president and the military, the disrespect for elders, the indulgence of feminists and black nationalists, and the refusal to submit to the draft. The hard hats' sudden notoriety represented a genuine and growing sentiment—the monumental desire in the country for normalcy and the restoration of authority.

The Republican Party would cleverly exploit that yearning in the midterm elections of 1970, luring many working-class Americans away from their traditional home in the Democratic Party. James Buckley, younger brother of the well-known conservative William F. Buckley Jr., ran for U.S. senator from New York as an independent, facing Charles Goodell, a dovish Republican, and Democrat Richard Ottinger, an antiwar congressman. With the conservative side of the electorate all to himself, Buckley hit strongly on the themes of patriotism and class resentment, building successfully on the rift the hard hats had helped open. In upstate New York he was greeted warmly in appearances at factories, even though he supported right-to-work laws, the termination of unions' tax-exempt status for meddling in politics, and other anti-labor views. In the election, he was able to pry enough blue-collar workers from their traditional Democratic roost, and won the Senate seat.

At the same time across the country in California, Republican governor Ronald Reagan, an arch conservative and heir to the Barry Goldwater wing of the party, was challenged by Jesse M. Unruh, a Democratic state politician and confidant of Robert Kennedy's, who accused Reagan of being indifferent to the state's rising unemployment rate. Reagan, ringing the chimes of patriotism and law and order, won reelection with substantial labor support.

Both these elections were closely monitored by the Nixon White House as it eyed its own upcoming reelection bid in 1972. Determined to similarly pursue working-class support, the Nixon administration in December 1971 commuted the sentence of Jimmy Hoffa, who had served four and a half years of a thirteen-year term in federal prison, helping to secure the endorsement of the Teamsters. By contrast, the AFL-CIO refused to endorse the Democratic candidate, George McGovern, because of his dovish views on the war, a startling break from federation tradition. McGovern was a decorated combat veteran of the Second World War and a man so attuned to the historic difficulties of organized labor he had recently coauthored a well-regarded book about the Ludlow Massacre of 1914; on Election Day, America rejected him overwhelmingly.

ONE POSITIVE OUTCOME of the Republican determination to identify with the concerns of working families was the passage in 1970 of the landmark Occupational Safety and Health Act (OSHA), which for the first time established a federal apparatus for the creation of health and safety standards for the workplace and the monitoring of related illnesses and injuries. President Nixon had only narrowly beat Hubert Humphrey in the bitterly fought election of 1968, and had reason to think he would face the popular Democratic senator again in 1972, so he saw political advantage in taking the initiative on workplace safety, just the kind of bread-and-butter issue with which Humphrey was identified, and which Republicans were intent on poaching.

In addition to enjoying substantial labor support, the OSHA legislation was also very much of the moment culturally, part of a wave of new environmental and public health–related laws including the Wilderness Act (1964), the National Environmental Policy Act (1969), which created the Environmental Protection Agency, the Clean Air Act (1970), and the celebration of the first Earth Day, April 22, 1970. This surge in environmental awareness was a response to diverse influences—the back-to-the-land ethos of the sixties' counterculture; a reawakened reverence for nature and wilderness, as well as troubling headlines about mercury poisoning in seafood, Southern California smog alerts, and the industrial pollution of the nation's urban waterways. The new importance of man's environment had been reinforced by recent photographs from outer space that for the first time allowed humanity to gaze back in awe at its sole planetary home, and by the general precariousness of the atomic age. Concerns about atomic radiation from bomb tests and nuclear reactor sites led inevitably to questions about other potentially harmful man-made substances that lingered in nature.

The publication in 1962 of Rachel Carson's *Silent Spring*, a meticulously prepared account of the dangers of the commonly used pesticide DDT, served as a template for inquiry into other industrial products like leaded gasoline and food additives. Three years later another landmark book—Ralph Nader's *Unsafe at Any Speed*—exposed the inherent risks built into automobiles, eventually influencing laws and attitudes as had no other work since Upton Sinclair's *The Jungle* a half century before. Venerable organizations like the Sierra Club, the National Wildlife Federation, and the Audubon Society, and more recent arrivals such as Friends of the Earth and Zero Population Growth, were energized by a new sense of mission, while a tide of techno/environmental mass market paperbacks such as *The Population Bomb* by Paul Ehrlich, R. Buckminster Fuller's *Operating Manual for Spaceship Earth*, and Wesley Marx's *The Frail Ocean* overnight became essential campus reading, joining *Walden* by Henry

David Thoreau and Aldo Leopold's *A Sand County Almanac*. The concept of environmental public interest law—that citizens have legal standing to defend the environment in court—emerged from the seminal 1965 ruling in *Scenic Hudson Preservation Conference v. Federal Power Commission*, in which concerned residents of Cornwall-on-Hudson, New York, won the right to challenge Consolidated Edison's plans to build a power plant at Storm King Mountain in the pristine lower Hudson River Valley. All these developments contributed to the dawning idea that citizens, consumers, and workers had the right, even the obligation, to question the potentially detrimental effects of industry and public utilities, what they produced, and how they produced it, in the context of public health and safety as well as any aesthetic or environmental impacts.

The invigorated concern for public health and the environment that produced OSHA in the late 1960s had been decades in the making. Devotion to what could be made better, faster, and with the utmost profit had almost always trumped attempts to rein in new products, challenge their potentially hazardous side effects, or question the faith in technology generally. A sensational early example was the so-called Looney Gas Scare of the 1920s, in which industrial health experts Alice Hamilton of the Harvard Medical School and Yandell Henderson of Yale University squared off against the combined might of DuPont, General Motors, and the Standard Oil Company of New Jersey over the manufacture and sale of lead-doped gasoline, marketed as Ethyl. Workers at DuPont who handled a concentrated form of tetraethyl lead had begun experiencing severe neurological problems (some had died or committed suicide). Once Ethyl went on sale, it was feared, millions of automobiles would begin belching leaded exhaust fumes that might be especially dangerous in enclosed areas such as tunnels or busy city streets.

Newspaper accounts of the DuPont employees who had gone mad or become incapacitated from exposure to tetraethyl lead stirred considerable worry among the public, and a federal commission was appointed to look into the matter. Hamilton and Henderson's warnings about the risks of leaded gasoline before the inquiry were, as it turned out, prophetic, but the day was won by the corporations, which held out the availability of lead gasoline additives as "a gift from God" in terms of their potential to improve automotive acceleration and make possible the manufacture of bigger cars. The panel, and society at large, was seduced by the evidence that America was living through a dynamic age of invention and technology, and that the fruits of these endeavors were to be developed without succumbing to the paranoid warnings of "health cranks."

To the frustration of Frances Perkins and other reformers from the factory safety movement who graduated to positions in the Roosevelt administration, the Depression also proved an inopportune time to advance workers' health issues, as they were shunted aside for more pressing economic concerns. It required an especially horrific 1936 industrial health scandal from West Virginia to grab the attention of Congress and the nation. Near the village of Gauley Bridge, about twenty-five miles southeast of Charleston, several thousand black and white laborers worked for as little as 30 cents an hour on the Hawk's Nest Tunnel, a Union Carbide project to divert water from the New River to create hydroelectric power. The workers called Hawk's Nest "the Tunnel of Death" due to the prevalence of silicosis, a lethal respiratory disease they contracted because the three-mile-long excavation was being bored through rock, the drilling churning up fine silica dust against which the workers had inadequate protection. "The dust was so thick that workers sometimes could see barely ten feet in the train headlights," reads one account. "Instead of waiting thirty minutes after blasting, as required by state law, workers were herded back into the tunnel immediately, often beaten by foremen with pick handles."[86] They also were warned never to speak of the company's authoritarian methods. But employees knew of an unmarked mass grave in the nearby town of Summerville where the bodies of the dead were interred, "their only gravestones cornstalks waving in the wind, their shrouds the overalls in which they died," according to a labor newspaper.[87] "I don't know what's wrong but I'm a-goin' to die," one young tunnel worker confided to his mother. "I think it's from my work. I want you to have me cut open. If you can get anything from the company, go ahead."[88]

The situation at Hawk's Nest went unnoticed for the same reasons government has always been challenged to adequately monitor workplace health and safety—the difficulty of gaining access to job sites for inspection, and the perennial lack of regulatory law backed by sufficient funding and manpower. The Walsh-Healey Act of 1936 gave Washington the right to establish safety rules for companies that had contracts worth more than $10,000 with the federal government, but fewer than 5 percent of the seventy-five thousand workplaces eligible under Walsh-Healey were ever examined.[89] Inspections were procedurally involved and required a committed budget, and there were simply too many risks—poisons, explosives, industrial compounds, faulty machinery—for any single agency to fully catalog and investigate them. And while some issues were easy to spot, such as loose flooring in a factory, others might be slow in showing their detrimental effect; indeed, many workers' health conditions—from inhaling cotton dust in textile mills, coal dust in deep mines, or "phossy jaw" from the manufacturing of matches—might take seven or eight years to develop, long after an individual worker had left the employ of a particular mine or factory, making the assignment of culpability difficult. Employers and employer associations also found the means to finesse these issues by supporting weak state enforcement and inspection regimes, or by funding their own scientific specialists to write articles or appear before government panels to counter the claims of safety and industrial health reformers.

The president of Rinehart & Dennis, Union Carbide's chief contractor, dismissed the West Virginia silicosis allegations as "gross misrepresentation and falsehood," but Congress would later determine that as many as 476 men had died and another 1,500 were severely stricken by silicosis at the Gauley Bridge tunnel. It also found that while tunnel inspectors were issued masks before entering the site, none had been given to the workers.[90] A lawsuit against Rinehart & Dennis resulted in payments of between $80 and $250 for blacks and $250 and $1,000 for whites stricken with the disease, although many long-term sufferers were denied compensation because the West Virginia statute of limitations had expired. In the wake of the Gauley Bridge hearings of 1936, Secretary Perkins sug-

gested that other states act at once to investigate and produce legislation to address silicosis, but the main result of her pleadings proved to
be the creation by industry of a pseudoscientific front group, the Industrial Health Foundation, designed to use "expert medical testimony and
advice" to fend off claims of injury and inhibit reform.[91]

In lieu of sweeping measures on worker health and safety from the
federal government, Perkins did bring about the creation in 1934 of the
Division of Labor Standards (DLS), which sought to educate workers
and labor unions about industrial hazards. The DLS had an activist bent,
pushing organized labor to include health and safety demands in their
bargaining efforts with employers, and assisting unions directly by giving
them information on specific health issues. It also compiled fact sheets
and wrote sample legislation for the states, urging them to increase factory inspections and retrain injured workers, while putting in place codes
of workplace safety and health that would match those in the most Progressive states such as New York.[92]

Authentic industry compliance with Perkins's DLS would not come
until the onset of the Second World War, when the National Committee for the Conservation of Manpower in Defense Industries began sending volunteer inspectors into defense-related plants under the terms of
the Walsh-Healey Act. Even formerly uncooperative plant managers had
begun to display concern about health and safety issues due to the pressures of war production, and because many wartime personnel—women,
blacks, and other unskilled workers—were entering factories for the first
time.[93] By war's end the DLS had prompted the inspection of twenty-one
thousand job sites, with many positive changes seen in on-site safety.[94]

I N THE POSTWAR ERA management resumed its resistance to government or employee intervention, business seeming to abhor health
and safety regulation much as it did the threat of the closed shop. Reformers had to be content with occasional wildcat strikes or newspaper expo-
sés related to specific problems such as poor mine ventilation. In 1952,
however, Hubert Humphrey introduced a bill in Congress for the setting

of national work safety standards and the provision of federal workplace inspectors, legislation that received the backing of the CIO. The press was generally supportive, one article noting that in the entire United States there were only sixteen hundred state workplace inspectors, half the number of fish and game wardens. But the Humphrey initiative was curtailed by a resistant AFL, which still favored a state-based approach; business lobbyists revealingly explained they opposed a federal solution because the risks involved in the nation's industry were so numerous, as many as ten thousand inspectors would be required to investigate them; some manufacturing operations, they complained, would require a full-time inspector.[95] Another familiar employer argument—that state safety laws might vary so greatly, they would "cripple" a business by forcing it to adopt costly measures a competitor across state lines could avoid—also served in fact as a strong rationale for uniform national standards.

The concept of a federal regulatory mechanism received a boost at the end of the decade, when an inquiry into previously mandated safety standards for longshoremen and harbor workers, occupations with unusually high levels of workplace injury, found that industry compliance had brought a sharp decrease in injuries. The dockworkers' example moved the Labor Department in 1960 to announce that states would have to adhere to new, more stringent federal safety guidelines when inspecting any job site involved with a federal defense contract. Cries of outrage were heard from the Chamber of Commerce and the National Safety Council, infuriated they had been bypassed in the shaping of so consequential an edict, but the pressure for federal legislation continued to grow. In 1965 the Public Health Service (PHS) reported to the Surgeon General that a new chemical entered the workplace every twenty minutes, that some of these substances were carcinogenic, and recommended the PHS establish a program to reduce occupational health dangers.[96] Organized labor, increasingly taking an interest in the possibility of a sweeping federal role and impressed by the PHS claims, urged the Surgeon General to pursue the matter. By May 1966 President Johnson added his voice to the demand for workplace health standards, assigning the task to Health, Education and Welfare Secretary John Gardner. Coal miners, hard hit by a respiratory ailment known as black lung, and uranium workers, diagnosed with workplace-related cancer, were also beginning to speak out. In March 1967 the *Washington Post* reported that as many as one hundred uranium miners had died of lung cancer in recent years and that as many as one thousand more such deaths might be expected. Uranium mining had begun in Colorado during the Second World War under the auspices of the Atomic Energy Commission (AEC), but all relevant federal agencies had missed dealing with the industry's health problems: the AEC neglected workers' health issues in general, the Bureau of Mines did not inspect uranium mines, and the Labor Department had kept hands off despite the fact that Walsh-Healey permitted it to oversee safety in government-contract work. Secretary of Labor Willard Wirtz was moved by the *Post*'s exposé to replace the AEC's standards for safety in uranium mining with much tougher ones designed by his department. The problems facing uranium miners remained in the news for years as miners sought relief at the state and federal levels.[97]

Unions across the nation including the UAW and the Steelworkers began stepping up their efforts on workplace health. In the late 1960s Tony Mazzocchi of the Oil, Chemical and Atomic Workers (OCAW) started visiting workplaces in the company of a physician to discuss with workers the health risks of industrial toxins that had the potential to harm them and their families. These were information-gathering encounters for Mazzocchi, who listened to myriad workers' tales of recurrent respiratory problems, cancer clusters, mysterious illnesses, even the deaths of coworkers. Mazzocchi had begun his labor career in a perfume factory in Long Island City as a "colonizer," a worker who takes a job with the intent to organize others, and was thus familiar with the lack of knowledge and safety protections among workers who spent their days handling, mixing, and transporting chemicals and industrial compounds. Mazzocchi tried where possible to stir up press interest in the stories he heard and urged stricken workers to write to their congressmen. He also encouraged labor to ally with the burgeoning environmental movement, disavowing the oft-cited antagonism between the two forces centered on the fear of job loss in industries affected by environmental restrictions. "We're making the point that you can't be concerned about the general environment unless you're concerned about the industrial environment, because the two are inseparable," he said in an appearance on NBC's *Today* program. He also reminded industrial workers of their larger connection to the environment, in that most pollutants found there originated in factories. "Let's face it," he said, "*we* are responsible . . . *we* make them. When you . . . see what we're putting into the water, which we ultimately have to drink and depend upon for life, and what we introduce into the air, you have a very frightening picture."[98]

In January 1968 President Johnson, calling it shameful that fourteen thousand American workers were killed on the job each year and more than 2 million injured or sickened, told Congress that the time had come to produce comprehensive federal workplace safety legislation.[99] Labor Secretary Wirtz proved a strong advocate in congressional hearings, urging efforts "to stop a carnage" that continues because people "can't see the blood on the food that they eat, on the things that they buy, and on the service they get."[100] Most major unions voiced support for the bill, as did Ralph Nader, while industry spokesmen complained that such measures would hand excessive regulatory powers to the federal government. As Congress took up the matter, however, the Labor Department made an unfortunate stumble, publishing a booklet, titled *On the Job Slaughter*, that contained disturbing images of a variety of workplace injuries. The photographs were meant to shock, but business pounced on and trumpeted the fact that most of the photographs appeared to be at least thirty years old. The bill the president had encouraged and organized labor had backed did not make it out of committee.

Mazzocchi believed the legislation had died largely for want of public pressure, and after President Nixon took office in January 1969 Mazzocchi helped orchestrate a greater lobbying effort by the Steelworkers, OCAW, and other unions. The new round of congressional hearings focused on a more conservative bill, suggestive of a greater advisory and less regulatory role for government. A key point of disagreement was the extent to which the Labor Department would control the program. Unions wanted both standard-making and enforcement functions to remain in the department, while industry asked for two separate and independent boards to administer these functions, not trusting the Labor Department to be a fair arbiter of management's interests. Organized labor feared this possibility because the choice of appointees to an independent agency would be too easily influenced by whoever sat in the White House. After several versions of the bill had been debated and amendments considered, it was agreed that the Labor Department would retain the important role of establishing standards and inspections, and a separate commission would hear violations and complaints and levy fines. A research entity, the National Institute for Occupational Safety and Health (NIOSH), was created to conduct objective studies that would determine the severity of workplace threats.

Thus, somewhat nervously supported by business forces such as the Chamber of Commerce, which understood some kind of legislation was inevitable and preferred it come from a Republican administration, and backed solidly by OCAW, the UAW, the Steelworkers, and the AFL-CIO, the Occupational Safety and Health Act was signed into law by President Nixon in late December 1970. Hailed as a "safety bill of rights," it extended federal protections for the first time to 56 million U.S. private sector workers. The new law gave the federal government the right to establish standards through a comment and review process, inspect workplaces, issue violations, and obtain court injunctions to close plants; it was also allowed to respond to workers' demand for an OSHA inspection without prior notice to management, with employees gaining the right to accompany an OSHA inspector on company premises to ensure he or she observed all suspected violations.

The first several years of OSHA governance were far from encouraging. Underfinanced and overwhelmed by the tasks it faced, by mid-1971 only ninety-three hundred out of 4 million workplaces had been inspected; of these, only 20 percent were found to be violation-free, suggesting that many violations awaited discovery and enforcement. Soon after, during a nine-month period in 1971–1972, OSHA was able to inspect 20,688 plants, 77 percent of which were found not to be in compliance.[101] Some representatives of organized labor fretted about the snail-like pace of reform, but as Ralph Nader pointed out in summer 1972, even they were having difficulty adjusting to the heightened focus on factory health and safety oversight. "Not one union has a physician, or engineer, or scientist, or lawyer working full time in Washington on the problem," Nader complained.[102] Things moved slowly on the standard-setting end as well. Of the fifteen thousand hazardous chemicals known to be used in U.S. industry, by August 1972 OSHA had set standards for only five hundred, a serious shortfall, as OSHA, since opening for business, had been inundated by worker complaints and questions from across the country about routinely handled chemical compounds. As an article in *Today's Health* reminded the government officials among its readers, "It is not the rickety banister but the deadly vapor that worries the working man most."[103]

T HE DISTRESSING STORY of a young female technician at a nuclear materials processing facility in Oklahoma helped bring the issue into tighter focus. Karen Silkwood, twenty-eight years old in 1974 and a divorced mother of three, had started work at the Kerr-McGee Nuclear Corporation two years earlier. The plant was located in the town of Crescent, not far from Oklahoma City, and belonged to Kerr-McGee's constellation of energy interests in oil, coal, uranium, timber, and chemicals. Robert S. Kerr, a governor and U.S. senator known for his larger-than-life personality as "the Big Boom from Oklahoma," had helped found the company in 1929; Dean A. McGee, a famously gifted explorer of valuable oil sites, joined in 1938. Kerr-McGee was one of the better-paying employers in the Oklahoma City area, and Silkwood felt fortunate to have a job there, particularly one that drew on her expertise, having attended Lamar University in Beaumont, Texas, on a science scholarship. She was paid $3.45 an hour, a slightly higher wage than that received by her coworkers.

The facility in Crescent manufactured plutonium pellets that were assembled into eight-foot-long fuel rods to be used in an experimental fast breeder reactor being built for the AEC near Richland, Washington. Plutonium, a by-product of neutron-bombarded uranium, made its first appearance in 1945 when it was used in the atomic bomb dropped by the United States on Nagasaki, Japan. Because the substance is highly radioactive, Kerr-McGee gave extra attention to how it was handled. Silkwood's job was to perform quality-control tests on the pellets as well as the finished rods to make sure the welds were perfect.

In fall 1972, shortly after she came to Kerr-McGee, Karen joined OCAW Local 5–283 in a strike for higher wages. The company, financially secure and able to find eager replacement workers from economically struggling Oklahoma farms, held out for several months. Of the original one hundred OCAW strikers who struck Kerr-McGee, only twenty, including Silkwood, withstood the urge to return without a contract. The firm eventually did agree to a new pact with the workers, bringing her back to work, but she had become politicized by her experience on the picket line.

There was little about Silkwood's background to suggest a role as a rebellious workplace advocate; relatively unworldly, she had come of age in the small-town environment of Texas and Oklahoma. But she was known to her friends and family as outspoken and stubborn, and as events would demonstrate, she could be, in the words of one biographer, "as tenacious as an abalone on a rock."[104] One colleague later recalled hearing her tell a superior, "Goddamit, I am right and you are wrong. If you want to tell me what to do, you oughta learn how to do the job right."[105] Drawn deeper into work with her OCAW local, Silkwood soon began curtailing many of her social activities, causing some coworkers to regard her with suspicion.

In spring 1974 the pace of work at the plant was stepped up, schedules were lengthened, and—most disturbing to Karen—the already mediocre plant radiation safety measures were relaxed. She was particularly worried about the young men Kerr-McGee had hired as replacements during the strike, many right off the farm. Having received a shortened version of the usual safety training, they were largely ignorant of radiation's dangers. The plant's new safety director, also hired at the time of the strike, held a degree in poultry science. Around the same time the usually upbeat Karen, who only a couple of years earlier had told a boyfriend, "I feel like I'm in love with the whole world," began to experience bouts of depression. After working her twelve-hour night shift at the plant she often found it hard to sleep, so a physician prescribed for her a new muscle relaxant known as Quaalude, upon which she soon grew reliant.[106] On July 31, 1974, Silkwood was mildly contaminated in a work incident. It did not appear to seriously threaten her health, but when a coworker was also contaminated a short time later, she expressed her concern about lax safety precautions to the company.

Later that summer Karen's local tapped her to be one of three employees on an OCAW bargaining committee. Kerr-McGee had called for a National Labor Review Board–monitored election for October 16 to challenge whether OCAW had enough support at the Crescent site to continue to represent its workers, an effort known as decertification. Winning the election, maintaining the union's NLRB certification as the designated bargaining representative for Kerr-McGee employees, was crucial to Silkwood and her cohorts, as a new contract was due to be negotiated later that fall and, for the first time, safety measures were to be a key issue. One of her colleagues, Jack Tice, had written to OCAW headquarters in Washington to complain that safety practices were not all they should be at the plant, and union vice president Elwood Swisher wrote back advising Tice to closely monitor the methods in question and then come to Washington to report. Karen began taking meticulous notes of safety violations she observed.

The local's chances in the decertification election were not terribly good, as many of the original OCAW workers had departed during the 1972 strike and their jobs were now held permanently by the nonunion replacements. Nationally OCAW had 185,000 members, but the group at Kerr-McGee was small, and Oklahoma City was remote from other locals around the country. To Jack Tice, Karen Silkwood, and Jerry Brewer—the three members of the bargaining unit—it seemed likely the local's chances would be improved if their efforts on plant safety could be shown to bear fruit, and it was with this in mind that the three left Oklahoma secretly for Washington on September 26 to meet with OCAW officials. They were also to meet with representatives of the AEC. It was Karen's first time on an airplane.

Greeting them in the union's Washington office was Tony Mazzocchi, the former New York chemical worker who had led OCAW's lobbying efforts in the lead-up to OSHA, and now headed the union's legislative office, and Steve Wodka, the union's legislative assistant. Mazzocchi was at the time busy with asbestos-related illness issues, but he nodded with understanding as the three visitors recounted the safety abuses at Kerr-McGee. When Mazzocchi explained that plutonium was one of the most highly carcinogenic substances known to mankind, Silkwood and her cohorts were shocked: no one at Kerr-McGee had ever warned workers that the material they handled each day could cause cancer.

During a break, when her two coworkers were out of earshot, Silkwood confided to Mazzocchi that Kerr-McGee was not simply negligent in its safety efforts, but that she believed workers occasionally cheated at quality control, passing along plutonium rods that were not safe. Mazzocchi was stunned. Such an allegation went well beyond workplace health concerns, since leaking fuel rods might potentially cause a meltdown or explosion at a nuclear plant, putting the public at risk. These were serious charges, and before they could be shared with the AEC, Mazzocchi and Wodka quietly instructed Silkwood "to go back to the plant, to find out who was falsifying the records, who was ordering it and to document everything in specific detail."[107] Mazzocchi asked Silkwood not to mention the quality-control cheating issue to anyone, as it was a grave allegation and would require hard facts to prove. If she could get evidence of her claims, he promised, he would get David Burnham, a reporter he knew at the *New York Times*, to look into the story.

Before the visitors returned to Oklahoma, Mazzocchi also suggested that OCAW arrange for scientists to come to the Crescent plant to inform the workers about the dangers of plutonium. Not only was this the right thing to do, he said, it would enhance the union's stature with the workers as the decertification election neared. Accordingly, six days before the election, on October 10, two scientists dispatched by OCAW arrived in Crescent to describe the risks of cancer to about fifty interested Kerr-McGee workers. They detailed how fine plutonium dust could get inside one's lungs, stomach, and esophagus. On October 16 the workers voted 80–61 to retain OCAW as their bargaining agent.

Now what remained was for Silkwood to get the evidence that Mazzocchi needed to expose safety cheating at Kerr-McGee. Karen was alone in this effort and not having an easy time. At work, she experienced three episodes of contamination and began suffering other health and emotional problems. She was by now using Quaaludes habitually, and had begun losing weight (she was down to ninety-four pounds); she'd also grown concerned, she told some close friends, that someone was after her, trying to hurt her, and that they had come into her home and put plutonium there. A Kerr-McGee team sent to her home found extremely high radiation readings, especially on a bologna sandwich in her refrigerator. A fecal test showed that Silkwood had ingested plutonium, and it also appeared that someone had placed plutonium in her urine-sample kit at work.

"Several people conceivably had motives for intimidating her," investigative reporter Howard Kohn would write later in *Rolling Stone*, "a plant supervisor worried about being found out for falsifying records, a higher-up who feared a scandal, a coworker concerned that she would cost others their jobs." Despite Mazzocchi's strict warning to Silkwood not to tell anyone of her suspicions about safety cheating, it came to light that she had confided her undercover inquiries to at least one colleague. Wodka later theorized that word had gotten out what she was doing, or that she had been seen taking notes about the falsifying, and that in order to scare her and perhaps force her to quit the plant, someone poisoned the food in her refrigerator and also contaminated her urine samples.[108]

An AEC inquiry that followed Kerr-McGee's own investigation confirmed that Silkwood had ingested plutonium and that her urine samples had been tampered with after they'd been excreted. Her roommate Sherri Ellis was also found to have been contaminated, likely by plutonium in their apartment. Kerr-McGee, disavowing knowledge of any clandestine effort to smear Silkwood's reputation or contaminate her, suggested that she had for some reason carried plutonium out of the plant and taken it home.[109]

Karen, in long-distance phone calls to OCAW's Steve Wodka, with whom she'd had a casual affair while in Washington, admitted being frightened, but said she had managed to gather information on Kerr-McGee's falsifying of quality-control measures. He arranged to come to Oklahoma City on November 13, bringing along reporter David Burnham to meet her and see the evidence. That night the two men were waiting several miles away at a motel north of the city for Silkwood, who was to come there directly after attending an OCAW local meeting at a café in downtown Crescent. Silkwood never arrived. Driving alone on Highway 74 south toward the city, her car veered off the road, crossed the median, and struck a culvert on the opposite shoulder. She was killed instantly.

Because there were no skid marks to suggest she had tried to brake, police deduced that Silkwood had fallen asleep at the wheel. This conclusion sounded unlikely to those who knew Karen, and particularly to Wodka, who doubted she would doze off given the importance of her meeting with Burnham and the risks she was taking. It simply seemed out of character. Critically, the manila folder stuffed with documents Karen intended to give the reporter, and that others had seen her holding at the OCAW meeting at the restaurant, was missing from the crash site and never found. Unhappy with the official police version of her death, the union hired veteran Texas accident investigator A. O. Pipkin to examine the crash. Pipkin, who had handled two thousand such inquiries in his long career, explained that when a driver falls asleep at the wheel their car usually drifts to the right, not the left, as Karen's had; he also hypothesized that from the tracks the vehicle had left, as well as indications she was gripping the steering wheel tightly at the moment of impact, she had not fallen asleep as she drove. He offered the alternative theory that her car had been rammed from behind, forcing her to lose control.

Despite the scrutiny of Pipkin, other experts, journalists, and investigators over the years, and recollections offered by colleagues, friends, and family, the case of Karen Silkwood has never been fully explained. Was she overly eager to embarrass her employer on behalf of her OCAW local or in the interest of publicizing the dangers of plutonium? Did her emotional state and her reliance on painkillers lead her to make irrational statements? Did she bring plutonium into her own home? Or was she the victim of a corporate conspiracy or a vendetta by a fellow employee?

While such questions will likely never be answered, Silkwood was correct that Kerr-McGee had failed to provide workers with adequate information about the risks of plutonium-related illness, and right to be alarmed by the corner-cutting she'd perceived in quality and safety control (some of her claims were later substantiated, but not all were as serious as she had believed). Whatever the circumstances of her death, she was a martyr to the principle that workers have a right to be fully informed about dangers in their place of work, and that employers have a moral duty to protect them.[110] As her mother suggested, months after laying her daughter to rest, "We never did appreciate Karen as much as we should have. Look what she did. She gave her life to save others."[111]

CHAPTER ELEVEN

A TIME FOR CHOOSING

ABRAHAM LINCOLN VALUED ORGANIZED LABOR; Grover Cleveland sent the army to suppress it; Harry Truman challenged the right to strike in coal, rail, and steel; Lyndon Johnson acted on issues of workplace health. But it was left to Ronald Reagan, the nation's fortieth president, to do what none had done before: destroy a labor union. Reagan's decimation in 1981 of the Professional Air Traffic Controllers Organization (PATCO) would prove a seminal failure of labor-management relations in America, one from which the labor movement has never fully recovered. Coming early in his initial term, the showdown with the nation's air traffic controllers would reveal the extent to which the ground had weakened under labor's feet and would offer a first, and to many an unpleasant, glimpse at Reagan's presidential mien.

As he never tired of reminding people, Reagan was a former president of the Screen Actors Guild (SAG) and the first member of the AFL to occupy the White House. Even the unionized air traffic controllers had been impressed enough with Reagan's labor bona fides—and by a statement of support he gave the union while a candidate—to buck the trend of the wider labor movement and endorse him over incumbent Jimmy Carter in the election of 1980. But despite Reagan's union affiliation in Hollywood and his oft-cited admiration for Franklin D. Roosevelt, he had in fact never been entirely comfortable with either the collective nature of labor organizations or the means by which they sought their objectives.

Reagan's SAG experience during the 1940s was strongly influenced by contemporary political currents as well as the troubled status of unionization in the film industry. Los Angeles was not particularly union-friendly, due to the pressure of a continual stream of job seekers from elsewhere, a large local unemployed class, and an historic contempt for radicalism of any kind. Movie studios were perpetually strained by tight budgets and schedules, and viewed work stoppages as potentially calamitous, while the industry's transience resulted in nonstandardized hiring practices and harsh working conditions, as well as an inhibition against labor organizing.

Concern among studio heads intensified in the late 1920s with the advent of sound motion pictures, as hundreds of stage actors, many of them members of Actors Equity, which had won a closed shop on Broadway, began making their way to California. In 1927 Louis B. Mayer, head of Metro-Goldwyn-Mayer (MGM), formed a company union, the Academy of Motion Picture Arts and Sciences (later sponsors of the Academy Awards), intended to thwart the formation of independent unions. The Academy succeeded at gathering numerous Hollywood professionals under its umbrella, and did produce labor contracts, but it also enforced management-friendly regulations including salary caps, limits on the activities of talent agents, and rules prohibiting studios from poaching one another's stars.

When, in 1933, in response to the Depression, the Academy moved to impose a 50 percent wage cut on actors' salaries, resentment boiled over, and a contingent broke away to found the Screen Actors Guild (SAG). With the almost simultaneous passage of the NIRA and its Section 7(a), there occurred, as historian Garry Wills notes, "a stampede of stars out of the Academy and into the Guild."[1] SAG's first success was shaking free of the controlling rules the Academy had put in place limiting actors' freedom to chart their own careers. The next year SAG and Actors Equity agreed to peacefully coexist, and SAG was accepted into the AFL.[2]

Reagan joined the West Coast film colony in 1937. A radio sportscaster with the Chicago Cubs, he had come to California on a spring training trip with the team, and while in Hollywood arranged to be screen-tested. Warner Bros. liked what it saw in the affable young man from Illinois and offered a seven-year contract. Reagan's film career, which spanned fifty-three movies, would be spent almost exclusively in second-tier productions such as *Love Is on the Air* (1937), *Dark Victory* in 1939 with Bette Davis, *Santa Fe Trail* (1940), *Knute Rockne All American* (1940), and *This Is the Army* (1943). He joined SAG and in 1941 was elected to its board; in 1947, after stateside service in the Second World War, he became the union's president, a position he would hold until 1952, and then again briefly in 1959.

One of his first experiences with union politics came during the war, when SAG was drawn into a dispute involving the Conference of Studio Unions (CSU), a coalition of technical workers' labor groups that included some members of the Communist Party, and the reigning AFL-affiliated technicians' union, the International Association of Theatrical and Stage Employees (IATSE). Reagan was part of a SAG team that met for months with the disputants in what proved a futile effort to resolve the standoff, and he came away disgusted by the process. "Some days I'd go home after hours of negotiations and think we'd made some progress toward a settlement," he later wrote. "But the next morning we'd meet again and the strikers would walk into the room with their lawyers and 27 new demands we'd never discussed before, which they said had to be settled before they'd call off the strike."[3] Becoming impatient with so much pointless discussion, which he characterized as "a basketful of words," Reagan concluded that the CSU's implacability derived from communistic influence. In the years immediately following the war Reagan's concern about Communism deepened, as he came to believe leftist unions were trying to impact Hollywood generally. "American movies occupied 70 percent of all the playing time on the world's movie screens in those first years after World War II," he would later write, "and, as was to become more and more apparent to me, Joseph Stalin had set out to make Hollywood an instrument of propaganda of Soviet expansionism aimed at communizing the world."[4]

Such a suspicion on Reagan's part might have been attributable to his own wartime work in U.S. propaganda films, but he was hardly alone in holding this extreme view. Anti-Communist fervor was pervasive enough in the movie colony to infect everyone from cartoonist Walt Disney to gossip columnists Hedda Hopper and Louella Parsons, as well as Reagan's own brother, Neil. Neil Reagan, along with Hopper and Parsons, was recruited by FBI director J. Edgar Hoover to gather information about questionable local lefties. Neil at one point warned his brother to terminate his membership in the Hollywood Independent Citizens Committee of the Arts, Sciences, and Professions (HICCASP), founded in 1944 to support President Roosevelt's reelection, because it had become a "suspect" organization. The group did have Communists as members but was not dominated by them. Although Reagan took Neil's advice and resigned from HICCASP (along with friend and fellow member Olivia de Havilland), the future president was himself inquired after by the FBI because he had attended meetings of liberal organizations, including one opposed to aiding Chinese Nationalist Chiang Kai-shek.

In order to join the fight against malignant Soviet influence, and to protect his career, Reagan turned FBI informant. Assigned an informer's code number, T-10, he secretly provided to the FBI the names of SAG members he thought had Communist sympathies, and in 1947 he testified before the House Un-American Activities Committee (HUAC), although he did not name names in that appearance.[5]

Reagan, like many in Hollywood, was wary initially of the coming of television—he feared its incessant need for content would create an inferior product and ruin the experience of moviegoing—but he and the new medium proved a highly successful match. In the early 1950s he became a familiar presence in American homes as the host and occasional star of television's *General Electric Theater*. General Electric, which was in the process of diversifying its operations and opening autonomous plants across the country, sent Reagan on the road each year to make promotional appearances at new GE sites. He worked hard to perfect his standard anecdote-filled speech, which, "couched in uncomplicated *Reader's Digest* prose," was "a primer of conservative doctrine," touting free enterprise, criticizing the excesses of the New Deal, and warning about the dangers posed by the Soviet Union.[6] Reagan was often called upon to give the address twice in one day—to GE workers, then again later in a public hall or school auditorium.

Reagan did this for eight years, later claiming to have visited all 135 General Electric facilities. The speech, which came to be called "A Time for Choosing," depicted an America endangered; the enemy at the gates was collectivism in the form of big government, and each citizen would need to count himself ready to meet the challenge. "We have come to a time for choosing," Reagan offered. "Either we accept the responsibility for our own destiny, or we abandon the American Revolution and confess that an intellectual belief in a far-distant capital (Washington) can plan our lives for us better than we can plan them ourselves."[7]

His relationship with GE ended in 1962 when the firm canceled the *General Electric Theater*. There were whispers the company had pulled the plug on the show partly out of concern its spokesman had gone over the edge politically, but by then Reagan was enough in demand as a speaker that he could carry on even without GE's sponsorship, although he also continued to pick up sporadic work in Hollywood, appearing in his last film, *The Killers*, in 1964, and serving through 1965 as the host of the televised western series *Death Valley Days*.

Reagan's formal coming-out as a political figure is usually associated with an October 27, 1964, appearance he made on behalf of Republican presidential candidate Barry Goldwater, at which he delivered his signature talk and raised $1 million for the Goldwater campaign.[8] Reagan, however, was by then part of a crusade far grander than Goldwater's election hopes (which against popular incumbent Lyndon Johnson were slim). A fringe but powerful New Right coalition had been germinating ever since the 1952 Republican Party Convention, where conservative senator Bob Taft, coauthor of the Taft-Hartley Bill, had been rejected as a presidential candidate in favor of Dwight Eisenhower. Taft himself died in 1953, but his brand of isolationism, anti-Communism, and anti–New Deal rhetoric survived among other influential figures such as Phyllis Schlafly, author of *A Choice Not an Echo*; Robert Welch (who would soon found the John Birch Society); and Goldwater himself, whose 1960 book, *The Conscience of a Conservative*, was a bestseller. The surge of New Right activity also produced John A. Stormer's 1964 *None Dare Call It Treason*, which alleged Communist influence over the American media.

Goldwater, as expected, lost to Johnson in a landslide, but the seeds of the coming conservative revolution had been sown, Reagan one of its most promising figures. It had long been assumed in California that a career in politics was his for the taking, and he had been approached about running for the U.S. Senate or the governorship. It was to this latter office that Reagan successfully ascended in 1966, the first step on his journey to the presidency and his confrontation with the nation's air traffic controllers.

FROM THE BOSTON POLICE STRIKE of 1919 to the Memphis Sanitation Strike of 1968, there had long been disagreement about the labor rights of government employees at the municipal, state, and also the national level. In January 1962 President John F. Kennedy issued an executive order allowing federal employees to form unions and collectively bargain, and the Postal Reorganization Act, passed in 1969, established a means for binding arbitration in the face of labor stalemates involving postal employees. While these steps signaled acceptance by the federal government of its employees' rights to organize and negotiate their demands, the Taft-Hartley Act and later the Civil Service Reform Act of 1978 prohibited federal workers from striking. But could Americans in the nation's employ really be expected to forgo so fundamental a weapon?

At what point would even they deserve the right to strike? By 1981 the no-strike concept had begun to appear particularly anachronistic because the government was increasingly hiring contract services from the private sector, meaning that at some work sites a federal employee who was not at liberty to strike might work side by side with a colleague who was free to do so.[9]

The seventeen thousand members of the Professional Air Traffic Controllers Organization (PATCO), founded in 1968, exhibited from the start a determination to defy such constraints. Unable to formally strike, they found various other means to make their grievances known. In the year of its founding the union launched what it slyly dubbed Operation Air Safety, a deliberate slowdown of traffic at the nation's hub airports; the following year its members staged a three-day sick-out. Concerned by the unmistakable signs of PATCO insurrection, Transportation Secretary John Volpe asked former journalist and veteran presidential adviser John J. Corson to investigate. Corson's report, issued in January 1970, detailed a poor working relationship between PATCO and the Federal Aviation Administration (FAA), which governed the work conditions of the controllers and managed their daily schedules and prospects for promotion. It also cited the confusion resulting from the fact that Congress, not the FAA, established the controllers' benefits and rates of pay. "Members of this committee have never previously observed a situation in which there is as much mutual resentment and antagonism between management and its employees," said the report.[10] The Corson Committee also noted that controllers were frustrated by "their inability to communicate upwards," and that those who spoke out about on-site problems or equipment failures feared endangering their chances of advancement.[11]

One persistent anxiety among the controllers was that the physical and psychological demands of the job were so great, they would never manage to remain at it long enough to earn a decent retirement. FAA data indicates that "between 1976 and 1979 about 8 percent of U.S. controllers who retired did so for medical reasons before they were eligible for full retirement benefits."[12] Controllers felt that the position's extreme difficulty was not taken seriously by management. Most had not forgotten (or forgiven) previous FAA head Langhorne Bond's thoughtless observation that air traffic control was no more stressful than driving a bus in New York City.[13] More welcomed were the conclusions of investigating Boston University psychiatrist Robert Rose, who reported frequent occurrence of hypertension, job stress, and psychiatric problems among as many as 50 percent of the controllers examined.[14] Senator Daniel Fong, a member of a Senate civil service committee, found it ironic that "a blackjack card dealer in Las Vegas is generally relieved from his duty after 40 minutes of dealing because of the monotony and mental stress of keeping up with a deck of cards, while an air traffic controller responsible for moving airplanes in and out of a busy airport will frequently remain on the radar-scope for four hours without relief."[15]

Juggling as many as thirty planes at a time through three-dimensional space, the controllers functioned in "a world not of mundane routine, but of intense emotions," writes anthropologist Katherine Newman, "of adrenalin rushes and gnawing tension, interspersed with boredom."[16] One controller reported, "Some days I go home and walk in the door and my wife takes one look at my face—and my clothes, which are sweated through from the neck down—and she doesn't say a word. She sends my son to his room and she makes me a drink and we don't talk for two hours."[17]

Their work's uniqueness created militancy among the controllers as well as a distinct sense of pride. Most had developed their skills in the military, many in Vietnam, and the FAA training they experienced included an eighteen-week training course so rigorous a significant percentage of trainees were eliminated. The controllers, even as they resented being taken for granted, saw themselves as elite, excelling at a job few people could or would do.[18]

In March 1970, when twenty-two hundred controllers staged a massive sick-out that lasted for twenty days, the Air Transport Association (ATA), representing the major airlines, obtained a court order sending the controllers back to work under the threat of lawsuits and fines. The

ATA stopped short of demanding the fines, but as part of the negotiated settlement, PATCO was forced to accept a permanent federal injunction forbidding the union from engaging in concerted actions such as strikes, stoppages, or slowdowns. In the event of any such stoppage, the union could be fined $25,000 per day.

The disgruntled controllers quickly found ways to defy the injunction. One effective yet entirely legal means involved their insisting on the mandated five-mile horizontal flight separation between aircraft. It was well known in the flying business that controllers at busy hubs routinely shortened the separation space to three miles or less in order to facilitate more takeoffs and landings. The airlines knew of and benefited from this practice. But controllers could insist on the standard required spacing, and when they did, the resulting delays hurt the airlines' reputations with consumers and wasted as much as $1 million a day in fuel as planes idled on runways.

In the spirit of the ATA settlement, Transportation Secretary Volpe had agreed to rehire some of the controllers fired over the illegal sick-out. However, despite the permanent injunction, stoppages occurred in 1976 over salary issues and in 1978 because international airlines ceased offering controllers the cherished perks known as "fam flights," in which a controller was allowed a free ride in a plane's cockpit in order to become familiar with pilot-to-ground communications. Everyone in the industry knew the privilege was abused for the controllers' personal travel, but it was nonetheless seen as disrespectful when it was taken away.

PATCO did have some success, with the help of the Corson Report and other publications, in educating Washington and the public to the idea that air traffic controllers deserved special consideration because their jobs were both crucial to the public and extremely high-stress. By 1980 the controllers had won from Congress the ability to retire at age fifty with full benefits if they had twenty years of service. PATCO had also amassed a $5 million nest egg based on dues income as well as a separate "subsistence" trust worth almost as much, which was, albeit not in name, a strike fund. In anticipation of a scheduled renegotiation of its contract the following year, PATCO's executive board in June 1980 ousted the union's genial president, John Leyden, who had headed PATCO for ten years, and installed the younger, more militant Robert Poli, who had been a vice president. Poli, a former air force controller who had worked in the FAA's Cleveland center, moved quickly to replace top union staff and attorneys with his own loyalists.

T HE CHANCES FOR THE AIR TRAFFIC CONTROLLERS, were they to strike, did not appear half bad. PATCO had the distinction of being the only federal workers' union to endorse Reagan in the recent 1980 election. This had not been solely a strategic move, for many of the controllers were Republicans and genuinely liked the conservative California governor. Candidate Reagan had, in turn, written a letter to PATCO on October 20, 1980, informing its members that he was aware of "the deplorable state of our nation's air traffic control system . . . that too few people working unreasonable hours with obsolete equipment has placed the nation's air travelers in unwarranted danger." He assured them that, as president of the United States, he would "take whatever steps are necessary to provide our air traffic controllers with the most modern equipment available and to adjust staff levels and work days so that they are commensurate with achieving a maximum degree of public safety."[19] Robert Poli had the letter framed and hung on the wall above his desk at PATCO headquarters in Washington.

Reagan had met privately with Poli on October 23 to accept PATCO's endorsement, and Poli had come away believing his union had Reagan's support. The PATCO leader, along with most Americans, then watched approvingly as the newly inaugurated president hailed the valiant struggle of the Polish shipyard workers' movement, *Solidarność*, led by Lech Walesa. Emulating the Polish unionists, PATCO members adopted the term "solidarity" and began referring to fellow members as "brother" and "sister."

The controllers could also look with hope at one of the last major labor actions involving federal workers, a 1970 wildcat postal strike in which 175,000 of the nation's 600,000 postal workers walked off the job, and the precedent set at the time by President Nixon. Federalizing National Guard soldiers to deliver the mail in place of the missing mailmen, Nixon did not invoke the laws that would have declared the strikers felons nor threaten to fire them. Instead, his secretary of labor, George P. Shultz—with the AFL-CIO's George Meany serving in an advisory capacity—sat down and hammered out terms for better wages and a restructuring of management-employee relations in the postal system. The striking workers returned to their mail routes.[20] More recently, when in 1980 controllers at Chicago's O'Hare Airport staged a slowdown because the FAA had refused to pay them a special "stress bonus," the administration of President Jimmy Carter did not enforce the permanent injunction or seek to fine PATCO.

But what Poli and his fellow PATCO executives had not adequately considered was Reagan's basic antipathy for unions. The president's kindly words for PATCO had in no way constituted an assurance that he intended to bargain over wages or allow strikes, and among his inner circle of aides and advisers there was not a single labor-friendly figure, someone who might be expected to soothe and troubleshoot a crisis as Shultz had for Nixon.[21] Ray Donovan, whom Reagan had appointed secretary of labor, was a former vice president for labor relations at a construction firm and held views antithetical to unionism, while Reagan's secretary of transportation, Andrew "Drew" Lewis Jr., was a businessman and staunch Reagan loyalist whose chief credential was having managed the president's election campaign in Pennsylvania. There were other warning signs. In February 1981, soon after Reagan took power, Lewis's department had hired the law firm of Morgan, Lewis & Bockius, which had a record of working against unions, to lead the contract negotiations with PATCO; then, in March, Reagan named J. Lynn Helms, the former head of Piper Aircraft and a known union-buster, to be the FAA administrator. The FAA had never taken seriously, or at least had never acted on, the troubling information contained in the Corson and Rose reports about the conditions and attitudes among air traffic controllers; instead it geared up for the coming negotiations by examining ways to undermine PATCO. "Rather than correcting management inadequacies," historians Richard Hurd and Jill Kriesky wrote, "if the agency could weather the strike, PATCO would be destroyed and the problems would disappear."[22]

PATCO had also been inattentive about establishing a reliable base of allies. Deposed president John Leyden had worked over the years to maintain favorable relations with key figures in organized labor, but Poli and his renegade forces had done little to reassure or cultivate these potential sources of support. Indeed, so badly handled had been the ouster of Leyden and his lieutenants, some had filed unfair labor practices complaints with the NLRB.[23]

On June 22, 1981, Poli and Secretary Lewis discussed a provisional new contract package for the controllers. Lewis described it as the best the administration could do, since Reagan was seeking to reduce government spending. It offered a raise of $4,000 per year to each controller, technical improvements in their workplaces, steeper raises for controllers who also served as instructors, a night shift raise, and time and a half after thirty-six hours of work in any given week. Other benefits offered included the proviso that controllers sidelined by medical conditions would receive paid retraining for less stressful jobs within the system. Poli termed the offer "fair."[24] Later he said he was inclined to accept it because, by PATCO's own rules, a vote of 80 percent of all controllers was required to stage a walkout, and in an earlier vote only 75 percent had approved such a potential action. Had the PATCO members accepted the deal as offered, estimated to be worth about $40 million, and Congress had then approved it, the agreement would have represented a significant union victory, since PATCO would walk away with an expanded wage-and-benefits package. But the members soundly rejected the pact Lewis had outlined, voting 13,495–616 against ratification.

This lopsided vote suggests not only the high level of unhappiness among controllers, but that wages were not the lead motivation for the strike. Many controllers were reported to be displeased that the contract offer failed to address their request that the standard workweek be reduced from forty to thirty-two hours. Poli himself later explained that "the strike was called because of early burnout, because U.S. controllers work more hours than controllers in other free-world countries, because wages do not keep up with inflation and because of management attitudes that ridicule our profession and turn deaf ears to our input into aviation safety."[25] Poli was correct in citing the number of hours worked; American controllers, averaging forty hours per week, were well above comparable rates for France (thirty-two hours), West Germany (thirty-three), or Australia (thirty-five), and received fewer vacation or paid sick days than controllers in major systems worldwide.[26]

What exactly led PATCO to reject the deal has never been entirely clear; some historians suggest that a "good cop, bad cop" scenario was planned all along to make it appear that the government's offer had at least received a hearing. Poli, speaking before a union gathering shortly after pronouncing Lewis's offer "fair," was welcomed with a standing ovation by fellow PATCO executives, yet at the same meeting, when the union's board refused ratification, hundreds of attendees jumped to their feet, chanting "Strike! Strike! Strike!"[27] Ultimately, the government and PATCO were too far apart for negotiations to have much effect. PATCO wanted a package worth about $740 million. Lewis, who continued to meet with Poli, offered ways the $40 million package could be reconfigured, but refused to enlarge upon the deal itself.

The PATCO leadership set a strike deadline for August 3, at the same time making new demands that included the thirty-two-hour workweek and a $10,000-per-person across-the-board wage hike. Lewis, calling the demands "nothing short of outrageous,"[28] warned there would be no more concessions. Attorney General William French Smith then informed Poli and other PATCO officers that they as well as the heads of striking PATCO locals would be prosecuted "to the fullest extent of the law" in case of a walkout. In Congress, fifty-five senators signed a letter accusing PATCO of threatening to force concessions from the government by punishing air travelers, and warned that Congress would not be "receptive to any demands negotiated by force." Most significantly, it vowed to back Reagan if he chose "to use the full force of the law to protect the public interest."[29] A similar letter was circulated in the House of Representatives.

Poli remained confident, believing that the prospect of a controllers' strike's crippling the nation's air transport system would leave the opposition no choice but to renegotiate, and that Reagan would ultimately make good on his implied promise of support. Yet when Lewis told Reagan PATCO was set to strike, the president instructed Labor Secretary Ray Donovan "to advise the union's leaders that, as a former union president, I was probably the best friend [the] organization ever had in the White House, but I could not countenance an illegal strike nor permit negotiations to take place as long as one was in progress."[30] Reagan called a White House staff briefing (set, appropriately, beneath a portrait of President Calvin Coolidge). Echoing Coolidge's famous edict that "there is no right to strike against the public safety by anybody, anywhere, any time," Reagan told his aides that where PATCO was concerned, "Dammit, the law is the law, and the law says they cannot strike. If they strike, they quit their jobs."[31]

The president was as good as his word. Late on the morning of August 3, four hours after the strike was officially called, Reagan issued an ultimatum from the Rose Garden stating that striking controllers would be fired if they did not return to their jobs within forty-eight hours. "Let me make one thing plain," Reagan told the nation. "I respect the right of workers in the private sector to strike. Indeed as president of my own union I led the first strike ever called by that union. . . . But we cannot compare labor management relations in the private sector with government. Government cannot close down the assembly line; it has to provide without interruption the protective services which are government's reason for being."[32] Seconding his boss's remarks, Drew Lewis assured reporters, "I don't care whether it's 9,000 or 12,000 or 100,000—whoever is not at work will be fired."[33]

Attorney General Smith also followed up on his earlier warning. His Justice Department hit PATCO immediately with $4.4 million in fines for violating the back-to-work order, and filed felony charges against seventy-two PATCO local leaders in twenty cities. Poli predicted that he would be arrested but the government chose not to make a martyr of him, although five executives of PATCO locals were taken into custody. "There's more effort going into busting our union than there is into fighting drug abuse or organized crime," griped Poli after news photos showed PATCO officers in handcuffs. But he insisted the controllers' spirit would not be broken. "PATCO is more than a name," he stated defiantly. "PATCO is more than a union—it's a religion."[34]

DESPITE SUCH SPIRITED TALK, PATCO's leaders appeared to have badly misjudged the controllers' indispensability, and had not fully appreciated how swiftly press and public would turn against them. "The air controllers have no right to hold up the nation," observed the *New York Times*. "President Reagan's tough threat to fire workers . . . is appropriate. A settlement that rewards them for illegally withholding vital services would be a serious mistake."[35] Travelers inconvenienced at the nation's airports also tended to support the White House. "I think they [the strikers] were very foolish . . . [they] are in danger of losing everything," observed Eric Peterson, seventy-four, of Orlando. "I have been a union man myself for 35 years so I should know. I sure do think the president did the right thing."[36] Policeman William Hoy, on duty at O'Hare Airport in Chicago, said, "Sure, they have a right to strike, and they have the right to get fired, too. I can't feel sorry for them. Reagan has to draw the line somewhere."[37] A *Newsweek* poll conducted the week of August 17 found that 57 percent of Americans backed Reagan's action, and only 29 percent did not.[38] This broad public support included even many working-class citizens, suggesting that the president had tapped into a wide vein of antiunion feeling. The National Association of Manufacturers, smelling the blood of all organized labor in Reagan's tough stance, overnight launched a committee to advocate for "a union-free environment."

The president did not have everyone in his corner. "It seems to me particularly embarrassing to see pictures in the media of the PATCO strikers being escorted to jail in leg irons and manacles, while we were all cheering lustily the courage of Lech Walesa and Solidarity," said Congressman William D. Ford. "I suspect that if the equivalent of PATCO went on strike in Russia tomorrow, we would have parades in the streets in support of them."[39] There were also expressions of disappointment that Reagan refused to make even an attempt at bargaining. "What is absolutely without precedent, at least in modern times," observed John Dunlop, secretary of labor in the administration of President Gerald Ford and a coauthor of New York State's Taylor Law, which prohibits public workers from striking but allows for methods to soothe labor-management tensions, "is that [the Reagan administration] has brought in no outside, dispassionate group to look at the problem. That ain't right. The administration has decided . . . to leave no avenue of escape for the union. You just don't do that."[40]

The union had probably missed a chance to gain public support when it failed to adequately publicize the safety and working conditions that motivated the strike; instead, most coverage featured their steep wage and benefits demands. Inflation was a major policy issue at the time, and the emphasis everywhere was on saving money and trimming government waste. In a year in which the country saw the end to the sixteen-month trauma of Americans being held hostage by Iranian Revolutionary Guards, and Reagan had himself almost been assassinated, the idea of well-paid controllers grounding air travel because they wanted more money simply proved not to be a winning or compelling crusade. Reagan's "political prowess is the skill with which he picks his battles," wrote the New Republic in a piece that argued PATCO had failed to gain the moral high ground by going on strike. "[He] appears to have been spoiling for a fight with organized labor, and the controllers handed him a perfect opportunity."[41]

In practical terms the strike was probably lost the moment it became evident the controllers were not indispensable, for the impact of the strike on the nation's commercial airlines was far less profound than PATCO had hoped. Initially it grounded about half the nation's fifteen thousand commercial flights, causing cancellations and difficulties at several major hubs. But the Reagan administration had, in anticipation of a strike, and apparently unbeknownst to PATCO, obtained an improved strike contingency plan from the FAA to replace one drawn up during the Carter years. The new plan managed air traffic by reducing it 25 percent overall through a method known as "flow control," wherein takeoffs at one airport are closely coordinated with the volume of landings elsewhere, thus reducing the strain on controllers. The FAA also temporarily grounded all noncommercial and nonessential forms of aviation. In addition to the controllers who were either not in the union or did not strike, about one thousand PATCO strikers had heeded Reagan's forty-eight-hour ultimatum and returned to work, and many supervisors as well as military controllers also filled in where needed. Meanwhile, the FAA's air controller training facility in Oklahoma City reported that seventy-seven thousand job applications had poured in during the first several days of the standoff.

One reason the disruptions were taken in stride was that the PATCO shutdown was, to an extent, a crisis the major airlines welcomed. Due to the 1978 deregulation of the airline industry, which had allowed for the emergence of low-price airline competitors like People Express and New York Air, the industry was suffering from numerous flight redundancies. The need to reduce the number of aircraft aloft for safe handling by the replacement controller force gave the airlines the opportunity to sift through presently scheduled flights and suspend those that were least profitable.

Conspicuously unhelpful were the Air Line Pilots Association (ALPA), as well as other airline unions such as the machinists and flight attendants, who refused to go out in sympathy with PATCO; most of their members crossed PATCO's picket lines to report to work. There were a number of reasons for this. Unlike the controllers, other workers more directly affiliated with the airlines were private sector unions and governed by the Railway Labor Act; since the controllers' strike was illegal, they could not join it without risking damage suits from the airlines. And as with the general public, the relatively high pay received by the controllers created minimal sympathy among lower-paid airline workers.[42] In addition, pilots saw potential harm to their own jobs in that the controllers' strike was allowing the government and the airlines to trim flight schedules. John J. O'Donnell, ALPA president, told the executive council of the AFL-CIO "that his members would have him thrown out of office if he attempted to insist that they respect the controllers' picket lines." The failure of ALPA's forty thousand pilots to stand with PATCO was perhaps the biggest strategic blow to the controllers' strike, since a combined walkout of the two unions could not have failed to shut down the nation's air travel network. The best ALPA could do was to encourage the White House to rehire the fired controllers.[43] "If the airline pilots had refused to cross the picket lines, the strike would have been a success," lamented a controller years later. "They made a mistake and they're paying for it now. Labor made a mistake."[44]

From the perspective of much of the labor movement, however, it appeared that it had been PATCO that had miscalculated. The headstrong controllers had been warned a strike would possibly be "suicidal," and, as a clear result of the shift from the Leyden to the Poli administration, it had failed to consult adequately with other airline-related unions in advance.[45] To be sure, some labor support did emerge. On August 15, four hundred teachers, autoworkers, firemen, and transit workers joined striking controllers on picket lines at New York's John F. Kennedy Airport. Carrying hand-lettered signs, they chanted "Tell Ronald Reagan to stop all his fussing, 'cause there ain't gonna be no union-busting." New York City transit employee Tom Spence told a reporter, "Any self-respecting trade unionist should be here supporting PATCO because the administration's attack on PATCO is a threat to all unions." Another, Larry Ingram, suggested, "It's like the quote that goes something like this—'First they came after the Communists, and I wasn't a Communist, so I didn't do anything. Then they came after the trade unionists and again, I did nothing. Then they came after the Jews and because I wasn't a Jew, I did nothing. And finally, when they came for me, there was no one left.' Well, it's better to fight for *their* jobs than to have to fight for mine."[46]

On August 16 the Coalition of Flight Attendants took out a full-page ad in the *New York Times* reprinting Reagan's October 1980 letter to PATCO in which he had vowed his concern for the outdated equipment and punishing work schedules controllers dealt with, and the ramifications for air safety. Reagan had ended his letter with the words, "I pledge to you that my administration will work very closely with you to bring about a spirit of cooperation between the President and the air traffic controllers." The flight attendants admonished Reagan "to honor his pledge to the air traffic controllers and return to the bargaining table with PATCO."[47]

The community of international air traffic controllers also offered support. The Canadian controllers' union refused for two days to clear flights emanating from the United States, and Portuguese controllers based in the Azores staged a two-day stoppage. Both efforts caused some disruption and delays on transatlantic routes but were largely symbolic (the two stoppages were not coordinated, which would have had a far more devastating effect).[48] On August 13 the sixty-one-country International Federation of Air Traffic Controllers' Associations, meeting in Amsterdam, voted not to back the striking U.S. controllers, although like other labor bodies it urged Reagan to reopen talks with PATCO.

Thus, one part of PATCO's strategy—that the strike would hobble the nation's airways—was only minimally successful. There was also a morally reprehensible element to the controllers' action that reflected negatively on them: the appearance that they had forced the White House into a game of chicken using the lives of innocent air travelers. As everyone knew, some sort of incident—a near miss involving two planes, or worse—would offer convincing proof of the controllers' indispensability, while each hour that passed safely tended to underscore the Reagan administration's vow that the system could function without them. While there were air fatalities during the era around the strike, including the January 1982 crash of an Air Florida plane into the Potomac River in Washington, in which seventy-eight people died, none could be linked to air controller failure. Flights were canceled and delayed, and some passengers refused to fly out of concern for their safety in the hands of inexperienced controllers, but in fact the air transport system responded well to the emergency. "The president was a lucky man during this episode of American history," writes historian Willis Nordlund, "in that there were no large air disasters that could have been attributed to a less than perfectly functioning air traffic control system."[49] Within days, flights were back to a 70 percent level,[50] the quick adjustment encouraging the president to suggest that "before the strike, the air traffic control system had about six thousand more controllers than it really needed to operate safely."[51]

Ultimately, of course, the real problem for the controllers was that they had not anticipated Reagan's readiness to break with White House practice and insist on firmly enforcing the letter of the laws governing federal workers. These laws expressed the idea that employees' right to organize was in the public interest, so even though Reagan could legally fire the strikers who spurned his forty-eight-hour deadline, he himself was failing to honor the law's broader implication. Many observers thought there was sufficient precedent, such as Nixon's handling of the 1970 postal strike, to make it incumbent on the White House to at least try for mediated solutions, instead of Reagan's "carpet bombing" approach, as Lane Kirkland, Meany's successor at the AFL-CIO, termed it.[52] Of course any comparison between the two strikes broke down when one considered the numbers involved—175,000 striking postal workers versus eleven thousand defiant controllers—and the fact that, unlike postal employees, who were visible, familiar figures "in their communities . . . few Americans have ever met, let alone know, an air traffic controller."[53]

Compounding the loss of their jobs was the government's effort to wreak havoc on the controllers' lives. It saw to PATCO's decertification, thus denying the now ex-controllers their organization, and "took special actions to completely prevent fired controllers from having access to unemployment benefits, housing subsidies, and other federal benefit programs."[54] Lane Kirkland pointed out to reporters that the president's cruel actions were reminiscent of the Danbury Hatters case of 1908, in which severe financial penalties were levied against striking workers, even to the point of attaching their homes and bank accounts.[55] One singular problem for the controllers was that their skills were not easily transferable to other kinds of employment. Civilian air traffic control was a highly specialized calling, "a working-class dream," notes anthropologist Katherine Newman, in that it came with status and was relatively well paid, yet "required no educational credentials beyond a high school diploma. There was a catch, however. Only one civilian employer could make the dream come true: the federal government."[56]

THERE WERE CLEARLY grave implications for organized labor in what had transpired. Not only had Reagan fired eleven thousand government employees, he had turned his back on eight decades of labor progress by whatever name it had ever aspired to be known, from industrial democracy to collective bargaining. Reagan "wanted to send a strong, unambiguous message to organized labor," Nordlund recounts. "That message . . . was that organized labor—unionism—was essentially incompatible with the emerging free-market philosophy of the administration."[57] Democratic House Speaker Thomas P. "Tip" O'Neill Jr., with grudging respect, conceded that the president was "a tough two-fisted person. . . . My brief dealings with [him] this year show he doesn't know the art of compromise."[58]

It was vintage Reagan—the defining of a controversy in simplistic moral extremes, a refusal to examine nuanced opinions or alternatives, a lack of interest in bargaining, and the adoption of a political stance that was admired for its intransigence alone. Some of Reagan's appeal all along had been that he was resolute, certainly more so than Jimmy Carter, who had appeared equivocating in the face of the Iran hostage crisis. Already, only seven months along in his presidency, Reagan had brought the hostages home, survived an assassination attempt, pushed his budget through Congress, de-funded everything from school lunches to disability programs, and smashed a union of federal employees by selling the action as a matter of law and order.

Of course one reason Reagan's policies had begun to stir so much concern was that the old GE pitchman was proving so adept at promoting them. His practiced but homespun words and the smoothness of his political salesmanship were anathema to progressives; they perceived in him a compelling phony whose popularity was especially maddening in that, as Kirkland complained, "he claims his victims as his allies [and makes] working people accomplices in his assault on their interests." It gave labor leaders fits to know that 44 percent of labor households had voted for Reagan in the 1980 election despite most unions' backing of Carter, and that he got away with claiming a special understanding of working people even though during his much-vaunted days as a "trade unionist" in Hollywood he had earned $150,000 per year and informed on his union colleagues to the FBI.[59]

Reagan's firing of the air controllers was a bold statement, but of a piece with his approach to conservative governance. It was the beginning of the Reagan Revolution, shifting wealth from the middle class to the rich through tax cuts, moving government money out of social entitlement programs and into the military. To labor professionals, of course, the PATCO firings threatened to embolden further antiunion actions not only from government, but from employers generally. Much as Franklin D. Roosevelt's signature on New Deal labor legislation had been a "signal on a hill" to the nation's workers, freeing them from hesitation about organizing, so would Reagan's action now inspire antiunion retribution from management.[60] Retired labor writer A. H. Raskin wrote that one likely result of Reagan's handling of the PATCO situation would be the "costly spread of labor-management turmoil over broad sectors of public and private employment as governors, mayors, school boards and corporations seek to copy [Reagan's] blitz tactics." As AFL-CIO secretary-treasurer Thomas R. Donahue asked, "Breathes there a city manager with soul so dead that he will not want to look like a hero when he sees the President of the United States being applauded for being tough and closing every door to a settlement in defiance of all the civilized rules of collective bargaining?"[61]

Forced to acknowledge the likelihood of the trend cited by Raskin and Donahue, other voices belatedly reconsidered the wisdom of the controller firings. On August 30 the *New York Times*, having supported Reagan's tough stance initially, suggested that since the president had "proved that [PATCO] could not extort a favorable wage settlement by stopping the planes . . . it's time to change strategy. Everyone's interest—that of the president, the strikers and the public—would now be served by offering to rehire the controllers—on the government's terms." The paper cited polls showing "that most Americans are behind the president, but are uneasy about the harshness of his actions."[62] But Reagan turned a deaf ear to any second-guessing, and, still on the offensive, went out of his way to disrupt labor's efforts to lick its wounds. When one hundred thousand union workers, including many fired air traffic controllers and their families, surged down Fifth Avenue in New York's Labor Day parade on September 7, Reagan was nearby at Gracie Mansion, presenting a symbolic cardboard check to Mayor Ed Koch for federal funding of the long-delayed Westway development project, which would create thousands of construction jobs in the city. "A gimmick to give the appearance [he favors] the working man," Lane Kirkland said in dismissing Reagan's gesture.[63] When Mayor Koch later joined the parade he was loudly booed and heckled. "That's OK," the ebullient mayor told a reporter. "It's like being at Yankee Stadium. The boos are really cheers."[64]

Two weeks later in Washington, the antipathy toward the president over the PATCO firings helped bring about the first large public outpouring of dissatisfaction with the Reagan presidency. On September 19 the AFL-CIO coordinated a massive rally in the nation's capital conspicuously dubbed Solidarity Day. The day was warm and sunny as the participants flooded into the city by bus, train, and car from all parts of the United States. A crowd estimated at 260,000 (larger than had attended either the March on Washington in 1963 or the anti-Vietnam War Moratorium in November 1969) gathered around the base of the Washington Monument before moving slowly toward the Capitol, taking three hours to traverse the distance. As many as two hundred diverse labor-affiliated organizations were represented. Five years earlier the notion of George Meany's labor federation leading an antiadministration protest in the nation's capital would have been unthinkable, but now there was no such hesitation. Union leaders from across the country, many bitter about the thrashing PATCO had taken, were determined to make a strong showing, and rank-and-file workers from both independent and public service unions were joined by thousands of ordinary citizens, eager to show their disdain for the president. Many were taking part in their first protest. Most cited revulsion for the president's assault on the working people, his brusque style of governance and lack of substance as having motivated their decision to attend.

"I'm not a radical. But Ronald Reagan made me come here," remarked Mildred Donahue, a librarian who had flown in from Connecticut.[65] Woodrow Wellington, a sixty-eight-year-old retired maintenance man from Newark, Delaware, expressed a common disappointment. "He made out like he was this big labor person. But I don't think he ever did much work but play with that toy pistol on 'Death Valley Days.'" Another attendee, John Richardson of New York, said he had gone through job training in a Comprehensive Employment and Training Act (CETA) program and had attained a job through it, but that under Reagan CETA had been canceled. Many of his coworkers had been in the program for five years; some had gotten married, thinking they would have job security. "But there's no security now," Richardson reported.[66]

Simply to have mounted such an ambitious event, stage-managing the tens of thousands of participants, seemed proof of labor's vitality, and it was an energized Kirkland who took to the podium to declare:

> Reagan has told us that he alone speaks for the working people
> of this country. . . . But if you believe that governments are raised
> by the people, not as their enemies but as their instruments,
> to promote the general welfare, look about you. You are not
> alone. . . . You are the people that do the work of America. You
> run its factories and offices, work its farms, transport its produce,

maintain its buildings, teach its children, nurse its sick, clean its streets and fight in its defense. When something goes wrong in America, you feel it first—before the politicians or the more securely placed. Something has gone wrong and you know it all too well.[67]

Many op-ed page editors, even conservative columnist William Safire, scolded Reagan for avoiding Solidarity Day by slipping out of town to Camp David. Presidents from Abraham Lincoln to Richard Nixon had remained in the capital to face protestors or at least hear their chants, but Reagan, who very rarely assented to hold a press conference, Safire wrote, "has evidently decided to conduct his presidency one step removed from the public. He wants to avoid having his scripted generalities challenged in the give-and-take of hard questioning."[68]

While the sentiments of Solidarity Day left a warm glow, labor's agenda remained short on specifics. The threat Reaganism posed was unmistakable, yet it was unclear what form resistance should take, or how it might be implemented by so diverse a constituency. If labor intended to confront the nation's "ascendant conservatism," it needed something more substantive than what one paper termed "a Quixotic wish list" of demands for "safety in the workplace" and "jobs and justice for all Americans—voiced by a parade of assorted workers and unhappy liberals."[69]

Reagan never repudiated his actions toward PATCO, although in the short term his efforts failed to conform to his reputation for slashing government spending. His unforgiving stance toward the union probably wound up costing the United States and the airlines around $30 billion, or $1.5 billion per month over the twenty months it took to get the air traffic control system back to full strength.[70] Training new replacement controllers alone cost the government $2 billion.[71] As Nordlund reports, between 1981 and 1985 the number of flights in the United States had grown from 66.7 million to 71.4 million (and to 80.4 million by 1988), yet in 1985 there were almost five thousand fewer controllers on the job than in 1981. "After almost ten years of turmoil, the expenditure of billions of dollars, the destruction of homes, families, and careers . . . little real improvement occurred."[72]

In the coming years, as had been predicted, his hard-line example inspired employers generally to take a tougher approach to labor relations—ordering lockouts, suppressing collective bargaining, and further legitimizing "replacement workers" as the tonic for troublesome workplace stoppages. Unions have always been sustained by society's disapproval of those who cross a picket line. "After God had finished the rattlesnake, the toad and the vampire, he had some awful substance left with which he made a strikebreaker," author Jack London had believed along with many of his countrymen. But an unwholesome effect of the PATCO affair was that the entire nation saw the president defy the oldest taboo in America's culture of work; in doing so he contributed to murdering the very idea of collective bargaining, since negotiations of any kind are naturally compromised when management can readily fill "open" jobs with nonunion replacements. "[Reagan] will be remembered for many things," asserts Nordlund, "but the one event that remains in the psyche of every American is the discharge of federal air traffic controllers for failure to follow a presidential directive to return to work. . . . There will be PATCO scars on the American labor movement for many decades to come."[73]

L ABOR WAS WAKING UP with a headache each morning, and an antiunion White House was only one of the sources of the discomfort. Social and economic adjustments under way since the Second World War had accelerated—suburbanization, the transition from manufacturing to service jobs, the decline of large urban manufacturing centers, and the growth of trade unions into mighty business enterprises. Looming over all such changes was globalization—the dispersal of the world's trade and finances through advances in shipping, air freight, telecommunications, and computerized banking and money exchanges, which allowed U.S. businesses access to lower-cost workers and production overseas—a trend that accelerated when the Soviet Union collapsed in 1989, bringing down the iron curtain and opening new markets as well as cheap labor to global producers. This development was exacerbated by the surging economies of China and India, which offered the world new consumers as well as legions of less expensive workers. American unionists facing contract negotiations or contemplating a strike were now dealing with factors utterly beyond their control.

Nor was the "barren marriage" between the labor movement and the Democratic Party, as author Mike Davis has termed it, proving to be of much help. Despite Lane Kirkland's advice to organized labor to rally around Democratic candidates in the November 1982 midterm elections, the long alliance between the two had for the past decade seemed more a stopgap than a fulfilling collaboration. Certainly many Democrats still had their hearts in the right places. Senator Edward Kennedy accused the Republicans of trying to "dismantle our federal government and all it stands for,"[74] and laid into Reagan for pursuing "the discredited and disastrous ideas of the 1920s,"[75] while House Speaker O'Neill spoke wistfully of the New Deal, when "together the Democrats and labor made a middle-class America . . . thirty of the greatest, fruitful and beneficial years that a democracy ever had."[76] But the Party of Roosevelt had long ago ceased being a reliable companion. When the Democrats split over civil rights in 1948, the labor movement found itself tied to the liberal wing of the party and ultimately on the losing end of the conservative wave that crested in 1968 with the election of law-and-order candidate Richard Nixon. Jimmy Carter, a Democratic president with control of Congress, had faced such stiff conservative opposition from within his own party that even his mild labor program had been largely nullified, and after twelve years of further retrenchment with first Reagan and then George H. W. Bush in command, labor—left with "only a token role in setting party policy"[77]—watched as President Bill Clinton led the country into international trade agreements harmful to domestic labor and, under pressure from congressional conservatives, curtailed welfare for the country's poorest demographic.

For a movement that knew in its bones the vital necessity of having leverage with which to bring opponents into line, labor came to occupy a position in which it had almost none. It had linked its fate to the activism of a political party that was far from activist, that largely took labor's support for granted; there seemed little real pressure on the Democrats to deliver for labor when it knew, everyone knew, that labor had nowhere else to go.

To a degree labor had become a victim of its own success, lulled for a generation by the view that the struggle for worker dignity and decent hours and conditions had ended, that victory had been secured by heroes with names like Gompers, Powderly, Jones, Lewis, and Reuther. With the securing of fat contracts in major industries, and the abandonment of class-based politics by even the most liberal unions, many workers seemed to have become complacent and comfortable. Some looked back ruefully at the labor movement's decided anti-Communism of the 1940s and 1950s. "Had organized labor resisted joining the Cold War consensus," scholar Kevin Boyle muses, "had it refused to accept a formal position in the Democratic Party, had it continued to promote a social democratic agenda, perhaps it might have won enough political and economic power to have withstood the conservative onslaught of the Reagan years."[78] But even had that come to pass it would have still been hard for labor to anticipate and prepare adequately for the seismic changes in the global economy and the impact they would have on the American corporation.

So it was that after PATCO labor seemed to settle into what might be termed a managed retreat. Increasingly it negotiated not for better terms but for tolerable adjustments—wage concessions, early retirements, and reduced benefits—that were believed necessary to help employers stay afloat and keep jobs viable. Meanwhile, the increasing use of replacement workers was soon joined by other nefarious personnel "innovations" such as the large-scale hiring of temporary and part-time employees, as opposed to full-time employment with benefits, which management defended as a cost-saving measure but that hindered both collective bargaining and member recruitment. All the issues confronting organized labor—from globalization to the use of these "contingent" workers—would factor in pivotal confrontations at Hormel Foods in 1985–1986, Caterpillar in 1994, and United Parcel Service in 1997. One would play out as a painful community melodrama pitting neighbor against neighbor, one would become a prized, exceptional victory; all were significant in revealing labor's disorientation before large baleful market forces. What was remarkable, however, was that they gave evidence of a pulse—a sign that at some elemental level labor retained its healthy insurgent heart and a capacity for sacrifice and principle.

HORMEL FOODS, famous for its Spam, Wrangler Sausages, and Dinty Moore Beef Stew, was one of the country's best-known manufacturers of supermarket canned meats. Its plant in the small southeast Minnesota city of Austin, started as a family business in 1891, had by 1984 come to employ sixteen hundred men and women; other Hormel slaughtering and manufacturing facilities opened elsewhere in the Upper Midwest. The firm built a new $100 million factory in Austin in the early 1980s, which, operating at full capacity, slaughtered 2 million hogs each year and produced 440 cans of Spam per minute; by 1985 Hormel provided a livelihood directly or indirectly for a quarter of the town's twenty-three thousand inhabitants. The founder, George A. Hormel, and his son, Jay, had worked to make the company a trusted community institution; it was a source of pride that the company's workers, foremen, executives, and their families sat side by side at church suppers and PTA meetings, watched their sons play Little League baseball together, and exchanged greetings at the gas pump.

After the new plant opened, however, workers sensed a change in the company's demeanor, as a corps of professional leadership filled the top positions and a stricter work environment took hold, with greater demands on efficiency and production. The company also began attending more seriously to its bottom line; in 1985 it announced it would seek concessions from the Austin-based Local P-9 of the United Food and Commercial Workers (UFCW) in the form of a reduction of the average wage at the plant, from $10.69 per hour down to $8.25. The step was necessary, management explained, in order for Hormel to stay competitive with other regional meatpacking plants that were nonunion and paid their employees as little as $6.00 an hour.

Local P-9 members took the news as an affront, as it was rumored Hormel's profits were still solid. When talks between Hormel and the national UFCW proved fruitless, P-9 hired a controversial New York labor consultant, Ray Rogers. Nicknamed "the Muscleman of Labor" for his daily weight-lifting regimen, Rogers had the youthful good looks of a freshman congressman and was known to play by his own rules. He had become identified with a new strategy of labor resistance called the "corporate campaign," which was designed to unnerve employers by exposing their corporate profile—their finances and anything potentially humiliating about their partnerships, investments, or stockholders. Rogers had grown up in a blue-collar family in coastal Massachusetts and was a veteran labor activist, having joined VISTA, the domestic Peace Corps, right out of college in 1967 and served in Appalachia. Following the triple homicide in 1969 that took the lives of UMW leader Joseph "Jock" Yablonski and his wife and daughter on the order of miners' president Anthony "Tough Tony" Boyle, Rogers had helped union reformer Arnold Miller and others within the UMW to expel Boyle, who along with three other men went to prison for their roles in the crime. Rogers was also involved in the lengthy North Carolina textile workers' campaign against J. P. Stevens & Co. that inspired *Norma Rae*, the popular 1979 Hollywood film starring Sally Fields.

P-9's bringing of so aggressive a labor advocate into a stoic heartland community like Austin was questioned at the Washington headquarters of the UFCW, which opposed Rogers's style of confrontation because it appeared to leave employers no room for compromise; the UFCW also worried that if Austin's workers failed to take seriously the concessions Hormel asked—the kinds manufacturers were demanding all across the country—they would resist themselves right out of their jobs. As for the residents of Austin, many were made uncomfortable by the fact that, seemingly through Rogers's influence, the standoff between P-9 and Hormel soon took on a nasty edge, neighbor siding against neighbor. A small embattled meatpacking local waging a lonely fight for worker dignity against a food industry Goliath made a good story, however, and attracted national media attention and wider labor movement support, even as it prompted concern that P-9's president, James Guyette, and other union leaders would become mesmerized by the spotlight and lose perspective. This fear seemed to be confirmed when Hormel offered to raise the reduced wage to as high as $10 an hour, in the eyes of many observers a reasonable compromise, and P-9's members, disregarding the advice of the national UFCW, rejected it by a vote of 775–540.[79]

After the strike began on August 17, 1985, management kept the plant running at a minimal production level through the fall using supervisory staff. In January 1986, however, frustrated with the impasse, Hormel announced it would reopen at full production, offering any workers who chose to return the $10-per-hour wage and $8 to new hires. This caused immediate friction among the townspeople, for while there was considerable loyalty to P-9 in Austin, there were also a large number of people eager for work. "If the President of the United States can replace strikers," noted one observer of the Hormel crisis, "this must be socially acceptable, politically acceptable, and we can do it, also."[80] About two thousand men and women applied for the $8-an-hour jobs. Distressing scenes occurred at the plant gates as infuriated strikers challenged their would-be replacements, many of whom they recognized as friends, neighbors, even relatives; there were shouting matches and cries of "Shame!" and "Scab!" At one point strikers blocked the plant entrance with their automobiles, briefly forcing Hormel to shut down and leading Minnesota governor Rudy Perpich to dispatch the National Guard.

The P-9 strikers hunkered down in the face of intensified opposition. Exhibiting a degree of militancy reminiscent of the UAW sit-downers of 1937, the P-9 workers kept themselves and their families together with organized food drives, pooled child care duties, the sharing of meals, and even the free exchange of services such as auto repair. But the cause was not free of dissent. Some members concluded independently that P-9's position was hopeless and returned to their jobs; others, remaining loyal to the union, nonetheless began to question whether it made sense to prolong a strike that increasingly appeared unwinnable. Townspeople upset at the upheaval the strike had created accused Rogers of being a charlatan and Guyette of having succumbed to the glare of momentary national fame; both of them, it was feared, shared a messiah complex and were willing to go down in glorious defeat for the sake of some vague labor movement martyrdom. The Austin city council weighed in, urging P-9 to end the strike "before this town is destroyed."[81]

Although Rogers, Guyette, and others were buoyed by the support of countless activists from across the country, including the Reverend Jesse Jackson, who came to Austin, the leadership of the country's mainstream labor movement concurred with the UFCW that continuing the strike would be a mistake; in disregarding others' well-meant advice, it seemed, P-9 was acting as a renegade union. When in late February 1986 Guyette and a small group of colleagues traveled to the AFL-CIO annual meeting in Bal Harbour, Florida, they received a chilly reception from Lane Kirkland and other officials. Guyette made an uncomfortable situation worse by telling reporters that AFL-CIO leaders were out of touch with America's workers and that "we feel confident that we can win with the support of the labor movement who is not down here in Bal Harbour out on the golf course or in the jewelry shops." UFCW official Lewie Anderson scolded Guyette for taking a cheap shot at the nation's labor leaders, saying, "Clearly they've lost the strike, it's a colossal failure"; Anderson suggested that at a time when organized labor generally was under attack, it was a pity that P-9's leaders were "going around saying such horrible things."[82] P-9 warned the AFL-CIO that the defeat of the Hormel strikers would stand, like PATCO, as a traumatic loss for all of organized labor, but Kirkland's reaction was to endorse a UFCW statement depicting Austin as "a story of inexperienced, misguided leadership and false prophets."[83]

The UFCW's irritation grew substantially when P-9 began orchestrating demonstrations and encouraging work stoppages at other Hormel facilities in the Midwest, and Rogers led demonstrations in Austin at First

Bank, which he deemed "the real power structure" behind Hormel, urging workers to withdraw their accounts. UFCW president William Wynn meanwhile advised his union's workers at Hormel sites across the country not to become "innocent victims of Local P-9's extremist actions." Criticizing P-9's all-or-nothing approach as "mass suicide," Wynn complained that "[Ray] Rogers has anointed himself the Ayatollah of Austin and is making hostages of our members at other Hormel plants."[84] Rogers retaliated by characterizing Wynn as complacent and out of touch with workingmen and -women, calling him "one of the most anti-union people I have ever come across."[85] The *New York Times* concurred with Wynn's assessment, however, terming the Hormel strike a "sad and highly publicized failure . . . less a labor action than a defiant shaking of fists at large economic forces."[86] The relationship between the Austin local and its national parent became so strained it began to appear the UFCW likely shared Hormel's interest in crushing the strike. Hormel meanwhile had filed charges against P-9 with the NLRB and obtained an injunction against picketing outside the Austin plant; it was an alleged violation of this injunction that led to the arrest of twenty-seven individuals, including Ray Rogers.[87]

The UFCW, its own credibility on the line, eventually placed Local P-9 into receivership and ceased making strike payments of between $40–$65 per week to each worker. Now at least formally in charge of the wayward local, it gave one final directive to P-9 to suspend the strike, which was ignored, at which point the UFCW fired both Guyette and Rogers. The strike thus officially ended with the remaining nine hundred strikers out of their jobs, their positions having been filled by replacements.

The Hormel strike had become, as its own leaders knew, a largely symbolic act, an expression of anger at the corporate diminishment of workers' status and at labor's weakness before demands for employee concessions. Hormel, an historically benign employer up against new competitive forces—global markets, faster means of transport, and the availability of cheap labor—had encountered a group of workers unwilling to suffer the effects of that transition. The strikers of P-9, in embracing principle, rejected the retreat culture of labor in the post-PATCO era, and paid the price.

T HE LESSON OF THE PATCO AND HORMEL STRIKES—that a large employer could effectively, and with little public or official disapproval, replace its workforce—was not lost on employees at Caterpillar, the world's largest manufacturer of construction equipment, located in Peoria, Illinois. Caterpillar's arrival in the Peoria-Decatur region in the 1950s had proven a significant economic boon to rural central Illinois. By the late 1980s, however, after decades of steady growth, the firm's profits declined, and by 1991 it had sliced its workforce, leaving only twelve thousand workers, down from twenty thousand in 1980. "The Cat" blamed some of its problems on the fact that it was now selling as much as 59 percent of its equipment overseas, where it found itself in fierce competition with the Japanese equipment-maker Komatsu Ltd. To better direct the struggle, Caterpillar in 1990 selected Don Fites, a veteran salesman, to be its CEO. Fites had spent many years selling for Caterpillar in Japan, and his global perspective and experience were expected to be a key asset in keeping the firm in the race with Komatsu. Fites was known to admire the way Japanese companies managed to dominate their labor unions.

In 1991 the firm sought a new six-year contract with its workers, who were represented by the UAW. One bit of belt-tightening the company proposed was to cease paying guards and janitors the $17.00 an hour wage it paid more skilled workers; it also sought a lower pay tier of $8.50 an hour for new hires. The contract offer, which covered a longer term than any previous pact, held out no pay increases to unskilled workers, only cost-of-living adjustments, and failed to renew a guarantee the company had with the UAW to keep a minimum number of workers on salary. More fundamentally, in proposing this new contract Caterpillar was announcing its wish to depart from the more traditional negotiation the UAW preferred, known as pattern bargaining, in which a union emulates a contract negotiated by workers at a similar enterprise, in this case Deere & Company, another large Midwestern farm implement manufacturer.

"Pattern bargaining is an outdated concept that makes no sense in a global economy," opined Gerald S. Flaherty, a Caterpillar vice president. "We need an agreement that makes sense for our employees and enables Caterpillar to continue providing high-quality jobs here in the United States. We also need an agreement that will allow us to sell products against non–United States competitors around the world."[88] The UAW had its own agenda: it wanted to safeguard pattern bargaining as a favored method of labor negotiations for possible use in upcoming talks with the Big Three automakers, which employed four hundred thousand UAW members.

The talks that commenced between Caterpillar and the UAW, stricken by disagreement about what form they should take, predictably went nowhere. When UAW members walked off at some Caterpillar facilities, the firm locked out employees at several others. Continuing efforts to restart discussions proved futile, and in April 1992 the company informed the strikers they must return in a week or lose their jobs, as it had already begun advertising for new hires. This threat was more serious at Caterpillar than at other employers because many of the company's workers were in their forties, and their chances of finding comparable employment in a depressed economy were slim. The unfavorable condition of the regional economy also meant that the firm would have no trouble finding applicants eager to apply for any replacement jobs; indeed, the company reported having received forty thousand responses about available jobs from across the country almost overnight. Faced with the near-certain loss of their jobs and with no progress in sight in the negotiations, the UAW froze their strike and ordered its members back to work. "Who's next?" a UAW officer complained to a reporter. "If they can do it at Caterpillar, what's going to stop Ford, General Motors, and Chrysler from doing it to us?"[89]

In one sense the predicament at Caterpillar was a worse sign for U.S. labor than Reagan's firing of the air traffic controllers a decade earlier. Not much love was lost between the government and the controllers, but Caterpillar was a regional anchor employer with deep roots in the community; there was something disturbing about its willingness to use scabs to oust the union with whom it had a long relationship, essentially tossing its veteran workforce out in the cold. Labor officials viewed it as a new low in corporate disloyalty, UAW president Owen Bieber decrying the idea that Caterpillar had no choice in the matter. "I'm getting a little sick of hearing the word 'global,'" he told the Detroit Economic Club. "Simply put, Caterpillar's anti-worker, anti-union takeaway strategy is a crime of domestic opportunity—not a legitimate struggle over global economic survival."[90]

Bieber was correct that Caterpillar saw the use of replacements less as a temporary fix and more as part of a long-term adaptation. That year the firm had joined two hundred other companies to create the Alliance to Keep Americans Working, whose first order of business was to defeat a bill working its way through Congress that would reverse the NLRB's ruling in *Harter Equipment* and ban the use of replacement workers in a lockout. In that 1986 case, which involved the Harter Equipment Company of New Jersey, the NLRB had ruled that employers who locked out striking workers could hire replacements in order to keep their businesses running, so long as there was no evidence of "anti-union motivation." Critics charged that such a right given to employers inherently defied workers' rights, since it rendered useless the threat of a strike. Labor had put up only a halfhearted effort to win support for the bill, thinking it stood little chance because President George H. W. Bush had threatened to veto it; in the end the legislation cleared the House but fell short in the Senate. "Within the AFL-CIO, serious misgivings had been expressed about risking organized labor's already beaten-down image in another losing battle," according to historian Stephen Franklin. "Organized labor did not do well in Congress, and had not won a major legislative battle in years. Stuck in its downward spiral . . . its defeat [in the replacement bill] was a self-fulfilled prophecy."[91]

Advocates for the legislation tried again early in Bill Clinton's first term, buffing up the image of what had been called the Striker Replacement Bill by renaming it the Workplace Fairness Bill, and later, after the death of the legendary farmworkers' leader in April 1993, the César Chávez Workplace Fairness Bill. Senator Edward Kennedy told his colleagues that most industrialized countries did not allow the hiring of replacement workers, and Representative Major Owens of Brooklyn defended the bill as essential to labor because "if you can be replaced, you don't have the right to strike." Republicans such as Senator Nancy Kassenbaum, however, complained that unless workers know they might lose their jobs to replacements, "there is little incentive for labor to make demands that are reasonable and reflect market realities." The legislation survived labor committees in both houses of Congress and passed in the House, but once again failed to garner enough votes in the Senate to overcome the Republicans' 60-vote filibuster.[92]

Although the UAW workers returned to their jobs at Caterpillar in spring 1992 in response to the company's ultimatum, many took up a kind of disruptive guerrilla warfare within the plant walls, carrying on what labor tacticians call "inside games"—worker slowdowns, holding union meetings in company lunchrooms, demonstrating outside Caterpillar's offices, and wearing anticorporate buttons and T-shirts that read YOU ARE ENTERING A WAR ZONE: CATERPILLAR V. ITS UAW EMPLOYEES. The company fought back with tightened discipline and selected firings.[93]

A three-day walkout was staged in November 1993, but the major renewed strike showdown came in June 1994. The UAW had amassed an impressive strike fund and appeared set to go the distance. "The Cat" was ready, too, however; when the workers went out the firm arranged to stay fully operational using temporary employees, white-collar personnel, and new hires, thoroughly frustrating the union's aim of crippling production. By now, the UAW was in an even weaker position in terms of public opinion regarding replacement workers, as replacements had been used that summer in a Major League Baseball strike. The use of replacements had become so common, the *New York Times* noted, a union's only chance of combating the tactic was to time strikes to coincide with periods of peak employer need, when the hiring of scabs would be too inconvenient. The paper also observed that the professional baseball players' union was unique in its ability to defy management's use of scabs, since the star athletes' celebrated talents and popularity with fans gave them "immunity to being replaced."[94]

The baseball strike again served as an analogy when, on March 8, 1995, President Bill Clinton signed an executive order denying federal contracts to firms that used replacement workers during strikes. "We don't want the industrial equivalent of minor leaguers and rookies making the tires for the next Desert Storm," said White House spokesman Mike McCurry, referring to the U.S. military engagement in Iraq and a current strike at Bridgestone-Firestone in which twenty-three hundred scabs had taken the jobs of striking rubber workers.[95] Conservative business groups vied to fight the executive order's application in court, while the order itself, offered chiefly as an olive branch to labor by Clinton to cool unions' irritation over the administration's approval of the North American Free Trade Agreement (NAFTA), was expected to affect only a modest number of employers.

The Caterpillar workers, however, were not athletes; their work did not require them to hit, catch, or pitch into the late innings; they possessed no virtue or talent more exceptional than simply having been loyal employees attempting to exercise the fundamental rights of collective bargaining. The strike at Caterpillar lingered halfheartedly for eighteen months, as UAW members crossed picket lines and returned to work or quit the union entirely; by December 1995 the UAW had no option but to admit defeat.

T HREE YEARS LATER the labor movement regained some ground, and got a much-needed morale boost, as the result of a 1997 Teamsters strike at United Parcel Service (UPS). The victory was cherished not because it triumphed over a badly behaving corporation—UPS had a fairly decent reputation for management-employee relations—but rather because the union challenged and won out against the insidious problem of "contingent" or "two-tier" employment, in which an employer cuts costs by relying on temporary and part-time workers. UPS was also attempting to change the structure of the workers' pension program, removing it from a multiemployer plan so as to place more control in the company's hands. The Teamsters resisted the idea because UPS was the richest member of the multiemployer group, and if it withdrew, fellow Teamsters at other, less endowed transportation firms might lose out. But staging a strike for any reason had become a risky undertaking, and also rare. Work stoppages in America declined from 3,111 in 1977 to only 385 by 1995, even as real wages lost 15 percent of their value—data that, as if on a diagnostic chart, revealed an ailing U.S. labor movement.[96]

Based in Atlanta, UPS was the nation's largest shipping company, with 302,000 American employees at twenty-four hundred sites and annual earnings of $1.1 billion. As many as 80 percent of the company's new hires were part-time, which allowed UPS to deny them full benefits and pay them $9 an hour in contrast to the $20 it paid full-timers. UPS defended the practice for two reasons—to stay competitive (its chief rival, Federal Express, had a lower-paid workforce, union-free except for its pilots), but also because the workday schedule at UPS was sporadic, with intense periods of loading and sorting followed by lulls in which few if any workers were needed. "We go in and out of business several times a day," one executive characterized it, explaining the preference for part-time employees.[97]

But the Teamsters complained that workers were kept at part-time status for years without promotion, and that as many as ten thousand part-timers actually worked full-time hours, although they received the lower, part-time rate. "In the corporate suite, that is called smart management," noted *New York Times* columnist Bob Herbert. "In other places, it is called ripping people off."[98]

UPS opened contract negotiations by offering to move eight hundred part-time workers to full time over the coming four years, while the union demanded that ten thousand make that leap in the same period. When no deal could be obtained, the union struck on August 4. The two thousand pilots who flew UPS planes agreed to honor the strike as 185,000 Teamsters walked off the job. The company made sure the media knew about a scandal involving Teamsters president Ron Carey, who faced charges that he'd illegally used union funds as "campaign contributions" in his recent narrow election over James Hoffa Jr. UPS alleged that Carey had forced the strike when he did to distract attention from his legal troubles. But by and large the union had the public on its side, and the press was also sympathetic. Polls showed the public supported the UPS strikers by a margin of 55 percent to 27 percent, and that people saw the issues of downsizing and contingent employees as a nationwide problem. The Teamsters' assertion that the two-tier method denied workers a middle-class existence rang true with many Americans, no doubt because by 1997 contingent work had become so ubiquitous virtually everyone knew a friend or family member trapped in the two-tier system as temps or part-timers, working at reduced pay, with marginal perks and nonexistent health coverage. In place of "the old ideal of job security," wrote Herbert, had come "permanent employment anxiety."[99]

While it was of limited solace, the fact that by 1997 most Americans took offense at the idea of a job without reliable benefits was in itself a tribute to the historic attainments of organized labor. Indeed the level of public empathy for the UPS walkout became news; in the 1981 PATCO strike 51 percent of Americans had backed President Reagan and only 40 percent the air traffic controllers; in the 1982 football players strike and the 1994 baseball players strike, respondents had sided with management by a margin of 43 percent to 22 percent. But the UPS workers, who enjoyed a 55 percent approval rate, were by far more familiar figures to most Americans than air traffic controllers or professional athletes, and there was a common perception that the men and women in brown uniforms seen toting packages in and out of the nation's businesses all day worked hard for their pay. As one pollster noted, there was also by 1997 a "very strong perception that management is less fair and less loyal to workers than it used to be."[100]

More crucially the UPS workers, unlike the PATCO controllers, benefited from the solidarity shown by the company's pilots; and unlike the Hormel strike, the Teamsters enjoyed the support of the rest of the labor movement, which perceived the strike as an important test of whether two-tier downsizing could be curbed. UPS was, after all, "a textbook example of the new economy, a service sector industry that's highly computerized, that's based on information, organization and smarts," said an economist. "If this kind of company cannot offer workers middle-class wages, if it pays $8.50 an hour instead of $20, that's a bad omen for the future."[101]

The AFL-CIO had even stepped forward to offer financial resources for the Teamsters strike fund. "Because their fight is our fight," federation president John Sweeney explained, "we are making this strike our strike."[102] Such cooperation was a reflection of the shake-up at the AFL-CIO in 1995, the first major reorientation of the 14-million-member organization since its inception forty years earlier. Disappointed over the passage of NAFTA in 1993 and angry that, following the 1994 midterm elections, President Clinton and the Democrats had shifted to the right and trimmed the country's welfare entitlement, the federation leadership had passed to Sweeney, the head of the Service Employees (SEIU). Sweeney brought a "rank and file" spirit to the job, a stark change from the executive-style leadership of Lane Kirkland. "I decided to run for president of the AFL-CIO because organized labor is the only voice of American workers and their families, and because the silence was deafening," Sweeney said.[103]

One innovative bit of activism the Teamsters pursued against UPS was to call on their friends around the world. While UPS was dominant in the shipping industry in America, it was still in an expansion mode in Europe. The Teamsters had links with transport unions in Europe, and so as union and UPS representatives sat across the bargaining table from one another in America, the European unions, as part of what was called UPS World Action Day, staged brief demonstrations or work stoppages. The message to UPS was clear: a failure to resolve the Teamsters strike on terms acceptable to workers might bring global consequences.

With the forces of big labor, public opinion, and coordinated sympathy strikes breaking out as far away as Orly Airport in Paris, UPS had its back to the wall. In this instance its own size and dominance of America's shipping business began to work against it. Because even the efforts of all its competitors, including FedEx and the U.S. Postal Service, could not pick up the slack created by the sudden disappearance of the familiar brown UPS trucks from the nation's streets, the firm came under immediate pressure from its customers, particularly retailers and catalog companies, to settle.[104] UPS also had exceptional vulnerability to a protracted strike, in that as a shipping business it made its money by providing a daily service and, unlike a manufacturer like Caterpillar, was not protected by its back inventory. President Clinton and his labor secretary, Alexis Herman, also pitched in, keeping the two parties at the bargaining table despite the sluggish pace of the talks, and at one point rejecting out of hand UPS's request for a court injunction against the Teamsters.

Fifteen days after the walkout began UPS capitulated, agreeing to shift ten thousand part-time workers to full time within five years and raise part-time salaries 37 percent during that period, full-timers by 15 percent. The company also agreed to maintain the present pension arrangement. Teamsters president Carey was exultant. "I remember in the 1980s when the air traffic controllers' union was wiped out," he said. "For 15 years after that, employers all across the country cut jobs, cut pensions, cut health coverage, and stepped on workers' rights. Working people were on the run, but not anymore. This strike marks a new era."[105] Labor scholar Nelson Lichtenstein concurred, noting that the Teamsters' win over UPS ended "the PATCO syndrome."[106] If anything, what the victory showed was that to succeed, a strike in the era of globalization must be vigorously supported by allies near and far and exceptionally well managed. The union had run such a strike, and it had won.

Economists, naturally, warned against jubilation. The overall trend of globalization and the pressures of intensified competition on employers, they explained, as well as the ever-broadening pool of cheaper workers, still augured poorly for labor. More factories would vanish in Ohio and Pennsylvania and reappear in Mexico, China, or Indonesia; at home the difficult problem of replacement workers and contingent workers would in all likelihood remain.

But no professional doubters were to deny organized labor its moment. The Teamsters, so recently the bad boy of American unionism, had shown it was still possible to rally against capital and win, and it had done so with the venerable AFL-CIO looking on with pride and approval. "What we have is a more aggressive labor movement," even the dour National Association of Manufacturers was forced to concede. "Whether we have a more effective one remains to be seen."[107]

I N NOVEMBER 2009 the U.S. sportswear company Russell Athletic made a startling announcement: it would reopen one of its Honduran clothing factories that it had closed ten months earlier in reaction to the unionization of the plant's twelve hundred workers. It took this unusual step, which included rehiring the workers, as the direct result of a national campaign by the United Students Against Sweatshops, youthful American activists who had pressured Boston College, Columbia, Harvard, New York University, and ninety-two other colleges to suspend the lucrative sportswear licensing agreements that allowed Russell to imprint sweatshirts and other clothing with the schools' names and logos. The students targeted not only college retailers and administrators but also picketed major college sporting events. As part of Russell's settlement, the company agreed to cease its antiunion activities at other plants in the Central American nation, leading a Honduran labor official to comment, "We are impressed by the social conscience of the students in the United States."[108]

What was particularly encouraging about the anti-sweatshop group's effort was that it had overcome perhaps the main obstacle that thwarts U.S. labor organizing today, the power of American corporations to disperse their operations to developing countries where there are cheaper workers and few if any labor regulations. Since the early 1990s U.S. firms have been all too glad to exchange a labor base that costs, for example, $5 million a year to maintain for one that will cost a fifth as much, and is less organized, more desperate, and hence more docile. The result of course is a significant loss of leverage on the part of unions and American workers.

The question is how readily organized labor can, like the United

Students Against Sweatshops, pivot to confront similar challenges. Some labor historians make the point that it has managed equally dramatic shifts before. "Just like capitalism," Ronaldo Munck insists, "trade unions as a social movement are capable of mutation, transformation, and regeneration."[109] When the apprentice-journeyman-master tradition was threatened by the manufacturing system, labor formed workingmen's associations; when industry became national in scope it evolved into sprawling trade union federations and later industrial unions; when management was at its most rapacious and brutal during the Gilded Age, elements of labor sought alternative means of economic organization, or staged massive strikes; when labor policy began to emanate from Washington, unions developed advocacy skills and the ability to affect elections.

Those who see reason for hope are encouraged by the possibility that organized labor can reinvent itself simply because it has done it before. "The reports on the death of the labor movement are not just premature but wrong," contends scholar Stanley Aronowitz. "As long as people procure their livelihood by working for wages and salaries, they will recognize, sooner or later, the futility of appealing to their employers as individuals. For most workers," suggests Aronowitz, "there is no alternative to collective action."[110] In 1986, only five years after PATCO's demise, he observes that the nonunion replacement air traffic controllers had themselves organized as the National Air Traffic Controllers Association, and had begun to echo many of the same grievances voiced by their predecessors.[111]

But does the American labor movement remain relevant enough to transition as it must? Today, in the new labor-management dynamic impacted by globalization—and the related loss of manufacturing, long-term full-time jobs, pension, and health benefits—overall union membership has shrunk to about a fifth of the percentage of U.S. workers it had in the mid-1950s, with only 11.9 percent belonging to a labor union. There are today 7.6 million unionized public sector workers (36.2 percent of the total number of government employees) and 7.1 million union members in the private sphere (6.9 percent of all such workers).

Meanwhile, there are tens of thousands of transnational corporations, controlling 75 percent of world trade and upward of 150 million jobs worldwide.[112] And much as large-scale industrial capital got the jump on organized labor in the early nineteenth century, so again during recent years has it leaped forward into global markets, rewriting or abandoning what was once viewed as a covenant with American workers, well ahead of labor's mostly gradual efforts to keep up. Is the cause of workers' rights somehow so timeless and universal that it can be expected, against such odds, to sustain or re-create itself through some inherent force of necessity?

WHILE GLOBALIZATION'S IMPACT on U.S. workers has been both substantial and insidious, wreaking havoc in ways large and small, not every setback can be laid at its door. Among other factors that have influenced the downward trend in unionism since the late 1970s must be included a popular disenchantment with workaday life itself. The general rise in education levels and the diverse cultural influences of recent decades combined to elevate individual expectations regarding the way one earned a living. Along with an increased desire for work that holds intrinsic interest and offers variety and challenge had come a disdain for the traditional "good job" in an office or factory. Indeed, many large firms themselves no longer encourage or make it possible for employees to stay put in one job over long periods of time, and workers enjoy such innovations as the four-day workweek, telecommuting, and the semi-independence of serving as a consultant or surviving as an artisan or entrepreneur.

Those escaping the nine-to-five grind, sometimes described as the "creative classes," are generally college-educated individuals who support themselves as graphic artists, freelance writers, Web designers, Internet publishers, interior decorators, photographers, food specialists, or public relations consultants. Some make ends meet with temporary jobs. Ironically, while such status confers tremendous freedom and mobility, it has largely removed its practitioners from the sphere of potential labor organization, and most, despite their credentials and qualifications, are in fact locked in a struggle to make a living different only in style from the plight of nonunionized workers a century ago. With no employer health coverage, no workplace safety protections, no employer-managed benefits, pension, or 401(k), no sick pay or vacation pay, not even the opportunity of collective bargaining, many are for all their worldliness a voiceless "Precariate," as scholar Andrew Ross has dubbed them, cut off from society's traditional sources of livelihood security.

Even for full-time employees, rights and security have sharply eroded, including the issue that historically was most dearly fought for—reasonable hours of work, so that laboring people would have a life beyond factory walls. This is not due solely to the disappearance of the union shop steward who kept an eye on the clock, but by the pressures of the contemporary workplace and its supposed conveniences of voice mail, e-mail, and laptop computers—an "electronic collar" that holds workers accountable twenty-four hours a day, seven days a week.

The deterioration of pensions and retirement health care has also been a significant problem. First offered by stagecoach operator American Express in 1875, pensions became a common feature of the welfare capitalist employment landscape of the 1920s, were reflected in the old-age and unemployment guarantees of the New Deal, then grew rapidly in popularity during the Second World War, when government wage controls made them an attractive wage-alternative to lure employees. By 1949, inspired by the decision of a Federal District Court the previous year in the case of *Inland Steel Co. v. National Labor Relations Board*, which had affirmed that the right to bargain for work conditions under Wagner included the right to bargain for retirement benefits, pension and benefits packages were won in steel, coal, and the auto industry, and the expectation of a comfortable retirement as a reward for one's working life became a staple of American culture. In the 1949 case *W. W. Cross & Co. v. National Labor Relations Board* similar bargaining rights were secured for health benefits. Employers lowered their own tax burden through pension contributions, and employees also got a tax break by having some of their income deferred to retirement, when they'd have less income overall. The Taft-Hartley Act, in order to limit the investing clout of unions, had directed that the responsibility for employee pension funds remain with management, although the act allowed for some joint union-employer control, an option that Thomas Geoghegan suggests unions erred in not pursuing more vigorously, as such oversight would have greatly empowered labor organizations financially.[113]

The notion of corporate-managed pensions went awry in 1963, when automaker Studebaker suddenly went broke, stranding the company's forty-one hundred workers with only 15 percent of their retirement funds. Alarm spread nationwide about the possible fallibility of the system, leading to the passage in 1974 of the Employee Retirement Income Security Act (ERISA), which mandated that firms have enough money on hand to cover their pension obligations. ERISA also established the Pension Benefit Guaranty Corporation (PBGC) to back up worker pensions where firms went belly-up, although the PBGC could guarantee only a certain percentage on the dollar, meaning long-term employees caught in a corporate bankruptcy would be the losers.

The crisis first glimpsed at Studebaker proved the start of what by the 1980s became determined corporate backpedaling away from pension management. In the tightening global economy, CEOs had come to see that the obligation of making monthly payments to retirees over many years in what was known as the defined-benefit system, which is based on years of employee service and other factors, would be financially ruinous, particularly as the average life span of former employees and their spouses lengthened. United Airlines, US Airways, and Bethlehem Steel all dumped their costly pension burdens on the PBGC and the federal government, and the number of traditional pension arrangements held by U.S. companies overall fell from 115,000 in 1985 to 31,000 in 2005, as corporations pursued what *New York Times* labor reporter Steven Greenhouse termed "an unhealthy race to the bottom on retirement benefits."[114] Other firms disappointed older workers by reconfiguring their defined-benefits programs, changing over to what is known as a "cash-balance" system, calculating retirement benefits on an employee's entire length of service, rather than allowing greater benefits to accrue more steeply in a worker's final years, as had previously been the case. The cash-balance formula in some instances reduced the employee's retirement pension by as much as half, thus seriously altering expectations and retirement planning. To some it meant that full retirement was no longer an option.

The 1990s bull market proved an ideal time to sell employees on another retirement innovation, the 401(k) account, which allowed the employer to shift responsibility to what is called a defined-contribution plan in which both employer and employee contribute to investment funds that are essentially managed by the employee. These individualized investment accounts not only required less of an employer contribution, saving companies millions of dollars a year, but freed them from having to arrange for the payout of retirement and health care benefits. With this method it was not the employer's money but the worker's that was subject to fluctuations in the investment market, although there was widespread faith that the nation's economy would continue to expand, making investment in stocks and bonds a more dynamic route to future security than a standard company pension, while an economic reversal or seizure on the scale of the Great Depression was deemed impossible.

The reality proved much different. Individual employees turned out in many instances to be reckless investors. Some placed too many of their chips on aggressive but risky stocks; others depleted their 401(k)s or cashed them out when switching jobs; the most distressing stories were those of workers who loyally invested their 401(k)s exclusively in their own company's stock, only to see their retirement nest egg obliterated when firms such as Enron tanked. Then, in the economic crises of 2001 and 2008, holders of these accounts learned that the value of even "solid" stock and bond portfolios can diminish or disappear overnight. Whether employees have used their 401(k) accounts wisely or not, the wide variation in the results obtained by individual employee-investors defies the notion of guaranteed retirement income inherent in the original movement toward pension savings.

All of these adjustments to the U.S. corporate pension system, as well as substantial increases in health care costs to individuals, have had the effect of making retirement as it was once viewed—an opportunity for travel, greater leisure time, perhaps relocation to the "retirement belt" of Florida, Arizona, or Southern California—increasingly obsolete. Vast numbers of Americans find the luxury of not working something they simply can't afford. Many now either delay retirement or arrange to earn part-time income during what were to have been their golden years.

Where the phaseout of traditional corporate retirement benefits gets particularly messy is when a company's benefits obligations are bound by union contract. It has become an article of faith among conservative critics of labor that it is the highly favorable wage and benefits pacts brokered by powerful labor unions that are to blame for U.S. firms losing ground to foreign manufacturers. This narrative has been recycled recently in the controversy over the federal government's bailout of the U.S. auto industry, where considerable blame was laid at the feet of the UAW for having secured "sweetheart contracts" over the years with the Big Three automakers. Beginning in the late 1940s and 1950s, when auto manufacturing was in a growth phase and U.S.-made cars ruled the roads, the UAW negotiated a number of exemplary contracts, securing good wages, cost-of-living increases, and fat health care and retirement payments. Detroit signed on to these long-term arrangements because times were flush, assembly lines were humming, and they offered a means of saving money in immediate wage hikes at the bargaining table. As Greenhouse writes, the irony is that many of the current problems with, for example, General Motors' benefits burden, often blamed on the UAW, came about simply because the union did a superb job at negotiating, winning for its members—and by extension all U.S. blue-collar workers—a shot at a middle-class lifestyle.[115]

Because of these generous pacts, however, GM had as of 2009 paid out $100 billion in retirement and health benefits over the past fifteen years, adding almost $2,000 to the cost of each new car. Even as its actual workforce fell to seventy-four thousand workers from four hundred thousand in 1970, the company was paying health benefits for 340,000 GM retirees and their spouses. Another frequently cited example of alleged union excess was the Jobs Bank, a twenty-five-year-old system by which UAW workers whose factories had closed were kept on salary (the program was dropped in 2009 in response to criticism).

The UAW feels unfairly singled out on the benefits issue. "Our contracts with Chrysler, Ford and GM represent only 10 per cent of the cost of assembling of a vehicle," UAW head Ron Gettelfinger told *Time* magazine in 2009. "But most days it seems like we get 110% of the attention."[116]

Where the UAW does deserve some blame for the auto industry meltdown is in its having sided with automakers in opposing more rigid fuel-efficiency standards, thus enabling Detroit to continue with the manufacture of gas-guzzling SUVs, earning short-term profits but neglecting to adapt to the market demand for smaller, more fuel-efficient vehicles.

ORGANIZED LABOR SHARES with environmentalism the willingness to challenge the actions of industry, but as in the UAW fuel efficiency controversy, the two do frequently lock horns over the impact of environmental regulations on jobs and economic growth. Some of the best-known struggles have involved federal listings under the Endangered Species Act that affect the logging industry in the Pacific Northwest, the banning of insecticides in agriculture, and the draining of wetlands for residential and commercial development.

The UAW has historically exercised an outsize impact on policies emanating from Washington because autoworkers constitute a massive voting bloc in Ohio and Michigan, states that are almost evenly divided between Republicans and Democrats and are thus fiercely contested politically. A modest financial contributor to the first Earth Day, the UAW initially appeared sympathetic to environmental concerns; but after siding with Congress in 1975 to raise automobile fuel-efficiency standards, the union did an abrupt about-face when data suggested the new standards were impeding the sale of Detroit cars. Beginning in the late 1970s, the UAW joined the Big Three automakers in opposing more regulations, and when in 1990 Congress again made a serious effort to tackle the problem by establishing "corporate average fuel economy" requirements, known as CAFÉ standards, in a bill sponsored by Senator Richard Bryan of Nevada, the UAW worked with automakers to defeat it. While the auto companies granted UAW members extended coffee breaks if they would use company phones to call their congressmen, UAW president Owen Bieber flew to Washington to stand with a Chrysler lobbyist in the hallway outside the Senate chamber, grabbing key senators to remind them that automakers and autoworkers alike were interested to know who would help defend their industry. The Bryan bill was defeated by a slim margin.

The Big Three automakers and the UAW were equally alarmed when Democrats Bill Clinton and Al Gore ran for the White House in 1992, vowing to address the fuel-efficiency issue. Clinton, an Arkansas native, was little known to autoworkers, but Gore had recently published a popular book, *Earth in the Balance*, warning of the effect the internal combustion engine had on global warming. The Republican Bush/Quayle ticket played on the UAW's fears, running an ad in Detroit newspapers that read, "If Bill Clinton has his way 40,000 Michigan autoworkers will go from the assembly line to the unemployment line."[117] Once Clinton was elected, the UAW lobbied him hard not to act rashly on fuel efficiency; Clinton, deferring legislative action, instead established a task force to examine the "next generation" of American automobiles, and after Republicans seized control of Congress in 1994 fuel reforms became more or less a dead letter. In 1997, when the Clinton administration was preparing for international global climate change talks in Kyoto, the UAW again cautioned the president against commitments that would unfairly hamstring the U.S. auto industry and possibly result in layoffs.[118]

While the UAW maneuvering took place at the highest levels of government, a more familiar, everyday version of the labor-environmentalist rift occurs almost daily in city council and community planning meetings across the country, where building trades unions seeking construction jobs face off against forces opposed to excessive or inappropriate development. With the advent of green technology in building and energy design, as well as the initiation of forest stewardship programs by environmental groups like the Natural Resources Defense Council (NRDC), the argument that doing right by the environment costs people their jobs has lost some of its former intensity, and in many urban areas progressive forces have joined with labor to advocate for manufacturing retention—to save jobs, but also because keeping manufacturing in or close to cities is seen as energy efficient and a way to reduce transport-related pollution. Many environmentalists have countered labor's anxiety about job loss by positing that the stewardship of natural resources and cleaner and more efficient forms of technology will not necessarily bring economic deprivation, but that newer green technology will itself produce enough jobs to offset those lost to the old.

At the same time, in response to the public's greater awareness of the imperative of environmental action, many large businesses like Exxon, Shell, British Petroleum, and DuPont have learned the efficacy of publicizing their own environmental efforts, such as the creation of dedicated corporate energy-saving programs or research scholarships. Some of these efforts may be inspired by genuine concern and have positive results; many are derided by critics as stunts or "green-washing." As far as organized labor's occasional resistance to environmental reform, it's worth noting that it generally pales in scope compared to the well-oiled reaction of the corporations and their conservative handmaidens, full-time business lobbyists like the Chamber of Commerce and issue-oriented conservative front groups such as the Alliance for Responsible CFC Policy, the Coalition for Vehicle Choice, or Nevadans for Fair Fuel Economy Standards.

THE WAY FORWARD FOR LABOR must involve global networks or coalitions of wage earners to match the power of transnational firms, and that will require nothing less than new ways of thinking and new means of coordination. Just as the issues of ozone depletion and global warming that emerged in the 1980s awakened scientists, environmentalists, and government agencies to the urgent need for global cooperation, so now do global labor economics compel a similar reorientation for labor. To follow the metaphor a step further, much as the release of industrial chemicals into the atmosphere by one nation impacts the residents of all nations, so do the wages paid textile workers in Honduras or Indonesia bear on the lives of textile mill employees in northern Mexico or North Carolina. What the United Students Against Sweatshops demonstrated in 2009 by successfully addressing the unfair treatment of foreign workers was the potential strength in unity of workers coordinating across national borders.

"Trade is global, capital is global, and labor too must become global," insists Andy Stern, former president of the Service Employees International Union (SEIU), which, with 1.8 million members, is one of the nation's fastest-growing unions, focusing on grassroots organizing at home and on organizing building and janitorial services, hospitals, and care providers. But the means of accomplishing or even beginning such an effort remains unclear. How does one organize labor under global circumstances, when the political, social, and economic contexts in which men and women (and children) go to work each day, the wages they receive, the protections they enjoy, are so dissimilar? How would one begin to write some sort of global Wagner Act, an international baseline of workers' rights, let alone enact and enforce it?

The steps being taken in this direction have some of their philosophical grounding in the vigorous protests that met the November 1999 meeting of the World Trade Organization (WTO) in Seattle, and which have recurred at similar gatherings. While in the 1990s international trade pacts were negotiated with inadequate attention given to labor and environmental concerns, today such agreements and the powerful bodies that create them are monitored and sometimes checked by opposition from labor and consumer advocates, environmentalists, and human rights activists. "The labor movement's message from Seattle could not have been clearer," comments Jay Mazur of the Union of Needle Trades, Industrial and Textile Employees (UNITE). "The era of trade negotiations conducted by sheltered elites balancing competing commercial interests behind closed doors is over."[119]

Labor's historic affiliation with the Democratic Party also has come under renewed scrutiny. The relationship, despite the Democrats' clear superiority to the Republicans on labor issues, has over the long term often been disappointing. By placing expectations for needed reforms on the shoulders of elected officials, labor's own motivation to act as an agent of social change has diminished, and when Democrats fail to deliver on labor's hopes, the movement faces the demoralizing fact that it has only its "friends" to criticize. As early as 1940 John L. Lewis had begun to fear the labor movement's adherence to the party of the New Deal and lawmakers in general. Certainly the risk of ceding the independence and fighting instinct of labor to a regime of government-derived and -enforced "labor practices" became apparent in the era of Taft-Hartley, when Congress pulled the rug out from under many of the labor protections won in 1935, a move even the combined efforts of labor and the Democratic Truman administration could not deter. By 1953, the outlines of Lewis's earlier premonition had become so clear, he told a Senate committee that as far as he was concerned not only Taft-Hartley but even the Wagner Act should be repealed. "This would give to this country, its employers and employees," he insisted, "an opportunity . . . to practice for a season true, free and genuine collective bargaining without government interference, free from the brooding shadows which presently hover over all bargaining tables."[120] Even when Democrats supported by labor have won control of the White House and both houses of Congress, as in the Johnson, Carter, and early Clinton administrations, obtaining labor reforms has proven a daunting and at times insurmountable challenge.

Labor organizations accordingly have come to treat seriously the need for unionized workers to be aware of the larger political and economic forces affecting today's global markets, and to know labor history itself. While the visionary labor ideologies of a century ago may appear quaint and even misguided today, there is no denying they were about connecting labor's daily experience to larger themes and world-size challenges. That impulse was reinvigorated by Walter Reuther and the UAW during the 1960s, but it has been chiefly in the past two decades that unions have launched deliberate efforts to educate their members (and the public) about social and economic forces relevant to the workplace, such as the conditions in foreign sweatshops, free trade product alternatives, the rights of women workers, and concepts such as industrial retention and green technology. This isn't to imply that people need indoctrination or to be taught new slogans, but rather that the use of unions' programmatic dollars on member education regarding labor issues is essential.[121]

Unions have also retooled structurally for global action. "Not so long ago, a major union's international activity could be carried out by a single person who might even have had other organizational responsibilities," explains Mazur. "This is no longer possible." Because almost all labor-industrial conflicts have an international aspect, "the most advanced unions now involve many of their departments—organizing, research, political action, public relations, education, legal, health and safety, and corporate affairs—in diverse strategies. In turn, these strategies forge effective links with overseas partners, coordinate industrial actions, lobby governments, take legal action, and simultaneously publicize all this activity in more than one country."[122]

However, activists hoping to work cooperatively with their counterparts in developing nations will need to be mindful of the negative impression left by decades of American labor's harmful meddling—the conspiring of Jay Lovestone and the CIA, ersatz U.S. Agency for International Development (USAID) "training" programs, and the undermining of labor unions and whole governments. In some instances, foreign trade unions with which American organizations might now seek alliance are the very ones plotted against by the AFL-CIO during the cold war, or they exist in countries where our own actions enabled the government to create means of suppressing independent labor unions. "By working to make the world safe for U.S. business in the 1950s, 1960s, and 1970s," says labor scholar Gregory Mantsios, "the AFL-CIO laid the ground for labor's current predicament: the world became all too safe for U.S. corporations interested in cheap labor and unregulated environments."[123]

What has differentiated America from other industrialized nations since the Second World War is not that some industries have become obsolete or that others have emerged—that was bound to occur—but that this process and the related need to confront globalization and the energy crisis have not been adequately met by coordinated economic or energy planning. The collective aspect of industrial self-control, as Geoghegan relates, such as a tax on oil consumption proposed by the Carter administration, failed to win broad support, even from organized labor, for all the old reasons of Americans' "excess of individualism," the nation's "short-sighted brand of liberal capitalism," and the lack of a "constituency with an interest in the long term, or in visionary economic planning." Participation in such an undertaking would be, under ideal circumstances, a natural calling for a reinvigorated labor movement.[124]

The question of how labor organizes has itself been the focus in recent years of the Employee Free Choice Act (EFCA), legislation which has languished in Congress. Labor wants a "card check" system that will allow workers to simply sign a card stating they want union representation, at which point an employer would have to recognize and bargain with the union that a majority of the workers have chosen. It would replace the existing arrangement, often abused by management, in which an NLRB election to certify a union is held once 30 percent of workers sign cards expressing a desire for a union's representation. Such elections are scheduled at the employer's discretion, allowing opportunity for management to propagandize against unionization and harass or even fire labor organizers. While such firings are illegal, employers know only too well that the process by which unfairly terminated workers must seek reinstatement under the National Labor Relations Act is nearly hopeless; indeed, firms have mastered a bag of tricks they can deploy to stall and hinder union representation elections, some of which become drawn out as long as ten or fifteen years. And as in the conservatives' historic use of the argument for the greater "freedom" of the open shop, employers' advocates take refuge behind the notion that employees' rights will be voided by the card check process since it would deny them the opportunity to vote their conscience freely in a secret-ballot election.[125]

Responding to an early 2010 Bureau of Labor Statistics report that indicated union members tend to earn more than nonunionized workers, Labor Secretary Hilda Solis suggested that enacting EFCA would have the salutary effect of enabling "more American workers to access the benefits of union membership," although—in comments suggestive of a deeply entrenched opposition—J. Justin Wilson, managing director of the business-supported Center for Union Facts, quickly dismissed the idea that unionized employees are better paid, terming membership in unions "an outdated concept for most working Americans" and "a relic of Depression-era labor-management relations."[126]

It is doubtful many people would describe themselves as optimistic about the present state of organized labor. The labor movement described in this book, a cause that "uniquely embodied a vision, a generosity of spirit, and the political courage to rescue society from selfishness, exploitation, and organized violence,"[127] now belongs to history, and for every expression of faith in the universal and timeless nature of worker solidarity there stands an illustration of its opposite: the eternalness of labor exploitation and abuse. Hispanic women suffer conditions and indignities in textile sweatshops in Los Angeles today that would be entirely recognizable to the Yiddish-speaking garment workers of the Lower East Side in 1909, or even to the New England mill hands who entrusted their ardor and youth to the Lowell Miracle. Gone missing is the communal purpose that animated America in the mid-twentieth century, leading workers into unions and creating fundamental trust in government sufficient to bring about not only the benefits of the New Deal but the advances of the 1960s, such as the Civil Rights Act, the Voting Rights Act, Medicare, Medicaid, and the National Endowment for the Arts, among many other programs.[128]

P ADLOCKED FACTORY GATES have become a familiar image in news or magazine stories about the decline of industrial America. Equally poignant is a spectacle less often glimpsed by the public—the physical dismantling of the machinery that once powered U.S. industry—as giant metal stamp presses, pieces of assembly lines, and other equipment are sold to manufacturers in Mexico, India, Brazil, the hardware of America's great industrial age following where America's jobs already have gone. Writer Paul Clemens, who witnessed the disassembling of two-story-tall stamping presses at the venerable ThyssenKrupp Budd auto parts factory in Detroit in 2007, described the knot of attending Mexican and German engineers watching closely as the presses were prepared for removal to Mexico, where a Spanish auto supplier would install the machines. "Their role is to stand there, in awe, and hope they can put it back together when they get it to Mexico," Clemens quoted an American electrician involved in the handoff.[129]

Not every machine or every factory gets a second life. Many once-valued pieces of industrial machinery are sold for scrap or lie abandoned, orange with rust, in the weeds behind long-shuttered factories; some old nineteenth-century buildings, however, especially the sturdy redbrick textile mills of New England, have been renovated for use as outlet stores or condominiums. To walk today among these structures in Lawrence, Lowell, and Fall River is to imagine how imposing they must have seemed in their heyday, tens of thousands of workers entering their portals each dawn, work bells summoning an entire town to labor. That ordinary workingmen and -women ever organized to defy these behemoths and the captains of fortune who ran them seems remarkable, yet we know that they did.

We know also that they went on to affirm a civil war for emancipation and free labor, formed national unions and federations, stayed corporate supremacy and abuse, and helped order the modern workplace. It was they who gave workers a voice on issues of war and economic justice, resisted the internal suppression of political freedom and free speech, inspired crusades for suffrage, equal rights, and education, and demanded the exercise of good government. Their words—rung in public squares, conventions, and union halls—spread from New England and New York to Appalachia, Detroit, to the timber stands of the Pacific Northwest and into the barrios of the Imperial Valley.

Of that bygone era's leading protagonists many left their life's battle unfinished. Eugene Debs expired in 1926, his body frail and worn down by years of incarceration; Mother Jones lived a full century before finding her rest in a miners' cemetery in rural Illinois; Joseph Ettor came into a small inheritance and moved to California to operate a wine business. John Reed, Big Bill Haywood, and Elizabeth Gurley Flynn died in Russia; Flynn's great love, Carlo Tresca, was assassinated on a New York street corner in 1943, his enemies so numerous even the hundred police detectives assigned to the case failed to find anyone to indict. John L. Lewis lived until 1969, long enough to see the UMW he'd nurtured for four decades slip into a bitter power struggle between two of his own former lieutenants, one of whom would soon order the murder of the other; Jimmy Hoffa vanished in 1975, the suspected victim of a Mafia hit. Visitors still come to Chicago's Waldheim Cemetery to honor the Haymarket martyrs; the immortal Joe Hill lives on in song; while the names Robert F. Wagner, George Meany, and Walter Reuther adorn major national labor archives.

Of course the real monument to what these individuals and millions of others achieved is not stored in a library or carved on a plaque. It's the freedoms and protections we take for granted—reasonable hours, on-the-job safety, benefits, and the bedrock notion that employees have the right to bargain for the value of their labor; it's also the knowledge that such rights were not handed down by anyone or distributed ready-made, but were organized around, demanded, and won by workers themselves. UNION FOR POWER—POWER TO BLESS HUMANITY read the banner that mill worker Sarah Bagley presented to the workingmen of New England nearly two centuries ago. That fabled relic, one hopes, was never discarded but is still with us somewhere in America; surely its author would be curious to know if its message had endured, and if the words she so carefully chose remain immutable.

★ ACKNOWLEDGMENTS ★

This book would not exist without the guidance of my friend and literary agent Scott Moyers of the Wylie Agency, who helped shape the book's premise and introduced me to Gerry Howard, an executive editor at Doubleday. Gerry has a deserved reputation as one of the top publishers in the business and I was pleased when he acquired the project. He has been a superb muse and collaborator.

Labor scholars Les Leopold, Seth Rockman, and especially Laura Wolf-Powers have been generous with their time. I am grateful to a number of historians whose work informs these pages, including Melvyn Dubofsky, Foster Rhea Dulles, Eric Foner, Philip S. Foner, Steven Fraser, Thomas Geoghegan, Elliott J. Gorn, Richard A. Greenwald, Nelson Lichtenstein, and Christine Stansell. The Tamiment Labor Archives at New York University were invaluable. Brian Berger, historian of all things Brooklyn, shared research ideas. In Providence, friends Angel Dean and Jonathan Thomas kindly provided a place to stay during my New England research (thank you for waiting until morning to mention the guest room is haunted).

I am indebted to Ted Widmer of the John Carter Brown Library at Brown University, who welcomed me to the center's resident fellowship program, where I spent a productive and enjoyable month writing labor history. Thanks also to Stephanie Steiker, Marisa Bowe, and my wife Lianne Smith for their concern and support, and to the highly professional staff at Doubleday, including editorial assistant Hannah Wood, production editor Nora Reichard, book designer Pei Loi Koay, and cover designer Emily Mahon.

★ NOTES ★

INTRODUCTION

1   *New York Times*, Jan. 6–7, 1874.
2   David T. Burbank, *Reign of Rabble: The St. Louis General Strike of 1877* (New York: Augustus M. Kelley, 1966), p. 6.
3   Franklin Folsom, *Impatient Armies of the Poor: The Story of Collective Action of the Unemployed, 1808–1942* (Niwat: University of Colorado Press, 1991), p. 117.
4   *New York Times*, Jan. 14, 1874.
5   Ibid.
6   Ibid.
7   *New York Tribune*, Jan. 31, 1874, and *New York Times*, Jan. 31, 1874.
8   *New York Times*, Jan. 31, 1874.
9   Ibid.
10 The phrase "an irrepressible conflict" as an allusion to the coming civil war originated with Senator William Seward (later Lincoln's secretary of state), and has often been invoked to describe the struggle between capital and organized labor. For one example see *Literary Digest*, Nov. 8, 1919.
11 *New York Tribune*, Jan. 14, 1874.
12 Gompers called Schwab's establishment "the post office and information center for the underground of revolution." See Franklin Folsom, *Impatient Armies of the Poor*, p. 121.
13 A similar point is made in Nelson Lichtenstein, *State of the Union: A Century of American Labor* (Princeton, N.J.: Princeton University Press, 2002), p. 18.
14 Lichtenstein, *State of the Union*, pp. 106–7.
15 Thomas Geoghegan, *Which Side Are You On?: Trying to Be for Labor When It's Flat on Its Back* (New York: New Press, 2004; originally published 1991), p. 6.

CHAPTER ONE: THE OPPRESSING HAND OF AVARICE

1   Benita Eisler, ed., *The Lowell Offering: Writings by New England Mill Women, 1840–1845* (New York: W. W. Norton & Co., 1998; originally published 1977), pp. 66–73; Sarah Bagley, "Tales of Factory Life, No 1, and No 2," in *The Lowell Offering*, ed. Benita Eisler, vol. 1, 1841.
2   Lucy Larcom, "Among Lowell Mill Girls: A Reminiscence," *Atlantic Monthly*, Nov. 1881.
3   Harriet H. Robinson, *Loom and Spindle, or Life Among the Early Mill Girls* (Kailua, Hawaii: Press Pacifica, 1976; originally published 1898), p. 59.

4 Hannah Josephson, *The Golden Threads: New England's Mill Girls and Magnates* (New York: Duell, Sloan, and Pearce, 1949), p. 190.

5 Eisler, *Lowell Offering*, pp. 63–65; Sarah Bagley, "Pleasures of Factory Life," in *The Lowell Offering*, vol. 1, 1840.

6 Jefferson as quoted in Leo Marx, *The Machine in the Garden: Technology and the Pastoral Ideal in America* (New York: Oxford University Press, 1964), pp. 124–25.

7 Doron S. Ben-Atar, *Trade Secrets: Intellectual Piracy and the Origins of American Industrial Power* (New Haven, Conn.: Yale University Press, 2004), p. 120.

8 Stephen Yafa, *Cotton: The Biography of a Revolutionary Fiber* (New York: Penguin Books, 2006), p. 73.

9 Marx, *Machine in the Garden*, p. 133; Jefferson to William Bingham, Sept. 25, 1789, quoted in Ben-Atar, *Trade Secrets*, p. 124.

10 Although such restrictions were often ignored (by 1774 there were forty-three hat makers in Philadelphia alone).

11 Jefferson letter to Benjamin Austin, Jan. 19, 1816, quoted in Marx, *Machine in the Garden*, p. 139.

12 Tench Coxe, *An Address to an Assembly of the Friends of American Manufactures* (Philadelphia: R. Aitkin & Son, 1787), p. 4.

13 Tench Coxe, *A View of the United States of America* (Philadelphia: William Hall, 1794), p. 42.

14 Ibid., p. 53.

15 Ibid., p. 42; see also Ben-Atar, *Trade Secrets*, p. 158.

16 A speech Coxe gave in June 1787 at the home of Benjamin Franklin, titled "An Enquiry into the Principle on Which a Commercial System for the United States of America Shall Be Founded," was published and dedicated to members of the Constitutional Convention. See Marx, *Machine in the Garden*, p. 152.

17 Michael Folsom and Steven Lubar, *The Philosophy of Manufactures: Early Debates over Industrialization in the United States* (Cambridge, Mass.: MIT Press, 1982), p. 90.

18 British authorities were also cautious about allowing those who had worked in England's cotton mills to immigrate to America. Samuel Slater, who opened one of America's first mills in Pawtucket, Rhode Island, in 1789, had dressed as a farmer in order to avoid suspicion when departing his native land. See Yafa, *Cotton: The Biography of a Revolutionary Fiber*, p. 77.

19 Bruce Watson, *Bread and Roses: Mills, Migrants, and the Struggle for the American Dream* (New York: Penguin Books, 2005), pp. 29–30.

20 Harriet H. Robinson, *Loom and Spindle*, pp. 5–6.

21 Teresa Anne Murphy, *Ten Hours Labor: Religion, Reform, and Gender in Early New England* (Ithaca, N.Y.: Cornell University Press, 1992), pp. 208–9.

22 On April 11, 1837, Boott tumbled from his carriage, dead from a cerebral hemorrhage at age forty-six.

23 *Lowell Courier*, Jan. 27, 1842.

24 Thomas Dublin, "Women, Work, and the Family: Female Operatives in the Lowell Mills, 1830–1860," *Feminist Studies*, vol. 3, nos. 1–2 (Autumn 1975).

25 Nancy Zaroulis, "Daughters of Freemen: The Female Operatives and the Beginning of the Labor Movement," in *Cotton Was King: History of Lowell, Massachusetts*, ed. Arthur L. Eno Jr. (Lowell, Mass.: Lowell Historical Society, 1976), p. 111.

26 Factory owner Zachary Allen quoted in Michael Folsom and Steven Lubar, *Philosophy of Manufactures*, p. xxii.

27 Alexander Hamilton, *Report on the Subject of Manufactures* (Philadelphia: William Brown, Printer, 1827; originally published 1797), p. 21.

28 Ann Sweet Appleton to Sarah Appleton, Jan. 8, 1847; quoted in Eisler, *Lowell Offering*, p. 19.

29 Harriet H. Robinson, *Loom and Spindle*, pp. 38 and 45.

30 Tom Juravich, William F. Hartford, and James R. Green, *Commonwealth of Toil: Chapters in the History of Massachusetts Workers and Their Unions* (Amherst: University of Massachusetts Press, 1996), p. 8.

31 Anthony Trollope, *North America*, vol. 1 (New York: Augustus M. Kelley, 1970; originally published 1862), p. 309. The author conducted more than just a cursory tour of Lowell, closely examining the boardinghouses, inquiring into the mills' output, and interviewing the factory owners. Astonished by the robust health and spirit of the young mill hands, he concluded the town functioned more as a "philanthropical manufacturing college" than a business enterprise, and in its superiority to anything comparable in England he declared it "the realization of a commercial Utopia." He cautioned, however, that changes in the availability of Southern cotton and a transition from water to steam power might soon render conditions at Lowell less satisfactory. See Trollope, *North America*, vol. 1, pp. 304–14.

32 *Massachusetts Spy*, March 8, 1820; quoted in Caroline F. Ware, *The Early New England Cotton Manufacture: A Study in Industrial Beginnings* (Boston: Houghton Mifflin, 1931), p. 203.

33 " 'She has worked in a factory' is sufficient to damn to infamy the most worthy and virtuous girl"—Orestes Brownson quoted in Zaroulis, "Daughters of Freemen," p. 110.

34 Larcom, "Among the Mill Girls: A Reminiscence." Larcom, who was a favorite of the poet John Greenleaf Whittier, went on to a distinguished career as a poet and essayist. Her 1889 memoir, "A New England Girlhood," became a classic account of childhood in the nineteenth century. A mountain in New Hampshire was named in her honor.

35 Edward Everett, "Fourth of July at Lowell (1830)," in *The Philosophy of Manufactures: Early Debates over Industrialization in the United States*, by Michael Folsom and Steven Lubar (Cambridge, Mass.: MIT Press, 1982), pp. 281–94. The factory experience, it was thought, also made Lowell girls superior wives. Everett, known as a brilliant orator and the first American to obtain a Ph.D., went on to be a U.S. senator, a secretary of state, and the governor of Massachusetts. Called to the consecration of a military cemetery after the Battle of Gettysburg in July 1863, he is remembered for having given the two-hour speech that immediately preceded Lincoln's eloquent three-minute Gettysburg Address, which Everett later acknowledged had been superior to his own.

36 Josephson, *Golden Threads*, p. 181.

37 Louis Taylor Merrill, "Mill Town on the Merrimack," in *New England Quarterly*, vol. 19, no. 1 (March 1946).

38 Josephson, *Golden Threads*, pp. 179–83.

39 The *Offering* was not the sole literary magazine to emerge from the New England mills; Chicopee had *The Olive Leaf and Factory Girls' Repository*; Newmarket had *The Factory Girl*; and Exeter its *Factory Girls' Garland*, but the *Offering* was the only one fully written and edited by mill workers in an era when few women were active in publishing or prominent in literary affairs. (Perhaps the most famous woman editor in America at the time was Lydia Maria Child at the *Anti-Slavery Standard*.) Some observers assumed the *Offering*—in its demonstration that mill girls who toiled twelve and fourteen hours a day could enjoy an active life of the mind—was a promotional tool sponsored by the mill owners, but only once, in buying a large number of unsold copies, did the corporation financially prop up the magazine. The mill owners understood that the journal's appeal lay in readers' certainty that young women workers were its prime movers.

40 Harriet H. Robinson, *Loom and Spindle*, p. 64.

41 Harriet Farley to Sarah Bagley, *Lowell Advertiser*, July 15, 1845, in Philip S. Foner, *The Factory Girls: A Collection of Writings on Life and Struggle in the New England Factories of the 1840s* (Urbana: University of Illinois Press, 1977), pp. 63–64.

42 Juravich, Hartford, and Green, *Commonwealth of Toil*, p. 20.

43 Eisler, *Lowell Offering*, vol. 1, pp. 112–13.

44 Josephine L. Baker, "A Second Peep at Factory Life," in *The Lowell Offering: Writings by New England Mill Women, 1840–1845*, ed. Benita Eisler (New York: W. W. Norton & Co., 1998; originally published 1977), vol. 5, 1845, pp. 77–82.

45 Yafa, *Cotton: The Biography of a Revolutionary Fiber*, pp. 95–96.

46 Alan MacDonald, "Lowell: A Commercial Utopia," *New England Quarterly*, vol. 10, no. 1 (March 1937).

47 Rosalyn Baxandall and Linda Gordon, eds., *America's Working Women, 1600 to the Present* (New York: W. W. Norton & Co., 1976), p. 70.

48 Pervis Sibley Andrews diary, Nov. 2, 1851, quoted in Laurel Ulrich, *The Age of Homespun: Objects and Stories in the Creation of an American Myth* (New York: Alfred A. Knopf, 2001), pp. 395–96.

49 Lise Vogel, "Hearts to Feel and Tongues to Speak: New England Mill Women in the Early Nineteenth Century," in *Class, Sex, and the Woman Worker*, ed. M. Cantor (Westport, Conn.: Greenwood Press, 1977), pp. 72–73; see also Ware, *Early New England Cotton Manufacture*, pp. 266–67.

50 There had been two earlier female strikes in New England. The first was in Pawtucket, Rhode Island, in 1824, when Samuel Slater threatened to reduce wages and extend work hours. Women mill hands walked out, gaining the sympathy of their male counterparts, and also the town itself, since most of the workers were locals. At Dover, New Hampshire, in 1828, about four hundred women textile workers, angry about new company restrictions on their personal time, left work and paraded around the town. They also reportedly fired off gunpowder outside the mill. The owner retaliated by advertising in a local newspaper for "better behaved women," while a newspaper from Philadelphia that learned of the event mocked the determination of the fairer "Yankee sex" and wondered if the governor of Massachusetts might be required to "call out the militia to prevent a gynecocracy." See Baxandall and Gordon, *America's Working Women*, pp. 68–69.

51 *Lowell Journal* reprinted in *Boston Transcript*, Feb. 14, 1834.

52 Cited in Thomas Dublin, *Women at Work: The Transformation of Work and Community in Lowell, Massachusetts, 1826–1860* (New York: Columbia University Press, 1979), pp. 96–97.

53 *Boston Transcript*, Feb. 17, 1834; see also Dublin, *Women at Work*, p. 91.

54 Juravich, Hartford, and Green, *Commonwealth of Toil*, p. 9.

55 See Ulrich, *Age of Homespun*, p. 392.

56 Lawrence Manufacturing Co. Records, Correspondence, vol. MAB-1, March 4 and March 9, 1834, at Baker Library, Harvard Business School, quoted in Thomas Dublin, "Women, Work, and Protest in the Early Lowell Mills: 'The Oppressing Hand of Avarice Would Enslave Us,'" in *Class, Sex, and the Woman Worker*, ed. M. Cantor (Westport, Conn.: Greenwood Press, 1977), p. 52.

57 *The Mechanic*, Nov. 30, 1844; italics in original.

58 *Awl*, Dec. 21, 1844.

59 Josephson, *Golden Threads*, p. 238.

60 *Boston Transcript*, Oct. 6, 1836.

61 Joseph H. Allen, *Our Liberal Movement in Theology* (Boston: Roberts Brothers, 1882), p. 71; Philip F. Gura, *American Transcendentalism: A History* (New York: Hill and Wang, 2007), p. 18.

62 Charles M. Ellis, *An Essay on Transcendental Boston* (Boston: Crocker and Ruggles, 1842), p. 11; see Gura, *American Transcendentalism*, p. 11.

63 *Voice of Industry*, June 12, 1845.

64 Eric Foner, *Free Soil, Free Labor, Free Men: The Ideology of the Republican Party Before the Civil War* (New York: Oxford University Press, 1970), p. 21.

65 Larcom, "Among Lowell Mill Girls: A Reminiscence."

66 Yafa, *Cotton: The Biography of a Revolutionary Fiber*, p. 122.

67   *Liberator*, Jan. 1, 1831.

68   Ibid., Jan. 29, 1831.

69   Ibid.

70   *Liberator*, Feb. 5, 1831.

71   Fitzhugh's books are *Sociology in the South* (1854) and *Cannibals All!* (1857).

72   Undated article from *Boston Bee* reprinted in *Awl*, Sept. 4, 1844.

73   Juravich, Hartford, and Green, *Commonwealth of Toil*, p. 23.

74   Margaret Crawford, *Building the Workingman's Paradise: The Design of American Company Towns* (New York: Verso, 1995), p. 27.

75   *Voice of Industry*, Sept. 18, 1845.

76   Gura, *American Transcendentalism*, p. 161.

77   Brisbane, in presenting Fourier's idea in America, emphasized his economic proposals while conveniently leaving out some of his teacher's flakier notions, such as the possibility that the moon and the stars would be so gratified by the harmony of man's reordered civilization that they would propagate in the heavens. Ralph Waldo Emerson dismissed such ideas but admired Fourier as someone who "carried a whole French Revolution in his head" and had created a set of theories that linked man's individual nature and spiritual need to economics and the survival in the real world. As Emerson had intuited, Fourier's notions of improved social beings uniting their individual passions with work in a collective environment struck less of a chord with Americans than the more practical aspects of economic cooperation. Emerson is quoted in Gura, *American Transcendentalism*, p. 169.

78   Another correspondent appearing in the *Tribune* at Greeley's invitation was Karl Marx.

79   1911 *Encyclopedia Britannica* entry for Brook Farm, see http://en.wikisource.org/wiki/1911_EncyclopA/dia_Britannica_Brook_Farm.

80   Eric Foner, *Free Soil, Free Labor, Free Men*, p. 21. The Lowell women also responded to the need for more comfortable women's clothing being promoted by newspaper editor Amelia Jenks Bloomer. One Fourth of July saw a contingent of Lowell women parade to the town common in their "Bloomers," loose trousers topped by a skirt or vest. "For myself, I confess to a liking for bloomers," labor leader Eugene V. Debs later remarked. "They seem cool and comfortable and there is something about the air of the girl who wears them that reminds me of the Declaration of Independence."

81   Sean Wilentz, *Chants Democratic: New York City and the Rise of the American Working Class, 1788–1850* (New York: Oxford University Press, 1984), p. 336.

82   Foster Rhea Dulles, *Labor in America: A History* (New York: Thomas Y. Crowell Co., 1966), p. 81.

83   Eric Foner, *Forever Free: The Story of Emancipation and Reconstruction* (New York: Alfred A. Knopf, 2005), pp. 26–27.

84   Wilentz, *Chants Democratic*, p. 338.

85   In May 1862, the South having seceded from the Union, Congress passed and President Lincoln signed the Homestead Act, which offered 50- to 160-acre plots of public western land to any adult citizen who had not taken up arms against the Union, and who would cultivate the land for five years.

86   Henry A. Miles, *Lowell, As It Was, and As It Is* (New York: Arno Reprint, 1972; originally published 1845), p. 2.

87   *Factory Girl*, Exeter, New Hampshire, March 1, 1843, quoted in Vogel, "Hearts to Feel and Tongues to Speak," pp. 76–77.

88   Eric Foner, *The Story of American Freedom* (New York: W. W. Norton & Co., 1998), p. 62.

89   The pattern repeated itself in other cities, most notably New York, where in 1829 six thousand skilled workers launched the New York City Working Man's Party. The mechanics' associations that sprang up in this era were characterized by workers' desire to win reforms related to their employ as well as broader social advances, such as an

end to debtors being sent to jail, stricter regulation of convict labor and financial institutions, and free public schools.

90   Third Grand Rally of the Workingmen of Charleston, Mass., Held Oct. 23, 1840, Kress Library, Harvard Business School (emphasis supplied), quoted in Christopher L. Tomlins, *Law, Labor, and Ideology in the Early American Republic* (New York: Cambridge University Press, 1993), pp. 308–9.

91   "Preamble and Constitution of the Lowell Female Labor Reform Association," *Voice of Industry*, Feb. 27, 1846.

92   *Voice of Industry*, June 5, 1845.

93   Ibid., Jan. 2, 1846, quoted in Eisler, *Lowell Offering*, pp. 39–40.

94   Josephson, *Golden Threads*, p. 248.

95   *Voice of Industry*, Jan. 2, 1846.

96   Ibid., July 10, 1845.

97   *Lowell Advertiser*, July 26, 1845, in Philip S. Foner, *Factory Girls*, p. 67.

98   *Voice of Industry*, July 17, 1845.

99   Eisler, *Lowell Offering*, p. 41.

100   Robin K. Berson, *Marching to a Different Drummer: Unrecognized Heroes of American History* (Westport, Conn.: Greenwood Press, 1994), p. 212.

101   Juravich, Hartford, and Green, *Commonwealth of Toil*, p. 22.

102   Berson, *Marching to a Different Drummer*, p. 215.

103   Juravich, Hartford, and Green, *Commonwealth of Toil*, p. 14.

104   Seth Luther, "Address Delivered Before the Mechanics and Workingmen of Brooklyn, (1836)," cited in Tomlins, *Law, Labor, and Ideology*, p. 198.

105   Frederick Robinson quoted in Tomlins, *Law, Labor, and Ideology*, p. 195.

106   Merle E. Curti, "Robert Rantoul, Jr., the Reformer in Politics," *New England Quarterly*, vol. 5 (1932).

107   Leonard W. Levy, *The Law of the Commonwealth and Chief Justice Shaw* (Cambridge, Mass.: Harvard University Press, 1957), p. 193; also see Robert Rantoul Jr., "Oration at Scituate, Massachusetts, 4 July, 1836," quoted in Levy, *Law of the Commonwealth*, p. 197.

108   Juravich, Hartford, and Green, *Commonwealth of Toil*, pp. 12–13.

109   Judge Thacher quoted in Levy, *Law of the Commonwealth*, p. 187.

110   Elias Lieberman, *Unions Before the Bar* (New York: Harper & Brothers, 1950), pp. 21–22.

111   Levy, *Law of the Commonwealth*, pp. 190–91.

112   *Commonwealth v. Hunt* (1842) quoted in Levy, *Law of the Commonwealth*, p. 188.

113   Lieberman, *Unions Before the Bar*, p. 26.

114   Levy, *Law of the Commonwealth*, p. 183; Tomlins, *Law, Labor, and Ideology*, p. 209.

115   *Voice of Industry*, Oct. 10, 1845.

116   Ibid., Jan. 2, 1846.

117   Dublin, *Women at Work*, p. 119.

118   Dulles, *Labor in America*, p. 85.

119   *Voice of Industry*, June 11 and 18, 1847.

120   Miles, *Lowell, As It Was, and As It Is*, pp. 124–25.

121   Massachusetts House Document No. 50, March 1845, in *A Documentary History of American Industrial Society*, ed. John R. Commons, vol. 8 (New York: Russell & Russell, 1958), pp. 133–51.

122   *Operative*, Dec. 28, 1844, in Dublin, *Women at Work*, pp. 115–16.

123   *Voice of Industry*, March 13, 1846.

124   Juravich, Hartford, and Green, *Commonwealth of Toil*, p. 26; *Voice of Industry*, June 12, 1845. Schouler several years later regained his seat in the legislature.

125   Dulles, *Labor in America*, p. 86.

126   *Voice of Industry*, March 13, 1846.

127   Elizabeth Cady Stanton, *Eighty Years and More: Reminiscences, 1815–1897* (New York: Schocken Books, 1971; originally published 1898), p. 149.

128 Only one signer of the resolution at Seneca Falls, factory worker Charlotte Wood-
      ward, lived long enough to cast a vote after women's suffrage was granted seventy-two
      years later with the ratification of the Nineteenth Amendment in 1920. See Kath-
      ryn Cullen-DuPont, "Seneca Falls Convention," *Encyclopedia of Women's History in
      America*, 2nd ed. (New York: Facts on File, 2000), American Women's History Online,
      Facts on File, Inc., http://www.foweb.com/activelink2.asp?.

129 Baxandall and Gordon, *America's Working Women*, pp. 78–79.

130 Seth Luther, a counterpart to Bagley as perhaps New England's best-known labor
      orator and provocateur, had a far less happy end. He was drawn in 1842 to join and
      eventually help lead a suffrage crusade in his native Rhode Island, where a government
      charter dating from 1663 skewed voting in favor of rural owners of property and effec-
      tively disenfranchised the growing number of landless factory employees. A nascent
      People's Party, formed to protest the restrictions, elected its own governor, Thomas
      Dorr, and proceeded even after its activities were declared illegal to claim election by
      votes the authorities technically ignored. Arrested and charged with treason, Luther
      made an eloquent defense in court, but it was not enough to escape a prison sentence.
      A most uncooperative convict, incarceration left him broken in body and mind, and
      after a brief reimmersion in labor politics, he spent the rest of his life in various New
      England mental asylums. See Berson, *Marching to a Different Drummer*, pp. 216–17;
      see also Louis Hartz, "Seth Luther: The Story of a Working-Class Rebel," *New England
      Quarterly*, vol. 13, no. 3 (Sept. 1940); Marvin E. Gettleman, *The Dorr Rebellion: A Study
      in American Radicalism, 1833–1849* (New York: Random House, 1973); and the UMass
      Library website subject "Dorr Rebellion," http://library.uml.edu.

131 Josephson, *Golden Threads*, p. 181.

132 Dublin, "Women, Work, and Protest in the Early Lowell Mills," p. 51; see also Eisler,
      Lowell Offering, p. 29.

133 Ray Ginger, "Labor in a Massachusetts Cotton Mill, 1853–1860," *Business History Review*,
      vol. 28, no. 1 (March 1954).

CHAPTER TWO: HELL WITH THE LID OFF

1   Foster Rhea Dulles, *Labor in America: A History* (New York: Thomas Y. Crowell Co.,
      1966), p. 90.

2   Alan Dawley, *Class and Community: The Industrial Revolution in Lynn* (Cambridge,
      Mass.: Harvard University Press, 1976), p. 77.

3   Paul Faler, "Cultural Aspects of the Industrial Revolution: Lynn, Massachusetts,
      Shoemakers and Industrial Morality, 1826–1860," *Labor History*, vol. 15 (Summer 1974).
      Faler uses the term "industrial morality" to describe "a tightening up of the moral code
      through either the abolition or drastic alteration of those customs, traditions, and
      practices that interfered with productive labor."

4   Faler, "Cultural Aspects of the Industrial Revolution."

5   Dawley, *Class and Community*, p. 84.

6   *Bay State*, April 12, 1860.

7   *Boston Transcript*, Feb. 25, 1860.

8   *New York Times*, Feb. 25, 1860.

9   *Bay State*, March 1, 1860.

10   Ibid., March 8, 1860.

11   Tom Juravich, William F. Hartford, and James R. Green, *Commonwealth of Toil: Chap-
      ters in the History of Massachusetts Workers and Their Unions* (Amherst: University of
      Massachusetts Press, 1996), p. 37.

12   *Bay State*, March 22, 1860.

13   Ibid., March 29, 1860.

14 Draper, thirty years old, was, according to the *New York Times*, "a man of some little education, (who) has at times taught writing, bookkeeping, and, we believe, French." Although not a shoemaker himself, he was the editor of a labor paper, the *New England Mechanic*. See *New York Times*, Feb. 25, 1860. The *Lynn Daily Advertiser* reported that Draper had "an indisposition to hard labor" and was a "dangerous influence" on the Lynn shoemakers. Reprinted in *Boston Transcript*, Feb. 24, 1860.

15 *New York Times*, Feb. 29, 1860.

16 Molly Stark was the mother of eleven children with John Stark. Molly was highly regarded for her service as a nurse during the war and for opening her house as a hospital for her husband's troops at the time of a smallpox epidemic; see *Boston Herald*, Feb. 24, 1860.

17 *New York Times*, Feb. 29, 1860.

18 *Boston Herald*, Feb. 28, 1860; see also *New York Times*, Feb. 29, 1860, and *Boston Journal*, Feb. 28, 1860.

19 *New York Times*, March 6, 1860.

20 Ibid.

21 *New York Times*, March 9, 1860.

22 Dawley, *Class and Community*, p. 80.

23 *Lynn Reporter*, March 31, 1860.

24 *Bay State*, March 29, 1860.

25 Lincoln quoted in Juravich, Hartford, and Green, *Commonwealth of Toil*, p. 40.

26 Dawley, *Class and Community*, p. 238.

27 Richard O. Boyer and Herbert M. Morais, *Labor's Untold Story* (New York: United Electrical, Radio & Machine Workers of America, 1972; originally published 1955), p. 25.

28 *Fincher's Trades' Review*, Aug. 29, 1863.

29 Ralph Korngold, *Two Friends of Man: The Story of William Lloyd Garrison and Wendell Phillips* (Boston: Little, Brown and Co., 1950), p. 369. Phillips ran for governor of Massachusetts in 1871 on the Labor-Reform ticket, demanding that government aid laboring men's cooperatives much as the state had earlier helped corporations and railroads, while also advocating a Progressive taxation policy.

30 Korngold, *Two Friends of Man*, p. 365.

31 Boyer and Morais, *Labor's Untold Story*, pp. 31–32.

32 Quoted in Eric Foner, *Free Soil, Free Labor, Free Men: The Ideology of the Republican Party Before the Civil War* (New York: Oxford University Press, 1970), p. 20.

33 *New York Tribune*, Jan. 6, 1855, cited in Eric Foner, *Free Soil, Free Labor, Free Men*, p. 20.

34 James C. Sylvis, *The Life, Speeches, Labors and Essays of William H. Sylvis* (Philadelphia: Claxton, Remsen, and Haffelfinger, 1872), pp. 78–79.

35 Boyer and Morais, *Labor's Untold Story*, p. 23.

36 William Sylvis, "Address to the Iron Molders International Union Convention," Buffalo, New York, 1864, quoted in Charlotte Todes, *William H. Sylvis and the National Labor Union* (New York: International Publishers, 1942), pp. 40–41.

37 *Fincher's Trades' Review*, Oct. 8 and 31, 1863.

38 Sylvis, *Life, Speeches, Labors and Essays of William H. Sylvis*, p. 15.

39 Boyer and Morais, *Labor's Untold Story*, p. 26.

40 Jonathan P. Grossman, *William Sylvis: Pioneer of American Labor* (New York: Octagon Books, 1972), p. 108.

41 Ibid., p. 240.

42 Grant's proclamation, dated May 19, 1869, appears in *The Papers of Ulysses S. Grant*, ed. John Y. Simon, vol. 19 (Carbondale: Southern Illinois University Press, 1995), p. 189; Letter from Sylvis to Grant of May 27, 1869, is in *Papers of Ulysses S. Grant*, pp. 190–91.

43 E. L. Godkin, "Cooperation," *North American Review*, Jan. 1868.

44 Ibid.

45 *Fincher's Trades' Review*, March 25, 1865.

46 *New York Times*, Aug. 21, 1869, in Todes, *William H. Sylvis and the National Labor Union*, p. 107.

47 Godkin, "Cooperation."

48 Ibid.

49 Boyer and Morais, *Labor's Untold Story*, p. 33.

50 Grossman, *William Sylvis: Pioneer of American Labor*, p. 227.

51 *New York Herald*, Sept. 22, 1868.

52 *New York Times*, Sept. 23, 1868.

53 *New York World*, Sept. 23, 1868, in Israel Kugler, "The Trade Union Career of Susan B. Anthony," *Labor History*, vol. 2, no. 1 (Winter 1961).

54 *Proceedings of the National Labor Union, Second Annual Session, Philadelphia, 1868*, Philadelphia, p. 23, in Kugler, "Trade Union Career of Susan B. Anthony."

55 *Revolution*, Oct. 8, 1868, in Kugler, "Trade Union Career of Susan B. Anthony."

56 *New York World*, Aug. 17, 1869.

57 Todes, *William H. Sylvis and the National Labor Union*, p. 74.

58 Rayford Logan, *The Betrayal of the Negro from Rutherford B. Hayes to Woodrow Wilson* (New York: Da Capo Press, 1997; originally published 1954), p. 142.

59 Indeed, race riots sparked by employment issues were almost as old as the country. In 1829 numerous blacks were killed in Cincinnati in a fracas over jobs; whites then attacked the black community itself, prompting two thousand black residents to decamp for Canada. In Philadelphia there were many such riots in the generation before the Civil War; one in 1834 lasted three days, while another outbreak in 1842 was halted only when the militia showed up bearing artillery. See W. E. B. Du Bois, *Black Reconstruction in America, 1860–1880* (New York: Free Press, 1998; originally published 1935), p. 18.

60 Sylvis, *Life, Speeches, Labors and Essays of William H. Sylvis*, p. 233; Todes, *William H. Sylvis and the National Labor Union*, p. 76.

61 Du Bois, *Black Reconstruction in America*, pp. 354–55.

62 Ibid., p. 355.

63 Ibid., pp. 357–58.

64 Quoted in ibid., p. 364.

65 Grossman, *William Sylvis: Pioneer of American Labor*, pp. 262–63.

66 Edward Pinkowski, *John Siney: The Miners' Martyr* (Philadelphia: Sunshine Press, 1963), p. 51.

67 "Don't Go Down in the Mines, Dad," from "A Discography of American Coal Miners Songs," *Labor History*, vol. 2, no. 1 (Winter 1961).

68 Louis Adamic, *Dynamite!: A Century of Class Violence in America* (New York: Viking Books, 1934), p. 12.

69 Kevin Kenny, *Making Sense of the Molly Maguires* (New York: Oxford University Press, 1998), p. 139.

70 Ibid., p. 146.

71 Pinkowski, *John Siney: The Miners' Martyr*, pp. 200–202.

72 Kenny, *Making Sense of the Molly Maguires*, pp. 145–47.

73 Ibid., p. 151.

74 *Miners Journal*, March 12, 1864, in Marvin Schlegel, *Ruler of the Reading: The Life of Franklin B. Gowen, 1836–1889* (Harrisburg, Pa.: Archives Publishing, 1947), p. 89.

75 In 1866 Pinkerton wrote and published *The History and Evidence of the Passage of Abraham Lincoln from Harrisburg, Pa., to Washington, DC on the 22nd and 23rd of February 1861*, the first of fifteen gripping detective yarns published under his name.

76 For background on Allan Pinkerton see Frank Morn, *The Eye That Never Sleeps: A History of the Pinkerton National Detective Agency* (Bloomington: Indiana University Press, 1982), pp. 17–52.

77 Allan Pinkerton, *Strikers, Communists, Tramps, and Detectives* (New York: G. W. Dillingham Publishing, 1906), p. 16.

78 *Miners Journal*, Jan. 13, 1866, in Schlegel, *Ruler of the Reading*, p. 91.

79 Allan Pinkerton, *The Molly Maguires and the Detectives* (New York: G. W. Carleton Publishing, 1877), pp. 14–15.

80 Alan Hynd, "With the Pinkertons, Through the Labyrinth of Death," *True Detective Mysteries Magazine*, Nov. 1940.

81 *Shenandoah Herald*, Sept. 28, 1875, in Schlegel, *Ruler of the Reading*, pp. 111–12.

82 Schlegel, *Ruler of the Reading*, p. 124.

83 Morn, *Eye That Never Sleeps*, p. 95.

84 Robert V. Bruce, *1877: Year of Violence* (Indianapolis, Ind.: Bobbs-Merrill Co., 1959), p. 39.

85 Quoted in Schlegel, *Ruler of the Reading*, pp. 130–31.

86 Boyer and Morais, *Labor's Untold Story*, p. 55.

87 Ibid., p. 56.

88 *New York Times*, June 21, 1877.

89 Today much local pride in Schuylkill County surrounds what could be considered an antidote to the Mollie legacy, the Pottsville Maroons, an independent professional football team that won a disputed NFL championship in 1925. The Maroons booked an unauthorized exhibition game in Philadelphia against an all-star team of former Notre Dame players. The game was ordered canceled by NFL president Joe Carr, and when the Pottsville team played it anyway their franchise was suspended, sacrificing the title.

90 Quoted in David T. Burbank, *Reign of Rabble: The St. Louis General Strike of 1877* (New York: Augustus M. Kelley, 1966), pp. 4–5.

91 *New York Times*, Jan. 14, 1874.

92 Ibid., July 30, 1877.

93 Quoted in David O. Stowell, *Streets, Railroads, and the Great Strike of 1877* (Chicago: University of Chicago Press, 1999), p. 2.

94 Bruce, *1877: Year of Violence*, p. 44.

95 *New York Times*, March 29, 1874.

96 Governor J. F. Hartranft to W. J. Falkenburg, March 29, 1874, in *New York Times*, March 30, 1874.

97 See Herbert G. Gutman, *Work, Culture & Society in Industrializing America* (New York: Alfred A. Knopf, 1976), pp. 301–17.

98 Quoted in David O. Stowell, *Streets, Railroads, and the Great Strike of 1877*, p. 5.

99 *New York Times*, Dec. 31, 1876, and Jan. 1, 1877.

100 *Munn v. Illinois*, 94 U.S. 113 (1877).

101 Bruce, *1877: Year of Violence*, pp. 36–41.

102 *Irish World*, June 30, 1877, in Bruce, *1877: Year of Violence*, p. 67.

103 *Wheeling Register*, July 18, 1877, in Bruce, *1877: Year of Violence*, p. 85.

104 The compromise that "solved" the disputed election of 1876 involved the Republican promise to place a Southerner in the cabinet (David Key of Tennessee), the withdrawal of the United States Army from the Reconstruction South, and "internal improvements of a national character," in effect a much-lobbied-for congressional subsidy for Tom Scott's planned transcontinental Texas & Pacific Railroad.

105 President Lincoln faced the issue during the war when printers went on strike and General William Rosecrans dispatched troopers to confront them. The printers sent word to Lincoln, reminding him of his praise for the Lynn shoemakers—"Thank God, we have a system where there can be a strike." Lincoln then ordered Rosecrans to desist, saying, "Servants of the federal government should not interfere with the legitimate demands of labor." Due to the exigencies of war, however, soldiers were deployed as replacement workers or guarded scabs when strikes impacted the war effort, and in some instances, strike leaders had been detained. See Todes, *William H. Sylvis and the National Labor Union*, p. 44.

106 Bruce, *1877: Year of Violence*, p. 91. Hayes may have also been moved to assist because Tom Scott, president of the Pennsylvania Railroad, had been instrumental in clear-

ing the way for Hayes's assumption of the presidency. Hayes had thus far not followed through with the promised effort to aid Scott's Texas and Pacific Railroad.

107 Jeremy Brecher, *Strike!* (Boston: South End Press, 1984; originally published 1972), p. 7.
108 Bruce, *1877: Year of Violence*, pp. 118–19.
109 Ibid., p. 120.
110 Ibid., pp. 135–36, in Brecher, *Strike!* p. 11. President Andrew Jackson in 1834 sent soldiers to deal with a turnout at a construction site of the Chesapeake and Ohio Canal.
111 *Harper's Weekly*, Aug. 18, 1877.
112 Bruce, *1877: Year of Violence*, p. 125.
113 *New York Times*, July 22, 1877.
114 Boyer and Morais, *Labor's Untold Story*, p. 62.
115 *Report of the Committee Appointed to Investigate the Railroad Riots in July 1877*, pp. 907–10.
116 James Green, *Death in the Haymarket: A Story of Chicago, the First Labor Movement, and the Bombing That Divided Gilded Age America* (New York: Pantheon Books, 2006), p. 76; Alan Calmer, *Labor Agitator: The Biography of Albert R. Parsons* (New York: International Publishers, 1937), p. 29.
117 *Harper's Weekly*, Aug. 18, 1877.
118 Ray Ginger, *Altgeld's America: The Lincoln Ideal Versus Changing Realities* (New York: Funk & Wagnalls, 1958), p. 39; Lucy Parsons, *The Life of Albert Parsons* (Chicago: Lucy Parsons Publisher, 1903), p. xxvi.
119 Burbank, *Reign of Rabble*, p. 11.
120 Ibid., p. 5.
121 Ibid., p. 53; Brecher, *Strike!* p. 19.
122 *Chicago Times*, July 25, 1877, in Bruce, *1877: Year of Violence*, p. 243.
123 Burbank, *Reign of Rabble*, p. 12.
124 Bruce, *1877: Year of Violence*, pp. 225–26.
125 *Harper's Weekly*, Aug. 18, 1877.
126 Dave Rodeiger and Franklin Rosemont, eds., *Haymarket Scrapbook* (Chicago: Charles H. Kerr Publishing Co., 1986), p. 81.
127 Bruce, *1877: Year of Violence*, p. 314.
128 *Harper's Weekly*, Aug. 18, 1877.
129 Bruce, *1877: Year of Violence*, p. 314.
130 Ibid.
131 Ibid., p. 315.

CHAPTER THREE: WE MEAN TO HAVE EIGHT HOURS

1   Harry J. Carman, ed., *The Path I Trod: The Autobiography of Terence V. Powderly* (New York: Columbia University Press, 1940), p. 35.
2   Some vocations, such as lawyer, doctor, banker, stockbroker, or anyone involved in selling or manufacturing liquor, were excluded from membership in the Knights.
3   Foster Rhea Dulles, *Labor in America: A History* (New York: Thomas Y. Crowell Co., 1966), p. 135.
4   Ibid.
5   Ibid., p. 142.
6   Ibid., p. 144.
7   Gompers. "What Does Labor Want?" AFL pamphlet (1893), reprinted in Pamphlets in American History series, Microfilming Corp. of America, Sanford, N.C., 1979.
8   Dave Rodeiger and Franklin Rosemont, eds., *Haymarket Scrapbook* (Chicago: Charles H. Kerr Publishing Co., 1986), p. 13.
9   Dulles, *Labor in America*, p. 146.
10 Lucy Parsons, *The Life of Albert Parsons* (Chicago: Lucy Parsons Publisher, 1903), p. 24.

11   Ibid., p. 15.

12   Ibid., p. 16.

13   Ibid., pp. 17–19.

14   *Alarm*, Dec. 21, 1887.

15   Ibid., Dec. 13, 1884.

16   Alan Calmer, *Labor Agitator: The Biography of Albert R. Parsons* (New York: International Publishers, 1937), pp. 57–59.

17   Louis Adamic, *Dynamite!: A Century of Class Violence in America* (New York: Viking Books, 1934), pp. 45–46.

18   Calmer, *Labor Agitator: The Biography of Albert R. Parsons*, pp. 60–61.

19   *Alarm*, Feb. 6, 1886.

20   Frederic Trautmann, *The Voice of Terror: A Biography of Johann Most* (Westport, Conn.: Greenwood Press, 1980), pp. 5–7.

21   Paul Avrich, *The Haymarket Tragedy* (Princeton, N.J.: Princeton University Press, 1984), p. 164.

22   *Alarm*, Jan. 13, 1885.

23   Richard Drinnon, ed., *Emma Goldman: Anarchism and Other Essays* (New York: Dover Books, 1969; originally published 1917), p. 50.

24   Miriam Brody, "Introduction," in *Living My Life*, by Emma Goldman (New York: Penguin Books, 2006; originally published 1931), p. xiv.

25   Ibid., p. xv.

26   Nicola Sacco and Bartolomeo Vanzetti, *The Letters of Sacco and Vanzetti*, ed. Marion Denman Frankfurter and Gardner Jackson (New York: Viking Press, 1928), p. 308.

27   Miriam Brody, "Introduction," p. xvii.

28   *Harper's Weekly*, May 15, 1886.

29   *Alarm*, Dec. 31, 1887.

30   Calmer, *Labor Agitator: The Biography of Albert R. Parsons*, p. 70.

31   Parsons linked the paper's name to the philosopher Edmund Burke, who had written, "I love clamor when there is an abuse. The alarm disturbs the slumber of the inmates, but it awakens them to the dangers that threaten." See *Alarm*, Nov. 19, 1887.

32   *Alarm*, Oct. 11, 1884.

33   Ibid., Dec. 13, 1884.

34   Ibid., May 20, 1885.

35   Ray Ginger, *Altgeld's America: The Lincoln Ideal Versus Changing Realities* (New York: Funk & Wagnalls, 1958), p. 41.

36   Avrich, *Haymarket Tragedy*, p. 173.

37   Richard O. Boyer and Herbert M. Morais, *Labor's Untold Story* (New York: United Electrical, Radio & Machine Workers of America, 1972; originally published 1955), p. 69.

38   Avrich, *Haymarket Tragedy*, p. 176.

39   *Chicago Tribune*, Nov. 23, 1875.

40   Rodeiger and Rosemont, *Haymarket Scrapbook*, p. 78.

41   *Alarm*, April 18, 1885.

42   Adamic, *Dynamite!* p. 66.

43   Claudius O. Johnson, *Carter H. Harrison I* (Chicago: University of Chicago Press, 1928), p. 120.

44   Harrison would serve five terms as Chicago's mayor. He was shot to death in his home on October 23, 1893, during the Chicago World's Fair, after admitting a frustrated office seeker named Prendergast, "a man of the Guiteau stamp . . . impelled to his deed by vague semi-political promptings." His son, Carter Harrison IV, later served multiple terms as mayor. See William Abbot, ed., *Carter H. Harrison, A Memoir* (New York: Dodd, Mead & Co., 1895).

45   *Alarm*, July 11, 1885.

46   George Schilling, in Parsons, *Life of Albert Parsons*, p. xxxii.

47   Rodeiger and Rosemont, *Haymarket Scrapbook*, p. 138.

48   *Alarm*, Sept. 5, 1885.

49   *New York Times*, Sept. 4–6, 1882; *New York Tribune*, Sept. 5, 1882. Previously, Washington's Birthday (Feb. 22) and July Fourth had served as occasions for displays of labor solidarity; March 18 had come to be honored as the anniversary of the Paris Commune, and in Illinois May 1, a day of ritualistic observance pagan in origin, was also occasionally used as a day of protest. In 1889, three years after the May 1 strike for the eight-hour day, May Day was declared a Socialist labor holiday by the Second International. By that same year the popularity of Labor Day, the first Monday of September, had also spread widely, as it was supported by both the Knights of Labor and the emerging labor federation that would become the AFL. Celebrated by 1890 in four hundred U.S. cities, Labor Day was established as a legal holiday by Congress in 1894.

50   *Alarm*, Feb. 20, 1886.

51   Calmer, *Labor Agitator: The Biography of Albert R. Parsons*, pp. 46–47.

52   Ibid., pp. 46–47; Parsons, *Life of Albert Parsons*, p. 25.

53   *Alarm*, April 24, 1886.

54   *Chicago Mail*, May 1, 1886, in *Alarm*, Dec. 31, 1887.

55   Boyer and Morais, *Labor's Untold Story*, p. 94.

56   Rodeiger and Rosemont, *Haymarket Scrapbook*, p. 14.

57   Captain William Ward report to Frederick Ebersold, General Supervisor of Police, May 30, 1886; Chicago Police Department Reports, Haymarket Affair Digital Collection (http://www.chicagohs.org/hadc/manuscripts/m03/MO3.htm).

58   Inspector John Bonfield report to Frederick Ebersold, General Supervisor of Police, May 30, 1886; Chicago Police Department Reports, Haymarket Affair Digital Collection (http://www.chicagohs.org/hadc/manuscripts/m03/MO3.htm).

59   James Green, *Death in the Haymarket: A Story of Chicago, the First Labor Movement, and the Bombing That Divided Gilded Age America* (New York: Pantheon Books, 2006), p. 208.

60   *New York Times*, May 5, 1886.

61   *Harper's Weekly*, May 15, 1886.

62   Melville E. Stone, *Fifty Years a Journalist* (Garden City, N.Y.: Doubleday, 1921), pp. 172–73.

63   *New York Times*, May 8, 1886.

64   Henry David, *The History of the Haymarket Affair* (New York: Farrar & Rinehart, 1936), p. 183.

65   *Alarm*, Dec. 17, 1887.

66   *New York Times*, Nov. 11, 1887.

67   Schnaubelt, who left Chicago and eventually sailed to England, wrote two letters from London insisting that he was not the bomb thrower. He died in 1901. A 1908 novel by Frank Harris, *The Bomb*, opens with a scene in which Schnaubelt confesses on his deathbed; the book was widely denounced by Schnaubelt's friends and former Chicago colleagues.

68   *New York Times*, May 6, 1886.

69   Ibid., May 5, 1886.

70   James Green, *Death in the Haymarket*, p. 213.

71   *Alarm*, Jan. 14, 1888.

72   Melville E. Stone, *Fifty Years a Journalist*, p. 173.

73   Boyer and Morais, *Labor's Untold Story*, p. 97.

74   Quoted in James Green, *Death in the Haymarket*, p. 214.

75   *Alarm*, Feb. 7, 1885, and May 30, 1885.

76   Boyer and Morais, *Labor's Untold Story*, p. 98.

77   Ray Ginger, *Altgeld's America*, p. 54.

78   Boyer and Morais, *Labor's Untold Story*, pp. 99–100.

79   Cited in David, *History of Haymarket*, p. 186.

80   Avrich, *Haymarket Tragedy*, pp. 162–63.

81   *Chicago Tribune*, Aug. 20, 1886.

82   *New York Times*, Aug. 21, 1886.

83   See "Meet the Haymarket Defendants," http://www.law.umkc.edu/faculty/projects/
     haymarketdefendants.html.

84   *Chicago Express*, Aug. 28, 1886.

85   *The Famous Speeches of the Eight Chicago Anarchists on October 7th, 8th, and 9th* (Chi-
     cago: Socialist Publishing Co., 1886), p. 10; also in James Green, *Death in the Haymar-
     ket*, p. 233.

86   James Green, *Death in the Haymarket*, pp. 234–37.

87   Boyer and Morais, *Labor's Untold Story*, pp. 101–2.

88   Ray Ginger, *Altgeld's America*, p. 58. Melville Stone claims to have been instrumental in
     convincing Schwab and Fielden to recant, and in delivering word of their intentions to
     Governor Oglesby. He also relates that, in a meeting with Parsons to discuss the matter,
     Parsons, who refused to recant, assaulted Stone and had to be restrained by a bailiff.
     See Melville E. Stone, *Fifty Years a Journalist*, pp. 175–77.

89   Adamic, *Dynamite!* p. 80.

90   Ibid.

91   Letter from Adolph Fischer to Johann Most, Nov. 5, 1887, in *Alarm*, Nov. 19, 1887.

92   *Alarm*, Nov. 19, 1887.

93   Ibid., Dec. 3, 1887.

94   Ibid., Nov. 19, 1887.

95   Ibid.

96   Dulles, *Labor in America*, p. 125.

97   *Alarm*, Dec. 3, 1887.

98   Rodeiger and Rosemont, *Haymarket Scrapbook*, p. 136.

99   Adamic, *Dynamite!* p. 84.

100 Dulles, *Labor in America*, p. 153.

101 Rodeiger and Rosemont, *Haymarket Scrapbook*, p. 12.

102 Harold C. Livesay, *Samuel Gompers and Organized Labor in America* (Prospect Heights,
     Ill.: Waveland Press, 1993; originally published 1978), p. 79.

103 Dulles, *Labor in America*, p. 159.

104 Livesay, *Samuel Gompers and Organized Labor in America*, p. 7.

105 Ibid., p. 39.

106 Dulles, *Labor in America*, p. 154.

107 Livesay, *Samuel Gompers and Organized Labor in America*, p. 70.

108 *U.S. Strike Commission Report—Chicago Strike of June–July 1894* (1895), p. 195.

109 Livesay, *Samuel Gompers and Organized Labor in America*, p. 45.

110 Ibid., p. 46.

111 Samuel Gompers, *Seventy Years of Life and Labor* (New York: E. P. Dutton & Co., 1925),
     p. 250.

112 *New York Standard*, Oct. 8, 1887.

113 Opponents of the reforms were equally devious. When the bill came up for review
     in the state legislature, they simply stole the original copy, thus delaying any possible
     action. The bill was eventually passed with the help of a young state assemblyman
     named Theodore Roosevelt, but enforcement proved difficult and the law was eventu-
     ally thrown out by the New York Court of Appeals, which was unwilling to accept the
     argument that public health concerns could trump private property rights.

114 *Alarm*, Sept. 5, 1885.

115 Livesay, *Samuel Gompers and Organized Labor in America*, p. 5.

CHAPTER FOUR: PULLMAN'S TOWN

1   Harold C. Livesay, *Samuel Gompers and Organized Labor in America* (Prospect Heights, Ill.: Waveland Press, 1993; originally published 1978), p. 119.
2   *New York Herald*, July 10, 1892; Paul Krause, *The Battle for Homestead, 1880–1892* (Pittsburgh, Pa.: University of Pittsburgh Press, 1992), p. 42.
3   *New York Times*, June 13, 1892.
4   Krause, *Battle for Homestead*, pp. 16–18.
5   Myron R. Stowell, *"Fort Frick," or the Siege of Homestead* (Pittsburgh, Pa.: Pittsburgh Printing Co., 1893), p. 52.
6   Krause, *Battle for Homestead*, pp. 21–25.
7   Ibid., p. 32.
8   Ibid., pp. 79–80.
9   Fosta Rhea Dulles, *Labor in America: A History* (New York: Thomas Y. Crowell Co., 1966), p. 171.
10   Krause, *Battle for Homestead*, pp. 39–40.
11   Leon Wolff, *Lockout: The Story of the Homestead Strike of 1892* (New York: Harper & Row, 1965), p. 164.
12   Jeremy Brecher, *Strike!* (Boston: South End Press, 1984; originally published 1972), pp. 62–63.
13   Alexander Berkman, *Prison Memoirs of an Anarchist* (Pittsburgh, Pa.: Frontier Press, 1970), pp. 6–7.
14   Emma Goldman, *Living My Life* (New York: Penguin Books, 2006; originally published 1931), p. 60.
15   Ibid., pp. 64–66.
16   Berkman, *Prison Memoirs of an Anarchist*, pp. 9–10.
17   Ibid., p. 37.
18   *New York Times*, July 24, 1892.
19   Ibid., July 25, 1892.
20   Ibid.
21   Goldman, *Living My Life*, pp. 73–74.
22   Ibid., p. 75.
23   *St. Louis Post-Dispatch* editorial is quoted in Charles R. Morris, *The Tycoons: How Andrew Carnegie, John D. Rockefeller, Jay Gould, and J. P. Morgan Invented the American Supereconomy* (New York: Henry Holt, 2005), p. 206.
24   The case was *Plessy v. Ferguson*, 163 U.S. 357 (1896).
25   Rayford Logan, *The Betrayal of the Negro from Rutherford B. Hayes to Woodrow Wilson* (New York: Da Capo Press, 1997; originally published 1954), p. 140.
26   It was reportedly feared by some employers that blacks were too neglectful to be around complicated machinery, or that its humming sound would have a lulling effect on their concentration, perhaps even putting them to sleep.
27   Gompers quoted in Herbert Hill, "The Real Practices of Organized Labor—The Age of Gompers and After," in *Employment, Race, and Poverty*, ed. Arthur M. Ross and Herbert Hill (New York: Harcourt, Brace and World, 1967), p. 367.
28   *Proceedings of the AFL, 1881–1888*, p. 14.
29   *Locomotive Firemen's Magazine*, July 1896, quoted in Hill, "The Real Practices of Organized Labor," p. 369.
30   Hill, "The Real Practices of Organized Labor," p. 370.
31   Ibid.
32   John M. Callahan to Samuel Gompers, Nov. 7, 1892, quoted in Philip S. Foner, *Organized Labor and the Black Worker, 1619–1973* (New York: Praeger, 1974), p. 68.
33   Brecher, *Strike!* pp. 64–66.
34   Hill, "The Real Practices of Organized Labor," pp. 371–72.

35   Ibid., p. 379. When Du Bois, as part of a study he was writing about black workers, wrote to the heads of several labor unions seeking information about their racial policies, Gompers scolded the scholar for being "pessimistic" and "unwilling to give credit where credit is due," before advising Du Bois, "Let me say further, that I have more important work to attend to than correct 'copy' for your paper." Hill, "The Real Practices of Organized Labor," pp. 379–80.

36   Philip S. Foner, *Organized Labor and the Black Worker*, p. 65.

37   Ibid., p. 72.

38   Logan, *Betrayal of the Negro*, p. 150.

39   Booker T. Washington, "The Negro and the Labor Unions," *Atlantic Monthly*, June 1913.

40   *New York Times*, June 29, 1894.

41   Some historians contend that the story that the "Pioneer" was in Lincoln's funeral train was invented later as a sales promotion, and that there was no way existing railway platforms between Chicago and Springfield could have been widened in time to accommodate the car. But Pullman himself and others insisted that with the cooperation of James H. Bowen, president of the Third National Bank of Chicago (and a friend and supporter of Pullman's efforts), as well as the Chicago, Alton and St. Louis Railroad, last-minute adjustments were made to prune the station platforms and that the "Pioneer" did indeed make the journey south from Chicago with the train carrying Lincoln's body. For discussion see L. E. Leyendecker, *Palace Car Prince: A Biography of George Mortimer Pullman* (Niwot: University Press of Colorado, 1992), pp. 77–78.

42   Stanley Buder, *Pullman: An Experiment in Industrial Order and Community Planning 1880–1930* (New York: Oxford University Press, 1967), pp. 5–6.

43   Ibid., p. 37.

44   Ibid., p. 148.

45   Ibid., p. 149.

46   Samuel Gompers, "The Lesson of the Recent Strikes," in *The Pullman Boycott of 1894: The Problem of Federal Intervention*, ed. Colston E. Warne (Boston: D. C. Heath, 1955).

47   "Statement from the Pullman Strikers to the Convention of the American Railway Union, June 15, 1894," in *The Pullman Boycott of 1894: The Problem of Federal Intervention*, ed. Colston E. Warne (Boston: D. C. Heath, 1955).

48   Leyendecker, *Palace Car Prince*, p. 235.

49   "Statement from the Pullman Strikers to the Convention of the American Railway Union, June 15, 1894."

50   Ray Ginger, *Altgeld's America: The Lincoln Ideal Versus Changing Realities* (New York: Funk & Wagnalls, 1958), p. 149.

51   Ibid., p. 151.

52   The sole precursor for the idea of expansive, direct government aid was the Bureau of Refugees, Freedmen, and Abandoned Lands (known as the Freedmen's Bureau) that Congress had created in March 1865 to deal with the aftermath of the Civil War by offering basic services to both blacks and whites striving to re-create a functioning society in the postwar South. The bureau's officers enforced emancipation and often monitored the first work contracts between freedmen and their former masters. But the agency was unpopular, particularly in the region it was meant to serve, where it was frequently savaged in broadsides and editorials, and was soon abandoned by Congress, as was eventually most of the federal effort to reconstruct the South.

53   Richard O. Boyer and Herbert M. Morais, *Labor's Untold Story* (New York: United Electrical, Radio & Machine Workers of America, 1972; originally published 1955), pp. 120–21.

54   Quoted in Carlos Schwantes, *Coxey's Army: An American Odyssey* (Lincoln: University of Nebraska Press, 1985), pp. 18–19.

55   One of the witnesses to Coxey's march on Washington was the author Lyman Frank Baum, who would later use it as the basis for his popular book *The Wonderful Wizard of Oz* (1900). In Baum's children's story, the innocent Dorothy sets out on a pilgrim-

age with the Scarecrow (a farmer), the Tin Man (a worker), and the Cowardly Lion (a politician) to seek the aid and guidance of the Wizard (President Cleveland).

56 *Tacoma News*, April 16, 1894, in Schwantes, *Coxey's Army*, p. 261.

57 Robert V. Bruce, *1877: Year of Violence* (Indianapolis, Ind.: Bobbs-Merrill Co., 1959), pp. 68–69.

58 Ray Ginger, *Altgeld's America*, p. 41.

59 Schwantes, *Coxey's Army*, p. 271.

60 See ibid., pp. 275–79.

61 Ray Ginger, *Altgeld's America*, p. 152; Dulles, *Labor in America*, p. 175.

62 Boyer and Morais, *Labor's Untold Story*, p. 122.

63 Debs in *Locomotive Firemen's Magazine*, Sept. 1892

64 Ray Ginger, *The Bending Cross: A Biography of Eugene Victor Debs* (New Brunswick, N.J.: Rutgers University Press, 1949), p. 106.

65 Ibid., pp. 97–98.

66 Ibid., p. 155.

67 "Statement from the Pullman Strikers to the Convention of the American Railway Union, June 15, 1894," in *The Pullman Boycott 1894: The Problem of Federal Intervention*, ed. Colston E. Warne (Boston: D. C. Heath, 1955).

68 Ray Ginger, *Bending Cross*, p. 113.

69 Ibid., p. 117.

70 David Montgomery, "The Pullman Boycott and the Making of Modern America," in *The Pullman Strike and the Crisis of the 1890s*, ed. Richard Schneirov (Urbana: University of Illinois Press, 1999).

71 Boyer and Morais, *Labor's Untold Story*, p. 125.

72 *New York Times*, June 28, 1894.

73 Montgomery, "The Pullman Boycott and the Making of Modern America."

74 *New York Times*, June 28 and 29, 1894.

75 Eugene Debs, "The Federal Government and the Chicago Strike," in *The Pullman Boycott 1894: The Problem of Federal Intervention*, ed. Colston E. Warne (Boston: D. C. Heath, 1955).

76 *New York Times*, July 5, 1894.

77 Dulles, *Labor in America*, p. 177.

78 *New York Times*, July 4, 1894.

79 Ray Ginger, *Bending Cross*, p. 145.

80 *New York Times*, July 9, 1894.

81 Ibid.

82 The blaring headlines of anarchy set loose were likely inspired in part by news of the assassination, only a few days earlier, of French president Sadi Carnot. See Ray Ginger, *Bending Cross*, p. 123.

83 *New York Times*, July 5, 1894.

84 Taft quoted in Melvyn Dubofsky, "The Federal Judiciary, Free Labor, and Equal Rights," in *The Pullman Strike and the Crisis of the 1890s*, ed. Richard Schneirov (Urbana: University of Illinois Press, 1999).

85 Gerald Eggert, *Railroad Labor Disputes: The Beginnings of Federal Strike Policy* (Ann Arbor: University of Michigan Press, 1967), p. 172.

86 Ray Ginger, *Bending Cross*, p. 137.

87 *New York Times*, June 29, 1894.

88 Ray Ginger, *Altgeld's America*, p. 161.

89 Ray Ginger, *Bending Cross*, p. 130.

90 Ray Ginger, *Altgeld's America*, p. 160.

91 John P. Altgeld, "Comment on the Supreme Court Decision," in *The Pullman Boycott 1894: The Problem of Federal Intervention*, ed. Colston E. Warne (Boston: D. C. Heath, 1955).

92 Boyer and Morais, *Labor's Untold Story*, p. 113.

93   See *New York Times*, June 27, 1893; *Chicago Tribune*, June 27, 1893; also Ray Ginger, *Altgeld's America*, p. 87.

94   Henry David, *The History of the Haymarket Affair* (New York: Farrar & Rinehart, 1936), pp. 479–503.

95   *Chicago Tribune*, June 27, 1893.

96   Ray Ginger, *Altgeld's America*, pp. 85–86.

97   *New York Times*, June 27, 1893.

98   Ibid., June 28, 1893.

99   *Philadelphia Times*, undated excerpt quoted in *New York Times*, July 8, 1894.

100 Ray Ginger, *Bending Cross*, p. 94.

101 *Baltimore Sun*, undated excerpt quoted in *New York Times*, July 8, 1894.

102 *New York Times*, July 3, 1894.

103 Willard King, "The Debs Case," in *The Pullman Boycott 1894: The Problem of Federal Intervention*, ed. Colston E. Warne (Boston: D. C. Heath, 1955).

104 Grover Cleveland, "The Government in the Chicago Strike of 1894," in *The Pullman Boycott 1894: The Problem of Federal Intervention*, ed. Colston E. Warne (Boston: D. C. Heath, 1955).

105 Ray Ginger, *Bending Cross*, p. 140.

106 Louis Adamic, *Dynamite!: A Century of Class Violence in America* (New York: Viking Books, 1934), p. 119.

107 *New York Times*, July 5, 1894.

108 Debs, "The Federal Government and the Chicago Strike"; see also Ray Ginger, *Bending Cross*, p. 139.

109 Ray Ginger, *Altgeld's America*, p. 161.

110 *U.S. Strike Commission Report: The Chicago Strike of June–July 1894* (1895), p. 192. See also Ray Ginger, *Bending Cross*, p. 149.

111 William D. Haywood, *Bill Haywood's Book: The Autobiography of William D. Haywood* (New York: International Publishers, 1929), p. 77.

112 Letter from Eugene Debs to his parents, July 16, 1894, The Papers of Eugene V. Debs, Tamiment Labor Archives, New York University.

113 *Chicago Inter-Ocean*, Nov. 21, 1892, cited in Edward Berman, *Labor and the Sherman Act* (New York: Harper & Brothers, 1930), p. 6.

114 *United States v. Workingmen's Amalgamated Council of New Orleans*, Eastern District Court of Louisiana, 54 Fed. 994, 996 (1893), cited in Edward Berman, p. 7.

115 *United States v. Patterson*, 55 Fed 605, 641 (1893), cited in Edward Berman, pp. 61–63.

116 *United States v. Debs*, 64 Fed. 724, 744–745 (1894). This interpretation was echoed in the first USSC decision on the Sherman Act in 1908, *Loewe v. Lawlor*, 208 U.S. 274, 301; see Edward Berman, pp. 7–8.

117 See *United States v. E. C. Knight Co.*, 156 U.S. 1 (1895).

118 Senator Robert Wagner quoted in *Congressional Record*, U.S. Senate, 74th Cong., 1st sess., May 15, 1936, p. 7565.

119 See *Standard Oil Co. of New Jersey v. United States*, 221 U.S. (1911).

120 *Standard Oil Co. of New Jersey v. United States*, 221 U.S. (1911). Two years later, in 1913, Standard Oil declared a 60 percent stock dividend and in 1922 a 400 percent stock dividend. See Patrick Renshaw, *The Wobblies: The Story of Syndicalism in the United States* (New York: Doubleday, 1967), p. 23. The court in 1911 also fulfilled Harlan's fears in its ruling in *United States v. American Tobacco Co.*, wherein it refused to demand the dissolution of a tobacco trust by rejecting the terms of the Sherman Act as written. American Tobacco had bought out 250 smaller firms and was prosecuted along with 65 of them for violating Sherman. Again Harlan made sharp dissenting comments, accusing his colleagues of second-guessing Congress and ignoring the statute's clear import. See *United States v. American Tobacco Co.*, 221 U.S. 189–93 (1911).

121   Adamic, *Dynamite!* p. 123.

122   Ray Ginger, *Bending Cross*, p. 150.

123   *U.S. Strike Commission Report: The Chicago Strike of June–July 1894 (1895)*, p. 76.

124   Ray Ginger, *Bending Cross*, pp. 109–10.

125   Margaret Crawford, *Building the Workingman's Paradise: The Design of American Company Towns* (New York: Verso, 1995), p. 45.

126   Ray Ginger, *Bending Cross*, p. 156.

127   *U.S. Strike Commission Report: The Chicago Strike of June–July 1894*, pp. xlvii–xlviii.

128   Ibid., pp. lii–liv.

129   Leyendecker, *Palace Car Prince*, p. 264.

130   The Reading had fired Gowen in 1886 for poor financial management. Dismissing rumors he'd been murdered by vengeful Mollies, his relations said that he'd been "acting queerly for some time and that there was a strain of hereditary insanity in the family." See James D. Horan and Howard Swiggett, *The Pinkerton Story* (New York: Atheneum, 1968), pp. 158–59.

131   Leyendecker, *Palace Car Prince*, p. 258; the preparations were finalized none too soon: Pullman succumbed to a heart attack in fall 1897 at the age of sixty-six.

132   Ray Ginger, *Bending Cross*, p. 151.

133   See *In re Debs*, 158 U.S. 564 (1895).

134   Eugene V. Debs letter to his father, Jan. 1, 1895, in Papers of Eugene V. Debs, Tamiment Labor Archives, New York University.

135   Ray Ginger, *Bending Cross*, pp. 176–78; *Chicago Tribune*, Nov. 23, 1895.

136   *U.S. Strike Commission Report: The Chicago Strike of June–July 1894*, p. 163.

CHAPTER FIVE: INDUSTRIAL DEMOCRACY

1   Foster Rhea Dulles, *Labor in America: A History* (New York: Thomas Y. Crowell Co., 1966), p. 184.

2   Richard Hofstadter, *The Age of Reform* (New York: Random House, 1955), p. 177.

3   Ibid., p. 205n.

4   Nelson Lichtenstein, *State of the Union: A Century of American Labor* (Princeton, N.J.: Princeton University Press, 2002), p. 6.

5   Hofstadter, *Age of Reform*, pp. 240–41n.

6   Louis Adamic, *Dynamite!: A Century of Class Violence in America* (New York: Viking Books, 1934), p. 131.

7   Hofstadter, *Age of Reform*, p. 240.

8   Richard A. Greenwald, *The Triangle Fire, the Protocols of Peace, and Industrial Democracy in Progressive Era New York* (Philadelphia: Temple University Press, 1988), pp. 10–11.

9   Ibid., p. 13.

10   Margaret Crawford, *Building the Workingman's Paradise: The Design of American Company Towns* (New York: Verso, 1995), p. 50.

11   Sanford M. Jacoby, *Employing Bureaucracy: Managers, Unions, and the Transformation of Work in American Industry, 1900–1945* (New York: Columbia University Press, 1985), p. 55.

12   Frederick W. Taylor, *The Principles of Scientific Management* and *Shop Management* (London: Routledge, 1993; originally published 1911), p. 11.

13   Sudhir Kakar, *Frederick Taylor: A Study in Personality and Innovation* (Cambridge, Mass.: MIT Press, 1970), pp. 175–76.

14   Charles R. Morris, *The Tycoons: How Andrew Carnegie, John D. Rockefeller, Jay Gould, and J. P. Morgan Invented the American Supereconomy* (New York: Henry Holt, 2005), p. 307.

15   Ibid., p. 308.

16   Kakar, *Frederick Taylor: A Study in Personality and Innovation*, p. 185.

17   Ibid., p. 54; Kakar, *Frederick Taylor: A Study in Personality and Innovation*, pp. 182–83, 185–86.

18   Morris, *Tycoons*, p. 309.

19   Ibid., p. 298.

20   Michael McGerr, *A Fierce Discontent: The Rise and Fall of the Progressive Movement in America, 1870–1920* (New York: Free Press, 2003), pp. 120–21.

21   Robert H. Wiebe, "The Anthracite Strike of 1902: A Record of Confusion," *Mississippi Valley Historical Review*, vol. 48, no. 2 (Sept. 1961).

22   Elting E. Morrison, ed., *The Letters of Theodore Roosevelt*, vol. 3 (New York: Cambridge University Press, 1951), p. 515.

23   McGerr, *Fierce Discontent*, p. 125.

24   Ibid., pp. 119–20.

25   Adamic, *Dynamite!* p. 134.

26   Selig Perlman, *A History of Trade Unionism in the United States* (New York: Macmillan, 1922), p. 177.

27   Wiebe, "Anthracite Strike of 1902."

28   Frederic W. Unger, "George F. Baer: Master-Spirit of the Anthracite Industry," *American Monthly Review of Reviews*, vol. 33 (1966), p. 545.

29   *American Federationist*, vol. 12 (1905), p. 221, quoted in Jerome L. Toner, *The Closed Shop* (Washington, D.C.: American Council on Public Affairs, 1942), p. 6.

30   Dulles, *Labor in America*, p. 191; in 1905 Baer would again offend the labor movement with a biblical allusion, remarking, "Strikes began with Genesis. . . . Cain was the first striker, and he killed Abel because Abel was the more prosperous fellow." See Unger, "George F. Baer: Master-Spirit of the Anthracite Industry."

31   Wiebe, "Anthracite Strike of 1902."

32   *New York Times*, Oct. 3, 1902.

33   The resolution by the Reverend Thomas Slicer was quoted in the *New York Times*, Oct. 4, 1902.

34   Theodore Roosevelt letter to W. M. Crane, Governor of Massachusetts, Oct. 22, 1902, in Morrison, *Letters of Theodore Roosevelt*, vol. 3, p. 360.

35   *New York Times*, Oct. 4, 1902.

36   Ibid.

37   Ibid.

38   Dulles, *Labor in America*, p. 192.

39   Roosevelt had also managed to elbow aside the powerful Hanna, whose presidential ambitions never picked up momentum (indeed, "Dollar Mark" contracted typhoid fever and died prematurely in February 1904).

40   *Boston Herald*, Dec. 5, 1902, in Philippa Strum, *Louis D. Brandeis: Justice for the People* (Cambridge, Mass.: Harvard University Press, 1984), p. 105.

41   Henry James, *Richard Olney and His Public Service* (Boston: Houghton Mifflin, 1923), p. 61.

42   Olney quoted in Gerald Eggert, *Richard Olney: Evolution of a Statesman* (University Park: Pennsylvania State University Press, 1974), pp. 157–58. Another jurist associated with the Pullman Strike, Peter Grosscup of the U.S. Circuit Court of Appeals, published an article in *McClure's Magazine* in 1905 against weighting the struggle between labor and capital too much on the corporate side. He worried that making it impossible for the common man to acquire property would stunt the country's moral growth and that "the loss that republican America now confronts is the loss of individual hope and prospect—the suppression of the instinct that . . . has made us a nation of individually independent and prosperous people." See Peter Grosscup, "How to Save the Corporation," *McClure's Magazine*, vol. 24 (Feb. 1905), cited in Hofstadter, *Age of Reform*, pp. 223–24.

43 Industrial Commission, Final Report of the Industrial Commission, 57th Cong., 1st sess., 1902, House Document 380.

44 See *Slaughterhouse Cases*, 16 Wall (83 U.S.) 36 (1873); see Paul Krens article on *Lochner* in Kermit L. Hall, ed., *Oxford Guide to U.S. Supreme Court Decisions* (New York: Oxford University Press, 1999), pp. 161–63. "Substantive due process" has proven something of a legal minefield, as critics allege it leads courts to usurp the privileges and power of legislatures, and that such "judicial activism" warps the original words of the Constitution to extend rights not articulated there. In addition to extending "freedom of contract" rights to employers and thus denying workers legislative remedies, substantive due process rulings have figured historically in cases related to the right to individual privacy as well as the disputed government "taking" of private property for regulatory purposes. See, for example, *Griswold v. Connecticut*, 381 U.S. 479 (1965) and *Roe v. Wade*, 410 U.S. 113 (1973).

45 See Herbert Croly, *The Promise of American Life*, chap. 12, quoted in Hofstadter, *Age of Reform*, pp. 246–47.

46 *U.S. Strike Commission Report—The Chicago Strike of June–July 1894*, p. 203.

47 See *Adair v. United States*, 208 U.S. 161 (1908).

48 Richard Olney, "Discrimination Against Union Labor—Legal?" *American Law Review* (March–April 1908), quoted in James, *Richard Olney and His Public Service*, p. 69.

49 Paul Krens article on *Lochner* in Kermit L. Hall, *Oxford Guide to U.S. Supreme Court Decisions*, pp. 161–63. See *Lochner v. New York*, 198 U.S. 45 (1905).

50 See *Loewe v. Lawlor*, 208 U.S. 274 (1908).

51 John Mitchell, *Organized Labor: Its Problems, Purposes and Ideals and the Present and Future of American Wage Earners* (Philadelphia: American Book and Bible House, 1903), p. 336.

52 Lichtenstein, *State of the Union*, pp. 30–31.

53 Walter Reuther quoted in Lichtenstein, *State of the Union*, p. 103.

54 Mother "Mary Harris" Jones, *The Autobiography of Mother Jones* (Chicago: Charles Kerr Publishing Co., 1990; originally published 1925), pp. 14–23.

55 Elizabeth Gurley Flynn, *I Speak My Own Piece* (New York: Masses and Mainstream, 1955), p. 81.

56 Elliott J. Gorn, *Mother Jones: The Most Dangerous Woman in America* (New York: Hill and Wang, 2001), p. 135.

57 Jones, *Autobiography of Mother Jones*, pp. 80–81; see Gorn, *Mother Jones*, p. 137.

58 Gorn, *Mother Jones*, p. 140; see also Jones, *Autobiography of Mother Jones*, pp. 71–83.

59 Sarah N. Cleghorn, *Portraits and Protests* (New York: Henry Holt, 1917), p. 75.

60 Melvyn Dubofsky, "Abortive Reform: The Wilson Administration and Organized Labor, 1913–1920," in *Work, Community, and Power: The Experience of Labor in Europe and America, 1900–1925*, ed. James E. Cronin and Carmen Sirianni (Philadelphia: Temple University Press, 1983).

61 *Duplex Printing Press Co. v. Deering*, 254 U.S. 443 (1921).

62 Dubofsky, "Abortive Reform."

63 Christine Stansell, *American Moderns: Bohemian New York and the Creation of a New Century* (New York: Metropolitan Books, 2000), p. 21.

64 Ann Schofield, "The Uprising of the 20,000: The Making of a Labor Legend," in *A Needle, a Bobbin, a Strike: Women Needleworkers in America*, ed. Joan M. Jensen and Sue Davidson (Philadelphia: Temple University Press, 1984).

65 *Collier's*, Dec. 25, 1909.

66 Schofield, "Uprising of the 20,000."

67 *New York Times*, Nov. 5, 1909.

68 Ibid., Nov. 6, 1909.

69 Ibid.

70 Leon Stein, *The Triangle Fire* (Ithaca, N.Y.: Cornell University Press, 2001), p. 167.

71   *New York World*, Nov. 23, 1909; Greenwald, *Triangle Fire, the Protocols of Peace, and Industrial Democracy*, p. 32; see also Françoise Basch, "The Shirtwaist Girls at Home and at Work," in *The Diary of a Shirtwaist Striker*, by Thersa Malkiel (Ithaca, N.Y.: Cornell University Press, 1990).

72   *Collier's*, Dec. 25, 1909.

73   *New York Times*, Nov. 27, 1909.

74   *New York Times*, Jan. 8, 1910.

75   Quoted in Basch, "The Shirtwaist Girls at Home and at Work." Perhaps no one illustrated the openness of the reform scene better than Rose Pastor, a young Jewish cigar maker who became known as "the Cinderella of the Tenements" after her marriage to Graham Phelps Stokes, a Yale-educated settlement house worker from an established New York family. Rose Pastor Stokes remained committed to the labor struggle. When asked by a reporter, "Are the strikers unreasonable in nothing?" Stokes famously replied, "My dear! The working people can make no unreasonable demand." See *Collier's*, Dec. 25, 1909.

76   *New York Times*, Dec. 6, 1909.

77   Ibid., Dec. 20, 1909.

78   Greenwald, *Triangle Fire, the Protocols of Peace, and Industrial Democracy*, pp. 46–48.

79   Strum, *Louis D. Brandeis*, pp. 108–9.

80   *American Cloak and Suit Review*, Sept. 1911, cited in Strum, *Louis D. Brandeis*, p. 177.

81   Strum, *Louis D. Brandeis*, p. 95.

82   Ibid., p. 96.

83   Ibid., p. 102.

84   Taylor, *Principles of Scientific Management*, p. 10.

85   *Muller v. Oregon*, 208 U.S. 412 (1908).

86   Greenwald, *Triangle Fire, the Protocols of Peace, and Industrial Democracy*, p. 70.

87   *New York World*, March 27, 1911.

88   "The Triangle Fire," speech by Rose Schneiderman in honor of the twenty-fifth anniversary of the Triangle Fire, March 25, 1936. Rose Schneiderman Papers, Tamiment Labor Archives, New York University.

89   Stein, *Triangle Fire*, p. 21.

90   Ibid., p. 168.

91   Shaw quoted in Seth Cagin and Philip Dray, *Between Earth and Sky: How CFCs Changed Our World* (New York: Pantheon Books, 1993), p. 43.

92   Robin K. Berson, *Marching to a Different Drummer: Unrecognized Heroes of American History* (Westport, Conn.: Greenwood Press, 1994), pp. 283–84.

93   Ibid., p. 284.

94   Greenwald, *Triangle Fire, the Protocols of Peace, and Industrial Democracy*, pp. 151–52.

95   John F. Witt, *The Accidental Republic: Crippled Workingmen, Destitute Widows, and the Remaking of American Labor* (Cambridge, Mass.: Harvard University Press, 2004), p. 13.

96   Ibid., pp. 3–4.

97   Patrick Renshaw, *The Wobblies: The Story of Syndicalism in the United States* (New York: Doubleday, 1967), p. 24.

98   Daniel Berman, *Death on the Job: Occupational Health and Safety Struggles in the United States* (New York: Monthly Review Press, 1978), pp. 19–20.

99   David Von Drehle, *Triangle: The Fire That Changed America* (New York: Atlantic Monthly Press, 2003), p. 207.

100   Florence Kelley, *Annals of the American Academy of Political and Social Science*, July 1911.

101   Frances Perkins, *The Roosevelt I Knew* (New York: Viking Press, 1946), pp. 22–23; see also Greenwald, *Triangle Fire, the Protocols of Peace, and Industrial Democracy*, p. 174.

102   Greenwald, *Triangle Fire, the Protocols of Peace, and Industrial Democracy*, p. 161.

103   Hamilton quoted in Cagin and Dray, *Between Earth and Sky*, p. 41.

104   Greenwald, *Triangle Fire, the Protocols of Peace, and Industrial Democracy*, pp. 218–20.

CHAPTER SIX: WE SHALL BE ALL

1   Melvyn Dubofsky, *We Shall Be All: A History of the Industrial Workers of the World*, abridged ed. (Urbana: University of Illinois Press, 2000), pp. 81–83.

2   Howard Kimeldorf, *Battling for American Labor: Wobblies, Craft Workers, and the Making of the Union Movement* (Berkeley: University of California Press, 1999), pp. 12–13.

3   William D. Haywood, *Bill Haywood's Book: The Autobiography of William D. Haywood* (New York: International Publishers, 1929), p. 73.

4   Anne Huber Tripp, *The IWW and the Paterson Silk Strike of 1913* (Urbana: University of Illinois Press, 1987), p. 6.

5   *American Federationist*, no. 12, Aug. 1905, in Tripp, *IWW and the Paterson Silk Strike*, p. 10.

6   Dubofsky, *We Shall Be All*, pp. 90–91.

7   Len De Caux, *The Living Spirit of the Wobblies* (New York: International Publishers, 1978), p. 16. The IWW acronym itself invariably became, in the hands of the organization's critics, "I Want Whiskey," "I Won't Work," and, when the Wobblies were accused of furthering the enemy's agenda during the First World War, "Imperial Wilhelm's Warriors." See Patrick Renshaw, *The Wobblies: The Story of Syndicalism in the United States* (New York: Doubleday, 1967), pp. 1–2.

8   Howard Kimeldorf, *Battling for American Labor: Wobblies, Craft Workers, and the Making of the Union Movement* (Berkeley: University of California Press, 1999), p. 3.

9   Renshaw, *Wobblies: Story of Syndicalism*, p. 1.

10   Dubofsky, *We Shall Be All*, pp. 87–88.

11   Tripp, *IWW and the Paterson Silk Strike*, p. 3.

12   Dubofsky, *We Shall Be All*, p. 50.

13   Louis Adamic, *Dynamite!: A Century of Class Violence in America* (New York: Viking Books, 1934), pp. 126–27.

14   De Caux, *Living Spirit of the Wobblies*, p. 31.

15   John Reed, "War in Paterson, June 1913," *The Masses*, June 1913.

16   Helen C. Camp, *Iron in Her Soul: Elizabeth Gurley Flynn and the American Left* (Pullman: Washington State University Press, 1995), p. 28.

17   *Outlook* quoted in Haywood, *Bill Haywood's Book*, p. 248.

18   Haywood, *Bill Haywood's Book*, p. 200.

19   Adamic, *Dynamite!* p. 149.

20   Ibid., p. 151.

21   Ibid.

22   Haywood, *Bill Haywood's Book*, p. 210.

23   Bruce Watson, *Bread and Roses: Mills, Migrants, and the Struggle for the American Dream* (New York: Penguin Books, 2005), p. 95.

24   Haywood, *Bill Haywood's Book*, p. 215.

25   *Independent*, vol. 74, Jan. 9, 1913, in Tripp, *IWW and the Paterson Silk Strike*, p. 132.

26   Haywood, *Bill Haywood's Book*, p. 223.

27   Adamic, *Dynamite!* p. 185.

28   Tripp, *IWW and the Paterson Silk Strike*, pp. 9–10.

29   *American Mercury*, Dec. 1926.

30   Camp, *Iron in Her Soul*, p. xxiii.

31   De Caux, *Living Spirit of the Wobblies*, p. 21.

32   Elizabeth Gurley Flynn, *I Speak My Own Piece* (New York: Masses and Mainstream, 1955), p. 51.

33   Ibid., pp. 54–55.

34   Ibid., pp. 53–54.

35   Camp, *Iron in Her Soul*, pp. 10, 15.

36   Dubofsky, *We Shall Be All*, p. 103.

37   Camp, *Iron in Her Soul*, pp. 23–24.

38   Adamic, *Dynamite!* p. 210.

39   Ibid., p. 216.

40   Ibid., pp. 229–30.

41   *San Diego Tribune*, March 4, 1912, in Renshaw, *Wobblies: Story of Syndicalism*, p. 89.

42   Goldman had met Czolgosz briefly on one occasion and had not conspired with or instructed him to target McKinley; the assassin, however, had told authorities of his admiration for her—hence the source of the rumor of her complicity. It was peculiar that Goldman's complicity in Alexander Berkman's assault on Henry Clay Frick had been overlooked, while the far less accurate Czolgosz allegation stuck to her for the rest of her life.

43   Dubofsky, *We Shall Be All*, p. 110.

44   Ibid., pp. 106–8.

45   The Lawrence struggle became famous in labor movement lore as "the Bread and Roses strike" for its emphasis on the fundamentals of decent pay and humane hours of work, as well as the large role played in the strike by both women and children. The phrase "bread and roses" had originated as a labor movement term in a poem written the year before the strike by James Oppenheim: "As we come marching, marching, in the beauty of the day / A million darkened kitchens, a thousand mill-lofts gray / Are touched with all the radiance that a sudden sun discloses / For the people hear us singing, 'Bread and Roses, Bread and Roses.'" See James Oppenheim, "Bread and Roses," *The American Magazine* 73 (Dec. 1911).

46   Watson, *Bread and Roses*, pp. 74–75.

47   Testimony of Frank Sherman, Report on the Lawrence Strike, U.S. House, p. 39.

48   *Lawrence Evening Tribune*, Jan. 12, 1912.

49   Watson, *Bread and Roses*, pp. 23–24.

50   It was not uncommon for parents in the Lawrence mills to procure false identity papers for their children, so that the underage could enter the mills and contribute to the family's income.

51   Trustees of the White Fund, The Report of the Lawrence Survey, 1912, pp. 111–13.

52   *Boston Globe*, Jan. 19, 1912. Wood was an Americanized immigrant and a successful wool salesman. He had made a fortuitous marriage to Ellen Ayer, daughter of a prosperous Rhode Island factory owner.

53   Watson, *Bread and Roses*, p. 53.

54   Industrial Workers of the World, "Ettor and Giovannitti Before the Jury at Salem MA, Nov. 23, 1912" [booklet] (Chicago: IWW Publishing, 1913), p. 8.

55   *Lawrence Telegram*, Jan. 16, 1912.

56   Flynn, *I Speak My Own Piece*, p. 120.

57   Renshaw, *Wobblies: Story of Syndicalism*, pp. 99–100.

58   *Pawtucket Evening Times*, Jan. 25, 1912.

59   *Boston Globe*, Jan. 16, 1912.

60   *Lawrence Evening Tribune*, Jan. 17, 1912.

61   *Boston Globe*, Jan. 19, 1912.

62   *Lawrence Evening Tribune*, Jan. 24, 1912.

63   Dubofsky, *We Shall Be All*, p. 140.

64   Ernest Pitman, a contractor who later confessed to supplying Breen with the dynamite, committed suicide in August 1912, but not before suggesting to investigators that Billy Wood was involved in the affair. Wood was indicted in the plot along with two other men, Frederick H. Atteaux and D. J. Collins, but was ultimately cleared, although Collins was found guilty. Breen got off with a $500 fine. Few observers believed Wood innocent of involvement in the scheme.

65   *American Mercury*, Dec. 1926.

66   Adamic, *Dynamite!* pp. 168–69.

67   Watson, *Bread and Roses*, p. 132.

68   *New York Times*, Feb. 11, 1912.

69   Ibid.

70   Ibid., Feb. 13, 1912.

71   Dubofsky, *We Shall Be All*, p. 146.

72   Haywood, *Bill Haywood's Book*, p. 249.

73   *Lawrence Evening Tribune*, Feb. 24, 1912.

74   *New York Tribune*, Feb. 26, 1912.

75   *New York Sun* quoted in *Literary Digest*, March 9, 1912.

76   *New York Tribune* quoted in *Literary Digest*, March 9, 1912.

77   *Industrial Worker*, June 27, 1912, in Watson, *Bread and Roses*, p. 214.

78   William Cahn, *Lawrence 1912: The Bread and Roses Strike* (New York: Pilgrim Press, 1980; originally published 1954), p. 2.

79   *Atlantic Monthly*, May 1912.

80   Watson, *Bread and Roses*, 205; *Lawrence Tribune*, March 14, 1912; *New York Tribune*, March 11, 1912; *Boston Evening Transcript*, March 11, 1912.

81   *Journal of Commerce and Commercial Bulletin*, Feb. 1, 1912.

82   *Atlantic Monthly*, May 1912.

83   Donald B. Cole, *Immigrant City: Lawrence, Massachusetts, 1845–1921* (Chapel Hill: University of North Carolina Press, 1963), p. 6.

84   Renshaw, *Wobblies: Story of Syndicalism*, pp. 107–8.

85   Camp, *Iron in Her Soul*, p. 34.

86   Ibid., p. 46.

87   Ibid., p. 40.

88   Indeed, when the next year someone tried to hang a similar banner during the IWW's Paterson Strike Pageant, it was torn down and crumpled at once by Wobbly leader Patrick Quinlan, to cheers from the audience; Quinlan assured reporters the IWW considered the banner "an infernal outrage." See *New York Times*, June 8, 1913.

89   Camp, *Iron in Her Soul*, p. 36.

90   Watson, *Bread and Roses*, pp. 225–40.

91   *Boston Globe*, Nov. 26, 1912.

92   Hamilton and Coxe, acting through the government-sponsored Society for Useful Manufactures, engaged L'Enfant, who had designed the new capital city of Washington, to similarly craft at Paterson a stunning industrial town that would reflect an enlightened approach to industry. The endeavor was well capitalized but ran aground after L'Enfant fell out with the leaders of the society and Paterson locals began to have second thoughts. See Margaret Crawford, *Building the Workingman's Paradise: The Design of American Company Towns* (New York: Verso, 1995), pp. 13–15.

93   Renshaw, *Wobblies: Story of Syndicalism*, pp. 112–13.

94   Flynn, *I Speak My Own Piece*, p. 143.

95   Dubofsky, *When Workers Organize*, p. 124.

96   Camp, *Iron in Her Soul*, pp. 45–46.

97   Flynn, *I Speak My Own Piece*, p. 141; Camp, *Iron in Her Soul*, p. 40.

98   *American Mercury*, Dec. 1926.

99   Christine Stansell, *American Moderns: Bohemian New York and the Creation of a New Century* (New York: Metropolitan Books, 2000), p. 112.

100   Ibid., p. 16.

101   Robert Rosenstone, *Romantic Revolutionary: A Biography of John Reed* (New York: Alfred A. Knopf, 1975), p. 125.

102   *American Mercury*, Dec. 1926; see Tripp, *IWW and the Paterson Silk Strike*, p. 118.

103   *Paterson Evening News*, March 14, 1913, in Tripp, *IWW and the Paterson Silk Strike*, pp. 87–88.

104   Tripp, *IWW and the Paterson Silk Strike*, p. 90.

105 Camp, *Iron in Her Soul*, p. 53.

106 Ibid., quotation on frontispiece.

107 Christopher Lasch, *The New Radicalism in America, 1889–1963* (Cambridge, Mass.: MIT Press, 1965), p. 128, in Tripp, *IWW and the Paterson Silk Strike*, p. 137.

108 Camp, *Iron in Her Soul*, p. 48.

109 *New York Times*, June 15, 1913.

110 Rosenstone, *Romantic Revolutionary*, p. 129; Steve Golin, *The Fragile Bridge: Paterson Silk Strike, 1913* (Philadelphia: Temple University Press, 1988), p. 169.

111 Tripp, *IWW and the Paterson Silk Strike*, p. 151.

112 Flynn, *I Speak My Own Piece*, p. 155.

113 Ibid., p. 156.

114 *New York Times*, June 24, 1913.

115 Golin, *Fragile Bridge*, p. 164.

116 Ibid., pp. 209–11.

117 Dubofsky, *We Shall Be All*, pp. 166–67.

118 Reprinted in *Solidarity*, Aug. 30, 1913, quoted in Golin, *Fragile Bridge*, pp. 210–11.

119 Rosenstone, *Romantic Revolutionary*, p. 131.

120 *New York Times*, June 24, 1913.

121 Reed, "The Colorado War," *Metropolitan*, July 1914.

122 Ibid.

123 Adamic, *Dynamite!* p. 258.

124 Rosenstone, *Romantic Revolutionary*, pp. 172–73.

125 Reed, "The Colorado War."

126 Ibid.

127 *New York Times*, May 8, 1914.

128 Ralph Chaplin, *When the Leaves Come Out and Other Rebel Verses* (self-published, 1917), p. 31; appears in Robert M. Smith, *From Blackjacks to Briefcases: A History of Commercialized Strikebreaking and Unionbusting in the United States* (Athens: Ohio University Press, 2003), p. 26.

129 In the First Balkan War (1912–1913), Greece joined with Serbia, Bulgaria, and Montenegro to drive from Europe the remnants of the Turkish Ottoman Empire.

130 Elliott J. Gorn, *Mother Jones: The Most Dangerous Woman in America* (New York: Hill and Wang, 2001), p. 202.

131 Ibid., p. 203.

132 Caleb Crain, "There Was Blood: The Ludlow Massacre Revisited," *The New Yorker*, Jan. 19, 2009.

133 Elias M. Ammons, "The Colorado Strike," *North American Review*, July 1914.

134 Ibid.

135 Reed, "The Colorado War."

136 Gorn, *Mother Jones*, p. 177.

137 *New York Times*, March 14 and 23, 1914.

138 Scott Martelle, *Blood Passion: The Ludlow Massacre and Class War in the American West* (New Brunswick, N.J.: Rutgers University Press, 2007), pp. 153–54; see also Reed, "The Colorado War."

139 Martelle, *Blood Passion*, p. 151; see also Crain, "There Was Blood: The Ludlow Massacre Revisited."

140 George S. McGovern and Leonard F. Guttridge, *The Great Coalfield War* (Boston: Houghton Mifflin, 1972), pp. 213–14.

141 Ibid., p. 229.

142 *New York Times*, May 3, 1914; Martelle, *Blood Passion*, p. 181.

143 *New York Times*, April 23, 1914.

144 Adamic, *Dynamite!* p. 260.

145 *New York Times*, May 16, 1914.

146 Ibid., May 8, 1914.
147 Cited in McGovern and Guttridge, *Great Coalfield War*, p. 270.
148 Ammons, "The Colorado Strike."
149 Martelle, *Blood Passion*, p. 2.
150 Gorn, *Mother Jones*, p. 206.
151 *New York Times*, May 17, 1914.
152 Ibid., May 15, 1914; McGovern and Guttridge, *Great Coalfield War*, p. 284.
153 Mabel Dodge Luhan, *Movers and Shakers* (Albuquerque: University of New Mexico Press, 1985; originally published 1936), p. 98.
154 *Mother Earth*, July 1914.
155 Luhan, *Movers and Shakers*, p. 112. After serving his time, Tannenbaum left the labor movement to pursue an academic career at Columbia University.
156 Luhan, *Movers and Shakers*, p. 117.
157 McGovern and Guttridge, *Great Coalfield War*, p. 277.
158 Ibid., p. 278.
159 *New York Times*, May 2, 1914.
160 *Mother Earth*, June 1914.
161 Report on the Colorado Strike Investigation, House of Representatives, 63rd Cong., 3rd sess., 1915, p. 42.
162 McGovern and Guttridge, *Great Coalfield War*, pp. 289–91.
163 *Mother Earth*, July 1914. A woman named Marie Chavez, who lived in the next apartment and apparently had no connection to the bomb factory, was also killed in the blast.
164 *Mother Earth*, July 1914.
165 Quoted by Patrick Renshaw, *The Wobblies: The Story of Syndicalism in the United States* (New York: Doubleday, 1967), p. 43.
166 De Caux, *Living Spirit of the Wobblies*, pp. 100–101.
167 Joe Hill to *Salt Lake City Telegram*, August 15, 1915; appears in a bound scrapbook of letters titled "Joe Hill, 1879–1915: The Man Who Never Died: Letters, a Sampling" (S.I.; s.i.) 1990; New York Public Library.
168 *Appeal to Reason*, Aug. 15, 1915.
169 De Caux, *Living Spirit of the Wobblies*, p. 106.

CHAPTER SEVEN: DYNAMITE

1 Melvyn Dubofsky, *We Shall Be All: A History of the Industrial Workers of the World*, abridged ed. (Urbana: University of Illinois Press, 2000), p. 201.
2 Mary Heaton Vorse, *Triangle: The Fire That Changed America* (New York: Farrar and Rinehart, 1935), pp. 73–74; also in Steve Golin, *The Fragile Bridge: Paterson Silk Strike, 1913* (Philadelphia: Temple University Press, 1988), p. 227.
3 Victor G. Reuther, *The Brothers Reuther and the Story of the UAW* (Boston: Houghton Mifflin, 1976), p. 22.
4 Paul Avrich, *Sacco and Vanzetti: The Anarchist Background* (Princeton, N.J.: Princeton University Press, 1991), p. 93.
5 Katherine Benton-Cohen, *Borderline Americans: Racial Division and Labor Wars in the Arizona Borderlands* (Cambridge, Mass.: Harvard University Press, 2004), p. 218.
6 *New York Times*, July 13, 1917.
7 Ibid.
8 Ibid.
9 Ibid.
10 Ibid.
11 Ibid.

12   *New York Times*, July 14, 1917.

13   Ibid.

14   Benton-Cohen, *Borderline Americans*, p. 234. A civil suit against Phelps Dodge and the railroad that had provided the freight train used in the deportation also went nowhere. The federal inquiry found that of the 1,280 deported men (and three women), 426 were Wobblies, 351 belonged to the AFL, 360 were not in any union, 62 were military veterans, 205 owned Liberty Bonds, and 520 had donated to the Red Cross. See Patrick Renshaw, *The Wobblies: The Story of Syndicalism in the United States* (New York: Doubleday, 1967), p. 188.

15   William D. Haywood, *Bill Haywood's Book: The Autobiography of William D. Haywood* (New York: International Publishers, 1929), pp. 82–83.

16   *New York Times*, Aug. 2, 1917.

17   Renshaw, *Wobblies: Story of Syndicalism*, p. 163.

18   *New York Times*, Aug. 3, 1917.

19   Dubofsky, *We Shall Be All*, p. 227.

20   Haywood, *Bill Haywood's Book*, p. 302.

21   Ibid., p. 304.

22   Dubofsky, *We Shall Be All*, p. 243.

23   *The Liberator*, Sept. 1918.

24   Brazier, "The Mass IWW Trial of 1918: A Retrospect," *Labor History*, vol. 7, no. 2 (1966); see also Helen C. Camp, *Iron in Her Soul: Elizabeth Gurley Flynn and the American Left* (Pullman: Washington State University Press, 1995), p. 74.

25   Len De Caux, *The Living Spirit of the Wobblies* (New York: International Publishers, 1978), pp. 6–7. A related IWW tactic was known as "Hoosiering up," playing dumb about how a job was to be done in order to slow the pace of work. See also De Caux, *Living Spirit of the Wobblies*, p. 121.

26   Brazier, "The Mass IWW Trial of 1918: A Retrospect."

27   Dubofsky, *We Shall Be All*, pp. 248–49.

28   Haywood, *Bill Haywood's Book*, pp. 321–22.

29   Ibid., p. 322.

30   *New York Times*, Aug. 31, 1918; Brazier, "The Mass IWW Trial of 1918: A Retrospect."

31   Dubofsky, *We Shall Be All*, p. 254.

32   Melvyn Dubofsky and Warren Van Tine, *John L. Lewis: A Biography*, abridged ed. (Urbana: University of Illinois Press, 1986), p. 35.

33   Robert K. Murray, *Red Scare: A Study in National Hysteria, 1919–1920* (New York: McGraw-Hill, 1964; originally published 1955), pp. 10–11.

34   Woodrow Wilson quoted in Murray, *Red Scare*, p. 9.

35   Robert L. Friedheim, *The Seattle General Strike* (Seattle: University of Washington Press, 1964), p. 170.

36   Ibid., p. 169.

37   Melvyn Dubofsky, "Abortive Reform: The Wilson Administration and Organized Labor, 1913–1920," in *Work, Community, and Power: The Experience of Labor in Europe and America, 1900–1925*, ed. James E. Cronin and Carmen Sirianni (Philadelphia: Temple University Press, 1983).

38   *New York Times*, Feb. 9, 1919.

39   Ibid., Feb. 7, 1919.

40   Jeremy Brecher, *Strike!* (Boston: South End Press, 1984; originally published 1972), p. 113. The attempted repression of the IWW in the Seattle area had a long history, having flared into a murderous scuffle in November 1916 when the sheriff and employer-backed vigilantes in the nearby lumber town of Everett opened fire on a boatload of Wobblies as they arrived for a free speech rally. Five IWW members were slain and many roughed up. When the boat, the *Verona*, turned back to Seattle to warn a second vessel, the *Calista*, not to embark for the rally, Seattle cops descended on the

pier and arrested seventy-four men, accusing them of the murders of two vigilantes who had fallen in the fighting at Everett. At trial, the IWW emphasized the nonviolent nature of its members' activities and won acquittal for the accused, suggesting the deputies killed were probably hit by stray gunfire from their own side's chaotic discharge of weapons. See Renshaw, *Wobblies: Story of Syndicalism*, pp. 93–94.

41 Friedheim, *Seattle General Strike*, p. 175.

42 Howard Kimeldorf, *Battling for American Labor: Wobblies, Craft Workers, and the Making of the Union Movement* (Berkeley: University of California Press, 1999), pp. 14–15.

43 *New York Times*, Nov. 9, 1919.

44 Ibid., Feb. 11, 1919.

45 Friedheim, *Seattle General Strike*, p. 174.

46 *New York Times*, June 3, 1919.

47 *Manufacturers Record* quoted in *Literary Digest*, Nov. 8, 1919.

48 *Literary Digest*, Nov. 8, 1919.

49 *New York Times*, June 5, 1919.

50 *Boston Globe*, Sept. 9, 1919; an earlier effort at organization, the Boston Social Club, had been unable to gain the ear of management, as it was shunned by Commissioner Edwin Upton Curtis.

51 See *Boston Globe*, Sept. 6, 1919.

52 *Boston Globe*, Sept. 3, 1919.

53 Ibid., Sept. 8, 1919.

54 Ibid., Sept. 9, 1919.

55 Ibid., Sept. 10, 1919.

56 *Philadelphia Public Ledger*, quoted in *Literary Digest*, Sept. 27, 1919.

57 Murray, *Red Scare*, p. 130.

58 *Boston Globe*, Sept. 12, 1919.

59 Ibid., Sept. 13, 1919.

60 Ibid., Sept. 14, 1919.

61 Ibid., Sept. 15, 1919; Murray, *Red Scare*, p. 132.

62 *Literary Digest*, Nov. 15, 1919.

63 Foster Rhea Dulles, *Labor in America: A History* (New York: Thomas Y. Crowell Co., 1966), p. 233.

64 Dubofsky, "Abortive Reform: The Wilson Administration and Organized Labor, 1913–1920."

65 Ibid.

66 Emma Goldman, *Living My Life* (New York: Penguin Books, 2006; originally published 1931), p. 338.

67 Interchurch World Movement, *Report on the Steel Strike of 1919* (New York: Da Capo Press, 1970; originally published 1920), p. 148.

68 *New York Times*, Oct. 2, 1919.

69 Ibid., Oct. 4, 1919.

70 For the Gary-Rockefeller exchange see Raymond B. Fostick, *John D. Rockefeller, Jr.: A Portrait* (New York: Harper & Brothers, 1956), pp. 174–75.

71 Louis Adamic, *Dynamite!: A Century of Class Violence in America* (New York: Viking Books, 1934), pp. 280–81; Elliott J. Gorn, *Mother Jones: The Most Dangerous Woman in America* (New York: Hill and Wang, 2001), p. 260.

72 Interchurch World Movement, *Report on the Steel Strike of 1919*, p. 155.

73 Ibid., p. 39.

74 *New York Times*, Oct. 4, 1919.

75 *Memphis Commercial Appeal* and William Randolph Hearst quoted in *Literary Digest*, Nov. 8, 1919.

76 Dulles, *Labor in America*, p. 237.

77 *Seattle Times* quoted in *Literary Digest*, Nov. 8, 1919. The nation's coalfields continued

to produce the most violent labor confrontations. Shooting wars among miners, police, company detectives, and federal troops broke out in West Virginia, Kentucky, and Illinois in the early 1920s. In the West Virginia–Kentucky border town of Mattewan a gun battle in May 1920 killed the mayor, two miners, and seven Baldwin-Felts guards. In Mattewan in August a three-hour exchange of fire resulted in six more deaths. Finally tired of the bullying by mine owners and their enforcers, an "army" of four thousand miners, including many recent war veterans, marched from Mattewan into neighboring Logan County, where it was reported deputies had killed several miners. The marchers ignored a plea from President Warren Harding to turn back. In a scene reminiscent of the Colorado coalfield wars of 1914, fighting broke out over a two-mile front, as gunfire filled the hillsides and hollows. Only the arrival of federal troops with machine guns and airplanes brought the violence to a halt, with hundreds of the miners indicted (but never convicted) of treason. (In a similar open war between miners and strikebreakers in Illinois two years later, it was the miners who went airborne, renting a plane from which they heaved dynamite bombs out onto known strikebreaker defenses.) See Brecher, *Strike!* pp. 134–39.

78   Ralph Chaplin, *The Centralia Massacre* (Austin, Tex.: Workplace Publishing, 1971; originally published 1924), p. 33.

79   Elizabeth Gurley Flynn, *I Speak My Own Piece* (New York: Masses and Mainstream, 1955), p. 253.

80   Renshaw, *Wobblies: Story of Syndicalism*, p. 164.

81   See Friedheim, *Seattle General Strike*, p. 173.

82   Chaplin, *Centralia Massacre*, p. 59.

83   Renshaw, *Wobblies: Story of Syndicalism*, p. 165; Grimm, Hubbard, and two other American Legion men killed in the day's fighting were eulogized as the true heroes of Centralia's "Armistice Day Massacre," ambushed by cowardly reds as they marched in a patriotic parade. Words of praise were spoken on the floor of Congress and in the press for those who had defied the IWW's infiltration of the Northwest's lumber country, with little mention made of the Legion's possible precipitating role in the assault or the horrific death of Wesley Everest. No official inquiry was ever made into Everest's lynching, but ten Wobblies who had defended the IWW hall were put on trial for murder; seven were convicted and sent away for sentences of between twenty-five and forty years; two others were acquitted and one was declared insane. After the Federal Council of Churches looked into the Centralia affair in the 1930s (and even some American Legion men spoke out about the case's injustice), the IWW men were pardoned in 1936, having spent seventeen years in the state penitentiary at Walla Walla.

84   Justin Kaplan, *Lincoln Steffens: A Biography* (New York: Simon & Schuster, 1974), pp. 250–51; Robert Sobel, *Coolidge: An American Enigma* (Washington, D.C.: Regnery, 1998), p. 122.

85   *Congressional Record*, 66th Cong., 1st sess., p. 7063; see Murray, *Red Scare*, pp. 195–96.

86   Athan G. Theoharis and John S. Cox, *The Boss: J. Edgar Hoover and the Great American Inquisition* (Philadelphia: Temple University Press, 1988), pp. 59–61. The authors report that Hoover claimed to have engaged in conversations with both Goldman and Berkman after their arrests, and to have come away from the experience even more astounded at the depth of the anarchists' communistic fervor. No transcripts of these meetings exist, unfortunately. What is clear is that Hoover's "pursuit of (Goldman and Berkman's) enforced exile was remorseless right up to the moment of their departure."

87   Murray, *Red Scare*, pp. 193–94.

88   *New York Times*, Nov. 8, 1919.

89   *New York Call*, Jan. 1, 1929.

90   Unattributed in Robert W. Dunn, "The Palmer Raids" [booklet] (New York: International Publishers, 1948).

91   Murray, *Red Scare*, p. 206.

92 Richard Gid Powers, *Secrecy and Power: The Life of J. Edgar Hoover* (New York: Free Press, 1987), p. 78.

93 *New York Times*, Dec. 22, 1919.

94 Powers, *Secrecy and Power*, pp. 82–83. Before their departure Berkman and Goldman had been feted at a farewell banquet in Chicago on December 2. Henry Clay Frick had died of a heart attack earlier that day. Berkman noted that Frick had been "deported by God. I'm glad he left the country before me."

95 *New York Times*, Dec. 22, 1919.

96 Ibid.

97 Ibid.

98 Quoted in Theoharis and Cox, *Boss: J. Edgar Hoover and the Great American Inquisition*, p. 63.

99 Powers, *Secrecy and Power*, p. 88.

100 Louis F. Post, *The Deportations Delirium of 1920* (Chicago: Charles H. Kerr & Co., 1923), p. 94.

101 *New York Times*, April 14, 1920.

102 Ibid.

103 *New York Times*, April 1, 1920.

104 *Schenectady Citizen* quoted in *Literary Digest*, Jan. 24, 1920.

105 Murray, *Red Scare*, p. 209.

106 Camp, *Iron in Her Soul*, p. 98.

107 Murray, *Red Scare*, p. 208.

108 In that same March 1919 session the court upheld the conviction of Eugene Debs, leader of the Socialist Party, for violation of the Espionage Act. Debs had received a ten-year sentence for a wartime speech in Canton, Ohio, in which he criticized the government for its assaults on Socialists opposed to the war.

109 *Abrams v. United States*, 250 U.S. 616 (1919) and *Schenck v. United States*, 249 U.S. 47 (1919); see also Murray, *Red Scare*, pp. 224–25.

110 Murray, *Red Scare*, p. 248. Of the nearly 10,000 people picked up in the Palmer raids, only 591 were ultimately deported. See Murray, *Red Scare*, pp. 248–51; Camp, *Iron in Her Soul*, p. 101.

111 Camp, *Iron in Her Soul*, p. 100.

112 Powers, *Secrecy and Power*, p. 114.

113 Post, *Deportations Delirium of 1920*, pp. 308–9.

114 Ibid., p. 311.

115 Powers, *Secrecy and Power*, pp. 116–17.

116 *Christian Science Monitor*, June 25, 1920; Murray, *Red Scare*, p. 251.

117 *New York Times*, May 1, 1920.

118 Murray, *Red Scare*, p. 253.

119 Brown, *Report Upon the Illegal Practices*, p. 58.

120 Ibid., p. 3.

121 Walsh quoted in Theoharis and Cox, *Boss: J. Edgar Hoover and the Great American Inquisition*, pp. 69–70.

122 Powers, *Secrecy and Power*, p. 123. Transcripts of the Walsh hearings were kept by forces friendly to Palmer from appearing in the *Congressional Record* until 1923.

123 Camp, *Iron in Her Soul*, p. 101.

124 Mike Davis, *Buda's Wagon: A Brief History of the Car Bomb* (New York: Verso, 2007), pp. 1–3.

125 *Atlantic Monthly*, July 1920.

126 William Z. Foster, *The Great Steel Strike and Its Lessons* (New York: B. W. Huebsch Inc., 1920), pp. 256–65.

127 De Caux, *Living Spirit of the Wobblies*, p. 10.

128 Dubofsky, *We Shall Be All*, p. 261.

129   Ibid., p. 262.

130   Ibid. The Soviets made an attempt to arrange work for Haywood, and he married a Russian woman, but the rebel from the western silver mines was never entirely at home in the Russian system. He retired to his room at a Moscow hotel where he received visitors, many old colleagues, to drink and reminisce. Never in good health, he was in and out of the hospital and died there in May 1928. On December 15, 1923, President Coolidge had commuted the sentences of all remaining IWW prisoners.

131   Powers, *Secrecy and Power*, p. 125.

132   Richard O. Boyer and Herbert M. Morais, *Labor's Untold Story* (New York: United Electrical, Radio & Machine Workers of America, 1972; originally published 1955), pp. 225–26.

133   Bartolomeo Vanzetti to E. G. Flynn, Dec. 21, 1922, in Elizabeth Gurley Flynn, *The Rebel Girl: An Autobiography: My First Life (1906–1926)* (New York: International Publishers, 1973), p. 304; see also Camp, *Iron in Her Soul*, p. 107.

134   Leon Harris, *Upton Sinclair: American Rebel* (New York: Thomas Y. Crowell, 1975), p. 244.

135   Murray, *Red Scare*, pp. 266–67.

136   Adamic, *Dynamite!* pp. 314–15.

CHAPTER EIGHT: LET US HAVE PEACE AND MAKE CARS

1   Foster Rhea Dulles, *Labor in America: A History* (New York: Thomas Y. Crowell Co., 1966), p. 242.

2   David Brody, *Workers in Industrial America: Essays on the Twentieth Century Struggle* (New York: Oxford University Press, 1993), p. 50.

3   Charles Schwab quoted in David Brody, *Workers in Industrial America*, p. 53.

4   See George Elton Mayo, *The Human Problems of an Industrialized Society* (New York: Macmillan, 1933).

5   U.S. Steel Corporation Stockholders Meeting, April 16, 1923, quoted in David Brody, *Workers in Industrial America*, p. 55.

6   Dulles, *Labor in America*, p. 256.

7   Arthur M. Schlesinger Jr., *The Age of Roosevelt: The Coming of the New Deal* (Boston: Houghton Mifflin, 1958), p. 385.

8   Steven Fraser, *Labor Will Rule: Sidney Hillman and the Rise of American Labor* (Ithaca, N.Y.: Cornell University Press, 1991), p. 152.

9   Raymond B. Fostick, *John D. Rockefeller, Jr.: A Portrait* (New York: Harper & Brothers, 1956), pp. 177–78.

10   Arthur M. Schlesinger Jr., "Sources of the New Deal," in *The New Deal: The Critical Issues*, ed. Otis Graham Jr. (Boston: Little, Brown and Co., 1971).

11   David Brody, *Workers in Industrial America*, pp. 76–78.

12   Ibid., p. 73.

13   Irving Bernstein, *The Turbulent Years: A History of the American Worker, 1933–1941* (Boston: Houghton Mifflin, 1970), p. 2.

14   Quoted in Zinn, "The Conservative New Deal," in *The New Deal: The Critical Issues*, ed. Otis Graham Jr. (Boston: Little, Brown and Co., 1971).

15   Bernstein, *Turbulent Years*, pp. 4–5.

16   Schlesinger, "Sources of the New Deal."

17   Zinn, "The Conservative New Deal," p. 144.

18   Perkins quoted in Kirsten Downey, *The Woman Behind the New Deal: The Life of Frances Perkins* (New York: Doubleday, 2009), p. 32.

19   Nelson Lichtenstein, *State of the Union: A Century of American Labor* (Princeton, N.J.: Princeton University Press, 2002), p. 25.

20   Frances Perkins, *The Roosevelt I Knew* (New York: Viking Press, 1946), pp. 217–20.

21   Downey, *Woman Behind the New Deal*, pp. 203–4. For an account of the Homestead
      visit, see also *Washington Post*, Aug. 1, 1933.
22   Bernstein, *Turbulent Years*, p. 14.
23   Schlesinger, *Age of Roosevelt*, p. 137.
24   Dulles, *Labor in America*, p. 237.
25   Melvyn Dubofsky and Warren Van Tine, *John L. Lewis: A Biography*, abridged ed.
      (Urbana: University of Illinois Press, 1986), pp. 131–32; Section 7(a) read: (1) That
      employees shall have the right to organize and bargain collectively through repre-
      sentatives of their own choosing, and shall be free from the interference, restraint, or
      coercions of employers of labor, or their agents, in the designation of such representa-
      tives or in self-organization or in other concerted activities for the purpose of collective
      bargaining or other mutual aid or protection; (2) That no employee and no one seek-
      ing employment shall be required as a condition of employment to join any company
      union or to refrain from joining, organizing, or assisting a labor organization of his
      own choosing."
26   Joseph P. Lash, *Dealers and Dreamers: A New Look at the New Deal* (New York: Double-
      day, 1988), p. 424.
27   Dulles, *Labor in America*, p. 267.
28   Schlesinger, *Age of Roosevelt*, pp. 138–39.
29   Dulles, *Labor in America*, p. 268.
30   Louis Stark quoted in Downey, *Woman Behind the New Deal*, p. 207.
31   Irving Bernstein, *The Lean Years: A History of the American Worker, 1920–1933* (Boston:
      Houghton Mifflin, 1966), pp. 300, 319.
32   Fraser M. Ottanelli, *The Communist Party of the United States: From the Depression to
      World War II* (New Brunswick, N.J.: Rutgers University Press, 1991), pp. 27–28.
33   Ibid., p. 28.
34   Frances Fox Piven and Richard A. Cloward, *Poor People's Movements: Why They Suc-
      ceed, How They Fail* (New York: Pantheon Books, 1977), p. 58.
35   Len De Caux, *The Living Spirit of the Wobblies* (New York: International Publishers,
      1978), pp. 162–63.
36   *New York Times*, March 7, 1930.
37   Eric Foner, *The Story of American Freedom* (New York: W. W. Norton & Co., 1998), p. 212.
38   Ottanelli, *Communist Party of the United States*, p. 35.
39   Muste, a war resister during the First World War, had served as dean of Brookwood
      Labor College in Katonah, New York, founded in 1921 by William and Helen Fincke
      of the pacifistic Fellowship of Reconciliation; it was the first, but eventually one of
      several, labor training schools that appeared in the war years and early 1920s. The
      philosophy behind Brookwood was the "idea of surrounding the state apparatus with
      a counter-hegemony, a hegemony created by mass organization of the working class
      and by developing working class institutions and culture." The goal was not "a frontal
      attack on the state but . . . the foundation of a new culture" imbued with "the norms
      and values of a new, proletarian society." Muste also busied himself with his Confer-
      ence for Progressive Labor Action (CPLA), a reaction to both the Communist Party
      and the strict craft unionism of the AFL. CPLA members, known as Musteites, sought
      organizing along industrial lines; many went on to serve the CIO, or followed Muste
      into action in the Southern textile strike of 1929 and the Toledo Auto-Lite struggle
      of 1934, and helped organize branches of the Unemployed League. See Richard J.
      Altenbaugh, *Education for Struggle: The American Labor Colleges of the 1920s and 1930s*
      (Philadelphia: Temple University Press, 1990), pp. 3–15 and 71–75; see also the article on
      Brookwood in *New York Times*, June 16, 1921.
40   *New York Times*, July 5, 1934.
41   Ibid., July 6, 1934.
42   Perkins, *Roosevelt I Knew*, pp. 313–14.

43   Downey, *Woman Behind the New Deal*, p. 215.

44   Perkins, *Roosevelt I Knew*, p. 316; see also Downey, *Woman Behind the New Deal*, pp. 216–17.

45   *Minneapolis Tribune*, May 17, 1934.

46   Schlesinger, *Age of Roosevelt*, p. 386.

47   See Lois Quam and Peter J. Rachleff, "Keeping Minneapolis an Open-Shop Town: The Citizens' Alliance in the 1930's," *Minnesota History*, vol. 50, no. 3 (Fall 1986).

48   Eric Sevareid quoted in Farrell Dobbs, *Teamster Rebellion* (New York: Monad Press, 1972), p. 12.

49   Charles R. Walker, *American City: A Rank and File History of Minneapolis* (Minneapolis: University of Minnesota Press, 2005; originally published 1937), p. 108.

50   Dobbs, *Teamster Rebellion*, p. 83.

51   *New York Times*, May 23, 1934; Walker, *American City*, pp. 116–21.

52   Bernstein, *Turbulent Years*, p. 230.

53   Dobbs, *Teamster Rebellion*, pp. 127–29.

54   *New York Times*, July 21, 1934.

55   Quam and Rachleff, "Keeping Minneapolis an Open-Shop Town." The labor triumph in Minneapolis would be short-lived. Within five years the Trotskyists alarmed many by opposing intervention in the war in Europe, and a series of strikes by WPA workers in Minnesota angered the local federal prosecutor, Victor Anderson, who warned, "Minneapolis is not going to become the Moscow of America," as he indicted more than one hundred WPA strikers. The Dunne brothers and Carl Skoglund, as leaders of Minneapolis's "red" labor cause, were pursued under the terms of the Alien Registration Act of 1940 (known as the Smith Act after Congressman Howard W. Smith). Accused of fomenting a conspiracy to overthrow the government, eighteen defendants including Skoglund, Vincent Dunne, and Miles Dunne (brother Grant Dunne took his own life during the trial) went to federal prison in 1943. See Walker, *American City*, pp. 126–27.

56   David Rosner and Gerald Markowitz, eds., *Dying for Work: Workers' Safety and Health in Twentieth-Century America* (Bloomington: Indiana University Press, 1987), pp. 151–52.

57   Robert H. Zieger, *The CIO: 1933–1955* (Chapel Hill: University of North Carolina Press, 1995), p. 25.

58   Dubofsky and Van Tine, *John L. Lewis: A Biography*, p. 155.

59   Lewis quoted in David Brody, *Workers in Industrial America*, p. 93.

60   Schlesinger, *Age of Roosevelt*, p. 412.

61   *The Nation*, Oct. 28, 1944.

62   Dubofsky and Van Tine, *John L. Lewis: A Biography*, p. 161.

63   Schlesinger, *Age of Roosevelt*, p. 414.

64   Thomas Geoghegan, *Which Side Are You On?: Trying to Be for Labor When It's Flat on Its Back* (New York: New Press, 2004; originally published 1991), p. 48.

65   Dubofsky and Van Tine, *John L. Lewis: A Biography*, p. 208.

66   Ibid., p. 267.

67   Quoted in Lichtenstein, *State of the Union*, p. 46.

68   *Schechter Poultry Corp v. United States*, 295 U.S. 495 (1935).

69   Senator Robert Wagner quoted in *New York Times*, Feb. 16, 1936.

70   *The Nation*, Oct. 28, 1944.

71   Bernstein, *Turbulent Years*, p. 15. Wagner responded to criticisms that the act was harder on employers than workers by saying, "No one would assail the traffic laws because they regulate the speed at which automobiles travel, and not the speed at which pedestrians walk." See *New York Times*, July 25, 1937; J. Joseph Huttmacher, *Senator Robert F. Wagner and the Rise of Urban Liberalism* (New York: Atheneum, 1968), p. 234.

72   *Congressional Record*, U.S. Senate, 1st sess., May 15, 1935, p. 7569.

73   Ibid., p. 7570.
74   Lichtenstein, *State of the Union*, p. 32.
75   Fraser, *Labor Will Rule*, p. 331.
76   Downey, *Woman Behind the New Deal*, p. 219.
77   Perkins, *Roosevelt I Knew*, pp. 243–44.
78   Lash, *Dealers and Dreamers*, pp. 427–28.
79   *Congressional Record*, U.S. Senate, 74th Cong., 1st sess., May 15, 1936, p. 7573; see also *New York Times*, May 16, 1935.
80   *New York Times*, May 19, 1935.
81   Ibid.
82   Geoghegan, *Which Side Are You On?* p. 50.
83   *New York Times*, June 26, 1936.
84   Ibid.
85   William Leuchtenburg, *The Supreme Court Reborn: The Constitutional Revolution in the Age of Roosevelt* (New York: Oxford University Press, 1995), p. 99.
86   *National Labor Relations Board v. Jones & Laughlin Steel Corp.*, 301 U.S. 1 (1937).
87   Downey, *Woman Behind the New Deal*, pp. 264–65.
88   Ibid., pp. 234–36.
89   Dulles, *Labor in America*, p. 282.
90   Perkins, *Roosevelt I Knew*, pp. 253–55. Wagner was not the sponsor of the Fair Labor bill, but with his backing of so many of the New Deal's innovations and the survival of the Wagner Act at the Supreme Court in 1937, resentful conservative voices increasingly targeted him, and he was red-baited in his own successful reelection campaign in New York during the summer and fall of 1938. See Huttmacher, *Senator Robert F. Wagner and the Rise of Urban Liberalism*, pp. 249–55.
91   Saul D. Alinsky, *John L. Lewis: An Unauthorized Biography* (New York: Vintage Books, 1970; originally published 1949), p. 106.
92   Dubofsky and Van Tine, *John L. Lewis: A Biography*, p. 190.
93   Sidney Fine, *Sit-Down: The General Motors Strike of 1936–1937* (Ann Arbor: University of Michigan Press, 1969), p. 56.
94   Herbert Harris, *American Labor* (New Haven, Conn.: Yale University Press, 1939), p. 271.
95   Ruth McKenney, *Industrial Valley* (New York: Harcourt Brace and Co., 1939), pp. 261–62.
96   Fine, *Sit-Down: The General Motors Strike of 1936–1937*, p. 131.
97   *New York Times*, Jan. 2, 1937.
98   Alinsky, *John L. Lewis: An Unauthorized Biography*, p. 108.
99   Frank Cormier and William J. Eaton, *Reuther* (Englewood Cliffs, N.J.: Prentice-Hall, 1970), p. 79.
100 Fine, *Sit-Down: The General Motors Strike of 1936–1937*, p. 152.
101 Dulles, *Labor in America*, p. 304.
102 Cormier and Eaton, *Reuther*, p. 85.
103 Victor G. Reuther, *The Brothers Reuther and the Story of the UAW* (Boston: Houghton Mifflin, 1976), p. 156.
104 Fine, *Sit-Down: The General Motors Strike of 1936–1937*, pp. 3–4. The confrontation would enter labor movement lore as "The Battle of the Running Bulls."
105 Victor G. Reuther, *Brothers Reuther and Story of UAW*, p. 162.
106 Cormier and Eaton, *Reuther*, pp. 92–93.
107 Alinsky, *John L. Lewis: An Unauthorized Biography*, pp. 127–28; Dulles, *Labor in America*, p. 305.
108 Dubofsky and Van Tine, *John L. Lewis: A Biography*, p. 195.
109 Cormier and Eaton, *Reuther*, p. 94.
110 Victor G. Reuther, *Brothers Reuther and Story of UAW*, pp. 170–71.
111 *New York Times*, May 22, 1937.
112 *Harper's*, May 1937; *Time* quote in Melvyn Dubofsky, "Not So 'Turbulent Years':

Another Look at the American 1930's," in *The New Deal*, ed. Melvyn Dubofsky (New York: Garland Publishing, 1992). It was unclear at first if the sit-down would be used extensively. The AFL openly disavowed the tactic; the CIO never formally approved of it. Conservative congressmen denounced it as a dangerous form of labor radicalism and moved unsuccessfully in spring 1937 to legislate against it. The U.S. Senate approved a resolution citing sit-ins as a violation of private property rights, and courts showed themselves willing to look upon them as a form of criminal trespass. In 1939 the Supreme Court took up the matter in a case that had its origins in February 1937 at Fansteel, a Chicago manufacturer. Employees angry at the firm's rejection of worker grievances and efforts to bargain collectively declared a sit-down strike and seized two factory buildings. The NLRB agreed with the workers that their labor rights had been violated, but the Supreme Court reversed the board's decision, ruling in *National Labor Relations Board v. Fansteel Metallurgical Corporation* that sit-ins were "an illegal seizure of buildings in order to prevent their use by their employers in a lawful manner." Employees who "sat in" could be discharged; once discharged, they could be ousted as trespassers. Sit-ins soon became relatively obsolete, partly due to the expanded improvement of work conditions through the passage of the Fair Labor Standards Act, but beginning a decade later they would be revived by the Congress of Racial Equality (CORE) and used to sensational effect in the early phases of the modern civil rights movement. See *New York Times*, Feb. 28, 1939, and May 11, 1970.

113   Dulles, *Labor in America*, pp. 299–300.
114   In 1938 President Roosevelt sent Taylor to France to an international conference regarding the fate of Jewish refugees from Europe, and in 1939 made him an envoy and later the ambassador to the Vatican. Taylor is often credited with convincing Spanish leader Francisco Franco to not bring Spain into the Second World War on the side of the Axis Powers.
115   *New York Times*, June 1, 1937.
116   Ibid.
117   Ibid.
118   Cormier and Eaton, *Reuther*, p. 82.
119   Alinsky, *John L. Lewis: An Unauthorized Biography*, p. 165.
120   *New York Times*, June 30, 1937.
121   Ibid., Sept. 4, 1937.
122   Alinsky, *John L. Lewis: An Unauthorized Biography*, pp. 161–62.
123   Geoghegan, *Which Side Are You On?* p. 45.
124   See Dubofsky and Van Tine, *John L. Lewis: A Biography*, pp. 237–39; Perkins, *Roosevelt I Knew*, pp. 126–27.
125   Fraser, *Labor Will Rule*, p. 432.
126   Ibid., p. 493.
127   Ibid., p. 73.
128   Ibid., p. 449.
129   Dubofsky and Van Tine, *John L. Lewis: A Biography*, pp. 250–51.
130   Ibid., pp. 244–45.
131   Ibid., pp. 256–57.
132   Ibid., pp. 257–58. Robert Wagner said publicly that he believed Willkie had promised Lewis the position of secretary of labor, a rich plum to Lewis, who was still smarting over Roosevelt's selection of Sidney Hillman for wartime labor adviser to the administration. See Dubofsky and Van Tine, *John L. Lewis: A Biography*, p. 260.
133   Dubofsky and Van Tine, *John L. Lewis: A Biography*, p. 254.
134   John Barnard, *Walter Reuther and the Rise of the Auto Workers* (Boston: Little, Brown and Co., 1983), p. 73.
135   Melvyn Dubofsky, ed., *The New Deal: Conflicting Interpretations and Shifting Perspectives* (New York: Garland Publishing, 1992), p. 140.

136 Steven Watts, *The People's Tycoon: Henry Ford and the American Century* (New York: Random House, 2005), p. 449.

137 Ibid., p. 455.

138 Ibid., p. 195.

139 Ibid., pp. 197–98.

140 Cormier and Eaton, *Reuther*, p. 102.

141 Watts, *People's Tycoon*, pp. 453–54.

142 *New York Times*, May 28, 1937.

143 Victor G. Reuther, *Brothers Reuther and the Story of the UAW*, p. 204.

144 Cormier and Eaton, *Reuther*, p. 112.

145 Elias M. Auerbach, *Labor and Liberty: The La Follette Committee and the New Deal* (Indianapolis, Ind.: Bobbs-Merrill Co., 1966), pp. 8–9.

146 Dubofsky and Van Tine, *John L. Lewis: A Biography*, p. 188.

147 Doris Kearns Goodwin, *No Ordinary Time: Franklin and Eleanor Roosevelt: The Home Front in World War II* (New York: Simon & Schuster, 1994), p. 227.

148 *The Nation*, Dec. 14, 1940; Goodwin, *No Ordinary Time*, p. 227; Eleanor Roosevelt's column, "My Day," was syndicated in many of the nation's newspapers. See *Harper's*, May 1937.

149 Victor G. Reuther, *Brothers Reuther and the Story of the UAW*, p. 200.

150 Goodwin, *No Ordinary Time*, pp. 228–29.

151 *New York Times*, May 23, 1941.

152 Ibid.

153 Charles E. Sorensen and William Samuelson, *My Forty Years with Ford* (New York: W. W. Norton & Co., 1956), pp. 268–69; Watts, *People's Tycoon*, p. 462.

154 Sorensen and Samuelson, *My Forty Years with Ford*, pp. 268–71; Watts, *People's Tycoon*, p. 462.

CHAPTER NINE: SPIES, CROOKS, AND CONGRESSMEN

1 Melvyn Dubofsky and Warren Van Tine, *John L. Lewis: A Biography*, abridged ed. (Urbana: University of Illinois Press, 1986), pp. 304–5.

2 Kirsten Downey, *The Woman Behind the New Deal: The Life of Frances Perkins* (New York: Doubleday, 2009), p. 329.

3 Dubofsky and Van Tine, *John L. Lewis: A Biography*, p. 207.

4 *New York Times*, June 3, 1943.

5 Steven Fraser, *Labor Will Rule: Sidney Hillman and the Rise of American Labor* (Ithaca, N.Y.: Cornell University Press, 1991), p. 502.

6 Dubofsky and Van Tine, *John L. Lewis: A Biography*, p. 323.

7 Fraser, *Labor Will Rule*, p. 462.

8 *New York Times*, June 13, 1943.

9 Ibid.

10 *New York Times*, June 26, 1943.

11 Ibid., June 13, 1943.

12 Ibid.

13 Quoted in Fraser, *Labor Will Rule*, p. 503.

14 Foster Rhea Dulles, *Labor in America: A History* (New York: Thomas Y. Crowell Co., 1966), p. 345.

15 Ibid., pp. 345–46.

16 Fraser, *Labor Will Rule*, p. 525.

17 *New York Times*, July 25, 1944.

18 Fraser, *Labor Will Rule*, p. 529.

19 Ibid., p. 530.

20 Hillman was further vilified by allegations that he was linked to the 1936 murder of a trucking company operator, Joseph Rosen, who was suspected of servicing nonunion businesses. Gangster Louis Lepke of the notorious Murder Incorporated was convicted and sentenced to death for the slaying. Like any labor leader of his day, Hillman no doubt dealt with racketeers at times, but contract murder seems uncharacteristic of a man who valued his personal reputation as much as Hillman did. However, the rumor that Hillman had paid for the hit was heard not only from such reactionary voices as columnist Westbrook Pegler, but even Socialist presidential candidate Norman Thomas, who once observed, "I think that was very fortunate for Mr. Hillman that Mr. Lepke went to the electric chair without talking more than he did." See Fraser, *Labor Will Rule*, pp. 252–53.

21 Novelist Philip Roth, quoted in *Time* magazine, July 6, 2009.

22 Dulles, *Labor in America*, p. 347.

23 Senator Arthur H. Vandenberg quoted in R. Alton Lee, *Truman and Taft-Hartley: A Question of Mandate* (Lexington: University of Kentucky Press, 1966), p. 23.

24 R. Alton Lee, *Truman and Taft-Hartley: A Question of Mandate* (Lexington: University of Kentucky Press, 1966), p. 24.

25 *United States v. United Mine Workers*, 330 U.S. 258 (1947).

26 *Newsweek*, June 3, 1946; *U.S. News & World Report*, May 17, 1946.

27 *New York Times*, May 26, 1946.

28 *New Republic*, Feb. 11, 1946.

29 *New York Times*, May 29, 1946.

30 Ibid., May 31, 1946.

31 William White, *The Taft Story* (New York: Harper & Brothers, 1954), p. 57.

32 Sloan quoted in Nelson Lichtenstein, *State of the Union: A Century of American Labor* (Princeton, N.J.: Princeton University Press, 2002), p. 107.

33 White, *Taft Story*, p. 78.

34 Lee, *Truman and Taft-Hartley*, p. 63.

35 Robert D. Parmet, *The Master of Seventh Avenue: David Dubinsky and the American Labor Movement* (New York: New York University Press, 2005), p. 216.

36 Ibid., p. 217; Irving Richter, *Labor's Struggles: 1945–1950* (New York: Columbia University Press, 1994), p. vii.

37 *New York Times*, Oct. 2, 1949.

38 Ibid., Oct. 9, 1949.

39 Ibid., Oct. 17, 1949.

40 Ibid., Oct. 12, 1949.

41 Ibid., Nov. 1, 1949. The following year a federal court dealt Taft-Hartley a more direct blow when John L. Lewis grew concerned that his UMW miners were not receiving adequate benefits from the health and welfare fund administered by the mine operators. Cleverly avoiding a strike that might be termed illegal under Taft-Hartley, Lewis announced instead a series of "worker memorial days" to protest the mines' poor records on workplace injuries and work-related illness. The Truman administration won an injunction against the UMW for these stoppages under Taft-Hartley. When the union duly ordered miners to return to work in compliance with the injunction, most simply refused. Stymied, the government pursued contempt charges against UMW leaders for not being forceful enough in getting miners back on the job, but a federal court spurned the government's argument, thus rendering the injunctive power available in such circumstances ineffectual. When, in 1952, the steel unions struck again and 560,000 workers walked out, Truman—citing the needs of the Korean War—didn't bother seeking an injunction; he seized the steel plants. The Supreme Court, however, ruled the seizure an unconstitutional act of executive power; the plants were returned to private operation and the strike resumed. Truman was criticized for not going the route of Taft-Hartley, but he may have resisted such a move after his experience with

the UMW in 1950. Truman's successor, President Dwight D. Eisenhower, also tripped and stumbled over the new law. In 1953 the International Longshoremen's Association (ILA) and the employers' New York Shipping Association disputed wages and hiring on the New York waterfront. With shipping in the nation's largest port at a standstill, the AFL expelled the ILA, accusing it of racketeering, and chartered a new longshoremen's union. Eisenhower obtained an injunction under Taft-Hartley to ban all waterfront strikes, but the internecine complexities of the warring dockhands' unions in New York, and a series of wildcat strikes, made the situation nearly impossible to manage. Then, to the embarrassment of the AFL, NLRB elections vindicated the original ILA, which managed to come to terms with the employers; the White House came off as fumbling and poorly informed. A more personal crisis for the president arose when it became known that he had withdrawn his support from twenty union-friendly amendments proposed to Taft-Hartley by his own secretary of labor, former union official Martin J. Durkin, who resigned over his boss's change of heart, which appeared to have come about through the influence of business interests.

42   Barbara S. Griffith, *The Crisis of American Labor: Operation Dixie and the Defeat of the CIO* (Philadelphia: Temple University Press, 1988), pp. 24–25.

43   Lewis quoted in Fraser M. Ottanelli, *The Communist Party of the United States: From the Depression to World War II* (New Brunswick, N.J.: Rutgers University Press, 1991), p. 139.

44   Paul Buhle, *Taking Care of Business: Samuel Gompers, George Meany, Lane Kirkland, and the Tragedy of American Labor* (New York: Monthly Review Press, 1999), pp. 127–28. These unions were Mine, Mill and Smelter; Fur and Leather Workers; Food, Tobacco, and Allied Workers; Marine Cooks and Stewards' Association; Fishermen's Union; the International Longshoremen's and Warehousemen's Union; United Office and Professional Workers; the American Communications Association; National Furniture Workers; and the United Public Workers of America.

45   Griffith, *Crisis of American Labor*, p. 38.

46   Thomas Geoghegan, *Which Side Are You On?: Trying to Be for Labor When It's Flat on Its Back* (New York: New Press, 2004; originally published 1991), pp. 51–52.

47   *New York Times*, May 11, 1970.

48   *Harper's Magazine*, May 1942.

49   Valentine Reuther had run unsuccessfully for the West Virginia state legislature as a Socialist.

50   Victor G. Reuther, *The Brothers Reuther and the Story of the UAW* (Boston: Houghton Mifflin, 1976), p. 21.

51   Walter Reuther, "500 Planes a Day—A Program for the Utilization of the Automobile Industry for Mass Production of Defense Planes," in *Reuther, Selected Papers*, ed. Henry M. Christman (New York: Pyramid, 1964; originally published 1961).

52   *New York Times*, May 11, 1970.

53   Bruce Catton, *The War Lords of Washington* (New York: Greenwood Press, 1969; originally published 1948), p. 93.

54   Reuther made several other attention-getting proposals during the war—that the drive to collect scrap metal be publicized by scrapping the iron fence around the White House, that an armored suit called "the Portable Foxhole" be designed for infantrymen, and so on. More important, he saw to it that the UAW, except for a few localized walkouts, adhered to the wartime no-strike pledge.

55   Frank Cormier and William J. Eaton, *Reuther* (Englewood Cliffs, N.J.: Prentice-Hall, 1970), pp. 315–16.

56   Dulles, *Labor in America*, p. 374.

57   Ibid., p. 379. By 1964 this number had fallen to 16.8 million, or 30 percent. Various forces contributed to this: the inability of even the combined AFL-CIO to act as a union powerful enough to draw new members; blacks, day laborers, many unskilled

workers remained ununionized; white-collar and management jobs; 8 million unorganized farmworkers (ignored since the days of the Wobblies).

58   Andy Stern, *A Country That Works: Getting America Back on Track* (New York: Free Press, 2006), pp. 89–90.

59   Archie Robinson, *George Meany and His Times* (New York: Columbia University Press, 1994), pp. 132–33.

60   Fraser, *Labor Will Rule*, p. 556.

61   America hesitated to join the ILO because of its League of Nations affiliation, but Frances Perkins led a successful effort in 1934 to win congressional approval of U.S. entry into the ILO as a gesture of support for European workers because Mussolini and Hitler had shut down their nations' trade union movements. Because the Labor Department also oversaw immigration issues, Perkins was later involved in delicate negotiations to manipulate U.S. immigration quotas in order to make it possible to accept asylum requests from Jewish and other European trade unionists. This was opposed by both Congress and the U.S. State Department. In 1940 she was also active in arranging to relocate the ILO's headquarters temporarily to Montreal, the ILO's European staffers fleeing through Lisbon in a dramatic escape from the Nazis. All these efforts, as well as her support of the West Coast longshoreman Harry Bridges, would later be used by fierce anti-Communist forces in the United States to blacken Perkins's reputation. See Kirsten Downey, *The Woman Behind the New Deal: The Life of Frances Perkins* (New York: Doubleday, 2009), pp. 187–96, for a discussion of U.S.-ILO relations, Perkins, and the refugee issue.

62   Ted Morgan, *A Covert Life: Jay Lovestone—Communist, Anti-Communist, and Spymaster* (New York: Random House, 1999), p. 236.

63   Anthony Carew, "The American Labor Movement in Fizzland: The Free Trade Union Committee and the CIA," *Labor History*, vol. 39, no. 1 (1998).

64   Parmet, *Master of Seventh Avenue*, p. 225.

65   Victor G. Reuther, *Brothers Reuther and Story of UAW*, p. 332.

66   Parmet, *Master of Seventh Avenue*, pp. 229–30.

67   Morgan, *Covert Life: Jay Lovestone*, p. 199.

68   Ibid., pp. 197–98.

69   Walter Reuther, "How to Beat the Communists," *Collier's*, Feb. 28, 1948.

70   Parmet, *Master of Seventh Avenue*, p. 231.

71   Hugh Wilford, *The Mighty Wurlitzer: How the CIA Played America* (Cambridge, Mass.: Harvard University Press, 2008), p. 68.

72   Carew, "The American Labor Movement in Fizzland."

73   Both the expulsion of the leftist CIO unions and the merger of the AFL and CIO were engineered with the help of former OSS officer and CIO general counsel Arthur Goldberg, who was later secretary of labor, a justice of the U.S. Supreme Court, and the American ambassador to the United Nations.

74   John Barnard, *Walter Reuther and the Rise of the Auto Workers* (Boston: Little, Brown and Co., 1983), p. 134.

75   Arthur M. Schlesinger Jr., *Robert Kennedy and His Times* (Boston: Houghton Mifflin, 1978), p. 141.

76   Cormier and Eaton, *Reuther*, p. 322. Both Walter and Victor Reuther nearly paid with their lives for their independent ways. In April 1948 a shotgun was fired through the kitchen window of Walter's Detroit home, wounding him badly in the right arm. Victor was attacked a year later, also in a home assault, a sniper's bullet striking him in the face. Walter, his arm permanently disabled, moved his family out of Detroit to the suburbs and hired a bodyguard; Victor, who'd lost an eye to his would-be killer, relocated abroad, living in Paris for several years as an official with the CIO's international affairs division. Police never determined whether the brothers' would-be assassins were labor movement rivals, gangsters, or others. No one was ever prosecuted for either of the shootings.

77   Victor G. Reuther, *Brothers Reuther and Story of UAW*, pp. 416–17.

78   Fred Hirsch, *An Analysis of Our AFL-CIO Role in Latin America* (San Jose, Calif.:
      Self-published, 1974), pp. 42–43.

79   *New York Times*, Sept. 4, 1964.

80   Ibid., Sept. 1, 1964.

81   Similar revelations followed a few years later concerning the CIA's use of the National
      Student Association, a respected bastion of liberal idealism whose international pro-
      grams were shown to have been used as a CIA front. Lovestone, working closely with
      CIA counterintelligence man James J. Angleton, carried on his work for three decades,
      until he was dropped by the AFL-CIO in 1974 when his deep CIA links became known.

82   A. H. Raskin, "New Issue: Labor as Big Business," *New York Times Magazine*, Feb. 22,
      1959.

83   Barnard, *Walter Reuther and Rise of Auto Workers*, p. 156.

84   John Hutchinson, *The Imperfect Union: A History of Corruption in American Trade
      Unions* (New York: E. P. Dutton & Co., 1972), p. 382.

85   Howard Kimeldorf, *Battling for American Labor: Wobblies, Craft Workers, and the Mak-
      ing of the Union Movement* (Berkeley: University of California Press, 1999), p. 27.

86   Malcolm Johnson, *On the Waterfront: The Pulitzer Prize–Winning Article That Inspired
      the Classic Movie and Transformed the New York Waterfront* (New York: Penguin Group,
      2005), pp. vii, 6.

87   T. J. English, *Havana Nocturne: How the Mob Owned Cuba . . . and Then Lost It to the
      Revolution* (New York: William Morrow, 2008), p. 190.

88   Ibid., p. 76.

89   U.S. Congress, Senate, *Third Interim Report of the Special Committee to Investigate
      Organized Crime in Interstate Commerce* (Washington, D.C.: General Printing Office,
      1951); see also Thaddeus Russell, *Out of the Jungle: Jimmy Hoffa and the Remaking of the
      American Working Class* (New York: Alfred A. Knopf, 2001), p. 172.

90   Robert F. Kennedy, *The Enemy Within: The McClellan Committee's Crusade Against
      Jimmy Hoffa and Corrupt Labor Unions* (New York: Da Capo Press, 1994; originally
      published 1960), p. 251. After proving an uncooperative witness, Gallo nonetheless
      assured Kennedy, "I'll line up my people for your brother in 1960." See Schlesinger,
      Robert Kennedy and His Times, p. 164.

91   English, *Havana Nocturne*, p. 85.

92   Quoted in Russell, *Out of the Jungle*, p. 180.

93   Schlesinger, *Robert Kennedy and His Times*, pp. 137–38.

94   Russell, *Out of the Jungle*, p. 202.

95   Schlesinger, *Robert Kennedy and His Times*, p. 141. Robert Kennedy's zealous pursuit of
      union leaders did not sit altogether well with his father, Joseph Kennedy, who had had
      dealings with the Teamsters and worried that organized labor might take revenge by
      withholding support from John Kennedy if he chose to run for president.

96   Schlesinger, *Robert Kennedy and His Times*, p. 138.

97   Kennedy, *Enemy Within*, p. 5.

98   Hutchinson, *Imperfect Union*, p. 233.

99   Schlesinger, *Robert Kennedy and His Times*, p. 143.

100   A. H. Raskin, "The Moral Issue That Confronts Labor," *New York Times Magazine*,
      March 31, 1957.

101   Dave Beck was pardoned by President Gerald Ford in 1975.

102   Hutchinson, *Imperfect Union*, p. 255.

103   Kennedy, *Enemy Within*, p. 76.

104   Russell, *Out of the Jungle*, p. 178. The Father Barry character was based on a real-life
      "waterfront priest," Father John Corridan, who had worked among the toughs on the
      New York docks and been a source for Malcolm Johnson's series in the *Sun*. Johnson's
      exposé and the information provided by Corridan helped prompt the states of New

York and New Jersey to investigate and then coordinate reforms in the federal Water-front Commission Act of 1953, which targeted the shape-up, the payoffs, and the added expense to consumers that stemmed from entrenched dockside corruption. See *New York Times*, July 3, 1984.

105   Schlesinger, *Robert Kennedy and His Times*, p. 140. Teamsters vice president Harold Gibbons, questioned as to why so many ex-cons and gangsters gravitated toward the Teamsters, explained: "There is no mystery. We happen to be in a heavily or largely unskilled area. One does not have to have too many talents to drive a truck. So it is easy to place them, and we probably have an undue amount of calls from parole agents, from priests, from ministers, who are working with people trying to rehabilitate them. . . . I am very happy that unions are cooperating in this kind of work, otherwise we would be turning loose on society an awful lot of people who could only make their living by a gun." Hutchinson, *Imperfect Union*, p. 248.

106   Hutchinson, *Imperfect Union*, p. 268.

107   *New York Times*, June 7, 1968.

108   Kennedy, *Enemy Within*, p. 61.

109   Hutchinson, *Imperfect Union*, p. 258.

110   Ibid., p. 259.

111   Ibid., p. 267.

112   Nathan W. Shefferman, *The Man in the Middle* (Garden City, N.Y.: Doubleday, 1961), p. 50.

113   Acceptance Speech by James Hoffa, Folder 15, Box 353, Walter P. Reuther Collection, Archives of Labor and Urban Affairs, Wayne State University; in Russell, *Out of the Jungle*, p. 196.

114   Kennedy, *Enemy Within*, p. x.

115   Hutchinson, *Imperfect Union*, p. 267.

116   Schlesinger, *Robert Kennedy and His Times*, p. 168. Robert Kennedy would be key in convincing J. Edgar Hoover to commit the FBI to take the threat seriously, and in cooperating with other government agencies to suppress organized crime generally. One of the key breaks resulting from a ramped-up federal policy was the cooperation of Joseph M. Valachi, a thirty-three-year veteran Mafia soldier linked to the Genovese crime family, the first major mob figure to defy the tradition of noncooperation. Valachi's revelation of the workings of the major crime families changed thinking forever about the extensive reach of underworld crime.

117   Cormier and Eaton, *Reuther*, p. 342.

118   Ibid., p. 344.

119   Schlesinger, *Robert Kennedy and His Times*, p. 174.

120   Cormier and Eaton, *Reuther*, p. 344.

121   Ibid., pp. 347–48.

122   Schlesinger, *Robert Kennedy and His Times*, p. 181.

123   Robert Kennedy resigned as counsel to the McClellan Committee after the passage of Landrum-Griffin, but reinvigorated his crusade against organized crime soon after as attorney general. Within the Teamsters Hoffa's reputation only seemed enhanced by the government's efforts, but eventually his luck ran out; Kennedy's Justice Department found evidence that Hoffa had tried to bribe jurors in a trial in Tennessee. A trucking firm, Commercial Carriers, had set up a company named Test Fleet Corporation to lease trucks. Commercial gave the ownership of Test Fleet to Hoffa's wife and the wife of another labor leader. The women made an initial profit of $125,000 on an invest-ment of $4,000, and the money continued to roll in. As Hoffa himself was alleged to profit from his wife's earnings, this violated a law against labor union leaders benefit-ing from financial dealings with employers. The Test Fleet trial ended in a hung jury, but on March 4, 1964, he was convicted of jury tampering in the case and sentenced to eight years in prison; at Kennedy's insistence, Hoffa was also made to stand trial in Chi-

cago over the Sun Valley land scam, and Hoffa and several other Teamster chieftains were convicted of mail and wire fraud; Hoffa got five years, which, added to his eight, put him away for thirteen years. In 1967, having exhausted his appeals, Hoffa began his thirteen-year term at a federal penitentiary. He was pardoned by President Nixon in December 1971.

CHAPTER TEN: IF AMERICA'S SOUL BECOMES POISONED

1   Saul D. Alinsky, *Reveille for Radicals* (New York: Vintage Books, 1989; originally published 1946), p. 29.
2   Nelson Lichtenstein, *State of the Union: A Century of American Labor* (Princeton, N.J.: Princeton University Press, 2002), p. 164.
3   Ibid., pp. 119–21.
4   Foster Rhea Dulles, *Labor in America: A History* (New York: Thomas Y. Crowell Co., 1966), p. 403.
5   There have long been competing claims for Henry's existence; various legends have him toiling for the railroads in Virginia, West Virginia, and Alabama. See Guy B. Johnson, *John Henry: Tracking Down a Negro Legend* (Chapel Hill: University of North Carolina Press, 1929), and Scott Nelson, *Steel Drivin' Man: The Untold Story of an American Legend* (New York: Oxford University Press, 2006).
6   Franklin M. Fisher and Gerald Kraft, "The Effect of the Removal of the Firemen on Railroad Accidents, 1962–1967," *Bell Journal of Economics and Management Science*, vol. 2, no. 2 (Autumn 1971). Their study found that when a November 1963 arbitration board created by Congress allowed U.S. railroads to start removing firemen—a 20 percent decrease by 1964, 50 percent by 1967—the rate of railway accidents increased 50 percent.
7   Dulles, *Labor in America*, pp. 409–10.
8   John Gregory Dunne, *Delano: The Story of the California Grape Strike* (Berkeley: University of California Press, 2008; originally published 1967), p. 16.
9   The phrase "factories in the fields" is from the book of that title by Carey McWilliams.
10 Dunne, *Delano: Story of California Grape Strike*, p. 36.
11 Dan La Botz, *César Chávez and La Causa* (New York: Pearson Longman, 2006), pp. 39–41. Ford and Suhr each served twelve years for their role in the Wheatland Riot.
12 *San Diego Tribune* quoted in Dunne, *Delano: Story of California Grape Strike*, p. 41.
13 Kirsten Downey, *The Woman Behind the New Deal: The Life of Frances Perkins* (New York: Doubleday, 2009), pp. 201–2.
14 Dunne, *Delano: Story of California Grape Strike*, p. 50.
15 Ibid., p. 51.
16 Alinsky, *Reveille for Radicals*, p. 193.
17 La Botz, *César Chávez and La Causa*, p. 25.
18 Ibid., p. 61.
19 Ibid., p. 60.
20 Dunne, *Delano: Story of California Grape Strike*, p. 128.
21 Joseph C. Goulden, *Meany* (New York: Atheneum, 1972), p. 337.
22 Philip S. Foner, *U.S. Labor and the Vietnam War* (New York: International Publishers, 1989), p. 14.
23 Goulden, *Meany*, p. 383.
24 Victor G. Reuther, *The Brothers Reuther and the Story of the UAW* (Boston: Houghton Mifflin, 1976), p. 392.
25 Philip S. Foner, *U.S. Labor and the Vietnam War*, p. 23.
26 *New York Times*, April 18, 1965.
27 Rhodri Jeffrey-Jones, *Peace Now!: American Society and the Ending of the Vietnam War*

(New Haven, Conn.: Yale University Press, 1999), p. 184. The author reports that a Veterans Administration study later confirmed that nearly 70 percent of GIs in Vietnam were working-class or low-income.

28   *AFL-CIO News*, May 8, 1965.

29   Philip S. Foner, *U.S. Labor and the Vietnam War*, p. 29.

30   Ibid., pp. 30–31.

31   Mazey was among five hundred union members from thirty-eight states who met in Chicago in fall 1967 to found the Labor Leadership Assembly for Peace. They had to appear as individuals, for their unions still backed the war. "Some still treasured the idea that the labor movement could and would become a catalyst for peace," note Albert V. Lannon and Marvin Rogoff, witnesses to the Chicago meeting, and the LLAP gathered momentum in some places, but "it was marginalized, and could not break the Cold War consensus in the AFL-CIO." See Lannon and Rogoff, "We Shall Not Remain Silent: Building the Anti-Vietnam War Movement in the House of Labor."

32   Dunne, *Delano: Story of California Grape Strike*, p. 12.

33   Ibid., p. 111.

34   Ibid., p. 112.

35   Ibid., p. 104.

36   La Botz, *César Chávez and La Causa*, p. 76.

37   Dunne, *Delano: Story of California Grape Strike*, p. 136.

38   *New York Times*, April 9, 1966.

39   Dunne, *Delano: Story of California Grape Strike*, p. 153. Saul Alinsky later told Dunne that he thought an alliance between Hoffa and the Chávez forces might have been mutually beneficial. "I would have gone to Hoffa. I would have said, 'Listen, everyone thinks you're nothing but a goddam hoodlum. You need to pretty yourself up. And the way to do it is to help the poor migrant Mexican. You do it and people won't call you Hoodlum Hoffa any more. They'll be calling you *Huelga Hoffa*.' " See Dunne, *Delano: Story of California Grape Strike*, p. 171.

40   Kevin Boyle, *The UAW and the Heyday of American Liberalism, 1945–1968* (Ithaca, N.Y.: Cornell University Press, 1995), pp. 210–11.

41   Ibid., p. 207.

42   In response to Victor's outburst, former CIA man Thomas Braden reported that he had once given Walter Reuther $50,000 for distribution to U.S.-friendly German auto unions.

43   Paul Potter of SDS quoted by Boyle, *UAW and Heyday of American Liberalism*, p. 211. In addition, the "passion for respectability" that drove unions to support anti-Communist subterfuges abroad and purge left-leaning members at home was reinforced by the labor legislation from Congress, all of which, from the benevolence of the Wagner Act of 1935 to its harsh revisions in Taft-Hartley (1947) and Landrum-Griffin (1959), had the cumulative effect of bureaucratizing unionism. "By holding union leaders (and union treasurers) accountable for violations, the latter two measures, in particular, nurtured carefully defined, legalistic, centralized decision making," suggests economist Neil Chamberlain. See Leon Fink, *Workingmen's Democracy: Knights of Labor and American Politics* (Urbana: University of Illinois Press, 1982), p. 183.

44   Alinsky, *Reveille for Radicals*, p. 33.

45   Goulden, *Meany*, p. 353.

46   Philip S. Foner, *U.S. Labor and the Vietnam War*, p. 109.

47   Goulden, *Meany*, pp. 356–57.

48   Philip S. Foner, *U.S. Labor and the Vietnam War*, p. 65.

49   Goulden, *Meany*, p. 361.

50   *New York Times*, July 12, 1967.

51   Coxey had been arrested, while the fifteen thousand Bonus marchers had been driven from the capital's streets by U.S. Army troops.

52   *New York Times*, April 5, 1967.

53   David J. Garrow, *Bearing the Cross: Martin Luther King, Jr., and the Southern Christian Leadership Conference* (New York: William Morrow, 1986), pp. 576–77.

54   Ibid., p. 582.

55   Other members of the commission included Mayor John Lindsay of New York City, presidential aide Cyrus Vance, and Attorney General Ramsey Clark; the board's two black members were Senator Edward W. Brooke of Massachusetts and Roy Wilkins, executive secretary of the NAACP.

56   *New York Times*, Feb. 25, 1968, and March 1, 1968.

57   Ibid., March 14, 1968.

58   Frank Cormier and William J. Eaton, *Reuther* (Englewood Cliffs, N.J.: Prentice-Hall, 1970), p. 389.

59   Fink, *Workingmen's Democracy*, p. xiii.

60   *Newsweek*, April 22, 1968.

61   *Memphis Commercial Appeal*, Feb. 16, 1968.

62   *New York Times*, March 31, 1968.

63   Ibid., March 30, 1968.

64   Ibid.

65   David Levering Lewis, *King: A Biography* (Urbana: University of Illinois Press, 1978; originally published 1970), pp. 386–87.

66   Ibid., pp. 376–77. On April 8 the march in support of the strike went ahead as planned, King's widow, Coretta, along with Walter Reuther and other dignitaries, led more than forty thousand people in support of the sanitation workers. President Johnson, meanwhile, had dispatched Undersecretary of Labor James Reynolds to Memphis to resolve the strike. Mayor Loeb continued his obstinacy but in the wake of the King assassination he had lost the support of the white business community and was forced to settle with the union by April 16, granting formal recognition to the union and satisfying several other demands. For analysis of the Memphis strike see Millie Allen Beik, *Labor Relations* (Westport, Conn.: Greenwood Press, 2005), pp. 223–48.

67   Goulden, *Meany*, pp. 389–90, 395–96.

68   Boyle, *UAW and Heyday of American Liberalism*, p. 237.

69   Goulden, *Meany*, pp. 389–90, 395–96.

70   See *New York Times*, May 12, 14, 17, and 18, 1968.

71   *New York Times*, Nov. 20, 1969.

72   Ibid., Nov. 22, 1969.

73   Les Leopold, *The Man Who Hated Work and Loved Labor: The Life and Times of Tony Mazzocchi* (White River Junction, Vt.: Chelsea Green, 2007), p. 275.

74   Nixon's address of April 30, 1970, quoted in *New York Times*, May 1, 1970.

75   Philip S. Foner, *U.S. Labor and the Vietnam War*, pp. 112–13. One of the signatures was that of Warren K. Billings, who had been convicted along with Tom Mooney of bombing a San Francisco Preparedness Day parade in 1915, a conviction later overturned.

76   Philip S. Foner, *U.S. Labor and the Vietnam War*, p. 101. The accident was blamed on a faulty altimeter as the plane attempted to land in the rain at a small airfield at Pellston, Michigan. Three days later, as Reuther was memorialized in Detroit, the nation's auto assembly lines fell silent for three minutes in tribute.

77   *New York Times*, Jan. 2, 1966.

78   Lindsay's predecessor, Mayor Robert F. Wagner Jr., son of the famous New Deal solon, had issued an executive order in 1958 that allowed municipal unions the right of collective bargaining, although a state law forbade them from striking and Wagner had managed to keep labor peace with the TWU by befriending Quill and making a point to meet with him on a frequent basis. Wagner, upon relinquishing his office to Lindsay, however, had immediately left town for a vacation in Mexico, seemingly eager to put as much distance between him and the TWU walkout as possible. For further background

on the 1966 New York City transit strike see Vincent J. Cannato, *The Ungovernable City: John Lindsay and His Struggle to Save New York* (New York: Basic Books, 2001), pp. 78–93.

79   Pete Hamill, "The Revolt of the White Lower Middle Class," *New York Magazine*, April 1969.

80   Cannato, *Ungovernable City*, p. 396.

81   *New York Times*, May 9, 1970.

82   Ibid.

83   Philip S. Foner, *U.S. Labor and the Vietnam War*, p. 104.

84   *New York Times*, May 12, 1970.

85   Jeffrey-Jones, *Peace Now!* p. 200.

86   Ray M. Elling, *The Struggle for Workers' Health* (Farmingdale, N.Y.: Baywood Publishing Co., 1986), p. 25.

87   *New York Times*, Jan. 23, 1936; see also *People's Press*, Dec. 7, 1935, at historymatters.gmu.edu/d/5089.

88   *People's News*, pp. 127–35, National Archives Record Group 174, Department of Labor website, http://www.dol.gov/oasam/programs/history/osha.htm.

89   Eric Arneson, ed., *Encyclopedia of U.S. Labor and Working-Class History*, vol. 2 (New York: Routledge, 2007), pp. 1032–33.

90   *New York Times*, Jan. 18 and Jan. 23, 1936.

91   Daniel Berman, *Death on the Job: Occupational Health and Safety Struggles in the United States* (New York: Monthly Review Press, 1978), pp. 27–29.

92   David Rosner and Gerald Markowitz, eds., *Dying for Work: Workers' Safety and Health in Twentieth-Century America* (Bloomington: Indiana University Press, 1987), pp. 191–93.

93   Ibid., p. 14; see also p. 204.

94   Ibid.

95   Robert Asher, "Organized Labor and the Origins of the Occupation Safety and Health Act," *Labor's Heritage*, vol. 3, no. 1 (Jan. 1991).

96   Judson MacLaury, "The Job Safety Law of 1970: Its Passage Was Perilous," U.S. Department of Labor website, http://www.dol.gov/oasam/programs/history/osha.htm.

97   Daniel Berman, *Death on the Job*, pp. 31–32.

98   Leopold, *Man Who Hated Work and Loved Labor*, p. 272.

99   John Stender, "Enforcing the Occupational Safety and Health Act of 1970: The Federal Government as Catalyst," *Law and Contemporary Problems*, vol. 38, no. 4 (Summer–Autumn 1974).

100 MacLaury, "The Job Safety Law of 1970: Its Passage Was Perilous."

101 *Today's Health*, Aug. 1972.

102 Ibid.

103 Ibid.

104 Richard Rashke, *The Killing of Karen Silkwood* (Boston: Houghton Mifflin, 1981), p. 7. See also Leopold, *Man Who Hated Work and Loved Labor*, pp. 312–35.

105 *Rolling Stone*, March 27, 1975.

106 Ibid.

107 Ibid.

108 Ibid.

109 *New York Times*, Jan. 7, 1975.

110 Silkwood's father and her children later won a $10 million court settlement from the firm, later reduced to $1.38 million on appeal. Karen's allegations about negligence and fudging of records at Kerr-McGee received some confirmation when it was reported that a higher-than-normal percentage of rods produced at the Kerr-McGee plant were defective.

111 *Rolling Stone*, March 27, 1975.

CHAPTER ELEVEN: A TIME FOR CHOOSING

1   Garry Wills, *Reagan's America: Innocents at Home* (Garden City, N.Y.: Doubleday, 1987), p. 218.

2   Some SAG members, out of lingering bitterness toward the Academy, threatened to boycott the 1936 Academy Awards ceremony. Frank Capra, one of Hollywood's most respected directors and president of the Academy, averted the crisis by announcing that the awards event would be a salute to aging film pioneer D. W. Griffith, a tribute few in the film community could disrespect, regardless of union affiliation.

3   Ronald Reagan, *An American Life* (New York: Simon & Schuster, 1990), p. 109.

4   Ibid., p. 110.

5   Wills, *Reagan's America*, p. 249.

6   Michael Round, *Grounded: Reagan and the PATCO Crash* (New York: Garland Publishing, 1999), p. 82.

7   Ronald Reagan, "A Time for Choosing," in *Reagan Talks to America*, by Ronald Reagan (Old Greenwich, Conn.: Devon Adair Co., 1983).

8   Reagan liked to render his political coming-of-age story as one in which he awakened as a conservative after years of staunch liberalism, but the metamorphosis was well under way as early as his days at the helm of SAG. Although he remained a registered Democrat until 1962, he had been active a full decade earlier in a group calling itself "Democrats for Eisenhower," and endorsed Eisenhower against Democrat Adlai Stevenson in both 1952 and 1956. In 1960 he backed Republican and fellow Californian Richard Nixon for president and in 1962 finally switched his party affiliation, saying, "I didn't leave the Democratic Party. The Party left me." See *Los Angeles Times*, June 6, 2004.

9   *New York Times*, Aug. 16, 1981.

10 John J. Corson, *The Corson Committee Report: The Career of the Air Traffic Controller*, a/k/a Senate Committee on Post Office and Civil Service, Air Traffic Controllers, 91st Cong., 2nd sess., Calendar No. 1016, Report No. 91–1012 (Washington, D.C.: Government Printing Office, July 9, 1970).

11 Willis J. Nordlund, *Silent Skies: The Air Traffic Controllers' Strike* (Westport, Conn.: Praeger, 1998), p. 83.

12 Ibid., p. 98.

13 Corson, *Corson Committee Report: The Career of the Air Traffic Controller*.

14 Richard W. Hurd and Jill K. Kriesky, " 'The Rise and Demise of PATCO' Reconstructed," *Industrial and Labor Relations Review*, vol. 40, no. 1 (Oct. 1986).

15 Nordlund, *Silent Skies*, p. 98.

16 Katherine S. Newman, "PATCO Lives! Stigma, Heroism, and Symbolic Transformations," *Cultural Anthropology*, vol. 2, no. 3 (Aug. 1987).

17 *New York Times*, Aug. 13, 1981.

18 Newman, "PATCO Lives! Stigma, Heroism, and Symbolic Transformations."

19 Reagan to Robert E. Poli, Oct. 20, 1980, letter published in *New York Times*, Aug. 16, 1981.

20 *New York Times*, Aug. 16, 1981.

21 Round, *Grounded: Reagan and the PATCO Crash*, p. 37.

22 Hurd and Kriesky, " 'The Rise and Demise of PATCO' Reconstructed."

23 Herbert R. Northrup, "The Rise and Demise of PATCO," *Industrial and Labor Relations Review*, vol. 37, no. 2 (Jan. 1984).

24 *New York Times*, Aug. 2, 1981.

25 *Washington Post*, Oct. 13, 1981.

26 *New York Times*, Aug. 16, 1981.

27 *Daily Labor Reporter* No. 127, July 2, 1981, in Nordlund, *Silent Skies*, p. 94.

28 *New York Times*, Aug. 2, 1981.

29   Ibid., July 30, 1981.

30   Reagan, *An American Life*, p. 282.

31   *Newsweek*, Aug. 17, 1981.

32   *New York Times*, Aug. 4, 1981.

33   Ibid.

34   *Newsweek*, Aug. 17, 1981.

35   *New York Times*, Aug. 4, 1981.

36   Ibid., Aug. 7, 1981.

37   Ibid.

38   *Newsweek*, Aug. 17, 1981.

39   Nordlund, *Silent Skies*, p. 10.

40   *The Nation*, Dec. 26, 1981.

41   *New Republic*, Aug. 22 and 29, 1981.

42   The average base pay for a controller was $33,000, with those who worked at busy centers earning $39,000 and even as much as $50,000.

43   *New York Times*, Aug. 16, 1981. Some in-kind and financial support for the strikers came from other federal unions, including the American Federation of Government Employees, the National Treasury Employees Union, and two large postal unions. This help took the form of legal assistance and babysitting for picketing PATCO workers, as well as financial aid for strikers' families struggling with household expenses.

44   Katherine S. Newman, *Falling from Grace: Downward Mobility in the Age of Affluence* (Berkeley: University of California Press, 1988), pp. 170–71.

45   *New York Times*, Aug. 16, 1981.

46   Ibid.

47   Ibid.

48   Ibid.

49   Nordlund, *Silent Skies*, p. 2.

50   Northrup, "The Rise and Demise of PATCO."

51   Reagan, *An American Life*, p. 283.

52   *New York Times*, Aug. 16, 1981.

53   Nordlund, *Silent Skies*, p. 14.

54   Ibid., p. 8.

55   *New York Times*, Aug. 4, 1981.

56   Newman, *Falling from Grace*, p. 146. They were forced to scrounge work elsewhere, as clerks, salesmen, construction workers, usually at salaries well below what they had previously enjoyed. This came with a related toll in divorces, homes lost, college educations denied, and several suicides. Conservative by nature, the former controllers adjusted with difficulty to being perceived as unpatriotic, even criminal. As one controller lamented, "One of the saddest parts of this tragedy is that a group of people whom I know to be decent and generous will forever be branded as irreverent malcontents." See Newman, *Falling from Grace*, pp. 151–53.

57   Nordlund, *Silent Skies*, p. 14.

58   *New York Times*, Aug. 14, 1981.

59   Ibid., Sept. 6, 1981.

60   Thomas Geoghegan, *Which Side Are You On?: Trying to Be for Labor When It's Flat on Its Back* (New York: New Press, 2004; originally published 1991), p. 46.

61   *New York Times*, Sept. 1, 1981.

62   Ibid., Aug. 30, 1981.

63   Ibid., Sept. 7 and 8, 1981.

64   Ibid.

65   *New York Times*, Sept. 20, 1981.

66   *Washington Post*, Sept. 20, 1981.

67   *New York Times*, Sept. 20, 1981. In addition to Lane Kirkland, speakers included

Coretta Scott King, widow of the slain civil rights leader and cochairman of the Full Employment Action Council; Benjamin L. Hooks of the NAACP, Vernon Jordan of the National Urban League, Bayard Rustin, chairman of the A. Philip Randolph Institute, and Eleanor Smeal, president of the National Organization of Women. Senator Daniel Patrick Moynihan of New York was also in attendance.

68 *New York Times*, Sept. 20, 1981.

69 Ibid., Sept. 19, 1981.

70 *New Republic*, Aug. 22 and 29, 1981.

71 Nordlund, *Silent Skies*, p. 11.

72 Ibid., pp. 178–79. As early as the late 1980s there was talk at the FAA of experimenting with what is called "free flight," the concept that in the future the role of ground-based air traffic control will be diminished as more responsibility for charting courses and avoiding collisions is delegated to pilots.

73 Nordlund, *Silent Skies*, p. 201.

74 *New York Times*, Sept. 20, 1981.

75 Ibid., Nov. 19, 1981.

76 *Washington Post*, Nov. 18, 1981.

77 Kevin Boyle, *The UAW and the Heyday of American Liberalism, 1945–1968* (Ithaca, N.Y.: Cornell University Press, 1995), p. 2.

78 Ibid., p. 3.

79 *New York Times*, Jan. 14, 1986.

80 Ibid., Sept. 30, 1986.

81 Ibid., May 29, 1985.

82 Ibid., Feb. 20, 1986.

83 Ibid., Feb. 18, 1986.

84 Ibid., Feb. 1 and 16, 1986.

85 Ibid., Feb. 21, 1986.

86 Ibid., Feb. 14, 1986.

87 Bud Schultz and Ruth Schultz, *We Will Be Heard: Voices in the Struggle for Constitutional Rights* (London: Merrell, 2000), p. 184.

88 *New York Times*, April 7, 1992.

89 Ibid., April 16, 1992.

90 Stephen Franklin, *Three Strikes: Labor's Heartland Losses and What They Mean for Working Americans* (New York: Guilford Press, 2001), p. 108.

91 Ibid. See Harter Equipment Inc. and Local 825, International Union of Operating Engineers; Case 22-CA-11527; Decisions and Orders of the National Labor Relations Board, vol. 280 (1986).

92 *New York Times*, May 6, 1993; see also Geoghegan, *Which Side Are You On?* pp. 310–11.

93 Michael Ballot, *Labor-Management Relations in a Changing Environment* (New York: John Wiley & Sons, 1996), p. 418.

94 *New York Times*, Aug. 21, 1994.

95 The executive order, termed a "misguided presidential directive" by conservatives, was seen as a mostly symbolic act, an effort to win back unions' favor by a president who had signed the North American Free Trade Agreement (NAFTA), which organized labor had opposed. See *Newsday*, March 9, 1995.

96 Jeremy Brecher and Tim Costello, "A New Labor Movement in the Shell of the Old," in *A New Labor Movement for the New Century*, ed. Gregory Mantsios (New York: Monthly Review Press, 1998).

97 *New York Times*, Aug. 11, 1997.

98 Ibid., Aug. 7, 1997.

99 Ibid.

100 *New York Times*, Aug. 17, 1997.

101 Ibid., Aug. 5, 1997.

102   Ibid., Aug. 17, 1997.

103   Brecher and Costello, "A New Labor Movement in the Shell of the Old."

104   *New York Times*, Aug. 1, 1997.

105   Ibid., Aug. 20, 1997.

106   Ibid.

107   Ibid.

108   *New York Times*, Nov. 18, 2009.

109   Ronaldo Munck, *Globilisation and Labour: The New Great Transformation* (London: Zed Books Ltd., 2002), p. 190.

110   Stanley Aronowitz, *From the Ashes of the Old: American Labor and America's Future* (Boston: Houghton Mifflin, 1998), pp. 7–8.

111   Ibid.

112   Bureau of Labor Statistics, Union Members Summary, January 21, 2011; http://www.bls.gov/news.release/union2.nro.htm.

113   Geoghegan, *Which Side Are You On?* p. 246; see *Inland Steel Co. v. National Labor Relations Board*, 170 F. 2d 247 (7th Cir. 1948); and *W. W. Cross & Co. v. National Labor Relations Board*, 174 F. 2d 875 (1st Cir. 1949).

114   Steven Greenhouse, *The Big Squeeze: Tough Times for the American Worker* (New York: Anchor Books, 2009), p. 285.

115   Ibid., pp. 96–97.

116   *Time*, March 1, 2009.

117   Keith Bradsher, *High and Mighty: The Dangerous Rise of the SUV* (New York: Public Affairs, 2002), pp. 69–70.

118   See Bradsher, *High and Mighty*, pp. 25–26, 62–64, 252–53.

119   Jay Mazur, "Labor's New Internationalism," *Foreign Affairs*, vol. 79, no. 1 (Jan.–Feb. 2000).

120   Melvyn Dubofsky and Warren Van Tine, *John L. Lewis: A Biography*, abridged ed. (Urbana: University of Illinois Press, 1986), p. 340.

121   Brecher and Costello, "A New Labor Movement in the Shell of the Old."

122   Mazur, "Labor's New Internationalism."

123   Gregory Mantsios, "What Does Labor Stand For?" in *A New Labor Movement for the New Century*, ed. Gregory Mantsios (New York: Monthly Review Press, 1998).

124   Geoghegan, *Which Side Are You On?* pp. 222–26.

125   See *Wall Street Journal*, Oct. 12, 2009.

126   *New York Times*, Jan. 23, 2010; conservatives and business groups have also reacted negatively to a proposal by the administration of President Barack Obama to award government procurement contracts based in part on how well companies treat employees in terms of pay and benefits. According to the *New York Times*, administration officials perceive it as "a way to shape social policy and lift more families into the middle class." Those opposed decry the plan as "a gift to organized labor." See *New York Times*, Feb. 26, 2010.

127   Steven Fraser, *Labor Will Rule: Sidney Hillman and the Rise of American Labor* (Ithaca, N.Y.: Cornell University Press, 1991), p. 575.

128   See "Renewing an Old Idea: Common Good," *New York Times*, March 17, 2010.

129   *New York Times*, Sept. 28, 2007.

BOOKS

Adamic, Louis. *Dynamite!: A Century of Class Violence in America*. New York: Viking Books, 1934.

Alinsky, Saul D. *John L. Lewis: An Unauthorized Biography*. New York: Vintage Books, 1970; originally published 1949.

Alinsky, Saul D. *Reveille for Radicals*. New York: Vintage Books, 1989; originally published 1946.

Allen, Joseph H. *Our Liberal Movement in Theology*. Boston: Roberts Brothers, 1882.

Altenbaugh, Richard J. *Education for Struggle: The American Labor Colleges of the 1920s and 1930s*. Philadelphia: Temple University Press, 1990.

Arneson, Eric, ed. *Encyclopedia of U.S. Labor and Working-Class History*. New York: Routledge, 2007.

Aronowitz, Stanley. *From the Ashes of the Old: American Labor and America's Future*. Boston: Houghton Mifflin, 1998.

Arthur, Anthony. *Radical Innocent: Upton Sinclair*. New York: Random House, 2006.

Auerbach, Jerold S. *Labor and Liberty: The La Follette Committee and the New Deal*. Indianapolis, Ind.: Bobbs-Merrill Co., 1966.

Avrich, Paul. *The Haymarket Tragedy*. Princeton, N.J.: Princeton University Press, 1984.

Avrich, Paul. *Sacco and Vanzetti: The Anarchist Background*. Princeton, N.J.: Princeton University Press, 1991.

Bailey, Thomas A. *Woodrow Wilson and the Great Betrayal*. New York: Macmillan and Co., 1945.

Ballot, Michael. *Labor-Management Relations in a Changing Environment*. New York: John Wiley & Sons, 1996.

Barbash, Jack. *The Taft-Hartley Act in Action*. New York: League for Industrial Democracy, 1954.

Barnard, John. *Walter Reuther and the Rise of the Auto Workers*. Boston: Little, Brown and Co., 1983.

Baxandall, Rosalyn, and Linda Gordon, eds. *America's Working Women, 1600 to the Present*. New York: W. W. Norton & Co., 1976.

Beecher, Jonathan. *Charles Fourier: The Visionary and His World*. Berkeley: University of California Press, 1986.

Beik, Millie Allen. *Labor Relations*. Westport, Conn.: Greenwood Press, 2005.

Ben-Atar, Doron S. *Trade Secrets: Intellectual Piracy and the Origins of American Industrial Power*. New Haven, Conn.: Yale University Press, 2004.

Benton-Cohen, Katherine. *Borderline Americans: Racial Division and Labor Wars in the Arizona Borderlands*. Cambridge, Mass.: Harvard University Press, 2009.

Berkman, Alexander. *ABC of Anarchism*. London: Freedom Press, 1973; originally published 1929.

Berkman, Alexander. *Prison Memoirs of an Anarchist*. Pittsburgh, Pa.: Frontier Press, 1970.

Berman, Daniel. *Death on the Job: Occupational Health and Safety Struggles in the United States*. New York: Monthly Review Press, 1978.

Berman, Edward. *Labor and the Sherman Act*. New York: Harper & Brothers, 1930.

Bernstein, Irving. *The Lean Years: A History of the American Worker, 1920–1933*. Boston: Houghton Mifflin, 1966.

Bernstein, Irving. *The Turbulent Years: A History of the American Worker, 1933–1941*. Boston: Houghton Mifflin, 1970.

Berson, Robin K. *Marching to a Different Drummer: Unrecognized Heroes of American History*. Westport, Conn.: Greenwood Press, 1994.

Blewett, Mary H. *Surviving Hard Times: The Working People of Lowell*. Lowell, Mass.: The Lowell Museum, 1982.

Blewett, Mary H. *We Will Rise in Our Might: Working Women's Voices from Nineteenth-Century New England*. Ithaca, N.Y.: Cornell University Press, 1991.

Boyer, Richard O., and Herbert M. Morais. *Labor's Untold Story*. New York: United Electrical, Radio & Machine Workers of America, 1972; originally published 1955.

Boyle, Kevin. *The UAW and the Heyday of American Liberalism, 1945–1968*. Ithaca, N.Y.: Cornell University Press, 1995.

Bradsher, Keith. *High and Mighty: The Dangerous Rise of the SUV*. New York: Public Affairs, 2002.

Brecher, Jeremy. *Strike!* Boston: South End Press, 1984; originally published 1972.

Bridenbaugh, Carl. *The Colonial Craftsman*. New York: New York University Press, 1950.

Brody, David. *Workers in Industrial America: Essays on the Twentieth Century Struggle*. New York: Oxford University Press, 1993.

Brown, R. G., et al. *Report upon the Illegal Practices of the United States Department of Justice*. New York: American Civil Liberties Union Reprint, 1920.

Bruce, Robert V. *1877: Year of Violence*. Indianapolis, Ind.: Bobbs-Merrill Co., 1959.

Buder, Stanley. *Pullman: An Experiment in Industrial Order and Community Planning 1880–1930*. New York: Oxford University Press, 1967.

Buhle, Paul. *Taking Care of Business: Samuel Gompers, George Meany, Lane Kirkland, and the Tragedy of American Labor*. New York: Monthly Review Press, 1999.

Buhle, Paul, and Alan Dawley, eds. *Working for Democracy: American Workers from the Revolution to the Present*. Urbana: University of Illinois Press, 1985.

Burbank, David T. *Reign of Rabble: The St. Louis General Strike of 1877*. New York: Augustus M. Kelley, 1966.

Cagin, Seth, and Philip Dray. *Between Earth and Sky: How CFCs Changed Our World*. New York: Pantheon Books, 1993.

Cahn, William. *Lawrence 1912: The Bread and Roses Strike*. New York: Pilgrim Press, 1980; originally published 1954.

Calmer, Alan. *Labor Agitator: The Biography of Albert R. Parsons*. New York: International Publishers, 1937.

Camp, Helen C. *Iron in Her Soul: Elizabeth Gurley Flynn and the American Left*. Pullman: Washington State University Press, 1995.

Cannato, Vincent J. *The Ungovernable City: John Lindsay and His Struggle to Save New York*. New York: Basic Books, 2001.

Cantor, M., ed. *Class, Sex, and the Woman Worker*. Westport, Conn.: Greenwood Press, 1977.

Carman, Harry J., ed. *The Path I Trod: The Autobiography of Terence V. Powderly*. New York: Columbia University Press, 1940.

Catton, Bruce. *The War Lords of Washington*. Westport, Conn.: Greenwood Press, 1969; originally published 1948.

Chaplin, Ralph. *The Centralia Massacre*. Austin, Tex.: Workplace Publishing, 1971; originally published 1924.

Chesler, Ellen. *Woman of Valor: Margaret Sanger and the Birth Control Movement in America*. New York: Simon & Schuster, 1992.

Christman, Henry M., ed. *Selected Papers of Walter P. Reuther*. New York: Pyramid, 1961.

Cole, Donald B. *Immigrant City: Lawrence, Massachusetts, 1845–1921*. Chapel Hill: University of North Carolina Press, 1963.

Commons, John R., ed. *A Documentary History of American Industrial Society*. Volume 8. New York: Russell & Russell, 1958.

Cormier, Frank, and William J. Eaton. *Reuther*. Englewood Cliffs, N.J.: Prentice-Hall, 1970.

Coxe, Tench. *An Address to an Assembly of the Friends of American Manufactures*. Philadelphia: R. Aitkin & Son, 1787.

Coxe, Tench. *Observations on the Agriculture, Manufactures, and Commerce of the United States*. New York: Childs & Swaine, 1789.

Coxe, Tench. *A View of the United States of America*. Philadelphia: William Hall, 1794.

Crawford, Margaret. *Building the Workingman's Paradise: The Design of American Company Towns*. New York: Verso, 1995.

Dall, Caroline. *Women's Right to Labor*. Boston: Walker, Wise and Co., 1860.

Dalzell, Robert F. *Enterprising Elite: The Boston Associates and the World They Made*. Cambridge, Mass.: Harvard University Press, 1987.

David, Henry. *The History of the Haymarket Affair*. New York: Farrar & Rinehart, 1936.

Davis, Mike. *Buda's Wagon: A Brief History of the Car Bomb*. New York: Verso, 2007.

Davis, Mike. *Prisoners of the American Dream: Politics and Economy in the History of the U.S. Working Class*. London: Verso, 1986.

Dawley, Alan. *Class and Community: The Industrial Revolution in Lynn*. Cambridge, Mass.: Harvard University Press, 1976.

De Caux, Len. *The Living Spirit of the Wobblies*. New York: International Publishers, 1978.

Dobbs, Farrell. *Teamster Rebellion*. New York: Monad Press, 1972.

Downey, Kirsten. *The Woman Behind the New Deal: The Life of Frances Perkins*. New York: Doubleday, 2009.

Drinnon, Richard, ed. *Emma Goldman: Anarchism and Other Essays*. New York: Dover Books, 1969; originally published 1917.

Dublin, Thomas. *Lowell: Story of an Industrial City*. Washington, D.C.: National Park Service Division of Publications, 1992.

Dublin, Thomas. *Women at Work: The Transformation of Work and Community in Lowell, Massachusetts, 1826–1860*. New York: Columbia University Press, 1979.

Dubofsky, Melvyn, ed. *The New Deal: Conflicting Interpretations and Shifting Perspectives*. New York: Garland Publishing, 1992.

Dubofsky, Melvyn. *We Shall Be All: A History of the Industrial Workers of the World*. Abridged edition. Urbana: University of Illinois Press, 2000.

Dubofsky, Melvyn. *When Workers Organize: New York City in the Progressive Era*. Amherst: University of Massachusetts Press, 1968.

Dubofsky, Melvyn, and Warren Van Tine. *John L. Lewis: A Biography*. Abridged edition. Urbana: University of Illinois Press, 1986.

Du Bois, W. E. B. *Black Reconstruction in America, 1860–1880*. New York: Free Press, 1998; originally published 1935.

Dulles, Foster Rhea. *Labor in America: A History*. New York: Thomas Y. Crowell Co., 1966.

Dunne, John Gregory. *Delano: The Story of the California Grape Strike*. Berkeley: University of California Press, 2008; originally published 1967.

Eggert, Gerald. *Railroad Labor Disputes: The Beginnings of Federal Strike Policy*. Ann Arbor: University of Michigan Press, 1967.

Eggert, Gerald. *Richard Olney: Evolution of a Statesman*. University Park: Pennsylvania State University Press, 1974.

Eisler, Benita, ed. *The Lowell Offering: Writings by New England Mill Women, 1840–1845*. New York: W. W. Norton & Co., 1998; originally published 1977.

Elling, Ray M. *The Struggle for Workers' Health*. Farmingdale, N.Y.: Baywood Publishing Co., 1986.

Ellis, Charles M. *An Essay on Transcendental Boston*. Boston: Crocker and Ruggles, 1842.

English, T. J. *Havana Nocturne: How the Mob Owned Cuba . . . and Then Lost It to the Revolution*. New York: William Morrow, 2008.

Eno, Arthur L., Jr., ed. *Cotton Was King: History of Lowell, Massachusetts*. Lowell, Mass.: Lowell Historical Society, 1976.

Faler, Paul G. *Mechanics and Manufacturers in the Early Industrial Revolution*. Albany: State University of New York Press, 1981.

Fine, Sidney. *Sit-Down: The General Motors Strike of 1936–1937*. Ann Arbor: University of Michigan Press, 1969.

Fink, Leon. *Workingmen's Democracy: Knights of Labor and American Politics*. Urbana: University of Illinois Press, 1982.

Flynn, Elizabeth Gurley. *I Speak My Own Piece*. New York: Masses and Mainstream, 1955.

Flynn, Elizabeth Gurley. *The Rebel Girl: An Autobiography: My First Life (1906–1926)*. New York: International Publishers, 1973.

Folsom, Franklin. *Impatient Armies of the Poor: The Story of Collective Action of the Unemployed, 1808–1942*. Niwat: University of Colorado Press, 1991.

Folsom, Michael, and Steven Lubar. *The Philosophy of Manufactures: Early Debates over Industrialization in the United States*. Cambridge, Mass.: MIT Press, 1982.

Foner, Eric. *Forever Free: The Story of Emancipation and Reconstruction*. New York: Alfred A. Knopf, 2005.

Foner, Eric. *Free Soil, Free Labor, Free Men: The Ideology of the Republican Party Before the Civil War*. New York: Oxford University Press, 1970.

Foner, Eric. *The Story of American Freedom*. New York: W. W. Norton & Co., 1998.

Foner, Philip S., ed. *The Factory Girls: A Collection of Writings on Life and Struggle in the New England Factories of the 1840s*. Urbana: University of Illinois Press, 1977.

Foner, Philip S. *Organized Labor and the Black Worker, 1619–1973*. New York: Praeger, 1974.

Foner, Philip S. *U.S. Labor and the Vietnam War*. New York: International Publishers, 1989.

Foster, William Z. *The Great Steel Strike and Its Lessons*. New York: B. W. Huebsch Inc., 1920.

Fostick, Raymond B. *John D. Rockefeller, Jr.: A Portrait*. New York: Harper & Brothers, 1956.

Franklin, Stephen. *Three Strikes: Labor's Heartland Losses and What They Mean for Working Americans*. New York: Guilford Press, 2001.

Fraser, Steven. *Labor Will Rule: Sidney Hillman and the Rise of American Labor*. Ithaca, N.Y.: Cornell University Press, 1991.

Friedheim, Robert L. *The Seattle General Strike*. Seattle: University of Washington Press, 1964.

Garrow, David J. *Bearing the Cross: Martin Luther King, Jr., and the Southern Christian Leadership Conference*. New York: William Morrow, 1986.

Geoghegan, Thomas. *Which Side Are You On?: Trying to Be for Labor When It's Flat on Its Back*. New York: New Press, 2004; originally published 1991.

Ginger, Ann, and David Christiano, eds. *The Cold War Against Labor*. Volume 1. Berkeley, Calif.: Meiklejohn Civil Liberties Institute, 1987.

Ginger, Ray. *Altgeld's America: The Lincoln Ideal Versus Changing Realities*. New York: Funk & Wagnalls, 1958.

Ginger, Ray. *The Bending Cross: A Biography of Eugene Victor Debs*. New Brunswick, N.J.: Rutgers University Press, 1949.

Goldman, Emma. *Living My Life*. New York: Penguin Books, 2006; originally published 1931.

Golin, Steve. *The Fragile Bridge: Paterson Silk Strike, 1913*. Philadelphia: Temple University Press, 1988.

Gompers, Samuel. *Seventy Years of Life and Labor*. New York: E. P. Dutton & Co., 1925.

Goodwin, Doris Kearns. *No Ordinary Time: Franklin and Eleanor Roosevelt: The Home Front in World War II*. New York: Simon & Schuster, 1994.

Gorn, Elliott J. *Mother Jones: The Most Dangerous Woman in America*. New York: Hill and Wang, 2001.

Goulden, Joseph C. *Meany*. New York: Atheneum, 1972.

Green, Hardy. *On Strike at Hormel: The Struggle for a Democratic Labor Movement*. Philadelphia: Temple University Press, 1990.

Green, James. *Death in the Haymarket: A Story of Chicago, the First Labor Movement, and the Bombing That Divided Gilded Age America*. New York: Pantheon Books, 2006.

Green, Martin. *New York 1913: The Armory Show and the Paterson Strike Pageant*. New York: Collier Books, 1988.

Greenhouse, Steven. *The Big Squeeze: Tough Times for the American Worker*. New York: Anchor Books, 2009.

Greenwald, Richard A. *The Triangle Fire, the Protocols of Peace, and Industrial Democracy in Progressive Era New York*. Philadelphia: Temple University Press, 2005.

Griffith, Barbara S. *The Crisis of American Labor: Operation Dixie and the Defeat of the CIO*. Philadelphia: Temple University Press, 1988.

Grossman, Jonathan P. *William Sylvis: Pioneer of American Labor*. New York: Octagon Books, 1973.

Gura, Philip F. *American Transcendentalism: A History*. New York: Hill and Wang, 2007.

Gutman, Herbert G. *Work, Culture & Society in Industrializing America*. New York: Alfred A. Knopf, 1976.

Hage, Dave, and Paul Klauda. *No Retreat, No Surrender: Labor's War at Hormel*. New York: William Morrow, 1989.

Hall, Kermit L., ed. *Oxford Guide to U.S. Supreme Court Decisions*. New York: Oxford University Press, 1999.

Hamilton, Alexander. *Report on the Subject of Manufactures*. Philadelphia: William Brown, Printer, 1827; originally published 1797.

Hanson, Charles. *The Closed Shop: A Comparative Study in Public Policy and Trade Union Security in Britain, the United States, and West Germany*. New York: St. Martin's Press, 1981.

Harris, Herbert. *American Labor*. New Haven, Conn.: Yale University Press, 1939.

Harris, Leon. *Upton Sinclair: American Rebel*. New York: Crowell, 1975.

Haywood, William D. *Bill Haywood's Book: The Autobiography of William D. Haywood*. New York: International Publishers, 1929.

Hentoff, Nat. *Peace Agitator*. New York: Macmillan, 1963.

Hindle, Brooke, and Steven Lubar. *Engines of Change: The American Industrial Revolution, 1790–1860*. Washington, D.C.: Smithsonian Institution Press, 1986.

Hirsch, Fred. *An Analysis of Our AFL-CIO Role in Latin America*. San Jose, Calif.: Self-published, 1974.

Hofstadter, Richard. *The Age of Reform*. New York: Random House, 1955.

Horan, James D., and Howard Swiggett. *The Pinkerton Story*. New York: Putnam, 1951.

Hutchinson, John. *The Imperfect Union: A History of Corruption in American Trade Unions*. New York: E. P. Dutton & Co., 1972.

Huttmacher, J. Joseph. *Senator Robert F. Wagner and the Rise of Urban Liberalism*. New York: Atheneum, 1968.

Interchurch World Movement. *Report on the Steel Strike of 1919*. New York: Da Capo Press, 1970; originally published 1920.

Jacoby, Sanford M. *Employing Bureaucracy: Managers, Unions, and the Transformation of Work in American Industry, 1900–1945*. New York: Columbia University Press, 1985.

James, Henry. *Richard Olney and His Public Service*. Boston: Houghton Mifflin, 1923.

Jeffrey-Jones, Rhodri. *Peace Now!: American Society and the Ending of the Vietnam War*. New Haven, Conn.: Yale University Press, 1999.

Jensen, Joan M., and Sue Davidson, eds. *A Needle, a Bobbin, a Strike: Women Needleworkers in America*. Philadelphia: Temple University Press, 1984.

Johnson, Claudius O. *Carter H. Harrison I*. Chicago: University of Chicago Press, 1928.

Johnson, Malcolm. *On the Waterfront: The Pulitzer Prize-Winning Article That Inspired the Classic Movie and Transformed the New York Waterfront.* New York: Penguin Group, 2005.

Jones, Mother "Mary Harris." *The Autobiography of Mother Jones.* Chicago: Charles Kerr Publishing Co., 1990; originally published 1925.

Josephson, Hannah. *The Golden Threads: New England's Mill Girls and Magnates.* New York: Duell, Sloan, and Pearce, 1949.

Juravich, Tom, William F. Hartford, and James R. Green. *Commonwealth of Toil: Chapters in the History of Massachusetts Workers and Their Unions.* Amherst: University of Massachusetts Press, 1996.

Kakar, Sudhir. *Frederick Taylor: A Study in Personality and Innovation.* Cambridge, Mass.: MIT Press, 1970.

Kanigel, Robert. *The One Best Way: Frederick Winslow Taylor and the Enigma of Efficiency.* New York: Viking, 1997.

Kaplan, Justin. *Lincoln Steffens: A Biography.* New York: Simon & Schuster, 1974.

Kennedy, Robert F. *The Enemy Within: The McClellan Committee's Crusade Against Jimmy Hoffa and Corrupt Labor Unions.* New York: Da Capo Press, 1994; originally published 1960.

Kenny, Kevin. *Making Sense of the Molly Maguires.* New York: Oxford University Press, 1998.

Kimeldorf, Howard. *Battling for American Labor: Wobblies, Craft Workers, and the Making of the Union Movement.* Berkeley: University of California Press, 1999.

Kogan, Bernard, ed. *The Chicago Haymarket Riot: Anarchy on Trial.* Boston: D. C. Heath, 1959.

Korngold, Ralph. *Two Friends of Man: The Story of William Lloyd Garrison and Wendell Phillips.* Boston: Little, Brown and Co., 1950.

Korth, Philip. *Minneapolis Teamsters Strike of 1934.* East Lansing: Michigan State University Press, 1995.

Krause, Paul. *The Battle for Homestead, 1880–1892.* Pittsburgh, Pa.: University of Pittsburgh Press, 1992.

La Botz, Dan. *César Chávez and La Causa.* New York: Pearson Longman, 2006.

Lasch, Christopher. *The New Radicalism in America, 1889–1963.* Cambridge, Mass.: MIT Press, 1965.

Lash, Joseph P. *Dealers and Dreamers: A New Look at the New Deal.* New York: Doubleday, 1988.

Lee, R. Alton. *Truman and Taft-Hartley: A Question of Mandate.* Lexington: University of Kentucky Press, 1966.

Leopold, Les. *The Looting of America: How Wall Street's Game of Fantasy Finance Destroyed Our Jobs, Pensions, and Prosperity.* White River Junction, Vt.: Chelsea Green, 2009.

Leopold, Les. *The Man Who Hated Work and Loved Labor: The Life and Times of Tony Mazzocchi.* White River Junction, Vt.: Chelsea Green, 2007.

Leuchtenburg, William. *Franklin D. Roosevelt and the New Deal, 1932–1940.* New York: Harper & Row, 1963.

Leuchtenburg, William. *The Supreme Court Reborn: The Constitutional Revolution in the Age of Roosevelt.* New York: Oxford University Press, 1995.

Levy, Leonard W. *The Law of the Commonwealth and Chief Justice Shaw.* Cambridge, Mass.: Harvard University Press, 1957.

Lewis, David Levering. *King: A Biography.* Urbana: University of Illinois Press, 1978; originally published 1970.

Leyendecker, L. E. *Palace Car Prince: A Biography of George Mortimer Pullman.* Niwot: University Press of Colorado, 1992.

Lichtenstein, Nelson. *The Most Dangerous Man in Detroit: Walter Reuther and the Fate of American Labor.* New York: Basic Books, 1995.

Lichtenstein, Nelson. *State of the Union: A Century of American Labor.* Princeton, N.J.: Princeton University Press, 2002.

Lieberman, Elias. *Unions Before the Bar.* New York: Harper & Brothers, 1950.

Limerick, Patricia Nelson. *The Legacy of Conquest: The Unbroken Past of the American West.* New York: W. W. Norton & Co., 1987.

Lingenfelter, Richard E. *The Hardrock Miners: A History of the Mining Labor Movement in the American West.* Berkeley: University of California Press, 1974.

Litwicki, Ellen M. *America's Public Holidays, 1865–1920.* Washington, D.C.: Smithsonian Institution Press, 2000.

Livesay, Harold C. *Samuel Gompers and Organized Labor in America.* Prospect Heights, Ill.: Waveland Press, 1993; originally published 1978.

Logan, Rayford. *The Betrayal of the Negro from Rutherford B. Hayes to Woodrow Wilson.* New York: Da Capo Press, 1997; originally published 1954.

Long, Priscilla. *Where the Sun Never Shines: A History of America's Bloody Coal Industry.* New York: Paragon House, 1989.

Luhan, Mabel Dodge. *Movers and Shakers.* Albuquerque: University of New Mexico Press, 1985; originally published 1936.

Lukas, J. Anthony. *Big Trouble: A Murder in a Small Western Town Sets Off a Struggle for America.* New York: Simon & Schuster, 1997.

Luther, Seth. *An Address to the Workingmen of New England.* Boston: n.p., 1832.

Mantsios, Gregory, ed. *A New Labor Movement for the New Century.* New York: Monthly Review Press, 1998.

Marchalonis, S. *The Worlds of Lucy Larcom.* Athens: University of Georgia Press, 1989.

Marshall, Ray. *The Negro and Organized Labor.* New York: John Wiley & Sons, 1965.

Martelle, Scott. *Blood Passion: The Ludlow Massacre and Class War in the American West.* New Brunswick, N.J.: Rutgers University Press, 2007.

Marx, Leo. *The Machine in the Garden: Technology and the Pastoral Ideal in America.* New York: Oxford University Press, 1964.

Mayo, George Elton. *The Human Problems of an Industrialized Society.* New York: Macmillan, 1933.

McCulloch, Frank W., and Tim Bornstein. *The National Labor Relations Board.* New York: Praeger, 1974.

McGerr, Michael. *A Fierce Discontent: The Rise and Fall of the Progressive Movement in America, 1870–1920.* New York: Free Press, 2003.

McGovern, George S., and Leonard F. Guttridge. *The Great Coalfield War.* Boston: Houghton Mifflin, 1972.

McKenney, Ruth. *Industrial Valley.* New York: Harcourt Brace and Co., 1939.

McWilliams, Carey. *Factories in the Field: The Story of Migratory Farm Labor in California.* Boston: Little, Brown and Co., 1939.

Miles, Henry A. *Lowell, As It Was, and As It Is.* New York: Arno Reprint, 1972; originally published 1845.

Miller, Donald L. *The Kingdom of Coal: Work, Enterprise, and Ethnic Communities in the Mine Fields.* Philadelphia: University of Pennsylvania Press, 1985.

Mintz, Benjamin W. *OSHA: History, Law and Policy.* Washington, D.C.: Bureau of National Affairs, 1984.

Mitchell, John. *Organized Labor: Its Problems, Purposes and Ideals and the Present and Future of American Wage Earners.* Philadelphia: American Book and Bible House, 1903.

Moldea, Dan E. *The Hoffa Wars: Teamsters, Rebels, Politicians and the Mob.* New York: Paddington Press Ltd., 1978.

Moran, William. *The Belles of New England: The Women of the Textile Mills and the Families Whose Wealth They Wove.* New York: Thomas Dunne Books, 2002.

Morgan, Ted. *A Covert Life: Jay Lovestone—Communist, Anti-Communist, and Spymaster.* New York: Random House, 1999.

Morn, Frank. *The Eye That Never Sleeps: A History of the Pinkerton National Detective Agency.* Bloomington: Indiana University Press, 1982.

Morris, Charles R. *The Tycoons: How Andrew Carnegie, John D. Rockefeller, Jay Gould, and J. P. Morgan Invented the American Supereconomy.* New York: Henry Holt, 2005.

Morrison, Elting E., ed. *The Letters of Theodore Roosevelt.* New York: Cambridge University Press, 1951.

Munck, Ronaldo. *Globilisation and Labour: The New Great Transformation.* London: Zed Books Ltd., 2002.

Murphy, Teresa Anne. *Ten Hours Labor: Religion, Reform, and Gender in Early New England.* Ithaca, N.Y.: Cornell University Press, 1992.

Murray, Robert K. *Red Scare: A Study in National Hysteria, 1919–1920.* New York: McGraw-Hill, 1964; originally published 1955.

Newman, Katherine S. *Falling from Grace: Downward Mobility in the Age of Affluence.* Berkeley: University of California Press, 1988.

Nicholson, Philip Yale. *Labor's Story in the United States.* Philadelphia: Temple University Press, 2004.

Noble, David. *The Progressive Mind, 1890–1917.* Chicago: Rand McNally, 1970.

Nordlund, Willis J. *Silent Skies: The Air Traffic Controllers' Strike.* Westport, Conn.: Praeger, 1998.

Northrup, Herbert R. *Organized Labor and the Negro.* New York: Harper & Brothers, 1944.

Orbach, Brian K. *Labor and the Environmental Movement.* Cambridge, Mass.: MIT Press, 2004.

Ottanelli, Fraser M. *The Communist Party of the United States: From the Depression to World War II.* New Brunswick, N.J.: Rutgers University Press, 1991.

Parmet, Robert D. *The Master of Seventh Avenue: David Dubinsky and the American Labor Movement.* New York: New York University Press, 2005.

Parsons, Lucy. *The Life of Albert Parsons.* Chicago: Lucy Parsons Publisher, 1903.

Perkins, Frances. *The Roosevelt I Knew.* New York: Viking Press, 1946.

Perlman, Selig. *A History of Trade Unionism in the United States.* New York: Macmillan, 1922.

Pinkerton, Allan. *The Molly Maguires and the Detectives.* New York: G. W. Carleton Publishing, 1877.

Pinkerton, Allan. *Strikers, Communists, Tramps, and Detectives.* New York: G. W. Dillingham Publishing, 1906.

Pinkowski, Edward. *John Siney: The Miners' Martyr.* Philadelphia: Sunshine Press, 1963.

Piven, Frances Fox, and Richard A. Cloward. *Poor People's Movements: Why They Succeed, How They Fail.* New York: Pantheon Books, 1977.

Polenberg, Richard, ed. *The Era of Franklin D. Roosevelt, 1933–1945.* Boston: Bedford/St. Martin's, 2000.

Post, Louis F. *The Deportations Delirium of 1920.* Chicago: Charles H. Kerr & Co., 1923.

Powers, Richard Gid. *Secrecy and Power: The Life of J. Edgar Hoover.* New York: Free Press, 1987.

Preston, L. *Aliens and Dissenters: Federal Suppression of Radicals, 1903–1933.* Urbana: University of Illinois Press, 1944.

Przybyszewski, Linda. *The Republic According to John Marshall Harlan.* Chapel Hill: University of North Carolina Press, 1999.

Rashke, Richard. *The Killing of Karen Silkwood.* Boston: Houghton Mifflin, 1981.

Reagan, Ronald. *Ronald Reagan: A Life.* New York: Simon & Schuster, 1990.

Reagan, Ronald. *Ronald Reagan Talks to America.* Old Greenwich, Conn.: Devon Adair Co., 1983.

Renshaw, Patrick. *The Wobblies: The Story of Syndicalism in the United States.* New York: Doubleday, 1967.

Reuther, Victor G. *The Brothers Reuther and the Story of the UAW.* Boston: Houghton Mifflin, 1976.

Richter, Irving. *Labor's Struggles: 1945–1950.* New York: Columbia University Press, 1994.

Robinson, Archie. *George Meany and His Times.* New York: Simon & Schuster, 1981.

Robinson, Harriet H. *Loom and Spindle, or Life Among the Early Mill Girls.* Kailua, Hawaii: Press Pacifica, 1976; originally published 1898.

Roddy, Edward G. *Mills, Mansions, and Mergers: The Life of William W. Wood*. North Andover, Mass.: Merrimack Valley Textile Museum, 1982.

Roediger, Dave, and Franklin Rosemont, eds. *Haymarket Scrapbook*. Chicago: Charles H. Kerr Publishing Co., 1986.

Rosenstone, Robert A. *Romantic Revolutionary: A Biography of John Reed*. New York: Alfred A. Knopf, 1975.

Rosner, David, and Gerald Markowitz, eds. *Dying for Work: Workers' Safety and Health in Twentieth-Century America*. Bloomington: Indiana University Press, 1987.

Round, Michael. *Grounded: Reagan and the PATCO Crash*. New York: Garland Publishing, 1999.

Russell, Thaddeus. *Out of the Jungle: Jimmy Hoffa and the Remaking of the American Working Class*. New York: Alfred A. Knopf, 2001.

Sacco, Nicola, and Bartolomeo Vanzetti. *The Letters of Sacco and Vanzetti*. Edited by Marion Denman Frankfurter and Gardner Jackson. New York: Viking Press, 1928.

Salvatore, Nick. *Eugene V. Debs: Citizen and Socialist*. Urbana: University of Illinois Press, 1984.

Schlegel, Marvin. *Ruler of the Reading: The Life of Franklin B. Gowen, 1836–1889*. Harrisburg, Pa.: Archives Publishing, 1947.

Schlesinger, Arthur M., Jr. *The Age of Roosevelt: The Coming of the New Deal*. Boston: Houghton Mifflin, 1958.

Schlesinger, Arthur M., Jr. *Robert Kennedy and His Times*. Boston: Houghton Mifflin, 1978.

Schluter, Herman. *Lincoln, Labor, and Slavery*. New York: Socialist Literature Co., 1913.

Schultz, Bud, and Ruth Schultz. *We Will Be Heard: Voices in the Struggle for Constitutional Rights*. London: Merrell, 2000.

Schwantes, Carlos. *Coxey's Army: An American Odyssey*. Lincoln: University of Nebraska Press, 1985.

Selden, Bernice. *The Mill Girls: Lucy Larcom, Harriet Hanson Robinson, Sarah G. Bagley*. New York: Atheneum,1983.

Shefferman, Nathan W. *The Man in the Middle*. Garden City, N.Y.: Doubleday, 1961.

Shostak, Arthur B. *The Air Controllers Controversy: Lessons from the PATCO Strike*. New York: Human Sciences Press, 1986.

Siracusa, Carl. *A Mechanical People: Perceptions of the Industrial Order in Massachusetts, 1815–1880*. Middletown, Conn.: Wesleyan University Press, 1979.

Sloane, Arthur A. *Hoffa*. Cambridge, Mass.: MIT Press, 1991.

Smith, Robert M. *From Blackjacks to Briefcases: A History of Commercialized Strikebreaking and Unionbusting in the United States*. Athens: Ohio University Press, 2003.

Sobel, Robert. *Coolidge: An American Enigma*. Washington, D.C.: Regnery, 1998.

Sorensen, Charles E., and William Samuelson. *My Forty Years with Ford*. New York: W. W. Norton & Co., 1956.

Sperno, Sterling D., and Abram L. Harris. *The Black Worker: The Negro and the Labor Movement*. New York: Atheneum, 1972; originally published 1931.

Stansell, Christine. *American Moderns: Bohemian New York and the Creation of a New Century*. New York: Metropolitan Books, 2000.

Stanton, Elizabeth Cady. *Eighty Years and More: Reminiscences, 1815–1897*. New York: Schocken Books, 1971; originally published 1898.

Steel, Ronald. *In Love with Night: The American Romance with Robert Kennedy*. New York: Simon & Schuster, 2000.

Stein, Leon. *The Triangle Fire*. Ithaca, N.Y.: Cornell University Press, 2001.

Stern, Andy. *A Country That Works: Getting America Back on Track*. New York: Free Press, 2006.

Stone, Melville E. *Fifty Years a Journalist*. Garden City, N.Y.: Doubleday, 1921.

Stowell, David O. *Streets, Railroads, and the Great Strike of 1877*. Chicago: University of Chicago Press, 1999.

Stowell, Myron R. *"Fort Frick," or the Siege of Homestead*. Pittsburgh, Pa.: Pittsburgh Printing Co., 1893.

Strum, Philippa. *Louis D. Brandeis: Justice for the People*. Cambridge, Mass.: Harvard University Press, 1984.

Suggs, George G. *Colorado's War on Militant Unionism: James H. Peabody and the Western Federation of Miners*. Detroit: Wayne State University Press, 1972.

Sylvis, James C. *The Life, Speeches, Labors and Essays of William H. Sylvis*. Philadelphia: Claxton, Remsen, and Haffelfinger, 1872.

Taylor, Frederick W. *The Principles of Scientific Management*, and *Shop Management*. London: Routledge, 1993; originally published 1911.

Theoharis, Athan G., and John S. Cox. *The Boss: J. Edgar Hoover and the Great American Inquisition*. Philadelphia: Temple University Press, 1988.

Todes, Charlotte. *William H. Sylvis and the National Labor Union*. New York: International Publishers, 1942.

Tomlins, Christopher L. *Law, Labor, and Ideology in the Early American Republic*. New York: Cambridge University Press, 1993.

Toner, Jerome L. *The Closed Shop*. Washington, D.C.: American Council on Public Affairs, 1942.

Trautmannn, Frederic. *The Voice of Terror: A Biography of Johann Most*. Westport, Conn.: Greenwood Press, 1980.

Tripp, Anne Huber. *The IWW and the Paterson Silk Strike of 1913*. Urbana: University of Illinois Press, 1987.

Trollope, Anthony. *North America*. Volume 1. New York: Augustus M. Kelley, 1970; originally published 1862.

Tyler, Robert L. *Rebels of the Woods: The IWW in the Pacific Northwest*. Eugene: University of Oregon Books, 1967.

Ulrich, Laurel. *The Age of Homespun: Objects and Stories in the Creation of an American Myth*. New York: Alfred A. Knopf, 2001.

Velie, Lester. *Labor U.S.A.* New York: Harper, 1959.

Von Drehle, David. *Triangle: The Fire That Changed America*. New York: Atlantic Monthly Press, 2003.

Vorse, Mary Heaton. *A Footnote to Folly: Reminiscences of Mary Heaton Vorse*. New York: Farrar and Rinehart, 1935.

Walker, Charles R. *American City: A Rank and File History of Minneapolis*. Minneapolis: University of Minnesota Press, 2005; originally published 1937.

Ware, Caroline F. *The Early New England Cotton Manufacture: A Study in Industrial Beginnings*. Boston: Houghton Mifflin, 1931.

Warne, Colston E., ed. *The Pullman Boycott 1894: The Problem of Federal Intervention*. Boston: D. C. Heath, 1955.

Watson, Bruce. *Bread and Roses: Mills, Migrants, and the Struggle for the American Dream*. New York: Penguin Books, 2005.

Watts, Steven. *The People's Tycoon: Henry Ford and the American Century*. New York: Random House, 2005.

Weinstein, Irving. *Pie in the Sky: An American Struggle: The Wobblies and Their Times*. New York: Delacorte Press, 1969.

White, William. *The Taft Story*. New York: Harper & Brothers, 1954.

Wilentz, Sean. *The Age of Reagan: A History, 1974–2008*. New York: Harper, 2008.

Wilentz, Sean. *Chants Democratic: New York City and the Rise of the American Working Class, 1788–1850*. New York: Oxford University Press, 1984.

Wilford, Hugh. *The Mighty Wurlitzer: How the CIA Played America*. Cambridge, Mass.: Harvard University Press, 2008.

Wills, Garry. *Reagan's America: Innocents at Home*. Garden City, N.Y.: Doubleday, 1987.

Witt, John F. *The Accidental Republic: Crippled Workingmen, Destitute Widows, and the Remaking of American Labor*. Cambridge, Mass.: Harvard University Press, 2004.

Witte, Edwin E. *The Government in Labor Disputes*. New York: McGraw-Hill, 1932.

Wolff, David A. *Industrializing the Rockies: Growth, Competition, and Turmoil in the Coalfields of Colorado and Wyoming, 1868–1914.* Boulder: University Press of Colorado, 2003.

Wolff, Leon. *Lockout: The Story of the Homestead Strike of 1892.* New York: Harper & Row, 1965.

Yafa, Stephen. *Cotton: The Biography of a Revolutionary Fiber.* New York: Penguin Books, 2006.

Young, Marguerite. *Harp Song for a Radical: The Life and Times of Eugene Victor Debs.* New York: Alfred A. Knopf, 1999.

Zieger, Robert H. *The CIO: 1933–1955.* Chapel Hill: University of North Carolina Press, 1995.

Zinn, Howard, Dana Frank, and Robin D. G. Kelley. *Three Strikes: Miners, Musicians, Salesgirls, and the Fighting Spirit of Labor's Last Century.* Boston: Beacon Press, 2001.

ARTICLES AND PAMPHLETS

Abbott, Edith. "History of the Employment of Women in the American Cotton Mills, Part 2." *Journal of Political Economy*, vol. 16, no. 10 (Dec. 1908).

Allen, Harbor. "The Flynn." *American Mercury*, Dec. 1926.

Altgeld, John P. "Comment on the Supreme Court Decision." In *The Pullman Boycott of 1894: The Problem of Federal Intervention*, edited by Colston E. Warne. Boston: D. C. Heath, 1955.

Altgeld, John P. "Federal Interference in the Chicago Strike." In *The Pullman Boycott of 1894: The Problem of Federal Intervention*, edited by Colston E. Warne. Boston: D. C. Heath, 1955.

Ammons, Elias M. "The Colorado Strike." *North American Review*, July 1914.

Asher, Robert. "Organized Labor and the Origins of the Occupational Safety and Health Act." *Labor's Heritage*, vol. 3, no. 1 (Jan. 1991).

Basch, Francoise. "The Shirtwaist Girls at Home and at Work." In *The Diary of a Shirtwaist Striker*, by Thersa Malkiel. Ithaca, N.Y.: Cornell University Press, 1990.

Brazier, Richard. "The Mass IWW Trial of 1918: A Retrospect." *Labor History*, vol. 7, no. 2 (1966).

Brecher, Jeremy, and Tim Costello. "A New Labor Movement in the Shell of the Old." In *A New Labor Movement for the New Century*, edited by Gregory Mantsios. New York: Monthly Review Press, 1998.

Brody, Miriam. "Introduction." In *Living My Life*, by Emma Goldman. New York: Penguin Books, 2006; originally published 1931.

Carew, Anthony. "The American Labor Movement in Fizzland: The Free Trade Union Committee and the CIA." *Labor History*, vol. 39, no. 1 (1998).

Clark, George R. "The Strange Story of the Reuther Plan." *Harper's Magazine*, May 1942.

Claxton, Oliver. "The Janitor's Boy: Robert F. Wagner." *The New Yorker*, March 5, 1927.

Cleveland, Grover. "The Government in the Chicago Strike of 1894." In *The Pullman Boycott of 1894: The Problem of Federal Intervention*, edited by Colston E. Warne. Boston: D. C. Heath, 1955.

Cooper, Jerry M. "The Army as Strikebreaker—The Railroad Strikes of 1877 and 1894." *Labor History*, vol. 18, no. 2 (Spring 1977).

Crain, Caleb. "There Was Blood: The Ludlow Massacre Revisited." *The New Yorker*, Jan. 19, 2009.

Curti, Merle E. "Robert Rantoul, Jr., the Reformer in Politics." *New England Quarterly*, vol. 5 (1932).

Debs, Eugene. "The Federal Government and the Chicago Strike." In *The Pullman Boycott of 1894: The Problem of Federal Intervention*, edited by Colston E. Warne. Boston: D. C. Heath, 1955.

Deland, Lorin F. "The Lawrence Strike: A Study." *Atlantic Monthly*, May 1912.

Doherty, Thomas. "Frank Costello's Hands: Film, Television, and the Kefauver Crime Hearings." *Film History*, vol. 10, no. 3 (1998).

Dublin, Thomas. "Women, Work, and Protest in the Early Lowell Mills: 'The Oppressing Hand of Avarice Would Enslave Us.'" In *Class, Sex, and the Woman Worker*, edited by M. Cantor. Westport, Conn.: Greenwood Press, 1977.

Dublin, Thomas. "Women, Work, and the Family: Female Operatives in the Lowell Mills, 1830–1860." *Feminist Studies*, vol. 3, nos. 1–2 (Autumn 1975).

Dubofsky, Melvyn. "Abortive Reform: The Wilson Administration and Organized Labor, 1913–1920." In *Work, Community, and Power: The Experience of Labor in Europe and America, 1900–1925*, edited by James E. Cronin and Carmen Sirianni. Philadelphia: Temple University Press, 1983.

Dubofsky, Melvyn. "The Federal Judiciary, Free Labor, and Equal Rights." In *The Pullman Strike and the Crisis of the 1890s*, edited by Richard Schneirov. Urbana: University of Illinois Press, 1999.

Dubofsky, Melvyn. "Not So 'Turbulent Years': Another Look at the American 1930's." In *The New Deal*, edited by Melvyn Dubofsky. New York: Garland Publishing, 1992.

Dunn, Robert W. "The Palmer Raids" [booklet]. New York: International Publishers, 1948.

Everett, Edward. "Fourth of July at Lowell (1830)." In *The Philosophy of Manufactures: Early Debates over Industrialization in the United States*, by Michael Folsom and Steven Lubar. Cambridge, Mass.: MIT Press, 1982.

Faler, Paul. "Cultural Aspects of the Industrial Revolution: Lynn, Massachusetts, Shoemakers and Industrial Morality, 1826–1860." *Labor History*, vol. 15 (Summer 1974).

Faue, Elizabeth. "Hard-Pressed in the Heartland: The Hormel Strike and the Future of the Labor Movement." *Journal of American History*, vol. 81, no. 2 (Sept. 1994).

Fisher, Franklin M., and Gerald Kraft. "The Effect of the Removal of the Firemen on Railroad Accidents, 1962–1967." *Bell Journal of Economics and Management Science*, vol. 2, no. 2 (Autumn 1971).

Garland, Hamlin. "Homestead and Its Perilous Trades." *McClure's Magazine*, vol. 3, no. 1 (June 1894).

Gersuny, Carl. "A Biographical Note on Seth Luther." *Labor History*, vol. 18 (Spring 1977).

Ginger, Ray. "Labor in a Massachusetts Cotton Mill, 1853–1860." *Business History Review*, vol. 28, no. 1 (March 1954).

Godkin, E. L. "Cooperation." *North American Review*, Jan. 1868.

Goldman, Emma. "Johann Most." *American Mercury*, June 1926.

Gompers, Samuel. "The Lesson of the Recent Strikes." In *The Pullman Boycott of 1894: The Problem of Federal Intervention*, edited by Colston E. Warne. Boston: D. C. Heath, 1955.

Gompers, Samuel. "What Does Labor Want?" AFL pamphlet (1893), reprinted in Pamphlets in American History series, Microfilming Corp. of America, Sanford, N.C., 1979.

Hall, Jacquelyn Dowd, Robert Korstad, and James Leloudis. "Cotton Mill People: Work, Community, and Protest in the Textile South, 1880–1940." *American Historical Review*, vol. 91, no. 2 (April 1986).

Hamill, Pete. "The Revolt of the White Lower Middle Class." *New York Magazine*, April 1969.

Harmon, M. Judd. "The New Deal: A Revolution Consummated." Utah State Agriculture College Monograph Series, vol. 4, no. 1 (April 1956).

Hartz, Louis. "Seth Luther: The Story of a Working-Class Rebel." *New England Quarterly*, vol. 13, no. 3 (Sept. 1940).

Hill, Herbert. "The Real Practices of Organized Labor—The Age of Gompers and After." In *Employment, Race, and Poverty*, edited by Arthur M. Ross and Herbert Hill. New York: Harcourt, Brace and World, 1967.

Horowitz, Morris A. "The Diesel Firemen Issue on the Railroads." *Industrial and Labor Relations Review*, vol. 13, no. 4 (July 1960).

Hurd, Richard W. "How PATCO Was Led into a Trap." *The Nation*, Dec. 26, 1981.

Hurd, Richard W., and Jill K. Kriesky. "'The Rise and Demise of PATCO' Reconstructed." *Industrial and Labor Relations Review*, vol. 40, no. 1 (Oct. 1986).

Hynd, Alan. "With the Pinkertons, Through the Labyrinth of Death." *True Detective Mysteries Magazine*, Nov. 1940.

Industrial Workers of the World. "Ettor and Giovannitti Before the Jury at Salem MA, Nov. 23, 1912" (booklet). Chicago: IWW Publishing, 1913.

Jacobs, Paul. "Extracurricular Activities of the McClellan Committee." *California Law Review*, vol. 51, no. 2 (May 1963).

James, Henry. "A Defense of Richard Olney." In *The Pullman Boycott of 1894: The Problem of Federal Intervention*, edited by Colston E. Warne. Boston: D. C. Heath, 1955.

King, Willard. "The Debs Case." In *The Pullman Boycott of 1894: The Problem of Federal Intervention*, edited by Colston E. Warne. Boston: D. C. Heath, 1955.

Kugler, Israel. "The Trade Union Career of Susan B. Anthony." *Labor History*, vol. 2, no. 1 (Winter 1961).

Lannon, Albert V., and Martin Rogoff. "We Shall Not Remain Silent: Building the Anti-Vietnam War Movement in the House of Labor." *Science and Society*, vol. 66, no. 4 (Winter 2002–2003).

Larcom, Lucy. "Among Lowell Mill Girls: A Reminiscence." *Atlantic Monthly*, Nov. 1881.

Larned, J. N. "Prepare for Socialism." *Atlantic Monthly*, May 1911.

Levinson, Edward. "Labor on the March." *Harper's Magazine*, May 1937.

MacDonald, Allan. "Lowell: A Commercial Utopia." *New England Quarterly*, vol. 10, no. 1 (March 1937).

MacLaury, Judson. "The Job Safety Law of 1970: Its Passage Was Perilous." U.S. Department of Labor website, http://www.dol.gov/oasam/programs/history/osha.htm.

Mantsios, Gregory. "What Does Labor Stand For?" In *A New Labor Movement for the New Century*, edited by Gregory Mantsios. New York: Monthly Review Press, 1998.

Mazur, Jay. "Labor's New Internationalism." *Foreign Affairs*, vol. 79, no. 1 (Jan.–Feb. 2000).

Merrill, Louis Taylor. "Mill Town on the Merrimack." *New England Quarterly*, vol. 19, no. 1 (March 1946).

Montgomery, David. "The Pullman Strike and the Making of Modern America." In *The Pullman Strike and the Crisis of the 1890s*, edited by Richard Schneirov. Urbana: University of Illinois Press, 1999.

Newman, Katherine S. "PATCO Lives! Stigma, Heroism, and Symbolic Transformations." *Cultural Anthropology*, vol. 2, no. 3 (Aug. 1987).

Northrup, Herbert R. "Reply to 'The Rise and Demise of PATCO' Reconstructed." *Industrial and Labor Relations Review*, vol. 40, no. 1 (Oct. 1986).

Northrup, Herbert R. "The Rise and Demise of PATCO." *Industrial and Labor Relations Review*, vol. 37, no. 2 (Jan. 1984).

Quam, Lois, and Peter J. Rachleff. "Keeping Minneapolis an Open-Shop Town: The Citizens' Alliance in the 1930's." *Minnesota History*, vol. 50, no. 3 (Fall 1986).

Raskin, A. H. "The Moral Issue That Confronts Labor." *New York Times Magazine*, March 31, 1957.

Raskin, A. H. "New Issue: Labor as Big Business." *New York Times Magazine*, Feb. 22, 1959.

Reagan, Ronald. "A Time for Choosing." In *Reagan Talks to America*, by Ronald Reagan. Old Greenwich, Conn.: Devon Adair Co., 1983.

Reed, John. "The Colorado War." *Metropolitan*, July 1914.

Reed, John. "War in Paterson, June 1913." *The Masses*, June 1913.

Reuther, Walter. "500 Planes a Day—A Program for the Utilization of the Automobile Industry for Mass Production of Defense Planes." In *Reuther, Selected Papers*, edited by Henry M. Christman. New York: Pyramid, 1964; originally published 1961.

Reuther, Walter. "How to Beat the Communists." *Collier's*, Feb. 28, 1948.

Schlesinger, Arthur M., Jr. "Sources of the New Deal." In *The New Deal: The Critical Issues*, edited by Otis Graham Jr. Boston: Little, Brown and Co., 1971.

Schofield, Ann. "The Uprising of the 20,000: The Making of a Labor Legend." In *A Needle, a Bobbin, a Strike: Women Needleworkers in America*, edited by Joan M. Jensen and Sue Davidson. Philadelphia: Temple University Press, 1984.

Shailor, Barbara, and George Kourpias. "Developing and Enforcing International Labor Standards." In *A New Labor Movement for the New Century*, edited by Gregory Mantsios. New York: Monthly Review Press, 1998.

Shannon, Fred A. "The Homestead Act and the Labor Surplus." *American Historical Review*, vol. 14, no. 4 (July 1936).

Sherrill, Robert. "What's Behind the Failure to Protect the Health of American Workers." *Today's Health*, Aug. 1972.

Stender, John. "Enforcing the Occupational Safety and Health Act of 1970: The Federal Government as Catalyst." *Law and Contemporary Problems*, vol. 38, no. 4 (Summer–Autumn 1974).

Stone, I. F. "Robert F. Wagner." *The Nation*, Oct. 28, 1944.

Unger, Frederic W. "George F. Baer: Master-Spirit of the Anthracite Industry." *American Monthly Review of Reviews*, vol. 33 (1906).

Vogel, Lise. "Hearts to Feel and Tongues to Speak: New England Mill Women in the Early Nineteenth Century." In *Class, Sex, and the Woman Worker*, edited by M. Cantor. Westport, Conn.: Greenwood Press, 1977.

Washington, Booker T. "The Negro and the Labor Unions." *Atlantic Monthly*, June 1913.

Wiebe, Robert H. "The Anthracite Strike of 1902: A Record of Confusion." *Mississippi Valley Historical Review*, vol. 48, no. 2 (Sept. 1961).

Zaroulis, Nancy. "Daughters of Freemen: The Female Operatives and the Beginning of the Labor Movement." In *Cotton Was King: History of Lowell, Massachusetts*, edited by Arthur L. Eno Jr. Lowell, Mass.: Lowell Historical Society, 1976.

Zinn, Howard. "The Conservative New Deal." In *The New Deal: The Critical Issues*, edited by Otis Graham Jr. Boston: Little, Brown and Co., 1971.

GOVERNMENT DOCUMENTS

Pennsylvania General Assembly. *Report of the Committee Appointed to Investigate the Railroad Riots in July 1877*. Harrisburg, Pa., 1878.

U.S. Congress. Senate. *Investigation of the Labor Troubles at Homestead*. 52nd Cong., 2nd sess., 1893, #128.

U.S. Congress. Senate. U.S. Strike Commission. *Report on the Chicago Strike of June–July 1894*. Senate Executive Document No. 7. 53rd Cong., 3rd sess. Washington, D.C.: Government Printing Office, 1895.

U.S. Congress. House of Representatives. *Final Report of the Industrial Commission*. 57th Cong., 1st sess., 1902. House Document 380.

U.S. Congress. House Committee on Rules. *Report on the Lawrence Strike, U.S. House—The Strike at Lawrence, Massachusetts: Hearings before the Committee*. 62nd Cong., 2nd sess., March 1912.

U.S. Congress. House of Representatives. *Report on the Colorado Strike Investigation*. 63rd Cong, 3rd sess., 1915. House document 1630.

U.S. House of Representatives, Commission on Industrial Relations, 1912–1915; Final Report of the Commission, 64th Congress, 1st sess., Washington D.C.: Government Printing Office, 1916.

U.S. Congress. House of Representatives. *Attorney General A. Mitchell Palmer on Charges Made Against the Department of Justice by Louis F. Post and Others: Hearings Before the Committee on Rules*. 66th Cong., 2nd sess., 1920.

U.S. Congress. Senate. La Follette Committee, Subcommittee of the Senate Committee on Labor and Public Welfare. *Violations of Free Speech and Assembly and Interference with the Rights of Labor: Hearings*. 74th Cong., 2nd sess., 1936.

U.S. Congress. Senate. *Third Interim Report of the Special Committee to Investigate Organized Crime in Interstate Commerce*. Washington, D.C.: General Printing Office, 1951.

U.S. Senate, 82nd Congress, 2nd sess., Select Committee on Improper Activities in the Labor and Management Field (McClellan Committee Hearings, 1957). Washington D.C.: Bureau of National Affairs, 1958.

Corson, John J. *The Corson Committee Report: The Career of the Air Traffic Controller*, a/k/a Senate Committee on Post Office and Civil Service, Air Traffic Controllers, 91st Cong., 2nd sess., Calendar No. 1016, Report No. 91–1012. Washington, D.C.: Government Printing Office, July 9, 1970.

Harter Equipment Inc and Local 825, International Union of Operating Engineers; Case 22-CA-11527; Decisions and Orders of the National Labor Relations Board, vol. 280, 1986.

COURT CASES

Commonwealth v. Hunt, 45 Mass. 111, 4 Met. (1842).
Farwell v. Boston and Worcester Railroad Corporation, 45 Mass. 49 (Mass. 1842).
Scott v. Sandford, 19 How. (60 U.S.) 393 (1857).
Slaughterhouse Cases, 16 Wall (83 U.S.) 36 (1873).
Munn v. Illinois, 94 U.S. 113 (1877).
Civil Rights Cases, 109 U.S. 3 (1883).
United States v. Workingmen's Amalgamated Council of New Orleans, Eastern District Court of Louisiana, 54 Fed. 994, 996 (1893).
United States v. Patterson, 55 Fed. 605, 641 (1893).
United States v. Debs, 64 Fed. 724, 744–745 (1894).
United States v. E. C. Knight Co., 156 U.S. 1 (1895).
In re Debs, 158 U.S. 564 (1895).
Plessy v. Ferguson, 163 U.S. 537 (1896).
Lochner v. New York, 198 U.S. 45 (1905).
Loewe v. Lawlor, 208 U.S. 274 (1908).
Adair v. United States, 208 U.S. 161 (1908).
Muller v. Oregon, 208 U.S. 412 (1908).
Standard Oil Co. of New Jersey v. United States, 221 U.S. (1911).
United States v. American Tobacco Co., 221 U.S. 189–93 (1911).
Schenck v. United States, 249 U.S. 47 (1919).
Abrams v. United States, 250 U.S. 616 (1919).
Colyer v. Skeffington, 265 Fed. 17 (D. Mass. 1920).
Duplex Printing Press Co. v. Deering, 254 U.S. 443 (1921).
Schechter Poultry Corp. v. United States, 295 U.S. 495 (1935).
National Labor Relations Board v. Jones & Laughlin Steel Corp., 301 U.S. 1 (1937).
United States v. United Mine Workers, 330 U.S. 258 (1947).
Inland Steel Co. v. National Labor Relations Board, 170 F. 2d 247 (7th Cir. 1948).
W. W. Cross & Co. v. National Labor Relations Board, 174 F. 2d 875 (1st Cir. 1949).
Reapportionment Cases, 377 U.S. 633 (1964).

★ ILLUSTRATION CREDITS ★

INSERT I

Page 1
Courtesy of the author

Page 2
TOP: Courtesy of the author
BOTTOM: Library of Congress

Page 3
TOP: Library of Congress
BOTTOM: Library of Congress

Page 4
TOP: Library of Congress
BOTTOM: Courtesy of the author

Page 5
TOP: Library of Congress
BOTTOM: Courtesy of the author

Page 6
TOP: Courtesy of the author
BOTTOM: Library of Congress

Page 7
TOP, LEFT: Courtesy of the author
TOP, RIGHT: Courtesy of the author
CENTER, LEFT: Courtesy of the author
CENTER, RIGHT: Courtesy of the author
BOTTOM: Courtesy of the author

Page 8
TOP: Labadie Collection at the University of Michigan
BOTTOM: Labadie Collection at the University of Michigan

Page 9
TOP: Library of Congress
BOTTOM: Library of Congress

Page 10
TOP: Library of Congress
BOTTOM: Library of Congress

Page 11
TOP: Library of Congress
BOTTOM: Library of Congress

Page 12
TOP: Library of Congress
BOTTOM: Carnegie Library of Pittsburgh

Page 13
TOP: Library of Congress
BOTTOM: Library of Congress

Page 14
TOP: Library of Congress
BOTTOM: Library of Congress

Page 15
TOP: Labadie Collection at the University of Michigan
BOTTOM: Library of Congress

Page 16
TOP: Library of Congress
BOTTOM: Library of Congress

INSERT 2

Page 1
TOP: Library of Congress
CENTER: Labadie Collection at the University of Michigan
BOTTOM: Library of Congress

Page 2
TOP: Library of Congress
BOTTOM: Library of Congress

Page 3
TOP: Library of Congress
BOTTOM: Library of Congress

Page 4
TOP: Labadie Collection at the University of Michigan
BOTTOM: Labadie Collection at the University of Michigan

Page 5
TOP: Denver Public Library
BOTTOM, LEFT: Labadie Collection at the University of Michigan
BOTTOM, RIGHT: Labadie Collection at the University of Michigan

Page 6
TOP: Courtesy of the author
BOTTOM: Walter P. Reuther Library at Wayne State University

Page 7
TOP: Library of Congress
BOTTOM: Library of Congress

Page 8
TOP: Labadie Collection at the University of Michigan
BOTTOM: Labadie Collection at the University of Michigan

Page 9
TOP: Library of Congress
BOTTOM: Library of Congress

Page 10
TOP: Library of Congress
BOTTOM: *Native Land* (still)

Page 11
TOP: Library of Congress
BOTTOM: Library of Congress

Page 12
TOP: Walter P. Reuther Library at Wayne State University
BOTTOM: Walter P. Reuther Library at Wayne State University

Page 13
TOP: Walter P. Reuther Library at Wayne State University
CENTER: Library of Congress
BOTTOM: Courtesy of the author

Page 14
TOP: Library of Congress
CENTER: Library of Congress
BOTTOM: Getty TIME/LIFE

Page 15
TOP: Walter P. Reuther Library at Wayne State University
BOTTOM: Walter P. Reuther Library at Wayne State University

Page 16
TOP: Walter P. Reuther Library at Wayne State University
BOTTOM: © Jim West